Parag Sapre

µC/OS-III™
The Real-Time Kernel

Jean J. Labrosse

Micrium
Press

Weston, FL 33326

Micrium Press
1290 Weston Road, Suite 306
Weston, FL 33326
USA
www.micrium.com

Library of Congress Control Number: 2010922732

Library of Congress subject headings:

1. Embedded computer systems
2. Real-time data processing
3. Computer software - Development

For bulk orders, please contact Micrium Press at: +1 954 217 2036

ISBN: 978-0-9823375-6-1

100-uCOS-III-TI-LM3S9B92-001

To my loving and caring wife, Manon,
and our two children James and Sabrina.

Table of Contents

Part I: µC/OS-III – The Real-Time Kernel

Part II: µC/OS-III and the Texas Instruments LM3S9B92

Table of Contents

Foreword to µC/OS-III — by Jack Ganssle

Your system has to read a keyboard and update the display. That's pretty easy to handle in a simple loop.

Oh, wait, then there's the A/D converter which needs service once a millisecond. The data is noisy so ten samples must be averaged and the result fed into a computation which is sent to the display. But you can't do the math till the results of the encoder become available, and that can only be read on 20 msec intervals.

But don't forget to monitor the radiation source; if it goes out of limits a safety protocol has to be invoked to avoid harming users. That has to be monitored every 250 milliseconds.

How would one write this code? Sure, it's possible to write an interrupt handler that takes clock ticks and then, via a number of tortured loops, sequences off the proper activities. It'll be tough to debug and harder to maintain. You can be sure the boss will come in, red-faced, wondering why the heck the system only looks at safety parameters every quarter second when any idiot knows the rate should be 0.230 sec, no matter how he wrote the spec. The loops grow more complex and the program ever more convoluted.

This is a very old problem, one solved by the use of a Real-Time Operating System (RTOS). Write each activity as a separate task. The code is simple, crystal clear, and easy to change.

An old problem, yes. But there's surprisingly little written about the use of an RTOS. Jean Labrosse wrote one of the first and best books on the subject: the first edition of this volume. I'm told it, and the subsequent second edition, are the best selling books ever published about embedded systems, and I'm not surprised. Extremely-well written, they covered the subject in depth and with finesse. He wrote using the µC/OS and µC/OS-II RTOSes as examples.

Now Jean and the crew at Micriµm have a new and hugely improved version of that RTOS: µC/OS-III. Where µC/OS-II is a commercial quality product, one that even meets the highest safety-critical requirements, µC/OS-III takes that quality and reliability levels to even the most demanding applications.

Jean has supplemented the new RTOS with this book. It's much weightier than his previous RTOS books as this volume goes deeply in depth into the nuances of using an operating system in real applications. µC/OS-III lays out the rational behind an RTOS, and then in a very logical fashion presents each of the resources provided by an RTOS and how one goes about using those features in a product. Though µC/OS-III is used as an example, it is not presented as the canonical RTOS, and users of any real-time operating system will find this material immensely useable.

I have long counted Jean a friend, and have great respect for his perfectionism. That is clear when reading the µC/OS source code, which is probably the most beautiful code I have read, and, since it has been used in products certified to DO-178B level A, also works!

That perfectionism also manifests itself in this book, in which it's clear he has taken pains to get every fact right, every drawing clear, all while maintaining a very consistent style.

This is a book by an engineer, for engineers (including engineering students). Devoid of fluff, it's packed with information about using an RTOS in a real system... today. What do I need to do to get started? What are all those files? Where is the information I need located?

Are you using an RTOS? If so, read this book. If you're not using one, read this book; not every embedded system needs an operating system, but there are too many that have been cobbled together through the painful use of ad hoc loops that an RTOS would vastly improve.

Preface

WHAT IS µC/OS-III?

µC/OS-III (pronounced "Micro C O S Three) is a scalable, ROMable, preemptive real-time kernel that manages an unlimited number of tasks. µC/OS-III is a third-generation kernel and offers all of the services expected from a modern real-time kernel, such as resource management, synchronization, inter-task communications, and more. However, µC/OS-III offers many unique features not found in other real-time kernels, such as the ability to complete performance measurements at run-time, to directly signal or send messages to tasks, achieve pending on multiple kernel objects, and more.

WHY A NEW µC/OS VERSION?

The µC/OS series, first introduced in 1992, has undergone a number of changes over the years based on feedback from thousands of people using and deploying its evolving versions.

µC/OS-III is the sum of this feedback and experience. Rarely used µC/OS-II features were eliminated and newer, more efficient features and services, were added. Probably the most common request was to add round robin scheduling, which was not possible for µC/OS-II, but is now a feature of µC/OS-III.

µC/OS-III also provides additional features that better exploit the capabilities of today's newer processors. Specifically, µC/OS-III was designed with 32-bit processors in mind, although it certainly works well with 16- and even several 8-bit processors.

µC/OS-III GOALS

The main goal of µC/OS-III is to provide a best-in-class real-time kernel that literally shaves months of development time from an embedded-product schedule. Using a commercial real-time kernel such as µC/OS-III provides a solid foundation and framework to the design engineer dealing with the growing complexity of embedded designs.

Another goal for µC/OS-III, and therefore this book, is to explain inner workings of a commercial-grade kernel. This understanding will assist the reader in making logical design decisions and informed tradeoffs between hardware and software that make sense.

Introduction

Real-time systems are systems whereby the correctness of the computed values and their timeliness are at the forefront. There are two types of real-time systems, hard and soft real time.

What differentiates hard and soft real-time systems is their tolerance to missing deadlines and the consequences associated with those misses. Correctly computed values after a deadline has passed are often useless.

For hard real-time systems, missing deadlines is not an option. In fact, in many cases, missing a deadline often results in catastrophe, which may involve human lives. For soft real-time systems, however, missing deadlines is generally not as critical.

Real-time applications cover a wide range, but many real-time systems are embedded. An embedded system is a computer built into a system and not acknowledged by the user as being a computer. The following list shows just a few examples of embedded systems:

Aerospace
- Flight management systems
- Jet engine controls
- Weapons systems

Audio
- MP3 players
- Amplifiers and tuners

Automotive
- Antilock braking systems
- Climate control
- Engine controls
- Navigation systems (GPS)

Communications
- Routers
- Switches
- Cell phones

Computer peripherals
- Printers
- Scanners

Domestic
- Air conditioning units
- Thermostats
- White goods

Office automation
- FAX machines / copiers

Process control
- Chemical plants
- Factory automation
- Food processing

Robots

Video
- Broadcasting equipment
- HD Televisions

And many more

Real-time systems are typically more complicated to design, debug, and deploy than non-real-time systems.

1-1 FOREGROUND/BACKGROUND SYSTEMS

Small systems of low complexity are typically designed as foreground/background systems or super-loops. An application consists of an infinite loop that calls modules (i.e., tasks) to perform the desired operations (background). Interrupt Service Routines (ISRs) handle asynchronous events (foreground). Foreground is also called interrupt level; background is called task level.

Critical operations that should be performed at the task level must unfortunately be handled by the ISRs to ensure that they are dealt with in a timely fashion. This causes ISRs to take longer than they should. Also, information for a background module that an ISR makes available is not processed until the background routine gets its turn to execute, which is called the task-level response. The worst-case task-level response time depends on how long a background loop takes to execute since the execution time of typical code is not constant, the time for successive passes through a portion of the loop is nondeterministic. Furthermore, if a code change is made, the timing of the loop is affected.

Most high-volume and low-cost microcontroller-based applications (e.g., microwave ovens, telephones, toys, etc.) are designed as foreground/background systems.

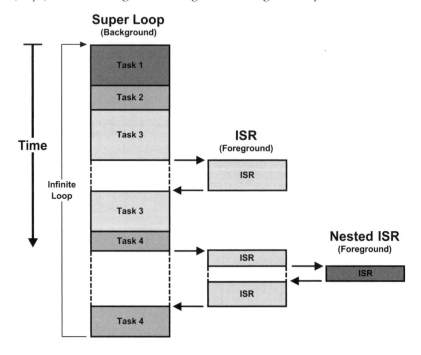

Figure 1-1 **Foreground/Background (SuperLoops) systems**

1-2 REAL-TIME KERNELS

A real-time kernel is software that manages the time and resources of a microprocessor, microcontroller or Digital Signal Processor (DSP).

The design process of a real-time application involves splitting the work into tasks, each responsible for a portion of the job. A task (also called a thread) is a simple program that thinks it has the Central Processing Unit (CPU) completely to itself. On a single CPU, only one task executes at any given time.

The kernel is responsible for the management of tasks. This is called multitasking. Multitasking is the process of scheduling and switching the CPU between several tasks. The CPU switches its attention between several sequential tasks. Multitasking provides the illusion of having multiple CPUs and maximizes the use of the CPU. Multitasking also helps in the creation of modular applications. One of the most important aspects of multitasking is that it allows the application programmer to manage the complexity inherent in real-time applications. Application programs are easier to design and maintain when multitasking is used.

µC/OS-III is a preemptive kernel, which means that µC/OS-III always runs the most important task that is ready to run as shown in Figure 1-2.

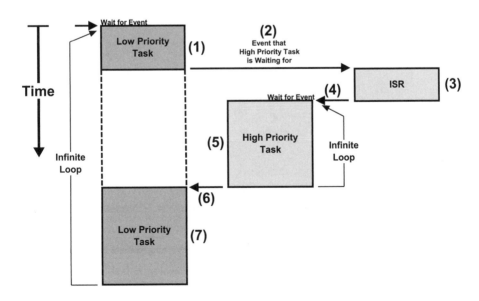

Figure 1-2 **µC/OS-III is a preemptive kernel**

FI-2(1)   A low-priority task is executing.

FI-2(2)   An interrupt occurs, and the CPU vectors to the ISR responsible for servicing the interrupting device.

FI-2(3)   The ISR services the interrupt device, but actually does very little work. The ISR will signal or send a message to a higher-priority task that will be responsible for most of the processing of the interrupting device. For example, if the interrupt comes from an Ethernet controller, the ISR simply signals a task, which will process the received packet.

FI-2(4)   When the ISR finishes, µC/OS-III notices that a more important task has been made ready to run by the ISR and will not return to the interrupted task, but instead context switch to the more important task.

FI-2(5)   The higher-priority task executes and performs the necessary processing in response to the interrupt device.

FI-2(6)   When the higher-priority task completes its work, it loops back to the beginning of the task code and makes a µC/OS-III function call to wait for the next interrupt from the device.

FI-2(7)   The low-priority task resumes exactly at the point where it was interrupted, not knowing what happened.

Kernels such as µC/OS-III are also responsible for managing communication between tasks, and managing system resources (memory and I/O devices).

A kernel adds overhead to a system because the services provided by the kernel require time to execute. The amount of overhead depends on how often these services are invoked. In a well-designed application, a kernel uses between 2% and 4% of a CPU's time. And, since µC/OS-III is software that is added to an application, it requires extra ROM (code space) and RAM (data space).

Low-end single-chip microcontrollers are generally not able to run a real-time kernel such as µC/OS-III since they have access to very little RAM. µC/OS-III requires between 1 Kbyte and 4 Kbytes of RAM, plus each task requires its own stack space. It is possible for µC/OS-III to work on processors having as little as 4 Kbytes of RAM.

Finally, µC/OS-III allows for better use of the CPU by providing approximately 70 indispensable services. After designing a system using a real-time kernel such as µC/OS-III, you will not return to designing a foreground/background system.

1-3 RTOS (REAL-TIME OPERATING SYSTEM)

A Real Time Operating System generally contains a real-time kernel and other higher-level services such as file management, protocol stacks, a Graphical User Interface (GUI), and other components. Most additional services revolve around I/O devices.

Micrium offers a complete suite of RTOS components including: µC/FS (an Embedded File System), µC/TCP-IP (a TCP/IP stack), µC/GUI (a Graphical User Interface), µC/USB (a USB device, host and OTG stack), and more. Most of these components are designed to work standalone. Except for µC/TCP-IP, a real-time kernel is not required to use the components in an application. In fact, users can pick and choose only the components required for the application. Contact Micrium (www.micrium.com) for additional details and pricing.

1-4 µC/OS-III

µC/OS-III is a scalable, ROMable, preemptive real-time kernel that manages an unlimited number of tasks. µC/OS-III is a third-generation kernel, offering all of the services expected from a modern real-time kernel including resource management, synchronization, inter-task communication, and more. However, µC/OS-III also offers many unique features not found in other real-time kernels, such as the ability to perform performance measurements at run time, directly signal or send messages to tasks, and pending (i.e., waiting) on such multiple kernel objects as semaphores and message queues.

Here is a list of features provided by µC/OS-III:

Source Code: µC/OS-III is provided in ANSI-C source form to licensees. The source code for µC/OS-III is arguably the cleanest and most consistent kernel code available. Clean source is part of the corporate culture at Micrium. Although many commercial kernel vendors provide source code for their products, unless the code follows strict coding standards and is accompanied by complete documentation with examples to show how the code works, these products may be cumbersome and difficult to harness. With this book, you will gain a deep understanding of the inner workings of µC/OS-III, which will protect your investment.

Intuitive Application Programming Interface (API): µC/OS-III is highly intuitive. Once familiar with the consistent coding conventions used, it is simple to predict the functions to call for the services required, and even predict which arguments are needed. For example, a pointer to an object is always the first argument, and a pointer to an error code is always the last one.

Preemptive multitasking: µC/OS-III is a preemptive multi-tasking kernel and therefore, µC/OS-III always runs the most important ready-to-run task.

Round robin scheduling of tasks at equal priority: µC/OS-III allows multiple tasks to run at the same priority level. When multiple tasks at the same priority are ready to run, and that priority level is the most important level, µC/OS-III runs each task for a user-specified time called a time quanta. Each task can define its own time quanta, and a task can also give up the CPU to another task at the same priority if it does not require the full time quanta.

Low interrupt disable time: µC/OS-III has a number of internal data structures and variables that it needs to access atomically. To ensure this, µC/OS-III is able to protect these critical regions by locking the scheduler instead of disabling interrupts. Interrupts are therefore disabled for very little time. This ensures that µC/OS-III is able to respond to some of the fastest interrupt sources.

Deterministic: Interrupt response with µC/OS-III is deterministic. Also, execution times of most services provided by µC/OS-III are deterministic.

Scalable: The footprint (both code and data) can be adjusted based on the requirements of the application. This assumes access to the source code for µC/OS-III since adding and removing features (i.e., services) is performed at compile time through approximately 40 #defines (see OS_CFG.H). µC/OS-III also performs a number of run-time checks on arguments passed to µC/OS-III services. Specifically, µC/OS-III verifies that the user is not passing NULL pointers, not calling task level services from ISRs, that arguments are within allowable range, and options specified are valid, etc.. These checks can be disabled (at compile time) to further reduce the code footprint and improve performance. The fact that µC/OS-III is scalable allows it to be used in a wide range of applications and projects.

Portable: µC/OS-III can be ported to a large number of CPU architectures. Most µC/OS-II ports are easily converted to work on µC/OS-III with minimal changes in just a matter of minutes and therefore benefit from more than 45 CPU architectures already supported by µC/OS-II.

ROMable: µC/OS-III was designed especially for embedded systems and can be ROMed along with the application code.

Run-time configurable: µC/OS-III allows the user to configure the kernel at run time. Specifically, all kernel objects such as tasks, stacks, semaphores, event-flag groups, message queues, number of messages, mutual exclusion semaphores, memory partitions and timers, are allocated by the user at run time. This prevents over-allocating resources at compile time.

Unlimited number of tasks: µC/OS-III supports an unlimited number of tasks. From a practical standpoint, however, the number of tasks is actually limited by the amount of memory (both code and data space) that the processor has access to. Each task requires its own stack space and, µC/OS-III provides features to allow stack growth of the tasks to be monitored at run-time.

µC/OS-III does not impose any limitations on the size of each task, except that there be a minimum size based on the CPU used.

Unlimited number of priorities: µC/OS-III supports an unlimited number of priority levels. However, configuring µC/OS-III for between 32 and 256 different priority levels is more than adequate for most applications.

Unlimited number of kernel objects: µC/OS-III allows for any number of tasks, semaphores, mutual exclusion semaphores, event flags, message queues, timers, and memory partitions. The user at run-time allocates all kernel objects.

Services: µC/OS-III provides all the services expected from a high-end real-time kernel, such as task management, time management, semaphores, event flags, mutexes, message queues, software timers, fixed-size memory pools, etc.

Mutual Exclusion Semaphores (Mutexes): Mutexes are provided for resource management. Mutexes are special types of semaphores that have built-in priority inheritance, which eliminate unbounded priority inversions. Accesses to a mutex can be nested and therefore, a task can acquire the same mutex up to 250 times. Of course, the mutex owner needs to release the mutex an equal number of times.

Nested task suspension: μC/OS-III allows a task to suspend itself or another task. Suspending a task means that the task will not be allowed to execute until the task is resumed by another task. Suspension can be nested up to 250 levels deep. In other words, a task can suspend another task up to 250 times. Of course, the task must be resumed an equal number of times for it to become eligible to run on the CPU.

Software timers: Define any number of "one-shot" and/or "periodic" timers. Timers are countdown counters that perform a user-definable action upon counting down to 0. Each timer can have its own action and, if a timer is periodic, the timer is automatically reloaded and the action is executed every time the countdown reaches zero.

Pend on multiple objects: μC/OS-III allows an application to wait (i.e., pend) on multiple events at the same time. Specifically, a task can wait on multiple semaphores and/or message queues to be posted. The waiting task wakes up as soon as one of the events occurs.

Task Signals: μC/OS-III allows an ISR or task to directly signal a task. This avoids having to create an intermediate kernel object such as a semaphore or event flag just to signal a task, and results in better performance.

Task Messages: μC/OS-III allows an ISR or a task to send messages directly to a task. This avoids having to create and use a message queue, and also results in better performance.

Task registers: Each task can have a user-definable number of "task registers." Task registers are different than CPU registers. Task registers can be used to hold "errno" type variable, IDs, interrupt disable time measurement on a per-task basis, and more.

Error checking: μC/OS-III verifies that **NULL** pointers are not passed, that the user is not calling task-level services from ISRs, that arguments are within allowable range, that options specified are valid, that a handler is passed to the proper object as part of the arguments to services that manipulate the desired object, and more. Each μC/OS-III API function returns an error code concerning the outcome of the function call.

Built-in performance measurements: μC/OS-III has built-in features to measure the execution time of each task, stack usage of each task, number of times a task executes, CPU usage, ISR-to-task and task-to-task response time, peak number of entries in certain lists, interrupt disable and scheduler lock time on a per-task basis, and more.

Can easily be optimized: µC/OS-III was designed so that it could easily be optimized based on the CPU architecture. Most data types used in µC/OS-III can be changed to make better use of the CPU's natural word size. Also, the priority resolution algorithm can easily be written in assembly language to benefit from special instructions such as bit set and clear, as well as count-leading-zeros (CLZ), or find-first-one (FF1) instructions.

Deadlock prevention: All of the µC/OS-III "pend" services include timeouts, which help avoid deadlocks.

Tick handling at task level: The clock tick manager in µC/OS-III is accomplished by a task that receives a trigger from an ISR. Handling delays and timeouts by a task greatly reduces interrupt latency. Also, µC/OS-III uses a hashed delta list mechanism, which further reduces the amount of overhead in processing delays and timeouts of tasks.

User definable hooks: µC/OS-III allows the port and application programmer to define "hook" functions, which are called by µC/OS-III. A hook is simply a defined function that allows the user to extend the functionality of µC/OS-III. One such hook is called during a context switch, another when a task is created, yet another when a task is deleted, etc.

Timestamps: For time measurements, µC/OS-III requires that a 16-bit or 32-bit free running counter be made available. This counter can be read at run time to make time measurements of certain events. For example, when an ISR posts a message to a task, the timestamp counter is automatically read and saved as part of the message posted. When the recipient receives the message, the timestamp is provided to the recipient, and by reading the current timestamp, the time it took for the message to be received can be determined.

Built-in support for Kernel Awareness debuggers: This feature allows kernel awareness debuggers to examine and display µC/OS-III variables and data structures in a user-friendly way, but only when the debugger hits a breakpoint. Instead of a static view of the environment the kernel awareness support in µC/OS-III is also used by µC/Probe to display the same information at run-time.

Object names: Each µC/OS-III kernel object can have a name associated with it. This makes it easy to recognize what the object is assigned to. Assign an ASCII name to a task, a semaphore, a mutex, an event flag group, a message queue, a memory partition, and a timer. The object name can have any length, but must be NUL terminated.

1-5 µC/OS, µC/OS-II AND µC/OS-III FEATURES COMPARISON

Table 1-1 shows the evolution of µC/OS over the years, comparing the features available in each version.

Feature	µC/OS	µC/OS-II	µC/OS-III
Year introduced	1992	1998	2009
Book	Yes	Yes	Yes
Source code available	Yes	Yes	Yes (Licensees only)
Preemptive Multitasking	Yes	Yes	Yes
Maximum number of tasks	64	255	Unlimited
Number of tasks at each priority level	1	1	Unlimited
Round Robin Scheduling	No	No	Yes
Semaphores	Yes	Yes	Yes
Mutual Exclusion Semaphores	No	Yes	Yes (Nestable)
Event Flags	No	Yes	Yes
Message Mailboxes	Yes	Yes	No (not needed)
Message Queues	Yes	Yes	Yes
Fixed Sized Memory Management	No	Yes	Yes
Signal a task without requiring a semaphore	No	No	Yes
Send messages to a task without requiring a message queue	No	No	Yes
Software Timers	No	Yes	Yes
Task suspend/resume	No	Yes	Yes (Nestable)
Deadlock prevention	Yes	Yes	Yes
Scalable	Yes	Yes	Yes
Code Footprint	3K to 8K	6K to 26K	6K to 20K
Data Footprint	1K+	1K+	1K+
ROMable	Yes	Yes	Yes

Feature	µC/OS	µC/OS-II	µC/OS-III
Run-time configurable	No	No	Yes
Compile-time configurable	Yes	Yes	Yes
ASCII names for each kernel object	No	Yes	Yes
Pend on multiple objects	No	Yes	Yes
Task registers	No	Yes	Yes
Built-in performance measurements	No	Limited	Extensive
User definable hook functions	No	Yes	Yes
Time stamps on posts	No	No	Yes
Built-in Kernel Awareness support	No	Yes	Yes
Optimizable Scheduler in assembly language	No	No	Yes
Tick handling at task level	No	No	Yes
Source code available	Yes	Yes	Yes
Number of services	~20	~90	~70
MISRA-C:1998	No	Yes (except 10 rules)	N/A
MISRA-C:2004	No	No	Yes (except 7 rules)
DO178B Level A and EUROCAE ED-12B	No	Yes	In progress
Medical FDA pre-market notification (510(k)) and pre-market approval (PMA)	No	Yes	In progress
SIL3/SIL4 IEC for transportation and nuclear systems	No	Yes	In progress
IEC-61508	No	Yes	In progress

Table 1-1 **µC/OS-II and µC/OS-III Features Comparison Chart**

1-6 HOW THE BOOK IS ORGANIZED

This book consists of two books in one.

Part I describes μC/OS-III and is not tied to any specific CPU architecture. Here, the reader will learn about real-time kernels through μC/OS-III. Specifically, critical sections, task management, the ready list, scheduling, context switching, interrupt management, wait lists, time management, timers, resource management, synchronization, memory management, how to use μC/OS-III's API, how to configure μC/OS-III, and how to port μC/OS-III to different CPU architectures, are all covered.

Part II describes the port of a popular CPU architecture. Here, learn about this CPU architecture and how μC/OS-III gets the most out of the CPU. Examples are provided to actually run code on the evaluation board that is available with this book.

As I just mentioned, this book assumes the presence of an evaluation board that allows the user to experiment with the wonderful world of real-time kernels, and specifically μC/OS-III. The book and board are complemented by a full set of tools that are provided free of charge either in a companion CD/DVD, or downloadable through the Internet. The tools and the use of μC/OS-III are free as long as they are used with the evaluation board, and there is no commercial intent to use them on a project. In other words, there is no additional charge except for the initial cost of the book, evaluation board and tools, as long as they are used for educational purposes.

The book also comes with a trial version of an award-winning tool from Micriµm called μC/Probe. The trial version allows the user to monitor and change up to five variables in a target system.

1-7 μC/PROBE

μC/Probe is a Microsoft Windows™ based application that enables the user to visualize variables in a target at run time. Specifically, display or change the value of any variable in a system while the target is running. These variables can be displayed using such graphical elements as gauges, meters, bar graphs, virtual LEDs, numeric indicators, and many more. Sliders, switches, and buttons can be used to change variables. This is accomplished without the user writing a single line of code!

µC/Probe interfaces to any target (8-, 16-, 32-, 64-bit, or even DSPs) through one of the many interfaces supported (J-Tag, RS-232C, USB, Ethernet, etc.). µC/Probe displays or changes any variable (as long as they are global) in the application, including µC/OS-III's internal variables.

µC/Probe works with any compiler/assembler/linker able to generate an ELF/DWARF or IEEE695 file. This is the exact same file that the user will download to the evaluation board or a final target. From this file, µC/Probe is able to extract symbolic information about variables, and determine where variables are stored in RAM or ROM.

µC/Probe also allows users to log the data displayed into a file for analysis of the collected data at a later time. µC/Probe also provides µC/OS-III kernel awareness as a built-in feature.

The trial version that accompanies the book is limited to the display or change of up to five variables.

µC/Probe is a tool that serious embedded software engineers should have in their toolbox. The full version of µC/Probe is included when licensing µC/OS-III. See www.micrium.com for more details.

1-8 CONVENTIONS

There are a number of conventions in this book.

First, notice that when a specific element in a figure is referenced, the element has a number next to it in parenthesis. A description of this element follows the figure and in this case, the letter "F" followed by the figure number, and then the number in parenthesis. For example, F3-4(2) indicates that this description refers to Figure 3-4 and the element (2) in that figure. This convention also applies to listings (starts with an "L") and tables (starts with a "T").

Second, notice that sections and listings are started where it makes sense. Specifically, do not be surprised to see the bottom half of a page empty. New sections begin on a new page, and listings are found on a single page, instead of breaking listings on two pages.

Third, code quality is something I've been avidly promoting throughout my whole career. At Micrium, we pride ourselves in having the cleanest code in the industry. Examples of this are seen in this book. I created and published a coding standard in 1992 that was published in the original µC/OS book. This standard has evolved over the years, but the spirit of the standard has been maintained throughout. The Micrium coding standard is available for download from the Micrium website, www.micrium.com

One of the conventions used is that all functions, variables, macros and **#define** constants are prefixed by "OS" (which stands for Operating System) followed by the acronym of the module (e.g., **Sem**), and then the operation performed by the function. For example **OSSemPost()** indicates that the function belongs to the OS (µC/OS-III), that it is part of the Semaphore services, and specifically that the function performs a **Post** (i.e., signal) operation. This allows all related functions to be grouped together in the reference manual, and makes those services intuitive to use.

Notice that signaling or sending a message to a task is called posting, and waiting for a signal or a message is called pending. In other words, an ISR or a task signals or sends a message to another task by using **OS???Post()**, where **???** is the type of service: **Sem**, **TaskSem**, **Flag**, **Mutex**, **Q**, and **TaskQ**. Similarly, a task can wait for a signal or a message by calling **OS???Pend()**.

1-9 CHAPTER CONTENTS

Figure 1-3 shows the layout and flow of Part I of the book. This diagram should be useful to understand the relationship between chapters. The first column on the left indicates chapters that should be read in order to understand µC/OS-III's structure. The second column shows chapters that are related to additional services provided by µC/OS-III. The third column relates to chapters that will help port µC/OS-III to different CPU architectures. The top of the fourth column explains how to obtain valuable run-time and compile-time statistics from µC/OS-III. This is especially useful if developing a kernel awareness plug-in for a debugger, or using µC/Probe. The middle of column four contains the µC/OS-III API and configuration manuals. Reference these sections regularly when designing a product using µC/OS-III. Finally, the bottom of the last column contains miscellaneous appendices.

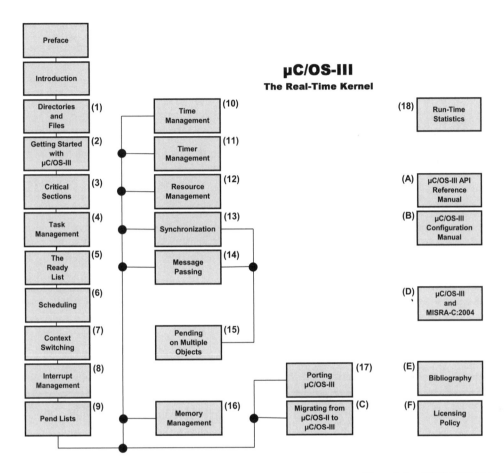

Figure 1-3 **µC/OS-III Book Layout**

Chapter 1, Directories and Files. This chapter explains the directory structure and files needed to build a µC/OS-III-based application. Learn about the files that are needed, where they should be placed, which module does what, and more.

Chapter 2, Getting Started with µC/OS-III. In this chapter, learn how to properly initialize and start a µC/OS-III-based application.

Chapter 3, Critical Sections. This chapter explains what critical sections are, and how they are protected.

Chapter 4, Task Management. This chapter is an introduction to one of the most important aspects of a real-time kernel, the management of tasks in a multitasking environment.

Chapter 5, The Ready List. In this chapter, learn how µC/OS-III efficiently keeps track of all of the tasks that are waiting to execute on the CPU.

Chapter 6, Scheduling. This chapter explains the scheduling algorithms used by µC/OS-III, and how it decides which task will run next.

Chapter 7, Context Switching. This chapter explains what a context switch is, and describes the process of suspending execution of a task and resuming execution of a higher-priority task.

Chapter 8, Interrupt Management. Here is how µC/OS-III deals with interrupts and an overview of services that are available from Interrupt Service Routines (ISRs). Learn how µC/OS-III supports nearly any interrupt controller.

Chapter 9, Pend Lists (or Wait Lists). Tasks that are not able to run are most likely blocked waiting for specific events to occur. Pend Lists (or wait lists), are used to keep track of tasks that are waiting for a resource or event. This chapter describes how µC/OS-III maintains these lists.

Chapter 10, Time Management. In this chapter, learn about µC/OS-III's services that allow users to suspend a task until some time expires. With µC/OS-III, specify to delay execution of a task for an integral number of clock ticks or until the clock-tick counter reaches a certain value. The chapter will also show how a delayed task can be resumed, and describe how to get the current value of the clock tick counter, or set this counter, if needed.

Chapter 11, Timer Management. µC/OS-III allows users to define any number of software timers. When a timer expires, a function can be called to perform some action. Timers can be configured to be either periodic or one-shot. This chapter also explains how the timer-management module works.

Chapter 12, Resource Management. In this chapter, learn different techniques so that tasks share resources. Each of these techniques has advantages and disadvantages that will be discussed. This chapter also explains the internals of semaphores, and mutual exclusion semaphore management.

Chapter 13, Synchronization. µC/OS-III provides two types of services for synchronization: semaphores and event flags and these are explained in this chapter, as well as what happens when calling specific services provided in this module.

Chapter 14, Message Passing. μC/OS-III allows a task or an ISR to send messages to a task. This chapter describes some of the services provided by the message queue management module.

Chapter 15, Pending on multiple objects. In this chapter, see how μC/OS-III allows an application to pend (or wait) on multiple kernel objects (semaphores or message queues) at the same time. This feature makes the waiting task ready to run as soon as any one of the objects is posted (i.e., OR condition), or a timeout occurs.

Chapter 16, Memory Management. Here is how μC/OS-III's fixed-size memory partition manager can be used to allocate and deallocate dynamic memory.

Chapter 17, Porting μC/OS-III. This chapter explains, in generic terms, how to port μC/OS-III to any CPU architecture.

Chapter 18, Run-Time Statistics. μC/OS-III provides a wealth of information about the run-time environment, such as number of context switches, CPU usage (as a percentage), stack usage on a per-task basis, μC/OS-III RAM usage, maximum interrupt disable time, maximum scheduler lock time, and more.

Appendix A, μC/OS-III API Reference Manual. This appendix provides a alphabetical reference for all user-available services provided by μC/OS-III.

Appendix B, μC/OS-III Configuration Manual. This appendix describes how to configure a μC/OS-III-based application. OS_CFG.H configures the μC/OS-III features (semaphores, queues, event flags, etc.), while OS_CFG_APP.H configures the run-time characteristics (tick rate, tick wheel size, stack size for the idle task, etc.).

Appendix C, Migrating from μC/OS-II to μC/OS-III. μC/OS-III has its roots in μC/OS-II and, in fact, most of the μC/OS-II ports can be easily converted to μC/OS-III. However, most APIs have changed from μC/OS-II to μC/OS-III, and this appendix describes some of the differences.

Appendix D, MISRA-C:2004 rules and μC/OS-III. μC/OS-III follows most of the MISRA-C:2004, except for 7 of these rules.

Appendix E, Bibliography.

Appendix F, Licensing μC/OS-III.

1-10 LICENSING

This book contains µC/OS-III precompiled in linkable object form, an evaluation board, and tools (compiler/assembler/linker/debugger). Use µC/OS-III for free, as long as it is only used with the evaluation board that accompanies this book. You will need to purchase a license when using this code in a commercial project, where the intent is to make a profit. Users do not pay anything beyond the price of the book, evaluation board and tools, as long as they are used for educational purposes.

You will need to license µC/OS-III if you intend to use µC/OS-III in a commercial product where you intend to make a profit. You need to purchase this license when you make the decision to use µC/OS-III in a design, not when you are ready to go to production.

If you are unsure about whether you need to obtain a license for your application, please contact Micriµm and discuss your use with a sales representative.

1-11 CONTACTING MICRIUM

Do not hesitate to contact Micriµm should you have any licensing questions regarding µC/OS-III.

Micriµm
1290 Weston Road, Suite 306
Weston, FL 33326

+1 954 217 2036
+1 954 217 2037 (FAX)

E-Mail: sales@micrium.com

Website: www.micrium.com

Directories and Files

µC/OS-III is fairly easy to use once it is understood exactly which source files are needed to make up a µC/OS-III-based application. This chapter will discuss the modules available for µC/OS-III and how everything fits together.

Figure 2-1 shows the µC/OS-III architecture and its relationship with hardware. Of course, in addition to the timer and interrupt controller, hardware would most likely contain such other devices as Universal Asynchronous Receiver Transmitters (UARTs), Analog to Digital Converters (ADCs), Ethernet controller(s) and more.

This chapter assumes development on a Windows®-based platform and makes references to typical Windows-type directory structures (also called Folder). However, since µC/OS-III is available in source form, it can also be used on Unix, Linux or other development platforms.

The names of the files are shown in upper case to make them "stand out". However, file names are actually lower case.

Figure 2-1 **µC/OS-III Architecture**

F2-1(1)   The application code consists of project or product files. For convenience, these are simply called **APP.C** and **APP.H**, however an application can contain any number of files that do not have to be called **APP.***. The application code is typically where one would find **main()**.

F2-1(2)   Semiconductor manufacturers often provide library functions in source form for accessing the peripherals on their CPU or MCU. These libraries are quite useful and often save valuable time. Since there is no naming convention for these files, ***.C** and ***.H** are assumed.

F2-1(3)   The Board Support Package (BSP) is code that is typically written to interface to peripherals on a target board. For example such code can turn on and off Light Emitting Diodes (LEDs), turn on and off relays, or code to read switches, temperature sensors, and more.

F2-1(4)   This is the µC/OS-III processor-independent code. This code is written in highly portable ANSI C and is available to µC/OS-III licensees only.

F2-1(5)   This is the µC/OS-III code that is adapted to a specific CPU architecture and is called a port. µC/OS-III has its roots in µC/OS-II and benefits from being able to use most of the 45 or so ports available for µC/OS-II. µC/OS-II ports, however, will require small changes to work with µC/OS-III. These changes are described in Appendix C, "Migrating from µC/OS-II to µC/OS-III" on page 607.

F2-1(6)   At Micriµm, we like to encapsulate CPU functionality. These files define functions to disable and enable interrupts, **CPU_???** data types to be independent of the CPU and compiler used, and many more functions.

F2-1(7)   µC/LIB is of a series of source files that provide common functions such as memory copy, string, and ASCII-related functions. Some are occasionally used to replace **stdlib** functions provided by the compiler. The files are provided to ensure that they are fully portable from application to application and especially, from compiler to compiler. µC/OS-III does not use these files, but µC/CPU does.

F2-1(8)   µC/OS-III configuration files defines µC/OS-III features (**OS_CFG.H**) to include in the application, and specifies the size of certain variables and data structures expected by µC/OS-III (**OS_CFG_APP.H**), such as idle task stack size, tick rate, size of the message pool, etc.

2-1 APPLICATION CODE

When Micriµm provides example projects, they are placed in a directory structure shown below. Of course, a directory structure that suits a particular project/product can be used.

```
\Micrium
    \Software
        \EvalBoards
            \<manufacturer>
                \<board_name>
                    \<compiler>
                        \<project name>
                            \*.*
```

\Micrium

This is where we place all software components and projects provided by Micriµm. This directory generally starts from the root directory of the computer.

\Software

This sub-directory contains all software components and projects.

\EvalBoards

This sub-directory contains all projects related to evaluation boards supported by Micriµm.

\<manufacturer>

This is the name of the manufacturer of the evaluation board. The "<" and ">" are not part of the actual name.

\<board name>

This is the name of the evaluation board. A board from Micriµm will typically be called **uC-Eval-xxxx** where "**xxxx**" represents the CPU or MCU used on the board. The "<" and ">" are not part of the actual name.

\<compiler>

This is the name of the compiler or compiler manufacturer used to build the code for the evaluation board. The "<" and ">" are not part of the actual name.

\<project name>

The name of the project that will be demonstrated. For example, a simple µC/OS-III project might have a project name of "**OS–Ex1**". The "**–Ex1**" represents a project containing only µC/OS-III. The project name **OS–Probe–Ex1** contains µC/OS-III and µC/Probe.

.

These are the project source files. Main files can optionally be called **APP*.***. This directory also contains configuration files **OS_CFG.H**, **OS_CFG_APP.H** and other required source files.

2-2 CPU

The directory where you will find semiconductor manufacturer peripheral interface source files is shown below. Any directory structure that suits the project/product may be used.

```
\Micrium
    \Software
        \CPU
            \<manufacturer>
                \<architecture>
                    \*.*
```

\Micrium

The location of all software components and projects provided by Micriµm.

\Software

This sub-directory contains all software components and projects.

\CPU

This sub-directory is always called CPU.

\<manufacturer>

Is the name of the semiconductor manufacturer providing the peripheral library.

\<architecture>

The name of the specific library, generally associated with a CPU name or an architecture.

.

Indicates library source files. The semiconductor manufacturer names the files.

2-3 BOARD SUPPORT PACKAGE (BSP)

The Board Support Package (BSP) is generally found with the evaluation or target board as it is specific to that board. In fact, when well written, the BSP should be used for multiple projects.

```
\Micrium
    \Software
        \EvalBoards
            \<manufacturer>
                \<board name>
                    \<compiler>
                        \BSP
                            \*.*
```

\Micrium

Contains all software components and projects provided by Micriµm.

\Software

This sub-directory contains all software components and projects.

\EvalBoards

This sub-directory contains all projects related to evaluation boards.

\<manufacturer>

The name of the manufacturer of the evaluation board. The "<" and ">" are not part of the actual name.

\<board name>

The name of the evaluation board. A board from Micriµm will typically be called **uC-Eval-xxxx** where "**xxxx**" is the name of the CPU or MCU used on the evaluation board. The "<" and ">" are not part of the actual name.

\<compiler>

The name of the compiler or compiler manufacturer used to build code for the evaluation board. The "<" and ">" are not part of the actual name.

\BSP

This directory is always called BSP.

.

The source files of the BSP. Typically all of the file names start with BSP. It is therefore normal to find **BSP.C** and **BSP.H** in this directory. BSP code should contain such functions as LED control functions, initialization of timers, interface to Ethernet controllers and more.

2-4 µC/OS-III, CPU INDEPENDENT SOURCE CODE

The files in these directories are available to µC/OS-III licensees (see Appendix F, "Licensing Policy" on page 653).

```
\Micrium
    \Software
        \uCOS-III
            \Cfg\Template
                \OS_APP_HOOKS.C
                \OS_CFG.H
                \OS_CFG_APP.H
            \Source
                \OS_CFG_APP.C
                \OS_CORE.C
                \OS_DBG.C
                \OS_FLAG.C
                \OS_INT.C
                \OS_MEM.C
                \OS_MSG.C
                \OS_MUTEX.C
                \OS_PEND_MULTI.C
                \OS_PRIO.C
                \OS_Q.C
                \OS_SEM.C
                \OS_STAT.C
                \OS_TASK.C
                \OS_TICK.C
                \OS_TIME.C
```

```
\OS_TMR.C
\OS_VAR
\OS.H
\OS_TYPE.H
```

\Micrium

Contains all software components and projects provided by Micriµm.

\Software

This sub-directory contains all software components and projects.

\uCOS-III

This is the main µC/OS-III directory.

\Cfg\Template

This directory contains examples of configuration files to copy to the project directory. You will then modify these files to suit the needs of the application.

OS_APP_HOOKS.C shows how to write hook functions that are called by µC/OS-III. Specifically, this file contains eight empty functions.

OS_CFG.H specifies which features of µC/OS-III are available for an application. The file is typically copied into an application directory and edited based on which features are required from µC/OS-III. If µC/OS-III is provided in linkable object code format, this file will be provided to indicate features that are available in the object file. See Appendix B, "µC/OS-III Configuration Manual" on page 587.

OS_CFG_APP.H is a configuration file to be copied into an application directory and edited based on application requirements. This file enables the user to determine the size of the idle task stack, the tick rate, the number of messages available in the message pool and more. See Appendix B, "µC/OS-III Configuration Manual" on page 587.

\Source

The directory containing the CPU-independent source code for µC/OS-III. All files in this directory should be included in the build (assuming you have the source code). Features that are not required will be compiled out based on the value of **#define** constants in OS_CFG.H and OS_CFG_APP.H.

OS_CFG_APP.C declares variables and arrays based on the values in **OS_CFG_APP.H**.

OS_CORE.C contains core functionality for µC/OS-III such as OSInit() to initialize µC/OS-III, OSSched() for the task level scheduler, OSIntExit() for the interrupt level scheduler, pend list (or wait list) management (see Chapter 10, "Pend Lists (or Wait Lists)" on page 185), ready list management (see Chapter 6, "The Ready List" on page 131), and more.

OS_DBG.C contains declarations of constant variables used by a kernel aware debugger or µC/Probe.

OS_FLAG.C contains the code for event flag management. See Chapter 14, "Synchronization" on page 259 for details about event flags.

OS_INT.C contains code for the interrupt handler task, which is used when

OS_CFG_ISR_POST_DEFERRED_EN (see **OS_CFG.H**) is set to 1. See Chapter 9, "Interrupt Management" on page 165 for details regarding the interrupt handler task.

OS_MEM.C contains code for the µC/OS-III fixed-size memory manager, see Chapter 17, "Memory Management" on page 331.

OS_MSG.C contains code to handle messages. µC/OS-III provides message queues and task specific message queues. **OS_MSG.C** provides common code for these two services. See Chapter 15, "Message Passing" on page 297.

OS_MUTEX.C contains code to manage mutual exclusion semaphores, see Chapter 13, "Resource Management" on page 217.

OS_PEND_MULTI.C contains the code to allow code to pend on multiple semaphores or message queues. This is described in Chapter 16, "Pending On Multiple Objects" on page 321.

OS_PRIO.C contains the code to manage the bitmap table used to keep track of which tasks are ready to run, see Chapter 6, "The Ready List" on page 131. This file can be replaced by an assembly language equivalent to improve performance if the CPU used provides bit set, clear and test instructions, and a count leading zeros instruction.

OS_Q.C contains code to manage message queues. See Chapter 15, "Message Passing" on page 297.

OS_SEM.C contains code to manage semaphores used for resource management and/or synchronization. See Chapter 13, "Resource Management" on page 217 and Chapter 14, "Synchronization" on page 259.

OS_STAT.C contains code for the statistic task, which is used to compute the global CPU usage and the CPU usage of each of tasks. See Chapter 5, "Task Management" on page 83.

OS_TASK.C contains code for managing tasks using `OSTaskCreate()`, `OSTaskDel()`, `OSTaskChangePrio()`, and many more. See Chapter 5, "Task Management" on page 83.

OS_TICK.C contains code to manage tasks that have delayed themselves or that are pending on a kernel object with a timeout. See Chapter 5, "Task Management" on page 83.

OS_TIME.C contains code to allow a task to delay itself until some time expires. See Chapter 11, "Time Management" on page 191.

OS_TMR.C contains code to manage software timers. See Chapter 12, "Timer Management" on page 201.

OS_VAR.C contains the µC/OS-III global variables. These variables are for µC/OS-III to manage and should not be accessed by application code.

OS.H contains the main µC/OS-III header file, which declares constants, macros, µC/OS-III global variables (for use by µC/OS-III only), function prototypes, and more.

OS_TYPE.H contains declarations of µC/OS-III data types that can be changed by the port designed to make better use of the CPU architecture. In this case, the file would typically be copied to the port directory and then modified. µC/OS-III in linkable object library format provides this file to enable the user to know what each data type maps to. See Appendix B, "µC/OS-III Configuration Manual" on page 587.

2-5 μC/OS-III, CPU SPECIFIC SOURCE CODE

The μC/OS-III port developer provides these files. See also Chapter 18, "Porting μC/OS-III" on page 343.

```
\Micrium
    \Software
        \uCOS-III
            \Ports
                \<architecture>
                    \<compiler>
                        \OS_CPU.H
                        \OS_CPU_A.ASM
                        \OS_CPU_C.C
```

\Micrium
Contains all software components and projects provided by Micriµm.

\Software
This sub-directory contains all software components and projects.

\uCOS-III
The main μC/OS-III directory.

\Ports
The location of port files for the CPU architecture(s) to be used.

\<architecture>
This is the name of the CPU architecture that μC/OS-III was ported to. The "<" and ">" are not part of the actual name.

\<compiler>
The name of the compiler or compiler manufacturer used to build code for the port. The "<" and ">" are not part of the actual name.

The files in this directory contain the μC/OS-III port, see Chapter 18, "Porting μC/OS-III" on page 343 for details on the contents of these files.

OS_CPU.H contains a macro declaration for OS_TASK_SW(), as well as the function prototypes for at least the following functions: OSCtxSw(), OSIntCtxSw() and OSStartHighRdy().

OS_CPU_A.ASM contains the assembly language functions to implement at least the following functions: OSCtxSw(), OSIntCtxSw() and OSStartHighRdy().

OS_CPU_C.C contains the C code for the port specific hook functions and code to initialize the stack frame for a task when the task is created.

2-6 µC/CPU, CPU SPECIFIC SOURCE CODE

µC/CPU consists of files that encapsulate common CPU-specific functionality and CPU and compiler-specific data types. See Chapter 18, "Porting µC/OS-III" on page 343.

```
\Micrium
    \Software
        \uC-CPU
            \CPU_CORE.C
            \CPU_CORE.H
            \CPU_DEF.H
            \Cfg\Template
                \CPU_CFG.H
            \<architecture>
                \<compiler>
                    \CPU.H
                    \CPU_A.ASM
                    \CPU_C.C
```

\Micrium
Contains all software components and projects provided by Micrium.

\Software
This sub-directory contains all software components and projects.

\uC-CPU

This is the main μC/CPU directory.

CPU_CORE.C contains C code that is common to all CPU architectures. Specifically, this file contains functions to measure the interrupt disable time of the CPU_CRITICAL_ENTER() and CPU_CRITICAL_EXIT() macros, a function that emulates a count leading zeros instruction and a few other functions.

CPU_CORE.H contains function prototypes for the functions provided in CPU_CORE.C and allocation of the variables used by the module to measure interrupt disable time.

CPU_DEF.H contains miscellaneous #define constants used by the μC/CPU module.

\Cfg\Template

This directory contains a configuration template file (**CPU_CFG.H**) that must be copied to the application directory to configure the μC/CPU module based on application requirements.

CPU_CFG.H determines whether to enable measurement of the interrupt disable time, whether the CPU implements a count leading zeros instruction in assembly language, or whether it will be emulated in C, and more.

\<architecture>

The name of the CPU architecture that μC/CPU was ported to. The "<" and ">" are not part of the actual name.

\<compiler>

The name of the compiler or compiler manufacturer used to build code for the μC/CPU port. The "<" and ">" are not part of the actual name.

The files in this directory contain the μC/CPU port, see Chapter 18, "Porting μC/OS-III" on page 343 for details on the contents of these files.

CPU.H contains type definitions to make μC/OS-III and other modules independent of the CPU and compiler word sizes. Specifically, one will find the declaration of the CPU_INT16U, CPU_INT32U, CPU_FP32 and many other data types. This file also specifies whether the CPU is a big or little endian machine, defines the CPU_STK data type used by μC/OS-III, defines the macros OS_CRITICAL_ENTER() and OS_CRITICAL_EXIT(), and contains function prototypes for functions specific to the CPU architecture, and more.

CPU_A.ASM contains the assembly language functions to implement code to disable and enable CPU interrupts, count leading zeros (if the CPU supports that instruction), and other CPU specific functions that can only be written in assembly language. This file may also contain code to enable caches, setup MPUs and MMU, and more. The functions provided in this file are accessible from C.

CPU_C.C contains C code of functions that are based on a specific CPU architecture but written in C for portability. As a general rule, if a function can be written in C then it should be, unless there is significant performance benefits available by writing it in assembly language.

2-7 μC/LIB, PORTABLE LIBRARY FUNCTIONS

μC/LIB consists of library functions meant to be highly portable and not tied to any specific compiler. This facilitates third-party certification of Micrium products. μC/OS-III does not use any μC/LIB functions, however the μC/CPU assumes the presence of **LIB_DEF.H** for such definitions as: DEF_YES, DEF_NO, DEF_TRUE, DEF_FALSE, DEF_ON, DEF_OFF and more.

```
\Micrium
    \Software
        \uC-LIB
            \LIB_ASCII.C
            \LIB_ASCII.H
            \LIB_DEF.H
            \LIB_MATH.C
            \LIB_MATH.H
            \LIB_MEM.C
            \LIB_MEM.H
            \LIB_STR.C
            \LIB_STR.H
            \Cfg\Template
                \LIB_CFG.H
            \Ports
                \<architecture>
                    \<compiler>
                        \LIB_MEM_A.ASM
```

\Micrium

Contains all software components and projects provided by Micriμm.

\Software

This sub-directory contains all software components and projects.

\uC-LIB

This is the main µC/LIB directory.

\Cfg\Template

This directory contains a configuration template file (**LIB_CFG.H**) that are required to be copied to the application directory to configure the µC/LIB module based on application requirements.

LIB_CFG.H determines whether to enable assembly language optimization (assuming there is an assembly language file for the processor, i.e., **LIB_MEM_A.ASM**) and a few other **#defines**.

2-8 SUMMARY

Below is a summary of all directories and files involved in a µC/OS-III-based project. The "<-Cfg" on the far right indicates that these files are typically copied into the application (i.e., project) directory and edited based on the project requirements.

```
\Micrium
    \Software
        \EvalBoards
            \<manufacturer>
                \<board name>
                    \<compiler>
                        \<project name>
                            \APP.C
                            \APP.H
                            \other
        \CPU
            \<manufacturer>
                \<architecture>
                    \*.*
```

```
\uCOS-III
   \Cfg\Template
      \OS_APP_HOOKS.C
      \OS_CFG.H                        <-Cfg
      \OS_CFG_APP.H                    <-Cfg
   \Source
      \OS_CFG_APP.C
      \OS_CORE.C
      \OS_DBG.C
      \OS_FLAG.C
      \OS_INT.C
      \OS_MEM.C
      \OS_MSG.C
      \OS_MUTEX.C
      \OS_PEND_MULTI.C
      \OS_PRIO.C
      \OS_Q.C
      \OS_SEM.C
      \OS_STAT.C
      \OS_TASK.C
      \OS_TICK.C
      \OS_TIME.C
      \OS_TMR.C
      \OS_VAR.C
      \OS.H
      \OS_TYPE.H                       <-Cfg
   \Ports
      \<architecture>
         \<compiler>
            \OS_CPU.H
            \OS_CPU_A.ASM
            \OS_CPU_C.C
\uC-CPU
   \CPU_CORE.C
   \CPU_CORE.H
   \CPU_DEF.H
   \Cfg\Template
      \CPU_CFG.H                       <-Cfg
```

```
\<architecture>
    \<compiler>
        \CPU.H
        \CPU_A.ASM
        \CPU_C.C
\uC-LIB
    \LIB_ASCII.C
    \LIB_ASCII.H
    \LIB_DEF.H
    \LIB_MATH.C
    \LIB_MATH.H
    \LIB_MEM.C
    \LIB_MEM.H
    \LIB_STR.C
    \LIB_STR.H
    \Cfg\Template
        \LIB_CFG.H                      <-Cfg
    \Ports
        \<architecture>
            \<compiler>
                \LIB_MEM_A.ASM
```

Chapter 2

3

Getting Started with µC/OS-III

µC/OS-III provides services to application code in the form of a set of functions that perform specific operations. µC/OS-III offers services to manage tasks, semaphores, message queues, mutual exclusion semaphores and more. As far as the application is concerned, it calls the µC/OS-III functions as if they were any other functions. In other words, the application now has access to a library of approximately 70 new functions.

In this chapter, the reader will appreciate how easy it is to start using µC/OS-III. Refer to Appendix A, "µC/OS-III API Reference Manual" on page 383, for the full description of several of the µC/OS-III services presented in this chapter.

It is assumed that the project setup (files and directories) is as described in the previous chapter, and that a C compiler exists for the target processor that is in use. However, this chapter makes no assumptions about the tools or the processor that is used.

3-1 SINGLE TASK APPLICATION

Listing 3-1 shows the top portion of a simple application file called **APP.C**.

```
/*
*********************************************************************************
*                               INCLUDE FILES
*********************************************************************************
*/
#include <app_cfg.h>                                                     (1)
#include <bsp.h>
#include <os.h>
/*
*********************************************************************************
*                           LOCAL GLOBAL VARIABLES
*********************************************************************************
*/
static   OS_TCB          AppTaskStartTCB;                                (2)
static   CPU_STK         AppTaskStartStk[APP_TASK_START_STK_SIZE];       (3)
/*
*********************************************************************************
*                             FUNCTION PROTOTYPES
*********************************************************************************
*/
static  void  AppTaskStart (void *p_arg);                                (4)
```

Listing 3-1 **APP.C (1st Part)**

L3-1(1)   As with any C programs, include the necessary headers to build the application.

APP_CFG.H.h is a header file that configures the application. For our example, APP_CFG.H contains #define constants to establish task priorities, stack sizes, and other application specifics.

BSP.H is the header file for the Board Support Package (BSP), which **defines** #defines and function prototypes, such as BSP_Init(), BSP_LED_On(), OS_TS_GET() and more.

OS.H is the main header file for µC/OS-III, and includes the following header files:

OS_CFG.H
CPU.H
CPU_CFG.H
CPU_CORE.H
OS_TYPE.H
OS_CPU.H

L3-1(2)   We will be creating an application task and it is necessary to allocate a task control block (OS_TCB) for this task.

L3-1(3)   Each task created requires its own stack. A stack must be declared using the CPU_STK data type. The stack can be allocated statically as shown here, or dynamically from the heap using malloc(). It should not be necessary to free the stack space, because the task should never be stopped, and the stack will always be used.

L3-1(4)   This is the function prototype of the task that we will create.

Most C applications start at main() as shown in Listing 3-2.

```
void  main (void)
{
    OS_ERR  err;

    BSP_IntDisAll();                                                   (1)
    OSInit(&err);                                                      (2)
    if (err != OS_ERR_NONE) {
        /* Something didn't get initialized correctly ...         */
        /* ... check OS.H for the meaning of the error code, see OS_ERR_xxxx */
    }
    OSTaskCreate((OS_TCB      *)&AppTaskStartTCB,                      (3)
                 (CPU_CHAR    *)"App Task Start",                     (4)
                 (OS_TASK_PTR )AppTaskStart,                          (5)
                 (void        *)0,                                    (6)
                 (OS_PRIO     )APP_TASK_START_PRIO,                   (7)
                 (CPU_STK     *)&AppTaskStartStk[0],                  (8)
                 (CPU_STK_SIZE)APP_TASK_START_STK_SIZE / 10,          (9)
                 (CPU_STK_SIZE)APP_TASK_START_STK_SIZE,               (10)
                 (OS_MSG_QTY  )0,
                 (OS_TICK     )0,
                 (void        *)0,
                 (OS_OPT      )(OS_OPT_TASK_STK_CHK | OS_OPT_TASK_STK_CLR),  (11)
                 (OS_ERR      *)&err);                                (12)
    if (err != OS_ERR_NONE) {
        /* The task didn't get created.  Lookup the value of the error code ... */
        /* ... in OS.H for the meaning of the error                   */
    }
    OSStart(&err);                                                    (13)
    if (err != OS_ERR_NONE) {
        /* Your code is NEVER supposed to come back to this point.     */
    }
}
```

Listing 3-2 **APP.C (2nd Part)**

L3-2(1)   Start **main()** by calling a BSP function that disables all interrupts. On most processors, interrupts are disabled at startup until explicitly enabled by application code. However, it is safer to turn off all peripheral interrupts during startup.

L3-2(2)   Call **OSInit()**, which is responsible for initializing µC/OS-III. **OSInit()** initializes internal variables and data structures, and also creates two (2) to five (5) internal tasks. At a minimum, µC/OS-III creates the idle task (**OS_IdleTask()**), which executes when no other task is ready to run. µC/OS-III also creates the tick task, which is responsible for keeping track of time.

Depending on the value of **#define** constants, µC/OS-III will create the statistic task (**OS_StatTask()**), the timer task (**OS_TmrTask()**), and the interrupt handler queue management task (**OS_IntQTask()**). Those are discussed in Chapter 5, "Task Management" on page 83.

Most of µC/OS-III's functions return an error code via a pointer to an **OS_ERR** variable, err in this case. If **OSInit()** was successful, err will be set to **OS_ERR_NONE**. If **OSInit()** encounters a problem during initialization, it will return immediately upon detecting the problem and set err accordingly. If this occurs, look up the error code value in **OS.H**. Specifically, all error codes start with **OS_ERR_**.

It is important to note that **OSInit()** must be called before any other µC/OS-III function.

L3-2(3)   Create a task by calling **OSTaskCreate()**. **OSTaskCreate()** requires 13 arguments. The first argument is the address of the **OS_TCB** that is declared for this task. Chapter 5, "Task Management" on page 83 provides additional information about tasks.

L3-2(4)   **OSTaskCreate()** allows a name to be assigned to each of the tasks. µC/OS-III stores a pointer to the task name inside the **OS_TCB** of the task. There is no limit on the number of ASCII characters used for the name.

L3-2(5)   The third argument is the address of the task code. A typical µC/OS-III task is implemented as an infinite loop as shown:

```
void  MyTask (void *p_arg)
{
    /* Do something with "p_arg".
    while (1) {
        /* Task body */
    }
}
```

The task receives an argument when it first starts. As far as the task is concerned, it looks like any other C function that can be called by the code. However, the code *must not* call **MyTask()**. The call is actually performed through µC/OS-III.

L3-2(6)   The fourth argument of **OSTaskCreate()** is the actual argument that the task receives when it first begins. In other words, the "**p_arg**" of **MyTask()**. In the example a **NULL** pointer is passed, and thus "**p_arg**" for **AppTaskStart()** will be a **NULL** pointer.

The argument passed to the task can actually be any pointer. For example, the user may pass a pointer to a data structure containing parameters for the task.

L3-2(7)   The next argument to **OSTaskCreate()** is the priority of the task. The priority establishes the relative importance of this task with respect to the other tasks in the application. A low-priority number indicates a high priority (or more important task). Set the priority of the task to any value between 1 and **OS_CFG_PRIO_MAX-2**, inclusively. Avoid using priority #0, and priority **OS_CFG_PRIO_MAX-1**, because these are reserved for μC/OS-III. **OS_CFG_PRIO_MAX** is a compile time configuration constant, which is declared in **OS_CFG.H**.

L3-2(8)   The sixth argument to **OSTaskCreate()** is the base address of the stack assigned to this task. The base address is always the lowest memory location of the stack.

L3-2(9)   The next argument specifies the location of a "watermark" in the task's stack that can be used to determine the allowable stack growth of the task. See Chapter 5, "Task Management" on page 83 for more details on using this feature. In the code above, the value represents the amount of stack space (in **CPU_STK** elements) before the stack is empty. In other words, in the example, the limit is reached when there is 10% of the stack left.

L3-2(10)   The eighth argument to **OSTaskCreate()** specifies the size of the task's stack in number of **CPU_STK** elements (not bytes). For example, if allocating 1 Kbyte of stack space for a task and the **CPU_STK** is a 32-bit word, then pass 256.

L3-2(11)   The next three arguments are skipped as they are not relevant for the current discussion. The next argument to **OSTaskCreate()** specifies options. In this example, we specify that the stack will be checked at run time (assuming the statistic task was enabled in **OS_CFG.H**), and that the contents of the stack will be cleared when the task is created.

L3-2(12)   The last argument of **OSTaskCreate()** is a pointer to a variable that will receive an error code. If **OSTaskCreate()** is successful, the error code will be **OS_ERR_NONE** otherwise, look up the value of the error code in **OS.H** (See **OS_ERR_xxxx**) to determine the problem with the call.

L3-2(13)   The final step in **main()** is to call **OSStart()**, which starts the multitasking process. Specifically, µC/OS-III will select the highest-priority task that was created before calling **OSStart()**. The highest-priority task is always **OS_IntQTask()** if that task is enabled in **OS_CFG.H** (through the **OS_CFG_ISR_POST_DEFERRED_EN** constant). If this is the case, **OS_IntQTask()** will perform some initialization of its own and then µC/OS-III will switch to the next most important task that was created.

A few important points are worth noting. For one thing, create as many tasks as you want before calling **OSStart()**. However, it is recommended to only create one task as shown in the example because, having a single application task allows µC/OS-III to determine how fast the CPU is, in order to determine the percentage of CPU usage at run-time. Also, if the application needs other kernel objects such as semaphores and message queues then it is recommended that these be created prior to calling **OSStart()**. Finally, notice that that interrupts are not enabled. This will be discussed next by examining the contents of **AppTaskStart()**, which is shown in Listing 3-3.

```
static  void  AppTaskStart (void *p_arg)                          (1)
{
    OS_ERR  err;


    p_arg = p_arg;
    BSP_Init();                                                   (2)
    CPU_Init();                                                   (3)
    BSP_Cfg_Tick();                                               (4)
    BSP_LED_Off(0);                                               (5)
    while (1) {                                                   (6)
        BSP_LED_Toggle(0);                                        (7)
        OSTimeDlyHMSM((CPU_INT16U)  0,                            (8)
                      (CPU_INT16U)  0,
                      (CPU_INT16U)  0,
                      (CPU_INT32U)100,
                      (OS_OPT    )OS_OPT_TIME_HMSM_STRICT,
                      (OS_ERR    *)&err);
        /* Check for 'err' */
    }
}
```

Listing 3-3 **APP.C (3rd Part)**

L3-3(1)   As previously mentioned, a task looks like any other C function. The argument "**p_arg**" is passed to **AppTaskStart()** by **OSTaskCreate()**, as discussed in the previous listing description.

L3-3(2)   **BSP_Init()** is a Board Support Package (BSP) function that is responsible for initializing the hardware on an evaluation or target board. The evaluation board might have General Purpose Input Output (GPIO) lines that might need to be configured, relays, sensors and more. This function is found in a file called **BSP.C**.

L3-3(3)   **CPU_Init()** initializes the µC/CPU services. µC/CPU provides services to measure interrupt latency, receive time stamps, and provides emulation of the count leading zeros instruction if the processor used does not have that instruction and more.

L3-3(4)   **BSP_Cfg_Tick()** sets up the µC/OS-III tick interrupt. For this, the function needs to initialize one of the hardware timers to interrupt the CPU at a rate of: **OSCfg_TickRate_Hz**, which is defined in **OS_CFG_APP.H** (See **OS_CFG_TICK_RATE_HZ**).

L3-3(5)   **BSP_LED_Off()** is a function that will turn off all LEDs because the function is written so that a zero argument means all the LEDs.

L3-3(6)   Most µC/OS-III tasks will need to be written as an infinite loop.

L3-3(7)   This BSP function toggles the state of the specified LED. Again, a zero indicates that all the LEDs should be toggled on the evaluation board. Simply change the zero to 1 and this will cause LED #1 to toggle. Exactly which LED is LED #1? That depends on the BSP developer. Specifically, encapsulate access to LEDs through such functions as **BSP_LED_On()**, **BSP_LED_Off()** and **BSP_LED_Toggle()**. Also, we prefer to assign LEDs logical values (1, 2, 3, etc.) instead of specifying which port and which bit on each port.

L3-3(8)   Finally, each task in the application must call one of the µC/OS-III functions that will cause the task to "wait for an event." The task can wait for time to expire (by calling **OSTimeDly()**, or **OSTimeDlyHMSM()**), or wait for a signal or a message from an ISR or another task. Chapter 11, "Time Management" on page 191 provides additional information about time delays.

3-2 MULTIPLE TASKS APPLICATION WITH KERNEL OBJECTS

The code of Listing 3-4 through Listing 3-8 shows a more complete example and contains three tasks: a mutual exclusion, semaphore, and a message queue.

```
/*
*********************************************************************************
*                               INCLUDE FILES
*********************************************************************************
*/
#include <app_cfg.h>
#include <bsp.h>
#include <os.h>
/*
*********************************************************************************
*                            LOCAL GLOBAL VARIABLES
*********************************************************************************
*/
static  OS_TCB          AppTaskStartTCB;                            (1)
static  OS_TCB          AppTask1_TCB;
static  OS_TCB          AppTask2_TCB;
static  OS_MUTEX        AppMutex;                                   (2)
static  OS_Q            AppQ;                                       (3)
static  CPU_STK         AppTaskStartStk[APP_TASK_START_STK_SIZE];   (4)
static  CPU_STK         AppTask1_Stk[128];
static  CPU_STK         AppTask2_Stk[128];
/*
*********************************************************************************
*                             FUNCTION PROTOTYPES
*********************************************************************************
*/
static  void  AppTaskStart (void *p_arg);                          (5)
static  void  AppTask1     (void *p_arg);
static  void  AppTask2     (void *p_arg);
```

Listing 3-4 **APP.C (1st Part)**

L3-4(1)   Allocate storage for the **OS_TCB**s of each task.

L3-4(2)   A mutual exclusion semaphore (a.k.a. a mutex) is a kernel object (a data structure) that is used to protect a shared resource from being accessed by more than one task. A task that wants to access the shared resource must obtain the mutex before it is allowed to proceed. The owner of the resource relinquishes the mutex when it has finished accessing the resource. This process is demonstrated in this example.

L3-4(3)   A message queue is a kernel object through which Interrupt Service Routines (ISRs) and/or tasks send messages to other tasks. The sender "formulates" a message and sends it to the message queue. The task(s) wanting to receive these messages wait on the message queue for messages to arrive. If there are already messages in the message queue, the receiver immediately retrieves those messages. If there are no messages waiting in the message queue, then the receiver will be placed in a wait list associated with the message queue. This process will be demonstrated in this example.

L3-4(4)   Allocate a stack for each task.

L3-4(5)   The user must prototype the tasks.

Listing 3-5 shows the entry point for C, **main()**.

```
void  main (void)
{
    OS_ERR  err;

    BSP_IntDisAll();
    OSInit(&err);
    /* Check for 'err' */

    OSMutexCreate((OS_MUTEX  *)&AppMutex,                                    (1)
                  (CPU_CHAR  *)"My App. Mutex",
                  (OS_ERR    *)&err);
    /* Check for 'err' */

    OSQCreate    ((OS_Q      *)&AppQ,                                        (2)
                  (CPU_CHAR  *)"My App Queue",
                  (OS_MSG_QTY )10,
                  (OS_ERR    *)&err);
    /* Check for 'err' */

    OSTaskCreate((OS_TCB     *)&AppTaskStartTCB,                             (3)
                 (CPU_CHAR   *)"App Task Start",
                 (OS_TASK_PTR )AppTaskStart,
                 (void       *)0,
                 (OS_PRIO    )APP_TASK_START_PRIO,
                 (CPU_STK    *)&AppTaskStartStk[0],
                 (CPU_STK_SIZE)APP_TASK_START_STK_SIZE / 10,
                 (CPU_STK_SIZE)APP_TASK_START_STK_SIZE,
                 (OS_MSG_QTY )0,
                 (OS_TICK    )0,
                 (void       *)0,
                 (OS_OPT     )(OS_OPT_TASK_STK_CHK | OS_OPT_TASK_STK_CLR),
                 (OS_ERR     *)&err);
    /* Check for 'err' */

    OSStart(&err);
    /* Check for 'err' */
}
```

Listing 3-5 **APP.C (2nd Part)**

L3-5(1)   Creating a mutex is simply a matter of calling **OSMutexCreate()**. Specify the address of the **OS_MUTEX** object that will be used for the mutex. Chapter 13, "Resource Management" on page 217 provides additional information about mutual exclusion semaphores.

You can assign an ASCII name to the mutex, which is useful when debugging.

L3-5(2)   Create the message queue by calling **OSQCreate()** and specifying the address of the **OS_Q** object. Chapter 15, "Message Passing" on page 297 provides additional information about message queues.

Assign an ASCII name to the message queue.

Specify how many messages the message queue is allowed to receive. This value must be greater than zero. If the sender sends messages faster than they can be consumed by the receiving task, messages will be lost. This can be corrected by either increasing the size of the message queue, or increasing the priority of the receiving task.

L3-5(3)   The first application task is created.

Listing 3-6 shows how to create other tasks once multitasking as started.

```
static  void  AppTaskStart (void *p_arg)
{
    OS_ERR  err;


    p_arg = p_arg;
    BSP_Init();
    CPU_Init();
    BSP_Cfg_Tick();
    OSTaskCreate((OS_TCB    *)&AppTask1_TCB,                                     (1)
                 (CPU_CHAR  *)"App Task 1",
                 (OS_TASK_PTR )AppTask1,
                 (void      *)0,
                 (OS_PRIO   )5,
                 (CPU_STK   *)&AppTask1_Stk[0],
                 (CPU_STK_SIZE)0,
                 (CPU_STK_SIZE)128,
                 (OS_MSG_QTY )0,
                 (OS_TICK   )0,
                 (void      *)0,
                 (OS_OPT    )(OS_OPT_TASK_STK_CHK | OS_OPT_TASK_STK_CLR),
                 (OS_ERR    *)&err);

    OSTaskCreate((OS_TCB    *)&AppTask2_TCB,                                     (2)
                 (CPU_CHAR  *)"App Task 2",
                 (OS_TASK_PTR )AppTask2,
                 (void      *)0,
                 (OS_PRIO   )6,
                 (CPU_STK   *)&AppTask2_Stk[0],
                 (CPU_STK_SIZE)0,
                 (CPU_STK_SIZE)128,
                 (OS_MSG_QTY )0,
                 (OS_TICK   )0,
                 (void      *)0,
                 (OS_OPT    )(OS_OPT_TASK_STK_CHK | OS_OPT_TASK_STK_CLR),
                 (OS_ERR    *)&err);
    BSP_LED_Off(0);
    while (1) {
        BSP_LED_Toggle(0);
        OSTimeDlyHMSM((CPU_INT16U)  0,
                      (CPU_INT16U)  0,
                      (CPU_INT16U)  0,
                      (CPU_INT32U)100,
                      (OS_OPT    )OS_OPT_TIME_HMSM_STRICT,
                      (OS_ERR    *)&err);
    }
}
```

Listing 3-6 **APP.C (3rd Part)**

L3-6(1)   Create Task #1 by calling **OSTaskCreate()**. If this task happens to have a
          higher priority than the task that creates it, µC/OS-III will immediately start
          Task #1. If the created task has a lower priority, **OSTaskCreate()** will return to
          AppTaskStart() and continue execution.

L3-6(2)   Task #2 is created and if it has a higher priority than **AppTaskStart()**,
          µC/OS-III will immediately switch to that task.

```c
static void AppTask1 (void *p_arg)
{
    OS_ERR   err;
    CPU_TS   ts;


    p_arg = p_arg;
    while (1) {
        OSTimeDly ((OS_TICK   )1,                          (1)
                   (OS_OPT    )OS_OPT_TIME_DLY,
                   (OS_ERR   *)&err);
        OSQPost   ((OS_Q     *)&AppQ,                      (2)
                   (void     *)1;
                   (OS_MSG_SIZE)sizeof(void *),
                   (OS_OPT    )OS_OPT_POST_FIFO,
                   (OS_ERR   *)&err);
        OSMutexPend((OS_MUTEX *)&AppMutex,                 (3)
                   (OS_TICK   )0,
                   (OS_OPT    )OS_OPT_PEND_BLOCKING;
                   (CPU_TS   *)&ts,
                   (OS_ERR   *)&err);
        /* Access shared resource */                       (4)
        OSMutexPost((OS_MUTEX *)&AppMutex,                 (5)
                   (OS_OPT    )OS_OPT_POST_NONE,
                   (OS_ERR   *)&err);
    }
}
```

Listing 3-7 **APP.C (4th Part)**

L3-7(1)   The task starts by waiting for one tick to expire before it does anything useful.
          If the µC/OS-III tick rate is configured for 1000 Hz, the task will execute every
          millisecond.

L3-7(2)   The task then sends a message to another task using the message queue AppQ. In this case, the example shows a fixed message "1," but the message could have consisted of the address of a buffer, the address of a function, or whatever would need to be sent.

L3-7(3)   The task then waits on the mutual exclusion semaphore since it needs to access a shared resource with another task. If the resource is already owned by another task, **AppTask1()** will wait forever for the mutex to be released by its current owner. The forever wait is specified by passing 0 as the second argument of the call.

L3-7(4)   When **OSMutexPend()** returns, the task owns the resource and can therefore access the shared resource. The shared resource may be a variable, an array, a data structure, an I/O device, etc.

L3-7(5)   When the task is done with the shared resource, it must call **OSMutexPost()** to release the mutex.

```
static  void  AppTask2 (void *p_arg)
{
    OS_ERR        err;
    void          *p_msg;
    OS_MSG_SIZE   msg_size;
    CPU_TS        ts;
    CPU_TS        ts_delta;


    p_arg = p_arg;
    while (1) {
        p_msg = OSQPend((OS_Q         *)&AppQ,                          (1)
                        (OS_MSG_SIZE *)&msg_size,
                        (OS_TICK     )0,
                        (OS_OPT      )OS_OPT_PEND_BLOCKING,
                        (CPU_TS      *)&ts,
                        (OS_ERR      *)&err);
        ts_delta = OS_TS_GET() - ts;                                   (2)
        /* Process message received */                                 (3)
    }
}
```

Listing 3-8 **APP.C (5th Part)**

L3-8(1)   Task #2 starts by waiting for messages to be sent through the message queue AppQ. The task waits forever for a message to be received because the third argument specifies an infinite timeout.

When the message is received **p_msg** will contain the message (i.e., a pointer to "something"). Both the sender and receiver must agree as to the meaning of the message. The size of the message received is saved in "**msg_size**". Note that "**p_msg**" could point to a buffer and "**msg_size**" would indicate the size of this buffer.

Also, when the message is received, "**ts**" will contain the timestamp of when the message was sent. A timestamp is the value read from a fairly fast free-running timer. The timestamp is typically an unsigned 32-bit (or more) value.

L3-8(2)   Knowing when the message was sent allows the user to determine how long it took this task to get the message. Reading the current timestamp and subtracting the timestamp of when the message was sent allows users to know how long it took for the message to be received. Note that the receiving task may not get the message immediately since ISRs or other higher-priority tasks might execute before the receiver gets to run.

L3-8(3)   Proceed with processing the received message.

Critical Sections

A critical section of code, also called a *critical region*, is code that needs to be treated indivisibly. There are many critical sections of code contained in μC/OS-III. If a critical section is accessible by an Interrupt Service Routine (ISR) and a task, then disabling interrupts is necessary to protect the critical region. If the critical section is only accessible by task level code, the critical section may be protected through the use of a *preemption lock*.

Within μC/OS-III, the critical section access method depends on which ISR post method is used by interrupts (see Chapter 9, "Interrupt Management" on page 165). If OS_CFG_ISR_POST_DEFERRED_EN is set to 0 (see OS_CFG.H) then μC/OS-III will disable interrupts when accessing internal critical sections. If OS_CFG_ISR_POST_DEFERRED_EN is set to 1 then μC/OS-III will lock the scheduler when accessing most of its internal critical sections.

Chapter 9, "Interrupt Management" on page 165 discusses how to select the method to use.

μC/OS-III defines one macro for entering a critical section and two macros for leaving:

```
OS_CRITICAL_ENTER(),
OS_CRITICAL_EXIT() and
OS_CRITICAL_EXIT_NO_SCHED()
```

These macros are internal to μC/OS-III and must not be invoked by the application code. However, if you need to access critical sections in your application code, consult Chapter 13, "Resource Management" on page 217.

4-1 DISABLING INTERRUPTS

When setting OS_CFG_ISR_POST_DEFERRED_EN to 0, µC/OS-III will disable interrupts before entering a critical section and re-enable them when leaving the critical section.

OS_CRITICAL_ENTER() invokes the µC/CPU macro CPU_CRITICAL_ENTER() that, in turn, calls CPU_SR_Save(). CPU_SR_Save() is a function typically written in assembly language that saves the current interrupt disable status and then disables interrupts. The saved interrupt disable status is returned to the caller and in fact, it is stored onto the caller's stack in a variable called "cpu_sr".

OS_CRITICAL_EXIT() and OS_CRITICAL_EXIT_NO_SCHED() both invoke the µC/CPU macro CPU_CRITICAL_EXIT(), which maps to CPU_SR_Restore(). CPU_SR_Restore() is passed the value of the saved "cpu_sr" variable to re-establish interrupts the way they were prior to calling OS_CRITICAL_ENTER().

The typical code for the macros is shown in Listing 4-1.

```
#define   OS_CRITICAL_ENTER()         { CPU_CRITICAL_ENTER(); }
#define   OS_CRITICAL_EXIT()          { CPU_CRITICAL_EXIT();  }
#define   OS_CRITICAL_EXIT_NO_SCHED() { CPU_CRITICAL_EXIT();  }
```

Listing 4-1 **Critical section code – Disabling interrupts**

4-1-1 MEASURING INTERRUPT DISABLE TIME

µC/CPU provides facilities to measure the amount of time interrupts are disabled. This is done by setting the configuration constant CPU_CFG_TIME_MEAS_INT_DIS_EN to 1 in CPU_CFG.H.

The measurement is started each time interrupts are disabled and ends when interrupts are re-enabled. The measurement keeps track of two values: a global interrupt disable time, and an interrupt disable time for each task. Therefore, it is possible to know how long a task disables interrupts, enabling the user to better optimize their code.

The per-task interrupt disable time is saved in the task's OS_TCB during a context switch (see OSTaskSwHook() in OS_CPU_C.C and described in Chapter 8, "Context Switching" on page 155).

The unit of measure for the measured time is in CPU_TS (timestamp) units. It is necessary to find out the resolution of the timer used to measure these timestamps. For example, if the timer used for the timestamp is incremented at 1 MHz then the resolution of **CPU_TS** is 1 microsecond.

Measuring the interrupt disable time obviously adds measurement artifacts and thus increases the amount of time the interrupts are disabled. However, as far as the measurement is concerned, measurement overhead is accounted for and the measured value represents the actual interrupt disable time as if the measurement was not present.

Interrupt disable time is obviously greatly affected by the speed at which the processor accesses instructions and thus, the memory access speed. In this case, the hardware designer might have introduced wait states to memory accesses, which affects overall performance of the system. This may show up as unusually long interrupt disable times.

4-2 LOCKING THE SCHEDULER

When setting **OS_CFG_ISR_POST_DEFERRED_EN** to 1, µC/OS-III locks the scheduler before entering a critical section and unlocks the scheduler when leaving the critical section.

OS_CRITICAL_ENTER() simply increments **OSSchedLockNestingCtr** to lock the scheduler. This is the variable the scheduler uses to determine whether or not the scheduler is locked. It is locked when the value is non-zero.

OS_CRITICAL_EXIT() decrements **OSSchedLockNestingCtr** and when the value reaches zero, invokes the scheduler.

OS_CRITICAL_EXIT_NO_SCHED() also decrements **OSSchedLockNestingCtr**, but does not invoke the scheduler when the value reaches zero.

The code for the macros is shown in Listing 4-2.

```
#define  OS_CRITICAL_ENTER()            {                                          \
                                        CPU_CRITICAL_ENTER();                      \
                                        OSSchedLockNestingCtr++;                   \
                                        CPU_CRITICAL_EXIT();                       \
                                        }
#define  OS_CRITICAL_EXIT()             {                                          \
                                        CPU_CRITICAL_ENTER();                      \
                                        OSSchedLockNestingCtr--;                   \
                                        if (OSSchedLockNestingCtr == (OS_NESTING_CTR)0) {  \
                                            CPU_CRITICAL_EXIT();                   \
                                            OSSched();                             \
                                        } else {                                   \
                                            CPU_CRITICAL_EXIT();                   \
                                        }                                          \
                                        }
#define  OS_CRITICAL_EXIT_NO_SCHED()    {                                          \
                                        CPU_CRITICAL_ENTER();                      \
                                        OSSchedLockNestingCtr--;                   \
                                        CPU_CRITICAL_EXIT();                       \
                                        }
```

Listing 4-2 **Critical section code – Locking the Scheduler**

4-2-1 MEASURING SCHEDULER LOCK TIME

µC/OS-III provides facilities to measure the amount of time the scheduler is locked. This is done by setting the configuration constant **OS_CFG_SCHED_LOCK_TIME_MEAS_EN** to 1 in **OS_CFG.H**.

The measurement is started each time the scheduler is locked and ends when the scheduler is unlocked. The measurement keeps track of two values: a global scheduler lock time, and a per-task scheduler lock time. It is therefore possible to know how long each task locks the scheduler allowing the user to better optimize code.

The per-task scheduler lock time is saved in the task's **OS_TCB** during a context switch (see **OSTaskSwHook()** in **OS_CPU_C.C** and described in Chapter 8, "Context Switching" on page 155).

The unit of measure for the measured time is in **CPU_TS** (timestamp) units so it is necessary to find the resolution of the timer used to measure the timestamps. For example, if the timer used for the timestamp is incremented at 1 MHz then the resolution of **CPU_TS** is 1 microsecond.

Measuring the scheduler lock time adds measurement artifacts and thus increases the amount of time the scheduler is actually locked. However, measurement overhead is accounted for and the measured value represents the actual scheduler lock time as if the measurement was not present.

4-3 µC/OS-III FEATURES WITH LONGER CRITICAL SECTIONS

Table 4-1 shows several µC/OS-III features that have potentially longer critical sections. Knowledge of these will help the user decide whether to direct µC/OS-III to use one critical section over another.

Feature	Reason
Multiple tasks at the same priority	Although this is an important feature of µC/OS-III, multiple tasks at the same priority create longer critical sections. However, if there are only a few tasks at the same priority, interrupt latency would be relatively small. If multiple tasks are not created at the same priority, use the interrupt disable method.
Event Flags Chapter 14, "Synchronization" on page 259	If multiple tasks are waiting on different events, going through all of the tasks waiting for events requires a fair amount of processing time, which means longer critical sections. If only a few tasks (approximately one to five) are waiting on an event flag group, the critical section would be short enough to use the interrupt disable method.
Pend on multiple objects Chapter 16, "Pending On Multiple Objects" on page 321	Pending on multiple objects is probably the most complex feature provided by µC/OS-III, requiring interrupts to be disabled for fairly long periods of time should the interrupt disable method be selected. If pending on multiple objects, it is highly recommended that the user select the scheduler-lock method. If the application does not use this feature, the interrupt disable method is an alternative.
Broadcast on Post calls See OSSemPost() and OSQPost() descriptions in Appendix A, "µC/OS-III API Reference Manual" on page 383.	µC/OS-III disables interrupts while processing a post to multiple tasks in a broadcast. When not using the broadcast option, you can use the interrupt disable method.

Table 4-1 **Disabling interrupts or locking the Scheduler**

4-4 SUMMARY

µC/OS-III needs to access critical sections of code, which it protects by either disabling interrupts (OS_CFG_ISR_POST_DEFERRED_EN set to 0 in OS_CFG.H), or locking the scheduler (OS_CFG_ISR_POST_DEFERRED_EN set to 1 in OS_CFG.H).

The application code must not use:

```
OS_CRITICAL_ENTER()
OS_CRITICAL_EXIT()
OS_CRITICAL_EXIT_NO_SCHED()
```

When setting CPU_CFG_TIME_MEAS_INT_DIS_EN in CPU_CFG.H, µC/CPU measures the maximum interrupt disable time. There are two values available, one for the global maximum and one for each task.

When setting OS_CFG_SCHED_LOCK_TIME_MEAS_EN to 1 in OS_CFG.H, µC/OS-III will measure the maximum scheduler lock time.

Chapter

5

Task Management

The design process of a real-time application generally involves splitting the work to be completed into tasks, each responsible for a portion of the problem. µC/OS-III makes it easy for an application programmer to adopt this paradigm. A task (also called a *thread*) is a simple program that thinks it has the Central Processing Unit (CPU) all to itself. On a single CPU, only one task can execute at any given time.

µC/OS-III supports multitasking and allows the application to have any number of tasks. The maximum number of task is actually only limited by the amount of memory (both code and data space) available to the processor. Multitasking is the process of *scheduling* and *switching* the CPU between several tasks (this will be expanded upon later). The CPU switches its attention between several *sequential* tasks. Multitasking provides the illusion of having multiple CPUs and, actually maximizes the use of the CPU. Multitasking also helps in the creation of modular applications. One of the most important aspects of multitasking is that it allows the application programmer to manage the complexity inherent in real-time applications. Application programs are typically easier to design and maintain when multitasking is used.

Tasks are used for such chores as monitoring inputs, updating outputs, performing computations, control loops, update one or more displays, reading buttons and keyboards, communicating with other systems, and more. One application may contain a handful of tasks while another application may require hundreds. The number of tasks does not establish how good or effective a design may be, it really depends on what the application (or product) needs to do. The amount of work a task performs also depends on the application. One task may have a few microseconds worth of work to perform while another task may require tens of milliseconds.

Tasks look like just any other C function except for a few small differences. There are two types of tasks: run-to-completion (Listing 5-1) and infinite loop (Listing 5-2). In most embedded systems, tasks typically take the form of an infinite loop. Also, no task is allowed to return as other C functions can. Given that a task is a regular C function, it can declare local variables.

5

When a µC/OS-III task begins executing, it is passed an argument, **p_arg**. This argument is a pointer to a **void**. The pointer is a universal vehicle used to pass your task the address of a variable, a structure, or even the address of a function, if necessary. With this pointer, it is possible to create many identical tasks, that all use the same code (or task body), but, with different run-time characteristics. For example, one may have four asynchronous serial ports that are each managed by their own task. However, the task code is actually identical. Instead of copying the code four times, create the code for a "generic" task that receives a pointer to a data structure, which contains the serial port's parameters (baud rate, I/O port addresses, interrupt vector number, etc.) as an argument. In other words, instantiate the same task code four times and pass it different data for each serial port that each instance will manage.

A run-to-completion task must *delete* itself by calling **OSTaskDel()**. The task starts, performs its function, and terminates. There would typically not be too many such tasks in the embedded system because of the overhead associated with "creating" and "deleting" tasks at run-time. In the task body, one can call most of µC/OS-III's functions to help perform the desired operation of the task.

```
void MyTask (void *p_arg)
{
    OS_ERR  err;
    /* Local variables                                        */


    /* Do something with 'p_arg'                              */
    /* Task initialization                                    */
    /* Task body ... do work!                                 */
    OSTaskDel((OS_TCB *)0, &err);
}
```

Listing 5-1 **Run-To-Completion task**

With µC/OS-III, call either C or assembly language functions from a task. In fact, it is possible to call the same C function from different tasks as long as the functions are reentrant. A *reentrant* function is a function that does not use static or otherwise global variables unless they are protected (µC/OS-III provides mechanisms for this) from multiple access. If shared C functions only use local variables, they are generally reentrant (assuming that the compiler generates reentrant code). An example of a non-reentrant function is the famous strtok() provided by most C compilers as part of the standard library. This function is used to parse an ASCII string for "tokens." The first time you call this function, you specify the ASCII string to parse and what constitute tokens. As soon as the function finds the first token, it returns. The function "remembers" where it was last so when called again, it can extract additional tokens, which is clearly non-reentrant.

The use of an infinite loop is more common in embedded systems because of the repetitive work needed in such systems (reading inputs, updating displays, performing control operations, etc.). This is one aspect that makes a task different than a regular C function. Note that one could use a "`while (1)`" or "`for (;;)`" to implement the infinite loop, since both behave the same. The one used is simply a matter of personal preference. At Micrium, we like to use "`while (DEF_ON)`". The infinite loop **must** call a µC/OS-III service (i.e., function) that will cause the task to wait for an event to occur. It is important that each task wait for an event to occur, otherwise the task would be a true infinite loop and there would be no easy way for other tasks to execute. This concept will become clear as more is understood regarding µC/OS-III.

```
void MyTask (void *p_arg)
{
    /* Local variables                                          */


    /* Do something with "p_arg"                                */
    /* Task initialization                                      */
    while (DEF_ON) {        /* Task body, as an infinite loop.  */
        :
        /* Task body ... do work!                               */
        :
        /* Must call one of the following services:             */
        /*      OSFlagPend()                                     */
        /*      OSMutexPend()                                    */
        /*      OSPendMulti()                                    */
        /*      OSQPend()                                        */
        /*      OSSemPend()                                      */
        /*      OSTimeDly()                                      */
        /*      OSTimeDlyHMSM()                                  */
        /*      OSTaskQPend()                                    */
        /*      OSTaskSemPend()                                  */
        /*      OSTaskSuspend()       (Suspend self)             */
        /*      OSTaskDel()           (Delete  self)             */
        :
        /* Task body ... do work!                               */
        :
    }
}
```

Listing 5-2 **Infinite Loop task**

5

The event the task is waiting for may simply be the passage of time (when **OSTimeDly()** or **OSTimeDlyHMSM()** is called). For example, a design may need to scan a keyboard every 100 milliseconds. In this case, simply delay the task for 100 milliseconds then see if a key was pressed on the keyboard and, possibly perform some action based on which key was pressed. Typically, however, a keyboard scanning task should just buffer an "identifier" unique to the key pressed and use another task to decide what to do with the key(s) pressed.

Similarly, the event the task is waiting for could be the arrival of a packet from an Ethernet controller. In this case, the task would call one of the **OS???Pend()** calls (pend is synonymous with wait). The task will have nothing to do until the packet is received. Once the packet is received, the task processes the contents of the packet, and possibly moves the packet along a network stack.

It's important to note that when a task waits for an event, it does not consume CPU time.

Tasks must be created in order for µC/OS-III to know about tasks. Create a task by simply calling **OSTaskCreate()**. The function prototype for **OSTaskCreate()** is shown below:

```
void OSTaskCreate (OS_TCB        *p_tcb,
                   OS_CHAR       *p_name,
                   OS_TASK_PTR    p_task,
                   void          *p_arg,
                   OS_PRIO        prio,
                   CPU_STK       *p_stk_base,
                   CPU_STK_SIZE   stk_limit,
                   CPU_STK_SIZE   stk_size,
                   OS_MSG_QTY     q_size,
                   OS_TICK        time_slice,
                   void          *p_ext,
                   OS_OPT         opt,
                   OS_ERR        *p_err)
```

A complete description of **OSTaskCreate()** and its arguments is provided in Appendix A, "µC/OS-III API Reference Manual" on page 383. However, it is important to understand that a task needs to be assigned a *Task Control Block* (i.e., TCB), a stack, a priority and a few other parameters which are initialized by **OSTaskCreate()**, as shown in Figure 5-1.

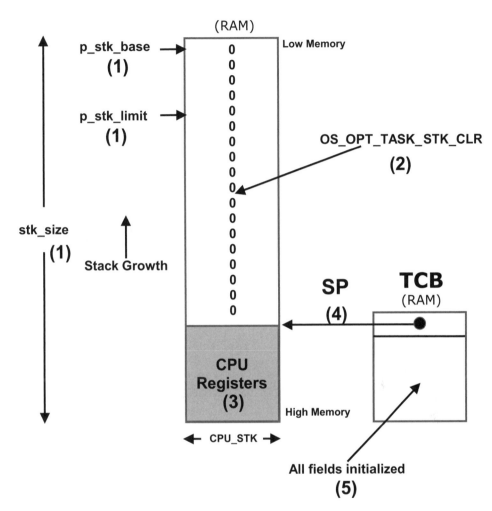

Figure 5-1 **OSTaskCreate() initializes the task's TCB and stack**

F5-1(1)   When calling **OSTaskCreate()**, one passes the base address of the stack (**p_stk_base**) that will be used by the task, the watermark limit for stack growth (**stk_limit**) which is expressed in number of **CPU_STK** entries before the stack is empty, and the size of that stack (**stk_size**), also in number of **CPU_STK** elements.

F5-1(2)   When specifying **OS_OPT_TASK_STK_CHK** + **OS_OPT_TASK_STK_CLR** in the opt argument of **OSTaskCreate()**, µC/OS-III initializes the task's stack with all zeros.

87

F5-1(3)   µC/OS-III then initializes the top of the task's stack with a copy of the CPU registers in the same stacking order as if they were all saved at the beginning of an ISR. This makes it easy to perform context switches as we will see when discussing the context switching process. For illustration purposes, the assumption is that the stack grows from high memory to low memory, but the same concept applies for CPUs that use the stack in the reverse order.

F5-1(4)   The new value of the stack pointer (SP) is saved in the TCB. Note that this is also called the **top-of-stack**.

F5-1(5)   The remaining fields of the TCB are initialized: task priority, task name, task state, internal message queue, internal semaphore, and many others.

Next, a call is made to a function that is defined in the CPU port, **OSTaskCreateHook()** (see **OS_CPU_C.C**). **OSTaskCreateHook()** is passed the pointer to the new TCB and this function allows you (or the port designer) to extend the functionality of **OSTaskCreate()**. For example, one could printout the contents of the fields of the newly created TCB onto a terminal for debugging purposes.

The task is then placed in the ready-list (see Chapter 6, "The Ready List" on page 131) and finally, if multitasking has started, µC/OS-III will invoke the scheduler to see if the created task is now the highest priority task and, if so, will context switch to this new task.

The body of the task can invoke other services provided by µC/OS-III. Specifically, a task can create another task (i.e., call **OSTaskCreate()**), suspend and resume other tasks (i.e., call **OSTaskSuspend()** and **OSTaskResume()** respectively), post signals or messages to other tasks (i.e., call **OS??Post()**), share resources with other tasks, and more. In other words, tasks are not limited to only make "wait for an event" function calls.

Figure 5-2 shows the resources with which a task typically interacts.

Figure 5-2 **Tasks interact with resources**

F5-2(1)   An important aspect of a task is its code. As previously mentioned, the code looks like any other C function, except that it is typically implemented as an infinite loop. Also, a task is not allowed to return.

F5-2(2)   Each task is assigned a priority based on its importance in the application. µC/OS-III's job is to decide which task will run on the CPU. The general rule is that µC/OS-III will run the most important *ready-to-run* task (highest priority).

With µC/OS-III, a low priority number indicates a high priority. In other words, a task at priority 1 is more important than a task at priority 10.

µC/OS-III supports a compile-time user configurable number of different priorities (see **OS_PRIO_MAX** in **OS_CFG.H**). Thus, µC/OS-III allows the user to determine the number of different priority levels the application is allowed to use. Also, µC/OS-III supports an unlimited number of tasks at the same priority. For example, µC/OS-III can be configured to have 64 different priority levels and one can assign dozens of tasks at each priority level.

See section 5-1 "Assigning Task Priorities" on page 92.

F5-2(3)   A task has its own set of CPU registers. As far as a task is concerned, the task thinks it has the actual CPU all to itself.

F5-2(4)   Because µC/OS-III is a preemptive kernel, each task must have its own stack area. The stack always resides in RAM and is used to keep track of local variables, function calls, and possibly ISR (Interrupt Service Routine) nesting.

Stack space can be allocated either statically (at compile-time) or dynamically (at run-time). A static stack declaration is shown below. This declaration is made outside of a function.

```
static  CPU_STK MyTaskStk[???];
```

or,

```
CPU_STK MyTaskStk[???];
```

Note that "**???**" indicates that the size of the stack (and thus the array) depends on the task stack requirements. Stack space may be allocated dynamically by using the C compiler's heap management function (i.e., **malloc()**) as shown below. However, care must be taken with fragmentation. If creating and deleting tasks, the process of allocating memory might not be able to provide a stack for the task(s) because the heap will eventually become fragmented. For this reason, allocating stack space dynamically in an embedded system is typically allowed but, once allocated, stacks should not be deallocated. Said another way, it's fine to create a task's stack from the heap as long as you don't free the stack space back to the heap.

```
void SomeCode (void)
{
    CPU_STK *p_stk;
    :
    :
    p_stk = (CPU_STK *)malloc(stk_size);
    if (p_stk != (CPU_STK *)0) {
        Create the task and pass it "p_stk" as the base address of the stack;
    }
    :
    :
}
```

See section 5-2 "Determining the Size of a Stack" on page 94.

F5-2(5)   A task can also have access to global variables. However, because µC/OS-III is a preemptive kernel care must be taken with code when accessing such variables as they may be shared between multiple tasks. Fortunately, µC/OS-III provides mechanisms to help with the management of such shared resources (semaphores, mutexes and more).

F5-2(6)   A task may also have access to one or more Input/Output (I/O) devices (also known as *peripherals*). In fact, it is common practice to assign tasks to manage I/O devices.

5

5-1 ASSIGNING TASK PRIORITIES

Sometimes task priorities are both obvious and intuitive. For example, if the most important aspect of the embedded system is to perform some type of control and it is known that the control algorithm must be responsive then it is best to assign the control task(s) a high priority while display and operator interface tasks are assigned low priority. However, most of the time, assigning task priorities is not so cut and dry because of the complex nature of real-time systems. In most systems, not all tasks are considered critical, and non-critical tasks should obviously be given low priorities.

An interesting technique called rate monotonic scheduling (RMS) assigns task priorities based on how often tasks execute. Simply put, tasks with the highest rate of execution are given the highest priority. However, RMS makes a number of assumptions, including:

■ All tasks are periodic (they occur at regular intervals).

■ Tasks do not synchronize with one another, share resources, or exchange data.

■ The CPU must always execute the highest priority task that is ready to run. In other words, preemptive scheduling must be used.

Given a set of **n** tasks that are assigned RMS priorities, the basic RMS theorem states that all task hard real-time deadlines are always met if the following inequality holds true:

$$\sum_i \frac{E_i}{T_i} \leq n \left(2^{1/n} - 1 \right)$$

Where **Ei** corresponds to the maximum execution time of task **i**, and **Ti** corresponds to the execution period of task **i**. In other words, **Ei/Ti** corresponds to the fraction of CPU time required to execute task **i**.

Table 5-1 shows the value for size $n(2^{1/n} - 1)$ based on the number of tasks. The upper bound for an infinite number of tasks is given by **ln(2)**, or **0.693**, which means that meeting all hard real-time deadlines based on RMS, CPU use of all time-critical tasks should be less than 70 percent!

Note that one can still have (and generally does) non time-critical tasks in a system and thus use close to 100 percent of the CPU's time. However, using 100 percent of your CPU's time is not a desirable goal as it does not allow for code changes and added features. As a rule of thumb, always design a system to use less than 60 to 70 percent of the CPU.

RMS says that the highest rate task has the highest priority. In some cases, the highest rate task might not be the most important task. The application dictates how to assign priorities. However, RMS is an interesting starting point.

Number of Tasks	$n(2^{1/n}-1)$
1	1.00
2	0.828
3	0.779
4	0.756
5	0.743
:	:
:	:
:	:
Infinite	0.693

Table 5-1 **Allowable CPU usage based on number of tasks**

5

5-2 DETERMINING THE SIZE OF A STACK

The size of the stack required by the task is application specific. When sizing the stack, however, one must account for the nesting of all the functions called by the task, the number of local variables to be allocated by all functions called by the task, and the stack requirements for all nested interrupt service routines. In addition, the stack must be able to store all CPU registers and possibly Floating-Point Unit (FPU) registers if the processor has a FPU. As a general rule in embedded systems, avoid writing recursive code.

It is possible to manually figure out the stack space needed by adding all the memory required by all function call nesting (1 pointer each function call for the return address), plus all the memory required by all the arguments passed in those function calls, plus storage for a full CPU context (depends on the CPU), plus another full CPU context for each nested ISRs (if the CPU doesn't have a separate stack to handle ISRs), plus whatever stack space is needed by those ISRs. Adding all this up is a tedious chore and the resulting number is a minimum requirement. Most likely one would not make the stack size that precise in order to account for "surprises." The number arrived at should probably be multiplied by some safety factor, possibly 1.5 to 2.0. This calculation assumes that the exact path of the code is known at all times, which is not always possible. Specifically, when calling a function such as **printf()** or some other library function, it might be difficult or nearly impossible to even guess just how much stack space **printf()** will require. In this case, start with a fairly large stack space and monitor the stack usage at run-time to see just how much stack space is actually used after the application runs for a while.

There are really cool and clever compilers/linkers that provide this information in a link map. For each function, the link map indicates the worst-case stack usage. This feature clearly enables one to better evaluate stack usage for each task. It is still necessary to add the stack space for a **full CPU** context plus, another **full CPU** context for each nested ISR (if the CPU does not have a separate stack to handle ISRs), plus whatever stack space is needed by those ISRs. Again, allow for a safety net and multiply this value by some factor.

Always monitor stack usage at run-time while developing and testing the product as stack overflows occur often and can lead to some curious behaviors. In fact, whenever someone mentions that his or her application behaves "strangely," insufficient stack size is the first thing that comes to mind.

5-3 DETECTING TASK STACK OVERFLOWS

1) Using an MMU or MPU

Stack overflows are easily detected if the processor has a Memory Management Unit (MMU) or a Memory Protection Unit (MPU). Basically, MMUs and MPUs are special hardware devices integrated alongside the CPU that can be configured to detect when a task attempts to access invalid memory locations, whether code, data, or stack. Setting up an MMU or MPU is well beyond the scope of this book.

2) Using a CPU with stack overflow detection

Some processors, however, do have simple stack pointer overflow detection registers. When the CPU's stack pointer goes below (or above depending on stack growth) the value set in this register, an exception is generated and the exception handler ensures that the offending code does not do further damage (possibly issue a warning about the faulty code). The `.StkLimitPtr` field in the `OS_TCB` (see Task Control Blocks) is provided for this purpose as shown in Figure 5-3. Note that the position of the stack limit is typically set at a valid location in the task's stack with sufficient room left on the stack to handle the exception itself (assuming the CPU does not have a separate exception stack). In most cases, the position can be fairly close to `&MyTaskStk[0]`.

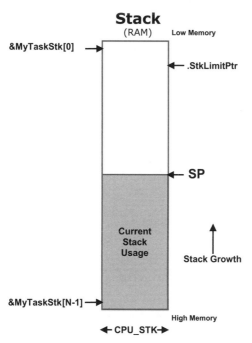

Figure 5-3 **Hardware detection of stack overflows**

5

As a reminder, the location of the `.StkLimitPtr` is determined by the "`stk_limit`" argument passed to `OSTaskCreate()`, when the task is created as shown below:

```
OS_TCB  MtTaskTCB;
CPU_STK MyTaskStk[1000];


OSTaskCreate(&MyTaskTCB,
            "MyTaskName",
            MyTask,
            &MyTaskArg,
            MyPrio,
            &MyTaskStk[0],    /* Stack base address                              */
            100,              /* Set .StkLimitPtr to trigger exception at stack usage > 90% */
            1000,             /* Total stack size (in CPU_STK elements)          */
            MyTaskQSize,
            MyTaskTimeQuanta,
            (void *)0,
            MY_TASK_OPT,
            &err);
```

Of course, the value of `.StkLimitPtr` used by the CPU's stack overflow detection hardware needs to be changed whenever µC/OS-III performs a context switch. This can be tricky because the value of this register may need to be changed so that it first points to **NULL**, then change the CPU's stack pointer, and finally set the value of the stack checking register to the value saved in the TCB's `.StkLimitPtr`. Why? Because if the sequence is not followed, the exception could be generated as soon as the stack pointer or the stack overflow detection register is changed. One can avoid this problem by first changing the stack overflow detection register to point to a location that ensures the stack pointer is never invalid (thus the **NULL** as described above). Note that I assumed here that the stack grows from high memory to low memory but the concept works in a similar fashion if the stack grows in the opposite direction.

3) Software-based stack overflow detection

Whenever µC/OS-III switches from one task to another, it calls a "hook" function (`OSTaskSwHook()`), which allows the µC/OS-III port programmer to extend the capabilities of the context switch function. So, if the processor doesn't have hardware stack pointer overflow detection, it's still possible to "simulate" this feature by adding code in the context switch hook function and, perform the overflow detection in software. Specifically, before a task is *switched* in, the code should ensure that the stack pointer to load into the CPU does not exceed the "limit" placed in `.StkLimitPtr`. Because the software implementation

cannot detect the stack overflow "as soon" as the stack pointer exceeds the value of
.StkLimitPtr, it is important to position the value of **.StkLimitPtr** in the stack fairly far from
&MyTaskStk[0], as shown in Figure 5-4. A software implementation such as this is not as
reliable as a hardware-based detection mechanism but still prevents a possible stack
overflow. Of course, the **.StkLimitPtr** field would be set using **OSTaskCreate()** as shown
above but this time, with a location further away from &MyTaskStk[0].

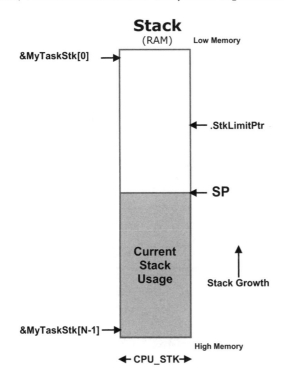

Figure 5-4 **Software detection of stack overflows, monitoring .StkLimitPtr**

4) Counting the amount of free stack space

Another way to check for stack overflows is to allocate more stack space than is anticipated
to be used for the stack, then, monitor and possibly display actual maximum stack usage at
run-time. This is fairly easy to do. First, the task stack needs to be cleared (i.e., filled with
zeros) when the task is created. Next, a low priority task *walks the stack* of each task
created, from the bottom (&MyTaskStk[0]) towards the top, counting the number of zero
entries. When the task finds a non-zero value, the process is stopped and the usage of the
stack can be computed (in number of bytes used or as a percentage). Then, adjust the size
of the stacks (by recompiling the code) to allocate a more *reasonable* value (either increase
or decrease the amount of stack space for each task). For this to be effective, however, run

the application long enough for the stack to grow to its highest value. This is illustrated in Figure 5-5. μC/OS-III provides a function that performs this calculation at run-time, OSTaskStkChk( ) and in fact, this function is called by OS_StatTask( ) to compute stack usage for every task created in the application (to be described later).

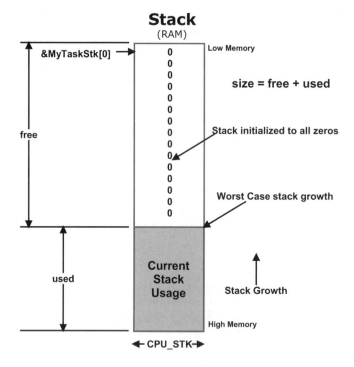

Figure 5-5 **Software detection of stack overflows, walking the stack**

5-4 TASK MANAGEMENT SERVICES

µC/OS-III provides a number of task-related services to call from the application. These services are found in **OS_TASK.C** and they all start with **OSTask???()**. The type of service they perform groups task-related services:

Group	Functions
General	OSTaskCreate()
	OSTaskDel()
	OSTaskChangePrio()
	OSTaskRegSet()
	OSTaskRegGet()
	OSTaskSuspend()
	OSTaskResume()
	OSTaskTimeQuantaSet()
Signaling a Task (See also Chapter 14, "Synchronization" on page 259)	OSTaskSemPend()
	OSTaskSemPost()
	OSTaskSemPendAbort()
Sending Messages to a Task (See also Chapter 15, "Message Passing" on page 297)	OSTaskQPend()
	OSTaskQPost()
	OSTaskQPendAbort()
	OSTaskQFlush()

Table 5-2 **Task Management Services**

A complete description of all µC/OS-III task related services is provided in Appendix A, "µC/OS-III API Reference Manual" on page 383.

5

5-5 TASK MANAGEMENT INTERNALS

5-5-1 TASK STATES

From a µC/OS-III user point of view, a task can be in any one of five states as shown in Figure 5-6. Internally, µC/OS-III does not need to keep track of the dormant state and the other states are tracked slightly differently. This will be discussed after a discussion on task states from the user's point of view. Figure 5-6 also shows which µC/OS-III functions are used to move from one state to another. The diagram is actually simplified as state transitions are a bit more complicated than this.

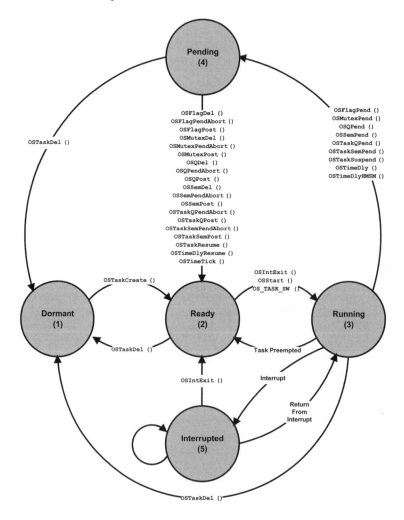

Figure 5-6 **Five basic states of a task**

F5-6(1)   The *Dormant* state corresponds to a task that resides in memory but has not been made available to µC/OS-III.

A task is made available to µC/OS-III by calling a function to create the task, **OSTaskCreate()**. The task code actually resides in code space but µC/OS-III needs to be informed about it.

When it is no longer necessary for µC/OS-III to manage a task, call the task delete function, **OSTaskDel()**. **OSTaskDel()** does not actually delete the code of the task, it is simply not eligible to access the CPU.

F5-6(2)   The *Ready* state corresponds to a ready-to-run task, but is not the most important task ready. There can be any number of tasks ready and µC/OS-III keeps track of all ready tasks in a **ready list** (discussed later). This list is sorted by priority.

F5-6(3)   The most important ready-to-run task is placed in the *Running* state. On a single CPU, only one task can be running at any given time.

The task selected to run on the CPU is *switched in* by µC/OS-III from the ready state when the application code calls **OSStart()**, or when µC/OS-III calls either **OSIntExit()** or **OS_TASK_SW()**.

As previously discussed, tasks must wait for an event to occur. A task waits for an event by calling one of the functions that brings the task to the pending state if the event has not occurred.

F5-6(4)   Tasks in the *Pending* state are placed in a special list called a *pend-list* (or wait list) associated with the event the task is waiting for. When waiting for the event to occur, the task does not consume CPU time. When the event occurs, the task is placed back into the ready list and µC/OS-III decides whether the newly readied task is the most important ready-to-run task. If this is the case, the currently running task will be preempted (placed back in the ready list) and the newly readied task is given control of the CPU. In other words, the newly readied task will run immediately if it is the most important task.

Note that the **OSTaskSuspend()** function unconditionally blocks a task and this task will not actually wait for an event to occur but in fact, waits until another task calls **OSTaskResume()** to make the task ready to run.

F5-6(5)   Assuming that CPU interrupts are enabled, an interrupting device will suspend execution of a task and execute an Interrupt Service Routine (ISR). ISRs are typically events that tasks wait for. Generally speaking, an ISR should simply notify a task that an event occurred and let the task process the event. ISRs should be as short as possible and most of the work of handling the interrupting devices should be done at the task level where it can be managed by µC/OS-III. ISRs are only allowed to make "Post" calls (i.e., **OSFlagPost()**, **OSQPost()**, **OSSemPost()**, **OSTaskQPost()** and **OSTaskSemPost()**). The only post call not allowed to be made from an ISR is OSMutexPost() since mutexes, as will be addressed later, are assumed to be services that are only accessible at the task level.

As the state diagram indicates, an interrupt can interrupt another interrupt. This is called **interrupt nesting** and most processors allow this. However, interrupt nesting easily leads to stack overflow if not managed properly.

Internally, µC/OS-III keeps track of task states using the state machine shown in Figure 5-7. The task state is actually maintained in a variable that is part of a data structure associated with each task, the task's TCB. The task state diagram was referenced throughout the design of µC/OS-III when implementing most of µC/OS-III's services. The number in parentheses is the state number of the task and thus, a task can be in any one of eight (8) states (see **OS.H, OS_TASK_STATE_???**).

Note that the diagram does not keep track of a dormant task, as a dormant task is not known to µC/OS-III. Also, interrupts and interrupt nesting is tracked differently as will be explained further in the text.

This state diagram should be quite useful to understand how to use several functions and their impact on the state of tasks. In fact, I'd highly recommend that the reader bookmark the page of the diagram.

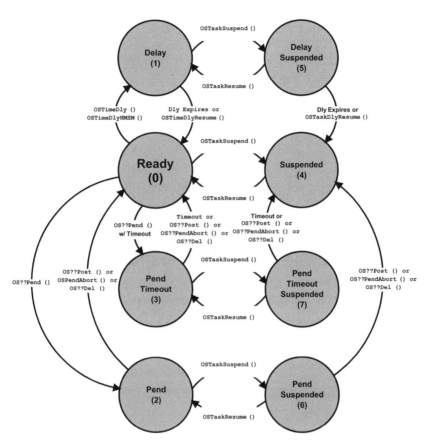

Figure 5-7 **µC/OS-III's internal task state machine**

F5-7(1)   State 0 occurs when a task is ready to run. Every task "wants" to be ready to run as that is the only way it gets to perform their duties.

F5-7(2)   A task can decide to wait for time to expire by calling either **OSTimeDly()** or **OSTimeDlyHMSM()**. When the time expires or the delay is cancelled (by calling **OSTimeDlyResume()**), the task returns to the ready state.

F5-7(3)   A task can wait for an event to occur by calling one of the pend (i.e., wait) functions (**OSFlagPend()**, **OSMutexPend()**, **OSQPend()**, **OSSemPend()**, **OSTaskQPend()**, or **OSTaskSemPend()**), and specify to wait forever for the event to occur. The pend terminates when the event occurs (i.e., a task or an ISR performs a "post"), the awaited object is deleted or, another task decides to abort the pend.

F5-7(4)   A task can wait for an event to occur as indicated, but specify that it is willing to wait a certain amount of time for the event to occur. If the event is not posted within that time, the task is readied, then the task is notified that a timeout occurred. Again, the pend terminates when the event occurs (i.e., a task or an ISR performs a "post"), the object awaited is deleted or, another task decides to abort the pend.

F5-7(5)   A task can suspend itself or another task by calling **OSTaskSuspend()**. The only way the task is allowed to resume execution is by calling **OSTaskResume()**. Suspending a task means that a task will not be able to run on the CPU until it is resumed by another task.

F5-7(6)   A delayed task can also be suspended by another task. In this case, the effect is additive. In other words, the delay must complete (or be resumed by **OSTimeDlyResume()**) and the suspension must be removed (by another task which would call **OSTaskResume()**) in order for the task to be able to run.

F5-7(7)   A task waiting on an event to occur may be suspended by another task. Again, the effect is additive. The event must occur and the suspension removed (by another task) in order for the task to be able to run. Of course, if the object that the task is pending on is deleted or, the pend is aborted by another task, then one of the above two condition is removed. The suspension , however, must be explicitly removed.

F5-7(8)   A task can wait for an event, but only for a certain amount of time, and the task could also be suspended by another task. As one might expect, the suspension must be removed by another task (or the same task that suspended it in the first place), and the event needs to either occur or timeout while waiting for the event.

5-5-2 TASK CONTROL BLOCKS (TCBs)

A task control block (TCB) is a data structure used by kernels to maintain information about a task. Each task requires its own TCB and, for µC/OS-III, the user assigns the TCB in user memory space (RAM). The address of the task's TCB is provided to µC/OS-III when calling task-related services (i.e., **OSTask???()** functions). The task control block data structure is declared in **OS.H** as shown in Listing 5-3. Note that the fields are actually commented in **OS.H**, and some of the fields are conditionally compiled based on whether or not certain features are desired. Both are not shown here for clarity.

Also, it is important to note that even when the user understands what the different fields of the **OS_TCB** do, the application code must never directly access these (especially change them). In other words, **OS_TCB** fields must only be accessed by µC/OS-III and not the code.

```
struct os_tcb {
    CPU_STK          *StkPtr;
    void             *ExtPtr;
    CPU_STK          *StkLimitPtr;
    OS_TCB           *NextPtr;
    OS_TCB           *PrevPtr;
    OS_TCB           *TickNextPtr;
    OS_TCB           *TickPrevPtr;
    OS_TICK_SPOKE    *TickSpokePtr;
    OS_CHAR          *NamePtr;
    CPU_STK          *StkBasePtr;
    OS_TASK_PTR       TaskEntryAddr;
    void             *TaskEntryArg;
    OS_PEND_DATA     *PendDataTblPtr;
    OS_OBJ_QTY        PendDataEntries;
    CPU_TS            TS;
    void             *MsgPtr;
    OS_MSG_SIZE       MsgSize;
    OS_MSG_Q          MsgQ;
    CPU_TS            MsgQPendTime;
    CPU_TS            MsgQPendTimeMax;
    OS_FLAGS          FlagsPend;
    OS_OPT            FlagsOpt;
    OS_FLAGS          FlagsRdy;
```

```
        OS_REG                 RegTbl[OS_TASK_REG_TBL_SIZE];
        OS_SEM_CTR             SemCtr;
        CPU_TS                 SemPendTime;
        CPU_TS                 SemPendTimeMax;
        OS_NESTING_CTR         SuspendCtr;
        CPU_STK_SIZE           StkSize;
        CPU_STK_SIZE           StkUsed;
        CPU_STK_SIZE           StkFree;
        OS_OPT                 Opt;
        OS_TICK                TickCtrPrev;
        OS_TICK                TickCtrMatch;
        OS_TICK                TickRemain;
        OS_TICK                TimeQuanta;
        OS_TICK                TimeQuantaCtr;
        OS_CPU_USAGE           CPUUsage;
        OS_CTX_SW_CTR          CtxSwCtr;
        CPU_TS                 CyclesDelta;
        CPU_TS                 CyclesStart;
        OS_CYCLES              CyclesTotal;
        CPU_TS                 IntDisTimeMax;
        CPU                    SchedLockTimeMax;
        OS_STATE               PendOn;
        OS_STATUS              PendStatus;
        OS_STATE               TaskState;
        OS_PRIO                Prio;
        OS_TCB                 DbgNextPtr;
        OS_TCB                 DbgPrevPtr;
        CPU_CHAR               DbgNamePtr;
};
```

Listing 5-3 **OS_TCB Data Structure**

.StkPtr

This field contains a pointer to the current top-of-stack for the task. µC/OS-III allows each task to have its own stack and each stack can be any size. **.StkPtr** should be the only field in the **OS_TCB** data structure accessed from assembly language code (for the context-switching code). This field is therefore placed as the first entry in the structure making access easier from assembly language code (it will be at offset zero in the data structure).

.ExtPtr

This field contains a pointer to a user-definable pointer to extend the TCB as needed. This pointer is easily accessible from assembly language.

.StkLimitPtr

The field contains a pointer to a location in the task's stack to set a *watermark* limit for stack growth and is determined from the value of the "**stk_limit**" argument passed to **OSTaskCreate()**. Some processors have special registers that automatically check the value of the stack pointer at run-time to ensure that the stack does not overflow. **.StkLimitPtr** may be used to set this register during a context switch. Alternatively, if the processor does not have such a register, this can be "simulated" in software. However, it is not as reliable as a hardware solution. If this feature is not used then the value of "**stk_limit**" can be set to 0 when calling **OSTaskCreate()**. See also section 5-3 "Detecting Task Stack Overflows" on page 95).

.NextPtr and .PrevPtr

These pointers are used to doubly link **OS_TCBs** in the ready list. A doubly linked list allows **OS_TCBs** to be quickly inserted and removed from the list.

.TickNextPtr and .TickPrevPtr

These pointers are used to doubly link **OS_TCBs** in the list of tasks waiting for time to expire or to timeout from pend calls. Again, a doubly linked list allows **OS_TCBs** to be quickly inserted and removed from the list.

.TickSpokePtr

This pointer is used to know which spoke in the "tick wheel" the task is linked to. The tick wheel will be described in "Chapter 9, "Interrupt Management" on page 165."

.NamePtr

This pointer allows a name (an ASCII string) to be assigned to each task. Having a name is useful when debugging, since it is user friendly compared to displaying the address of the OS_TCB. Storage for the ASCII string is assumed to be in user space in code memory (ASCII string declared as a const) or in RAM.

.StkBasePtr

This field points to the base address of the task's stack. The stack base is typically the lowest address in memory where the stack for the task resides. A task stack is declared as follows:

```
CPU_STK MyTaskStk[???];
```

CPU_STK is the data type you must use to declare task stacks and ??? is the size of the stack associated with the task. The base address is always &MyTaskStk[0].

.TaskEntryAddr

This field contains the entry address of the task. As previously mentioned, a task is declared as shown below and this field contains the address of MyTask.

```
void  MyTask (void *p_arg);
```

.TaskEntryArg

This field contains the value of the argument that is passed to the task when the task starts. As previously mentioned, a task is declared as shown below and this field contains the value of p_arg.

```
void  MyTask (void *p_arg);
```

.PendDataTblPtr

μC/OS-III allows the task to pend on any number of semaphores or message queues simultaneously. This pointer points to a table containing information about the pended objects.

.PendDataEntries

This field works with the .PendDataTblPtr, indicating the number of objects a task is pending on at the same time.

.TS

This field is used to store a "time stamp" of when an event that the task was waiting on occurred. When the task resumes execution, this time stamp is returned to the caller.

.MsgPtr

When a message is sent to a task, this field contains the message received. This field only exists in a TCB if message queue services (**OS_CFG_Q_EN** is set to 1 in **OS_CFG.H**), or task message queue services, are enabled (**OS_CFG_TASK_Q_EN** is set to 1 in **OS_CFG.H**) at compile time.

.MsgSize

When a message is sent to a task, this field contains the size (in number of bytes) of the message received. This field only exists in a TCB if message queue services (**OS_CFG_Q_EN** is set to 1 in **OS_CFG.H**), or task message queue services, (**OS_CFG_TASK_Q_EN** is set to 1 in **OS_CFG.H**) are enabled at compile time.

.MsgQ

µC/OS-III allows tasks or ISRs to send messages directly to tasks. Because of this, a message queue is actually built into each TCB. This field only exists in a TCB if task message queue services are enabled at compile time (**OS_CFG_TASK_Q_EN** is set to 1 in **OS_CFG.H**). .MsgQ is used by the **OSTaskQ???()** services.

.MsgQPendTime

This field contains the amount of time for a message to arrive. When **OSTaskQPost()** is called, the current time stamp is read and stored in the message. When **OSTaskQPend()** returns, the current time stamp is read again and the difference between the two times is stored in this variable. A debugger or µC/Probe can be used to indicate the time taken for a message to arrive by displaying this field.

This field is only available if setting **OS_CFG_TASK_PROFILE_EN** to 1 in **OS_CFG.H**.

.MsgQPendTimeMax

This field contains the maximum amount of time it takes for a message to arrive. It is a peak detector of the value of **.MsgQPendTime**. The peak can be reset by calling **OSStatReset()**.

This field is only available if setting OS_CFG_TASK_PROFILE_EN to 1 in OS_CFG.H.

.FlagsPend

When a task pends on event flags, this field contains the event flags (i.e., bits) that the task is pending on. This field only exists in a TCB if event flags services are enabled at compile time (OS_CFG_FLAG_EN is set to 1 in OS_CFG.H).

.FlagsOpt

When a task pends on event flags, this field contains the type of pend (pend on any event flag bit specified in **.FlagsPend** or all event flag bits specified in **.FlagsPend**). This field only exists in a TCB if event flags services are enabled at compile time (OS_CFG_FLAG_EN is set to 1 in OS_CFG.H).

.FlagsRdy

This field contains the event flags that were posted and that the task was waiting on. In other words, it allows a task to know which event flags made the task ready to run. This field only exists in a TCB if event flags services are enabled at compile time (OS_CFG_FLAG_EN is set to 1 in OS_CFG.H).

.RegTbl[]

This field contains a table of "registers" that are task-specific. These registers are different than CPU registers. Task registers allow for the storage of such task-specific information as task ID, "**errno**" common in some software components, and more. Task registers may also store task-related data that needs to be associated with the task at run time. Note that the data type for elements of this array is OS_REG, which can be declared at compile time to be nearly anything. However, all registers must be of this data type. This field only exists in a TCB if task registers are enabled at compile time (OS_CFG_TASK_REG_TBL_SIZE is greater than 0 in OS_CFG.H).

.SemCtr

This field contains a semaphore counter associated with the task. Each task has its own semaphore built-in. An ISR or another task can signal a task using this semaphore. **.SemCtr** is therefore used to keep track of how many times the task is signaled. **.SemCtr** is used by **OSTaskSem???()** services.

.SemPendTime

This field contains the amount of time taken for the semaphore to be signaled. When OSTaskSemPost() is called, the current time stamp is read and stored in the OS_TCB (see .TS). When OSTaskSemPend() returns, the current time stamp is read again and the difference between the two times is stored in this variable. This field can be displayed by a debugger or µC/Probe to indicate how much time it took for the task to be signaled.

This field is only available when setting OS_CFG_TASK_PROFILE_EN to 1 in OS_CFG.H.

.SemPendTimeMax

This field contains the maximum amount of time it took for the task to be signaled. It is a peak detector of the value of .SemPendTime. The peak can be reset by calling OSStatReset().

This field is only available if setting OS_CFG_TASK_PROFILE_EN to 1 in OS_CFG.H.

.SuspendCtr

This field is used by OSTaskSuspend() and OSTaskResume() to keep track of how many times a task is suspended. Task suspension can be nested. When .SuspendCtr is 0, all suspensions are removed. This field only exists in a TCB if task suspension is enabled at compile time (OS_CFG_TASK_SUSPEND_EN is set to 1 in OS_CFG.H).

.StkSize

This field contains the size (in number of CPU_STK elements) of the stack associated with the task. Recall that a task stack is declared as follows:

```
CPU_STK MyTaskStk[???];
```

.StkSize is the value of ??? in the above array.

.StkUsed and .StkFree

µC/OS-III is able to compute (at run time) the amount of stack space a task actually uses and how much stack space remains. This is accomplished by a function called OSTaskStkChk(). Stack usage computation assumes that the task's stack is "cleared" when the task is created. In other words, when calling OSTaskCreate(), it is expected that the following options be specified: OS_TASK_OPT_STK_CLR and OS_TASK_OPT_STK_CHK. OSTaskCreate() will then clear all the RAM used for the task's stack.

µC/OS-III provides an internal task called **OS_StatTask()** that checks the stack of each of the tasks at run-time. **OS_StatTask()** typically runs at a low priority so that it does not interfere with the application code. **OS_StatTask()** saves the value computed for each task in the TCB of each task in these fields, which represents the maximum number of stack bytes used and the amount of stack space still unused by the task. These fields only exist in a TCB if the statistic task is enabled at compile time (**OS_CFG_STAT_TASK_STK_CHK_EN** is set to 1 in **OS_CFG.H**).

.Opt

This field saves the "options" passed to **OSTaskCreate()** when the task is created (see **OS_TASK_OPT_???** in **OS.H**). Note that task options are additive.

.TickCtrPrev

This field stores the previous value of **OSTickCtr** when **OSTimeDly()** is called with the **OS_OPT_TIME_PERIODIC** option.

.TickCtrMatch

When a task is waiting for time to expire, or pending on an object with a timeout, the task is placed in a special list of tasks waiting for time to expire. When in this list, the task waits for **.TickCtrMatch** to match the value of the "tick counter" (**OSTickCtr**). When a match occurs, the task is removed from that list.

.TickRemain

This field is computed at run time by **OS_TickTask()** to compute the amount of time (expressed in "ticks") left before a delay or timeout expires. This field is useful for debuggers or run-time monitors for display purposes.

.TimeQuanta and .TimeQuantaCtr

These fields are used for time slicing. When multiple tasks are ready to run at the same priority, **.TimeQuanta** determines how much time (in ticks) the task will execute until it is preempted by µC/OS-III so that the next task at the same priority gets a chance to execute. **.TimeQuantaCtr** keeps track of the remaining number of ticks for this to happen and is loaded with **.TimeQuanta** at the beginning of the task's time slice.

.CPUUsage

This field is computed by **OS_StatTask()** if **OS_CFG_TASK_PROFILE_EN** is set to 1 in **OS_CFG.H**. **.CPUUsage** contains the CPU usage of a task in percent (0 to 100%).

.CtxSwCtr

This field keeps track of how often the task has executed (not how long it has executed). This field is generally used by debuggers or run-time monitors to see if a task is executing (the value of this field would be non-zero and would be incrementing). The field is enabled at compile time when OS_CFG_TASK_PROFILE_EN is set to 1.

.CyclesDelta

.CyclesDelta is computed during a context switch and contains the value of the current time stamp (obtained by calling OS_TS_GET()) minus the value of .CyclesStart. This field is generally used by debuggers or a run-time monitor to see how long a task takes to execute. The field is enabled at compile time when OS_CFG_TASK_PROFILE_EN is set to 1.

.CyclesStart

This field is used to measure the execution time of a task. .CyclesStart is updated when µC/OS-III performs a context switch. .CyclesStart contains the value of the current time stamp (it calls OS_TS_GET()) when a task switch occurs. This field is generally used by debuggers or a run-time monitor to see how long a task takes to execute. The field is enabled at compile time when OS_CFG_TASK_PROFILE_EN is set to 1.

.CyclesTotal

This field accumulates the value of .CyclesDelta, so it contains the total execution time of a task. This is typically a 64-bit value because of the accumulation of cycles over time. Using a 64-bit value ensures that we can accumulate CPU cycles for almost 600 years even if the CPU is running at 1 GHz! Of course, it's assumed that the compiler supports 64-bit data types.

.IntDisTimeMax

This field keeps track of the maximum interrupt disable time of the task. The field is updated only if µC/CPU supports interrupt disable time measurements. This field is available only if setting OS_CFG_TASK_PROFILE_EN to 1 in OS_CFG.H and µC/CPU's CPU_CFG_TIME_MEAS_INT_DIS_EN is defined in CPU_CFG.H.

.SchedLockTimeMax

The field keeps track of the maximum scheduler lock time of the task.

This field is available only if you set OS_CFG_TASK_PROFILE_EN to 1 and OS_CFG_SCHED_LOCK_TIME_MEAS_EN is set to 1 in OS_CFG.H.

5

.PendOn

This field indicates upon what the task is pending and contains OS_TASK_PEND_ON_??? (see OS.H).

.PendStatus

This field indicates the outcome of a pend and contains OS_STATUS_PEND_??? (see OS.H).

.TaskState

This field indicates the current state of a task and contains one of the eight (8) task states that a task can be in, see OS_TASK_STATE_??? (see OS.H).

.Prio

This field contains the current priority of a task. .Prio is a value between 0 and OS_CFG_PRIO_MAX-1. In fact, the idle task is the only task at priority OS_CFG_PRIO_MAX-1.

.DbgNextPtr

This field contains a pointer to the next OS_TCB in a doubly linked list of OS_TCBs. OS_TCBs are placed in this list by OSTaskCreate(). This field is only present if OS_CFG_DBG_EN is set to 1 in OS_CFG.H. the current priority of a task.

.DbgPrevPtr

This field contains a pointer to the previous OS_TCB in a doubly linked list of OS_TCBs. OS_TCBs are placed in this list by OSTaskCreate(). This field is only present if OS_CFG_DBG_EN is set to 1 in OS_CFG.H.

.DbgNamePtr

This field contains a pointer to the name of the object that the task is pending on when the task is pending on an event flag group, a semaphore, a mutual exclusion semaphore or a message queue. This information is quite useful during debugging and thus, this field is only present if OS_CFG_DBG_EN is set to 1 in OS_CFG.H.

5-6 INTERNAL TASKS

During initialization, µC/OS-III creates a minimum of two (2) internal tasks (OS_IdleTask() and OS_TickTask()) and, three (3) optional tasks (OS_StatTask(), OS_TmrTask() and OS_IntQTask()). The optional tasks are created based on the value of compile-time #defines found in OS_CFG.H.

5-6-1 THE IDLE TASK (OS_IdleTask())

OS_IdleTask() is the very first task created by µC/OS-III and always exists in a µC/OS-III-based application. The priority of the idle task is always set to OS_CFG_PRIO_MAX-1. In fact, OS_IdleTask() is the only task that is ever allowed to be at this priority and, as a safeguard, when other tasks are created, OSTaskCreate() ensures that there are no other tasks created at the same priority as the idle task. The idle task runs whenever there are no other tasks that are ready to run. The important portions of the code for the idle task are shown below (refer to OS_CORE.C for the complete code).

```
void  OS_IdleTask (void *p_arg)
{
    while (DEF_ON) {                    (1)
        OS_CRITICAL_ENTER();
        OSIdleTaskCtr++;               (2)
        OSTaskStatCtr++;
        OS_CRITICAL_EXIT();
        OSIdleTaskHook();              (3)
    }
}
```

Listing 5-4 **Idle Task**

L5-4(1)   The idle task is a "true" infinite loop that never calls functions to "wait for an event". This is because, on most processors, when there is "nothing to do," the processor still executes instructions. When µC/OS-III determines that there is no other higher-priority task to run, µC/OS-III "parks" the CPU in the idle task. Instead of having an empty "for loop" doing nothing, this "idle" time is used to do something useful.

L5-4(2)   Two counters are incremented whenever the idle task runs.

OSIdleTaskCtr is typically defined as a 32-bit unsigned integer (see OS.H). OSIdleTaskCtr is reset once when µC/OS-III is initialized. OSIdleTaskCtr is used to indicate "activity" in the idle task. In other words, if one monitors and displays OSIdleTaskCtr, one should expect to see a value between 0x00000000 and 0xFFFFFFFF. The rate at which OSIdleTaskCtr increments depend on how busy the CPU is at running the application code. The faster the increment, the less work the CPU has to do in application tasks.

OSStatTaskCtr is also typically defined as a 32-bit unsigned integer (see **OS.H**) and is used by the statistic task (described later) to get a sense of CPU utilization at run time.

L5-4(3) Every time through the loop, **OS_IdleTask()** calls **OSIdleTaskHook()**, which is a function that is declared in the μC/OS-III port for the processor used. **OSIdleTaskHook()** allows the implementer of the μC/OS-III port to perform additional processing during idle time. It is very important for this code to not make calls that would cause the idle task to "wait for an event". This is generally not a problem as most programmers developing μC/OS-III ports know to follow this simple rule.

OSIdleTaskHook() may be used to place the CPU in low-power mode for battery-powered applications or to simply not waste energy as shown in the pseudo-code below. However, doing this means that **OSStatTaskCtr** cannot be used to measure CPU utilization (described later).

```
void  OSIdleTaskHook (void)
{
    /* Place the CPU in low power mode */
}
```

Typically, most processors exit low-power mode when an interrupt occurs. Depending on the processor, however, the Interrupt Service Routine (ISR) may have to write to "special" registers to return the CPU to its full or desired speed. If the ISR wakes up a high-priority task (every task is higher in priority than the idle task) then the ISR will not immediately return to the interrupted idle task, but instead switch to the higher-priority task. When the higher-priority task completes its work and waits for its event to occur, μC/OS-III causes a context switch to return to **OSIdleTaskHook()** just "after" the instruction that caused the CPU to enter low-power mode. In turn, **OSIdleTaskHook()** returns to **OS_IdleTask()** and causes another iteration through the "for loop."

5

5-6-2 THE TICK TASK (OS_TickTask())

Nearly every RTOS requires a periodic time source called a *Clock Tick* or *System Tick* to keep track of time delays and timeouts. µC/OS-III's clock tick handling is encapsulated in the file OS_TICK.C.

OS_TickTask() is a task created by µC/OS-III and its priority is configurable by the user through µC/OS-III's configuration file OS_CFG_APP.H (see OS_CFG_TICK_TASK_PRIO). Typically OS_TickTask() is set to a relatively high priority. In fact, the priority of this task is set slightly lower than the most important tasks.

OS_TickTask() is used by µC/OS-III to keep track of tasks waiting for time to expire or, for tasks that are pending on kernel objects with a timeout. OS_TickTask() is a periodic task and it waits for signals from the tick ISR (described in Chapter 9, "Interrupt Management" on page 165) as shown in Figure 5-8.

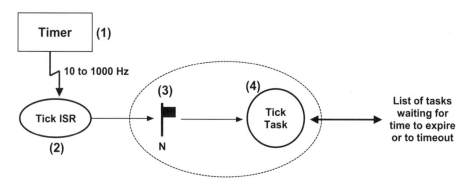

Figure 5-8 **Tick ISR and Tick Task relationship**

F5-8(1)   A hardware timer is generally used and configured to generate an interrupt at a rate between 10 and 1000 Hz (see OS_CFG_TICK_RATE in OS_CFG_APP.H). This timer is generally called the *Tick Timer*. The actual rate to use depends on such factors as: processor speed, desired time resolution, and amount of allowable overhead to handle the tick timer, etc.

The tick interrupt does not have to be generated by a timer and, in fact, it can come from other regular time sources such as the power-line frequency (50 or 60 Hz), which are known to be fairly accurate over long periods of time.

F5-8(2)   Assuming CPU interrupts are enabled, the CPU accepts the tick interrupt, preempts the current task, and vectors to the tick ISR. The tick ISR must call **OSTimeTick()** (see **OS_TIME.C**), which accomplishes most of the work needed by µC/OS-III. The tick ISR then clears the timer interrupt (and possibly reloads the timer for the next interrupt). However, some timers may need to be taken care of prior to calling **OSTimeTick()** instead of after as shown below.

```
void  TickISR (void)
{
    OSTimeTick();
    /* Clear tick interrupt source             */
    /* Reload the timer for the next interrupt */
}
```

or,

```
void  TickISR (void)
{
    /* Clear tick interrupt source             */
    /* Reload the timer for the next interrupt */
    OSTimeTick();
}
```

OSTimeTick() calls **OSTimeTickHook()** at the very beginning of **OSTimeTick()** to give the opportunity to the µC/OS-III port developer to react as soon as possible upon servicing the tick interrupt.

F5-8(3)   **OSTimeTick()** calls a service provided by µC/OS-III to signal the tick task and make that task ready to run. The tick task executes as soon as it becomes the most important task. The reason the tick task might not run immediately is that the tick interrupt could have interrupted a task higher in priority than the tick task and, upon completion of the tick ISR, µC/OS-III will resume the interrupted task.

F5-8(4)   When the tick task executes, it goes through a list of all tasks that are waiting for time to expire or are waiting on a kernel object with a timeout. From this point forward, this will be called the tick list. The tick task will make ready to run all of the tasks in the tick list for which time or timeout has expired. The process is explained below.

μC/OS-III may need to place literally hundreds of tasks (if an application has that many tasks) in the tick list. The tick list is implemented in such a way that it does not take much CPU time to determine if time has expired for those tasks placed in the tick list and, possibly makes those tasks ready to run. The tick list is implemented as shown in Figure 5-9.

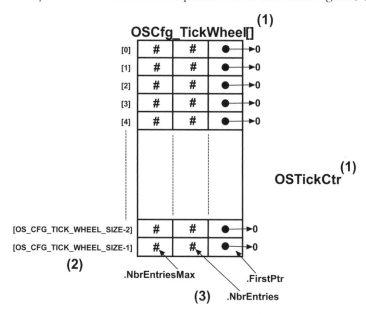

Figure 5-9 **Empty Tick List**

F5-9(1)   The tick list consists of a table (OSCfg_TickWheel[]) and a counter (OSTickCtr).

F5-9(2)   The table contains up to **OS_CFG_TICK_WHEEL_SIZE** entries, which is a compile time configuration value (see **OS_CFG_APP.H**). The number of entries depends on the amount of memory (RAM) available to the processor and the maximum number of tasks in the application. A good starting point for **OS_CFG_TICK_WHEEL_SIZE** may be: **#Tasks / 4**. It is recommended not to make **OS_CFG_TICK_WHEEL_SIZE** an even multiple of the tick rate. If the tick rate is 1000 Hz and one has 50 tasks in the application, avoid setting **OS_CFG_TICK_WHEEL_SIZE** to 10 or 20 (use 11 or 23 instead). Actually, prime numbers are good choices. Although it is not really possible to plan at compile time what will happen at run time, ideally, the number of tasks waiting in each entry of the table will be distributed uniformly.

5

F5-9(3)   Each entry in the table contains three fields: **.NbrEntriesMax**, **.NbrEntries** and **.FirstPtr**.

.NbrEntries indicates the number of tasks linked to this table entry.

.NbrEntriesMax keeps track of the highest number of entries in the table. This value is reset when the application code calls **OSStatReset()**.

.FirstPtr contains a pointer to a doubly linked list of tasks (through the tasks **OS_TCB**) belonging to the list, at that table position.

The counter is incremented by **OS_TickTask()** each time the task is signaled by the tick ISR.

Tasks are automatically inserted in the tick list when the application programmer calls a **OSTimeDly???()** function, or when an **OS???Pend()** call is made with a non-zero timeout value.

Example 5-1

Using an example to illustrate the process of inserting a task in the tick list, let's assume that the tick list is completely empty, **OS_CFG_TICK_WHEEL_SIZE** is configured to 12, and the current value of **OSTickCtr** is 10 as shown in Figure 5-10. A task is placed in the tick list when **OSTimeDly()** is called and assume **OSTimeDly()** is called as follows:

```
    :
    OSTimeDly(1, OS_OPT_TIME_DLY, &err);
    :
```

Referring to the µC/OS-III reference manual in Appendix A, notice that this action indicates to µC/OS-III to delay the current task for 1 tick. Since **OSTickCtr** has a value of 10, the task will be put to sleep until **OSTickCtr** reaches 11 or at the very next clock tick interrupt. Tasks are inserted in the **OSCfg_TickWheel[]** table using the following equation:

```
MatchValue                 = OSTickCtr + dly
Index into OSCfg_TickWheel[] = MatchValue % OS_CFG_TICK_WHEEL_SIZE
```

Where "**dly**" is the value passed in the first argument of **OSTimeDly()** or, 1 in this example. We therefore obtain the following:

```
MatchValue                        =  10 + 1
Index into OSCfg_TickWheel[] = (10 + 1) % 12
```

or,

```
MatchValue                        = 11
Index into OSCfg_TickWheel[] = 11
```

Because of the "circular" nature of the table (a modulo operation using the size of the table), the table is referred to as a *tick wheel* and each entry is a *spoke* in the wheel.

The OS_TCB of the task being delayed is entered at index 11 in OSCfg_TickWheel[] (i.e., spoke 11 using the wheel analogy). The OS_TCB of the task is inserted in the first entry of the list (i.e., pointed to by OSCfg_TickWheel[11].FirstPtr), and the number of entries at spoke 11 is incremented (i.e., OSCfg_TickWheel[11].NbrEntries will be 1). Notice that the OS_TCB also links back to &OSCfg_TickWheel[11] and the "MatchValue" are placed in the OS_TCB field .TickCtrMatch. Since this is the first task inserted in the tick list at spoke 11, the .TickNextPtr and .TickPrevPtr both point to NULL.

Figure 5-10 **Inserting a task in the tick list**

5

OSTimeDly() takes care of a few other details. Specifically, the task is removed from µC/OS-III's ready list (described in Chapter 6, "The Ready List" on page 131) since the task is no longer eligible to run (because it is waiting for time to expire). Also, the scheduler is called because µC/OS-III will need to run the next most important ready-to-run task.

If the next task to run also happens to call **OSTimeDly()** "before" the next tick arrives and calls **OSTimeDly()** as follows:

```
    :
    OSTimeDly(13, OS_OPT_TIME_DLY, &err);
    :
```

µC/OS-III will calculate the match value and spoke as follows:

```
MatchValue                    =  10 + 13
OSCfg_TickWheel[] spoke number = (10 + 13) % 12
```

or,

```
MatchValue                    =  23
OSCfg_TickWheel[] spoke number =  11
```

The "second task" will be inserted at the same table entry as shown in Figure 5-11. Tasks sharing the same spoke are sorted in ascending order such that the task with the least amount of time remaining is placed at the head of the list.

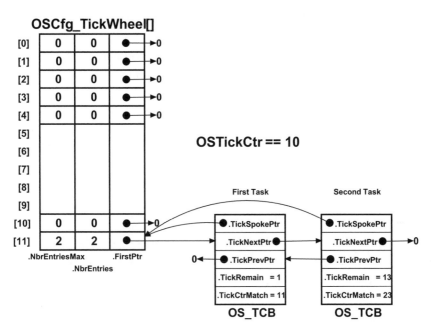

Figure 5-11 **Inserting a second task in the tick list**

When the tick task executes (see OS_TickTask() and also OS_TickListUpdate() in OS_TICK.C), it starts incrementing OSTickCtr and determines which table entry (i.e., which spoke) needs to be processed. Then, if there are tasks in the list at this entry (i.e., .FirstPtr is not NULL), each OS_TCB is examined to determine whether the .TickCtrMatch value "matches" OSTickCtr and, if so, we remove the OS_TCB from the list. If the task is only waiting for time to expire, it will be placed in the ready list (described later). If the task is pending on an object, not only will the task be removed from the tick list, but it will also be removed from the list of tasks waiting on that object. The search through the list terminates as soon as OSTickCtr does not match the task's .TickCtrMatch value; since there is no point in looking any further in the list.

Note that OS_TickTask() does most of its work in a critical section when the tick list is updated. However, because the list is sorted, the critical section has a chance to be fairly short.

5

5-6-3 THE STATISTIC TASK (OS_StatTask())

μC/OS-III contains an internal task that provides such run-time statistics as overall CPU utilization (0 to 100%), per-task CPU utilization (0-100%), and per-task stack usage.

The statistic task is optional in a μC/OS-III application and its presence is controlled by a compile-time configuration constant OS_CFG_STAT_TASK_EN defined in OS_CFG.H. Specifically, the code is included in the build when OS_CFG_STAT_TASK_EN is set to 1.

Also, the priority of this task and the location and size of the statistic task's stack is configurable via OS_CFG_APP.H (OS_CFG_STAT_TASK_PRIO).

If the application uses the statistic task, it should call OSStatTaskCPUUsageInit() from the first, and only the application task created in the **main()** function as shown in Listing 5-5. The startup code should create only one task before calling OSStart(). The single task created is, of course, allowed to create other tasks, but only after calling OSStatTaskCPUUsageInit().

```
void main (void)                        (1)
{
    OS_ERR  err;
    :
    OSInit(&err);                       (2)
    if (err != OS_ERR_NONE) {
        /* Something wasn't configured properly, µC/OS-III not properly initialized  */
    }
    /* (3) Create ONE task (we'll call it AppTaskStart() for sake of discussion)     */
    :
    OSStart(&err);                      (4)
}


void AppTaskStart (void *p_arg)
{
    OS_ERR  err;
    :
    /* (5) Initialize the tick interrupt                                            */
#if OS_CFG_STAT_TASK_EN > 0
    OSStatTaskCPUUsageInit(&err);       (6)
#endif
    :
    /* (7) Create other tasks                                                       */
    while (DEF_ON) {
        /* AppTaskStart() body                                                      */
    }
}
```

Listing 5-5 **Proper startup for computing CPU utilization**

L5-5(1)   The C compiler should start up the CPU and bring it to **main()** as is typical in
            most C applications.

L5-5(2)   **main()** calls **OSInit()** to initialize µC/OS-III. It is assumed that the statistics
            task is enabled by setting **OS_CFG_STAT_TASK_EN** to 1 in **OS_CFG_APP.H**.
            Always examine µC/OS-III's returned error code to make sure the call was
            done properly. Refer to **OS.H** for a list of possible errors, **OS_ERR_???**.

L5-5(3)   As the comment indicates, creates a single task called **AppTaskStart()** in the
            example (its name is left to the creator's discretion). When creating this task,
            give it a fairly high priority (do not use priority 0 since it's reserved for
            µC/OS-III).

5

Normally, µC/OS-III allows the user to create as many tasks as are necessary prior to calling **OSStart()**. However, when the statistic task is used to compute overall CPU utilization, it is necessary to create only one task.

L5-5(4) Call **OSStart()** to let µC/OS-III start the highest-priority task which, should be **AppTaskStart()**. At this point, there should be either four or five tasks created (the timer task is optional): µC/OS-III creates up to four tasks (**OS_IdleTask()**, **OS_TickTask()**, **OS_StatTask()** and **OS_TaskTmr()**), and now **AppTaskStart()**.

L5-5(5) The start task should then configure and enable tick interrupts. This most likely requires that the user initialize the hardware timer used for the clock tick and have it interrupt at the rate specified by **OS_CFG_STAT_TASK_RATE** (see **OS_CFG_APP.H**). Additionally, Micriµm provides sample projects that include a basic board-support package (BSP). The BSP initializes many aspects of the CPU as well as the periodic time source required by µC/OS-III. If available, the user may utilize BSP services by calling **BSP_Init()** from the startup task. After this point, no further time source initialization is required by the user.

L5-5(6) Call **OSStatTaskCPUUsageInit()**. This function determines the maximum value that **OSStatTaskCtr** (see **OS_IdleTask()**) can count up to for 1/OS_CFG_STAT_TASK_RATE second when there are no other tasks running in the system (apart for the other µC/OS-III tasks). For example, if the system does not contain an application task and **OSStatTaskCtr** counts from 0 to 10,000,000 for 1/OS_CFG_STAT_TASK_RATE second, when adding tasks, and the test is redone every 1/OS_CFG_STAT_TASK_RATE second, the **OSStatTaskCtr** will not reach 10,000,000 and actual CPU utilization is determined as follows:

$$CPU\_Utilization_\% = \left(100 - \frac{100 \times OSTaskStatCtr}{OSTaskStatCtr_{Max}}\right)$$

For example, if when redoing the test, **OSStatTaskCtr** reaches 7,500,000 the CPU is busy 25% of its time running application tasks:

$$25\% = \left(100 - \frac{100 \times 7,500,000}{10,000,000}\right)$$

L5-5(7)   **AppTaskStart()** can then create other application tasks as needed.

As previously described, µC/OS-III stores run-time statistics for a task in each task's **OS_TCB**.

OS_StatTask() also computes stack usage of all created tasks by calling **OSTaskStkChk()** and stores the return values of this function (free and used stack space) in the **.StkFree** and **.StkUsed** field of the task's **OS_TCB**, respectively.

5-6-4 THE TIMER TASK (OS_TmrTask())

µC/OS-III provides timer services to the application programmer. Code to handle timers is found in **OS_TMR.C**.

The timer task is optional in a µC/OS-III application and its presence is controlled by the compile-time configuration constant **OS_CFG_TMR_EN** defined in **OS_CFG.H**. Specifically, the code is included in the build when **OS_CFG_TMR_EN** is set to 1.

Timers are countdown counters that perform an action when the counter reaches zero. The action is provided by the user through a callback function. A callback function is a function that the user declares and that will be called when the timer expires. The callback can thus be used to turn on or off a light, a motor, or perform whatever action needed. It is important to note that the callback function is called from the context of the timer task. The application programmer may create an unlimited number of timers (limited only by the amount of available RAM). Timer management is fully described in Chapter 12, "Timer Management" on page 201 and the timer services available to the application programmer are described in Appendix A, "µC/OS-III API Reference Manual" on page 383.

OS_TmrTask() is a task created by µC/OS-III (this assumes setting **OS_CFG_TMR_EN** to 1 in **OS_CFG.H**) and its priority is configurable by the user through µC/OS-III's configuration file **OS_CFG_APP.H** (see **OS_CFG_TMR_TASK_PRIO**). **OS_TmrTask()** is typically set to a medium priority.

OS_TmrTask( ) is a periodic task using the same interrupt source that was used to generate clock ticks. However, timers are generally updated at a slower rate (i.e., typically 10 Hz) and the timer tick rate is divided down in software. In other words, if the tick rate is 1000 Hz and the desired timer rate is 10 Hz, the timer task will be signaled every 100th tick interrupt as shown in Figure 5-12.

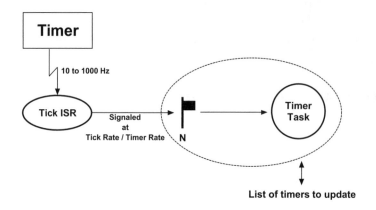

Figure 5-12 **Tick ISR and Timer Task relationship**

5-6-5 THE ISR HANDLER TASK (OS_IntQTask())

When setting the compile-time configuration constant OS_CFG_ISR_POST_DEFERRED_EN in OS_CFG.H to 1, µC/OS-III creates a task (called OS_IntQTask()) responsible for "deferring" the action of OS service post calls from ISRs.

As described in Chapter 4, "Critical Sections" on page 77, µC/OS-III manages critical sections either by disabling/enabling interrupts, or by locking/unlocking the scheduler. If selecting the latter method (i.e., setting OS_CFG_ISR_POST_DEFERRED_EN to 1), µC/OS-III "post" functions called from interrupts are not allowed to manipulate such internal data structures as the ready list, pend lists, and others.

When an ISR calls one of the "post" functions provided by µC/OS-III, a copy of the data posted and the desired destination is placed in a special "holding" queue. When all nested ISRs complete, µC/OS-III context switches to the ISR handler task (OS_IntQTask()), which "re-posts" the information placed in the holding queue to the appropriate task(s). This extra step is performed to reduce the amount of interrupt disable time that would otherwise be necessary to remove tasks from wait lists, insert them in the ready list, and perform other time-consuming operations.

Figure 5-13 **ISR Handler Task**

`OS_IntQTask()` is created by µC/OS-III and always runs at priority 0 (i.e., the highest priority). If `OS_CFG_ISR_POST_DEFERRED_EN` is set to 1, no other task will be allowed to use priority 0.

5-7 SUMMARY

A task is a simple program that thinks it has the CPU all to itself. On a single CPU, only one task executes at any given time. µC/OS-III supports multitasking and allows the application to have any number of tasks. The maximum number of tasks is actually only limited by the amount of memory (both code and data space) available to the processor.

A task can be implemented as a run-to-completion task in which the task deletes itself when it is finished or more typically as an infinite loop, waiting for events to occur and processing those events.

A task needs to be created. When creating a task, it is necessary to specify the address of an `OS_TCB` to be used by the task, the priority of the task, and an area in RAM for the task's stack. A task can also perform computations (CPU bound task), or manage one or more I/O (Input/Output) devices.

µC/OS-III creates up to five internal tasks: the idle task, tick task, ISR handler task, statistics task, and timer task. The idle and tick tasks are always created while statistics and timer tasks are optional.

5

6

The Ready List

Tasks that are ready to execute are placed in the Ready List. The ready list consists of two parts: a bitmap containing the priority levels that are ready and a table containing pointers to all the tasks ready.

6-1 PRIORITY LEVELS

Figures 5-1 to 5-3 show the bitmap of priorities that are ready. The "width" of the table depends on the data type **CPU_DATA** (see **CPU.H**), which can either be 8-, 16- or 32-bits. The width depends on the processor used.

µC/OS-III allows up to **OS_CFG_PRIO_MAX** different priority levels (see **OS_CFG.H**). In µC/OS-III, a low-priority number corresponds to a high-priority level. Priority level zero (0) is thus the highest priority level. Priority **OS_CFG_PRIO_MAX-1** is the lowest priority level. µC/OS-III uniquely assigns the lowest priority to the idle task. No other tasks are allowed at this priority level. If there are tasks that are ready-to-run at a given a priority level, then its corresponding bit is set (i.e., 1) in the bitmap table. Notice in Figures 5-1 to 5-3 that "priority levels" are numbered from left to right and, the priority level increases (moves toward lower priority) with an increase in table index. The order was chosen to be able to use a special instruction called Count Leading Zeros (CLZ), which is found on many modern processors. This instruction greatly accelerates the process of determining the highest priority level.

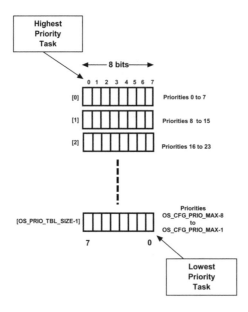

Figure 6-1 **CPU_DATA declared as a CPU_INT08U**

6

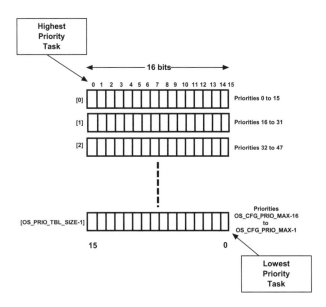

Figure 6-2 **CPU_DATA declared as a CPU_INT16U**

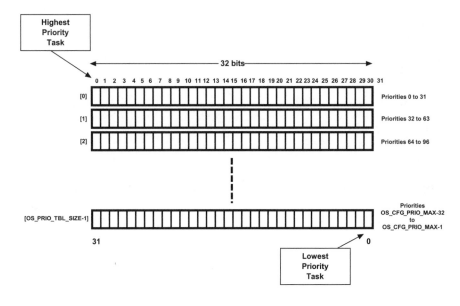

Figure 6-3 **CPU_DATA declared as a CPU_INT32U**

OS_PRIO.C contains the code to set, clear, and search the bitmap table. These functions are internal to μC/OS-III and are placed in OS_PRIO.C to allow them to be optimized in assembly language by replacing OS_PRIO.C with an assembly language equivalent OS_PRIO.ASM, when necessary.

Function	Description
OS_PrioGetHighest()	Find the highest priority level
OS_PrioInsert()	Set bit corresponding to priority level in the bitmap table
OS_PrioRemove()	Clear bit corresponding to priority level in the bitmap table

Table 6-1 **Priority Level access functions**

To determine the highest priority level that contains ready-to-run tasks, the bitmap table is scanned until the first bit set in the lowest bit position is found using OS_PrioGetHighest(). The code for this function is shown in Listing 6-1.

```
OS_PRIO  OS_PrioGetHighest (void)
{
    CPU_DATA  *p_tbl;
    OS_PRIO    prio;


    prio  = (OS_PRIO)0;
    p_tbl = &OSPrioTbl[0];
    while (*p_tbl == (CPU_DATA)0) {              (1)
        prio += sizeof(CPU_DATA) * 8u;           (2)
        p_tbl++;
    }
    prio += (OS_PRIO)CPU_CntLeadZeros(*p_tbl);   (3)
    return (prio);
}
```

Listing 6-1 **Finding the highest priority level**

L6-1(1)   OS_PrioGetHighest() scans the table from OSPrioTbl[] until a non-zero entry is found. The loop will always terminate because there will always be a non-zero entry in the table because of the idle task.

L6-1(2)   Each time a zero entry is found, we move to the next table entry and increment "**prio**" by the width (in number of bits) of each entry. If each entry is 32-bits wide, "**prio**" is incremented by 32.

L6-1(3)   Once the first non-zero entry is found, the number of "**leading zeros**" of that entry is simply added and return the priority level back to the caller. Counting the number of zeros is a CPU-specific function so that if a particular CPU has a built-in CLZ instruction, it is up to the implementer of the CPU port to take advantage of this feature. If the CPU used does not provide that instruction, the functionality must be implemented in C.

The function **CPU_CntLeadZeros()** simply counts how many zeros there are in a **CPU_DATA** entry starting from the left (i.e., most significant bit). For example, assuming 32 bits, **0xF0001234** results in 0 leading zeros and **0x00F01234** results in 8 leading zeros.

At first view, the linear path through the table might seem inefficient. However, if the number of priority levels is kept low, the search is quite fast. In fact, there are several optimizations to streamline the search. For example, if using a 32-bit processor and you are satisfied with limiting the number of different priority levels to 64, the above code can be optimized as shown in Listing 6-2. In fact, some processors have built-in "Count Leading Zeros" instructions and thus, the code can be written with just a few lines of assembly language. Remember that with µC/OS-III, 64 priority levels does not mean that the user is limited to 64 tasks since with µC/OS-III, any number of tasks are possible at a given priority level.

```
OS_PRIO  OS_PrioGetHighest (void)
{
    OS_PRIO  prio;


    if (OSPrioTbl[0] != (OS_PRIO_BITMAP)0) {
        prio = OS_CntLeadingZeros(OSPrioTbl[0]);
    } else {
        prio = OS_CntLeadingZeros(OSPrioTbl[1]) + 32;
    }
    return (prio);
}
```

Listing 6-2 **Finding the highest priority level within 64 levels**

6

6-2 THE READY LIST

Tasks that are ready to run are placed in the Ready List. As shown in Figure 6-1, the ready list is an array (OSRdyList[ ]) containing OS_CFG_PRIO_MAX entries, with each entry defined by the data type OS_RDY_LIST (see OS.H). An OS_RDY_LIST entry consists of three fields: .Entries, .TailPtr and .HeadPtr.

.Entries contains the number of ready-to-run tasks at the priority level corresponding to the entry in the ready list. .Entries is set to zero (0) if there are no tasks ready to run at a given priority level.

.TailPtr and .HeadPtr are used to create a doubly linked list of all the tasks that are ready at a specific priority. .HeadPtr points to the head of the list and .TailPtr points to its tail.

The "index" into the array is the priority level associated with a task. For example, if a task is created at priority level 5 then it will be inserted in the table at OSRdyList[5] if that task is ready to run.

Table 6-2 shows the functions that μC/OS-III uses to manipulate entries in the ready list. These functions are internal to μC/OS-III and the application code must never call them.

Function	Description
OS_RdyListInit()	Initialize the ready list to "empty" (see Figure 6-4)
OS_RdyListInsert()	Insert a TCB into the ready list
OS_RdyListInsertHead()	Insert a TCB at the head of the list
OS_RdyListInsertTail()	Insert a TCB at the tail of the list
OS_RdyListMoveHeadToTail()	Move a TCB from the head to the tail of the list
OS_RdyListRemove()	Remove a TCB from the ready list

Table 6-2 **Ready List access functions**

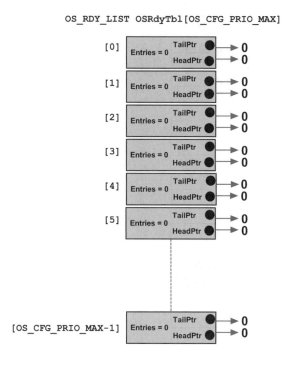

OS_RDY_LIST OSRdyTbl[OS_CFG_PRIO_MAX]

Figure 6-4 **Empty Ready List**

Assuming all internal μC/OS-III's tasks are enabled, Figure 6-5 shows the state of the ready list after calling **OSInit()** (i.e., μC/OS-III's initialization). It is assumed that each μC/OS-III task had a unique priority. With μC/OS-III, this does not have to be the case.

F6-4(1)   There is only one entry in **OSRdyList[OS_CFG_PRIO_MAX-1]**, the idle task.

F6-4(2)   The list points to OS_TCBs. Only relevant fields of the TCB are shown. The **.PrevPtr** and **.NextPtr** are used to form a doubly linked list of **OS_TCBs** associated to tasks at the same priority. For the idle task, these fields always point to **NULL**.

F6-4(3)   **Priority** 0 is reserved to the ISR handler task when **OS_CFG_ISR_DEFERRED_EN** is set to 1 in **OS_CFG.H**. In this case, this is the only task that can run at priority 0.

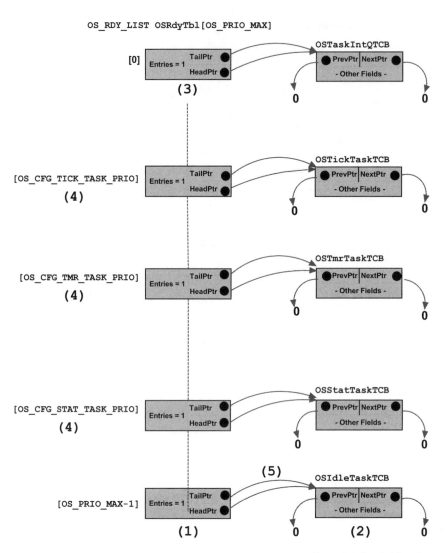

Figure 6-5 **Ready List after calling OSInit()**

F6-5(1)   The tick task and the other two optional tasks have their own priority level, as shown. µC/OS-III enables the user to have multiple tasks at the same priority and thus, the tasks could be set up as shown. Typically, one would set the priority of the tick task higher than the timer task and, the timer task higher in priority than the statistic task.

F6-5(2)   Both the tail and head pointers point to the same TCB when there is only one TCB at a given priority level.

6-3 ADDING TASKS TO THE READY LIST

Tasks are added to the ready list by a number of µC/OS-III services. The most obvious service is **OSTaskCreate()**, which always creates a task in the ready-to-run state and adds the task to the ready list. As shown in Figure 6-6, when creating a task, and specifying a priority level where tasks already exist (two in this example) in the ready list at that priority level, **OSTaskCreate()** will insert the new task at the end of the list of tasks at that priority level.

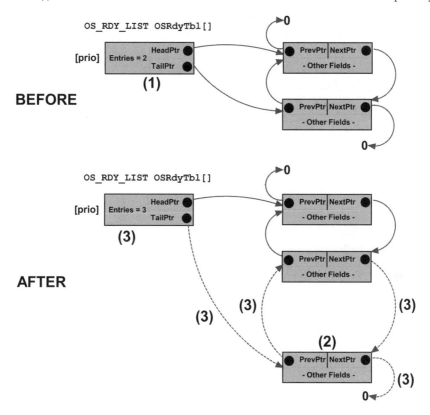

Figure 6-6 **Inserting a newly created task in the ready list**

F6-6(1)   Before calling **OSTaskCreate()** (in this example), two tasks were in the ready list at priority "**prio**".

F6-6(2)   A new TCB is passed to **OSTaskCreate()** and, µC/OS-III initialized the contents of that TCB.

6

F6-6(3)   `OSTaskCreate()` calls `OS_RdyListInsertTail()`, which links the new TCB to the ready list by setting up four pointers and also incrementing the .Entries field of `OSRdyList[prio]`. Not shown in Figure 6-6 is that `OSTaskCreate()` also calls `OS_PrioInsert()` to set the bit in the bitmap table. Of course, this operation is not necessary as there are already entries in the list at this priority. However, `OS_PrioInsert()` is a very fast call and thus it should not affect performance.

The reason the new TCB is added to the end of the list is that the current head of the list could be the task creator and, at the same priority, there is no reason to make the new task the next task to run. In fact, a task being made ready will be inserted at the tail of the list if the current task is at the same priority. However, if a task is being made ready at a different priority than the current task, it will be inserted at the head of the list.

6-4 SUMMARY

µC/OS-III supports any number of different priority levels. However, 256 different priority levels should be sufficient for the most complex applications and most systems will not require more than 64 levels.

The ready list consist of two data structures: a bitmap table that keeps track of which priority level is ready, and a table containing a list of all the tasks ready at each priority level.

Processors having "count leading zeros" instructions can accelerate the table lookup process used in determining the highest priority task.

Chapter

7

Scheduling

The scheduler, also called the dispatcher, is a part of µC/OS-III responsible for determining which task runs next. µC/OS-III is a *preemptive, priority-based kernel*. Each task is assigned a priority based on its importance. The priority for each task depends on the application, and µC/OS-III supports multiple tasks at the same priority level.

The word preemptive means that when an event occurs, and that event makes a more important task ready to run, then µC/OS-III will immediately give control of the CPU to that task. Thus, when a task signals or sends a message to a higher-priority task, the current task is suspended and the higher-priority task is given control of the CPU. Similarly, if an Interrupt Service Routine (ISR) signals or sends a message to a higher priority task, when the message is completed, the interrupted task remains suspended, and the new higher priority task resumes.

7-1 PREEMPTIVE SCHEDULING

µC/OS-III handles event posting from interrupts using two different methods: Direct and Deferred Post. These will be discussed in greater detail in Chapter 9, "Interrupt Management" on page 165. From a scheduling point of view, the end result of the two methods is the same; the highest priority and ready task will receive the CPU as shown in Figures 6-1 and 6-2.

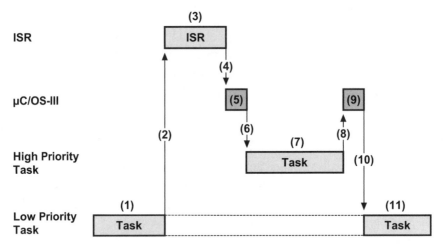

Figure 7-1 **Preemptive scheduling – Direct Method**

F7-1(1)   A low priority task is executing, and an interrupt occurs.

F7-1(2)   If interrupts are enabled, the CPU vectors (i.e., jumps) to the ISR that is responsible for servicing the interrupting device.

F7-1(3)   The ISR services the device and signals or sends a message to a higher-priority task waiting to service this device. This task is thus ready to run.

F7-1(4)   When the ISR completes its work it makes a service call to µC/OS-III.

F7-1(5)
F7-1(6)   Since there is a more important ready-to-run task, µC/OS-III decides to not return to the interrupted task but switches to the more important task. See Chapter 8, "Context Switching" on page 155 for details on how this works.

F7-1(7)

F7-1(8)   The higher priority task services the interrupting device and, when finished, calls µC/OS-III asking it to wait for another interrupt from the device.

F7-1(9)

F7-1(10)   µC/OS-III blocks the high-priority task until the next device interrupts. Since the device has not interrupted a second time, µC/OS-III switches back to the original task (the one that was interrupted).

F7-1(11)   The interrupted task resumes execution, exactly at the point where it was interrupted.

Figure 7-2 shows that µC/OS-III performs a few extra steps when it is configured for the Deferred Post method. Notice that the end results is the same; the high-priority task preempts the low-priority one.

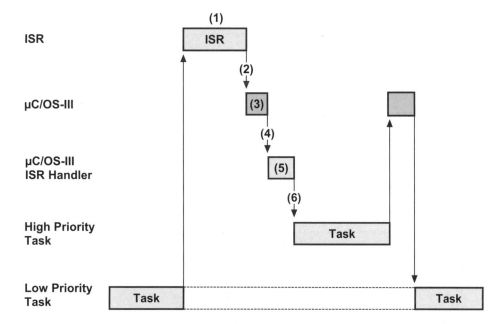

Figure 7-2 **Preemptive scheduling – Deferred Post Method**

F7-2(1)   The ISR services the device and, instead of signaling or sending the message to the task, μC/OS-III (through the POST call) places the post call into a special queue and makes a very high-priority task (actually the highest-possible priority) ready to run. This task is called the *ISR Handler Task*.

F7-2(2)   When the ISR completes its work, it makes a service call to μC/OS-III.

F7-2(3)
F7-2(4)   Since the ISR made the ISR Handler Task ready to run, μC/OS-III switches to that task.

F7-2(5)
F7-2(6)   The ISR Handler Task then removes the post call from the message queue and reissues the post. This time, however, it does it at the task level instead of the ISR level. The reason this extra step is performed is to keep interrupt disable time as small as possible. See Chapter 9, "Interrupt Management" on page 165 to find out more on the subject. When the queue is emptied, μC/OS-III removes the ISR Handler Task from the ready list and switches to the task that was signaled or sent a message.

7-2 SCHEDULING POINTS

Scheduling occurs at scheduling points and nothing special must be done in the application code since scheduling occurs automatically based on the conditions described below.

A task signals or sends a message to another task:
This occurs when the task signaling or sending the message calls one of the post services, OS???Post(). Scheduling occurs towards the end of the OS???Post() call. Note that scheduling does not occur if one specifies (as part of the post call) to not invoke the scheduler (i.e., set the option argument to OS_OPT_POST_NO_SCHED).

A task calls OSTimeDly() or OSTimeDlyHMSM():
If the delay is non-zero, scheduling always occurs since the calling task is placed in a list waiting for time to expire. Scheduling occurs as soon as the task is inserted in the wait list.

A task waits for an event to occur and the event has not yet occurred:
This occurs when one of the OS???Pend() functions are called. The task is placed in the wait list for the event and, if a non-zero timeout is specified, then the task is also inserted in the list of tasks waiting to timeout. The scheduler is then called to select the next most important task to run.

If a task aborts a pend:
A task is able to abort the wait (i.e., pend) of another task by calling OS???PendAbort(). Scheduling occurs when the task is removed from the wait list for the specified kernel object.

If a task is created:
The newly created task may have a higher priority than the task's creator. In this case, the scheduler is called.

If a task is deleted:
When terminating a task, the scheduler is called if the current task is deleted.

If a kernel object is deleted:
If you delete an event flag group, a semaphore, a message queue, or a mutual exclusion semaphore, if tasks are waiting on the kernel object, those tasks will be made ready to run and the scheduler will be called to determine if any of the tasks have a higher priority than the task that deleted the kernel object.

A task changes the priority of itself or another task:
The scheduler is called when a task changes the priority of another task (or itself) and the new priority of that task is higher than the task that changed the priority.

A task suspends itself by calling OSTaskSuspend():
The scheduler is called since the task that called OSTaskSuspend() is no longer able to execute, and must be resumed by another task.

A task resumes another task that was suspended by OSTaskSuspend():
The scheduler is called if the resumed task has a higher priority than the task that calls OSTaskResume().

At the end of all nested ISRs:

The scheduler is called at the end of all nested ISRs to determine whether a more important task is made ready to run by one of the ISRs. The scheduling is actually performed by `OSIntExit()` instead of `OSSched()`.

The scheduler is unlocked by calling OSSchedUnlock():

The scheduler is unlocked after being locked. Lock the scheduler by calling `OSSchedLock()`. Note that locking the scheduler can be nested and the scheduler must be unlocked a number of times equal to the number of locks.

A task gives up its time quanta by calling OSSchedRoundRobinYield():

This assumes that the task is running alongside with other tasks at the same priority and the currently running task decides that it can give up its time quanta and let another task run.

The user calls OSSched():

The application code can call `OSSched()` to run the scheduler. This only makes sense if calling `OS???Post()` functions and specifying `OS_OPT_POST_NO_SCHED` so that multiple posts can be accomplished without running the scheduler on every post. Of course, in the above situation, the last post can be a post without the `OS_OPT_POST_NO_SCHED` option.

7-3 ROUND-ROBIN SCHEDULING

When two or more tasks have the same priority, μC/OS-III allows one task to run for a predetermined amount of time (called a *Time Quanta*) before selecting another task. This process is called *Round-Robin Scheduling* or *Time Slicing*. If a task does not need to use its full time quanta it can voluntarily give up the CPU so that the next task can execute. This is called *Yielding*. μC/OS-III allows the user to enable or disable round robin scheduling at run time.

Figure 7-3 shows a timing diagram with tasks running at the same priority. There are three tasks that are ready to run at priority "X". For sake of illustration, the time quanta occurs every 4th clock tick. This is shown as a darker tick mark.

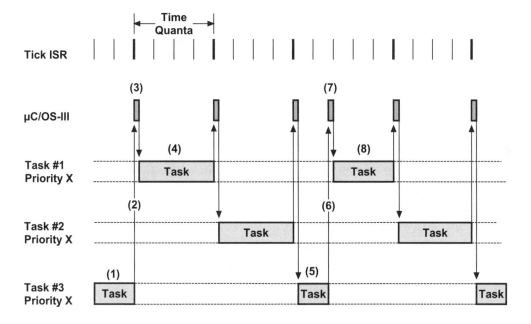

Figure 7-3 **Round Robin Scheduling**

F7-3(1)   Task #3 is executing. During that time, tick interrupts occur but the time quanta have not expired yet for Task #3.

F7-3(2)   On the 4th tick interrupt, the time quanta for Task #3 expire.

F7-3(3)   µC/OS-III resumes Task #1 since it was the next task in the list of tasks at priority "X" that was ready to run.

F7-3(4)   Task #1 executes until its time quanta expires (i.e., after four ticks).

7

F7-3(5)

F7-3(6)

F7-3(7)   Here Task #3 executes but decides to give up its time quanta by calling the µC/OS-III function **OSSchedRoundRobinYield()**, which causes the next task in the list of tasks ready at priority "X" to execute. An interesting thing occurred when µC/OS-III scheduled Task #1. It reset the time quanta for that task to four ticks so that the next time quanta will expire four ticks from this point.

F7-3(8)   Task #1 executes for its full time quanta.

µC/OS-III allows the user to change the time quanta at run time through the **OSSchedRoundRobinCfg()** function (see Appendix A, "µC/OS-III API Reference Manual" on page 383). This function also allows round robin scheduling to be enabled/disabled, and the ability to change the default time quanta.

µC/OS-III also enables the user to specify the time quanta on a per-task basis. One task could have a time quanta of 1 tick, another 12, another 3, and yet another 7, etc. The time quanta of a task is specified when the task is created. The time quanta of a task may also be changed at run time through the function **OSTaskTimeQuantaSet()**.

7-4 SCHEDULING INTERNALS

Scheduling is performed by two functions: OSSched() and OSIntExit(). OSSched() is called by task level code while OSIntExit() is called by ISRs. Both functions are found in OS_CORE.C.

Figure 7-1 illustrates the two sets of data structures that the scheduler uses; the priority ready bitmap and the ready list as described in Chapter 6, "The Ready List" on page 131.

Figure 7-4 **Priority ready bitmap and Ready list**

7-4-1 OSSched()

The pseudo code for the task level scheduler, **OSSched()** is shown in Listing 7-1.

```
void  OSSched (void)
{
    Disable interrupts;
    if (OSIntNestingCtr > 0) {                              (1)
        return;
    }
    if (OSSchedLockNestingCtr > 0) {                        (2)
        return;
    }
    Get highest priority ready;                             (3)
    Get pointer to OS_TCB of next highest priority task;   (4)
    if (OSTCBNHighRdyPtr != OSTCBCurPtr) {                  (5)
        Perform task level context switch;
    }
    Enable interrupts;
}
```

Listing 7-1 **OSSched() pseudocode**

L7-1(1)   **OSSched()** starts by making sure it is not called from an ISR as **OSSched()** is the task level scheduler. Instead, an ISR must call OSIntExit(). If **OSSched()** is called by an ISR, **OSSched()** simply returns.

L7-1(2)   The next step is to make sure the scheduler is not locked. If the code calls **OSSchedLock()** the user does not want to run the scheduler and the function just returns.

L7-1(3)   **OSSched()** determines the priority of the highest priority task ready by scanning the bitmap **OSPrioTbl[]** as described in Chapter 6, "The Ready List" on page 131.

L7-1(4)   Once it is known which priority is ready, index into the **OSRdyList[]** and extract the **OS_TCB** at the head of the list (i.e., **OSRdyList[highest priority].HeadPtr**). At this point, it is known which **OS_TCB** to switch to and which **OS_TCB** to save to as this was the task that called **OSSched()**. Specifically, **OSTCBCurPtr** points to the current task's **OS_TCB** and **OSTCBHighRdyPtr** points to the new **OS_TCB** to switch to.

L7-1(5)   If the user is not attempting to switch to the same task that is currently running, OSSched() calls the code that will perform the context switch (see Chapter 8, "Context Switching" on page 155). As the code indicates, however, the task level scheduler calls a task-level function to perform the context switch.

Notice that the scheduler and the context switch runs with interrupts disabled. This is necessary because this process needs to be atomic.

7-4-2 OSIntExit()

The pseudo code for the ISR level scheduler, OSIntExit() is shown in Listing 7-2. Note that interrupts are assumed to be disabled when OSIntExit() is called.

```
void  OSIntExit (void)
{
    if (OSIntNestingCtr == 0) {                          (1)
        return;
    }
    OSIntNestingCtr--;
    if (OSIntNestingCtr > 0) {                           (2)
        return;
    }
    if (OSSchedLockNestingCtr > 0) {                     (3)
        return;
    }
    Get highest priority ready;                          (4)
    Get pointer to OS_TCB of next highest priority task; (5)
    if (OSTCBHighRdyPtr != OSTCBCurPtr) {                (6)
        Perform ISR level context switch;
    }
}
```

Listing 7-2 **OSIntExit() pseudocode**

L7-2(1)   OSIntExit() starts by making sure that the call to OSIntExit() will not cause OSIntNestingCtr to wrap around. This would be extremely and unlikely occurrence, but not worth taking a chance that it might.

L7-2(2)   OSIntExit() decrements the nesting counter as OSIntExit() is called at the end of an ISR. If all ISRs have not nested, the code simply returns. There is no need to run the scheduler since there are still interrupts to return to.

7

L7-2(3)   OSIntExit() checks to see that the scheduler is not locked. If it is, OSIntExit() does not run the scheduler and simply returns to the interrupted task that locked the scheduler.

L7-2(4)   Finally, this is the last nested ISR (we are returning to task-level code) and the scheduler is not locked. Therefore, we need to find the highest priority task that needs to run.

L7-2(5)   Again, we extract the highest priority OS_TCB from OSRdyList[].

L7-2(6)   If the highest-priority task is not the current task µC/OS-III performs an ISR level context switch. The ISR level context switch is different as it is assumed that the interrupted task's context was saved at the beginning of the ISR and it is only left to restore the context of the new task to run. This is described in Chapter 8, "Context Switching" on page 155.

7-4-3 OS_SchedRoundRobin()

When the time quanta for a task expires and there are multiple tasks at the same priority, µC/OS-III will select and run the next task that is ready to run at the current priority. OS_SchedRoundRobin() is the code used to perform this operation. OS_SchedRoundRobin() is either called by OSTimeTick() or OS_IntQTask(). OS_SchedRoundRobin() is found in OS_CORE.C.

OS_SchedRoundRobin() is called by OSTimeTick() when you selected the Direct Method of posting (see Chapter 9, "Interrupt Management" on page 165). OS_SchedRoundRobin() is called by OS_IntQTask() when selecting the Deferred Post Method of posting, described in Chapter 8.

The pseudo code for the round-robin scheduler is shown in Listing 7-3.

```
void  OS_SchedRoundRobin (void)
{
    if (OSSchedRoundRobinEn != TRUE) {              (1)
        return;
    }
    if (Time quanta counter > 0) {                  (2)
        Decrement time quanta counter;
    }
    if (Time quanta counter > 0) {
        return;
    }
    if (Number of OS_TCB at current priority level < 2) {   (3)
        return;
    }
    if (OSSchedLockNestingCtr > 0) {                (4)
        return;
    }
    Move OS_TCB from head of list to tail of list;  (5)
    Reload time quanta for current task;            (6)
}
```

Listing 7-3 **OS_SchedRoundRobin() pseudocode**

L7-3(1)   **OS_SchedRoundRobin()** starts by making sure that round robin scheduling is
            enabled. Recall that to enable round robin scheduling, one must call
            OSSchedRoundRobinCfg().

L7-3(2)   The time quanta counter, which resides inside the **OS_TCB** of the running task, is
            decremented. If the value is still non-zero then **OS_SchedRoundRobin()** returns.

L7-3(3)   Once the time quanta counter reaches zero, check to see that there are other
            ready-to-run tasks at the current priority. If there are none, return. Round robin
            scheduling only applies when there are multiple tasks at the same priority and
            the task doesn't completes its work within its time quanta.

L7-3(4)   **OS_SchedRoundRobin()** also returns if the scheduler is locked.

L7-3(5)   Next, **OS_SchedRoundRobin()** move the **OS_TCB** of the current task from the
            head of the ready list to the end.

L7-3(6)   The time quanta for the task at the head of the list are loaded. Each task may specify its own time quanta when the task is created or through **OSTaskTimeQuantaSet()**. If specifying 0, µC/OS-III assumes the default time quanta, which corresponds to the value in the variable **OSSchedRoundRobinDfltTimeQuanta**.

7-5 SUMMARY

µC/OS-III is a preemptive scheduler so it will always execute the highest priority task that is ready to run.

µC/OS-III allows for multiple tasks at the same priority. If there are multiple ready-to-run tasks, µC/OS-III will round robin between these tasks.

Scheduling occurs at specific scheduling points, when the application calls µC/OS-III functions.

µC/OS-III has two schedulers: **OSSched()**, which is called by task-level code, and **OSIntExit()** called at the end of each ISR.

Chapter

8

Context Switching

When μC/OS-III decides to run a different task (see Chapter 7, "Scheduling" on page 141), it saves the current task's context, which typically consists of the CPU registers, onto the current task's stack and restores the context of the new task and resumes execution of that task. This process is called a *Context Switch*.

Context switching adds overhead. The more registers a CPU has, the higher the overhead. The time required to perform a context switch is generally determined by how many registers must be saved and restored by the CPU.

The context switch code is generally part of a processor's *port* of μC/OS-III. A port is the code needed to adapt μC/OS-III to the desired processor. This code is placed in special C and assembly language files: **OS_CPU.H**, **OS_CPU_C.C** and **OS_CPU_A.ASM**. Chapter 18, "Porting μC/OS-III" on page 343, Porting μC/OS-III provides more details on the steps needed to port μC/OS-III to different CPU architectures.

In this chapter, we will discuss the context switching process in generic terms using a fictitious CPU as shown in Figure 8-1. Our fictitious CPU contains 16 integer registers (R0 to R15), a separate ISR stack pointer, and a separate status register (SR). Every register is 32 bits wide and each of the 16 integer registers can hold either data or an address. The program counter (or instruction pointer) is R15 and there are two separate stack pointers labeled R14 and R14". R14 represents a task stack pointer (TSP), and R14" represents an ISR stack pointer (ISP). The CPU automatically switches to the ISR stack when servicing an exception or interrupt. The task stack is accessible from an ISR (i.e., we can push and pop elements onto the task stack when in an ISR), and the interrupt stack is also accessible from a task.

Figure 8-1 **Fictitious CPU**

In µC/OS-III, the stack frame for a ready task is always setup to look as if an interrupt has just occurred and all processor registers were saved onto it. Tasks enter the ready state upon creation and thus their stack frames are pre-initialized by software in a similar manner. Using our fictitious CPU, we'll assume that a stack frame for a task that is ready to be restored is shown in Figure 8-2.

The task stack pointer points to the last register saved onto the task's stack. The program counter and status registers are the first registers saved onto the stack. In fact, these are saved automatically by the CPU when an exception or interrupt occurs (assuming interrupts are enabled) while the other registers are pushed onto the stack by software in the exception handler. The stack pointer (R14) is not actually saved on the stack but instead is saved in the task's OS_TCB.

The interrupt stack pointer points to the current top-of-stack for the interrupt stack, which is a different memory area. When an ISR executes, the processor uses R14" as the stack pointer for function calls and local arguments.

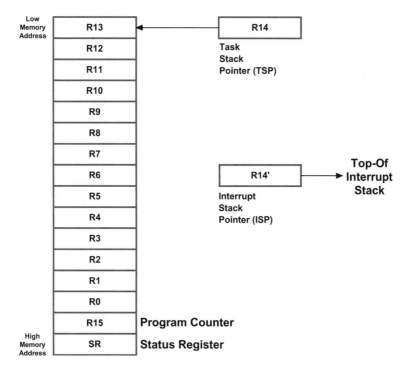

Figure 8-2 **CPU register stacking order of ready task**

There are two types of context switches: one performed from a task and another from an ISR. The task level context switch is implemented by the code in **OSCtxSw()**, which is actually invoked by the macro **OS_TASK_SW()**. A macro is used as there are many ways to invoke **OSCtxSw()** such as software interrupts, trap instructions, or simply calling the function.

The ISR context switch is implemented by **OSIntCtxSw()**. The code for both functions is typically written in assembly language and is found in a file called **OS_CPU_A.ASM**.

8-1 OSCtxSw()

OSCtxSw() is called when the task level scheduler (OSSched()) determines that a new high priority task needs to execute. Figure 8-3 shows the state of several µC/OS-III variables and data structures just prior to calling OSCtxSw().

Figure 8-3 **Variables and data structures prior to calling OSCtxSw()**

F8-3(1)   OSTCBCurPtr points to the OS_TCB of the task that is currently running and that called OSSched().

F8-3(2)   OSSched() finds the new task to run by having OSTCBHighRdyPtr point to its OS_TCB.

F8-3(3)   **OSTCBHighRdyPtr->StkPtr** points to the top of stack of the new task to run.

F8-3(4)   When μC/OS-III creates or suspends a task, it always leaves the stack frame to look as if an interrupt just occurred and all the registers saved onto it. This represents the expected state of the task so it can be resumed.

F8-3(5)   The CPU's stack pointer points within the stack area (i.e., RAM) of the task that called **OSSched()**. Depending on how **OSCtxSw()** is invoked, the stack pointer may be pointing at the return address of **OSCtxSw()**.

Figure 8-4 shows the steps involved in performing the context switch as implemented by **OSCtxSw()**.

Figure 8-4 **Operations performed by OSCtxSw()**

8

F8-4(1)   **OSCtxSw()** begins by saving the status register and program counter of the current task onto the current task's stack. The saving order of register depends on how the CPU expects the registers on the stack frame when an interrupt occurs. In this case, it is assumed that the SR is stacked first. The remaining registers are then saved onto the stack.

F8-4(2)   **OSCtxSw()** saves the contents of the CPU's stack pointer into the **OS_TCB** of the task being suspended. In other words, **OSTCBCurPtr->StkPtr = R14**.

F8-4(3)   **OSCtxSw()** then loads the CPU stack pointer with the saved top-of-stack from the new task's **OS_TCB**. In other words, **R14 = OSTCBHighRdyPtr->StkPtr**.

F8-4(4)   Finally, **OSCtxSw()** retrieves the CPU register contents from the new stack. The program counter and status registers are generally retrieved at the same time by executing a return from interrupt instruction.

8-2 OSIntCtxSw()

OSIntCtxSw() is called when the ISR level scheduler (OSIntExit()) determines that a new high priority task is ready to execute. Figure 8-5 shows the state of several µC/OS-III variables and data structures just prior to calling OSIntCtxSw().

Figure 8-5 **Variables and data structures prior to calling OSIntCtxSw()**

µC/OS-III assumes that CPU registers are saved onto the task's stack at the beginning of an ISR (see Chapter 9, "Interrupt Management" on page 165). Because of this, notice that OSTCBCurPtr->StkPtr contains a pointer to the top-of-stack pointer of the task being suspended (the one on the left). OSIntCtxSw() does not have to worry about saving the CPU registers of the suspended task since that is already finished.

Figure 8-6 shows the operations performed by `OSIntCtxSw()` to complete the second half of the context switch. This is exactly the same process as the second half of `OSCtxSw()`.

Figure 8-6 **Operations performed by OSIntCtxSw()**

F8-6(1)   `OSIntCtxSw()` loads the CPU stack pointer with the saved top-of-stack from the new task's `OS_TCB`. R14 = `OSTCBHighRdyPtr->StkPtr`.

F8-6(2)   `OSIntCtxSw()` then retrieves the CPU register contents from the new stack. The program counter and status registers are generally retrieved at the same time by executing a return from interrupt instruction.

8-3 SUMMARY

A context switch consists of saving the context (i.e., CPU registers) associated with one task and restoring the context of a new, higher-priority task.

The new task to be switched to is determined by **OSSched()** when a context switch is initiated by task level code, and **OSIntExit()** when initiated by an ISR.

OSCtxSw() performs the context switch for **OSSched()** and **OSIntCtxSw()** performs the context switch for **OSIntExit()**. However, **OSIntCtxSw()** only needs to perform the second half of the context switch because it is assumed that the ISR saved CPU registers upon entry to the ISR.

8

8

9

Interrupt Management

An *interrupt* is a hardware mechanism used to inform the CPU that an asynchronous event occurred. When an interrupt is recognized, the CPU saves part (or all) of its context (i.e., registers) and jumps to a special subroutine called an *Interrupt Service Routine* (ISR). The ISR processes the event, and – upon completion of the ISR – the program either returns to the interrupted task, or the highest priority task, if the ISR made a higher priority task ready to run.

Interrupts allow a microprocessor to process events when they occur (i.e., asynchronously), which prevents the microprocessor from continuously *polling* (looking at) an event to see if it occurred. Task level response to events is typically better using interrupt mode as opposed to polling mode, however at the possible cost of increased interrupt latency. Microprocessors allow interrupts to be ignored or recognized through the use of two special instructions: disable interrupts and enable interrupts, respectively.

In a real-time environment, interrupts should be disabled as little as possible. Disabling interrupts affects interrupt latency possibly causing interrupts to be missed.

Processors generally allow interrupts to be nested, which means that while servicing an interrupt, the processor recognizes and services other (more important) interrupts.

One of the most important specifications of a real-time kernel is the maximum amount of time that interrupts are disabled. This is called *interrupt disable time*. All real-time systems disable interrupts to manipulate critical sections of code and re-enable interrupts when critical sections are completed. The longer interrupts are disabled, the higher the interrupt latency.

Interrupt response is defined as the time between the reception of the interrupt and the start of the user code that handles the interrupt. Interrupt response time accounts for the entire overhead involved in handling an interrupt. Typically, the processor's context (CPU registers) is saved on the stack before the user code is executed.

Interrupt recovery is defined as the time required for the processor to return to the interrupted code or to a higher priority task if the ISR made such a task ready to run.

Task latency is defined as the time it takes from the time the interrupt occurs to the time task level code resumes.

9-1 HANDLING CPU INTERRUPTS

There are many popular CPU architectures on the market today, and most processors typically handle interrupts from a multitude of sources. For example, a UART receives a character, an Ethernet controller receives a packet, a DMA controller completes a data transfer, an Analog-to-Digital Converter (ADC) completes an analog conversion, a timer expires, *etc.*

In most cases, an *interrupt controller* captures all of the different interrupts presented to the processor as shown in Figure 9-1 (note that the "CPU Interrupt Enable/Disable" is typically part of the CPU, but is shown here separately for sake of the illustration).

Interrupting devices signal the interrupt controller, which then prioritizes the interrupts and presents the highest-priority interrupt to the CPU.

Figure 9-1 **Interrupt controllers**

Modern interrupt controllers have built-in intelligence that enable the user to prioritize interrupts, remember which interrupts are still pending and, in many cases, have the interrupt controller provide the address of the ISR (also called the vector address) directly to the CPU.

9

If "global" interrupts (i.e., the switch in Figure 9-1) are disabled, the CPU will ignore requests from the interrupt controller, but they will be held pending by the interrupt controller until the CPU re-enables interrupts.

CPUs deal with interrupts using one of two models:

1   All interrupts *vector* to a single interrupt handler.

2   Each interrupt *vectors* directly to an interrupt handler.

Before discussing these two methods, it is important to understand how µC/OS-III handles CPU interrupts.

9-2 TYPICAL µC/OS-III INTERRUPT SERVICE ROUTINE (ISR)

µC/OS-III requires that an interrupt service routine be written in assembly language. However, if a C compiler supports in-line assembly language, the ISR code can be placed directly into a C source file. The pseudo-code for a typical ISR when using µC/OS-III is shown in Listing 9-1.

```
MyISR:                                               (1)
    Disable all interrupts;                          (2)
    Save the CPU registers;                          (3)
    OSIntNestingCtr++;                               (4)
    if (OSIntNestingCtr == 1) {                      (5)
        OSTCBCurPtr->StkPtr = Current task's CPU stack pointer register value;
    }
    Clear interrupting device;                       (6)
    Re-enable interrupts (optional);                 (7)
    Call user ISR;                                   (8)
    OSIntExit();                                     (9)
    Restore the CPU registers;                       (10)
    Return from interrupt;                           (11)
```

Listing 9-1 **ISRs under µC/OS-III (assembly language)**

9

L9-1(1)   As mentioned above, an ISR is typically written in assembly language. **MyISR** corresponds to the name of the handler that will handle the interrupting device.

L9-1(2)   It is important that all interrupts are disabled before going any further. Some processors have interrupts disabled whenever an interrupt handler starts. Others require the user to explicitly disable interrupts as shown here. This step may be tricky if a processor supports different interrupt priority levels. However, there is always a way to solve the problem.

L9-1(3)   The first thing the interrupt handler must do is save the context of the CPU onto the interrupted task's stack. On some processors, this occurs automatically. However, on most processors it is important to know how to save the CPU registers onto the task's stack. Save the full "context" of the CPU, which may also include Floating-Point Unit (FPU) registers if the CPU used is equipped with an FPU.

Certain CPUs also automatically switch to a special stack just to process interrupts (i.e., an interrupt stack). This is generally beneficial as it avoids using up valuable task stack space. However, for μC/OS-III, the context of the interrupted task needs to be saved onto that task's stack.

If the processor does not have a dedicated stack pointer to handle ISRs then it is possible to implement one in software. Specifically, upon entering the ISR, simply save the current task stack, switch to a dedicated ISR stack, and when done with the ISR switch back to the task stack. Of course, this means that there is additional code to write, however the benefits are enormous since it is not necessary to allocate extra space on the task stacks to accommodate for worst case interrupt stack usage including interrupt nesting.

L9-1(4)   Next, either call **OSIntEnter()**, or simply increment the variable **OSIntNestingCtr** in assembly language. This is generally quite easy to do and is more efficient than calling **OSIntEnter()**. As its name implies, **OSIntNestingCtr** keeps track of the interrupt nesting level.

L9-1(5)   If this is the first nested interrupt, save the current value of the stack pointer of the interrupted task into its **OS_TCB**. The global pointer **OSTCBCurPtr** conveniently points to the interrupted task's OS_TCB. The very first field in

OS_TCB is where the stack pointer needs to be saved. In other words, OSTCBCurPtr->StkPtr happens to be at offset 0 in the OS_TCB (this greatly simplifies assembly language).

L9-1(6)   At this point, clear the interrupting device so that it does not generate another interrupt until it is ready to do so. The user does not want the device to generate the same interrupt if re-enabling interrupts (refer to the next step). However, most people defer the clearing of the source and prefer to perform the action within the user ISR handler in "C."

L9-1(7)   At this point, it is safe to re-enable interrupts if the developer wants to support nested interrupts. This step is optional.

L9-1(8)   At this point, further processing can be deferred to a C function called from assembly language. This is especially useful if there is a large amount of processing to do in the ISR handler. However, as a general rule, keep the ISRs as short as possible. In fact, it is best to simply signal or send a message to a task and let the task handle the details of servicing the interrupting device.

The ISR must call one of the following functions: OSSemPost(), OSTaskSemPost(), OSFlagPost(), OSQPost() or OSTaskQPost(). This is necessary since the ISR will notify a task, which will service the interrupting device. These are the only functions able to be called from an ISR and they are used to signal or send a message to a task. However, if the ISR does not need to call one of these functions, consider writing the ISR as a "Short Interrupt Service Routine," as described in the next section.

L9-1(9)   When completing the ISR, the user must call OSIntExit() to tell µC/OS-III that the ISR has completed. OSIntExit() simply decrements OSIntNestingCtr and, if OSIntNestingCtr goes to 0, this indicates that the ISR will return to task-level code (instead of a previously interrupted ISR). µC/OS-III will need to determine whether there is a higher priority task that needs to run because of one of the nested ISRs. In other words, the ISR might have signaled or sent a message to a higher- priority task waiting for this signal or message. In this case, µC/OS-III will context switch to this higher priority task instead of returning to the interrupted task. In this latter case, OSIntExit() does not actually return, but takes a different path.

L9-1(10)   If the ISR signaled or sent a message to a lower-priority task than the interrupted task, **OSIntExit()** returns. This means that the interrupted task is still the highest-priority task to run and it is important to restore the previously saved registers.

L9-1(11)   The ISR performs a return from interrupts and so resumes the interrupted task.

NOTE: From this point on, (1) to (6) will be referred to as the *ISR Prologue* and (9) to (11) as the ISR Epilogue.

9-3 SHORT INTERRUPT SERVICE ROUTINE (ISR)

The above sequence assumes that the ISR signals or sends a message to a task. However, in many cases, the ISR may not need to notify a task and can simply perform all of its work within the ISR (assuming it can be done quickly). In this case, the ISR will appear as shown in Listing 9-2.

```
MyShortISR:                                             (1)
    Save enough registers as needed by the ISR;         (2)
    Clear interrupting device;                          (3)
    DO NOT re-enable interrupts;                         (4)
    Call user ISR;                                       (5)
    Restore the saved CPU registers;                    (6)
    Return from interrupt;                               (7)
```

Listing 9-2 **Short ISRs with µC/OS-III**

L9-2(1)   As mentioned above, an ISR is typically written in assembly language. **MyShortISR** corresponds to the name of the handler that will handle the interrupting device.

L9-2(2)   Here, save sufficient registers as required to handle the ISR.

L9-2(3)   The user may want to clear the interrupting device to prevent it from generating the same interrupt once the ISR returns.

L9-2(4)   *Do not* re-enable interrupts at this point since another interrupt could make μC/OS-III calls, forcing a context switch to a higher-priority task. This means that the above ISR would complete, but at a much later time.

L9-2(5)   Now take care of the interrupting device in assembly language or call a C function, if necessary.

L9-2(6)   Once finished, simply restore the saved CPU registers.

L9-2(7)   Perform a return from interrupt to resume the interrupted task.

Short ISRs, as described above, should be the exception and not the rule since μC/OS-III has no way of knowing when these ISRs occur.

9-4 ALL INTERRUPTS VECTOR TO A COMMON LOCATION

Even though an interrupt controller is present in most designs, some CPUs still vector to a common interrupt handler, and an ISR queries the interrupt controller to determine the source of the interrupt. At first glance, this might seem silly since most interrupt controllers are able to force the CPU to jump directly to the proper interrupt handler. It turns out, however, that for μC/OS-III, it is easier to have the interrupt controller vector to a single ISR handler than to vector to a unique ISR handler for each source. Listing 9-3 describes the sequence of events to be performed when the interrupt controller forces the CPU to vector to a single location.

```
An interrupt occurs;                                    (1)
The CPU vectors to a common location;                   (2)
The ISR code performs the "ISR prologue"                (3)
The C handler performs the following:                   (4)
    while (there are still interrupts to process) {     (5)
        Get vector address from interrupt controller;
        Call interrupt handler;
    }
The "ISR epilogue" is executed;                         (6)
```

Listing 9-3 **Single interrupt vector for all interrupts**

L9-3(1)   An interrupt occurs from any device. The interrupt controller activates the interrupt pin on the CPU. If there are other interrupts that occur after the first one, the interrupt controller will latch them and properly prioritize the interrupts.

L9-3(2)   The CPU vectors to a single interrupt handler address. In other words, all interrupts are to be handled by this one interrupt handler.

L9-3(3)   Execute the "ISR prologue" code needed by µC/OS-III. as previously described. This ensures that all ISRs will be able to make µC/OS-III "post" calls.

L9-3(4)   Call a µC/OS-III C handler, which will continue processing the ISR. This makes the code easier to write (and read). Notice that interrupts are not re-enabled.

L9-3(5)   The µC/OS-III C handler then interrogates the interrupt controller and asks it: "Who caused the interrupt?" The interrupt controller will either respond with a number (1 to N) or with the address of the interrupt handler for the interrupting device. Of course, the µC/OS-III C handler will know how to handle the specific interrupt controller since the C handler is written specifically for that controller.

If the interrupt controller provides a number between 1 and N, the C handler simply uses this number as an index into a table (in ROM or RAM) containing the address of the interrupt service routine servicing the interrupting device. A RAM table is handy to change interrupt handlers at run-time. For many embedded systems, however, the table may also reside in ROM.

If the interrupt controller responds with the address of the interrupt service routine, the C handler only needs to call this function.

In both of the above cases, all interrupt handlers need to be declared as follows:

```
void MyISRHandler (void);
```

There is one such handler for each possible interrupt source (obviously, each having a unique name).

The "**while**" loop terminates when there are no other interrupting devices to service.

L9-3(6)   The µC/OS-III "ISR epilogue" is executed to see if it is necessary to return to the interrupted task, or switch to a more important one.

A couple of interesting points to notice:

■   If another device caused an interrupt before the C handler had a chance to query the interrupt controller, most likely the interrupt controller will capture that interrupt. In fact, if that second device happens to be a higher-priority interrupting device, it will most likely be serviced first, as the interrupt controller will prioritize the interrupts.

■   The loop will not terminate until all pending interrupts are serviced. This is similar to allowing nested interrupts, but better, since it is not necessary to redo the ISR prologue and epilogue.

The disadvantage of this method is that a high priority interrupt that occurs after the servicing of another interrupt that has already started must wait for that interrupt to complete before it will be serviced. So, the latency of any interrupt, regardless of priority, can be as long as it takes to process the longest interrrupt.

9-5 EVERY INTERRUPT VECTORS TO A UNIQUE LOCATION

If the interrupt controller vectors directly to the appropriate interrupt handler, each of the ISRs must be written in assembly language as described in section 9-2 "Typical µC/OS-III Interrupt Service Routine (ISR)" on page 167. This, of course, slightly complicates the design. However, copy and paste the majority of the code from one handler to the other and just change what is specific to the actual device.

If the interrupt controller allows the user to query it for the source of the interrupt, it may be possible to simulate the mode in which all interrupts vector to the same location by simply setting all vectors to point to the same location. Most interrupt controllers that vector to a unique location, however, do not allow users to query it for the source of the interrupt since, by definition, having a unique vector for all interrupting devices should not be necessary.

9-6 DIRECT AND DEFERRED POST METHODS

µC/OS-III handles event posting from interrupts using two different methods: Direct and Deferred Post. The method used in the application is selected by changing the value of OS_CFG_ISR_POST_DEFERRED_EN in OS_CFG.H (this assumes you have access to µC/OS-III's source code). When set to 0, µC/OS-III uses the Direct Post Method and when set to 1, µC/OS-III uses the Deferred Post Method.

As far as application code and ISRs are concerned, these two methods are completely transparent. It is not necessary to change anything except the configuration value OS_CFG_ISR_POST_DEFERRED_EN to switch between the two methods. Of course, changing the configuration constant will require recompiling the product and µC/OS-III.

Before explaining why to use one versus the other, let us review their differences.

9-6-1 DIRECT POST METHOD

The Direct Post Method is used by µC/OS-II and is replicated in µC/OS-III. Figure 9-2 shows a task diagram of what takes place in a Direct Post.

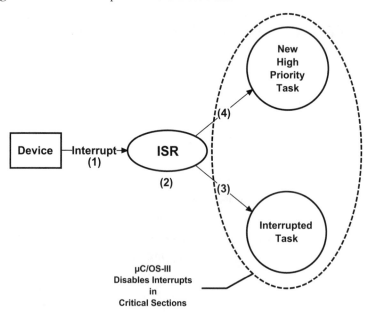

Figure 9-2 **Direct Post Method**

F9-2(1)   A device generates an interrupt.

F9-2(2)   The Interrupt Service Routine (ISR) responsible to handle the device executes (assuming interrupts are enabled). The device interrupt is generally the event a task is waiting for. The task waiting for this interrupt to occur either has a higher priority than the interrupted task, or lower (or equal) in priority.

F9-2(3)   If the ISR made a lower (or equal) priority task ready to run then upon completion of the ISR, μC/OS-III returns to the interrupted task exactly at the point the interrupt occurred.

F9-2(4)   If the ISR made a higher priority task ready to run, μC/OS-III will context switch to the new higher-priority task since the more important task was waiting for this device interrupt.

F9-2(5)   In the Direct Post Method, μC/OS-III must protect critical sections by disabling interrupts as some of these critical sections can be accessed by ISRs.

The above discussion assumed that interrupts were enabled and that the ISR could respond quickly to the interrupting device. However, if the application code makes μC/OS-III service calls (and it will at some point), it is possible that interrupts would be disabled. When `OS_CFG_ISR_POST_DEFERRED_EN` is set to 0, μC/OS-III disables interrupts while accessing critical sections. Thus, interrupts will not be responded to until μC/OS-III re-enables interrupts. Of course, attempts were made to keep interrupt disable times as short as possible, but there are complex features of μC/OS-III that disable interrupts for a longer period than the user would like.

The key factor in determining whether to use the Direct Post Method is generally the μC/OS-III interrupt disable time. This is fairly easy to determine since the μC/CPU files provided with the μC/OS-III port for the processor used includes code to measure maximum interrupt disable time. This code can be enabled (assumes you have the source code) for testing purposes and removed when ready to deploy the product. The user would typically not want to leave measurement code in production code to avoid introducing measurement artifacts. Once instrumented, let the application run for sufficiently long and read the variable `CPU_IntDisMeasMaxRaw_cnts`. The resolution (in time) of this variable depends on the timer used during the measurement.

9

Determine the interrupt latency, interrupt response, interrupt recovery, and task latency by adding the execution times of the code involved for each, as shown below.

Interrupt Latency   = Maximum interrupt disable time;

Interrupt Response = Interrupt latency
                      + Vectoring to the interrupt handler
                      + ISR prologue;

Interrupt Recovery = Handling of the interrupting device
                      + Posting a signal or a message to a task
                      + OSIntExit()
                      + OSIntCtxSw();

Task Latency   = Interrupt response
                      + Interrupt recovery
                      + Time scheduler is locked;

The execution times of the µC/OS-III ISR prologue, ISR epilogue, OSIntExit(), and OSIntCtxSw(), can be measured independently and should be fairly constant.

It should also be easy to measure the execution time of a post call by using OS_TS_GET().

In the Direct Post Method, the scheduler is locked only when handling timers and therefore, task latency should be fast if there are not too many timers with short callbacks expiring at the same time. See Chapter 12, "Timer Management" on page 201. µC/OS-III is also able to measure the amount of time the scheduler is locked, providing task latency.

9-6-2 DEFERRED POST METHOD

In the Deferred Post Method (**OS_CFG_ISR_POST_DEFERRED_EN** is set to 1), instead of disabling interrupts to access critical sections, μC/OS-III locks the scheduler. This avoids having other tasks access critical sections while allowing interrupts to be recognized and serviced. In the Deferred Post Method, interrupts' are almost never disabled. The Deferred Post Method is, however, a bit more complex as shown in Figure 9-3.

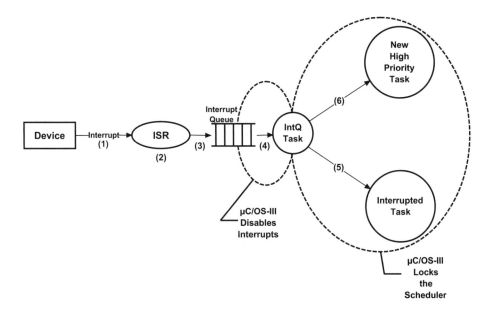

Figure 9-3 **Deferred Post Method block diagram**

F9-3(1)   A device generates an interrupt.

F9-3(2)   The ISR responsible for handling the device executes (assuming interrupts are enabled). The device interrupt is the event that a task was waiting for. The task waiting for this interrupt to occur is either higher in priority than the interrupted task, lower, or equal in priority.

F9-3(3)   The ISR calls one of the post services to signal or send a message to a task. However, instead of performing the post operation, the ISR queues the actual post call along with arguments in a special queue called the *Interrupt Queue*. The ISR then makes the *Interrupt Queue Handler Task* ready to run. This task is internal to μC/OS-III and is always the highest priority task (i.e., Priority 0).

F9-3(4)   At the end of the ISR, µC/OS-III always context switches to the interrupt queue handler task, which then extracts the post command from the queue. We disable interrupts to prevent another interrupt from accessing the interrupt queue while the queue is being emptied. The task then re-enables interrupts, locks the scheduler, and performs the post call as if the post was performed at the task level all along. This effectively manipulates critical sections at the task level.

F9-3(5)   When the interrupt queue handler task empties the interrupt queue, it makes itself not ready to run and then calls the scheduler to determine which task must run next. If the original interrupted task is still the highest priority task, µC/OS-III will resume that task.

F9-3(6)   If, however, a more important task was made ready to run because of the post, µC/OS-III will context switch to that task.

All the extra processing is performed to avoid disabling interrupts during critical sections of code. The extra processing time only consist of copying the post call and arguments into the queue, extracting it back out of the queue, and performing an extra context switch.

Similar to the Direct Post Method, it is easy to determine interrupt latency, interrupt response, interrupt recovery, and task latency, by adding execution times of the pieces of code involved for each as shown below.

Interrupt Latency   =   Maximum interrupt disable time;

Interrupt Response   =   Interrupt latency
                          + Vectoring to the interrupt handler
                          + ISR prologue;

Interrupt Recovery   =   Handling of the interrupting device
                          + Posting a signal or a message to the Interrupt Queue
                          + OSIntExit()
                          + OSIntCtxSw() to Interrupt Queue Handler Task;

Task Latency   =   Interrupt response
                                   + Interrupt recovery
                                   + Re-issue the post to the object or task
                                   + Context switch to task
                                   + Time scheduler is locked;

The execution times of the µC/OS-III ISR prologue, ISR epilogue, `OSIntExit()`, and `OSIntCtxSw()`, can be measured independently and should be constant.

9

It should also be easy to measure the execution time of a post call by using `OS_TS_GET()`. In fact, the post calls should be short in the Deferred Post Method because it only involves copying the post call and its arguments into the interrupt queue.

The difference is that in the Deferred Post Method, interrupts are disabled for a very short amount of time and thus, the first three metrics should be fast. However, task latency is higher as µC/OS-III locks the scheduler to access critical sections.

9-7 DIRECT VS. DEFERRED POST METHOD

In the Direct Post Method, µC/OS-III disables interrupts to access critical sections. In comparison, while in the Deferred Post Method, µC/OS-III locks the scheduler to access the same critical sections.

In the Deferred Post Method, µC/OS-III must still disable interrupts to access the interrupt queue. However, the interrupt disable time is very short and fairly constant.

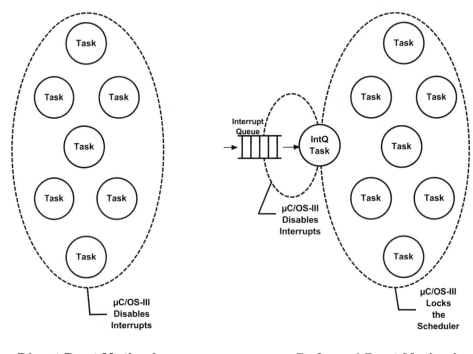

Direct Post Method   **Deferred Post Method**

Figure 9-4 **Direct vs. Deferred Post Methods**

If interrupt disable time is critical in the application because there are very fast interrupt sources and the interrupt disable time of µC/OS-III is not acceptable using the Direct Post Method, use the Deferred Post Method.

However, if you are planning on using the features listed in Table 9-1, consider using the Deferred Post Method, described in the next section.

Feature	Reason
Multiple tasks at the same priority	Although this is an important feature of µC/OS-III, multiple tasks at the same priority create longer critical sections. However, if there are only a few tasks at the same priority, interrupt latency will be relatively small. If the user does not create multiple tasks at the same priority, the Direct Post Method is recommended.
Event Flags Chapter 14, "Synchronization" on page 259	If multiple tasks are waiting on different events, going through all of the tasks waiting for events requires a fair amount of processing time, which means longer critical sections. If only a few tasks (approximately one to five) are waiting on an event flag group, the critical section will be short enough to use the Direct Post Method.
Pend on multiple objects Chapter 16, "Pending On Multiple Objects" on page 321	Pending on multiple objects is probably the most complex feature provided by µC/OS-III and requires interrupts to be disabled for fairly long periods of time when using the Direct Post Method. If pending on multiple objects, the Deferred Post Method is highly recommended. If the application does not use this feature, the user may select the Direct Post Method.
Broadcast on Post calls See OSSemPost() and OSQPost() descriptions.	µC/OS-III disables interrupts while processing a post to multiple tasks in a broadcast. If not using the broadcast option, use the Direct Post Method. Note that broadcasts only apply to semaphores and message queues.

Table 9-1 **µC/OS-III features to avoid when using the Direct Post Method**

9-8 THE CLOCK TICK (OR SYSTEM TICK)

µC/OS-III-based systems generally require the presence of a periodic time source called the *clock tick* or *system tick*.

A hardware timer configured to generate an interrupt at a rate between 10 and 1000 Hz provides the clock tick. A tick source may also be obtained by generating an interrupt from an AC power line (typically 50 or 60 Hz). In fact, one can easily derive 100 or 120 Hz by detecting zero crossings of the power line.

The clock tick interrupt can be viewed as the system's heartbeat. The rate is application specific and depends on the desired resolution of this time source. However, the faster the tick rate, the higher the overhead imposed on the system.

The clock tick interrupt allows µC/OS-III to delay tasks for an integral number of clock ticks and provide timeouts when tasks are waiting for events to occur.

The clock tick interrupt must call **OSTimeTick()**. The pseudocode for **OSTimeTick()** is shown in Listing 9-4.

```
void  OSTimeTick (void)
{
    OSTimeTickHook();                                       (1)
#if OS_CFG_ISR_POST_DEFERRED_EN > 0u
    Get timestamp;                                          (2)
    Post "time tick" to the Interrupt Queue;
#else
    Signal the Tick Task;                                   (3)
    Run the round-robin scheduling algorithm;              (4)
    Signal the timer task;                                  (5)
#endif
}
```

Listing 9-4 **OSTimeTick() pseudocode**

L9-4(1)   The time tick ISR starts by calling a hook function, **OSTimeTickHook()**. The hook function allows the implementer of the µC/OS-III port to perform additional processing when a tick interrupt occurs. In turn, the tick hook can call a user-defined tick hook if its corresponding pointer, **OS_AppTimeTickHookPtr**, is non-**NULL**. The reason the hook is called first is to give the application immediate access to this periodic time source. This can be useful to read sensors at a regular interval (not as subject to jitter), update Pulse Width Modulation (PWM) registers, and more.

L9-4(2)   If µC/OS-III is configured for the Deferred Post Method, µC/OS-III reads the current timestamp and defers the call to signal the tick task by placing an appropriate entry in the interrupt queue. The tick task will thus be signaled by the Interrupt Queue Handler Task.

L9-4(3)   If µC/OS-III is configured for the Direct Post Method, µC/OS-III signals the tick task so that it can process the time delays and timeouts.

L9-4(4)   µC/OS-III runs the round-robin scheduling algorithm to determine whether the time slot for the current task has expired.

L9-4(5)   The tick task is also used as the time base for the timers (see Chapter 13, "Resource Management" on page 217).

A common misconception is that a system tick is always needed with µC/OS-III. In fact, many low-power applications may not implement the system tick because of the power required to maintain the tick list. In other words, it is not reasonable to continuously power down and power up the product just to maintain the system tick. Since µC/OS-III is a preemptive kernel, an event other than a tick interrupt can wake up a system placed in low power mode by either a keystroke from a keypad or other means. Not having a system tick means that the user is not allowed to use time delays and timeouts on system calls. This is a decision required to be made by the designer of the low-power product.

9-9 SUMMARY

µC/OS-III provides services to manage interrupts. An ISR should be short in length, and signal or send a message to a task, which is responsible for servicing the interrupting device.

ISRs that are short and do not need to signal or send a message to a task, are not required to do so.

µC/OS-III supports processors that vector to a single ISR for all interrupting devices, or to a unique ISR for each device.

µC/OS-III supports two methods: Direct and Deferred Post. The Direct Post Method assumes that µC/OS-III critical sections are protected by disabling interrupts. The Deferred Post Method locks the scheduler when µC/OS-III accesses critical sections of code.

µC/OS-III assumes the presence of a periodic time source for applications requiring time delays and timeouts on certain services.

Chapter 9

9

Pend Lists (or Wait Lists)

A task is placed in a *Pend List* (also called a *Wait List*) when it is waiting on a semaphore to be signaled, a mutual exclusion semaphore to be released, an event flag group to be posted, or a message queue to be posted.

See ...	For ...	Kernel Object
Chapter 13, "Resource Management" on page 217	Semaphores Mutual Exclusion Semaphores	OS_SEM OS_MUTEX
Chapter 14, "Synchronization" on page 259	Semaphores Event Flags	OS_SEM OS_FLAG_GRP
Chapter 15, "Message Passing" on page 297	Message Queues	OS_Q

Table 10-1 **Kernel objects that have Pend Lists**

A pend list is similar to the *Ready List*, except that instead of keeping track of tasks that are ready-to-run, the pend list keeps track of tasks waiting for an object to be posted. In addition, the pend list is sorted by priority; the highest priority task waiting on the object is placed at the head of the list, and the lowest priority task waiting on the object is placed at the end of the list.

A pend list is a data structure of type **OS_PEND_LIST**, which consists of three fields as shown in Figure 10-1.

Figure 10-1 **Pend List**

`.NbrEntries`	Contains the current number of entries in the pend list. Each entry in the pend list points to a task that is waiting for the kernel object to be posted.
`.TailPtr`	Is a pointer to the last task in the list (i.e., the lowest priority task).
`.HeadPtr`	Is a pointer to the first task in the list (i.e., the highest priority task).

Figure 10-2 indicates that each kernel object using a pend list contains the same three fields at the beginning of the kernel object that we called an `OS_PEND_OBJ`. Notice that the first field is always a "Type" which allows µC/OS-III to know if the kernel object is a semaphore, a mutual exclusion semaphore, an event flag group, or a message queue object.

Figure 10-2 **OS_PEND_OBJ at the beginning of certain kernel objects**

Table 10-2 shows that the "Type" field of each of the above objects is initialized to contain four ASCII characters when the respective object is created. This allows the user to identify these objects when performing a memory dump using a debugger.

Kernel Object	**Type**
Semaphore	'S" "E" "M" "A"
Mutual Exclusion Semaphore	'M" "U" "T" "X"
Event Flag Group	'F" "L" "A" "G"
Message Queue	'Q" "U" "E" "U"

Table 10-2 **Kernel objects with initialized "Type" field**

A pend list does not actually point to a task's **OS_TCB**, but instead points to **OS_PEND_DATA** objects as shown in Figure 10-3. Also, an **OS_PEND_DATA** structure is allocated dynamically on the current task's stack when a task is placed on a pend list. This implies that a task stack needs to be able to allocate storage for this data structure.

OS_PEND_DATA

PrevPtr
NextPtr
TCBPtr
PendObjPtr
RdyObjPtr
RdyMsgPtr
RdyMsgSize
RdyTS

Figure 10-3 **Pend Data**

10

.PrevPtr

Is a pointer to an **OS_PEND_DATA** entry in the pend list. This pointer points to a higher or equal priority task waiting on the kernel object.

.NextPtr

Is a pointer to an **OS_PEND_DATA** entry in the pend list. This pointer points to a lower or equal priority task waiting on the kernel object.

.TCBPtr

Is a pointer to the **OS_TCB** of the task waiting on the pend list.

.PendObjPtr

Is a pointer to the kernel object that the task is pending on. In other words, this pointer can point to an **OS_SEM**, **OS_MUTEX**, **OS_FLAG_GRP** or **OS_Q** by using an **OS_PEND_OBJ** as the common data structure.

.RdyObjPtr

Is a pointer to the kernel object that is ready if the task actually waits for multiple kernel objects. See Chapter 16, "Pending On Multiple Objects" on page 321 for more on this.

.RdyMsgPtr   Is a pointer to the message posted through `OSQPost()` if the task is pending on multiple kernel objects. Again, see Chapter 16, "Pending On Multiple Objects" on page 321.

.RdyTS   Is a timestamp of when the kernel object was posted. This is used when a task pends on multiple kernel objects as described in Chapter 16, "Pending On Multiple Objects" on page 321.

Figure 10-4 exhibits how all data structures connect to each other when tasks are inserted in a pend list. This drawing assumes that there are two tasks waiting on a semaphore.

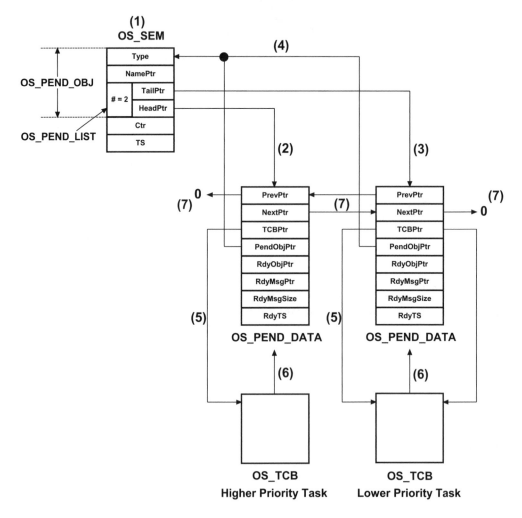

Figure 10-4 **Pend Data**

F9-4(1)   The **OS_SEM** data type contains an **OS_PEND_OBJ**, which in turn contains an **OS_PEND_LIST**. The **.NbrEntries** field in the pend list indicates that there are two tasks waiting on the semaphore.

F9-4(2)   The **.HeadPtr** field of the pend list points to the **OS_PEND_DATA** structure associated with the highest priority task waiting on the semaphore.

F9-4(3)   The **.TailPtr** field of the pend list points to the **OS_PEND_DATA** structure associated with the lowest priority task waiting on the semaphore.

F9-4(4)   Both **OS_PEND_DATA** structures in turn point back to the **OS_SEM** data structure. The pointers think they are pointing to an **OS_PEND_OBJ**. We know that the **OS_PEND_OBJ** is a semaphore by examining the **.Type** field of the **OS_PEND_OBJ**.

F9-4(5)   Each **OS_PEND_DATA** structure points to its respective **OS_TCB**. In other words, we know which task is pending on the semaphore.

F9-4(6)   Each task points back to the **OS_PEND_DATA** structure.

F9-4(7)   Finally, the **OS_PEND_DATA** structure forms a doubly linked list so that the µC/OS-III can easily add or remove entries in this list.

Although this may seem complex, the reasoning will become apparent in Chapter 16, "Pending On Multiple Objects" on page 321. For now, assume all of the links are necessary.

Table 10-3 shows the functions that µC/OS-III uses to manipulate entries in a pend list. These functions are internal to µC/OS-III and the application code must never call them. The code is found in **OS_CORE.C**.

10

Function	Description
OS_PendListChangePrio()	Change the priority of a task in a pend list
OS_PendListInit()	Initialize a pend list
OS_PendListInsertHead()	Insert an OS_PEND_DATA at the head of the pend list
OS_PendListInsertPrio()	Insert an OS_PEND_DATA in priority order in the pend list
OS_PendListRemove()	Remove multiple OS_PEND_DATA from the pend list
OS_PendListRemove1()	Remove single OS_PEND_DATA from the pend list

Table 10-3 **Pend List access functions**

10-1 SUMMARY

µC/OS-III keeps track of tasks waiting for semaphores, mutual exclusion semaphores, event flag groups and message queues using pend lists.

A pend list consists of a data structure of type **OS_PEND_LIST**. The pend list is further encapsulated into another data type called an **OS_PEND_OBJ**.

Tasks are not directly linked to the pend list but instead are linked through an intermediate data structure called an **OS_PEND_DATA** which is allocated on the stack of the task waiting on the kernel object.

Application code must not access pend lists, since these are internal to µC/OS-III.

Time Management

µC/OS-III provides time-related services to the application programmer.

In Chapter 9, "Interrupt Management" on page 165, it was established that µC/OS-III generally requires (as do most kernels) that the user provide a periodic interrupt to keep track of time delays and timeouts. This periodic time source is called a clock tick and should occur between 10 and 1000 times per second, or Hertz (see **OS_CFG_TICK_RATE_HZ** in **OS_CFG_APP.H**). The actual frequency of the clock tick depends on the desired tick resolution of the application. However, the higher the frequency of the ticker, the higher the overhead.

µC/OS-III provides a number of services to manage time as summarized in Table 11-1, and the code is found in **OS_TIME.C**.

Function Name	Operation
OSTimeDly()	Delay execution of a task for "n" ticks
OSTimeDlyHMSM()	Delay a task for a user specified time in HH:MM:SS.mmm
OSTimeDlyResume()	Resume a delayed task
OSTimeGet()	Obtain the current value of the tick counter
OSTimeSet()	Set the tick counter to a new value
OSTimeTick()	Signal the occurrence of a clock tick

Table 11-1 **Time Services API summary**

The application programmer should refer to Appendix A, "µC/OS-III API Reference Manual" on page 383 for a detailed description of these services.

11-1 **OSTimeDly()**

A task calls this function to suspend execution until some time expires. The calling function will not execute until the specified time expires. This function allows three modes: relative, periodic and absolute.

Listing 11-1 shows how to use **OSTimeDly()** in relative mode.

```
void  MyTask (void *p_arg)
{
    OS_ERR  err;
    :
    :
    while (DEF_ON) {
        :
        :
        OSTimeDly(2,                        (1)
                  OS_OPT_TIME_DLY,          (2)
                  &err);                    (3)
        /* Check "err" */                   (4)
        :
        :
    }
}
```

Listing 11-1 **OSTimeDly() - Relative**

L11-1(1)   The first argument specifies the amount of time delay (in number of ticks) from when the function is called. For example if the tick rate (**OS_CFG_TICK_RATE_HZ** in **OS_CFG_APP.H**) is set to 1000 Hz, the user is asking to suspend the current task for approximately 2 milliseconds. However, the value is not accurate since the count starts from the next tick which could occur almost immediately. This will be explained shortly.

L11-1(2)   Specifying **OS_OPT_TIME_DLY** indicates that the user wants to use "relative" mode.

L11-1(3)   As with most μC/OS-III services an error return value will be returned. The example should return **OS_ERR_NONE** as the arguments are all valid. Refer to Chapter 11, "Time Management" on page 191 for a list of possible error codes.

L11-1(4)   Always check the error code returned by µC/OS-III. If "**err**" does not contain OS_ERR_NONE, OSTimeDly() did not perform the intended work. For example, another task could remove the time delay suspension by calling OSTimeDlyResume() and when MyTask() returns, it would not have returned because the time had expired.

As mentioned above, the delay is not accurate. Refer to Figure 11-1 and its description below to understand why.

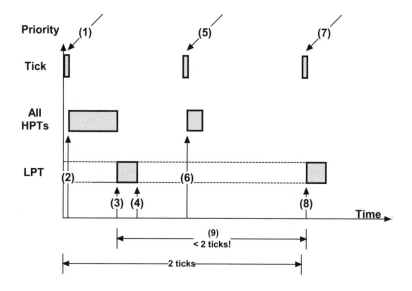

Figure 11-1 **OSTimeDly() - Relative**

F11-1(1)   We get a tick interrupt and µC/OS-III services the ISR.

F11-1(2)   At the end of the ISR, all Higher Priority Tasks (HPTs) execute. The execution time of HPTs is unknown and can vary.

F11-1(3)   Once all HPTs have executed, µC/OS-III runs the task that has called OSTimeDly() as shown above. For the sake of discussion, it is assumed that this task is a lower priority task (LPT).

F11-1(4)   The task calls **OSTimeDly()** and specifies to delay for two ticks in "relative" mode. At this point, μC/OS-III places the current task in the tick list where it will wait for two ticks to expire. The delayed task consumes zero CPU time while waiting for the time to expire.

F11-1(5)   The next tick occurs. If there are HPTs waiting for this particular tick, μC/OS-III will schedule them to run at the end of the ISR.

F11-1(6)   The HPTs execute.

F11-1(7)   The next tick interrupt occurs. This is the tick that the LPT was waiting for and will now be made ready to run by μC/OS-III.

F11-1(8)   Since there are no HPTs to execute on this tick, μC/OS-III switches to the LPT.

F11-1(9)   Given the execution time of the HPTs, the time delay is not exactly two ticks, as requested. In fact, it is virtually impossible to obtain a delay of exactly the desired number of ticks. One might ask for a delay of two ticks, but the very next tick could occur almost immediately after calling **OSTimeDly()**! Just imagine what might happen if all HPTs took longer to execute and pushed (3) and (4) further to the right. In this case, the delay would actually appear as one tick instead of two.

OSTimeDly() can also be called with the **OS_OPT_TIME_PERIODIC** option as shown in Listing 11-2. This option allows delaying the task until the tick counter reaches a certain periodic match value and thus ensures that the spacing in time is always the same as it is not subject to CPU load variations.

μC/OS-III determines the "match value" of **OSTickCtr** to determine when the task will need to wake up based on the desired period. This is shown in Figure 11-2. μC/OS-III checks to ensure that if the match is computed such that it represents a value that has already gone by then, the delay will be zero.

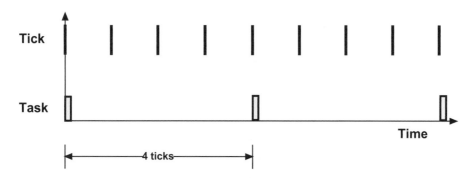

Figure 11-2 **OSTimeDly() - Periodic**

```
void  MyTask (void *p_arg)
{
    OS_ERR    err;
    :
    :
    while (DEF_ON) {
        OSTimeDly(4,                                (1)
                  OS_OPT_TIME_PERIODIC,             (2)
                  &err);
        /* Check "err" */                           (3)
        :
        :
    }
}
```

Listing 11-2 **OSTimeDly() - Periodic**

L11-2(1)   The first argument specifies the period for the task to execute, specifically every four ticks. Of course, if the task is a low-priority task, μC/OS-III only schedules and runs the task based on its priority relative to what else needs to be executed.

L11-2(2)   Specifying **OS_OPT_TIME_PERIODIC** indicates that the task is to be ready to run when the tick counter reaches the desired period from the previous call.

L11-2(3)   You should always check the error code returned by μC/OS-III.

Relative and Periodic modes might not look different, but they are. In Relative mode, it is possible to miss one of the ticks when the system is heavily loaded, missing a tick or more on occasion. In Periodic mode, the task may still execute later, but it will always be synchronized to the desired number of ticks. In fact, Periodic mode is the preferred mode to use to implement a time-of-day clock.

Finally, you can use the absolute mode to perform a specific action at a fixed time after power up. For example, turn off a light 10 seconds after the product powers up. In this case, you would specify **OS_OPT_TIME_MATCH** while "**dly**" actually corresponds to the desired value of **OSTickCtr** you want to reach.

To summarize, the task will wake up when **OSTickCtr** reaches the following value:

Value of "opt"	Task wakes up when
OS_OPT_TIME_DLY	OSTickCtr + dly
OS_OPT_TIME_PERIODIC	OSTCBCurPtr->TickCtrPrev + dly
OS_OPT_TIME_MATCH	dly

11-2 OSTimeDlyHMSM()

A task may call this function to suspend execution until some time expires by specifying the length of time in a more user-friendly way. Specifically, specify the delay in hours, minutes, seconds, and milliseconds (thus the HMSM). This function only works in "Relative" mode.

Listing 11-3 indicates how to use OSTimeDlyHMSM().

```
void  MyTask (void *p_arg)
{
    OS_ERR  err;
    :
    :
    while (DEF_ON) {
        :
        :
        OSTimeDlyHMSM(0,                              (1)
                      0,
                      1,
                      0,
                      OS_OPT_TIME_HMSM_STRICT,        (2)
                      &err);                          (3)
        /* Check "err" */
        :
        :
    }
}
```

Listing 11-3 **OSTimeDlyHMSM()**

L11-3(1)   The first four arguments specify the amount of time delay (in hours, minutes, seconds, and milliseconds) from this point in time. In the above example, the task should delay by 1 second. The resolution greatly depends on the tick rate. For example, if the tick rate (OS_CFG_TICK_RATE_HZ in OS_CFG_APP.H) is set to 1000 Hz there is technically a resolution of 1 millisecond. If the tick rate is 100 Hz then the delay of the current task is in increments of 10 milliseconds. Again, given the relative nature of this call, the actual delay may not be accurate.

L11-3(2)   Specifying OS_OPT_TIME_HMSM_STRICT verifies that the user strictly passes valid values for hours, minutes, seconds and milliseconds. Valid hours are 0 to 99, valid minutes are 0 to 59, valid seconds are 0 to 59, and valid milliseconds are 0 to 999.

11

If specifying **OS_OPT_TIME_HMSM_NON_STRICT**, the function will accept nearly any value for hours (between 0 to 999), minutes (from 0 to 9999), seconds (any value, up to **65,535**), and milliseconds (any value, up to **4,294,967,295**). **OSTimeDlyHMSM(203, 101, 69, 10000)** may be accepted. Whether or not this makes sense is a different story.

The reason hours is limited to 999 is that time delays typically use 32-bit values to keep track of ticks. If the tick rate is set at 1000 Hz then, it is possible to only track 4,294,967 seconds, which corresponds to 1,193 hours, and therefore 999 is a reasonable limit.

L11-3(3)   As with most μC/OS-III services the user will receive an error return value. The example should return **OS_ERR_NONE** since the arguments are all valid. Refer to Appendix A, "μC/OS-III API Reference Manual" on page 383 for a list of possible error codes.

Even though μC/OS-III allows for very long delays for tasks, it is actually not recommended to delay tasks for a long time. There is no indication that the task is actually "alive" unless it is possible to monitor the amount of time remaining for the delay. It is better to have the task wake up approximately every minute or so, and have it "tell you" that it is still ok.

OSTimeDly() and **OSTimeDlyHMSM()** are often used to create periodic tasks (tasks that execute periodically). For example, it is possible to have a task that scans a keyboard every 50 milliseconds and another task that reads analog inputs every 10 milliseconds, etc.

11-3 `OSTimeDlyResume()`

A task can resume another task that called `OSTimeDly()` or `OSTimeDlyHMSM()` by calling `OSTimeDlyResume()`. Listing 11-4 shows how to use `OSTimeDlyResume()`. The task that delayed itself will not know that it was resumed, but will think that the delay expired. Because of this, use this function with great care.

```
OS_TCB  MyTaskTCB;


void  MyTask (void *p_arg)
{
    OS_ERR  err;
    :
    :
    while (1) {
        :
        :
        OSTimeDly(10,
                  OS_OPT_TIME_DLY,
                  &err);
        /* Check "err" */
        :
        :
    }
}


void  MyOtherTask (void *p_arg)
{
    OS_ERR  err;
    :
    :
    while (1) {
        :
        :
        OSTimeDlyResume(&MyTaskTCB,
                        &err);
        /* Check "err" */
        :
        :
    }
}
```

Listing 11-4 **OSTimeDlyResume()**

11-4 `OSTimeSet()` **AND** `OSTimeGet()`

µC/OS-III increments a tick counter every time a tick interrupt occurs. This counter allows the application to make coarse time measurements and have some notion of time (after power up).

`OSTimeGet()` allows the user to take a snapshot of the tick counter. As shown in a previous section, use this value to delay a task for a specific number of ticks and repeat this periodically without losing track of time.

`OSTimeSet()` allows the user to change the current value of the tick counter. Although µC/OS-III allows for this, it is recommended to use this function with great care.

11-5 `OSTimeTick()`

The tick Interrupt Service Routine (ISR) must call this function every time a tick interrupt occurs. µC/OS-III uses this function to update time delays and timeouts on other system calls. OSTimeTick() is considered an internal function to µC/OS-III.

11-6 SUMMARY

µC/OS-III provides services to applications so that tasks can suspend their execution for user-defined time delays. Delays are either specified by a number of clock ticks or hours, minutes, seconds, and milliseconds.

Application code can resume a delayed task by calling `OSTimeDlyResume()`. However, its use is not recommended because resumed task will not know that they were resumed as opposed to the time delay expired.

µC/OS-III keeps track of the number of ticks occurring since power up or since the number of ticks counter was last changed by `OSTimeSet()`. The counter may be read by the application code using `OSTimeGet()`.

12

Timer Management

μC/OS-III provides timer services to the application programmer and code to handle timers is found in **OS_TMR.C**. Timer services are enabled when setting **OS_CFG_TMR_EN** to 1 in **OS_CFG.H**.

Timers are down counters that perform an *action* when the counter reaches zero. The user provides the action through a *callback* function (or simply *callback*). A callback is a user-declared function that will be called when the timer expires. The callback can be used to turn a light on or off, start a motor, or perform other actions. However, it is important to never make blocking calls within a callback function (i.e., call **OSTimeDly()**, **OSTimeDlyHMSM()**, **OS???Pend()**, or anything that causes the timer task to block or be deleted).

Timers are useful in protocol stacks (retransmission timers, for example), and can also be used to poll I/O devices at predefined intervals.

An application can have any number of timers (limited only by the amount of RAM available). Timer services in μC/OS-III start with the **OSTmr???()** prefix, and the services available to the application programmer are described in Appendix A, "μC/OS-III API Reference Manual" on page 383.

The resolution of all the timers managed by μC/OS-III is determined by the configuration constant: **OS_CFG_TMR_TASK_RATE_HZ**, which is expressed in Hertz (Hz). So, if the timer task (described later) rate is set to 10, all timers have a resolution of 1/10th of a second (ticks in the diagrams to follow). In fact, this is the typical recommended value for the timer task. Timers are to be used with "coarse" granularity.

μC/OS-III provides a number of services to manage timers as summarized in Table 12-1.

Function Name	Operation
OSTmrCreate()	Create and specify the operating mode of the timer.
OSTmrDel()	Delete a timer.
OSTmrRemainGet()	Obtain the remaining time left before the timer expires.
OSTmrStart()	Start (or restart) a timer.
OSTmrStateGet()	Obtain the current state of a timer.
OSTmrStop()	Stop the countdown process of a timer.

Table 12-1 **Timer API summary**

A timer needs to be created before it can be used. Create a timer by calling **OSTmrCreate()** and specify a number of arguments to this function based on how the timer is to operate. Once the timer operation is specified, its operating mode cannot be changed unless the timer is deleted and recreated. The function prototype for **OSTmrCreate()** is shown below as a quick reference:

```
void  OSTmrCreate (OS_TMR                 *p_tmr,           /* Pointer to timer      */
                   CPU_CHAR               *p_name,          /* Name of timer, ASCII */
                   OS_TICK                dly,              /* Initial delay         */
                   OS_TICK                period,           /* Repeat period         */
                   OS_OPT                 opt,              /* Options               */
                   OS_TMR_CALLBACK_PTR    p_callback,       /* Fnct to call at 0     */
                   void                   *p_callback_arg,  /* Arg. to callback      */
                   OS_ERR                 *p_err)
```

Once created, a timer can be started (or restarted) and stopped as often as is necessary. Timers can be created to operate in one of three modes: One-shot, Periodic (no initial delay), and Periodic (with initial delay).

12-1 ONE-SHOT TIMERS

As its name implies, a one-shot timer will countdown from its initial value, call the callback function when it reaches zero, and stop. Figure 12-1 shows a timing diagram of this operation. The countdown is initiated by calling OSTmrStart(). At the completion of the time delay, the callback function is called, assuming a callback function was provided when the timer was created. Once completed, the timer does not do anything unless restarted by calling OSTmrStart(), at which point the process starts over.

Terminate the countdown process of a timer (before it reaches zero) by calling OSTmrStop(). In this case, specify that the callback function be called or not.

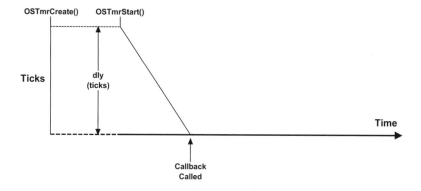

Figure 12-1 **One Shot Timers (dly > 0, period == 0)**

As shown in Figure 12-2, a one-shot timer is retriggered by calling OSTmrStart() before the timer reaches zero. This feature can be used to implement watchdogs and similar safeguards.

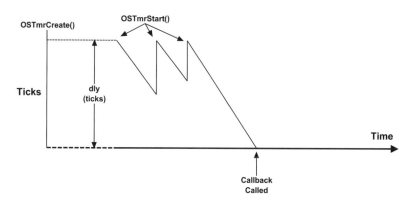

Figure 12-2 **Retriggering a One Shot Timer**

12-2 PERIODIC (NO INITIAL DELAY)

As indicated in Figure 12-3, timers can be configured for periodic mode. When the countdown expires, the callback function is called, the timer is automatically reloaded, and the process is repeated. If specifying a delay of zero (i.e., **dly == 0**) when the timer is created, when started, the timer immediately uses the "**period**" as the reload value. Calling **OSTmrStart()** at any point in the countdown restarts the process.

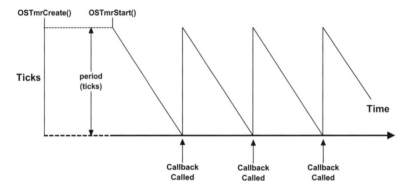

Figure 12-3 **Periodic Timers (dly == 0, period > 0)**

12-3 PERIODIC (WITH INITIAL DELAY)

As shown in Figure 12-4, timers can be configured for periodic mode with an initial delay that is different than its period. The first countdown count comes from the "**dly**" argument passed in the **OSTmrCreate()** call, and the reload value is the "**period**". Calling **OSTmrStart()** restarts the process including the initial delay.

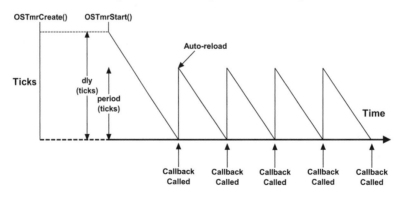

Figure 12-4 **Periodic Timers (dly > 0, period > 0)**

12-4 TIMER MANAGEMENT INTERNALS

12-4-1 TIMER MANAGEMENT INTERNALS - TIMERS STATES

Figure 12-5 shows the state diagram of a timer.

Tasks can call **OSTmrStateGet()** to find out the state of a timer. Also, at any time during the countdown process, the application code can call **OSTmrRemainGet()** to find out how much time remains before the timer reaches zero (0). The value returned is expressed in "timer ticks." If timers are decremented at a rate of 10 Hz then a count of 50 corresponds to 5 seconds. If the timer is in the stop state, the time remaining will correspond to either the initial delay (one shot or periodic with initial delay), or the period if the timer is configured for periodic without initial delay.

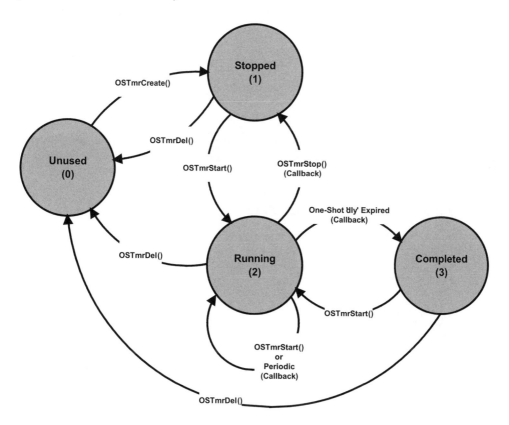

Figure 12-5 **Timer State Diagram**

205

F12-5(1)   The "Unused" state is a timer that has not been created or has been "deleted." In other words, µC/OS-III does not know about this timer.

F12-5(2)   When creating a timer or calling **OSTmrStop()**, the timer is placed in the "stopped" state.

F12-5(3)   A timer is placed in running state when calling **OSTmrStart()**. The timer stays in that state unless it's stopped, deleted, or completes its one shot.

F12-5(4)   The "Completed" state is the state a one-shot timer is in when its delay expires.

12-4-2 TIMER MANAGEMENT INTERNALS - OS_TMR

A timer is a kernel object as defined by the **OS_TMR** data type (see **OS.H**) as shown in Listing 12-1.

The services provided by µC/OS-III to manage timers are implemented in the file **OS_TMR.C**. A µC/OS-III licensee has access to the source code. In this case, timer services are enabled at compile time by setting the configuration constant **OS_CFG_TMR_EN** to 1 in **OS_CFG.H**.

```
typedef   struct   os_tmr   OS_TMR;                    (1)


struct   os_tmr {
    OS_OBJ_TYPE            Type;              (2)
    CPU_CHAR              *NamePtr;           (3)
    OS_TMR_CALLBACK_PTR   CallbackPtr;        (4)
    void                 *CallbackPtrArg;     (5)
    OS_TMR               *NextPtr;            (6)
    OS_TMR               *PrevPtr;
    OS_TICK               Match;             (7)
    OS_TICK               Remain;            (8)
    OS_TICK               Dly;               (9)
    OS_TICK               Period;           (10)
    OS_OPT                Opt;              (11)
    OS_STATE              State;            (12)
};
```

Listing 12-1 **OS_TMR data type**

L12-1(1) In µC/OS-III, all structures are given a data type. In fact, all data types start with "**OS_**" and are all uppercase. When a timer is declared, simply use **OS_TMR** as the data type of the variable used to declare the timer.

L12-1(2) The structure starts with a "**Type**" field, which allows it to be recognized by µC/OS-III as a timer. Other kernel objects will also have a "**Type**" as the first member of the structure. If a function is passed a kernel object, µC/OS-III is able to confirm that it is passed the proper data type. For example, if passing a message queue (**OS_Q**) to a timer service (for example **OSTmrStart()**) then µC/OS-III will be able to recognize that an invalid object was passed, and return an error code accordingly.

L12-1(3) Each kernel object can be given a name for easier recognition by debuggers or µC/Probe. This member is simply a pointer to an ASCII string which is assumed to be NUL terminated.

L12-1(4) The **.CallbackPtr** member is a pointer to a function that is called when the timer expires. If a timer is created and passed a **NULL** pointer, a callback would not be called when the timer expires.

L12-1(5) If there is a non-**NULL** **.CallbackPtr** then the application code could have also specified that the callback be called with an argument when the timer expires. This is the argument that would be passed in this call.

L12-1(6) **.NextPtr** and **.PrevPtr** are pointers used to link a timer in a doubly linked list. These are described later.

L12-1(7) A timer expires when the timer manager variable **OSTmrTickCtr** reaches the value stored in a timer's **.Match** field. This is also described later.

L12-1(8) The **.Remain** contains the amount of time remaining for the timer to expire. This value is updated once per **OS_CFG_TMR_WHEEL_SIZE** (see **OS_CFG_APP.H**) that the timer task executes (described later). The value is expressed in multiples of **1/OS_CFG_TMR_TASK_RATE_HZ** of a second (see **OS_CFG_APP.H**).

12

L12-1(9)   The **.Dly** field contains the one-shot time when the timer is configured (i.e., created) as a one-shot timer and the initial delay when the timer is created as a periodic timer. The value is expressed in multiples of 1/**OS_CFG_TMR_TASK_RATE_HZ** of a second (see **OS_CFG_APP.H**).

L12-1(10)   The **.Period** is the timer period when the timer is created to operate in periodic mode. The value is expressed in multiples of 1/**OS_CFG_TMR_TASK_RATE_HZ** of a second (see **OS_CFG_APP.H**).

L12-1(11)   The **.Opt** field contains options as passed to **OSTmrCreate()**.

L12-1(12)   The **.State** field represents the current state of the timer (see Figure 12-5).

Even if the internals of the **OS_TMR** data type are understood, the application code should never access any of the fields in this data structure directly. Instead, always use the Application Programming Interfaces (APIs) provided with µC/OS-III.

12-4-3 TIMER MANAGEMENT INTERNALS - TIMER TASK

OS_TmrTask() is a task created by µC/OS-III (assumes setting **OS_CFG_TMR_EN** to 1 in **OS_CFG.H**) and its priority is configurable by the user through µC/OS-III's configuration file **OS_CFG_APP.H** (see **OS_CFG_TMR_TASK_PRIO**). **OS_TmrTask()** is typically set to a medium priority.

OS_TmrTask() is a periodic task and uses the same interrupt source used to generate clock ticks. However, timers are generally updated at a slower rate (i.e., typically 10 Hz or so) and thus, the timer tick rate is divided down in software. If the tick rate is 1000 Hz and the desired timer rate is 10 Hz then the timer task will be signaled every 100th tick interrupt as shown in Figure 12-6.

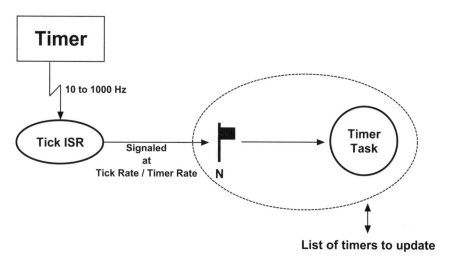

Figure 12-6 **Tick ISR and Timer Task relationship**

Figure 12-7 shows timing diagram associated with the timer management task.

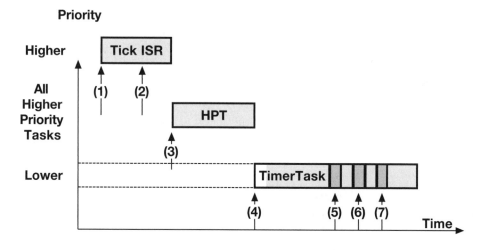

Figure 12-7 **Timing Diagram**

F12-7(1)   The tick ISR occurs and assumes interrupts are enabled and executes.

F12-7(2)   The tick ISR signals the tick task that it is time for it to update timers.

F12-7(3)   The tick ISR terminates, however there are higher priority tasks that need to execute (assuming the timer task has a lower priority). Therefore, μC/OS-III runs the higher priority task(s).

F12-7(4)   When all higher priority tasks have executed, μC/OS-III switches to the timer task and determines that there are three timers that expired.

F12-7(5)   The callback for the first timer is executed.

F12-7(6)   The callback for the second expired timer is executed.

F12-7(7)   The callback for the third expired timer is executed.

There are a few interesting things to notice:

■   Execution of the callback functions is performed within the context of the timer task. This means that the application code will need to make sure there is sufficient stack space for the timer task to handle these callbacks.

■   The callback functions are executed one after the other based on the order they are found in the timer list.

■   The execution time of the timer task greatly depends on how many timers expire and how long each of the callback functions takes to execute. Since the callbacks are provided by the application code they have a large influence on the execution time of the timer task.

■   The timer callback functions must never wait on events that would delay the timer task for excessive amounts of time, if not forever.

■   Callbacks are called with the scheduler locked, so you should ensure that callbacks execute as quickly as possible.

12-4-4 TIMER MANAGEMENT INTERNALS - TIMER LIST

μC/OS-III might need to literally maintain hundreds of timers (if an application requires that many). The timer list management needs to be implemented such that it does not take too much CPU time to update the timers. The timer list works similarly to a tick list as shown in Figure 12-8.

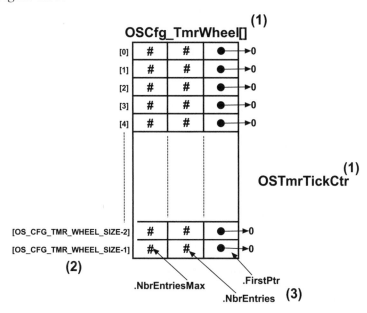

Figure 12-8 **Empty Timer List**

F12-8(1)   The timer list consists of a table (OSCfg_TmrWheel[]) and a counter (OSTmrTickCtr).

F12-8(2)   The table contains up to **OS_CFG_TMR_WHEEL_SIZE** entries, which is a compile time configuration value (see **OS_CFG_APP.H**). The number of entries depends on the amount of RAM available to the processor and the maximum number of timers in the application. A good starting point for **OS_CFG_TMR_WHEEL_SIZE** might be: **#Timers/4**. It is not recommended to make **OS_CFG_TMR_WHEEL_SIZE** an even multiple of the timer task rate. In other words, if the timer task is 10 Hz, avoid setting **OS_CFG_TMR_WHEEL_SIZE** to 10 or 100 (use 11 or 101 instead). Also, use prime numbers for the timer wheel size. Although it is not really possible to plan at compile time what will happen at run time, ideally the number of timers waiting in each entry of the table is distributed uniformly.

F12-8(3)   Each entry in the table contains three fields: **.NbrEntriesMax**, **.NbrEntries** and **.FirstPtr**. **.NbrEntries** indicates how many timers are linked to this table entry. **.NbrEntriesMax** keeps track of the highest number of entries in the table. Finally, **.FirstPtr** contains a pointer to a doubly linked list of timers (through the tasks **OS_TMR**) belonging into the list at that table position.

The counter is incremented by **OS_TmrTask()** every time the tick ISR signals the task.

Timers are inserted in the timer list by calling **OSTmrStart()**. However, a timer must be created before it can be used.

An example to illustrate the process of inserting a timer in the timer list is as follows. Let's assume that the timer list is completely empty, **OS_CFG_TMR_WHEEL_SIZE** is configured to 9, and the current value of **OSTmrTickCtr** is 12 as shown in Figure 12-9. A timer is placed in the timer list when calling **OSTmrStart()**, and assumes that the timer was created with a delay of 1 and that this timer will be a one-shot timer as follows:

```
OS_TMR  MyTmr1;
OS_TMR  MyTmr2;


void MyTask (void *p_arg)
{
    OS_ERR  err;


    while (DEF_ON) {
        :
        OSTmrCreate((OS_TMR             *)&MyTmr1,
                    (OS_CHAR            *)"My Timer #1",
                    (OS_TICK            )1,
                    (OS_TICK            )0,
                    (OS_OPT             )OS_OPT_TMR_ONE_SHOT,
                    (OS_TMR_CALLBACK_PTR)0;
                    (OS_ERR             *)&err;
        /* Check 'err" */
        OSTmrStart ((OS_TMR *)&MyTmr1,
                    (OS_ERR *)&err);
        /* Check "err" */
        // Continues in the next code listing!
```

Listing 12-2 **Creating and Starting a timer**

Since `OSTmrTickCtr` has a value of 12, the timer will expire when `OSTmrTickCtr` reaches 13, or during the next time the timer task is signaled. Timers are inserted in the `OSCfg_TmrWheel[]` table using the following equation:

```
MatchValue                    = OSTmrTickCtr + dly
Index into OSCfg_TmrWheel[]  = MatchValue % OS_CFG_TMR_WHEEL_SIZE
```

Where "`dly`" (in this example) is the value passed in the third argument of `OSTmrCreate()` (i.e., 1 in this example). Again, using the example, we arrive at the following:

```
MatchValue                    = 12 + 1
Index into OSCfg_TickWheel[] = 13 % 9
```

or,

```
MatchValue                    = 13
Index into OSCfg_TickWheel[] = 4
```

Because of the "circular" nature of the table (a modulo operation using the size of the table), the table is referred to as a timer wheel, and each entry is a spoke in the wheel.

The timer is entered at index 4 in the timer wheel, `OSCfg_TmrWheel[]`. In this case, the `OS_TMR` is placed at the head of the list (i.e., pointed to by `OSCfg_TmrWheel[4].FirstPtr`), and the number of entries at index 4 is incremented (i.e., `OSCfg_TmrWheel[4].NbrEntries` will be 1). "`MatchValue`" is placed in the `OS_TMR` field `.Match`. Since this is the first timer inserted in the timer list at index 4, the `.NextPtr` and `.PrevPtr` both point to `NULL`.

Figure 12-9 **Inserting a timer in the timer list**

The code below shows creating and starting another timer. This is performed "before" the timer task is signaled.

```
// Continuation of code from previous code listing.
:
:
OSTmrCreate((OS_TMR              *)&MyTmr2,
            (OS_CHAR             *)"My Timer #2",
            (OS_TICK             )10,
            (OS_TICK             )0,
            (OS_OPT              )OS_OPT_TMR_ONE_SHOT,
            (OS_TMR_CALLBACK_PTR)0;
            (OS_ERR              *)&err;
    /* Check 'err" */
    OSTmrStart ((OS_TMR *)&MyTmr,
                (OS_ERR *)&err);
    /* Check 'err" */
    }
}
```

Listing 12-3 **Creating and Starting a timer - continued**

µC/OS-III will calculate the match value and index as follows:

```
MatchValue                    = 12 + 10
Index into OSCfg_TmrWheel[] = 22 % 9
```

or,

```
MatchValue                    = 22
Index into OSCfg_TickWheel[] =  4
```

The "second timer" will be inserted at the same table entry as shown in Figure 12-10, but sorted so that the timer with the least amount of time remaining before expiration is placed at the head of the list, and the timer with the longest to wait at the end.

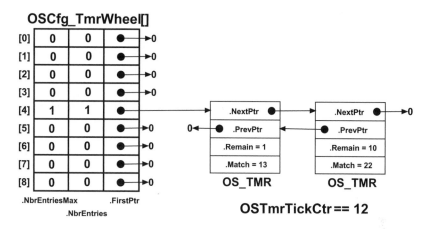

Figure 12-10 **Inserting a second timer in the tick list**

When the timer task executes (see OS_TmrTask() in OS_TMR.C), it starts by incrementing OSTmrTickCtr and determines which table entry (i.e., spoke) it needs to update. Then, if there are timers in the list at this entry (i.e., .FirstPtr is not NULL), each OS_TMR is examined to determine whether the .Match value "matches" OSTmrTickCtr and, if so, the OS_TMR is removed from the list and OS_TmrTask() calls the timer callback function, assuming one was defined when the timer was created. The search through the list terminates as soon as OSTmrTickCtr does not match the timer's .Match value. There is no point in looking any further in the list since the list is already sorted.

Note that OS_TmrTask() does most of its work with the scheduler locked. However, because the list is sorted, and the search through the list terminates as soon as there no longer is a match, the critical section should be fairly short.

215

12-5 SUMMARY

Timers are down counters that perform an action when the counter reaches zero. The action is provided by the user through a callback function.

µC/OS-III allows application code to create any number of timers (limited only by the amount of RAM available).

The callback functions are executed in the context of the timer task with the scheduler locked. Keep callback functions as short and as fast as possible and do not have the callbacks make blocking calls.

Chapter

13

Resource Management

This chapter will discuss services provided by μC/OS-III to manage shared resources. A shared resource is typically a variable (static or global), a data structure, table (in RAM), or registers in an I/O device.

When protecting a shared resource it is preferred to use mutual exclusion semaphores, as will be described in this chapter. Other methods are also presented.

Tasks can easily share data when all tasks exist in a single address space and can reference global variables, pointers, buffers, linked lists, ring buffers, etc. Although sharing data simplifies the exchange of information between tasks, it is important to ensure that each task has exclusive access to the data to avoid contention and data corruption.

For example, when implementing a module that performs a simple time-of-day algorithm in software, the module obviously keeps track of hours, minutes and seconds. The **TimeOfDay()** task may appear as that shown in Listing 13-1.

Imagine if this task was preempted by another task because an interrupt occurred, and, the other task was more important than the **TimeOfDay()** task) after setting the Minutes to 0. Now imagine what will happen if this higher priority task wants to know the current time from the time-of-day module. Since the Hours were not incremented prior to the interrupt, the higher-priority task will read the time incorrectly and, in this case, it will be incorrect by a whole hour.

The code that updates variables for the **TimeOfDay()** task must treat all of the variables indivisibly (or atomically) whenever there is possible preemption. Time-of-day variables are considered shared resources and any code that accesses those variables must have exclusive access through what is called a critical section. μC/OS-III provides services to protect shared resources and enables the easy creation of critical sections.

```
CPU_INT08U  Hours;
CPU_INT08U  Minutes;
CPU_INT08U  Seconds;


void  TimeOfDay (void *p_arg)
{
    OS_ERR  err;


    (void)&p_arg;
    while (DEF_ON) {
        OSTimeDlyHMSM(0,
                      0,
                      1,
                      0,
                      OS_OPT_TIME_HMSM_STRICT,
                      &err);
        /* Examine "err" to make sure the call was successful */
        Seconds++;
        if (Seconds > 59) {
            Seconds = 0;
            Minutes++;
            if (Minutes > 59) {
                Minutes = 0;
                Hours++;
                if (Hours > 23) {
                    Hours = 0;
                }
            }
        }
    }
}
```

Listing 13-1 **Faulty Time-Of-Day clock task**

The most common methods of obtaining exclusive access to shared resources and to create *critical sections* are:

- disabling interrupts

- disabling the scheduler

- using semaphores

- using mutual exclusion semaphores (a.k.a. a mutex)

The mutual exclusion mechanism used depends on how fast the code will access a shared resource, as shown in Table 13-1.

Resource Sharing Method	When should you use?
Disable/Enable Interrupts	When access to shared resource is very quick (reading from or writing to few variables) and access is faster than µC/OS-III's interrupt disable time. It is highly recommended to not use this method as it impacts interrupt latency.
Locking/Unlocking the Scheduler	When access time to the shared resource is longer than µC/OS-III's interrupt disable time, but shorter than µC/OS-III's scheduler lock time. Locking the scheduler has the same effect as making the task that locks the scheduler the highest-priority task. It is recommended not to use this method since it defeats the purpose of using µC/OS-III. However, it is a better method than disabling interrupts, as it does not impact interrupt latency.
Semaphores	When all tasks that need to access a shared resource do not have deadlines. This is because semaphores may cause unbounded priority inversions (described later). However, semaphore services are slightly faster (in execution time) than mutual-exclusion semaphores.
Mutual Exclusion Semaphores	This is the preferred method for accessing shared resources, especially if the tasks that need to access a shared resource have deadlines. Remember that µC/OS-III's mutual exclusion semaphores have a built-in priority inheritance mechanism, which avoids unbounded priority inversions. However, mutual exclusion semaphore services are slightly slower (in execution time) than semaphores since the priority of the owner may need to be changed, which requires CPU processing.

13

Table 13-1 **Resource sharing**

219

13-1 DISABLE/ENABLE INTERRUPTS

The easiest and fastest way to gain exclusive access to a shared resource is by disabling and enabling interrupts, as shown in the pseudo-code in Listing 13-2.

```
Disable Interrupts;
Access the resource;
Enable  Interrupts;
```

Listing 13-2 **Disabling and Enabling Interrupts**

μC/OS-III uses this technique (as do most, if not all, kernels) to access certain internal variables and data structures, ensuring that these variables and data structures are manipulated atomically. However, disabling and enabling interrupts are actually CPU-related functions rather than OS-related functions and functions in CPU-specific files are provided to accomplish this (see the CPU.H file of the processor being used). The services provided in the CPU module are called μC/CPU. Each different target CPU architecture has its own set of μC/CPU-related files.

```
void OS_Function (void)
{
    CPU_SR_ALLOC();                  (1)


    CPU_CRITICAL_ENTER();            (2)
    Access the resource;             (3)
    CPU_CRITICAL_EXIT();             (4)
}
```

Listing 13-3 **Using CPU macros to disable and enable interrupts**

L13-3(1)   The **CPU_SR_ALLOC()** macro is required when the other two macros that disable/enable interrupts are used. This macro simply allocates storage for a local variable to hold the value of the current interrupt disable status of the CPU. If interrupts are already disabled we do not want to enable them upon exiting the critical section.

L13-3(2)   **CPU_CRITICAL_ENTER( )** saves the current state of the CPU interrupt disable flag(s) in the local variable allocated by **CPU_SR_ALLOC( )** and disables all maskable interrupts.

L13-3(3)   The critical section of code is then accessed without fear of being changed by either an ISR or another task because interrupts are disabled. In other words, this operation is now atomic.

L13-3(4)   **CPU_CRITICAL_EXIT( )** restores the previously saved interrupt disable status of the CPU from the local variable.

CPU_CRITICAL_ENTER( ) and **CPU_CRITICAL_EXIT( )** are always used in pairs. Interrupts should be disabled for as short a time as possible as disabling interrupts impacts the response of the system to interrupts. This is known as interrupt latency. Disabling and enabling is used only when changing or copying a few variables.

Note, this is the only way that a task can share variables or data structures with an ISR. μC/CPU provides a way to actually measure interrupt latency.

When using μC/OS-III, interrupts may be disabled for as much time as μC/OS-III does, without affecting *interrupt latency*. Obviously, it is important to know how long μC/OS-III disables interrupts, which depends on the CPU used.

Although this method works, avoid disabling interrupts as it affects the responsiveness of the system to real-time events.

13

13-2 LOCK/UNLOCK

If the task does not share variables or data structures with an ISR, disable and enable µC/OS-III's scheduler while accessing the resource, as shown in Listing 13-4.

```
void OS_Function (void)
{
    CPU_SR_ALLOC();                 (1)
    CPU_CRITICAL_ENTER();           (2)
    Access the resource;            (3)
    CPU_CRITICAL_EXIT();            (4)
}
```

Listing 13-4 **Accessing a resource with the scheduler locked**

Using this method, two or more tasks share data without the possibility of contention. Note that while the scheduler is locked, interrupts are enabled and if an interrupt occurs while in the critical section, the ISR is executed immediately. At the end of the ISR, the kernel always returns to the interrupted task even if a higher priority task is made ready to run by the ISR. Since the ISR returns to the interrupted task, the behavior of the kernel is similar to that of a non-preemptive kernel (while the scheduler is locked).

OSSchedLock() and OSSchedUnlock() can be nested up to 250 levels deep. The scheduler is invoked only when OSSchedUnlock() is called the same number of times the application called OSSchedLock().

After the scheduler is unlocked, µC/OS-III performs a context switch if a higher priority task is ready to run.

µC/OS-III will not allow the user to make blocking calls when the scheduler is locked. If the application were able to make blocking calls, the application would most likely fail.

Although this method works well, avoid disabling the scheduler as it defeats the purpose of having a preemptive kernel. Locking the scheduler makes the current task the highest priority task.

13-3 SEMAPHORES

A semaphore originally was a mechanical signaling mechanism. The railroad industry used the device to provide a form of mutual exclusion for railroads tracks shared by more than one train. In this form, the semaphore signaled trains by closing a set of mechanical arms to block a train from a section of track that was currently in use. When the track became available, the arm would swing up and the waiting train would then proceed.

The notion of using a semaphore in software as a means of synchronization was invented by the Dutch computer scientist Edgser Dijkstra in 1959. In computer software, a semaphore is a protocol mechanism offered by most multitasking kernels. Semaphores, originally used to control access to shared resources, now are used for synchronization as described in Chapter 14, "Synchronization" on page 259. However, it is useful to describe how semaphores can be used to share resources. The pitfalls of semaphores will be discussed in a later section.

A semaphore was originally a "lock mechanism" and code acquired the key to this lock to continue execution. Acquiring the key means that the executing task has permission to enter the section of otherwise locked code. Entering a section of locked code causes the task to wait until the key becomes available.

Typically, two types of semaphores exist: binary semaphores and counting semaphores. As its name implies, a binary semaphore can only take two values: 0 or 1. A counting semaphore allows for values between 0 and 255, 65,535, or 4,294,967,295, depending on whether the semaphore mechanism is implemented using 8, 16, or 32 bits, respectively. For μC/OS-III, the maximum value of a semaphore is determined by the data type **OS_SEM_CTR** (see **OS_TYPE.H**), which can be changed as needed (assuming μC/OS-III's source code is available). Along with the semaphore's value, μC/OS-III also keeps track of tasks waiting for the semaphore's availability.

Only tasks are allowed to use semaphores when semaphores are used for sharing resources; ISRs are not allowed.

A semaphore is a kernel object defined by the **OS_SEM** data type, which is defined by the structure os_sem (see **OS.H**). The application can have any number of semaphores (limited only by the amount of RAM available).

13

There are a number of operations the application is able to perform on semaphores, summarized in Table 13-2. In this chapter, only three functions used most often are discussed: **OSSemCreate()**, **OSSemPend()**, and **OSSemPost()**. Other functions are described in Appendix A, "µC/OS-III API Reference Manual" on page 383. When semaphores are used for sharing resources, every semaphore function must be called from a task and never from an ISR. The same limitation does not apply when using semaphores for signaling, as described later in Chapter 13.

Function Name	Operation
OSSemCreate()	Create a semaphore.
OSSemDel()	Delete a semaphore.
OSSemPend()	Wait on a semaphore.
OSSemPendAbort()	Abort the wait on a semaphore.
OSSemPost()	Release or signal a semaphore.
OSSemSet()	Force the semaphore count to a desired value.

Table 13-2 **Semaphore API summary**

13-3-1 BINARY SEMAPHORES

A task that wants to acquire a resource must perform a Wait (or Pend) operation. If the semaphore is available (the semaphore value is greater than 0), the semaphore value is decremented, and the task continues execution (owning the resource). If the semaphore's value is 0, the task performing a Wait on the semaphore is placed in a waiting list. µC/OS-III allows a timeout to be specified. If the semaphore is not available within a certain amount of time, the requesting task is made ready to run, and an error code (indicating that a timeout has occurred) is returned to the caller.

A task releases a semaphore by performing a Signal (or Post) operation. If no task is waiting for the semaphore, the semaphore value is simply incremented. If there is at least one task waiting for the semaphore, the highest-priority task waiting on the semaphore is made ready to run, and the semaphore value is not incremented. If the readied task has a higher priority than the current task (the task releasing the semaphore), a context switch occurs and the higher-priority task resumes execution. The current task is suspended until it again becomes the highest-priority task that is ready to run.

13

The operations described above are summarized using the pseudo-code shown in Listing 13-5.

```
OS_SEM  MySem;                          (1)


void  main (void)
{
    OS_ERR  err;
    :

    :
    OSInit(&err);
    :
    OSSemCreate(&MySem,                 (2)
                "My Semaphore",         (3)
                1,                      (4)
                &err);                  (5)
    /* Check "err" */
    :
    /* Create task(s) */
    :
    OSStart(&err);
    (void)err;
}
```

Listing 13-5 **Using a semaphore to access a shared resource**

L13-5(1) The application must declare a semaphore as a variable of type **OS_SEM**. This variable will be referenced by other semaphore services.

L13-5(2) Create a semaphore by calling **OSSemCreate()** and pass the address to the semaphore allocated in (1). The semaphore must be created before it can be used by other tasks. Here, the semaphore is initialized in startup code (i.e., **main ()**), however it could also be initialized by a task (but it must be initialized before it is used).

L13-5(3) Assign an ASCII name to the semaphore, which can be used by debuggers or µC/Probe to easily identify the semaphore. Storage for the ASCII characters is typically in ROM, which is typically more plentiful than RAM. If it is necessary to change the name of the semaphore at runtime, store the characters in an array in RAM and simply pass the address of the array to **OSSemCreate()**. Of course, the array must be NUL terminated.

L13-5(4) Specify the initial value of the semaphore. Initialize the semaphore to 1 when the semaphore is used to access a single shared resource (as in this example).

L13-5(5) **OSSemCreate()** returns an error code based on the outcome of the call. If all the arguments are valid, err will contain **OS_ERR_NONE**. Refer to the description of **OSSemCreate()** in Appendix A, "µC/OS-III API Reference Manual" on page 383 for a list of other error codes and their meaning.

```
void Task1 (void *p_arg)
{
    OS_ERR   err;
    CPU_TS   ts;


    while (DEF_ON) {
        :
        OSSemPend(&MySem,                       (6)
                  0,                            (7)
                  OS_OPT_PEND_BLOCKING,         (8)
                  &ts,                          (9)
                  &err);                        (10)
        switch (err) {
            case OS_ERR_NONE:
                Access Shared Resource;         (11)
                OSSemPost(&MySem,               (12)
                          OS_OPT_POST_1,        (13)
                          &err);                (14)
                /* Check "err" */
                break;


            case OS_ERR_PEND_ABORT:
                /* The pend was aborted by another task   */
                break;


            case OS_ERR_OBJ_DEL:
                /* The semaphore was deleted              */
                break;


            default:
                /* Other errors                           */
        }
        :
    }
}
```

Listing 13-6 **Using a semaphore to access a shared resource**

L13-6(6)   The task pends (or waits) on the semaphore by calling OSSemPend(). The application must specify the desired semaphore to wait upon, and the semaphore must have been previously created.

L13-6(7)   The next argument is a timeout specified in number of clock ticks. The actual timeout depends on the tick rate. If the tick rate (see OS_CFG_APP.H) is set to 1000, a timeout of 10 ticks represents 10 milliseconds. Specifying a timeout of zero (0) means waiting forever for the semaphore.

L13-6(8)   The third argument specifies how to wait. There are two options: **OS_OPT_PEND_BLOCKING** and **OS_OPT_PEND_NON_BLOCKING**. The blocking option means that if the semaphore is not available, the task calling **OSSemPend()** will wait until the semaphore is posted or until the timeout expires. The non-blocking option indicates that if the semaphore is not available, **OSSemPend()** will return immediately and not wait. This last option is rarely used when using a semaphore to protect a shared resource.

L13-6(9)   When the semaphore is posted, μC/OS-III reads a "timestamp" and returns this timestamp when **OSSemPend()** returns. This feature allows the application to know "when" the post happened and the semaphore was released. At this point, **OS_TS_GET()** is read to get the current timestamp and compute the difference, indicating the length of the wait.

L13-6(10)   **OSSemPend()** returns an error code based on the outcome of the call. If the call is successful, err will contain **OS_ERR_NONE**. If not, the error code will indicate the reason for the error. See Appendix A, "μC/OS-III API Reference Manual" on page 383 for a list of possible error code for **OSSemPend()**. Checking for error return values is important since other tasks might delete or otherwise abort the pend. However, it is not a recommended practice to delete kernel objects at run time as the action may cause serious problems.

L13-6(11)   The resource can be accessed when **OSSemPend()** returns, if there are no errors.

L13-6(12)   When finished accessing the resource, simply call **OSSemPost()** and specify the semaphore to be released.

L13-6(13)   **OS_OPT_POST_1** indicates that the semaphore is signaling a single task, if there are many tasks waiting on the semaphore. In fact, always specify this option when a semaphore is used to access a shared resource.

L13-6(14)   As with most μC/OS-III functions, specify the address of a variable that will receive an error message from the call.

```
void  Task2 (void *p_arg)
{
    OS_ERR  err;
    CPU_TS  ts;


    while (DEF_ON) {
        :
        OSSemPend(&MySem,                          (15)
                  0,
                  OS_OPT_PEND_BLOCKING,
                  &ts,
                  &err);
        switch (err) {
            case OS_ERR_NONE:
                Access Shared Resource;
                OSSemPost(&MySem,
                          OS_OPT_POST_1,
                          &err);
                /* Check "err" */
                break;

            case OS_ERR_PEND_ABORT:
                /* The pend was aborted by another task    */
                break;

            case OS_ERR_OBJ_DEL:
                /* The semaphore was deleted               */
                break;

            default:
                /* Other errors                            */
        }
        :
    }
}
```

Listing 13-7 **Using a semaphore to access a shared resource**

L13-7(15)   Another task wanting to access the shared resource needs to use the same procedure to access the shared resource.

Semaphores are especially useful when tasks share I/O devices. Imagine what would happen if two tasks were allowed to send characters to a printer at the same time. The printer would contain interleaved data from each task. For instance, the printout from Task 1 printing "I am Task 1," and Task 2 printing "I am Task 2," could result in "I Ia amm T Tasask k1 2". In this case, use a semaphore and initialize it to 1 (i.e., a binary semaphore). The rule is simple: to access the printer each task must first obtain the resource's semaphore. Figure 13-1 shows tasks competing for a semaphore to gain exclusive access to the printer. Note that a key, indicating that each task must obtain this key to use the printer, represents the semaphore symbolically.

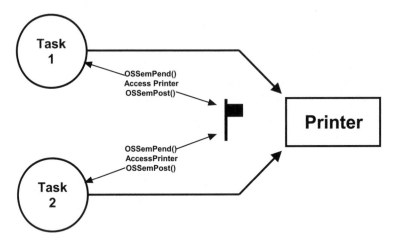

Figure 13-1 **Using a semaphore to access a printer**

The above example implies that each task knows about the existence of the semaphore to access the resource. It is almost always better to encapsulate the critical section and its protection mechanism. Each task would therefore not know that it is acquiring a semaphore when accessing the resource. For example, an RS-232C port is used by multiple tasks to send commands and receive responses from a device connected at the other end as shown in Figure 13-2.

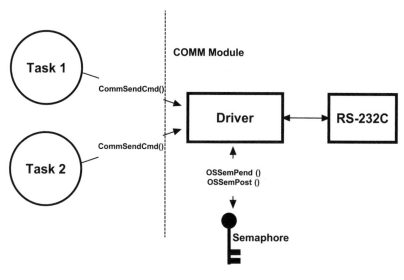

Figure 13-2 **Hiding a semaphore from a task**

The function **CommSendCmd()** is called with three arguments: the ASCII string containing the command, a pointer to the response string from the device, and finally, a timeout in case the device does not respond within a certain amount of time. The pseudo-code for this function is shown in Listing 13-8.

```
APP_ERR  CommSendCmd (CPU_CHAR  *cmd,
                      CPU_CHAR  *response,
                      OS_TICK    timeout)
{
    Acquire serial port's semaphore;
    Send "cmd" to device;
    Wait for response with "timeout";
    if (timed out) {
        Release serial port's semaphore;
        return (error code);
    } else {
        Release serial port's semaphore;
        return (no error);
    }
}
```

Listing 13-8 **Encapsulating the use of a semaphore**

Each task that needs to send a command to the device must call this function. The semaphore is assumed to be initialized to 1 (i.e., available) by the communication driver initialization routine. The first task that calls CommSendCmd() acquires the semaphore, proceeds to send the command, and waits for a response. If another task attempts to send a command while the port is busy, this second task is suspended until the semaphore is released. The second task appears simply to have made a call to a normal function that will not return until the function performs its duty. When the semaphore is released by the first task, the second task acquires the semaphore and is allowed to use the RS-232C port.

13-3-2 COUNTING SEMAPHORES

A counting semaphore is used when elements of a resource can be used by more than one task at the same time. For example, a counting semaphore is used in the management of a buffer pool, as shown in Figure 13-3. Assume that the buffer pool initially contains 10 buffers. A task obtains a buffer from the buffer manager by calling BufReq(). When the buffer is no longer needed, the task returns the buffer to the buffer manager by calling BufRel(). The pseudo-code for these functions is shown in Listing 13-9.

The buffer manager satisfies the first 10 buffer requests because the semaphore is initialized to 10. When all buffers are used, a task requesting a buffer is suspended until a buffer becomes available. Use µC/OS-III's OSMemGet() and OSMemPut() (see Chapter 17, "Memory Management" on page 331) to obtain a buffer from the buffer pool. When a task is finished with the buffer it acquired, the task calls BufRel() to return the buffer to the buffer manager and the buffer is inserted into the linked list before the semaphore is signaled. By encapsulating the interface to the buffer manager in BufReq() and BufRel(), the caller does not need to be concerned with actual implementation details.

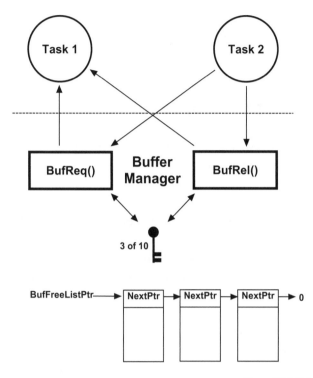

Figure 13-3 **Using a counting semaphore**

```
BUF  *BufReq (void)
{
    BUF  *ptr;


    Wait on semaphore;
    ptr = OSMemGet(...) ;                  /* Get a buffer      */
    return (ptr);
}


void  BufRel (BUF *ptr)
{
    OSMemPut(..., (void *)ptr, ...);       /* Return the buffer */
    Signal semaphore;
}
```

Listing 13-9 **Buffer management using a semaphore.**

Note that the details of creating the memory partition are removed since this is discussed in Chapter 17, "Memory Management" on page 331. The semaphore is used here to extend the memory management capabilities of µC/OS-III, and to provide it with a blocking mechanism. However, only tasks can make **BufReq()** and **BufRel()** calls.

13-3-3 NOTES ON SEMAPHORES

Using a semaphore to access a shared resource does not increase interrupt latency. If an ISR or the current task makes a higher priority task ready to run while accessing shared data, the higher priority task executes immediately.

An application may have as many semaphores as required to protect a variety of different resources. For example, one semaphore may be used to access a shared display, another to access a shared printer, another for shared data structures, and another to protect a pool of buffers, etc. However, it is preferable to use semaphores to protect access to I/O devices rather than memory locations.

Semaphores are often overused. The use of a semaphore to access a simple shared variable is overkill in most situations. The overhead involved in acquiring and releasing the semaphore consumes valuable CPU time. Perform the job more efficiently by disabling and enabling interrupts, however there is an indirect cost to disabling interrupts: even higher priority tasks that do not share the specific resource are blocked from using the CPU. Suppose, for instance, that two tasks share a 32-bit integer variable. The first task increments the variable, while the second task clears it. When considering how long a processor takes to perform either operation, it is easy to see that a semaphore is not required to gain exclusive access to the variable. Each task simply needs to disable interrupts before performing its operation on the variable and enable interrupts when the operation is complete. A semaphore should be used if the variable is a floating-point variable and the microprocessor does not support hardware floating-point operations. In this case, the time involved in processing the floating-point variable may affect interrupt latency if interrupts are disabled.

Semaphores are subject to a serious problem in real-time systems called priority inversion, which is described in section 13-3-5 "Priority Inversions" on page 240.

13-3-4 SEMAPHORE INTERNALS (FOR RESOURCE SHARING)

As previously mentioned, a semaphore is a kernel object as defined by the OS_SEM data type, which is derived from the structure os_sem (see OS.H) as shown in Listing 13-10.

The services provided by µC/OS-III to manage semaphores are implemented in the file OS_SEM.C. µC/OS-III licensees have access to the source code. In this case, semaphore services are enabled at compile time by setting the configuration constant OS_CFG_SEM_EN to 1 in OS_CFG.H.

```
typedef struct os_sem OS_SEM;            (1)


struct os_sem {
    OS_OBJ_TYPE         Type;            (2)
    CPU_CHAR            *NamePtr;        (3)
    OS_PEND_LIST        PendList;        (4)
    OS_SEM_CTR          Ctr;             (5)
    CPU_TS              TS;              (6)
};
```

Listing 13-10 **OS_SEM data type**

L13-10(1) In µC/OS-III, all structures are given a data type. All data types start with "OS_" and are uppercase. When a semaphore is declared, simply use OS_SEM as the data type of the variable used to declare the semaphore.

L13-10(2) The structure starts with a "Type" field, which allows it to be recognized by µC/OS-III as a semaphore. Other kernel objects will also have a ".Type" as the first member of the structure. If a function is passed a kernel object, µC/OS-III will confirm that it is being passed the proper data type. For example, if passing a message queue (OS_Q) to a semaphore service (for example OSSemPend()), µC/OS-III will recognize that an invalid object was passed, and return an error code accordingly.

L13-10(3) Each kernel object can be given a name for easier recognition by debuggers or µC/Probe. This member is simply a pointer to an ASCII string, which is assumed to be NUL terminated.

L13-10(4)   Since it is possible for multiple tasks to wait (or pend) on a semaphore, the semaphore object contains a pend list as described in Chapter 10, "Pend Lists (or Wait Lists)" on page 185.

L13-10(5)   A semaphore contains a counter. As explained above, the counter can be implemented as either an 8-, 16- or 32-bit value, depending on how the data type **OS_SEM_CTR** is declared in **OS_TYPE.H**.

μC/OS-III does not make a distinction between binary and counting semaphores. The distinction is made when the semaphore is created. If creating a semaphore with an initial value of 1, it is a binary semaphore. When creating a semaphore with a value > 1, it is a counting semaphore. In the next chapter, we discover that a semaphore is more often used as a signaling mechanism and therefore, the semaphore counter is initialized to zero.

L13-10(6)   A semaphore contains a timestamp used to indicate the last time the semaphore was posted. μC/OS-III assumes the presence of a free-running counter that allows the application to make time measurements. When the semaphore is posted, the free-running counter is read and the value is placed in this field, which is returned when **OSSemPend( )** is called. The value of this field is more useful when a semaphore is used as a signaling mechanism (see Chapter 14, "Synchronization" on page 259), as opposed to a resource-sharing mechanism.

Even if the user understands the internals of the **OS_SEM** data type, the application code should never access any of the fields in this data structure directly. Instead, always use the APIs provided with μC/OS-III.

As previously mentioned, semaphores must be created before they can be used by an application.

A task waits on a semaphore before accessing a shared resource by calling **OSSemPend( )** as shown in Listing 13-11 (see Appendix A, "μC/OS-III API Reference Manual" on page 383 for details regarding the arguments).

```
OS_SEM  MySem;


void MyTask (void *p_arg)
{
    OS_ERR  err;
    CPU_TS  ts;

        :
    while (DEF_ON) {
            :
        OSSemPend(&MySem,                   /* (1) Pointer to semaphore                        */
                  10,                       /*     Wait up until this time for the semaphore   */
                  OS_OPT_PEND_BLOCKING,     /*     Option(s)                                   */
                  &ts,                      /*     Returned timestamp of when sem. was released */
                  &err);                    /*     Pointer to Error returned                   */
            :
        /* Check "err" */                   /* (2)                                             */
            :
        OSSemPost(&MySem,                   /* (3) Pointer to semaphore                        */
                  OS_OPT_POST_1,            /*     Option(s) … always OS_OPT_POST_1            */
                  &err);                    /*     Pointer to Error returned                   */
        /* Check "err" */
            :
            :
    }
}
```

13

Listing 13-11 **Pending on and Posting to a Semaphore**

L13-11(1)   When called, **OSSemPend()** starts by checking the arguments passed to this function to make sure they have valid values.

If the semaphore counter (**.Ctr** of **OS_SEM**) is greater than zero, the counter is decremented and **OSSemPend()** returns. If **OSSemPend()** returns without error, then the task now owns the shared resource.

When the semaphore counter is zero, this indicates that another task owns the semaphore, and the calling task may need to wait for the semaphore to be released. If specifying **OS_OPT_PEND_NON_BLOCKING** as the option (the application does not want the task to block), **OSSemPend()** returns immediately to the caller and the returned error code indicates that the semaphore is unavailable. Use this option if the task does not want to wait for the resource to be available, and would prefer to do something else and check back later.

If specifying the **OS_OPT_PEND_BLOCKING** option, the calling task will be inserted in the list of tasks waiting for the semaphore to become available. The task is inserted in the list by priority order and therefore, the highest priority task waiting on the semaphore is at the beginning of the list.

If specifying a non-zero timeout, the task will also be inserted in the tick list. A zero value for a timeout indicates that the user is willing to wait forever for the semaphore to be released. Most of the time, specify an infinite timeout when using the semaphore in resource sharing. Adding a timeout may temporarily break a deadlock, however, there are better ways of preventing deadlock at the application level (e.g., never hold more than one semaphore at the same time; resource ordering; etc.).

The scheduler is called since the current task is no longer able to run (it is waiting for the semaphore to be released). The scheduler will then run the next highest-priority task that is ready to run.

When the semaphore is released and the task that called **OSSemPend()** is again the highest-priority task, µC/OS-III examines the task status to determine the reason why **OSSemPend()** is returning to its caller. The possibilities are:

1) The semaphore was given to the waiting task

2) The pend was aborted by another task

3) The semaphore was not posted within the specified timeout

4) The semaphore was deleted

When **OSSemPend()** returns, the caller is notified of the above outcome through an appropriate error code.

L13-11(2)   If **OSSemPend()** returns with err set to **OS_ERR_NONE**, assume that you now have access to the resource.

If err contains anything else, **OSSemPend()** either timed out (if the timeout argument was non-zero), the pend was aborted by another task, or the semaphore was deleted by another task. It is always important to examine the returned error code and not assume that everything went well.

L13-11(3)   When the task is finished accessing the resource, it needs to call **OSSemPost()** and specify the same semaphore. Again, **OSSemPost()** starts by checking the arguments passed to this function to make sure there are valid values.

OSSemPost() then calls **OS_TS_GET()** to obtain the current timestamp so it can place that information in the semaphore to be used by **OSSemPend()**.

OSSemPost() checks to see if any tasks are waiting for the semaphore. If not, **OSSemPost()** simply increments **p_sem->Ctr**, saves the timestamp in the semaphore, and returns.

If there are tasks waiting for the semaphore to be released, **OSSemPost()** extracts the highest-priority task waiting for the semaphore. This is a fast operation as the pend list is sorted by priority order.

When calling **OSSemPost()**, it is possible to specify as an option to not call the scheduler. This means that the post is performed, but the scheduler is not called even if a higher priority task waits for the semaphore to be released. This allows the calling task to perform other post functions (if needed) and make all posts take effect simultaneously without the possibility of context switching in between each post.

13

13-3-5 PRIORITY INVERSIONS

Priority inversion is a problem in real-time systems, and occurs only when using a priority-based preemptive kernel. Figure 13-4 illustrates a priority-inversion scenario. Task H (high priority) has a higher priority than Task M (medium priority), which in turn has a higher priority than Task L (low priority).

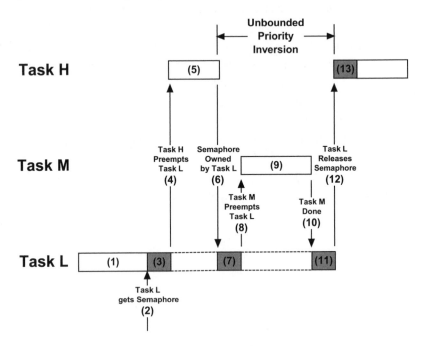

Figure 13-4 **Unbounded priority Inversion**

F13-4(1)   Task H and Task M are both waiting for an event to occur and Task L is executing.

F13-4(2)   At some point, Task L acquires a semaphore, which it needs before it can access a shared resource.

F13-4(3)   Task L performs operations on the acquired resource.

F13-4(4)   The event that Task H was waiting for occurs, and the kernel suspends Task L and start executing Task H since Task H has a higher priority.

F13-4(5)   Task H performs computations based on the event it just received.

F13-4(6)   Task H now wants to access the resource that Task L currently owns (i.e., it attempts to get the semaphore that Task L owns). Because Task L owns the resource, Task H is placed in a list of tasks waiting for the semaphore to be free.

F13-4(7)   Task L is resumed and continues to access the shared resource.

F13-4(8)   Task L is preempted by Task M since the event that Task M was waiting for occurred.

F13-4(9)   Task M handles the event.

F13-4(10)   When Task M completes, the kernel relinquishes the CPU back to Task L.

F13-4(11)   Task L continues accessing the resource.

F13-4(12)   Task L finally finishes working with the resource and releases the semaphore. At this point, the kernel knows that a higher-priority task is waiting for the semaphore, and a context switch takes place to resume Task H.

F13-4(13)   Task H has the semaphore and can access the shared resource.

So, what happened here is that the priority of Task H has been reduced to that of Task L since it waited for the resource that Task L owned. The trouble begins when Task M preempted Task L, further delaying the execution of Task H. This is called an *unbounded priority inversion*. It is unbounded because any medium priority can extend the time Task H has to wait for the resource. Technically, if all medium-priority tasks have known worst-case periodic behavior and bounded execution times, the priority inversion time is computable. This process, however, may be tedious and would need to be revised every time the medium priority tasks change.

This situation can be corrected by raising the priority of Task L, only during the time it takes to access the resource, and restore the original priority level when the task is finished. The priority of Task L should be raised up to the priority of Task H. µC/OS-III contains a special type of semaphore that does just that called a mutual-exclusion semaphore.

13

13-4 MUTUAL EXCLUSION SEMAPHORES (MUTEX)

μC/OS-III supports a special type of binary semaphore called a mutual exclusion semaphore (also known as a mutex) that eliminates unbounded priority inversions. Figure 13-5 shows how priority inversions are bounded using a Mutex.

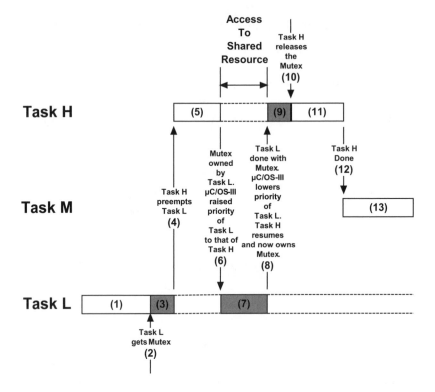

Figure 13-5 **Using a mutex to share a resource**

F13-5(1)   Task H and Task M are both waiting for an event to occur and Task L is executing.

F13-5(2)   At some point, Task L acquires a mutex, which it needs before it is able to access a shared resource.

F13-5(3)   Task L performs operations on the acquired resource.

F13-5(4)   The event that Task H waited for occurs and the kernel suspends Task L and begins executing Task H since Task H has a higher priority.

F13-5(5)   Task H performs computations based on the event it just received.

F13-5(6)   Task H now wants to access the resource that Task L currently owns (i.e., it attempts to get the mutex from Task L). Given that Task L owns the resource, µC/OS-III raises the priority of Task L to the same priority as Task H to allow Task L to finish with the resource and prevent Task L from being preempted by medium-priority tasks.

F13-5(7)   Task L continues accessing the resource, however it now does so while it is running at the same priority as Task H. Note that Task H is not actually running since it is waiting for Task L to release the mutex. In other words, Task H is in the mutex wait list.

F13-5(8)   Task L finishes working with the resource and releases the mutex. µC/OS-III notices that Task L was raised in priority and thus lowers Task L to its original priority. After doing so, µC/OS-III gives the mutex to Task H, which was waiting for the mutex to be released.

F13-5(9)   Task H now has the mutex and can access the shared resource.

F13-5(10)   Task H is finished accessing the shared resource, and frees up the mutex.

F13-5(11)   There are no higher-priority tasks to execute, therefore Task H continues execution.

F13-5(12)   Task H completes and decides to wait for an event to occur. At this point, µC/OS-III resumes Task M, which was made ready to run while Task H or Task L were executing.

F13-5(13)   Task M executes.

Note that there is no priority inversion, only resource sharing. Of course, the faster Task L accesses the shared resource and frees up the mutex, the better.

µC/OS-III implements full-priority inheritance and therefore if a higher priority requests the resource, the priority of the owner task will be raised to the priority of the new requestor.

A mutex is a kernel object defined by the **OS_MUTEX** data type, which is derived from the structure **os_mutex** (see **OS.H**). An application may have an unlimited number of mutexes (limited only by the RAM available).

Only tasks are allowed to use mutual exclusion semaphores (ISRs are not allowed).

μC/OS-III enables the user to nest ownership of mutexes. If a task owns a mutex, it can own the same mutex up to 250 times. The owner must release the mutex an equivalent number of times. In several cases, an application may not be immediately aware that it called **OSMutexPend()** multiple times, especially if the mutex is acquired again by calling a function as shown in Listing 13-12.

```
OS_MUTEX         MyMutex;
SOME_STRUCT      MySharedResource;


void  MyTask (void *p_arg)
{
    OS_ERR  err;
    CPU_TS  ts;


    :
    while (DEF_ON) {
        OSMutexPend((OS_MUTEX *)&MyMutex,                      (1)
                    (OS_TICK  )0,
                    (OS_OPT   )OS_OPT_PEND_BLOCKING,
                    (CPU_TS   *)&ts,
                    (OS_ERR   *)&err);
        /* Check 'err"                           */            (2)
        /* Acquire shared resource if no error   */
        MyLibFunction();                                       (3)
        OSMutexPost((OS_MUTEX *)&MyMutex,                      (7)
                    (OS_OPT   )OS_OPT_POST_NONE,
                    (OS_ERR   *)&err);
        /* Check "err"                           */
    }
}
```

```
void  MyLibFunction (void)
{
   OS_ERR  err;
   CPU_TS  ts;


   OSMutexPend((OS_MUTEX *)&MyMutex,                    (4)
               (OS_TICK  )0,
               (OS_OPT   )OS_OPT_PEND_BLOCKING,
               (CPU_TS   *)&ts,
               (OS_ERR   *)&err);
   /* Check "err"                     */
   /* Access shared resource if no error */            (5)
   OSMutexPost((OS_MUTEX *)&MyMutex,                    (6)
               (OS_OPT   )OS_OPT_POST_NONE,
               (OS_ERR   *)&err);
   /* Check "err"                     */
}
```

Listing 13-12 **Nesting calls to OSMutexPend()**

13

L13-12(1)   A task starts by pending on a mutex to access shared resources. **OSMutexPend()** sets a nesting counter to 1.

L13-12(2)   Check the error return value. If no errors exist, **MyTask()** owns **MySharedResource**.

L13-12(3)   A function is called that will perform additional work.

L13-12(4)   The designer of **MyLibFunction()** knows that, to access **MySharedResource**, it must acquire the mutex. Since the calling task already owns the mutex, this operation should not be necessary. However, **MyLibFunction()** could have been called by yet another function that might not need access to **MySharedResource**. µC/OS-III allows nested mutex pends, so this is not a problem. The mutex nesting counter is thus incremented to 2.

L13-12(5)   **MyLibFunction()** can access the shared resource.

L13-12(6)   The mutex is released and the nesting counter is decremented back to 1. Since this indicates that the mutex is still owned by the same task, nothing further needs to be done, and **OSMutexPost()** simply returns. **MyLibFunction()** returns to its caller.

L13-12(7)   The mutex is released again and, this time, the nesting counter is decremented back to 0 indicating that other tasks can now acquire the mutex.

Always check the return value of **OSMutexPend()** (and any kernel call) to ensure that the function returned because you properly obtained the mutex, and not because the return from **OSMutexPend()** was caused by the mutex being deleted, or because another task called **OSMutexPendAbort()** on this mutex.

As a general rule, do not make function calls in critical sections. All mutual exclusion semaphore calls should be in the leaf nodes of the source code (e.g., in the low level drivers that actually touches real hardware or in other reentrant function libraries).

There are a number of operations that can be performed on a mutex, as summarized in Table 13-3. However, in this chapter, we will only discuss the three functions that most often used: **OSMutexCreate()**, **OSMutexPend()**, and **OSMutexPost()**. Other functions are described in Appendix A, "µC/OS-III API Reference Manual" on page 383.

Function Name	Operation
OSMutexCreate()	Create a mutex.
OSMutexDel()	Delete a mutex.
OSMutexPend()	Wait on a mutex.
OSMutexPendAbort()	Abort the wait on a mutex.
OSMutexPost()	Release a mutex.

Table 13-3 **Mutex API summary**

13-4-1 MUTUAL EXCLUSION SEMAPHORE INTERNALS

A mutex is a kernel object defined by the **OS_MUTEX** data type, which is derived from the structure **os_mutex** (see **OS.H**) as shown in Listing 13-13:

```
typedef  struct  os_mutex  OS_MUTEX;          (1)


struct  os_mutex {
    OS_OBJ_TYPE         Type;                 (2)
    CPU_CHAR            *NamePtr;             (3)
    OS_PEND_LIST        PendList;             (4)
    OS_TCB              *OwnerTCBPtr;         (5)
    OS_PRIO             OwnerOriginalPrio;    (6)
    OS_NESTING_CTR      OwnerNestingCtr;      (7)
    CPU_TS              TS;                   (8)
};
```

Listing 13-13 **OS_MUTEX data type**

L13-13(1)   In µC/OS-III, all structures are given a data type. All data types begin with "OS_" and are uppercase. When a mutex is declared, simply use **OS_MUTEX** as the data type of the variable used to declare the mutex.

L13-13(2)   The structure starts with a "Type" field, which allows it to be recognized by µC/OS-III as a mutex. Other kernel objects may also have a ".**Type**" as the first member of the structure. If a function is passed a kernel object, µC/OS-III will be able to confirm that it is being passed the proper data type. For example, if passing a message queue (**OS_Q**) to a mutex service (for example **OSMutexPend()**), µC/OS-III will recognize that the application passed an invalid object and return an error code accordingly.

L13-13(3)   Each kernel object can be given a name to make them easier to recognize by debuggers or µC/Probe. This member is simply a pointer to an ASCII string, which is assumed to be **NUL** terminated.

L13-13(4)   Because it is possible for multiple tasks to wait (or pend on a mutex), the mutex object contains a pend list as described in Chapter 10, "Pend Lists (or Wait Lists)" on page 185.

L13-13(5) If the mutex is owned by a task, it will point to the **OS_TCB** of that task.

L13-13(6) If the mutex is owned by a task, this field contains the "original" priority of the task that owns the mutex. This field is required in case the priority of the task must be raised to a higher priority to prevent unbounded priority inversions.

L13-13(7) µC/OS-III allows a task to "acquire" the same mutex multiple times. In order for the mutex to be released, the owner must release the mutex the same number of times that it was acquired. Nesting can be performed up to 250-levels deep.

L13-13(8) A mutex contains a timestamp, used to indicate the last time it was released. µC/OS-III assumes the presence of a free-running counter that allows applications to make time measurements. When the mutex is released, the free-running counter is read and the value is placed in this field, which is returned when **OSMutexPend()** returns.

Application code should never access any of the fields in this data structure directly. Instead, always use the APIs provided with µC/OS-III.

A mutual exclusion semaphore (mutex) must be created before it can be used by an application. Listing 13-14 shows how to create a mutex.

```
OS_MUTEX  MyMutex;                        (1)


void  MyTask (void *p_arg)
{
    OS_ERR  err;
    :
    :
    OSMutexCreate(&MyMutex,               (2)
                  "My Mutex",             (3)
                  &err);                  (4)
    /* Check "err" */
    :
    :
}
```

Listing 13-14 **Creating a mutex**

L13-14(1)   The application must declare a variable of type **OS_MUTEX**. This variable will be referenced by other mutex services.

L13-14(2)   Create a mutex by calling **OSMutexCreate()** and pass the address to the mutex allocated in (1).

L13-14(3)   Assign an ASCII name to the mutex, which can be used by debuggers or µC/Probe to easily identify this mutex. There are no practical limits to the length of the name since µC/OS-III stores a pointer to the ASCII string, and not to the actual characters that makes up the string.

L13-14(4)   **OSMutexCreate()** returns an error code based on the outcome of the call. If all the arguments are valid, err will contain **OS_ERR_NONE**.

Note that since a mutex is always a binary semaphore, there is no need to initialize a mutex counter.

13

A task waits on a mutual exclusion semaphore before accessing a shared resource by calling **OSMutexPend()** as shown in Listing 13-15 (see Appendix A, "µC/OS-III API Reference Manual" on page 383 for details regarding the arguments).

```
OS_MUTEX  MyMutex;


void MyTask (void *p_arg)
{
    OS_ERR  err;
    CPU_TS  ts;
    :
    while (DEF_ON) {
        :
        OSMutexPend(&MyMutex,              /* (1) Pointer to mutex                          */
                    10,                    /*     Wait up until this time for the mutex     */
                    OS_OPT_PEND_BLOCKING, /*     Option(s)                                 */
                    &ts,                   /*     Timestamp of when mutex was released      */
                    &err);                 /*     Pointer to Error returned                 */
        :
        /* Check "err" */                  (2)                                            */
        :
        OSMutexPost(&MyMutex,              /* (3) Pointer to mutex                          */
                    OS_OPT_POST_NONE,
                    &err);                 /*     Pointer to Error returned                 */
        /* Check "err" */                                                                 */
        :
        :
    }
}
```

Listing 13-15 **Pending (or waiting) on a Mutual Exclusion Semaphore**

L13-15(1)   When called, **OSMutexPend()** starts by checking the arguments passed to this function to make sure they have valid values.

If the mutex is available, **OSMutexPend()** assumes the calling task is now the owner of the mutex and stores a pointer to the task's **OS_TCB** in **p_mutex->OwnerTCPPtr**, saves the priority of the task in **p_mutex->OwnerOriginalPrio**, and sets a mutex nesting counter to 1. **OSMutexPend()** then returns to its caller with an error code of **OS_ERR_NONE**.

If the task that calls **OSMutexPend()** already owns the mutex, **OSMutexPend()** simply increments a nesting counter. Applications can nest calls to **OSMutexPend()** up to 250-levels deep. In this case, the error returned will indicate **OS_ERR_MUTEX_OWNER**.

If the mutex is already owned by another task and OS_OPT_PEND_NON_BLOCKING is specified, OSMutexPend() returns since the task is not willing to wait for the mutex to be released by its owner.

If the mutex is owned by a lower-priority task, µC/OS-III will raise the priority of the owner to match the priority of the current task.

If specifying OS_OPT_PEND_BLOCKING as the option, the calling task will be inserted in the list of tasks waiting for the mutex to be available. The task is inserted in the list by priority order and the highest priority task waiting on the mutex is at the beginning of the list.

If further specifying a non-zero timeout, the task will also be inserted in the tick list. A zero value for a timeout indicates a willingness to wait forever for the mutex to be released.

The scheduler is then called since the current task is no longer able to run (it is waiting for the mutex to be released). The scheduler will then run the next highest-priority task that is ready to run.

When the mutex is finally released and the task that called OSMutexPend() is again the highest-priority task, a task status is examined to determine the reason why OSMutexPend() is returning to its caller. The possibilities are:

1) The mutex was given to the waiting task

2) The pend was aborted by another task

3) The mutex was not posted within the specified timeout

4) The mutex was deleted

When OSMutexPend() returns, the caller is notified of the outcome through an appropriate error code.

13

L13-15(2)   If OSMutexPend() returns with err set to OS_ERR_NONE, assume that the calling task now owns the resource and can proceed with accessing it. If err contains anything else, then OSMutexPend() either timed out (if the timeout argument was non-zero), the pend was aborted by another task, or the mutex was deleted by another task. It is always important to examine returned error codes and not assume everything went as planned.

If "err" is OS_ERR_NESTING_OWNER, then the caller attempted to pend on the same mutex.

L13-15(3)   When your task is finished accessing the resource, it must call OSMutexPost() and specify the same mutex. Again, OSMutexPost() starts by checking the arguments passed to this function to make sure they contain valid values.

OSMutexPost() now calls OS_TS_GET() to obtain the current timestamp and place that information in the mutex, which will be used by OSMutexPend().

OSMutexPost() decrements the nesting counter and, if still non-zero, OSMutexPost() returns to the caller. In this case, the current owner has not fully released the mutex. The error code will indicate OS_ERR_MUTEX_NESTING.

If there are no tasks waiting for the mutex, OSMutexPost() sets p_mutex->OwnerTCBPtr to a NULL pointer and clears the mutex nesting counter.

If μC/OS-III had to raise the priority of the mutex owner, it is returned to its original priority at this time.

The highest-priority task waiting on the mutex is then extracted from the pend list and given the mutex. This is a fast operation since the pend list is sorted by priority.

The scheduler is called to see if the new mutex owner has a higher priority than the current task. If so, μC/OS-III will switch context to the new mutex owner.

You should note that you should only acquire one mutex at a time. In fact, it's highly recommended that when you acquire a mutex, you don't acquire any other kernel objects.

13-5 SHOULD YOU USE A SEMAPHORE INSTEAD OF A MUTEX?

A semaphore can be used instead of a mutex if none of the tasks competing for the shared resource have deadlines to be satisfied.

However, if there are deadlines to meet, you should use a mutex prior to accessing shared resources. Semaphores are subject to unbounded priority inversions, while mutex are not.

13-6 DEADLOCKS (OR DEADLY EMBRACE)

A *deadlock*, also called a **deadly embrace**, is a situation in which two tasks are each unknowingly waiting for resources held by the other.

Assume Task T1 has exclusive access to Resource R1 and Task T2 has exclusive access to Resource R2 as shown in the pseudo-code of Listing 13-16.

13

```
void T1 (void *p_arg)
{
    while (DEF_ON) {
        Wait for event to occur;        (1)
        Acquire M1;                     (2)
        Access  R1;                     (3)
        :
        :
        \--------  Interrupt!           (4)
        :
        :                               (8)
        Acquire M2;                     (9)
        Access  R2;
    }
}
```

```
void  T2 (void *p_arg)
{
    while (DEF_ON) {
        Wait for event to occur;          (5)
        Acquire M2;                       (6)
        Access  R2;
        :
        :
        Acquire M1;                       (7)
        Access  R1;
    }
}
```

Listing 13-16 **Deadlock problem**

L13-16(1)   Assume that the event that task T1 is waiting for occurs and T1 is now the highest priority task that must execute.

L13-16(2)   Task T1 executes and acquires M1.

L13-16(3)   Resource R1 is accessed.

L13-16(4)   An interrupt occurs causing the CPU to switch to task T2 as T2 is now the highest-priority task. Actually, this could be a blocking call when the task is suspended and the CPU is given to another task.

L13-16(5)   The ISR is the event that task T2 was waiting for and therefore T2 resumes execution.

L13-16(6)   Task T2 acquires mutex M2 and is able to access resource R2.

L13-16(7)   Task T2 tries to acquire mutex M1, but µC/OS-III knows that mutex M1 is owned by another task.

L13-16(8)   µC/OS-III switches back to task T1 because Task T2 can no longer continue. It needs mutex M1 to access resource R1.

L13-16(9)   Task T1 now tries to access mutex M2 but, unfortunately, mutex M2 is owned by task T2. At this point, the two tasks are deadlocked.

Techniques used to avoid deadlocks are for tasks to:

- Never acquire more than one mutex at a time

- Never acquire a mutex directly (i.e., let them be hidden inside drivers and reentrant library calls)

- Acquire all resources before proceeding

- Always acquire resources in the same order

µC/OS-III allows the calling task to specify a timeout when acquiring a semaphore or a mutex. This feature allows a deadlock to be broken, but the same deadlock may then recur later, or many times later. If the semaphore or mutex is not available within a certain period of time, the task requesting the resource resumes execution. µC/OS-III returns an error code indicating that a timeout occurred. A return error code prevents the task from thinking it has properly obtained the resource.

13

The pseudo-code avoids deadlocks by first acquiring all resources as shown in Listing 13-17.

```
void T1 (void *p_arg)
{
    while (DEF_ON) {
        Wait for event to occur;
        Acquire M1;
        Acquire M2;
        Access  R1;
        Access  R2;
    }
}


void  T2 (void *p_arg)
{
    while (DEF_ON) {
        Wait for event to occur;
        Acquire M1;
        Acquire M2;
        Access  R1;
        Access  R2;
    }
}
```

Listing 13-17 **Deadlock avoidance – acquire all first and in the same order**

The pseudo-code to acquire all of the mutexes in the same order is shown in Listing 13-18. This is similar to the previous example, except that it is not necessary to acquire all the mutexes first, only to make sure that the mutexes are acquired in the same order for both tasks.

```
void T1 (void *p_arg){
    while (DEF_ON) {
        Wait for event to occur;
        Acquire M1;
        Access  R1;
        Acquire M2;
        Access  R2;
    }
}


void  T2 (void *p_arg)
{
    while (DEF_ON) {
        Wait for event to occur;
        Acquire M1;
        Access  R1;
        Acquire M2;
        Access  R2;
    }
}
```

Listing 13-18 **Deadlock avoidance – acquire in the same order**

13

13-7 SUMMARY

The mutual exclusion mechanism used depends on how fast code will access the shared resource, as shown in Table 13-4.

Resource Sharing Method	When should you use?
Disable/Enable Interrupts	When access to shared resource is very quick (reading from or writing to just a few variables) and the access is actually faster than µC/OS-III's interrupt disable time. It is highly recommended to not use this method as it impacts interrupt latency.
Locking/Unlocking the Scheduler	When access time to the shared resource is longer than µC/OS-III's interrupt disable time, but shorter than µC/OS-III's scheduler lock time. Locking the scheduler has the same effect as making the task that locks the scheduler the highest priority task. It is recommended to not use this method since it defeats the purpose of using µC/OS-III. However, it's a better method than disabling interrupts as it does not impact interrupt latency.
Semaphores	When all tasks that need to access a shared resource do not have deadlines. This is because semaphores can cause unbounded priority inversions. However, semaphore services are slightly faster (in execution time) than mutual exclusion semaphores.
Mutual Exclusion Semaphores	This is the preferred method for accessing shared resources, especially if the tasks that need to access a shared resource have deadlines. Remember that mutual exclusion semaphores have a built-in priority inheritance mechanism, which avoids unbounded priority inversions. However, mutual exclusion semaphore services are slightly slower (in execution time) than semaphores, because the priority of the owner may need to be changed, which requires CPU processing.

Table 13-4 **Resource sharing summary**

14

Synchronization

This chapter focuses on how tasks can synchronize their activities with Interrupt Service Routines (ISRs), or other tasks.

When an ISR executes, it can signal a task telling the task that an event of interest has occurred. After signaling the task, the ISR exits and, depending on the signaled task priority, the scheduler is run. The signaled task may then service the interrupting device, or otherwise react to the event. Serving interrupting devices from task level is preferred whenever possible, since it reduces the amount of time that interrupts are disabled and the code is easier to debug.

There are two basic mechanisms for synchronizations in µC/OS-III: semaphores and event flags.

14-1 SEMAPHORES

As defined in Chapter 13, "Resource Management" on page 217, a semaphore is a protocol mechanism offered by most multitasking kernels. Semaphores were originally used to control access to shared resources. However, better mechanisms exist to protect access to shared resources, as described in Chapter 12. Semaphores are best used to synchronize an ISR to a task, or synchronize a task with another task as shown in Figure 14-1.

Note that the semaphore is drawn as a flag to indicate that it is used to signal the occurrence of an event. The initial value for the semaphore is typically zero (0), indicating the event has not yet occurred.

The value "N" next to the flag indicates that the semaphore can accumulate events or credits. It is possible to initialize the semaphore with a value other than zero, indicating that the semaphore initially contains that number of events. An ISR (or a task) can post (or signal) multiple times to a semaphore and the semaphore will remember how many times it was posted.

Also, the small hourglass close to the receiving task indicates that the task has an option to specify a timeout. This timeout indicates that the task is willing to wait for the semaphore to be signaled (or posted to) within a certain amount of time. If the semaphore is not signaled within that time, µC/OS-III resumes the task and returns an error code indicating that the task was made ready to run because of a timeout and not the semaphore was signaled.

Figure 14-1 **µC/OS-III Semaphore Services**

There are a number of operations to perform on semaphores as summarized in Table 14-1 and Figure 14-1. However, in this chapter, we will only discuss the three functions used most often: **OSSemCreate()**, **OSSemPend()**, and **OSSemPost()**. The other functions are described in Appendix A, "µC/OS-III API Reference Manual" on page 383. Also note that every semaphore function is callable from a task, but only **OSSemPost()** can be called by an ISR

Function Name	Operation
OSSemCreate()	Create a semaphore.
OSSemDel()	Delete a semaphore.
OSSemPend()	Wait on a semaphore.
OSSemPendAbort()	Abort the wait on a semaphore.
OSSemPost()	Signal a semaphore.
OSSemSet()	Force the semaphore count to a desired value.

Table 14-1 **Semaphore API summary**

When used for synchronization, a semaphore keeps track of how many times it was signaled using a counter. The counter can take values between 0 and 255, 65,535, or 4,294,967,295, depending on whether the semaphore mechanism is implemented using 8, 16, or 32 bits, respectively. For µC/OS-III, the maximum value of a semaphore is determined by the data type **OS_SEM_CTR** (see **OS_TYPE.H**), which is changeable, as needed (assuming access to µC/OS-III's source code). Along with the semaphore's value, µC/OS-III keeps track of tasks waiting for the semaphore to be signaled.

14

14-1-1 UNILATERAL RENDEZVOUS

Figure 14-2 shows that a task can be synchronized with an ISR (or another task) by using a semaphore. In this case, no data is exchanged, however there is an indication that the ISR or the task (on the left) has occurred. Using a semaphore for this type of synchronization is called a unilateral rendezvous.

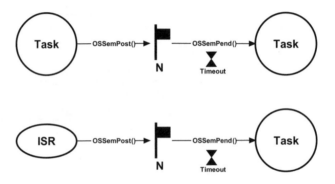

Figure 14-2 **Unilateral Rendezvous**

A unilateral rendezvous is used when a task initiates an I/O operation and waits (i.e., call OSSemPend()) for the semaphore to be signaled (posted). When the I/O operation is complete, an ISR (or another task) signals the semaphore (i.e., calls **OSSemPost()**), and the task is resumed. This process is also shown on the timeline of Figure 14-3 and described below. The code for the ISR and task is shown in Listing 14-1.

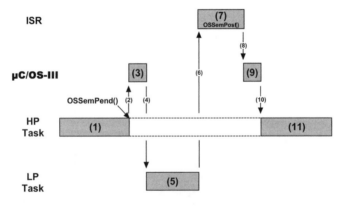

Figure 14-3 **Unilateral Rendezvous, Timing Diagram**

F14-3(1)   A high priority task is executing. The task needs to synchronize with an ISR (i.e., wait for the ISR to occur) and call **OSSemPend()**.

F14-3(2)
F14-3(3)
F14-3(4)   Since the ISR has not occurred, the task will be placed in the waiting list for the semaphore until the event occurs The scheduler in µC/OS-III will then select the next most important task and context switch to that task.

F14-3(5)   The low-priority task executes.

F14-3(6)   The event that the original task was waiting for occurs. The lower-priority task is immediately preempted (assuming interrupts are enabled), and the CPU vectors to the interrupt handler for the event.

F14-3(7)
F14-3(8)   The ISR handles the interrupting device and then calls **OSSemPost()** to signal the semaphore. When the ISR completes, µC/OS-III is called.

F14-3(9)
F14-3(10)   µC/OS-III notices that a higher-priority task is waiting for this event to occur and context switches back to the original task.

F14-3(11)   The original task resumes execution immediately after the call to **OSSemPend()**.

```
OS_SEM  MySem;


void MyISR (void)
{
    OS_ERR  err;


    /* Clear the interrupting device */
    OSSemPost(&MySem,                  (7)
             OS_OPT_POST_1,
             &err);
    /* Check "err" */
}


void MyTask (void *p_arg)
{
    OS_ERR  err;
    CPU_TS  ts;
    :
    :
    while (DEF_ON) {
        OSSemPend(&MySem,              (1)
                 10,
                 OS_OPT_PEND_BLOCKING,
                 &ts,
                 &err);
        /* Check "err" */             (11)
        :
        :
    }
}
```

Listing 14-1 **Pending (or waiting) on a Semaphore**

A few interesting things are worth noting about this process. First, the task does not need to know about the details of what happens behind the scenes. As far as the task is concerned, it called a function (OSSemPend()) that will return when the event it is waiting for occurs. Second, µC/OS-III maximizes the use of the CPU by selecting the next most important task, which executes until the ISR occurs. In fact, the ISR may not occur for many milliseconds and, during that time, the CPU will work on other tasks. As far as the task that is waiting for the semaphore is concerned, it does not consume CPU time while it is waiting. Finally, the task waiting for the semaphore will execute immediately after the event occurs (assuming it is the most important task that needs to run).

14-1-2 CREDIT TRACKING

As previously mentioned, a semaphore "remembers" how many times it was signaled (or posted to). In other words, if the ISR occurs multiple times before the task waiting for the event becomes the highest-priority task, the semaphore will keep count of the number of times it was signaled. When the task becomes the highest priority ready-to-run task, it will execute without blocking as many times as there were ISRs signaled. This is called Credit Tracking and is illustrated in Figure 14-4 and described below.

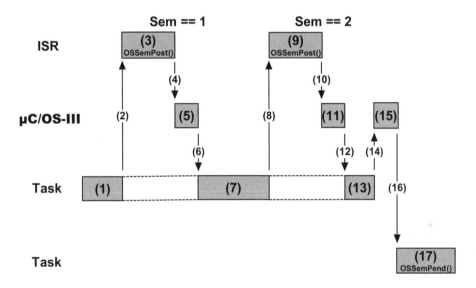

Figure 14-4 **Semaphore Credit Tracking**

F14-4(1)   A high-priority task is executing.

F14-4(2)

F14-4(3)   An event meant for a lower-priority task occurs which preempts the task (assuming interrupts are enabled). The ISR executes and posts the semaphore. At this point the semaphore count is 1.

F14-4(4)

F14-4(5)

F14-4(6)   µC/OS-III is called at the end of the ISR to see if the ISR caused a higher-priority task to be ready to run. Since the ISR was an event that a lower-priority task was waiting on, µC/OS-III will resume execution of the higher-priority task at the exact point where it was interrupted.

265

F14-4(7)   The high-priority task is resumed and continues execution.

F14-4(8)
F14-4(9)   The interrupt occurs a second time. The ISR executes and posts the semaphore. At this point the semaphore count is 2.

F14-4(10)
F14-4(11)
F14-4(12)   µC/OS-III is called at the end of the ISR to see if the ISR caused a higher-priority task to be ready to run. Since the ISR was an event that a lower-priority task was waiting on, µC/OS-III resumes execution of the higher-priority task at the exact point where it was interrupted.

F14-4(13)
F14-4(14)   The high-priority task resumes execution and actually terminates the work it was doing. This task will then call one of the µC/OS-III services to wait for "its" event to occur.

F14-4(15)
F14-4(16)   µC/OS-III will then select the next most important task, which happens to be the task waiting for the event and will context switch to that task.

F14-4(17)   The new task executes and will know that the ISR occurred twice since the semaphore count is two. The task will handle this accordingly.

14-1-3 MULTIPLE TASKS WAITING ON A SEMAPHORE

It is possible for more than one task to wait on the same semaphore, each with its own timeout as illustrated in Figure 14-5.

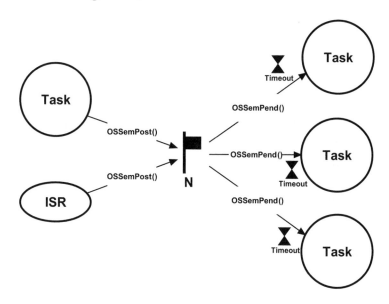

Figure 14-5 **Multiple Tasks waiting on a Semaphore**

When the semaphore is signaled (whether by an ISR or task), µC/OS-III makes the highest-priority task waiting on the semaphore ready to run. However, it is also possible to specify that all tasks waiting on the semaphore be made ready to run. This is called broadcasting and is accomplished by specifying `OS_OPT_POST_ALL` as an option when calling `OSSemPost()`. If any of the waiting tasks has a higher priority than the previously running task, µC/OS-III will execute the highest-priority task made ready by `OSSemPost()`.

Broadcasting is a common technique used to synchronize multiple tasks and have them start executing at the same time. However, some of the tasks that we want to synchronize might not be waiting for the semaphore. It is fairly easy to resolve this problem by combining semaphores and event flags. This will be described after examining event flags.

14-1-4 SEMAPHORE INTERNALS (FOR SYNCHRONIZATION)

Note that some of the material presented in this section is also contained in Chapter 13, "Resource Management" on page 217, as semaphores were also discussed in that chapter. However, the material presented here will be applicable to semaphores used for synchronization and thus will differ somewhat.

A counting semaphore allows values between 0 and 255, 65,535, or 4,294,967,295, depending on whether the semaphore mechanism is implemented using 8, 16, or 32 bits, respectively. For µC/OS-III, the maximum value of a semaphore is determined by the data type OS_SEM_CTR (see OS_TYPE.H), which can be changed as needed (assuming access to µC/OS-III's source code). Along with the semaphore's value, µC/OS-III keeps track of tasks waiting for the semaphore's availability.

The application programmer can create an unlimited number of semaphores (limited only by available RAM). Semaphore services in µC/OS-III start with the OSSem???() prefix, and services available to the application programmer are described in Appendix A, "µC/OS-III API Reference Manual" on page 383. Semaphore services are enabled at compile time by setting the configuration constant OS_CFG_SEM_EN to 1 in OS_CFG.H.

Semaphores must be created before they can be used by the application. Listing 14-3 shows how to create a semaphore.

As previously mentioned, a semaphore is a kernel object as defined by the OS_SEM data type, which is derived from the structure os_sem (see OS.H) as shown in Listing 14-2.

The services provided by µC/OS-III to manage semaphores are implemented in the file OS_SEM.C. µC/OS-III licensees, have access to the source code.

```
typedef  struct  os_sem  OS_SEM;                (1)


struct  os_sem {
    OS_OBJ_TYPE         Type;                   (2)
    CPU_CHAR            *NamePtr;               (3)
    OS_PEND_LIST        PendList;               (4)
    OS_SEM_CTR          Ctr;                    (5)
    CPU_TS              TS;                     (6)
};
```

Listing 14-2 **OS_SEM data type**

L14-2(1)   In µC/OS-III, all structures are given a data type. In fact, all data types start with "**OS_**" and are all uppercase. When a semaphore is declared, simply use **OS_SEM** as the data type of the variable used to declare the semaphore.

L14-2(2)   The structure starts with a "**Type**" field, which allows it to be recognized by µC/OS-III as a semaphore. In other words, other kernel objects will also have a "**Type**" as the first member of the structure. If a function is passed a kernel object, µC/OS-III will confirm that it is being passed the proper data type. For example, if passing a message queue (**OS_Q**) to a semaphore service (for example **OSSemPend()**), µC/OS-III will recognize that an invalid object was passed, and return an error code accordingly.

L14-2(3)   Each kernel object can be given a name to make them easier to be recognized by debuggers or µC/Probe. This member is simply a pointer to an ASCII string, which is assumed to be **NUL** terminated.

L14-2(4)   Since it is possible for multiple tasks to be waiting (or pending) on a semaphore, the semaphore object contains a pend list as described in Chapter 10, "Pend Lists (or Wait Lists)" on page 185.

L14-2(5)   A semaphore contains a counter. As explained above, the counter can be implemented as either an 8-, 16- or 32-bit value, depending on how the data type **OS_SEM_CTR** is declared in **OS_TYPE.H**.

             µC/OS-III keeps track of how many times the semaphore is signaled with this counter and this field is typically initialized to zero by **OSSemCreate()**.

14

L14-2(6)   A semaphore contains a time stamp, which is used to indicate the last time the semaphore was signaled (or posted to). μC/OS-III assumes the presence of a free-running counter that allows the application to make time measurements. When the semaphore is signaled, the free-running counter is read and the value is placed in this field, which is returned when **OSSemPend()** is called. This value allows the application to determine either when the signal was performed, or how long it took for the task to get control of the CPU from the signal. In the latter case, call **OS_TS_GET()** to determine the current timestamp and compute the difference.

Even for users who understand the internals of the **OS_SEM** data type, the application code should never access any of the fields in this data structure directly. Instead, always use the APIs provided with μC/OS-III.

Semaphores must be created before they can be used by an application. Listing 14-3 shows how to create a semaphore.

```
OS_SEM  MySem;                       (1)


void  MyCode (void)
{
    OS_ERR  err;
    :
    OSSemCreate(&MySem,              (2)
                "My Semaphore",      (3)
                (OS_SEM_CTR)0,       (4)
                &err);               (5)
    /* Check "err" */
    :

}
```

Listing 14-3 **Creating a Semaphore**

L14-3(1)   The application must declare a variable of type **OS_SEM**. This variable will be referenced by other semaphore services.

L14-3(2)   Create a semaphore by calling **OSSemCreate()** and pass the address to the semaphore allocated in (1).

14

L14-3(3)   Assign an ASCII name to the semaphore, which can be used by debuggers or μC/Probe to easily identify this semaphore.

L14-3(4)   Initialize the semaphore to zero (0) when using a semaphore as a signaling mechanism.

L14-3(5)   **OSSemCreate()** returns an error code based on the outcome of the call. If all arguments are valid, err will contain **OS_ERR_NONE**.

OSSemCreate() performs a check on the arguments passed to this function and only initializes the contents of the variable of type **OS_SEM** used for signaling.

A task waits for a signal from an ISR or another task by calling **OSSemPend()** as shown in Listing 14-4 (see Appendix A, "μC/OS-III API Reference Manual" on page 383 for details regarding the arguments).

```
OS_SEM  MySem;                        (1)


void  MyCode (void)
{
    OS_ERR  err;
    :
    OSSemCreate(&MySem,               (2)
                "My Semaphore",       (3)
                (OS_SEM_CTR)0,        (4)
                &err);                (5)
    /* Check "err" */
    :
}
```

Listing 14-4 **Pending (or waiting) on a Semaphore**

L14-4(1)   When called, **OSSemPend()** starts by checking the arguments passed to this function to make sure they have valid values.

If the semaphore counter (**.Ctr** of **OS_SEM**) is greater than zero, the counter is decremented and **OSSemPend()** returns, which indicates that the signal occurred. This is the outcome that the caller expects.

If the semaphore counter is zero, this indicates that the signal has not occurred and the calling task might need to wait for the semaphore to be released. If specifying OS_OPT_PEND_NON_BLOCKING as the option (the task is not to block), OSSemPend() returns immediately to the caller and the returned error code will indicate that the signal did not occur.

If specifying OS_OPT_PEND_BLOCKING as the option, the calling task will be inserted in the list of tasks waiting for the semaphore to be signaled. The task is inserted in the list by priority order with the highest priority task waiting on the semaphore at the beginning of the list as shown in Figure 14-6.

If further specifying a non-zero timeout, the task will also be inserted in the tick list. A zero value for a timeout indicates that the calling task is willing to wait forever for the semaphore to be signaled.

The scheduler is then called as the current task is not able to run (it is waiting for the semaphore to be signaled). The scheduler will then run the next highest-priority task that is ready to run.

When the semaphore is signaled and the task that called OSSemPend() is again the highest-priority task, a task status is examined to determine the reason why OSSemPend() is returning to its caller. The possibilities are:

1) The semaphore was signaled

2) The pend was aborted by another task

3) The semaphore was not signaled within the specified timeout

4) The semaphore was deleted

When OSSemPend() returns, the caller is notified of the above outcome through an appropriate error code.

L14-4(2)   If OSSemPend() returns with **err** set to OS_ERR_NONE, assume that the semaphore was signaled and the task can proceed with servicing the ISR or task that caused the signal. If **err** contains anything else, OSSemPend() either timed out (if the timeout argument was non-zero), the pend was aborted by another task, or the semaphore was deleted by another task. It is always important to examine returned error code and not assume everything went as expected.

To signal a task (either from an ISR or a task), simply call **OSSemPost()** as shown in Listing 14-5.

```
OS_SEM  MySem;


void MyISR (void)
{
    OS_ERR  err;
    :
    OSSemPost(&MySem,               (1)
              OS_OPT_POST_1,        (2)
              &err);                (3)
    /* Check "err" */
    :
    :
}
```

Listing 14-5 Posting (or signaling) a Semaphore

L14-5(1)   Your task signals (or posts to) the semaphore by calling **OSSemPost()**. Specify the semaphore to post by passing its address. The semaphore must have been previously created.

L14-5(2)   The next argument specifies how the task wants to post. There are a number of options to choose from.

Specify **OS_OPT_POST_1**, which indicates posting to only one task in case there are multiple tasks waiting on the semaphore. The task that will be made ready to run will be the highest-priority task waiting on the semaphore. If there are multiple tasks at the same priority, only one of them will be made ready-to-run. As shown in Figure 14-6, tasks waiting are in priority order (HPT means High Priority Task and LPT means Low Priority Task). It is a fast operation to extract the HPT from the list.

14

If specifying **OS_OPT_POST_ALL**, all tasks waiting on the semaphore will be posted and made ready to run.

The calling task can "add" the option **OS_OPT_POST_NO_SCHED** to either of the two previous options to indicate that the scheduler is not to be called at the end of **OSSemPost()**, possibly because additional postings will be performed, and rescheduling should take place when finished. This means that the signal is performed, but the scheduler is not called even if a higher-priority task was waiting for the semaphore to be signaled. This allows the calling task to perform other post functions (if needed) and make all the posts take effect simultaneously. Note that **OS_OPT_POST_NO_SCHED** is "additive," meaning that it can be used with either of the previous options. You can specify:

```
OS_OPT_POST_1
OS_OPT_POST_ALL
OS_OPT_POST_1   + OS_OPT_POST_NO_SCHED
OS_OPT_POST_ALL + OS_OPT_POST_NO_SCHED
```

Figure 14-6 **Tasks waiting for semaphore**

L14-5(3)   `OSSemPost()` returns an error code based on the outcome of the call. If the call was successful, err will contain **OS_ERR_NONE**. If not, the error code will indicate the reason for the error (see Appendix A, "µC/OS-III API Reference Manual" on page 383 for a list of possible error codes for `OSSemPost()`.

14-2 TASK SEMAPHORE

Signaling a task using a semaphore is a very popular method of synchronization and, in µC/OS-III, each task has its own built-in semaphore. This feature not only simplifies code, but is also more efficient than using a separate semaphore object. The semaphore, which is built into each task, is shown in Figure 14-7.

Task semaphore services in µC/OS-III start with the **OSTaskSem???()** prefix, and the services available to the application programmer are described in Appendix A, "µC/OS-III API Reference Manual" on page 383. Task semaphores are built into µC/OS-III and cannot be disabled at compile time as can other services. The code for task semaphores is found in **OS_TASK.C**.

Use this feature if the code knows which task to signal when the event occurs. For example, if receiving an interrupt from an Ethernet controller, signal the task responsible for processing the received packet as it is preferable to perform this processing using a task instead of the ISR.

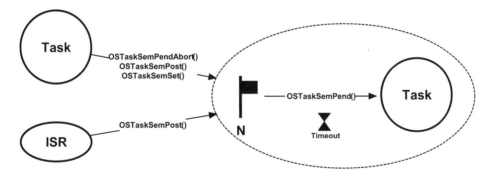

Figure 14-7 **Semaphore built-into a Task**

There are a number of operations to perform on task semaphores, summarized in Table 14-2.

Function Name	Operation
OSTaskSemPend()	Wait on a task semaphore.
OSTaskSemPendAbort()	Abort the wait on a task semaphore.
OSTaskSemPost()	Signal a task.
OSTaskSemSet()	Force the semaphore count to a desired value.

Table 14-2 **Task Semaphore API summary**

14-2-1 PENDING (i.e., WAITING) ON A TASK SEMAPHORE

When a task is created, it automatically creates an internal semaphore with an initial value of zero (0). Waiting on a task semaphore is quite simple, as shown in Listing 14-6.

```
void MyTask (void *p_arg)
{
    OS_ERR  err;
    CPU_TS  ts;
    :
    while (DEF_ON) {
        OSTaskSemPend(10,                       (1)
                      OS_OPT_PEND_BLOCKING,     (2)
                      &ts,                      (3)
                      &err);                    (4)
        /* Check "err" */
        :
        :
    }
}
```

Listing 14-6 **Pending (or waiting) on Task's internal semaphore**

L14-6(1)   A task pends (or waits) on the task semaphore by calling **OSTaskSemPend()**. There is no need to specify which task, as the current task is assumed. The first argument is a timeout specified in number of clock ticks. The actual timeout obviously depends on the tick rate. If the tick rate (see **OS_CFG_APP.H**) is set to 1000, a timeout of 10 ticks represents 10 milliseconds. Specifying a timeout of zero (0) means that the task will wait forever for the task semaphore.

L14-6(2)   The second argument specifies how to pend. There are two options: **OS_OPT_PEND_BLOCKING** and **OS_OPT_PEND_NON_BLOCKING**. The blocking option means that, if the task semaphore has not been signaled (or posted to), the task will wait until the semaphore is signaled, the pend is aborted by another task or, until the timeout expires.

L14-6(3)   When the semaphore is signaled, µC/OS-III reads a "timestamp" and places it in the receiving task's **OS_TCB**. When **OSTaskSemPend()** returns, the value of the timestamp is placed in the local variable "**ts**". This feature captures "when" the signal actually happened. Call **OS_TS_GET()** to read the current timestamp and compute the difference. This establishes how long it took for the task to receive the signal from the posting task or ISR.

L14-6(4)   **OSTaskSemPend()** returns an error code based on the outcome of the call. If the call was successful, err will contain **OS_ERR_NONE**. If not, the error code will indicate the reason of the error (see Appendix A, "µC/OS-III API Reference Manual" on page 383 for a list of possible error code for **OSTaskSemPend()**.

14-2-2 POSTING (i.e., SIGNALING) A TASK SEMAPHORE

An ISR or a task signals a task by calling **OSTaskSemPost()**, as shown in Listing 14-7.

```
OS_TCB  MyTaskTCB;


void MyISR (void *p_arg)
{
    OS_ERR  err;
    :
    OSTaskSemPost(&MyTaskTCB,            (1)
                  OS_OPT_POST_NONE,      (2)
                  &err);                 (3)
    /* Check "err" */
    :
    :
}
```

Listing 14-7 **Posting (or signaling) a Semaphore**

14

L14-7(1)   A task posts (or signals) the task by calling **OSTaskSemPost()**. It is necessary to pass the address of the desired task's **OS_TCB**. Of course, the task must exist.

L14-7(2)   The next argument specifies how the user wants to post. There are only two choices.

Specify **OS_OPT_POST_NONE**, which indicates the use of the default option of calling the scheduler after posting the semaphore.

Or, specify **OS_OPT_POST_NO_SCHED** to indicate that the scheduler is not to be called at the end of **OSTaskSemPost()**, possibly because there will be additional postings, and rescheduling would take place when finished (the last post would not specify this option).

L14-7(3)   **OSTaskSemPost()** returns an error code based on the outcome of the call. If the call was successful, err will contain **OS_ERR_NONE**. If not, the error code will indicate the reason of the error (see Appendix A, "µC/OS-III API Reference Manual" on page 383 for a list of possible error codes for **OSTaskSemPost()**.

14

14-2-3 BILATERAL RENDEZVOUS

Two tasks can synchronize their activities by using two task semaphores, as shown in Figure 14-8, and is called a *bilateral rendezvous*. A bilateral rendezvous is similar to a unilateral rendezvous, except that both tasks must synchronize with one another before proceeding. A bilateral rendezvous cannot be performed between a task and an ISR because an ISR cannot wait on a semaphore.

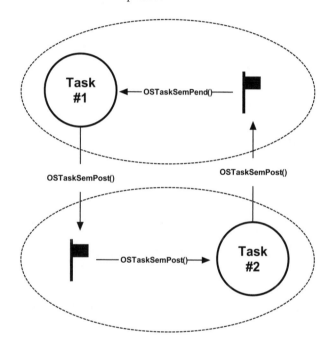

Figure 14-8 **Bilateral Rendezvous**

The code for a bilateral rendezvous is shown in Listing 14-8. Of course, a bilateral rendezvous can use two separate semaphores, but the built-in task semaphore makes setting up this type of synchronization quite straightforward.

14

```
OS_TCB  MyTask1_TCB;
OS_TCB  MyTask2_TCB;


void Task1 (void *p_arg)
{
    OS_ERR  err;
    CPU_TS  ts;

    while (DEF_ON) {
        :
        OSTaskSemPost(&MyTask2_TCB,              (1)
                      OS_OPT_POST_NONE,
                      &err);
        /* Check 'err" */
        OSTaskSemPend(0,                         (2)
                      OS_OPT_PEND_BLOCKING,
                      &ts,
                      &err);
        /* Check 'err" */
        :
    }
}


void Task2 (void *p_arg)
{
    OS_ERR  err;
    CPU_TS  ts;

    while (DEF_ON) {
        :
        OSTaskSemPost(&MyTask1_TCB,              (3)
                      OS_OPT_POST_NONE,
                      &err);
        /* Check 'err" */
        OSTaskSemPend(0,                         (4)
                      OS_OPT_PEND_BLOCKING,
                      &ts,
                      &err);
        /* Check 'err" */
        :
    }
}
```

Listing 14-8 **Tasks synchronizing their activities**

L14-8(1)   Task #1 is executing and signals Task #2's semaphore.

L14-8(2)   Task #1 pends on its internal semaphore to synchronize with Task #2. Because Task #2 has not executed yet, Task #1 is blocked waiting on its semaphore to be signaled. µC/OS-III context switches to Task #2.

L14-8(3)   Task #2 executes, and signals Task #1's semaphore.

L14-8(4)   Since it has already been signaled, Task #2 is now synchronized to Task #1. If Task #1 is higher in priority than Task #2, µC/OS-III will switch back to Task #1. If not, Task #2 continues execution.

14-3 EVENT FLAGS

Event flags are used when a task needs to synchronize with the occurrence of multiple events. The task can be synchronized when any of the events have occurred, which is called disjunctive synchronization (logical OR). A task can also be synchronized when all events have occurred, which is called conjunctive synchronization (logical AND). Disjunctive and conjunctive synchronization are shown in Figure 14-9.

The application programmer can create an unlimited number of event flag groups (limited only by available RAM). Event flag services in µC/OS-III start with the **OSFlag???()** prefix. The services available to the application programmer are described in Appendix A, "µC/OS-III API Reference Manual" on page 383.

The code for event flag services is found in the file **OS_FLAG.C**, and is enabled at compile time by setting the configuration constant **OS_CFG_FLAG_EN** to 1 in **OS_CFG.H**.

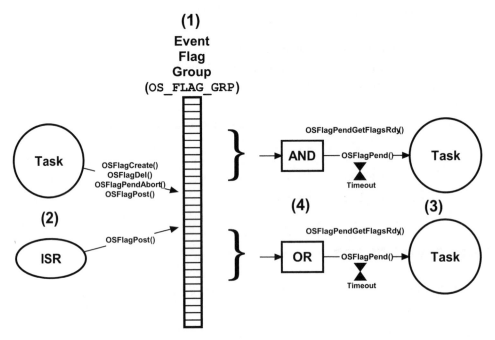

Figure 14-9 **Event Flags**

F14-9(1)   A µC/OS-III "event flag group" is a kernel object of type **OS_FLAG_GRP** (see **OS.H**), and consists of a series of bits (8-, 16- or 32-bits, based on the data type **OS_FLAGS** defined in **OS_TYPE.H**). The event flag group also contains a list of tasks waiting for some (or all) of the bits to be set (1) or clear (0). An event flag group must be created before it can be used by tasks and ISRs. Create event flags prior to starting µC/OS-III, or by a startup task in the application code.

F14-9(2)   Tasks or ISRs can post to event flags. In addition, only tasks can create, delete, and stop other task from pending on event flag groups.

F14-9(3)   A task can wait (i.e., pend) on any number of bits in an event flag group (i.e., a subset of all the bits). As with all µC/OS-III pend calls, the calling task can specify a timeout value such that if the desired bits are not posted within a specified amount of time (in ticks), the pending task is resumed and informed about the timeout.

F14-9(4)   The task can specify whether it wants to wait for "any" subset of bits (OR) to be set (or clear), or wait for "all" bits in a subset of bit (AND) to be set (or clear).

There are a number of operations to perform on event flags, as summarized in Table 14-3.

Table 14-3 **Event Flags API summary**

Function Name	Operation
OSFlagCreate()	Create an event flag group
OSFlagDel()	Delete an event flag group
OSFlagPend()	Pend (i.e., wait) on an event flag group
OSFlagPendAbort()	Abort waiting on an event flag group
OSFlagPendGetFlagsRdy()	Get flags that caused task to become ready
OSFlagPost()	Post flag(s) to an event flag group

14-3-1 USING EVENT FLAGS

When a task or an ISR posts to an event flag group, all tasks that have their wait conditions satisfied will be resumed.

It's up to the application to determine what each bit in an event flag group means and it is possible to use as many event flag groups as needed. In an event flag group you can, for example, define that bit #0 indicates that a temperature sensor is too low, bit #1 may indicate a low battery voltage, bit #2 could indicate that a switch was pressed, etc. The code (tasks or ISRs) that detects these conditions would set the appropriate event flag by calling **OSFlagPost()** and the task(s) that would respond to those conditions would call **OSFlagPend()**.

Listing 14-9 shows how to use event flags.

14

283

```
#define    TEMP_LOW   (OS_FLAGS)0x0001                          (1)
#define    BATT_LOW   (OS_FLAGS)0x0002
#define    SW_PRESSED (OS_FLAGS)0x0004

OS_FLAG_GRP  MyEventFlagGrp;                                     (2)

void main (void)
{
   OS_ERR  err;

   OSInit(&err);
   :
   OSFlagCreate(&MyEventFlagGrp,                                 (3)
             "My Event Flag Group",
             (OS_FLAGS)0,
             &err);
   /* Check 'err" */
   :
   OSStart(&err);
}


void  MyTask (void *p_arg)                                       (4)
{
   OS_ERR  err;
   CPU_TS  ts;

   while (DEF_ON) {
       OSFlagPend(&MyEventFlagGrp,                               (5)
             TEMP_LOW + BATT_LOW,
             (OS_TICK )0,
             (OS_OPT)OS_OPT_PEND_FLAG_SET_ANY,
             &ts,
             &err);
       /* Check 'err" */
       :
   }
}
```

```
void  MyISR (void)                                           (6)
{
    OS_ERR  err;
    :
    OSFlagPost(&MyEventFlagGrp,                               (7)
              BAT_LOW,
              (OS_OPT)OS_OPT_POST_FLAG_SET,
              &err);
    /* Check 'err" */
    :
}
```

Listing 14-9 **Using Event Flags**

L14-9(1)   Define some bits in the event flag group.

L14-9(2)   Declare an object of type **OS_FLAG_GRP**. This object will be referenced in all
            subsequent µC/OS-III calls that apply to this event flag group. For the sake of
            discussions, assume that event flags are declared to be 16-bits in **OS_TYPE.H**
            (i.e., of type **CPU_INT16U**).

L14-9(3)   Event flag groups must be "created" before they can be used. The best place to
            do this is in your startup code as it ensures that no tasks, or ISR, will be able to
            use the event flag group until µC/OS-III is started. In other words, the best
            place is to create the event flag group is in **main()**. In the example, the event
            flag was given a name and all bits start in their cleared state (i.e., all zeros).

L14-9(4)   Assume that the application created "**MyTask()**" which will be pending on the
            event flag group.

L14-9(5)   To pend on an event flag group, call **OSFlagPend()** and pass it the address of
            the desired event flag group.

            The second argument specifies which bits the task will be waiting to be set
            (assuming the task is triggered by set bits instead of cleared bits).

            Specify how long to wait for these bits to be set. A timeout value of zero (0)
            indicates that the task will wait forever. A non-zero value indicates the number
            of ticks the task will wait until it is resumed if the desired bits are not set.

Specifying **OS_OPT_FLAG_SET_ANY** indicates that the task will wake up if either of the two bits specified is set.

A timestamp is read and saved when the event flag group is posted to. This timestamp can be used to determine the response time to the event.

OSFlagPend() performs a number of checks on the arguments passed (i.e., did you pass **NULL** pointers, invalid options, etc.), and returns an error code based on the outcome of the call. If the call was successful "err" will be set to **OS_ERR_NONE**.

L14-9(6)   An ISR (it can also be a task) is setup to detect when the battery voltage of the product goes low (assuming the product is battery operated). The ISR signals the task, letting the task perform whatever corrective action is needed.

L14-9(7)   The desired event flag group is specified in the post call as well as which flag the ISR is setting. The third option specifies that the error condition will be "flagged" as a set bit. Again, the function sets "err" based on the outcome of the call.

Event flags are generally used for two purposes: status and transient events. Typically use different event flag groups to handle each of these as shown in Listing 14-10.

Tasks or ISRs can report status information such as a temperature that has exceeded a certain value, that RPM is zero on an engine or motor, or there is fuel in the tank, and more. This status information cannot be "consumed" by the tasks waiting for these events, because the status is managed by other tasks or ISRs. Event flags associated with status information are monitored by other task by using non-blocking wait calls.

Tasks will report transient events such as a switch was pressed, an object was detected by a motion sensor, an explosion occurred, etc. The task that responds to these events will typically block waiting for any of those events to occur and "consume" the event.

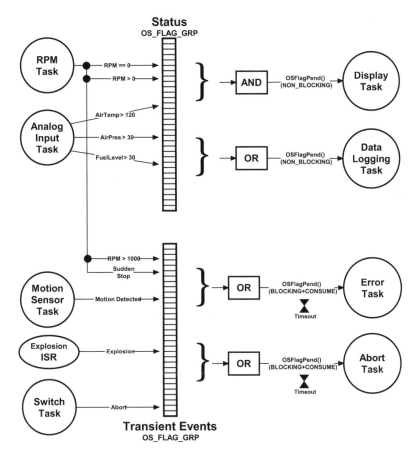

Figure 14-10 **Event Flags used for Status and Transient Events**

14-3-2 EVENT FLAGS INTERNALS

The application programmer can create an unlimited number of event flag groups (limited only by available RAM). Event flag services in µC/OS-III start with OSFlag and the services available to the application programmer are described in Appendix A, "µC/OS-III API Reference Manual" on page 383. Event flag services are enabled at compile time by setting the configuration constant OS_CFG_FLAG_EN to 1 in OS_CFG.H.

An event flag group is a kernel object as defined by the OS_FLAG_GRP data type, which is derived from the structure os_flag_grp (see OS.H) as shown in Listing 14-10.

The services provided by µC/OS-III to manage event flags are implemented in the file **OS_FLAG.C**. µC/OS-III licensees have access to the source code.

```
typedef  struct  os_flag_grp  OS_FLAG_GRP;      (1)


struct  os_flag_grp {
    OS_OBJ_TYPE           Type;                  (2)
    CPU_CHAR              *NamePtr;              (3)
    OS_PEND_LIST          PendList;             (4)
    OS_FLAGS              Flags;                (5)
    CPU_TS                TS;                   (6)
};
```

Listing 14-10 **OS_FLAG_GRP data type**

L14-10(1)   In µC/OS-III, all structures are given a data type. In fact, all data types start with "**OS_**" and are uppercase. When an event flag group is declared, simply use **OS_FLAG_GRP** as the data type of the variable used to declare the event flag group.

L14-10(2)   The structure starts with a "**Type**" field, which allows it to be recognized by µC/OS-III as an event flag group. In other words, other kernel objects will also have a "**Type**" as the first member of the structure. If a function is passed a kernel object, µC/OS-III will be able to confirm that it is being passed the proper data type. For example, if passing a message queue (**OS_Q**) to an event flag service (for example **OSFlagPend()**), µC/OS-III will be able to recognize that an invalid object was passed, and return an error code accordingly.

L14-10(3)   Each kernel object can be given a name to make them easier to be recognized by debuggers or µC/Probe. This member is simply a pointer to an ASCII string, which is assumed to be **NUL** terminated.

L14-10(4)   Because it is possible for multiple tasks to be waiting (or pending) on an event flag group, the event flag group object contains a pend list as described in Chapter 10, "Pend Lists (or Wait Lists)" on page 185.

14

L14-10(5)   An event flag group contains a series of flags (i.e., bits), and this member contains the current state of these flags. The flags can be implemented using either an 8-, 16- or 32-bit value depending on how the data type **OS_FLAGS** is declared in **OS_TYPE.H**.

L14-10(6)   An event flag group contains a timestamp used to indicate the last time the event flag group was posted to. µC/OS-III assumes the presence of a free-running counter that allows users to make time measurements. When the event flag group is posted to, the free-running counter is read and the value is placed in this field, which is returned when **OSFlagPend()** is called. This value allows an application to determine either when the post was performed, or how long it took for your the to obtain control of the CPU from the post. In the latter case, call **OS_TS_GET()** to determine the current timestamp and compute the difference.

Even if the user understands the internals of the **OS_FLAG_GRP** data type, application code should never access any of the fields in this data structure directly. Instead, always use the APIs provided with µC/OS-III.

Event flag groups must be created before they can be used by an application as shown in Listing 14-11.

```
OS_FLAG_GRP  MyEventFlagGrp;              (1)


void  MyCode (void)
{
    OS_ERR  err;
    :
    OSFlagCreate(&MyEventFlagGrp,         (2)
             "My Event Flag Group",       (3)
             (OS_FLAGS)0,                 (4)
             &err);                       (5)
    /* Check 'err" */
    :
}
```

Listing 14-11 **Creating a Event Flag Group**

L14-11(1)   The application must declare a variable of type **OS_FLAG_GRP**. This variable will be referenced by other event flag services.

L14-11(2)   Create an event flag group by calling **OSFlagCreate()** and pass the address to the event flag group allocated in (1).

L14-11(3)   Assign an ASCII name to the event flag group, which can be used by debuggers or µC/Probe to easily identify this event flag group. µC/OS-III stores a pointer to the name so there is no practical limit to its size, except that the ASCII string needs to be **NUL** terminated.

L14-11(4)   Initialize the flags inside the event flag group to zero (0) unless the task and ISRs signal events with bits cleared instead of bits set. If using cleared bits, initialize all the bits to ones (1).

L14-11(5)   **OSFlagCreate()** returns an error code based on the outcome of the call. If all the arguments are valid, err will contain **OS_ERR_NONE**.

A task waits for one or more event flag bits either from an ISR or another task by calling **OSFlagPend()** as shown in Listing 14-12 (see Appendix A, "µC/OS-III API Reference Manual" on page 383 for details regarding the arguments).

```
OS_FLAG_GRP  MyEventFlagGrp;


void MyTask (void *p_arg)
{
    OS_ERR  err;
    CPU_TS  ts;
    :
    while (DEF_ON) {
        :
        OSFlagPend(&MyEventFlagGrp,            /* (1) Pointer to event flag group     */
                    (OS_FLAGS)0x0F,            /*     Which bits to wait on            */
                    10,                        /*     Maximum time to wait             */
                    OS_OPT_PEND_BLOCKING +
                    OS_OPT_PEND_FLAG_SET_ANY,  /*     Option(s)                       */
                    &ts,                       /*     Timestamp of when posted to      */
                    &err);                     /*     Pointer to Error returned        */
        /* Check "err"                              (2)                                */
        :
        :
    }
}
```

Listing 14-12 **Pending (or waiting) on an Event Flag Group**

L14-12(1)   When called, **OSFlagPend()** starts by checking the arguments passed to this function to ensure they have valid values. If the bits the task is waiting for are set (or cleared depending on the option), **OSFlagPend()** returns and indicate which flags satisfied the condition. This is the outcome that the caller expects.

If the event flag group does not contain the flags that the caller is looking for, the calling task might need to wait for the desired flags to be set (or cleared). If specifying **OS_OPT_PEND_NON_BLOCKING** as the option (the task is not to block), **OSFlagPend()** returns immediately to the caller and the returned error code indicates that the bits have not been set (or cleared).

If specifying **OS_OPT_PEND_BLOCKING** as the option, the calling task will be inserted in the list of tasks waiting for the desired event flag bits. The task is not inserted in priority order but simply inserted at the beginning of the list. This is done because whenever bits are set (or cleared), it is necessary to examine all tasks in this list to see if their desired bits have been satisfied.

If further specifying a non-zero timeout, the task will also be inserted in the tick list. A zero value for a timeout indicates that the calling task is willing to wait forever for the desired bits.

The scheduler is then called since the current task is no longer able to run (it is waiting for the desired bits). The scheduler will run the next highest-priority task that is ready to run.

When the event flag group is posted to and the task that called **OSFlagPend()** has its desired bits set or cleared, a task status is examined to determine the reason why **OSFlagPend()** is returning to its caller. The possibilities are:

1) The desired bits were set (or cleared)

2) The pend was aborted by another task

3) The bits were not set (or cleared) within the specified timeout

4) The event flag group was deleted

When **OSFlagPend()** returns, the caller is notified of the above outcome through an appropriate error code.

L14-12(2)   If **OSFlagPend()** returns with err set to **OS_ERR_NONE**, assume that the desired bits were set (or cleared) and the task can proceed with servicing the ISR or task that created those events. If err contains anything else, **OSFlagPend()** either timed out (if the timeout argument was non-zero), the pend was aborted by another task or, the event flag group was deleted by another task. It is always important to examine the returned error code and not assume everything went as planned.

To set (or clear) event flags (either from an ISR or a task), simply call **OSFlagPost()**, as shown in Listing 14-13.

```
OS_FLAG_GRP  MyEventFlagGrp;

void MyISR (void)
{
    OS_ERR  err;
    :
    OSFlagPost(&MyEventFlagGrp,        (1)
                (OS_FLAGS)0x0C,         (2)
                OS_OPT_POST_FLAG_SET,   (3)
                &err);                  (4)
    /* Check 'err" */
    :
    :
}
```

Listing 14-13 **Posting flags to an Event Flag Group**

L14-13(1) A task posts to the event flag group by calling **OSFlagPost()**. Specify the desired event flag group to post by passing its address. Of course, the event flag group must have been previously created.

L14-13(2) The next argument specifies which bit(s) the ISR (or task) will be setting or clearing in the event flag group.

L14-13(3) Specify **OS_OPT_POST_FLAG_SET** or **OS_OPT_POST_FLAG_CLR**.

If specifying **OS_OPT_POST_FLAG_SET**, the bits specified in the second arguments will set the corresponding bits in the event flag group. For example, if **MyEventFlagGrp.Flags** contains 0x03, the code in Listing 14-13 will change **MyEventFlagGrp.Flags** to 0x0F.

If specifying **OS_OPT_POST_FLAG_CLR**, the bits specified in the second arguments will clear the corresponding bits in the event flag group. For example, if **MyEventFlagGrp.Flags** contains 0x0F, the code in Listing 14-13 will change **MyEventFlagGrp.Flags** to 0x03.

14

293

When calling **OSFlagPost()** specify as an option (i.e., **OS_OPT_POST_NO_SCHED**) to not call the scheduler. This means that the post is performed, but the scheduler is not called even if a higher-priority task was waiting for the event flag group. This allows the calling task to perform other post functions (if needed) and make all the posts take effect simultaneously.

L14-13(4)   **OSFlagPost()** returns an error code based on the outcome of the call. If the call was successful, err will contain **OS_ERR_NONE**. If not, the error code will indicate the reason of the error (see Appendix A, "µC/OS-III API Reference Manual" on page 383 for a list of possible error codes for **OSFlagPost()**.

14-4 SYNCHRONIZING MULTIPLE TASKS

Synchronizing the execution of multiple tasks by broadcasting to a semaphore is a commonly used technique. It may be important to have multiple tasks start executing at the same time. Obviously, on a single processor, only one task will actually execute at one time. However, the start of their execution will be synchronized to the same time. This is called a multiple task rendezvous. However, some of the tasks synchronized might not be waiting for the semaphore when the broadcast is performed. It is fairly easy to resolve this problem by combining semaphores and event flags, as shown in Figure 14-11. For this to work properly, the task on the left needs to have a lower priority than the tasks waiting on the semaphore.

Figure 14-11 **Multiple Task Rendezvous**

F14-11(1)   Each task that needs to synchronize at the rendezvous needs to set an event flag bit (and specify OS_OPT_POST_NO_SCHED).

F14-11(2)   The task needs to wait for the semaphore to be signaled.

F14-11(3)   The task that will be broadcasting must wait for "all" of the event flags corresponding to each task to be set.

F14-11(4)   When all waiting tasks are ready, the task that will synchronize the waiting task issues a broadcast to the semaphore.

14-5 SUMMARY

Three methods are presented to allow an ISR or a task to signal one or more tasks: semaphores, task semaphores, and event flags.

Both semaphores and task semaphores contain a counter allowing them to perform credit tracking and accumulate the occurrence of events. If an ISR or task needs to signal a single task (as opposed to multiple tasks when the event occurs), it makes sense to use a task semaphore since it prevents the user from having to declare an external semaphore object. Also, task semaphore services are slightly faster (in execution time) than semaphores.

Event flags are used when a task needs to synchronize with the occurrence of one or more events. However, event flags cannot perform credit tracking since a single bit (as opposed to a counter) represents each event.

14

15

Message Passing

It is sometimes necessary for a task or an ISR to communicate information to another task. This information transfer is called *inter-task* communication. Information can be communicated between tasks in two ways: through global data, or by sending messages.

As seen in Chapter 13, "Resource Management" on page 217, when using global variables, each task or ISR must ensure that it has exclusive access to variables. If an ISR is involved, the only way to ensure exclusive access to common variables is to disable interrupts. If two tasks share data, each can gain exclusive access to variables either by disabling interrupts, locking the scheduler, using a semaphore, or preferably, using a mutual-exclusion semaphore. Note that a task can only communicate information to an ISR by using global variables. A task is not aware when a global variable is changed by an ISR, unless the ISR signals the task, or the task polls the contents of a variable periodically.

Messages can either be sent to an intermediate object called a *message queue*, or directly to a task since in µC/OS-III, each task has its own built-in message queue. Use an external message queue if multiple tasks are to wait for messages. Send a message directly to a task if only one task will process the data received.

When a task waits for a message to arrive, it does not consume CPU time.

15-1 MESSAGES

A message consists of a pointer to data, a variable containing the size of the data being pointed to, and a timestamp indicating when the message was sent. The pointer can point to a data area or even a function. Obviously, the sender and the receiver must agree as to the contents and the meaning of the message. In other words, the receiver of the message will know the meaning of the message received to be able to process it. For example, an Ethernet controller receives a packet and sends a pointer to this packet to a task that knows how to handle the packet.

The message contents must always remain in scope since the data is actually sent by reference instead of by value. In other words, data sent is not copied. Consider using dynamically allocated memory as described in Chapter 17, "Memory Management" on page 331. Alternatively, pass pointers to a global variable, a global data structure, a global array, or a function, etc.

15-2 MESSAGE QUEUES

A message queue is a kernel object allocated by the application. In fact, you can allocate any number of message queues. The only limit is the amount of RAM available.

There are a number of operations that the user can perform on message queues, summarized in Figure 15-1. However, an ISR can only call OSQPost(). A message queue must be created before sending messages through it.

Figure 15-1 **Operations on message queue**

Message queues are drawn as a first-in, first-out pipe (FIFO). However, with µC/OS-III, it is possible to post messages in last-in, first-out order (LIFO). The LIFO mechanism is useful when a task or an ISR must send an "urgent" message to a task. In this case, the message bypasses all other messages already in the message queue. The size of the message queue is configurable at run time.

The small hourglass close to the receiving task indicates that the task has an option to specify a timeout. This timeout indicates that the task is willing to wait for a message to be sent to the message queue within a certain amount of time. If the message is not sent within that time, µC/OS-III resumes the task and returns an error code indicating that the task was made ready to run because of a timeout, and not because the message was received. It is possible to specify an infinite timeout and indicate that the task is willing to wait forever for the message to arrive.

The message queue also contains a list of tasks waiting for messages to be sent to the message queue. Multiple tasks can wait on a message queue as shown in Figure 15-2. When a message is sent to the message queue, the highest priority task waiting on the message queue receives the message. Optionally, the sender can *broadcast* a message to all tasks waiting on the message queue. In this case, if any of the tasks receiving the message from the broadcast has a higher priority than the task sending the message (or interrupted task, if the message is sent by an ISR), µC/OS-III will run the highest-priority task that is waiting. Notice that not all tasks must specify a timeout; some tasks may want to wait forever.

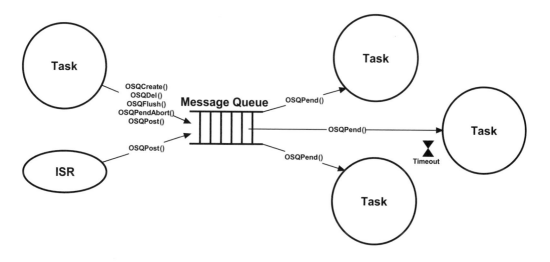

Figure 15-2 **Multiple tasks waiting on a message queue**

15-3 TASK MESSAGE QUEUE

It is fairly rare to find applications where multiple tasks wait on a single message queue. Because of this, a message queue is built into each task and the user can send messages directly to a task without going through an external message queue object. This feature not only simplifies the code but, is also more efficient than using a separate message queue object. The message queue that is built into each task is shown in Figure 15-3.

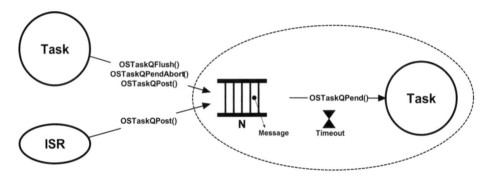

Figure 15-3 **Task message queue**

Task message queue services in µC/OS-III start with the **OSTaskQ???()** prefix, and services available to the application programmer are described in Appendix A, "µC/OS-III API Reference Manual" on page 383. Setting **OS_CFG_TASK_EN** in **OS_CFG.H** enables task message queue services. The code for task message queue management is found in **OS_TASK.C**.

Use this feature if the code knows which task to send the message(s) to. For example, if receiving an interrupt from an Ethernet controller, send the address of the received packet to the task that will be responsible for processing the received packet.

15-4 BILATERAL RENDEZVOUS

Two tasks can synchronize their activities by using two message queues, as shown in Figure 15-4. This is called a *bilateral rendezvous* and works the same as with semaphores except that both tasks may send messages to each other. A bilateral rendezvous cannot be performed between a task and an ISR since an ISR cannot wait on a message queue.

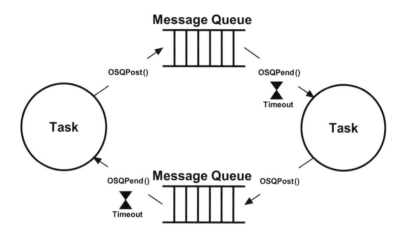

Figure 15-4 **Bilateral Rendezvous**

15

In a bilateral rendezvous, each message queue holds a maximum of one message. Both message queues are initially created empty. When the task on the left reaches the rendezvous point, it sends a message to the top message queue and waits for a message to arrive on the bottom message queue. Similarly, when the task on the right reaches its rendezvous point, it sends a message to the message queue on the bottom and waits for a message to arrive on the top message queue.

Figure 15-5 shows how to use task-message queues to perform a bilateral rendezvous.

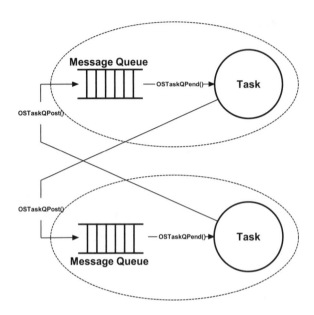

Figure 15-5 **Figure Bilateral Rendezvous with task message queues**

15-5 FLOW CONTROL

Task-to-task communication often involves data transfer from one task to another. One task produces data while the other *consumes* it. However, data processing takes time and consumers might not consume data as fast as it is produced. In other words, it is possible for the producer to overflow the message queue if a higher-priority task preempts the consumer. One way to solve this problem is to add flow control in the process as shown in Figure 15-6.

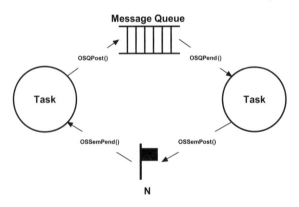

Figure 15-6 **Producer and consumer tasks with flow control**

Here, a counting semaphore is used, initialized with the number of allowable messages that can be sent by the consumer. If the consumer cannot queue more than 10 messages, the counting semaphore contains a count of 10.

As shown in the pseudo code of Listing 15-1, the producer must wait on the semaphore before it is allowed to send a message. The consumer waits for messages and, when processed, signals the semaphore.

```
Producer Task:
Pend on Semaphore;
Send message to message queue;

Consumer Task:
Wait for message from message queue;
Signal the semaphore;
```

Listing 15-1 **Producer and consumer flow control**

Combining the task message queue and task semaphores (see Chapter 14, "Synchronization" on page 259), it is easy to implement flow control as shown in Figure 15-7. In this case, however, **OSTaskSemSet()** must be called immediately after creating the task to set the value of the task semaphore to the same value as the maximum number of allowable messages in the task message queue.

15

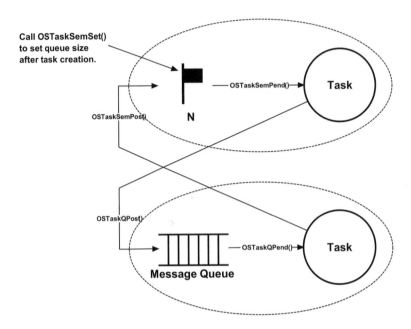

Call OSTaskSemSet()
to set queue size
after task creation.

OSTaskSemPend()→ **Task**

OSTaskSemPost()

N

OSTaskQPost()

OSTaskQPend()→ **Task**

Message Queue

Figure 15-7 **Flow control with task semaphore and task message queue**

15

15-6 KEEPING THE DATA IN SCOPE

The messages sent typically point to data structures, variables, arrays, tables, etc. However, it is important to realize that the data must remain static until the receiver of the data completes its processing of the data. Once sent, the sender must not touch the sent data. This seems obvious, however it is easy to forget.

One possibility is to use the fixed-size memory partition manager provided with µC/OS-III (see Chapter 17, "Memory Management" on page 331) to dynamically allocate and free memory blocks used to pass the data. Figure 15-8 shows an example. For sake of illustration, assume that a device is sending data bytes to the UART in packets using a protocol. In this case, the first byte of a packet is unique and the end-of-packet byte is also unique.

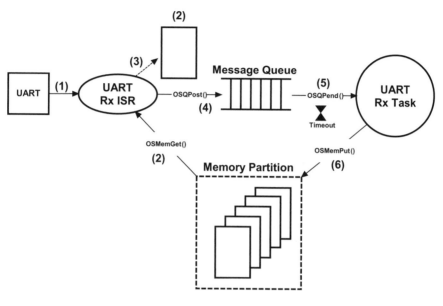

Figure 15-8 **Using memory partitions for message contents**

F15-8(1)   Here, a UART generates an interrupt when characters are received.

F15-8(2)   The pseudo-code in Listing 15-2 shows what the UART ISR code might look like. There are a lot of details omitted for sake of simplicity. The ISR reads the byte received from the UART and sees if it corresponds to a start of packet. If it is, a buffer is obtained from the memory partition.

F15-8(3)   The received byte is then placed in the buffer.

F15-8(4)   If the data received is an end-of-packet byte, simply post the address of the buffer to the message queue so that the task can process the received packet.

F15-8(5)   If the message sent makes the UART task the highest priority task, µC/OS-III will switch to that task at the end of the ISR instead of returning to the interrupted task. The task retrieves the packet from the message queue. Note that the OSQPend() call also returns the number of bytes in the packet and a time stamp indicating when the message was sent.

F15-8(6)   When the task is finished processing the packet, the buffer is returned to the memory partition it came from by calling OSMemPut().

15

```
void  UART_ISR (void)
{
    OS_ERR  err;


    RxData = Read byte from UART;
    if (RxData == Start of Packet) {            /* See if we need a new buffer    */
        RxDataPtr = OSMemGet(&UART_MemPool,     /* Yes                            */
                        &err);
        RxDataCtr = 0;
    } else {
        RxDataCtr++;                            /* Update number of bytes received */
    }
    if (RxData == End of Packet byte) {         /* See if we got a full packet    */
        OSQPost((OS_Q       *)&UART_Q,          /* Yes, post to task for processing */
                (void       *)RxDataPtr,
                (OS_MSG_SIZE)RxDataCtr,
                (OS_OPT     )OS_OPT_POST_FIFO,
                (OS_ERR     *)&err);
        RxDataPtr = NULL;                       /* Don't point to sent buffer     */
        RxDataCtr = 0;
    } else; {
        *RxDataPtr++ = RxData;                  /* Save the byte received         */
    }
}
```

Listing 15-2 **UART ISR Pseudo-code**

15-7 USING MESSAGE QUEUES

Table 15-1 shows a summary of message-queue services available from μC/OS-III. Refer to Appendix A, "μC/OS-III API Reference Manual" on page 383 for a full description on their use.

Function Name	Operation
OSQCreate()	Create a message queue.
OSQDel()	Delete a message queue.
OSQFlush()	Empty the message queue.
OSQPend()	Wait for a message.
OSQPendAbort()	Abort waiting for a message.
OSQPost()	Send a message through a message queue.

Table 15-1 **Message queue API summary**

Table 15-2 is a summary of task message queue services available from μC/OS-III. Refer to Appendix A, "μC/OS-III API Reference Manual" on page 383, for a full description on how to their use.

Function Name	Operation
OSTaskQPend()	Wait for a message.
OSTaskQPendAbort()	Abort the wait for a message.
OSTaskQPost()	Send a message to a task.
OSTaskQFlush()	Empty the message queue.

Table 15-2 **Task message queue API summary**

15

Figure 15-9 shows an example of using a message queue when determining the speed of a rotating wheel.

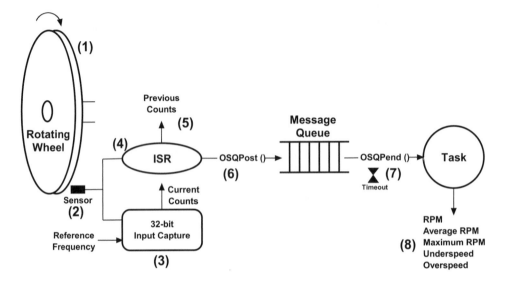

Figure 15-9 **Measuring RPM**

F15-9(1)   The goal is to measure the RPM of a rotating wheel.

F15-9(2)   A sensor is used to detect the passage of a hole in the wheel. In fact, to receive additional resolution, the wheel could contain multiple holes that are equally spaced.

F15-9(3)   A 32-bit input capture register is used to capture the value of a free-running counter when the hole is detected.

F15-9(4)   An interrupt is generated when the hole is detected. The ISR reads the current count of the input capture register and subtracts the value of the previous capture to receive the time it took for one rotation (assuming only a single hole).

```
Delta Counts    = Current Counts - Previous Counts;
Previous Counts = Current Counts;
```

F15-9(5)   The delta counts are sent to a message queue. Since a message is actually a pointer, if the pointer is 32-bits wide on the processor in use, simply cast the 32-bit delta counts to a pointer and send this through the message queue. A safer and more portable approach is to dynamically allocate storage to hold the delta counts using a memory block from µC/OS-III's memory management services (see Chapter 17, "Memory Management" on page 331) and send the address of the allocated memory block.

F15-9(6)   When the message is sent, the RPM measurement task wakes up and computes the RPM as follows:

```
RPM = 60 * Reference Frequency / Delta Counts;
```

The user may specify a timeout on the pend call and the task will wake up if a message is not sent within the timeout period. This allows the user to easily detect that the wheel is not rotating and therefore, the RPM is 0.

F15-9(7)   Along with computing RPM, the task can also compute average RPM, maximum RPM, and whether the speed is above or below thresholds, etc.

A few interesting things are worth noting about the above example. First, the ISR is very short; read the input capture and post the delta counts to the task to accomplish the time-consuming math. Second, with the timeout on the pend, it is easy to detect that the wheel is stopped. Finally, the task can perform additional calculations and can further detect such errors as the wheel spinning too fast or too slow. In fact, the task can notify other tasks about these errors, if needed.

Listing 15-3 shows how to implement the RPM measurement example using µC/OS-III's message queue services. Some of the code is pseudo-code, while the calls to µC/OS-III services are actual calls with their appropriate arguments.

15

```
OS_Q       RPM_Q;                                              (1)
CPU_INT32U DeltaCounts;
CPU_INT32U CurrentCounts;
CPU_INT32U PreviousCounts;


void main (void)
{
    OS_ERR  err ;
    :
    OSInit(&err) ;                                             (2)
    :
    OSQCreate((OS_Q     *)&RPM_Q,
              (CPU_CHAR *)"My Queue",
              (OS_MSG_QTY)10,
              (OS_ERR   *)&err);
    :
    OSStart(&err);
}


void RPM_ISR (void)                                            (3)
{
    OS_ERR  err;


    Clear the interrupt from the sensor;
    CurrentCounts  = Read the input capture;
    DeltaCounts    = CurrentCounts − PreviousCounts;
    PreviousCounts = CurrentCounts;
    OSQPost((OS_Q      *)&RPM_Q,                               (4)
            (void      *)DeltaCounts,
            (OS_MSG_SIZE)sizeof(void *),
            (OS_OPT     )OS_OPT_POST_FIFO,
            (OS_ERR    *)&err);
}
```

15

```
void RPM_Task (void *p_arg)
{
    CPU_INT32U   delta;
    OS_ERR       err;
    OS_MSG_SIZE  size;
    CPU_TS       ts;


    DeltaCounts    = 0;
    PreviousCounts = 0;
    CurrentCounts  = 0;
    while (DEF_ON) {
        delta = (CPU_INT32U)OSQPend((OS_Q        *)&RPM_Q,            (5)
                                    (OS_TICK      )OS_CFG_TICK_RATE * 10,
                                    (OS_OPT       )OS_OPT_PEND_BLOCKING,
                                    (OS_MSG_SIZE *)&size,
                                    (CPU_TS      *)&ts,
                                    (OS_ERR      *)&err);
        if (err == OS_ERR_TIMEOUT) {                                 (6)
            RPM = 0;
        } else {
            if (delta > 0u) {
                RPM = 60 * Reference Frequency / delta;              (7)
            }
        }
        Compute average RPM;                                         (8)
        Detect maximum RPM;
        Check for overspeed;
        Check for underspeed;
        :
        :
    }
}
```

Listing 15-3 **Pseudo-code of RPM measurement**

L15-3(1)   Variables are declared. Notice that it is necessary to allocate storage for the message queue itself.

L15-3(2)   Call **OSInit()** and create the message queue before it is used. The best place to do this is in startup code.

L15-3(3)   The RPM ISR clears the sensor interrupt and reads the value of the 32-bit input capture. Note that it is possible to read RPM if there is only a 16-bit input capture. The problem with a 16-bit input capture is that it is easy for it to overflow, especially at low RPMs.

The RPM ISR also computes delta counts directly in the ISR. It is just as easy to post the current counts and let the task compute the delta. However, the subtraction is a fast operation and does not significantly increase ISR processing time.

L15-3(4)   Send the delta counts to the RPM task, responsible for computing the RPM and perform additional computations. Note that the message gets lost if the queue is full when the user attempts to post. This happens if data is generated faster than it is processed. Unfortunately, it is not possible to implement flow control in the example because it is dealing with an ISR.

L15-3(5)   The RPM task starts by waiting for a message from the RPM ISR by pending on the message queue. The third argument specifies the timeout. In this case, ten seconds worth of timeout is specified. However, the value chosen depends on the requirements of an application.

Also notice that the ts variable contains the timestamp of when the post was completed. Determine the time it took for the task to respond to the message received by calling **OS_TS_GET( )**, and subtract the value of **ts**:

```
response_time = OS_TS_GET() - ts;
```

L15-3(6)   If a timeout occurs, assume the wheel is no longer spinning.

L15-3(7)   The RPM is computed from the delta counts received, and from the reference frequency of the free-running counter.

L15-3(8)   Additional computations are performed as needed. In fact, messages can be sent to different tasks in case error conditions are detected. The messages would be processed by the other tasks. For example, if the wheel spins too fast, another task can initiate a shutdown on the device that is controlling the wheel speed.

15

In Listing 15-4, **OSQPost()** and **OSQPend()** are replaced with **OSTaskQPost()** and **OSTaskQPend()** for the RPM measurement example. Notice that the code is slightly simpler to use and does not require creating a separate message queue object. However, when creating the RPM task, it is important to specify the size of the message queue used by the task and compile the application code with **OS_CFG_TASK_Q_EN** set to 1. The differences between using message queues and the task's message queue will be explained.

```
OS_TCB        RPM_TCB;                                          (1)
OS_STK        RPM_Stk[1000];
CPU_INT32U    DeltaCounts ;
CPU_INT32U    CurrentCounts ;
CPU_INT32U    PreviousCounts ;


void main (void)
{
    OS_ERR  err ;
    :
    OSInit(&err) ;
    :
    void  OSTaskCreate ((OS_TCB       *)&RPM_TCB,               (2)
                        (CPU_CHAR     *)"RPM Task",
                        (OS_TASK_PTR  )RPM_Task,
                        (void         *)0,
                        (OS_PRIO      )10,
                        (CPU_STK      *)&RPM_Stk[0],
                        (CPU_STK_SIZE )100,
                        (CPU_STK_SIZE )1000,
                        (OS_MSG_QTY   )10,
                        (OS_TICK      )0,
                        (void         *)0,
                        (OS_OPT       )(OS_OPT_TASK_STK_CHK + OS_OPT_TASK_STK_CLR),
                        (OS_ERR       *)&err);
    :
    OSStart(&err);
}
```

15

```
void RPM_ISR (void)
{
    OS_ERR  err;

    Clear the interrupting from the sensor;
    CurrentCounts  = Read the input capture;
    DeltaCounts    = CurrentCounts - PreviousCounts;
    PreviousCounts = CurrentCounts;
    OSTaskQPost((OS_TCB     *)&RPM_TCB,                                   (3)
                (void       *)DeltaCounts,
                (OS_MSG_SIZE)sizeof(DeltaCounts),
                (OS_OPT     )OS_OPT_POST_FIFO,
                (OS_ERR     *)&err);
}

void RPM_Task (void *p_arg)
{
    CPU_INT32U   delta;
    OS_ERR       err;
    OS_MSG_SIZE  size;
    CPU_TS       ts;


    DeltaCounts   = 0;
    PreviousCounts = 0;
    CurrentCounts = 0;
    while (DEF_ON) {
        delta = (CPU_INT32U)OSTaskQPend((OS_TICK      )OS_CFG_TICK_RATE * 10,  (4)
                                        (OS_OPT      )OS_OPT_PEND_BLOCKING,
                                        (OS_MSG_SIZE *)&size,
                                        (CPU_TS      *)&ts,
                                        (OS_ERR      *)&err);
        if (err == OS_ERR_TIMEOUT) {
            RPM = 0;
        } else {
            if (delta > 0u) {
                RPM = 60 * ReferenceFrequency / delta;
            }
        }
        Compute average RPM;
        Detect maximum RPM;
        Check for overspeed;
        Check for underspeed;
        :
        :
    }
}
```

Listing 15-4 **Pseudo-code of RPM measurement**

15

L15-4(1)   Instead of declaring a message queue, it is important to know the **OS_TCB** of the task that will be receiving messages.

L15-4(2)   The RPM task is created and a queue size of 10 entries is specified. Of course, hard-coded values should not be specified in a real application, but instead, use **#defines**. Fixed numbers are used here for sake of illustration.

L15-4(3)   Instead of posting to a message queue, the ISR posts the message directly to the task, specifying the address of the **OS_TCB** of the task. This is known since the **OS_TCB** is allocated when creating the task.

L15-4(4)   The RPM task starts by waiting for a message from the RPM ISR by calling **OSTaskQPend()**. This is an inherent call so it is not necessary to specify the address of the **OS_TCB** to pend on as the current task is assumed. The second argument specifies the timeout. Here, ten seconds worth of timeout is specified, which corresponds to 6 RPM.

15-8 CLIENTS AND SERVERS

Another interesting use of message queues is shown in Figure 15-10. Here, a task (the server) is used to monitor error conditions that are sent to it by other tasks or ISRs (clients). For example, a client detects whether the RPM of the rotating wheel has been exceeded, another client detects whether an over-temperature exists, and yet another client detects that a user pressed a shutdown button. When the clients detect error conditions, they send a message through the message queue. The message sent indicates the error detected, which threshold was exceeded, the error code that is associated with error conditions, or even suggests the address of a function that will handle the error, and more.

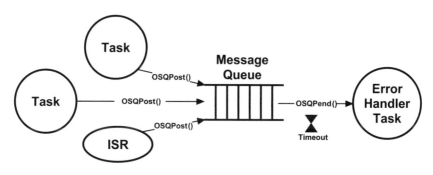

Figure 15-10 **Clients and Servers**

15-9 MESSAGE QUEUES INTERNALS

As previously described, a message consists of a pointer to actual data, a variable indicating the size of the data being pointed to and a timestamp indicating when the message was actually sent. When sent, a message is placed in a data structure of type OS_MSG, shown in Figure 15-11.

The sender and receiver are unaware of this data structure since everything is hidden through the APIs provided by µC/OS-III.

Figure 15-11 **OS_MSG structure**

µC/OS-III maintains a pool of free OS_MSGs. The total number of available messages in the pool is determined by the value of OS_CFG_MSG_POOL_SIZE found in OS_CFG_APP.H. When µC/OS-III is initialized, OS_MSGs are linked in a single linked list as shown in Figure 15-12. Notice that the free list is maintained by a data structure of type OS_MSG_POOL, which contains three fields: .NextPtr, which points to the free list; .NbrFree, which contains the number of free OS_MSGs in the pool; and finally .NbrUsed, which contains the number of OS_MSGs allocated to application.

Figure 15-12 **Pool of free OS_MSGs**

Messages are queued using a data structure of type **OS_MSG_Q**, as shown in Figure 15-13.

Figure 15-13 **OS_MSG_Q structure**

.InPtr   This field contains a pointer to where the next **OS_MSG** will be inserted in the queue. In fact, the **OS_MSG** will be inserted "after" the **OS_MSG** pointed to.

.OutPtr   This field contains a pointer to where the next **OS_MSG** will be extracted.

.NbrEntriesSize   This field contains the maximum number of **OS_MSGs** that the queue will hold. If an application attempts to send a message and the **.NbrEntries** matches this value, the queue is considered to be full and the **OS_MSG** will not be inserted.

.NbrEntries   This field contains the current number of **OS_MSGs** in the queue.

.NbrEntriesMax   This field contains the highest number of **OS_MSGs** existing in the queue at any given time.

A number of internal functions are used by µC/OS-III to manipulate the free list and messages. Specifically, **OS_MsgQPut()** inserts an **OS_MSG** in an **OS_MSG_Q**, **OS_MsgQGet()** extracts an **OS_MSG** from an **OS_MSG_Q**, and **OS_MsgQFreeAll()** returns all **OS_MSGs** in an **OS_MSG_Q** to the pool of free **OS_MSGs**. There are other **OS_MsgQ??()** functions in **OS_MSG.C** that are used during initialization.

15

Figure 15-14 shows an example of an OS_MSG_Q when four OS_MSGs are inserted.

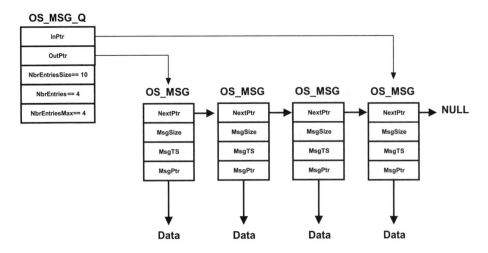

Figure 15-14 **OS_MSG_Q with four OS_MSGs**

OS_MSG_Qs are used inside two additional data structures: OS_Q and OS_TCB. Recall that an OS_Q is declared when creating a message queue object. An OS_TCB is a task control block and, as previously mentioned, each OS_TCB can have its own message queue when the configuration constant OS_CFG_TASK_Q_EN is set to 1 in OS_CFG.H. Figure 15-15 shows the contents of an OS_Q and partial contents of an OS_TCB containing an OS_MSG_Q. The OS_MSG_Q data structure is shown as an "exploded view" to emphasize the structure within the structure.

Figure 15-15 **OS_Q and OS_TCB each contain an OS_MSG_Q**

15-10 SUMMARY

Message queues are useful when a task or an ISR is to send data to another task. The data sent must remain in scope as it is actually sent by reference instead of by value. In other words, the data sent is not copied.

The task waiting for the data will not consume CPU time while waiting for a message to be sent to it.

If it is known which task is responsible for servicing messages sent by producers, use task message queue (i.e., **OSTaskQ???( )**) services since they are simple and fast. Task message queue services are enabled when **OS_CFG_TASK_Q_EN** is set to 1 in **OS_CFG.H**.

If multiple tasks must wait for messages from the same message queue, allocate an **OS_Q** and have the tasks wait for messages to be sent to the queue. Alternatively, broadcast special messages to all tasks waiting on a message queue. Regular message queue services are enabled when **OS_CFG_Q_EN** is set to 1 in **OS_CFG.H**.

Messages are sent using an **OS_MSG** data structure obtained by µC/OS-III from a pool. Set the maximum number of messages that can be sent to a message queue, or as many messages as are available in the pool.

15

15

Pending On Multiple Objects

In Chapter 10, "Pend Lists (or Wait Lists)" on page 185 we saw how multiple tasks can pend (or wait) on a single kernel object such as a semaphore, mutual exclusion semaphore, event flag group, or message queue. In this chapter, we will see how tasks can pend on multiple objects. However, µC/OS-III only allows for pend on multiple semaphores and/or message queues. In other words, it is not possible to pend on multiple event flag groups or mutual exclusion semaphores.

As shown in Figure 16-1, a task can pend on any number of semaphores or message queues at the same time. The first semaphore or message queue posted will make the task ready to run and compete for CPU time with other tasks in the ready list. As shown, a task pends on multiple objects by calling **OSPendMulti()** and specifies an optional timeout value. The timeout applies to all of the objects. If none of the objects are posted within the specified timeout, the task resumes with an error code indicating that the pend timed out.

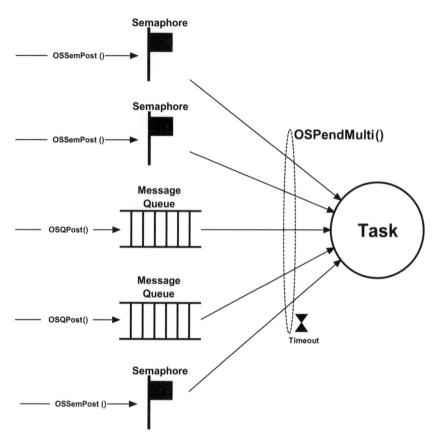

Figure 16-1 **Task pending on multiple objects**

Listing 16-1 shows the function prototype of **OSPendMulti()** and Figure 16-2 exhibits an array of **OS_PEND_DATA** elements.

```
OS_OBJ_QTY  OSPendMulti (OS_PEND_DATA  *p_pend_data_tbl,        (1)
                         OS_OBJ_QTY    tbl_size,                (2)
                         OS_TICK       timeout,                 (3)
                         OS_OPT        opt,                     (4)
                         OS_ERR        *p_err);                 (5)
```

Listing 16-1 **OSPendMulti() prototype**

Figure 16-2 **Array of OS_PEND_DATA**

16

L16-1(1)   **OSPendMulti()** is passed an array of **OS_PEND_DATA** elements. The caller must instantiate an array of **OS_PEND_DATA**. The size of the array depends on the total number of kernel objects that the task wants to pend on. For example, if the task wants to pend on three semaphores and two message queues then the array contains five **OS_PEND_DATA** elements as shown below:

```
OS_PEND_DATA   my_pend_multi_tbl[5];
```

The calling task needs to initialize the **.PendObjPtr** of each element of the array to point to each of the objects to be pended on. For example:

```
OS_SEM  MySem1;
OS_SEM  MySem2;
OS_SEM  MySem3;
OS_Q    MyQ1;
OS_Q    MyQ2;


void  MyTask (void)
{
    OS_ERR          err;
    OS_PEND_DATA  my_pend_multi_tbl[5];
    :
    while (DEF_ON) {
        :
        my_pend_multi_tbl[0].PendObjPtr = (OS_PEND_OBJ)&MySem1;       (6)
        my_pend_multi_tbl[1].PendObjPtr = (OS_PEND_OBJ)&MySem2;
        my_pend_multi_tbl[2].PendObjPtr = (OS_PEND_OBJ)&MySem3;
        my_pend_multi_tbl[3].PendObjPtr = (OS_PEND_OBJ)&MyQ1;
        my_pend_multi_tbl[4].PendObjPtr = (OS_PEND_OBJ)&MyQ2;
        OSPendMulti((OS_PEND_DATA *)&my_pend_multi_tbl[0],
                    (OS_OBJ_QTY    )5,
                    (OS_TICK       )0,
                    (OS_OPT        )OS_OPT_PEND_BLOCKING,
                    (OS_ERR       *)&err);
        /* Check 'err" */
        :
    }
}
```

L16-1(2)   This argument specifies the size of the **OS_PEND_DATA** table. In the above example, this is 5.

L16-1(3)   Specify whether or not to timeout in case none of the objects are posted within a certain amount of time. A non-zero value indicates the number of ticks to timeout. Specifying zero indicates the task will wait forever for any of the objects to be posted.

L16-1(4)   The "opt" argument specifies whether to wait for objects to be posted (set opt to **OS_OPT_PEND_BLOCKING**) or, not block if none of the objects have already been posted (set opt to **OS_OPT_PEND_NON_BLOCKING**).

F16-2(1)   As with most µC/OS-III function calls, specify the address of a variable that will receive an error code based on the outcome of the function call. See Appendix A, "µC/OS-III API Reference Manual" on page 383 for a list of possible error codes. As always, it is highly recommended to examine the error return code.

F16-2(2)   Note that all objects are cast to **OS_PEND_OBJ** data types.

When called, **OSPendMulti()** first starts by validating that all of the objects specified in the **OS_PEND_DATA** table are either an **OS_SEM** or an **OS_Q**. If not, an error code is returned.

Next, **OSPendMulti()** goes through the **OS_PEND_DATA** table to see if any of the objects have already posted. If so, **OSPendMulti()** fills the following fields in the table: **.RdyObjPtr**, **.RdyMsgPtr**, **.RdyMsgSize** and **.RdyTS**.

.RdyObjPtr   is a pointer to the object if the object has been posted. For example, if the first object in the table is a semaphore and the semaphore has been posted to, **my_pend_multi_tbl[0].RdyObjPtr** is set to **my_pend_multi_tbl[0].PendObjPtr**.

.RdyMsgPtr   is a pointer to a message if the object in the table at this entry is a message queue and a message was received from the message queue.

.RdyMsgSize   is the size of the message received if the object in the table at this entry is a message queue and a message was received from the message queue.

.RdyTS   is the timestamp of when the object posted. This allows the user to know when a semaphore or message queue posts.

If there are no objects posted, then **OSPendMulti()** places the current task in the wait list of all the objects that it is pending on. This is a complex and tedious process for **OSPendMulti()** since there can be other tasks in the pend list of some of these objects we are pending on.

To indicate how tricky things get, Figure 16-3 is an example of a task pending on two semaphores.

16

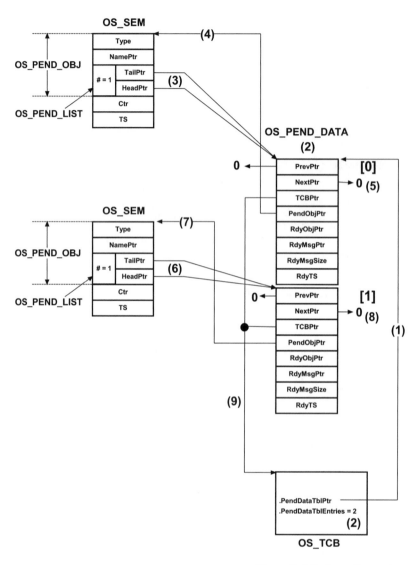

Figure 16-3 **Task pending on two semaphores**

F16-3(1)   A pointer to the base address of the **OS_PEND_DATA** table is placed in the **OS_TCB** of the task placed in the pend list of the two semaphores.

F16-3(2)   The numbers of entries in the **OS_PEND_DATA** table are also placed in the **OS_TCB**. Again, this task is waiting on two semaphores and therefore there are two entries in the table.

F16-3(3)   Entry [0] of the **OS_PEND_DATA** table is linked to the semaphore object specified by that entry's **.PendObjPtr**.

F16-3(4)   This pointer was specified by the caller of **OSPendMulti()**.

F16-3(5)   Since there is only one task in the pend list of the semaphore, the **.PrevPtr** and **.NextPtr** are pointing to **NULL**.

F16-3(6)   The second semaphore points to the second entry in the **OS_PEND_DATA** table.

F16-3(7)   This pointer was specified by the caller of **OSPendMulti()**.

F16-3(8)   The second semaphore only has one entry in its pend list. Therefore the **.PrevPtr** and **.NextPtr** both point to **NULL**.

F16-3(9)   **OSPendMulti()** links back each **OS_PEND_DATA** entry to the task that is waiting on the two semaphores.

Figure 16-4 is a more complex example where one task is pending on two semaphores while another task also pends on one of the two semaphores. The examples presented so far only show semaphores, but they could be combinations of semaphores and message queues.

16

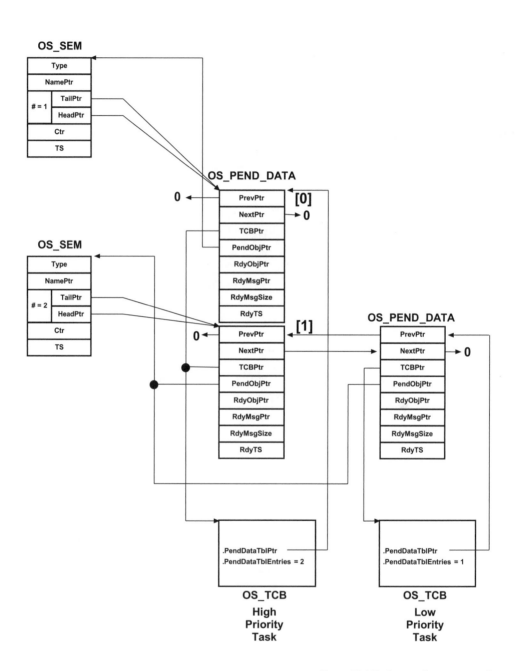

Figure 16-4 **Tasks pending on semaphores**

When either an ISR or a task signals or sends a message to one of the objects that the task is pending on, OSPendMulti() returns, indicating in the OS_PEND_DATA table which object was posted. This is done by only filling in "one" of the .RdyObjPtr entries, the one that corresponds to the object posted as shown in Figure 16-2.

Only one of the entries in the OS_PEND_DATA table will have a .RdyObjPtr with a non-NULL value while all the other entries have the .RdyObjPtr set to NULL. Going back to the case where a task waits on five semaphores and two message queues, if the first message queue is posted while the task is pending on all those objects, the OS_PEND_DATA table will be as shown in Figure 16-5.

	.PrevPtr	.NextPtr	.TCBPtr	.PendObjPtr	.RdyObjPtr	.RdyMsgPtr	.RdyMsgSize	.RdyTS
[0]	0	0	TCBPtr	PendObjPtr	0	0	0	0
[1]	0	0	TCBPtr	PendObjPtr	0	0	0	0
[2]	0	0	TCBPtr	PendObjPtr	0	0	0	0
[3]	0	0	TCBPtr	&MyQ1	&MyQ1	Msg Ptr	Msg Size	Timestamp
[4]	0	0	TCBPtr	PendObjPtr	0	0	0	0

Figure 16-5 **Message queue #1 posted before timeout expired**

16-1 SUMMARY

µC/OS-III allows tasks to pend on multiple kernel objects.

OSPendMulti() can only pend on multiple semaphores and message queues, not event flags and mutual-exclusion semaphores.

If the objects are already posted when OSPendMulti() is called, µC/OS-III will specify which of the objects in the list of objects have already been posted.

If none of the objects are posted, OSPendMulti() will place the calling task in the pend list of all the desired objects. OSPendMulti() will return as soon as one of the objects is posted. In this case, OSPendMulti() will indicate which object was posted.

OSPendMulti() is a complex function that has potentially long critical sections.

16

16

Chapter

17

Memory Management

An application can allocate and free dynamic memory using any ANSI C compiler's `malloc()` and `free()` functions, respectively. However, using `malloc()` and `free()` in an embedded real-time system may be dangerous. Eventually, it might not be possible to obtain a single contiguous memory area due to fragmentation. Fragmentation is the development of a large number of separate free areas (i.e., the total free memory is fragmented into small, non-contiguous pieces). Execution time of `malloc()` and `free()` is generally nondeterministic given the algorithms used to locate a contiguous block of free memory.

μC/OS-III provides an alternative to `malloc()` and `free()` by allowing an application to obtain fixed-sized memory blocks from a partition made from a contiguous memory area, as illustrated in Figure 17-1. All memory blocks are the same size, and the partition contains an integral number of blocks. Allocation and deallocation of these memory blocks is performed in constant time and is deterministic. The partition itself is typically allocated statically (as an array), but can also be allocated by using `malloc()` as long as it is never freed.

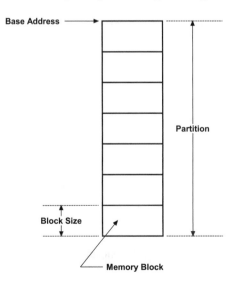

Figure 17-1 **Memory Partition**

As indicated in Figure 17-2, more than one memory partition may exist in an application and each one may have a different number of memory blocks and be a different size. An application can obtain memory blocks of different sizes based upon requirements. However, a specific memory block must always be returned to the partition that it came from. This type of memory management is not subject to fragmentation except that it is possible to run out of memory blocks. It is up to the application to decide how many partitions to have and how large each memory block should be within each partition.

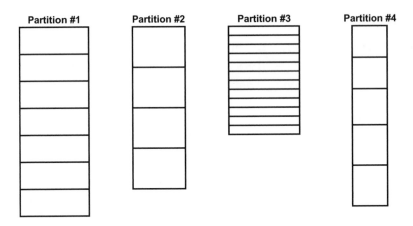

Figure 17-2 **Multiple Memory Partitions**

17-1 CREATING A MEMORY PARTITION

Before using a memory partition, it must be created. This allows µC/OS-III to know something about the memory partition so that it can manage their allocation and deallocation. Once created, a memory partition is as shown in Figure 17-3. Calling OSMemCreate() creates a memory partition.

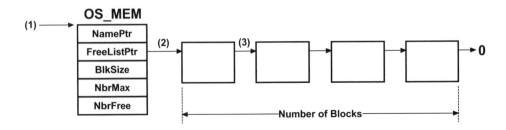

Figure 17-3 **Created Memory Partition**

F17-3(1) When creating a partition, the application code supplies the address of a memory partition control block (**OS_MEM**). Typically, this memory control block is allocated from static memory, however it can also be obtained from the heap by calling **malloc()**. The application code should however never deallocate it.

F17-3(2) **OSMemCreate()** organizes the continuous memory provided into a singly linked list and stores the pointer to the beginning of the list in the **OS_MEM** structure.

F17-3(3) Each memory block must be large enough to hold a pointer. Given the nature of the linked list, a block needs to be able to point to the next block.

Listing 17-1 indicates how to create a memory partition with µC/OS-III.

```
OS_MEM      MyPartition;                             (1)
CPU_INT08U  MyPartitionStorage[12][100];             (2)


void  main (void)                                    (3)
{
    OS_ERR  err;
    :
    :
    OSInit(&err);
    :
    OSMemCreate((OS_MEM     *)&MyPartition,           (4)
                (CPU_CHAR   *)"My Partition",         (5)
                (void       *)&MyPartitionStorage[0][0],  (6)
                (OS_MEM_QTY ) 12,                     (7)
                (OS_MEM_SIZE)100,                     (8)
                (OS_ERR     *)&err);                  (9)
    /* Check 'err" */
    :
    :
    OSStart(&err);
}
```

Listing 17-1 **Creating a memory partition**

L17-1(1) An application needs to allocate storage for a memory partition control block. This can be a static allocation as shown here or **malloc()** can be used in the code. However, the application code must not deallocate the memory control block.

L17-1(2)   The application also needs to allocate storage for the memory that will be split into memory blocks. This can also be a static allocation or **malloc()** can be used. The same reasoning applies. Do not deallocate this storage since other tasks may rely on the existence of this storage.

L17-1(3)   Memory partition must be created before allocating and deallocating blocks from the partition. One of the best places to create memory partitions is in **main()** prior to starting the multitasking process. Of course, an application can call a function from **main()** to do this instead of actually placing the code directly in **main()**.

L17-1(4)   Pass the address of the memory partition control block to **OSMemCreate()**. Never reference any of the internal members of the **OS_MEM** data structure. Instead, use µC/OS-III's API.

L17-1(5)   Assign a name to the memory partition. There is no limit to the length of the ASCII string as µC/OS-III saves a pointer to the ASCII string in the partition control block and not the actual characters.

L17-1(6)   Pass the base address of the storage area reserved for the memory blocks.

L17-1(7)   Specify how many memory blocks are available from this memory partition. Hard coded numbers are used for the sake of the illustration but one should instead use **#define** constants.

L17-1(8)   Specify the size of each memory block in the partition. Again, a hard coded value is used for illustration, which is not recommended in real code.

L17-1(9)   As with most µC/OS-III services, **OSMemCreate()** returns an error code indicating the outcome of the service. The call is successful if "**err**" contains **OS_ERR_NONE**.

Listing 17-2 shows how to create a memory partition with µC/OS-III, this time using **malloc()** to allocate storage. Do not deallocate the memory control block or the storage for the partition.

```
OS_MEM        *MyPartitionPtr;                              (1)


void  main (void)
{
    OS_ERR   err;
    void    *p_storage;
    :
    OSInit(&err);
    :
    MyPartitionPtr = (OS_MEM *)malloc(sizeof(OS_MEM));       (2)
    if (MyPartitionPtr != (OS_MEM *)0) {
        p_storage = malloc(12 * 100);                       (3)
        if (p_storage != (void *)0) {
            OSMemCreate((OS_MEM     *)MyPartitionPtr,        (4)
                        (CPU_CHAR  *)"My Partition",
                        (void      *)p_storage,             (5)
                        (OS_MEM_QTY ) 12,                   (6)
                        (OS_MEM_SIZE)100,                   (6)
                        (OS_ERR    *)&err);
            /* Check 'err" */
        }
    }
    :
    OSStart(&err);
}
```

Listing 17-2 **Creating a memory partition**

17

L17-2(1)   Instead of allocating static storage for the memory partition control block, assign a pointer that receives the **OS_MEM** allocated using `malloc()`.

L17-2(2)   The application allocates storage for the memory control block.

L17-2(3)   Allocate storage for the memory partition.

L17-2(4)   Pass a pointer to the allocated memory control block to `OSMemCreate()`.

L17-2(5)   Pass the base address of the storage used for the partition.

L17-2(6)   Finally, pass the number of blocks and the size of each block so that µC/OS-III creates the linked list of 12 blocks of 100 bytes each. Again, hard coded numbers are used, but these would typically be replaced by `#defines`.

17-2 GETTING A MEMORY BLOCK FROM A PARTITION

Application code can request a memory block from a partition by calling `OSMemGet()` as shown in Listing 17-3. The code assumes that the partition was already created.

```
OS_MEM      MyPartition;                                              (1)
CPU_INT08U *MyDataBlkPtr;


void  MyTask (void *p_arg)
{
    OS_ERR  err;


    :
    while (DEF_ON) {
        :
        MyDataBlkPtr = (CPU_INT08U *)OSMemGet((OS_MEM     *)&MyPartition,  (2)
                                    (OS_ERR    *)&err);
        if (err == OS_ERR_NONE) {                                    (3)
            /* You have a memory block from the partition */
        }
        :
        :
    }
}
```

Listing 17-3 **Obtaining a memory block from a partition**

L17-3(1)   The memory partition control block must be accessible by all tasks or ISRs that will be using the partition.

L17-3(2)   Simply call `OSMemGet()` to obtain a memory block from the desired partition. A pointer to the allocated memory block is returned. This is similar to `malloc()`, except that the memory block comes from a pool that is guaranteed to not fragment.

L17-3(3)   It is important to examine the returned error code to ensure that there are free memory blocks and that the application can start putting content in the memory blocks.

17-3 RETURNING A MEMORY BLOCK TO A PARTITION

The application code must return an allocated memory block back to the proper partition when finished. Do this by calling OSMemPut() as shown in Listing 17-4. The code assumes that the partition was already created.

```
OS_MEM        MyPartition;                                    (1)
CPU_INT08U   *MyDataBlkPtr;


void  MyTask (void *p_arg)
{
    OS_ERR  err;


    :
    while (DEF_ON) {
        :
        OSMemPut((OS_MEM  *)&MyPartition,                    (2)
                 (void     *)MyDataBlkPtr,                    (3)
                 (OS_ERR  *)&err);
        if (err == OS_ERR_NONE) {                            (4)
            /* You properly returned the memory block to the partition */
        }
        :
        :
    }
}
```

Listing 17-4 **Returning a memory block to a partition**

L17-4(1)   The memory partition control block must be accessible by all tasks or ISRs that will be using the partition.

L17-4(2)   Simply call OSMemPut() to return the memory block back to the memory partition. Note that there is no check to see whether the proper memory block is being returned to the proper partition (assuming you have multiple different partitions). It is therefore important to be careful (as is necessary when designing embedded systems).

L17-4(3)   Pass the pointer to the data area that is allocated so that it can be returned to the pool. Note that a "**void ***" is assumed.

L17-4(4)   Examine the returned error code to ensure that the call was successful.

17-4 USING MEMORY PARTITIONS

Memory management services are enabled at compile time by setting the configuration constant OS_CFG_MEM_EN to 1 in OS_CFG.H.

There are a number of operations to perform on memory partitions as summarized in Table 13-1.

Function Name	Operation
OSMemCreate()	Create a memory partition.
OSMemGet()	Obtain a memory block from a memory partition.
OSMemPut()	Return a memory block to a memory partition.

Table 17-1 **Memory Partition API summary**

OSMemCreate() can only be called from task-level code, but OSMemGet() and OSMemPut() can be called by Interrupt Service Routines (ISRs).

Listing 17-4 shows an example of how to use the dynamic memory allocation feature of µC/OS-III, as well as message-passing capabilities (see Chapter 15, "Message Passing" on page 297). In this example, the task on the left reads and checks the value of analog inputs (pressures, temperatures, and voltage) and sends a message to the second task if any of the analog inputs exceed a threshold. The message sent contains information about which channel had the error, an error code, an indication of the severity of the error, and other information.

Error handling in this example is centralized. Other tasks, or even ISRs, can post error messages to the error-handling task. The error-handling task could be responsible for displaying error messages on a monitor (a display), logging errors to a disk, or dispatching other tasks to take corrective action based on the error.

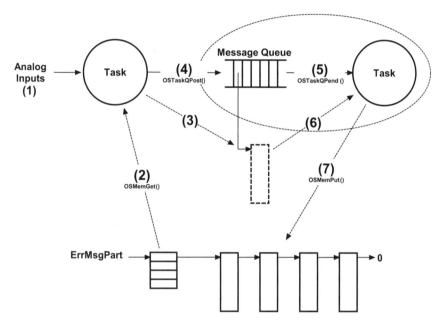

Figure 17-4 **Using a Memory Partition – non blocking**

F17-4(1)   The analog inputs are read by the task. The task determines that one of the inputs is outside a valid range and an error message needs to be sent to the error handler.

F17-4(2)   The task then obtains a memory block from a memory partition so that it can place information regarding the detected error.

F17-4(3)   The task writes this information to the memory block. As mentioned above, the task places the analog channel that is at fault, an error code, an indication of the severity, possible solutions, and more. There is no need to store a timestamp in the message, as time stamping is a built-in feature of µC/OS-III so the receiving task will know when the message was posted.

F17-4(4)   Once the message is complete, it is posted to the task that will handle such error messages. Of course the receiving task needs to know how the information is placed in the message. Once the message is sent, the analog input task is no longer allowed (by convention) to access the memory block since it sent it out to be processed.

F17-4(5)   The error handler task (on the right) normally pends on the message queue. This task will not execute until a message is sent to it.

F17-4(6)   When a message is received, the error handler task reads the contents of the message and performs necessary action(s). As indicated, once sent, the sender will not do anything else with the message.

F17-4(7)   Once the error handler task is finished processing the message, it simply returns the memory block to the memory partition. The sender and receiver therefore need to know about the memory partition or, the sender can pass the address of the memory partition as part of the message and the error handler task will know where to return the memory block.

Sometimes it is useful to have a task wait for a memory block in case a partition runs out of blocks. µC/OS-III does not support pending on partitions, but it is possible to support this requirement by adding a counting semaphore (see Chapter 13, "Resource Management" on page 217) to guard the memory partition. This is illustrated in Figure 17-5.

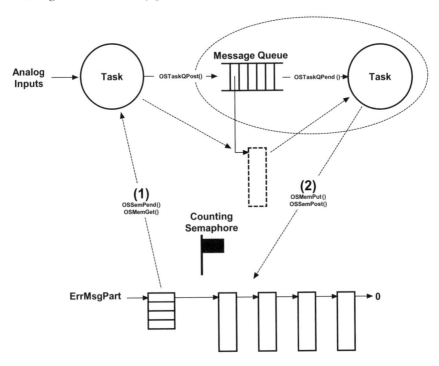

Figure 17-5 **Using a Memory Partition - blocking**

F17-5(1)   To obtain a memory block, simply obtain the semaphore by calling OSSemPend() and call OSMemGet() to receive the memory block.

F17-5(2)   To release a block, simply return the memory block by calling OSMemPut() and signal the semaphore by calling OSSemPost().

The above operations must be performed in order.

Note that the user may call OSMemGet() and OSMemPut() from an ISR since these functions do not block and in fact, execute very quickly. However, you cannot use blocking calls from ISRs.

17-5 SUMMARY

Do not use malloc() and free() in embedded systems since they lead to fragmentation.

It is possible to use malloc() to allocate memory from the heap, but do not deallocate the memory.

The application programmer can create an unlimited number of memory partitions (limited only by the amount of available RAM).

Memory partition services in µC/OS-III start with the OSMem???() prefix, and the services available to the application programmer are described in Appendix A, "µC/OS-III API Reference Manual" on page 383.

Memory management services are enabled at compile time by setting the configuration constant OS_CFG_MEM_EN to 1 in OS_CFG.H.

OSMemGet() and OSMemPut() can be called from ISRs.

17

17

18

Porting µC/OS-III

This chapter describes in general terms how to adapt µC/OS-III to different processors. Adapting µC/OS-III to a microprocessor or a microcontroller is called porting. Most of µC/OS-III is written in C for portability. However, it is still necessary to write processor-specific code in C and assembly language. µC/OS-III manipulates processor registers, which can only be done using assembly language. Porting µC/OS-III to different processors is relatively easy as µC/OS-III was designed to be portable and, since µC/OS-III is similar to µC/OS-II, the user can start from a µC/OS-II port. If there is already a port for the processor to be used, it is not necessary to read this chapter unless, of course, there is an interest in knowing how µC/OS-III processor-specific code works.

µC/OS-III can run on a processor if it satisfies the following general requirements:

■ The processor has an ANSI C compiler that generates reentrant code.

■ The processor supports interrupts and can provide an interrupt that occurs at regular intervals (typically between 10 and 1000 Hz).

■ Interrupts can be disabled and enabled.

■ The processor supports a hardware stack that accommodates a fair amount of data (possibly many kilobytes).

■ The processor has instructions to save and restore the stack pointer and other CPU registers, either on the stack or in memory.

■ The processor has access to sufficient RAM for µC/OS-III's variables and data structures as well as internal task stacks.

■ The compiler should support 64-bit data types (typically "long long").

Figure 18-1 shows the µC/OS-III architecture and its relationship with other software components and hardware. When using µC/OS-III in an application, the user is responsible for providing application software and µC/OS-III configuration sections.

Figure 18-1 **µC/OS-III architecture**

F18-1(1)   A µC/OS-III port consists of writing or changing the contents of three kernel-specific files: **OS_CPU.H**, **OS_CPU_A.ASM** and **OS_CPU_C.C**.

F18-1(2)   A port also involves writing or changing the contents of three CPU specific files: **CPU.H**, **CPU_A.ASM** and **CPU_CORE.C**.

F18-1(3)   A Board Support Package (BSP) is generally necessary to interface µC/OS-III to a timer (which is used for the clock tick) and an interrupt controller.

F18-1(4)   Some semiconductor manufacturers provide source and header files to access on-chip peripherals. These are contained in CPU/MCU specific files.

Porting µC/OS-III is quite straightforward once the subtleties of the target processor and the C compiler/assembler are understood. Depending on the processor, a port consists of writing or changing between 100 and 400 lines of code, which takes a few hours to a few days to accomplish. The easiest thing to do, however, is to modify an existing port from a processor that is similar to the one intended for use.

A µC/OS-III port looks very much like a µC/OS-II port. Since µC/OS-II was ported to well over 45 different CPU architectures it is easy to start from a µC/OS-II port. Converting a µC/OS-II port to µC/OS-III takes approximately an hour. The process is described in Appendix C, "Migrating from µC/OS-II to µC/OS-III" on page 607.

A port involves three aspects: CPU, OS and board-specific code. The board-specific code is often called a *Board Support Package* (BSP) and from µC/OS-III's point of view, requires very little.

18

18-1 μC/CPU

CPU-specific code is related to the CPU and the compiler in use, and less so with μC/OS-III. For example, disabling and enabling interrupts and the word width of the stack, whether the stack grows from high-to-low memory or from low-to-high memory and more are all CPU specific and not OS specific. Micrium encapsulates CPU functions and data types into a module called μC/CPU.

Table 18-1 shows the name of μC/CPU files and where they should be placed on the computer used to develop a μC/OS-III-based application.

File	Directory
CPU_DEF.H	\Micrium\Software\uC-CPU\
CPU.H	\Micrium\Software\uC-CPU\<processor>\<compiler>
CPU_C.C	\Micrium\Software\uC-CPU\<processor>\<compiler>
CPU_CFG.H	\Micrium\Software\uC-CPU\CFG\TEMPLATE
CPU_CORE.C	\Micrium\Software\uC-CPU\
CPU_CORE.H	\Micrium\Software\uC-CPU\
CPU_A.ASM	\Micrium\Software\uC-CPU\<processor>\<compiler>

Table 18-1 μC/CPU files and directories

Here, <processor> is the name of the processor that the **CPU*.*** files apply to, and <compiler> is the name of the compiler that these files assume because of different assembly language directives that different tool chains use.

The above source files for the CPU that came with this book are found when downloading the code from the Micrium website.

CPU_DEF.H
This file should not require any changes. **CPU_DEF.H** declares **#define** constants that are used by Micrium software components.

CPU.H

Many CPUs have different word lengths and **CPU.H** declares a series of type definitions that ensure portability. Specifically, at Micriµm, C data types **int**, **short**, **long**, **char**, *etc.*, are not used. Instead, clearer data types are defined. Consult compiler documentation to determine whether the standard declarations described below must be changed for the CPU/compiler used. When using a 32-bit CPU, the declarations below should work without change.

```
typedef            void       CPU_VOID;
typedef  unsigned  char       CPU_CHAR;
typedef  unsigned  char       CPU_BOOLEAN;
typedef  unsigned  char       CPU_INT08U;
typedef    signed  char       CPU_INT08S;
typedef  unsigned  short      CPU_INT16U;
typedef    signed  short      CPU_INT16S;
typedef  unsigned  int        CPU_INT32U;
typedef    signed  int        CPU_INT32S;
typedef  unsigned  long long  CPU_INT64U;
typedef    signed  long long  CPU_INT64S;
typedef            float      CPU_FP32;
typedef            double     CPU_FP64;
typedef  volatile  CPU_INT08U CPU_REG08;
typedef  volatile  CPU_INT16U CPU_REG16;
typedef  volatile  CPU_INT32U CPU_REG32;
typedef  volatile  CPU_INT64U CPU_REG64;
typedef            void       (*CPU_FNCT_VOID)(void);
typedef            void       (*CPU_FNCT_PTR )(void *);
typedef  CPU_INT32U           CPU_ADDR;
typedef  CPU_INT32U           CPU_DATA;
typedef  CPU_DATA             CPU_ALIGN;
typedef  CPU_ADDR             CPU_SIZE_T;
typedef  CPU_INT32U           CPU_STK;          (1)
typedef  CPU_ADDR             CPU_STK_SIZE;
typedef  CPU_INT16U           CPU_ERR;
typedef  CPU_INT32U           CPU_SR;           (2)
typedef  CPU_INT32U           CPU_TS;           (3)
```

18

(1)   Especially important for µC/OS-III is the definition of the **CPU_STK** data type, which sets the width of a stack entry. Specifically, is the width of data pushed to and popped from the stack 8 bits, 16 bits, 32 bits or 64 bits?

(2)   **CPU_SR** defines the data type for the processor's status register (SR) that generally holds the interrupt disable status.

(3)   The **CPU_TS** is a time stamp used to determine when an operation occurred, or to measure the execution time of code.

CPU.H also declares macros to disable and enable interrupts: CPU_CRITICAL_ENTER() and CPU_CRITICAL_EXIT(), respectively. Finally, CPU.H declares function prototypes for a number of functions found in either CPU_C.C or CPU_CORE.C.

CPU_C.C

This is an optional file containing CPU-specific functions to set the interrupt controller, timer prescalers, and more. Most implementations will not contain this file.

CPU_CFG.H

This is a configuration file to be copied into the product directory and changed based on the options to exercise in μC/CPU. The file contains #define constants that may need to be changed based on the desired use of μC/CPU. For example, to assign a "name" to the CPU, the name can be queried and displayed. Also, to name the CPU, one must specify the length of the ASCII string.

CPU_CORE.C

This file is generic and does not need to be changed. However it must be included in all builds. CPU_CORE.C defines such functions as CPU_Init(), CPU_CntLeadZeros(), and code to measure maximum CPU interrupt disable time.

CPU_Init() must be called before calling OSInit().

CPU_CntLeadZeros() is used by the μC/OS-III scheduler to find the highest priority ready task (see Chapter 7, "Scheduling" on page 141). CPU_CORE.C implements a count leading zeros in C. However, if the processor used provides a built-in instruction to count leading zeros, define

CPU_CFG_LEAD_ZEROS_ASM_PRESENT, and replace this function by an assembly language equivalent (in CPU_A.ASM). It is important to properly declare CPU_CFG_DATA_SIZE in CPU.H for this function to work.

CPU_CORE.C also includes code that allows you to read timestamps. μC/CPU timestamps (CPU_TS) are 32-bit values. However, μC/CPU can return a 64-bit timestamp since μC/CPU keeps track of overflows of the low part of the 64-bit timestamp. Also use timestamps to determine when events occur, or to measure the execution time of code. Timestamp support requires a 16- or 32-bit free-running counter/timer that can be read. The code to read this timer will be placed in the BSP (Board Support Package) of the evaluation board or target board used.

18

CPU_CORE.H

This header file is required by **CPU_CORE.C** to define function prototypes.

CPU_A.ASM

This file contains assembly language code to implement such functions as disabling and enabling interrupts, a more efficient count leading zeros function, and more. At a minimum, this file should implement **CPU_SR_Save()** and **CPU_SR_Restore()**.

CPU_SR_Save() reads the current value of the CPU status register where the current interrupt disable flag resides and returns this value to the caller. However, before returning, **CPU_SR_Save()** must disable all interrupts. **CPU_SR_Save()** is actually called by the macro **CPU_CRITICAL_ENTER()**.

CPU_SR_Restore() restores the CPU's status register to a previously saved value. **CPU_SR_Restore()** is called from the macro **CPU_CRITICAL_EXIT()**.

18-2 µC/OS-III PORT

Table 18-2 shows the name of µC/OS-III files and where they are typically found.

File	Directory
OS_CPU.H	\Micrium\Software\uCOS-III\Ports\<processor>\<compiler>\
OS_CPU_A.ASM	\Micrium\Software\uCOS-III\Ports\<processor>\<compiler>\
OS_CPU_C.C	\Micrium\Software\uCOS-III\Ports\<processor>\<compiler>\

Table 18-2 **µC/OS-III files and directories**

Here, <processor> is the name of the processor that the **OS_CPU*.*** files apply to, and <compiler> is the name of the compiler that these files assume because of the different assembly language directives that different tool chains use.

OS_CPU.H

This file must define the macro **OS_TASK_SW()**, which is called by **OSSched()** to perform a task-level context switch. The macro can translate directly to a call to **OSCtxSw()**, trigger a software interrupt, or a **TRAP**. The choice depends on the CPU architecture.

18

`OS_CPU.H` must also define the macro `OS_TS_GET()` which obtains the current time stamp. It is expected that the time stamp is type `CPU_TS`, which is typically declared as at least a 32-bit value.

`OS_CPU.H` also defines function prototypes for `OSCtxSw()`, `OSIntCtxSw()`, `OSStartHighRdy()` and possibly other functions required by the port.

OS_CPU_A.ASM
This file contains the implementation of the following assembly language functions:

> `OSStartHighRdy()`
> `OSCtxSw()`
> `OSIntCtxSw()`

and optionally,

> `OSTickISR()`

`OSTickISR()` may optionally be placed in `OS_CPU_A.ASM` if it does not change from one product to another. The functions in this file are implemented in assembly language since they manipulate CPU registers, which is typically not possible from C. The functions are described in Appendix A, "µC/OS-III API Reference Manual" on page 383.

OS_CPU_C.C
This file contains the implementation of the following C functions:

> `OSIdleTaskHook()`
> `OSInitHook()`
> `OSStatTaskHook()`
> `OSTaskCreateHook()`
> `OSTaskDelHook()`
> `OSTaskReturnHook()`
> `OSTaskStkInit()`
> `OSTaskSwHook()`
> `OSTimeTickHook()`

The functions are described in Appendix A, "µC/OS-III API Reference Manual" on page 383. `OS_CPU_C.C` can declare other functions as needed by the port, however the above functions are mandatory.

18-3 BOARD SUPPORT PACKAGE (BSP)

A board support package refers to code associated with the actual evaluation board or the target board used. For example, the BSP defines functions to turn LEDs on or off, reads push-button switches, initializes peripheral clocks, etc., providing nearly any functionality to multiple products/projects.

Names of typical BSP files include:

> BSP.C
> BSP.H
> BSP_INT.C
> BSP_INT.H

All files are generally placed in a directory as follows:

> \Micrium\Software\EvalBoards\<manufacturer>\
> <board_name>\<compiler>\BSP\

Here, <manufacturer> is the name of the evaluation board or target board manufacturer, <board_name> is the name of the evaluation or target board and <compiler> is the name of the compiler that these files assume, although most should be portable to different compilers since the BSP is typically written in C.

BSP.C and BSP.H

These files normally contain functions and their definitions such as BSP_Init(), BSP_LED_On(), BSP_LED_Off(), BSP_LED_Toggle(), BSP_PB_Rd(), and others. It is up to the user to decide if the functions in this file start with the prefix BSP_. In other words, use LED_On() and PB_Rd() if this is clearer. However, it is a good practice to encapsulate this type of functionality in a BSP type file.

In BSP.C, add CPU_TS_TmrInit() to initialize the µC/CPU timestamp feature. This function must return the number 16 if using a 16-bit timer and 0 for a 32-bit timer.

CPU_TS_TmrGet() is responsible for reading the value of a 16- or 32-bit free-running timer. If the timer is 16 bits, this function will need to return the value of the timer, but shifted to the left 16 places so that it looks like a 32-bit timer. If the timer is 32 bits, simply return the current value of the timer. Note that the timer is assumed to be an up counter. If the timer counts down, the BSP code will need to return the ones-complement of the timer value (prior to the shift).

BSP_INT.C and BSP_INT.H

These files are typically used to declare interrupt controller related functions. For example, code that enables or disables specific interrupts from the interrupt controller, acknowledges the interrupt controller, and code to handle all interrupts if the CPU vectors to a single location when an interrupt occurs (see Chapter 9, "Interrupt Management" on page 165). The pseudo code below shows an example of the latter.

```
void  BSP_IntHandler (void)                                        (1)
{
    CPU_FNCT_VOID    p_isr;

    while (interrupts being asserted) {                            (2)
        p_isr = Read the highest priority interrupt from the controller;  (3)
        if (p_isr != (CPU_FNCT_VOID)0) {                          (4)
            (*p_isr)();                                           (5)
        }
        Acknowledge interrupt controller;                         (6)
    }
}
```

(1)   Here assume that the handler for the interrupt controller is called from the assembly language code that saves the CPU registers upon entering an ISR (see Chapter 9, "Interrupt Management" on page 165).

(2)   The handler queries the interrupt controller to ask it for the address of the ISR that needs to be executed in response to the interrupt. Some interrupt controllers return an integer value that corresponds to the source. In this case, simply use this integer value as an index into a table (RAM or ROM) where those vectors are placed.

(3)   The interrupt controller is asked to provide the highest priority interrupt pending. It is assumed here that the CPU may receive multiple simultaneous interrupts (or closely spaced interrupts), and that the interrupt will prioritize the interrupts received. The CPU will then service each interrupt in priority order instead of on a first-come basis. However, the scheme used greatly depends on the interrupt controller itself.

(4)   Check to ensure that the interrupt controller did not return a **NULL** pointer.

(5)   Simply call the ISR associated with the interrupt device.

(6)   The interrupt controller generally needs to be acknowledged so that it knows that the interrupt presented is taken care of.

18-4 SUMMARY

A port involves three aspects: CPU, OS and board specific (BSP) code.

µC/OS-III port consists of writing or changing the contents of three kernel specific files: **OS_CPU.H**, **OS_CPU_A.ASM** and **OS_CPU_C.C**.

It is necessary to write or change the content of three CPU specific files: **CPU.H**, **CPU_A.ASM** and **CPU_C.C**.

Finally create or change a Board Support Package (BSP) for the evaluation board or target board being used.

A µC/OS-III port is similar to a µC/OS-II port, therefore start from one of the many µC/OS-II ports already available (see Appendix C, "Migrating from µC/OS-II to µC/OS-III" on page 607).

18

18

19

Run-Time Statistics

µC/OS-III performs substantial run-time statistics that can be displayed by kernel-aware debuggers and/or µC/Probe. Specifically, it is possible to ascertain the total number of context switches, maximum interrupt disable time, maximum scheduler lock time, CPU usage, stack space used on a per-task basis, the RAM used by µC/OS-III, and much more.

No other real-time kernel provides as much run-time information as µC/OS-III. This information is quite useful during debugging as it provides a sense of how well an application is running and the resources being used.

µC/OS-III also provides information about the configuration of the system. Specifically, the amount of RAM used by µC/OS-III, including all internal variables and task stacks.

The µC/OS-III variables described in this chapter should be displayed and never changed.

19-1 GENERAL STATISTICS – RUN-TIME

The following is a list of µC/OS-III variables that are not associated to any specific task:

OSCfg_TickWheel[i].NbrEntries
The tick wheel contains up to OS_CFG_TICK_WHEEL_SIZE "spokes" (see OS_CFG_APP.H), and each spoke contains the .NbrEntries field, which holds the current number of entries in that spoke.

OSCfg_TickWheel[i].NbrEntriesMax
The .NbrEntriesMax field holds the maximum (i.e., peak) number of entries in a spoke.

OSCfg_TmrWheel[i].NbrEntries
The tick wheel contains up to OS_CFG_TMR_WHEEL_SIZE "spokes" (see OS_CFG_APP.H), and each spoke contains the .NbrEntries field, which holds the current number of entries in that spoke.

OSCfg_TmrWheel[i].NbrEntriesMax
The .NbrEntriesMax field holds the maximum (i.e., peak) number of entries in a spoke.

OSIdleTaskCtr
This variable contains a counter that is incremented every time the idle task infinite loop runs.

OSIntNestingCtr
This variable contains the interrupt nesting level. 1 means servicing the first level of interrupt nesting, 2 means the interrupt was interrupted by another interrupt, etc.

OSIntDisTimeMax
This variable contains the maximum interrupt disable time (in CPU_TS units).

OSRunning
This variable indicates that multitasking has started.

OSIntQNbrEntries
This variable indicates the current number of entries in the interrupt handler queue.

OSIntQOvfCtr

This variable shows the number of attempts to post a message from an interrupt to the interrupt handler queue, and there was not enough room to place the post call. In other words, how many times an interrupt was not being able to be serviced by its corresponding task. This value should always be 0 if the interrupt handler queue is sized large enough. If the value is non-zero, increase the size of the interrupt handler queue. A non-zero value may also indicate that the processor is not fast enough.

OSIntQTaskTimeMax

This variable contains the maximum execution time of the Interrupt Queue Handler Task (in CPU_TS units).

OSFlagQty

This variable indicates the number of event flag groups created. This variable is only declared if OS_CFG_FLAG_EN is set to 1 in OS_CFG.H.

OSMemQty

This variable indicates the number of fixed-sized memory partitions created by the application. This variable is only declared if OS_CFG_MEM_EN is set to 1 in OS_CFG.H.

OSMsgPool.NbrFree

The variable indicates the number of free OS_MSGs in the message pool. This number should never be zero since that indicate that the application is no longer able to send messages. This variable is only declared if OS_CFG_Q_EN is set to 1, or OS_CFG_TASK_Q_EN is set to 1 in OS_CFG.H.

OSMsgPool.NbrUsed

This variable indicates the number of OS_MSGs currently used by the application. This variable is only declared if OS_CFG_Q_EN is set to 1, or OS_CFG_TASK_Q_EN is set to 1 in OS_CFG.H.

OSMutexQty

This variable indicates the number of mutual exclusion semaphores created by the application. This variable is only declared if OS_CFG_MUTEX_EN is set to 1 in OS_CFG.H.

OSRdyList[i].NbrEntries

It is useful to examine how many entries there are in the ready list at each priority.

19

OSSchedLockTimeMax

This variable indicates the maximum amount of time the scheduler was locked irrespective of which task did the locking. It represents the global scheduler lock time. This value is expressed in CPU_TS units. The variable is only declared if OS_CFG_SCHED_LOCK_TIME_MEAS_EN is set to 1 in OS_CFG.H.

OSSchedLockTimeMaxCur

This variable indicates the maximum amount of time the scheduler was locked. This value is expressed in CPU_TS units and is reset by the context switch code so that it can track the scheduler lock time on a per-task basis. This variable is only declared if OS_CFG_SCHED_LOCK_TIME_MEAS_EN is set to 1 in OS_CFG.H.

OSSchedLockNestingCtr

This variable keeps track of the nesting level of the scheduler lock.

OSSchedRoundRobinEn

This variable indicates whether or not round robin scheduling is enabled.

OSSemQty

This variable indicates the number of semaphores created by your application. This variable is only declared if OS_CFG_SEM_EN is set to 1 in OS_CFG.H.

OSStatTaskCPUUsage

This variable indicates the CPU usage of the application expressed as a percentage. A value of 10 indicates that 10% of the CPU is used, while 90% of the time the CPU is idling. This variable is only declared if OS_CFG_STAT_TASK_EN is set to 1 in OS_CFG.H.

OSStatTaskCtr

This variable contains a counter that is incremented every time the idle task infinite loop runs. This variable is only declared if OS_CFG_STAT_TASK_EN is set to 1 in OS_CFG.H.

OSStatTaskCtrMax

This variable contains the maximum number of times the idle task loop runs in 0.1 second. This value is used to measure the CPU usage of the application. This variable is only declared if OS_CFG_STAT_TASK_EN is set to 1 in OS_CFG.H.

OSStatTaskTimeMax

This variable contains the maximum execution time of the statistic task (in CPU_TS units). It is only declared if OS_CFG_STAT_TASK_EN is set to 1 in OS_CFG.H.

OSTaskCtxSwCtr

This variable accumulates the number of context switches performed by μC/OS-III.

OSTaskQty

The variable contains the total number of tasks created in the application.

OSTickCtr

This variable is incremented every time the tick task executes.

OSTickTaskTimeMax

This variable contains the maximum execution time of the tick task (in **CPU_TS** units).

OSTmrQty

This variable indicates the number of timers created by the application. It is only declared if OS_CFG_TMR_EN is set to 1 in OS_CFG.H.

OSTmrCtr

This variable is incremented every time the timer task executes.

OSTmrTaskTimeMax

This variable contains the maximum execution time of the timer task (in **CPU_TS** units). It is only declared if OS_CFG_TMR_EN is set to 1 in OS_CFG.H.

19

19-2 PER-TASK STATISTICS – RUN-TIME

µC/OS-III maintains statistics for each task at run-time. This information is saved in the task's **OS_TCB**.

.CPUUsage

This variable keeps track of CPU usage of the task as a percentage of the total CPU usage. For example if the task's **.CPUUsage** is 20%, and the total CPU usages from **OSTaskStatCPUUsage** is 10%, this variable represents 2% of total CPU usage.

The variable is only declared when **OS_CFG_TASK_PROFILE_EN** is set to 1 in **OS_CFG.H**.

.CtxSwCtr

This variable keeps track of the number of times a task is context switched to. This variable should increment. If it does not increment, the task is not running. At a minimum, the counter should at least have a value of one since a task is always created ready to run.

This variable is only declared when **OS_CFG_TASK_PROFILE_EN** is set to 1 in **OS_CFG.H**.

.IntDisTimeMax

This variable keeps track of the maximum interrupt disable time of a task (in **CPU_TS** units). This variable shows how each task affects interrupt latency.

The variable is only declared when **OS_CFG_TASK_PROFILE_EN** is set to 1 in **OS_CFG.H** and defines **CPU_CFG_INT_DIS_MEAS_EN** in **CPU_CFG.H**.

.MsgQ.NbrEntries

This variable indicates the number of entries currently waiting in the message queue of a task. This variable is only declared when **OS_CFG_TASK_Q_EN** is set to 1 in **OS_CFG.H**.

.MsgQ.NbrEntriesMax

This variable indicates the maximum number of entries placed in the message queue of a task. This variable is only declared when **OS_CFG_TASK_Q_EN** is set to 1 in **OS_CFG.H**.

.MsgQ.NbrEntriesSize

This variable indicates the maximum number of entries that a task message queue is able to accept before it is full.

This variable is only declared when **OS_CFG_TASK_Q_EN** is set to 1 in **OS_CFG.H**.

.MsgQ.PendTime

This variable indicates the amount of time it took for a task or an ISR to send a message to the task (in **CPU_TS** units).

The variable is only declared when **OS_CFG_TASK_PROFILE_EN** is set to 1 in **OS_CFG.H**.

.MsgQ.PendTimeMax

This variable indicates the maximum amount of time it took for a task or an ISR to send a message to the task (in **CPU_TS** units).

This variable is only declared when **OS_CFG_TASK_PROFILE_EN** is set to 1 in **OS_CFG.H**.

.PendOn

This variable indicates what a task is pending on if the task is in a pend state. Possible values are:

0	Nothing
1	Pending on an event flag group
2	Pending on the task's message queue
3	Pending on multiple objects
4	Pending on a mutual exclusion semaphore
5	Pending on a message queue
6	Pending on a semaphore
7	Pending on a task's semaphore

.Prio

This corresponds to the priority of the task. This might change at run time depending on whether or not the task owns a mutual exclusion semaphore, or the user changes the priority of the task by calling **OSTaskChangePrio()**.

.SchedLockTimeMax

This variable keeps track of the maximum time a task locks the scheduler (in **CPU_TS** units). This variable allows the application to see how each task affects task latency. The variable is declared only when **OS_CFG_TASK_PROFILE_EN** and **OS_CFG_SCHED_LOCK_TIME_MEAS_EN** are set to 1 in **OS_CFG.H**.

19

.SemPendTime

This variable indicates the amount of time it took for a task or ISR to signal the task (in CPU_TS units).

This variable is only declared when **OS_CFG_TASK_PROFILE_EN** is set to 1 in **OS_CFG.H**.

.SemPendTimeMax

This variable indicates the maximum amount of time it took for a task or an ISR to signal the task (in **CPU_TS** units).

This variable is only declared when **OS_CFG_TASK_PROFILE_EN** is set to 1 in **OS_CFG.H**.

.State

This variable indicates the current state of a task. The possible values are:

0	Ready
1	Delayed
2	Pending
3	Pending with Timeout
4	Suspended
5	Delayed and Suspended
6	Pending and Suspended
7	Pending, Delayed and Suspended

.StkFree

This variable indicates the amount of stack space (in bytes) unused by a task. This value is determined by the statistic task if **OS_CFG_TASK_STAT_STK_CHK_EN** is set to 1 in **OS_CFG.H**.

.StkUsed

This variable indicates the maximum stack usage (in bytes) of a task. This value is determined by the statistic task if **OS_CFG_TASK_STAT_STK_CHK_EN** is set to 1 in **OS_CFG.H**.

.TickRemain

This variable indicates the amount of time left (in clock ticks) until a task time delay expires, or the task times out waiting on a kernel object such as a semaphore, message queue, or other.

19-3 KERNEL OBJECT – RUN-TIME

It is possible to examine the run-time values of certain kernel objects as described below.

SEMAPHORES

.NamePtr
This is a pointer to an ASCII string used to provide a name to the semaphore. The ASCII string can have any length as long as it is NUL terminated.

.PendList.NbrEntries
Each semaphore contains a wait list of tasks waiting for the semaphore to be signaled. The variable represents the number of entries in the wait list.

.Ctr
This variable represents the current count of the semaphore.

.TS
This variable contains the timestamp of when the semaphore was last signaled.

MUTUAL EXCLUSION SEMAPHORES

.NamePtr
This is a pointer to an ASCII string used to provide a name to the mutual exclusion semaphore. The ASCII string can have any length as long as it is NUL terminated.

.PendList.NbrEntries
Each mutual exclusion semaphore contains a list of tasks waiting for the semaphore to be released. The variable represents the number of entries in the wait list.

.OwnerOriginalPrio
This variable holds the original priority of the task that owns the mutual exclusion semaphore.

.OwnerTCBPtr->Prio
Dereferencing the pointer to the OS_TCB of the mutual exclusion semaphore owner allows the application to determine whether a task priority was changed.

19

.OwnerNestingCtr

This variable indicates how many times the owner of the mutual exclusion semaphore requested the semaphore.

.TS

This variable contains the timestamp of when the mutual exclusion semaphore was last released.

MESSAGE QUEUES

.NamePtr

This is a pointer to an ASCII string used to provide a name to the message queue. The ASCII string can have any length, as long as it is **NUL** terminated.

.PendList.NbrEntries

Each message queue contains a wait list of tasks waiting for messages to be sent to the queue. The variable represents the number of entries in the wait list.

.MsgQ.NbrEntries

This variable represents the number of messages currently in the message queue.

.MsgQ.NbrEntriesMax

This variable represents the maximum number of messages ever placed in the message queue.

.MsgQ.NbrEntriesSize

This variable represents the maximum number of messages that can be placed in the message queue.

EVENT FLAGS

.NamePtr

This is a pointer to an ASCII string used to provide a name to the event flag group. The ASCII string can have any length, as long as it is **NUL** terminated.

.PendList.NbrEntries

Each event flag group contains a wait list of tasks waiting for event flags to be set or cleared. This variable represents the number of entries in the wait list.

.Flags

This variable contains the current value of the event flags in an event flag group.

.TS

This variable contains the timestamp of when the event flag group was last posted.

MEMORY PARTITIONS

.NamePtr

This is a pointer to an ASCII string that is used to provide a name to the memory partition. The ASCII string can have any length as long as it is **NUL** terminated.

.BlkSize

This variable contains the block size (in bytes) for the memory partition.

.NbrMax

This variable contains the maximum number of memory blocks belonging to the memory partition.

.NbrFree

This variable contains the number of memory blocks that are available from memory partition. The number of memory blocks in use is given by:

    .NbrMax - .NbrFree

19

19-4 OS_DBG.C – **STATIC**

OS_DBG.C is provided in µC/OS-III as some debuggers are not able to read the values of #define constants. Specifically, OS_DBG.C contains ROM variables initialized to #define constants so that users can read them with any debugger.

Below is a list of ROM variables provided in OS_DBG.C, along with their descriptions. These variables use approximately 100 bytes of code space.

The application code can examine these variables and you do not need to access them in a critical region as they reside in code space and are therefore not changeable.

ROM Variable	Data Type	Value
OSDbg_DbgEn	CPU_INT08U	OS_CFG_DBG_EN

When 1, this variable indicates that ROM variables in OS_DBG.C will be compiled. This value is set in OS_CFG.H.

ROM Variable	Data Type	Value
OSDbg_ArgChkEn	CPU_INT08U	OS_CFG_ARG_CHK_EN

When 1, this variable indicates that run-time argument checking is enabled. This means that µC/OS-III will check the validity of the values of arguments passed to functions. The feature is enabled in OS_CFG.H.

19

ROM Variable	Data Type	Value
OSDbg_AppHooksEn	CPU_INT08U	OS_CFG_DBG_EN

When 1, the variable indicates whether application hooks will be available to the application programmer, and the pointers listed below are declared. This value is set in **OS_CFG.H**.

```
OS_AppTaskCreateHookPtr;
OS_AppTaskDelHookPtr;
OS_AppTaskReturnHookPtr;
OS_AppIdleTaskHookPtr;
OS_AppStatTaskHookPtr;
OS_AppTaskSwHookPtr;
OS_AppTimeTickHookPtr;
```

ROM Variable	Data Type	Value
OSDbg_EndiannessTest	CPU_INT32U	0x12345678

This variable allows the kernel awareness debugger or μC/Probe to determine the endianness of the CPU. This is easily done by looking at the lowest address in memory where this variable is saved. If the value is 0x78 then the CPU is a little endian machine. If it's 0x12, it is a big endian machine.

ROM Variable	Data Type	Value
OSDbg_CalledFromISRChkEn	CPU_INT08U	OS_CFG_CALLED_FROM_ISR_CHK_EN

When 1, this variable indicates that μC/OS-III will perform run-time checking to see if a function that is not supposed to be called from an ISR, is called from an ISR. This value is set in **OS_CFG.H**.

19

ROM Variable	Data Type	Value
OSDbg_FlagEn	CPU_INT08U	OS_CFG_FLAG_EN

When 1, this variable indicates that µC/OS-III's event flag services are available to the application programmer. This value is set in **OS_CFG.H**.

ROM Variable	Data Type	Value
OSDbg_FlagDelEn	CPU_INT08U	OS_CFG_FLAG_DEL_EN

When 1, this variable indicates that the **OSFlagDel()** function is available to the application programmer. This value is set in **OS_CFG.H**.

ROM Variable	Data Type	Value
OSDbg_FlagModeClrEn	CPU_INT08U	OS_CFG_FLAG_MODE_CLR_EN

When 1, this variable indicates that cleared flags can be used instead of set flags when posting and pending on event flags. This value is set in **OS_CFG.H**.

ROM Variable	Data Type	Value
OSDbg_FlagPendAbortEn	CPU_INT08U	OS_CFG_FLAG_PEND_ABORT_EN

When 1, this variable indicates that the **OSFlagPendAbort()** function is available to the application programmer. This value is set in **OS_CFG.H**.

ROM Variable	Data Type	Value
OSDbg_FlagGrpSize	CPU_INT16U	sizeof(OS_FLAG_GRP)

This variable indicates the memory footprint (in RAM) of an event flag group (in bytes). This data type is declared in **OS.H**.

19

ROM Variable	Data Type	Value
OSDbg_FlagWidth	CPU_INT16U	sizeof(OS_FLAGS)

This variable indicates the word width (in bytes) of event flags. If event flags are declared as **CPU_INT08U**, this variable will be 1, if declared as a **CPU_INT16U**, this variable will be 2, etc. This data type is declared in **OS_TYPE.H**.

ROM Variable	Data Type	Value
OSDbg_IntQSize	CPU_INT16U	sizeof(OS_INT_Q)

This variable indicates the size of the **OS_INT_Q** data type, which is used to queue up deferred posts. The value of this variable is zero if **OS_CFG_ISR_POST_DEFERRED_EN** is 0 in **OS_CFG.H**.

ROM Variable	Data Type	Value
OSDbg_ISRPostDeferredEn	CPU_INT08U	OS_CFG_ISR_POST_DEFERRED_EN

When 1, this variable indicates that an ISR will defer posts to task-level code. This value is set in **OS_CFG.H**.

ROM Variable	Data Type	Value
OSDbg_MemEn	CPU_INT08U	OS_CFG_MEM_EN

When 1, this variable indicates that μC/OS-III's memory management services are available to the application. This value is set in **OS_CFG.H**.

ROM Variable	Data Type	Value
OSDbg_MemSize	CPU_INT16U	sizeof(OS_MEM)

This variable indicates the RAM footprint (in bytes) of a memory partition control block.

19

ROM Variable	Data Type	Value
OSDbg_MsgEn	CPU_INT08U	OS_CFG_MSG_EN

When 1, this variable indicates that the application either enabled message queues, or task message queues, or both. This value is set in OS_CFG.H by ORing the value of OS_CFG_Q_EN and OS_CFG_TASK_Q_EN.

ROM Variable	Data Type	Value
OSDbg_MsgSize	CPU_INT16U	sizeof(OS_MSG)

This variable indicates the RAM footprint (in bytes) of an OS_MSG data structure.

ROM Variable	Data Type	Value
OSDbg_MsgPoolSize	CPU_INT16U	sizeof(OS_MSG_POOL)

This variable indicates the RAM footprint (in bytes) of an OS_MSG_POOL data structure.

ROM Variable	Data Type	Value
OSDbg_MsgQSize	CPU_INT16U	sizeof(OS_MSG_Q)

This variable indicates the RAM footprint (in number of bytes) of an OS_MSG_Q data type.

ROM Variable	Data Type	Value
OSDbg_MutexEn	CPU_INT08U	OS_CFG_MUTEX_EN

When 1, this variable indicates that μC/OS-III's mutual exclusion semaphore management services are available to the application. This value is set in OS_CFG.H.

ROM Variable	Data Type	Value
OSDbg_MutexDelEn	CPU_INT08U	OS_CFG_MUTEX_DEL_EN

When 1, this variable indicates that the function OSMutexDel() is available to the application. This value is set in OS_CFG.H.

ROM Variable	Data Type	Value
OSDbg_MutexPendAbortEn	CPU_INT08U	OS_CFG_MUTEX_PEND_ABORT_EN

When 1, the variable indicates that the function OSMutexPendAbort() is available to the application. This value is set in OS_CFG.H.

ROM Variable	Data Type	Value
OSDbg_MutexSize	CPU_INT16U	sizeof(OS_MUTEX)

This variable indicates the RAM footprint (in number of bytes) of an OS_MUTEX data type.

ROM Variable	Data Type	Value
OSDbg_ObjTypeChkEn	CPU_INT08U	OS_CFG_OBJ_TYPE_CHK_EN

When 1, this variable indicates that µC/OS-III will check for valid object types at run time. µC/OS-III will make sure the application is accessing a semaphore if calling OSSem???() functions, accessing a message queue when calling OSQ???() functions, etc. This value is set in OS_CFG.H.

19

ROM Variable	Data Type	Value
OSDbg_PendMultiEn	CPU_INT08U	OS_CFG_PEND_MULTI_EN

When 1, this variable indicates that µC/OS-III's service to pend on multiple objects (semaphores or message queues) is available to the application. This value is set in OS_CFG.H.

ROM Variable	Data Type	Value
OSDbg_PendDataSize	CPU_INT16U	sizeof(OS_PEND_DATA)

This variable indicates the RAM footprint (in bytes) of an **OS_PEND_DATA** data type.

ROM Variable	Data Type	Value
OSDbg_PendListSize	CPU_INT16U	sizeof(OS_PEND_LIST)

This variable indicates the RAM footprint (in bytes) of an OS_PEND_LIST data type.

ROM Variable	Data Type	Value
OSDbg_PendObjSize	CPU_INT16U	sizeof(OS_PEND_OBJ)

This variable indicates the RAM footprint (in bytes) of an **OS_PEND_OBJ** data type.

ROM Variable	Data Type	Value
OSDbg_PrioMax	CPU_INT16U	OS_CFG_PRIO_MAX

This variable indicates the maximum number of priorities that the application will support.

ROM Variable	Data Type	Value
OSDbg_PtrSize	CPU_INT16U	sizeof(void *)

This variable indicates the size (in bytes) of a pointer.

ROM Variable	Data Type	Value
OSDbg_QEn	CPU_INT08U	OS_CFG_Q_EN

When 1, this variable indicates that µC/OS-III's message queue services are available to the application. This value is set in **OS_CFG.H**.

ROM Variable	Data Type	Value
OSDbg_QDelEn	CPU_INT08U	OS_CFG_Q_DEL_EN

When 1, this variable indicates that the function OSQDel() is available to the application. This value is set in OS_CFG.H.

ROM Variable	Data Type	Value
OSDbg_QFlushEn	CPU_INT08U	OS_CFG_Q_FLUSH_EN

When 1, this variable indicates that the function OSQFlush() is available to the application. This value is set in OS_CFG.H.

ROM Variable	Data Type	Value
OSDbg_QPendAbortEn	CPU_INT08U	OS_CFG_Q_PEND_ABORT_EN

When 1, this variable indicates that the function OSQPendAbort() is available to the application. This value is set in OS_CFG.H.

ROM Variable	Data Type	Value
OSDbg_QSize	CPU_INT16U	

This variable indicates the RAM footprint (in number of bytes) of an OS_Q data type.

ROM Variable	Data Type	Value
OSDbg_SchedRoundRobinEn	CPU_INT08U	OS_CFG_ROUND_ROBIN_EN

When 1, this variable indicates that the µC/OS-III round robin scheduling feature is available to the application. This value is set in OS_CFG.H.

19

ROM Variable	Data Type	Value
OSDbg_SemEn	CPU_INT08U	OS_CFG_SEM_EN

When 1, this variable indicates that μC/OS-III's semaphore management services are available to the application. This value is set in OS_CFG.H.

ROM Variable	Data Type	Value
OSDbg_SemDelEn	CPU_INT08U	OS_CFG_SEM_DEL_EN

When 1, this variable indicates that the function OSSemDel() is available to the application. This value is set in OS_CFG.H.

ROM Variable	Data Type	Value
OSDbg_SemPendAbortEn	CPU_INT08U	OS_CFG_SEM_PEND_ABORT_EN

When 1, this variable indicates that the function OSSemPendAbort() is available to the application. This value is set in OS_CFG.H.

ROM Variable	Data Type	Value
OSDbg_SemSetEn	CPU_INT08U	OS_CFG_SEM_SET_EN

When 1, this variable indicates that the function OSSemSet() is available to the application. This value is set in OS_CFG.H.

ROM Variable	Data Type	Value
OSDbg_RdyList	CPU_INT16U	sizeof(OS_RDY_LIST)

This variable indicates the RAM footprint (in bytes) of an OS_RDY_LIST data type.

ROM Variable	Data Type	Value
OSDbg_RdyListSize	CPU_INT32U	sizeof(OSRdyList)

This variable indicates the RAM footprint (in bytes) of the ready list.

ROM Variable	Data Type	Value
OSDbg_StkWidth	CPU_INT08U	sizeof(CPU_STK)

This variable indicates the word size of a stack entry (in bytes). If a stack entry is declared as **CPU_INT08U**, this value will be 1, if a stack entry is declared as **CPU_INT16U**, the value will be 2, etc.

ROM Variable	Data Type	Value
OSDbg_StatTaskEn	CPU_INT08U	OS_CFG_STAT_TASK_EN

When 1, this variable indicates that μC/OS-III's statistic task is enabled. This value is set in **OS_CFG.H**.

ROM Variable	Data Type	Value
OSDbg_StatTaskStkChkEn	CPU_INT08U	OS_CFG_STAT_TASK_STK_CHK_EN

When 1, this variable indicates that μC/OS-III will perform run-time stack checking by walking the stack of each task to determine the usage of each. This value is set in **OS_CFG.H**.

ROM Variable	Data Type	Value
OSDbg_TaskChangePrioEn	CPU_INT08U	OS_CFG_TASK_CHANGE_PRIO_EN

When 1, this variable indicates that the function **OSTaskChangePrio()** is available to the application. This value is set in **OS_CFG.H**.

19

ROM Variable	Data Type	Value
OSDbg_TaskDelEn	CPU_INT08U	OS_CFG_TASK_DEL_EN

When 1, this variable indicates that the function **OSTaskDel()** is available to the application. This value is set in **OS_CFG.H**.

ROM Variable	Data Type	Value
OSDbg_TaskQEn	CPU_INT08U	OS_CFG_TASK_Q_EN

When 1, this variable indicates that **OSTaskQ???()** services are available to the application. This value is set in **OS_CFG.H**.

ROM Variable	Data Type	Value
OSDbg_TaskQPendAbortEn	CPU_INT08U	OS_CFG_TASK_Q_PEND_ABORT_EN

When 1, this variable indicates that the function **OSTaskQPendAbort()** is available to the application. This value is set in **OS_CFG.H**.

ROM Variable	Data Type	Value
OSDbg_TaskProfileEn	CPU_INT08U	OS_CFG_TASK_PROFILE_EN

When 1, this variable indicates that task profiling is enabled, and that µC/OS-III will perform run-time performance measurements on a per-task basis. Specifically, when 1, µC/OS-III will keep track of how many context switches each task makes, how long a task disables interrupts, how long a task locks the scheduler, and more. This value is set in **OS_CFG.H**.

ROM Variable	Data Type	Value
OSDbg_TaskRegTblSize	CPU_INT16U	OS_CFG_TASK_REG_TBL_SIZE

This variable indicates how many entries each task register table can accept.

ROM Variable	Data Type	Value
OSDbg_TaskSemPendAbortEn	CPU_INT08U	OS_CFG_TASK_SEM_PEND_ABORT_EN

When 1, this variable indicates that the function **OSTaskSemPendAbort()** is available to the application. This value is set in **OS_CFG.H**.

ROM Variable	Data Type	Value
OSDbg_TaskSuspendEn	CPU_INT08U	OS_CFG_TASK_SUSPEND_EN

When 1, this variable indicates that the function **OSTaskSuspend()** is available to the application. This value is set in **OS_CFG.H**.

ROM Variable	Data Type	Value
OSDbg_TCBSize	CPU_INT16U	sizeof(OS_TCB)

This variable indicates the RAM footprint (in bytes) of an **OS_TCB** data structure.

ROM Variable	Data Type	Value
OSDbg_TickSpokeSize	CPU_INT16U	sizeof(OS_TICK_SPOKE)

This variable indicates the RAM footprint (in bytes) of an **OS_TICK_SPOKE** data structure.

19

ROM Variable	Data Type	Value
OSDbg_TimeDlyHMSMEn	CPU_INT08U	OS_CFG_TIME_DLY_HMSM_EN

When 1, this variable indicates that the function **OSTimeDlyHMSM()** is available to the application. This value is set in **OS_CFG.H**.

ROM Variable	Data Type	Value
OSDbg_TimeDlyResumeEn	CPU_INT08U	OS_CFG_TIME_DLY_RESUME_EN

When 1, this variable indicates that the function **OSTimeDlyResume()** is available to the application. This value is set in **OS_CFG.H**.

ROM Variable	Data Type	Value
OSDbg_TmrEn	CPU_INT08U	OS_CFG_TMR_EN

When 1, this variable indicates that **OSTmr???()** services are available to the application. This value is set in **OS_CFG.H**.

ROM Variable	Data Type	Value
OSDbg_TmrDelEn	CPU_INT08U	OS_CFG_TMR_DEL_EN

When 1, this variable indicates that the function **OSTmrDel()** is available to the application. This value is set in **OS_CFG.H**.

ROM Variable	Data Type	Value
OSDbg_TmrSize	CPU_INT16U	sizeof(OS_TMR)

This variable indicates the RAM footprint (in bytes) of an **OS_TMR** data structure.

ROM Variable	Data Type	Value
OSDbg_TmrSpokeSize	CPU_INT16U	sizeof(OS_TMR_SPOKE)

This variable indicates the RAM footprint (in bytes) of an **OS_TMR_SPOKE** data structure.

19

ROM Variable	Data Type	Value
OSDbg_VersionNbr	CPU_INT16U	OS_VERSION

This variable indicates the current version of µC/OS-III multiplied by 1000. For example version 3.00.4 will show as 3004.ZZ

ROM Variable	Data Type	Value
OSDbg_DataSize	CPU_INT32U	Size of all RAM variables

This variable indicates the RAM footprint (in bytes) of the internal µC/OS-III variables for the current configuration.

19-5 OS_CFG_APP.C – STATIC

As with OS_DBG.C, OS_CFG_APP.C defines a number of ROM variables. These variables, however, reflect the run-time configuration of an application. Specifically, the user will be able to know the RAM footprint (in bytes) of µC/OS-III task stacks, the message pool, and more.

Below is a list of ROM variables provided in OS_APP_CFG.C, along with their descriptions. These variables represent approximately 100 bytes of code space.

Application code can examine these variables and the application does not need to access them in a critical region since they reside in code space and are therefore not changeable.

ROM Variable	Data Type	Value
OSCfg_IdleTaskStkSizeRAM	CPU_INT32U	sizeof(OSCfg_IdleTaskStk)

This variable indicates the RAM footprint (in bytes) of the µC/OS-III idle task stack.

19

ROM Variable	Data Type	Value
OSCfg_IntQSizeRAM	CPU_INT32U	sizeof(OSCfg_IntQ)

This variable indicates the RAM footprint (in bytes) of the µC/OS-III interrupt handler task queue.

ROM Variable	Data Type	Value
OSCfg_IntQTaskStkSizeRAM	CPU_INT32U	sizeof(OSCfg_IntQTaskStk)

This variable indicates the RAM footprint (in bytes) of the µC/OS-III interrupt queue handler task stack.

ROM Variable	Data Type	Value
OSCfg_ISRStkSizeRAM	CPU_INT32U	sizeof(OSCfg_ISRStk)

This variable indicates the RAM footprint (in bytes) of the dedicated Interrupt Service Routine (ISR) stack.

ROM Variable	Data Type	Value
OSCfg_MsgPoolSizeRAM	CPU_INT32U	sizeof(OSCfg_MsgPool)

This variable indicates the RAM footprint (in bytes) of the message pool.

ROM Variable	Data Type	Value
OSCfg_StatTaskStkSizeRAM	CPU_INT32U	sizeof(OSCfg_StatTaskStk)

This variable indicates the RAM footprint (in bytes) of the µC/OS-III statistic task stack.

ROM Variable	Data Type	Value
OSCfg_TickTaskStkSizeRAM	CPU_INT32U	sizeof(OSCfg_TickTaskStk)

This variable indicates the RAM footprint (in bytes) of the µC/OS-III tick task stack.

19

ROM Variable	Data Type	Value
OSCfg_TickWheelSizeRAM	CPU_INT32U	sizeof(OSCfg_TickWheel)

This variable indicates the RAM footprint (in bytes) of the tick wheel.

ROM Variable	Data Type	Value
OSCfg_TmrWheelSizeRAM	CPU_INT32U	sizeof(OSCfg_TmrWheel)

This variable indicates the RAM footprint (in bytes) of the timer wheel.

ROM Variable	Data Type	Value
OSCfg_DataSizeRAM	CPU_INT32U	Total of all configuration RAM

This variable indicates the RAM footprint (in bytes) of all of the configuration variables declared in OS_CFG_APP.C.

19-6 SUMMARY

This chapter presented a number of variables that can be read by a debugger and/or µC/Probe.

These variables provide run-time and compile-time (static) information regarding µC/OS-III-based applications. The µC/OS-III variables allow users to monitor RAM footprint, task stack usage, context switches, CPU usage, the execution time of many operations, and more.

The application must never change (i.e., write to) any of these variables.

19

19

µC/OS-III API Reference Manual

This chapter provides a reference to µC/OS-III services. Each of the user-accessible kernel services is presented in alphabetical order. The following information is provided for each entry:

■ A brief description of the service

■ The function prototype

■ The filename of the source code

■ The #define constant required to enable code for the service

■ A description of the arguments passed to the function

■ A description of returned value(s)

■ Specific notes and warnings regarding use of the service

■ One or two examples of how to use the function

Many functions return error codes. These error codes should be checked by the application to ensure that the µC/OS-III function performed its operation as expected.

The next few pages summarizes most of the services provided by µC/OS-III. The function calls in bold are commonly used.

A-1 TASK MANAGEMENT

```
void
OSTaskChangePrio   (OS_TCB      *p_tcb,
                    OS_PRIO      prio,
                    OS_ERR      *p_err);
```

```
void
OSTaskCreate       (OS_TCB      *p_tcb,
                    CPU_CHAR    *p_name,
                    OS_TASK_PTR *p_task,
                    void        *p_arg,
                    OS_PRIO      prio,
                    CPU_STK     *p_stk_base,
                    CPU_STK_SIZE stk_limit,
                    CPU_STK_SIZE stk_size,
                    OS_MSG_QTY   q_size,
                    OS_TICK      time_quanta,
                    void        *p_ext,
                    OS_OPT       opt,
                    OS_ERR      *p_err);
```

Values for "opt":
  OS_OPT_TASK_NONE
  OS_OPT_TASK_STK_CHK
  OS_OPT_TASK_STK_CLR
  OS_OPT_TASK_SAVE_FP

```
void
OSTaskDel          (OS_TCB      *p_tcb,
                    OS_ERR      *p_err);
```

```
OS_REG
OSTaskRegGet       (OS_TCB      *p_tcb,
                    OS_REG_ID    id,
                    OS_ERR      *p_err);
```

```
void
OSTaskRegSet       (OS_TCB      *p_tcb,
                    OS_REG_ID    id,
                    OS_REG       value,
                    OS_ERR      *p_err);
```

```
void
OSTaskResume       (OS_TCB      *p_tcb,
                    OS_ERR      *p_err);
```

```
void
OSTaskSuspend      (OS_TCB      *p_tcb,
                    OS_ERR      *p_err);
```

```
void
OSTaskStkChk       (OS_TCB      *p_tcb,
                    CPU_STK_SIZE *p_free,
                    CPU_STK_SIZE *p_used,
                    OS_ERR      *p_err);
```

```
void
OSTaskTimeQuantaSet (OS_TCB      *p_tcb,
                     OS_TICK      time_quanta,
                     OS_ERR      *p_err);
```

A-2 TIME MANAGEMENT

```
void
OSTimeDly      (OS_TICK    dly,
                OS_OPT     opt,
                OS_ERR     *p_err);
```

```
void
OSTimeDlyHMSM  (CPU_INT16U  hours,
                CPU_INT16U  minutes,
                CPU_INT16U  seconds
                CPU_INT32U  milli,
                OS_OPT      opt,
                OS_ERR      *p_err);
```

Values for "opt":
  OS_OPT_TIME_HMSM_STRICT
  OS_OPT_TIME_HMSM_NON_STRICT

```
void
OSTimeDlyResume (OS_TCB    *p_tcb,
                 OS_ERR    *p_err);
```

```
OS_TICK
OSTimeGet       (OS_ERR    *p_err);
```

```
void
OSTimeSet       (OS_TICK    ticks,
                 OS_ERR     *p_err);
```

A-3 MUTUAL EXCLUSION SEMAPHORES – RESOURCE MANAGEMENT

```
void
OSMutexCreate    (OS_MUTEX   *p_mutex,
                  CPU_CHAR   *p_name,
                  OS_ERR     *p_err);
```

```
void
OSMutexDel      (OS_MUTEX   *p_mutex,
                 OS_OPT      opt,
                 OS_ERR     *p_err);
```

Values for "opt":
  OS_OPT_DEL_NO_PEND
  OS_OPT_DEL_ALWAYS

```
void
OSMutexPend      (OS_MUTEX   *p_mutex,
                  OS_TICK     timeout,
                  OS_OPT      opt,
                  CPU_TS     *p_ts,
                  OS_ERR     *p_err);
```

Values for "opt":
  OS_OPT_PEND_BLOCKING
  OS_OPT_PEND_NON_BLOCKING

```
OS_OBJ_QTY
OSMutexPendAbort (OS_MUTEX   *p_mutex,
                  OS_OPT      opt,
                  OS_ERR     *p_err);
```

Values for "opt":
  OS_OPT_PEND_ABORT_1
  OS_OPT_PEND_ABORT_ALL
  OS_OPT_POST_NO_SCHED (additive)

```
void
OSMutexPost      (OS_MUTEX   *p_mutex,
                  OS_OPT      opt,
                  OS_ERR     *p_err);
```

Values for "opt":
  OS_OPT_POST_NONE
  OS_OPT_POST_NO_SCHED

A-4 EVENT FLAGS – SYNCHRONIZATION

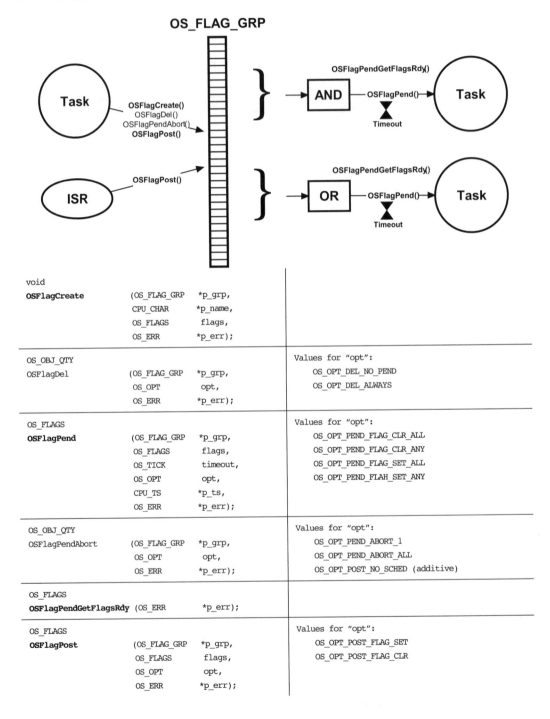

```
void
OSFlagCreate           (OS_FLAG_GRP   *p_grp,
                        CPU_CHAR      *p_name,
                        OS_FLAGS       flags,
                        OS_ERR        *p_err);
```

```
OS_OBJ_QTY                                          Values for "opt":
OSFlagDel              (OS_FLAG_GRP   *p_grp,          OS_OPT_DEL_NO_PEND
                        OS_OPT         opt,            OS_OPT_DEL_ALWAYS
                        OS_ERR        *p_err);
```

```
OS_FLAGS                                            Values for "opt":
OSFlagPend             (OS_FLAG_GRP   *p_grp,          OS_OPT_PEND_FLAG_CLR_ALL
                        OS_FLAGS       flags,          OS_OPT_PEND_FLAG_CLR_ANY
                        OS_TICK        timeout,        OS_OPT_PEND_FLAG_SET_ALL
                        OS_OPT         opt,            OS_OPT_PEND_FLAH_SET_ANY
                        CPU_TS        *p_ts,
                        OS_ERR        *p_err);
```

```
OS_OBJ_QTY                                          Values for "opt":
OSFlagPendAbort        (OS_FLAG_GRP   *p_grp,          OS_OPT_PEND_ABORT_1
                        OS_OPT         opt,            OS_OPT_PEND_ABORT_ALL
                        OS_ERR        *p_err);         OS_OPT_POST_NO_SCHED (additive)
```

```
OS_FLAGS
OSFlagPendGetFlagsRdy (OS_ERR        *p_err);
```

```
OS_FLAGS                                            Values for "opt":
OSFlagPost             (OS_FLAG_GRP   *p_grp,          OS_OPT_POST_FLAG_SET
                        OS_FLAGS       flags,          OS_OPT_POST_FLAG_CLR
                        OS_OPT         opt,
                        OS_ERR        *p_err);
```

A-5 SEMAPHORES – SYNCHRONIZATION

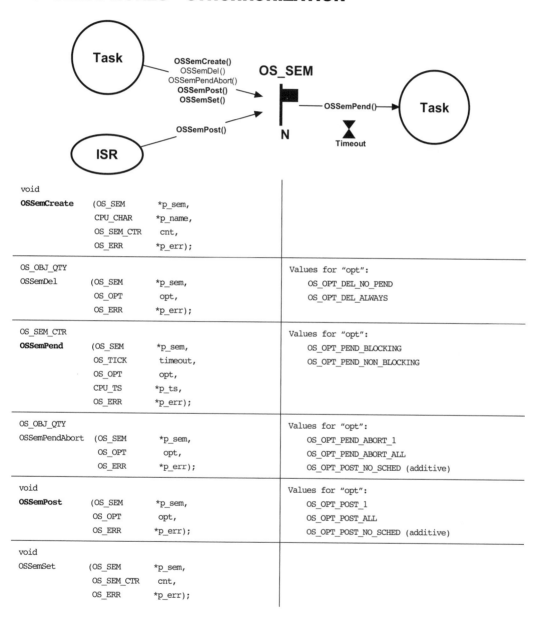

```
void
OSSemCreate     (OS_SEM       *p_sem,
                 CPU_CHAR     *p_name,
                 OS_SEM_CTR   cnt,
                 OS_ERR       *p_err);
```

```
OS_OBJ_QTY
OSSemDel        (OS_SEM       *p_sem,
                 OS_OPT       opt,
                 OS_ERR       *p_err);
```

Values for "opt":
    OS_OPT_DEL_NO_PEND
    OS_OPT_DEL_ALWAYS

```
OS_SEM_CTR
OSSemPend       (OS_SEM       *p_sem,
                 OS_TICK      timeout,
                 OS_OPT       opt,
                 CPU_TS       *p_ts,
                 OS_ERR       *p_err);
```

Values for "opt":
    OS_OPT_PEND_BLOCKING
    OS_OPT_PEND_NON_BLOCKING

```
OS_OBJ_QTY
OSSemPendAbort  (OS_SEM       *p_sem,
                 OS_OPT       opt,
                 OS_ERR       *p_err);
```

Values for "opt":
    OS_OPT_PEND_ABORT_1
    OS_OPT_PEND_ABORT_ALL
    OS_OPT_POST_NO_SCHED (additive)

```
void
OSSemPost       (OS_SEM       *p_sem,
                 OS_OPT       opt,
                 OS_ERR       *p_err);
```

Values for "opt":
    OS_OPT_POST_1
    OS_OPT_POST_ALL
    OS_OPT_POST_NO_SCHED (additive)

```
void
OSSemSet        (OS_SEM       *p_sem,
                 OS_SEM_CTR   cnt,
                 OS_ERR       *p_err);
```

A-6 TASK SEMAPHORES – SYNCHRONIZATION

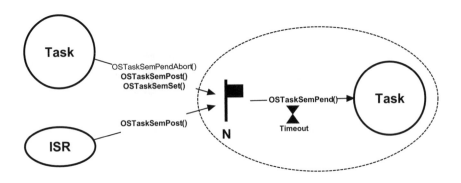

OS_SEM_CTR		Values for "opt":
OSTaskSemPend	(OS_TICK timeout,	OS_OPT_PEND_BLOCKING
	OS_OPT opt,	OS_OPT_PEND_NON_BLOCKING
	CPU_TS *p_ts,	
	OS_ERR *p_err);	
CPU_BOOLEAN		Values for "opt":
OSTaskSemPendAbort	(OS_TCB *p_tcb,	OS_OPT_POST_NONE
	OS_OPT opt,	OS_OPT_POST_NO_SCHED
	OS_ERR *p_err);	
OS_SEM_CTR		Values for "opt":
OSTaskSemPost	(OS_TCB *p_tcb,	OS_OPT_POST_NONE
	OS_OPT opt,	OS_OPT_POST_NO_SCHED
	OS_ERR *p_err);	
OS_SEM_CTR		
OSTaskSemSet	(OS_TCB *p_tcb,	
	OS_SEM_CTR cnt,	
	OS_ERR *p_err);	

A-7 MESSAGE QUEUES – MESSAGE PASSING

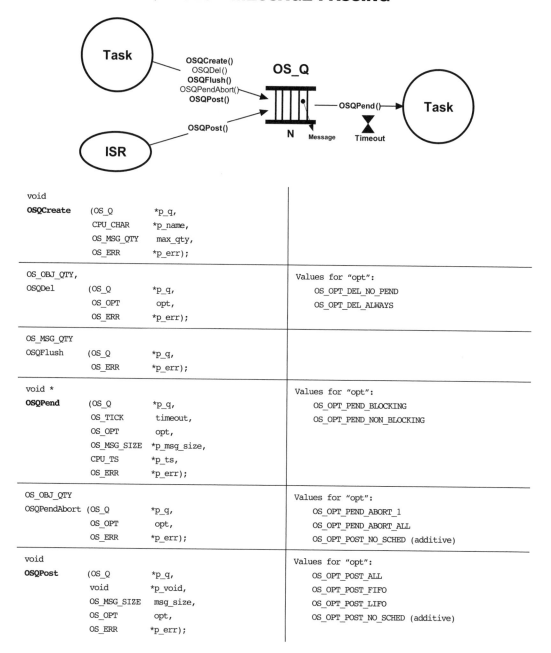

```
void
OSQCreate      (OS_Q        *p_q,
                CPU_CHAR     *p_name,
                OS_MSG_QTY    max_qty,
                OS_ERR       *p_err);
```

```
OS_OBJ_QTY,
OSQDel         (OS_Q        *p_q,
                OS_OPT       opt,
                OS_ERR       *p_err);
```

Values for "opt":
  OS_OPT_DEL_NO_PEND
  OS_OPT_DEL_ALWAYS

```
OS_MSG_QTY
OSQFlush       (OS_Q        *p_q,
                OS_ERR       *p_err);
```

```
void *
OSQPend        (OS_Q        *p_q,
                OS_TICK       timeout,
                OS_OPT        opt,
                OS_MSG_SIZE  *p_msg_size,
                CPU_TS       *p_ts,
                OS_ERR       *p_err);
```

Values for "opt":
  OS_OPT_PEND_BLOCKING
  OS_OPT_PEND_NON_BLOCKING

```
OS_OBJ_QTY
OSQPendAbort (OS_Q          *p_q,
                OS_OPT        opt,
                OS_ERR       *p_err);
```

Values for "opt":
  OS_OPT_PEND_ABORT_1
  OS_OPT_PEND_ABORT_ALL
  OS_OPT_POST_NO_SCHED (additive)

```
void
OSQPost        (OS_Q        *p_q,
                void         *p_void,
                OS_MSG_SIZE   msg_size,
                OS_OPT        opt,
                OS_ERR       *p_err);
```

Values for "opt":
  OS_OPT_POST_ALL
  OS_OPT_POST_FIFO
  OS_OPT_POST_LIFO
  OS_OPT_POST_NO_SCHED (additive)

A-8 TASK MESSAGE QUEUES – MESSAGE PASSING

```
OS_MSG_QTY
OSTaskQFlush      (OS_TCB       *p_tcb,
                   OS_ERR       *p_err);
```

```
void *
OSTaskQPend       (OS_TICK       timeout,
                   OS_OPT        opt,
                   OS_MSG_SIZE  *p_msg_size,
                   CPU_TS       *p_ts,
                   OS_ERR       *p_err);
```

Values for "opt":
   OS_OPT_PEND_BLOCKING
   OS_OPT_PEND_NON_BLOCKING

```
CPU_BOOLEAN
OSTaskQPendAbort (OS_TCB       *p_tcb,
                   OS_OPT        opt,
                   OS_ERR       *p_err);
```

Values for "opt":
   OS_OPT_POST_NONE
   OS_OPT_POST_NO_SCHED

```
void
OSTaskQPost       (OS_TCB       *p_tcb,
                   void         *p_void,
                   OS_MSG_SIZE   msg_size,
                   OS_OPT        opt,
                   OS_ERR       *p_err);
```

Values for "opt":
   OS_OPT_POST_FIFO
   OS_OPT_POST_LIFO
   OS_OPT_POST_NO_SCHED (additive)

A-9 PENDING ON MULTIPLE OBJECTS

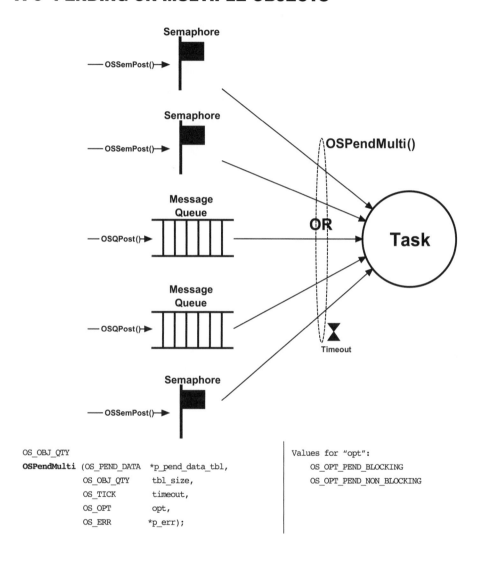

```
OS_OBJ_QTY
OSPendMulti (OS_PEND_DATA  *p_pend_data_tbl,
             OS_OBJ_QTY     tbl_size,
             OS_TICK        timeout,
             OS_OPT         opt,
             OS_ERR        *p_err);
```

```
Values for "opt":
    OS_OPT_PEND_BLOCKING
    OS_OPT_PEND_NON_BLOCKING
```

A-10 TIMERS

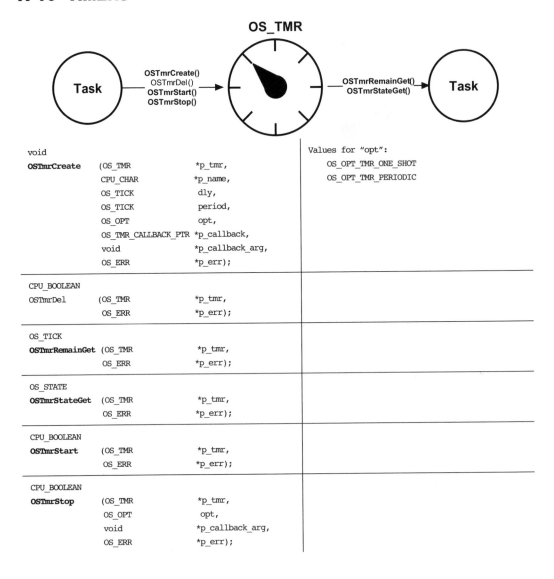

```
void
OSTmrCreate       (OS_TMR                *p_tmr,
                   CPU_CHAR              *p_name,
                   OS_TICK               dly,
                   OS_TICK                period,
                   OS_OPT                opt,
                   OS_TMR_CALLBACK_PTR *p_callback,
                   void                  *p_callback_arg,
                   OS_ERR                *p_err);
```

```
CPU_BOOLEAN
OSTmrDel          (OS_TMR                *p_tmr,
                   OS_ERR                *p_err);
```

```
OS_TICK
OSTmrRemainGet (OS_TMR                   *p_tmr,
                OS_ERR                   *p_err);
```

```
OS_STATE
OSTmrStateGet     (OS_TMR                *p_tmr,
                   OS_ERR                *p_err);
```

```
CPU_BOOLEAN
OSTmrStart        (OS_TMR                *p_tmr,
                   OS_ERR                *p_err);
```

```
CPU_BOOLEAN
OSTmrStop         (OS_TMR                *p_tmr,
                   OS_OPT                opt,
                   void                  *p_callback_arg,
                   OS_ERR                *p_err);
```

Values for "opt":

    OS_OPT_TMR_ONE_SHOT
    OS_OPT_TMR_PERIODIC

A-11 FIXED-SIZE MEMORY PARTITIONS – MEMORY MANAGEMENT

```
void
OSMemCreate (OS_MEM      *p_mem,
             CPU_CHAR    *p_name,
             void        *p_addr,
             OS_MEM_QTY  n_blks,
             OS_MEM_SIZE blk_size,
             OS_ERR      *p_err);
```

```
void *
OSMemGet    (OS_MEM      *p_mem,
             OS_ERR      *p_err);
```

```
void
OSMemPut    (OS_MEM      *p_mem,
             void        *p_blk,
             OS_ERR      *p_err);
```

OSCtxSw()

void   OSCtxSw (void)

File	Called from	Code enabled by
OS_CPU_A.ASM	OSSched()	N/A

OSCtxSw() is called from the macro OS_TASK_SW(), which in turn is called from OSSched() to perform a task-level context switch. Interrupts are disabled when OSCtxSw() is called.

Prior to calling OSCtxSw(), OSSched() sets OSTCBCurPtr to point at the OS_TCB of the task that is being switched out, and OSTCBHighRdyPtr to point at the OS_TCB of the task being switched in.

Arguments

None

Returned Values

None

Notes/Warnings

None

Example

The pseudocode for OSCtxSw() follows:

```
void  OSCtxSw (void)
{
    Save all CPU registers;                        (1)
    OSTCBCurPtr->StkPtr = SP;                       (2)
    OSTaskSwHook();                                 (3)
    OSPrioCur          = OSPrioHighRdy;             (4)
    OSTCBCurPtr        = OSTCBHighRdyPtr;           (5)
    SP                 = OSTCBHighRdyPtr->StkPtr;   (6)
    Restore all CPU registers;                      (7)
    Return from interrupt;                          (8)
}
```

(1)   **OSCtxSw()** must save all of the CPU registers onto the current task's stack. **OSCtxSw()** is called from the context of the task being switched out. Therefore, the CPU stack pointer is pointing to the proper stack. The user must save all of the registers in the same order as if an ISR started and all the CPU registers were saved on the stack. The stacking order should therefore match that of **OSTaskStkInit()**.

(2)   Save the current task's stack pointer into the current task's **OS_TCB**.

(3)   Next, **OSCtxSw()** must call **OSTaskSwHook()**.

(4)   Copy **OSPrioHighRdy** to **OSPrioCur**.

(5)   Copy **OSTCBHighRdyPtr** to **OSTCBCurPtr** since the current task is now the task being switched in.

(6)   Restore the stack pointer of the new task, which is found in the **OS_TCB** of the new task.

(7)   Restore all the CPU registers from the new task's stack.

(8)   Finally, **OSCtxSw()** must execute a return from interrupt instruction.

OSFlagCreate()

```
void  OSFlagCreate (OS_FLAG_GRP   *p_grp,
                    CPU_CHAR      *p_name,
                    OS_FLAGS       flags,
                    OS_ERR        *p_err)
```

File	Called from	Code enabled by
OS_FLAG.C	Task or startup code	OS_CFG_FLAG_EN

OSFlagCreate() is used to create and initialize an event flag group. µC/OS-III allows the user to create an unlimited number of event flag groups (limited only by the amount of RAM in the system).

Arguments

p_grp   is a pointer to an event flag group that must be allocated in the application. The user will need to declare a "global" variable as shown, and pass a pointer to this variable to **OSFlagCreate()**:

OS_FLAG_GRP   MyEventFlag;

p_name   is a pointer to an ASCII string used for the name of the event flag group. The name can be displayed by debuggers or by µC/Probe.

flags   contains the initial value of the flags to store in the event flag group.

p_err   is a pointer to a variable that is used to hold an error code. The error code can be one of the following:

OS_ERR_NONE	if the call is successful and the event flag group has been created.
OS_ERR_CREATE_ISR	if attempting to create an event flag group from an ISR, w is not allowed.
OS_ERR_NAME	if **p_name** is a **NULL** pointer.
OS_ERR_OBJ_CREATED	if the object passed has already been created.
OS_ERR_OBJ_PTR_NULL	if **p_grp** is a **NULL** pointer.

Returned Values

None

Notes/Warnings

1. Event flag groups must be created by this function before they can be used by the other event flag group services.

Example

```
OS_FLAG_GRP  EngineStatus;


void main (void)
{
    OS_ERR  err;

    OSInit(&err);                    /* Initialize µC/OS-III                            */
    :
    :
    OSFlagCreate(&EngineStatus,
                 "Engine Status",
                 (OS_FLAGS)0,
                 &err);              /* Create a flag grp containing the engine's status */
    /* Check "err" */
    :
    :
    OSStart();                       /* Start Multitasking                             */
}
```

OSFlagDel()

```
void OSFlagDel (OS_FLAG_GRP  *p_grp,
                OS_OPT        opt,
                OS_ERR       *p_err);
```

File	Called from	Code enabled by
OS_FLAG.C	Task	OS_CFG_FLAG_EN and OS_CFG_FLAG_DEL_EN

OSFlagDel() is used to delete an event flag group. This function should be used with care since multiple tasks may be relying on the presence of the event flag group. Generally, before deleting an event flag group, first delete all of the tasks that access the event flag group. Also, it is recommended that the user not delete kernel objects at run time.

Arguments

p_grp   is a pointer to the event flag group to delete.

opt   specifies whether the user wants to delete the event flag group only if there are no pending tasks (OS_OPT_DEL_NO_PEND), or whether the event flag group should always be deleted regardless of whether or not tasks are pending (OS_OPT_DEL_ALWAYS). In this case, all pending task are readied.

p_err   is a pointer to a variable used to hold an error code. The error code can be one of the following:

OS_ERR_NONE	if the call is successful and the event flag group has been deleted.
OS_ERR_DEL_ISR	if the user attempts to delete an event flag group from an ISR.
OS_ERR_OBJ_PTR_NULL	if p_grp is a NULL pointer.
OS_ERR_OBJ_TYPE	if p_grp is not pointing to an event flag group.
OS_ERR_OPT_INVALID	if the user does not specify one of the options mentioned in the opt argument.
OS_ERR_TASK_WAITING	if one or more tasks are waiting on the event flag group and OS_OPT_DEL_NO_PEND is specified.

Returned Values

0 if no task was waiting on the event flag group, or an error occurs.

> 0 if one or more tasks waiting on the event flag group are now readied and informed

Notes/Warnings

1. Use this call with care as other tasks might expect the presence of the event flag group.

Example

```
OS_FLAG_GRP  EngineStatusFlags;


void Task (void *p_arg)
{
    OS_ERR      err;
    OS_OBJ_QTY  qty;

    (void)&p_arg;
    while (DEF_ON) {
        :
        :
        qty = OSFlagDel(&EngineStatusFlags,
                        OS_OPT_DEL_ALWAYS,
                        &err);
        /* Check "err" */
        :
        :
    }
}
```

OSFlagPend()

```
OS_FLAGS  OSFlagPend (OS_FLAG_GRP *p_grp,
                      OS_FLAGS      flags,
                      OS_TICK       timeout,
                      OS_OPT        opt,
                      CPU_TS       *p_ts,
                      OS_ERR       *p_err)
```

File	Called from	Code enabled by
OS_FLAG.C	Task	OS_CFG_FLAG_EN

OSFlagPend() allows the task to wait for a combination of conditions (i.e., events or bits) to be set (or cleared) in an event flag group. The application can wait for any condition to be set or cleared, or for all conditions to be set or cleared. If the events that the calling task desires are not available, the calling task is blocked (optional) until the desired conditions are satisfied, the specified timeout expires, the event flag is deleted, or the pend is aborted by another task.

Arguments

p_grp   is a pointer to the event flag group.

flags   is a bit pattern indicating which bit(s) (i.e., flags) to check. The bits wanted are specified by setting the corresponding bits in flags. If the application wants to wait for bits 0 and 1 to be set, specify 0x03.

timeout   allows the task to resume execution if the desired flag(s) is(are) not received from the event flag group within the specified number of clock ticks. A timeout value of 0 indicates that the task wants to wait forever for the flag(s). The timeout value is not synchronized with the clock tick. The timeout count begins decrementing on the next clock tick, which could potentially occur immediately.

opt   specifies whether all bits are to be set/cleared or any of the bits are to be set/cleared. Specify the following arguments:

            OS_OPT_PEND_FLAG_CLR_ALL   Check all bits in flags to be clear (0)

            OS_OPT_PEND_FLAG_CLR_ANY   Check any bit in flags to be clear (0)

OS_OPT_PEND_FLAG_SET_ALL   Check all bits in flags to be set (1)

OS_OPT_PEND_FLAG_SET_ANY   Check any bit in flags to be set (1)

The user may also specify whether the flags are consumed by "adding" OS_OPT_PEND_FLAG_CONSUME to the opt argument. For example, to wait for any flag in a group and then clear the flags that satisfy the condition, set opt to:

OS_OPT_PEND_FLAG_SET_ANY + OS_OPT_PEND_FLAG_CONSUME

Finally, you can specify whether the user wants to block if the flag(s) are available or not. The user must "add" the following options:

OS_OPT_PEND_BLOCKING

OS_OPT_PEND_NON_BLOCKING

Note that the timeout argument should be set to 0 when specifying OS_OPT_PEND_NON_BLOCKING, since the timeout value is irrelevant using this option.

p_ts   is a pointer to a timestamp indicating when the flags were posted, the pend was aborted, or the event flag group was deleted. If passing a NULL pointer (i.e., (CPU_TS *)0), the user will not obtain the timestamp. Passing a NULL pointer is valid, and indicates that the user does not need the timestamp.

A timestamp is useful when the task desires to know when the event flag group was posted or how long it took for the task to resume after the event flag group was posted. In the latter case, the user must call OS_TS_GET() and compute the difference between the current value of the timestamp and *p_ts, as shown:

delta = OS_TS_GET() - *p_ts;

p_err   is a pointer to an error code and can be:

OS_ERR_NONE   No error.

OS_ERR_OBJ_PTR_NULL   if p_grp is a NULL pointer.

OS_ERR_OBJ_TYPE   p_grp is not pointing to an event flag group.

OS_ERR_OPT_INVALID   the user specified an invalid option.

OS_ERR_PEND_ABORT   the wait on the flags was aborted by another task that called OSFlagPendAbort().

`OS_ERR_PEND_ISR`	An attempt was made to call OSFlagPend from an ISR, which is not allowed.
`OS_ERR_SCHED_LOCKED`	When calling this function while the scheduler was locked.
`OS_ERR_PEND_WOULD_BLOCK`	**if** specifying non-blocking but the flags were not available and the call would block if the user had specified `OS_OPT_PEND_BLOCKING`.
`OS_ERR_TIMEOUT`	the flags are not available within the specified amount of time.

Returned Values

The flag(s) that cause the task to be ready, 0 if either none of the flags are ready, or indicate an error occurred.

Notes/Warnings

1. The event flag group must be created before it is used.

Example

```
#define  ENGINE_OIL_PRES_OK   0x01
#define  ENGINE_OIL_TEMP_OK   0x02
#define  ENGINE_START         0x04


OS_FLAG_GRP  EngineStatus;

void Task (void *p_arg)
{
    OS_ERR    err;
    OS_FLAGS  value;
    CPU_TS    ts;


    (void)&p_arg;
    while (DEF_ON) {
        value = OSFlagPend(&EngineStatus,
                           ENGINE_OIL_PRES_OK   + ENGINE_OIL_TEMP_OK,
                           OS_FLAG_WAIT_SET_ALL + OS_FLAG_CONSUME,
                           10,
                           OS_OPT_PEND_BLOCKING,
                           &ts,
                           &err);
        /* Check "err" */
        :
        :
    }
}
```

OSFlagPendAbort()

```
OS_OBJ_QTY  OSFlagPendAbort (OS_SEM  *p_grp,
                             OS_OPT   opt,
                             OS_ERR  *p_err)
```

File	Called from	Code enabled by
OS_FLAG.C	Task	OS_CFG_FLAG_EN and OS_CFG_FLAG_PEND_ABORT_EN

OSFlagPendAbort() aborts and readies any tasks currently waiting on an event flag group. This function should be used by another task to fault abort the wait on the event flag group, rather than to normally signal the event flag group via **OSFlagPost()**.

Arguments

p_grp   is a pointer to the event flag group for which pend(s) must be aborted.

opt   determines the type of abort performed.

OS_OPT_PEND_ABORT_1	Aborts the pend of only the highest priority task waiting on the event flag group.
OS_OPT_PEND_ABORT_ALL	Aborts the pend of all the tasks waiting on the event flag group.
OS_OPT_POST_NO_SCHED	Specifies that the scheduler should not be called even if the pend of a higher priority task is aborted. Scheduling will need to occur from another function. Use this option if the task calling **OSFlagPendAbort()** will perform additional pend aborts, rescheduling will take place at completion, and when multiple pend aborts are to take effect simultaneously.

p_err is a pointer to a variable that holds an error code. **OSFlagPendAbort()** sets ***p_err** to one of the following:

OS_ERR_NONE	at least one task waiting on the event flag group was readied and informed of the aborted wait. Check the return value for the number of tasks where a wait on the event flag group was aborted.
OS_ERR_OBJ_PTR_NULL	if **p_grp** is a **NULL** pointer.
OS_ERR_OBJ_TYPE	if **p_grp** is not pointing to an event flag group.
OS_ERR_OPT_INVALID	if specifying an invalid option.
OS_ERR_PEND_ABORT_ISR	This function cannot be called from an ISR.
OS_ERR_PEND_ABORT_NONE	No task was aborted since no task was waiting.

Returned Value

OSFlagPendAbort() returns the number of tasks made ready to run by this function. Zero indicates that no tasks were pending on the event flag group and thus this function had no effect.

Notes/Warnings

1. Event flag groups must be created before they are used.

Example

```
OS_FLAG_GRP  EngineStatus;


void Task (void *p_arg)
{
    OS_ERR     err;
    OS_OBJ_QTY nbr_tasks;


    (void)&p_arg;
    while (DEF_ON) {
        :
        :
        nbr_tasks = OSFlagPendAbort(&EngineStatus,
                                    OS_OPT_PEND_ABORT_ALL,
                                    &err);

        /* Check "err" */
        :
        :
    }
}
```

OSFlagPendGetFlagsRdy()

```
OS_FLAGS  OSFlagPendGetFlagsRdy (OS_ERR  *p_err)
```

File	Called from	Code enabled by
OS_FLAG.C	Task	OS_CFG_FLAG_EN

OSFlagPendGetFlagsRdy() is used to obtain the flags that caused the current task to be ready to run. This function allows the user to know "Who done it!"

Arguments

p_err   is a pointer to an error code and can be:

OS_ERR_NONE	No error.
OS_ERR_PEND_ISR	When attempting to call this function from an ISR.

Returned Value

The value of the flags that caused the current task to become ready to run.

Notes/Warnings

1. The event flag group must be created before it is used.

Example

```
#define  ENGINE_OIL_PRES_OK    0x01
#define  ENGINE_OIL_TEMP_OK    0x02
#define  ENGINE_START          0x04


OS_FLAG_GRP  EngineStatus;


void Task (void *p_arg)
{
    OS_ERR    err;
    OS_FLAGS  value;
    OS_FLAGS  flags_rdy;


    (void)&p_arg;
    while (DEF_ON) {
        value     = OSFlagPend(&EngineStatus,
                             ENGINE_OIL_PRES_OK  + ENGINE_OIL_TEMP_OK,
                             OS_FLAG_WAIT_SET_ALL + OS_FLAG_CONSUME,
                             10,
                             &err);
        /* Check "err" */
        flags_rdy = OSFlagPendGetFlagsRdy(&err);
        /* Check "err" */
        :
        :
    }
}
```

OSFlagPost()

```
OS_FLAGS  OSFlagPost (OS_FLAG_GRP  *p_grp,
                      OS_FLAGS      flags,
                      OS_OPT        opt,
                      OS_ERR        *p_err)
```

File	Called from	Code enabled by
OS_FLAG.C	Task or ISR	OS_CFG_FLAG_EN

Set or clear event flag bits by calling **OSFlagPost()**. The bits set or cleared are specified in a bit mask (i.e., the flags argument). **OSFlagPost()** readies each task that has its desired bits satisfied by this call. The user can set or clear bits that are already set or cleared.

Arguments

p_grp   is a pointer to the event flag group.

flags   specifies which bits to be set or cleared. If opt is **OS_OPT_POST_FLAG_SET**, each bit that is set in flags will set the corresponding bit in the event flag group. For example to set bits 0, 4, and 5, set flags to 0x31 (note that bit 0 is the least significant bit). If opt is **OS_OPT_POST_FLAG_CLR**, each bit that is set in flags will clear the corresponding bit in the event flag group. For example to clear bits 0, 4, and 5, specify flags as 0x31 (again, bit 0 is the least significant bit).

opt   indicates whether the flags are set (**OS_OPT_POST_FLAG_SET**) or cleared (**OS_OPT_POST_FLAG_CLR**).

             The user may also "add" **OS_OPT_POST_NO_SCHED** so that μC/OS-III will not call the scheduler after the post.

p_err   is a pointer to an error code and can be:

OS_ERR_NONE	the call is successful.
OS_ERR_FLAG_INVALID_OPT	specify an invalid option.
OS_ERR_OBJ_PTR_NULL	the user passed a **NULL** pointer.
OS_ERR_OBJ_TYPE	the user is not pointing to an event flag group.

Returned Value

The new value of the event flags.

Notes/Warnings

1   Event flag groups must be created before they are used.

2   The execution time of this function depends on the number of tasks waiting on the event flag group. However, the execution time is still deterministic.

3   Although the example below shows that we are posting from a task, **OSFlagPost()** can also be called from an ISR.

Example

```
#define  ENGINE_OIL_PRES_OK    0x01
#define  ENGINE_OIL_TEMP_OK    0x02
#define  ENGINE_START          0x04

OS_FLAG_GRP  EngineStatusFlags;


void  TaskX (void *p_arg)
{
    OS_ERR    err;
    OS_FLAGS  flags;


    (void)&p_arg;
    while (DEF_ON) {
        :
        :
        flags = OSFlagPost(&EngineStatusFlags,
                           ENGINE_START,
                           OS_OPT_POST_FLAG_SET,
                           &err);
        /* Check 'err" */
        :
        :
    }
}
```

OSIdleTaskHook()

```
void   OSIdleTaskHook (void);
```

File	Called from	Code enabled by
OS_CPU_C.C	OS_IdleTask() ONLY	N/A

This function is called by **OS_IdleTask()**.

OSIdleTaskHook() is part of the CPU port code and this function *must not* be called by the application code. **OSIdleTaskHook()** is used by the µC/OS-III port developer.

OSIdleTaskHook() runs in the context of the idle task so that it is important to make sure there is sufficient stack space in the idle task. **OSIdleTaskHook()** *must not* make any **OS???Pend()** calls, call **OSTaskSuspend()** or **OSTimeDly???()**. In other words, this function must never be allowed to make a blocking call.

Arguments

None

Returned Value

None

Notes/Warnings

1. Never make blocking calls from **OSIdleTaskHook()**.

2. *Do not* call this function from you application.

Example

The code below calls an application-specific hook that the application programmer can define. The user can simply set the value of **OS_AppIdleTaskHookPtr** to point to the desired hook function which in this case assumes s defined in **OS_APP_HOOKS.C**. The idle task calls **OSIdleTaskHook()** which in turns calls **App_OS_IdleTaskHook()** through **OS_AppIdleTaskHookPtr**.

This feature is very useful when there is a processor that can enter low-power mode. When µC/OS-III has no other task to run, the processor can be put to sleep waiting for an interrupt to wake it up.

```c
void  App_OS_IdleTaskHook (void)                          /* See OS_APP_HOOKS.C    */
{
    /* Your code goes here! */
    /* Put the CPU in low power mode (optional) */
}


void App_OS_SetAllHooks (void)                            /* OS_APP_HOOKS.C        */
{
    CPU_SR_ALLOC();

    CPU_CRITICAL_ENTER();
    :
    OS_AppIdleTaskHookPtr = App_OS_IdleTaskHook;
    :
    CPU_CRITICAL_EXIT();
}


void  OSIdleTaskHook (void)                               /* See OS_CPU_C.C        */
{
#if OS_CFG_APP_HOOKS_EN > 0u
    if (OS_AppIdleTaskHookPtr != (OS_APP_HOOK_VOID)0) {   /* Call application hook */
        (*OS_AppIdleTaskHookPtr)();
    }
#endif
}
```

OSInit()

```
void OSInit (OS_ERR *p_err);
```

File	Called from	Code enabled by
OS_CORE.C	Startup code only	N/A

OSInit() initializes µC/OS-III and it must be called prior to calling any other µC/OS-III function. Including OSStart()which will start multitasking.

Arguments

p_err   is a pointer to an error code and can be:

OS_ERR_NONE   initialization was successful.

OS_ERR_????   some other OS_ERR_???? value returned by a
                               sub-function of OSInit().

Returned Values
None

Notes/Warnings
1. OSInit() must be called before OSStart().

2. OSInit() returns as soon as it detects an error in any of the sub-functions it calls. For example, if OSInit() encounters a problem initializing the task manager, an appropriate error code will be returned and OSInit() will not go any further. It is therefore important that the user checks the error code before starting multitasking.

Example

```
void main (void)
{
    OS_ERR  err;

        :
    OSInit(&err);                   /* Initialize µC/OS-III           */
    /* Check "err" */
        :
        :
    OSStart(&err);                  /* Start Multitasking             */
    /* Check "err" */               /* Code not supposed to end up here! */
}
```

OSInitHook()

```
void OSInitHook (void);
```

File	Called from	Code enabled by
OS_CPU_C.C	OSInit()	Always enabled

OSInitHook() is a function that is called by µC/OS-III's initialization code, OSInit(). OSInitHook() is typically implemented by the port implementer for the processor used. This hook allows the port to be extended to do such tasks as setup exception stacks, floating-point registers, and more. OSInitHook() is called at the beginning of OSInit(), before any µC/OS-III task and data structure have been initialized.

Arguments

None

Returned Values

None

Notes/Warnings

None

Example

```
void  OSInitHook (void)                          /* See OS_CPU_C.C      */
{
    /* Perform any initialization code necessary by the port */
}
```

OSIntCtxSw()

void   OSIntCtxSw (void)

File	Called from	Code enabled by
OS_CPU_A.ASM	OSIntExit()	N/A

OSIntCtxSw() is called from OSIntExit() to perform a context switch when all nested interrupts have returned.

Interrupts are disabled when OSIntCtxSw() is called.

OSIntExit() sets OSTCBCurPtr to point at the OS_TCB of the task that is switched out and OSTCBHighRdyPtr to point at the OS_TCB of the task that is switched in.

Arguments
None

Returned Values
None

Notes/Warnings
None

Example

The pseudocode for OSIntCtxSw() is shown below. Notice that the code does only half of what OSCtxSw() did. The reason is that OSIntCtxSw() is called from an ISR and it is assumed that all of the CPU registers of the interrupted task were saved at the beginning of the ISR. OSIntCtxSw() therefore only must restore the context of the new, high-priority task.

```
void  OSIntCtxSw (void)
{
    OSTaskSwHook();                              (1)
    OSPrioCur          = OSPrioHighRdy;          (2)
    OSTCBCurPtr        = OSTCBHighRdyPtr;         (3)
    SP                 = OSTCBHighRdyPtr->StkPtr; (4)
    Restore all CPU registers;                   (5)
    Return from interrupt;                        (6)
}
```

(1)   OSIntCtxSw() must call OSTaskSwHook().

(2)   Copy OSPrioHighRdy to OSPrioCur.

(3)   Copy OSTCBHighRdyPtr to OSTCBCurPtr because the current task will now be the new task.

(4)   Restore the stack pointer of the new task, which is found in the OS_TCB of the new task.

(5)   Restore all the CPU registers from the new task's stack.

(6)   Execute a return from interrupt instruction.

OSIntEnter()

void OSIntEnter (void);

File	Called from	Code enabled by
OS_CORE.C	ISR only	N/A

OSIntEnter() notifies µC/OS-III that an ISR is being processed, which allows µC/OS-III to keep track of interrupt nesting. **OSIntEnter()** is used in conjunction with **OSIntExit()**. This function is generally called at the beginning of ISRs. Note that on some CPU architectures, it must be written in assembly language (shown below in pseudo code):

```
MyISR:
    Save CPU registers;
    OSIntEnter();              /* Or, OSIntNestingCtr++ */
        :
    Process ISR;
        :
    OSIntExit();
    Restore CPU registers;
    Return from interrupt;
```

Arguments
None

Returned Values
None

Notes/Warnings
1. This function must not be called by task-level code.

2. Iincrement the interrupt-nesting counter (OSIntNestingCtr) directly in the ISR to avoid the overhead of the function call/return. It is safe to increment OSIntNestingCtr in the ISR since interrupts are assumed to be disabled when OSIntNestingCtr is incremented. However, that is not true for all CPU architectures. Make sure interrupts are disabled in the ISR before directly incrementing OSIntNestingCtr.

3. It is possible to nest interrupts up to 250 levels deep.

OSIntExit()

void OSIntExit (void);

File	Called from	Code enabled by
OS_CORE.C	ISR only	N/A

OSIntExit() notifies µC/OS-III that an ISR is complete, which allows µC/OS-III to keep track of interrupt nesting. OSIntExit() is used in conjunction with OSIntEnter(). When the last nested interrupt completes, OSIntExit() determines if a higher priority task is ready to run. If so, the interrupt returns to the higher priority task instead of the interrupted task.

This function is typically called at the end of ISRs as follows, and on some CPU architectures, it must be written in assembly language (shown below in pseudo code):

```
MyISR:
    Save CPU registers;
    OSIntEnter();
        :
    Process ISR;
        :
    OSIntExit();
    Restore CPU registers;
    Return from interrupt;
```

Arguments
None

Returned Value
None

Notes/Warnings
1. This function must not be called by task-level code. Also, if directly incrementing OSIntNestingCtr, instead of calling OSIntEnter(), the user must still call OSIntExit().

OSMemCreate()

```
void  OSMemCreate (OS_MEM        *p_mem,
                   CPU_CHAR      *p_name,
                   void          *p_addr,
                   OS_MEM_QTY    n_blks,
                   OS_MEM_SIZE   blk_size,
                   OS_ERR        *p_err)
```

File	Called from	Code enabled by
OS_MEM.C	Task or startup code	OS_CFG_MEM_EN

OSMemCreate() creates and initializes a memory partition. A memory partition contains a user-specified number of fixed-size memory blocks. An application may obtain one of these memory blocks and, when completed, release the block back to the same partition where the block originated.

Arguments

p_mem   is a pointer to a memory partition control block that must be allocated in the application. It is assumed that storage will be allocated for the memory control blocks in the application. In other words, the user will declare a "global" variable as follows, and pass a pointer to this variable to OSMemCreate():

        OS_MEM MyMemPartition;

p_name   is a pointer to an ASCII string to provide a name to the memory partition. The name can be displayed by debuggers or µC/Probe.

p_addr   is the address of the start of a memory area used to create fixed-size memory blocks. Memory partitions may be created either using static arrays or malloc() during startup. Note that the partition *must* align on a pointer boundary. Thus, if a pointer is 16-bits wide. the partition must start on a memory location with an address that ends with 0, 2, 4, 6, 8, etc. If a pointer is 32-bits wide, the partition must start on a memory location with an address that ends in 0, 4, 8 of C. The easiest way to ensure this is to create a static array as follows:

        void *MyMemArray[N][M * sizeof(void *)]

Never deallocate memory blocks that were allocated from the heap to prevent fragmentation of your heap. It is quite acceptable to allocate memory blocks from the heap as long as the user does not deallocate them.

n_blks   contains the number of memory blocks available from the specified partition. Specify at least two memory blocks per partition.

blk_size   specifies the size (in bytes) of each memory block within a partition. A memory block must be large enough to hold at least a pointer. Also, the size of a memory block must be a multiple of the size of a pointer. If a pointer is 32-bits wide then the block size must be 4, 8, 12, 16, 20, etc. bytes (i.e., a multiple of 4 bytes).

p_err   is a pointer to a variable that holds an error code:

OS_ERR_NONE	if the memory partition is created successfully
OS_ERR_MEM_INVALID_BLKS	if the user does not specify at least two memory blocks per partition
OS_ERR_MEM_INVALID_P_ADDR	if specifying an invalid address (i.e., **p_addr** is a **NULL** pointer) or the partition is not properly aligned.
OS_ERR_MEM_INVALID_SIZE	if the user does not specify a block size that can contain at least a pointer variable, and if it is not a multiple of a pointer-size variable.

Returned Value

None

Notes/Warnings

1. Memory partitions must be created before they are used.

Example

```
OS_MEM      CommMem;
CPU_INT32U *CommBuf[16][32];             /* 16 buffers of 32 words of 32 bits */


void  main (void)
{
    OS_ERR  err;


    OSInit(&err);                        /* Initialize µC/OS-III              */
    :
    :
    OSMemCreate(&CommMem,
                "Comm Buffers",
                &CommBuf[0][0],
                16,
                32 * sizeof(CPU_INT32U),
                &err);
    /* Check "err" */
    :
    :
    OSStart(&err);                       /* Start Multitasking               */
}
```

OSMemGet()

```
void  *OSMemGet (OS_MEM  *p_mem,
                 OS_ERR  *p_err)
```

File	Called from	Code enabled by
OS_MEM.C	Task or ISR	OS_CFG_MEM_EN

OSMemGet() obtains a memory block from a memory partition. It is assumed that the application knows the size of each memory block obtained. Also, the application must return the memory block [using OSMemPut()] to the same memory partition when it no longer requires it. OSMemGet() may be called more than once until all memory blocks are allocated.

Arguments

p_mem   is a pointer to the desired memory partition control block.

p_err   is a pointer to a variable that holds an error code:

OS_ERR_NONE	if a memory block is available and returned to the application.
OS_ERR_MEM_INVALID_P_MEM	if p_mem is a NULL pointer.
OS_ERR_MEM_NO_FREE_BLKS	if the memory partition does not contain additional memory blocks to allocate.

Returned Value

OSMemGet() returns a pointer to the allocated memory block if one is available. If a memory block is not available from the memory partition, OSMemGet() returns a NULL pointer. It is up to the application to "cast" the pointer to the proper data type since OSMemGet() returns a void *.

Notes/Warnings

1. Memory partitions must be created before they are used.

2. This is a non-blocking call and this function can be called from an ISR.

Example

```
OS_MEM  CommMem;


void Task (void *p_arg)
{
    OS_ERR      err;
    CPU_INT08U  *p_msg;


    (void)&p_arg;
    while (DEF_ON) {
        p_msg = (CPU_INT08U *)OSMemGet(&CommMem,
                                       &err);
        /* Check "err" */
        :
        :
    }
}
```

OSMemPut()

```
void  OSMemPut (OS_MEM  *p_mem,
               void     *p_blk,
               OS_ERR   *p_err)
```

File	Called from	Code enabled by
OS_MEM.C	Task or ISR	OS_CFG_MEM_EN

OSMemPut() returns a memory block back to a memory partition. It is assumed that the user will return the memory block to the same memory partition from which it was allocated.

Arguments

p_mem   is a pointer to the memory partition control block.

p_blk   is a pointer to the memory block to be returned to the memory partition.

p_err   is a pointer to a variable that holds an error code:

OS_ERR_NONE	if a memory block is available and returned to the application.
OS_ERR_MEM_INVALID_P_BLK	if the user passed a NULL pointer for the memory block being returned to the memory partition.
OS_ERR_MEM_INVALID_P_MEM	if p_mem is a NULL pointer.
OS_ERR_MEM_MEM_FULL	if returning a memory block to an already full memory partition. This would indicate that the user freed more blocks that were allocated and potentially did not return some of the memory blocks to the proper memory partition.

Returned Value

None

Notes/Warnings

1. Memory partitions must be created before they are used.

2. Return a memory block to the proper memory partition.

3. Call this function from an ISR or a task.

Example

```
OS_MEM        CommMem;
CPU_INT08U  *CommMsg;


void Task (void *p_arg)
{
    OS_ERR err;


    (void)&p_arg;
    while (DEF_ON) {
        OSMemPut(&CommMem,
                 (void *)CommMsg,
                 &err);
        /* Check "err" */
        :
        :
    }
}
```

OSMutexCreate()

```
void  OSMutexCreate (OS_MUTEX   *p_mutex,
                     CPU_CHAR   *p_name,
                     OS_ERR     *p_err)
```

File	Called from	Code enabled by
OS_MUTEX.C	Task or startup code	OS_CFG_MUTEX_EN

OSMutexCreate() is used to create and initialize a mutex. A mutex is used to gain exclusive access to a resource.

Arguments

p_mutex   is a pointer to a mutex control block that must be allocated in the application. The user will need to declare a "global" variable as follows, and pass a pointer to this variable to OSMutexCreate():

            OS_MUTEX MyMutex;

p_name   is a pointer to an ASCII string used to assign a name to the mutual exclusion semaphore. The name may be displayed by debuggers or µC/Probe.

p_err   is a pointer to a variable that is used to hold an error code:

OS_ERR_NONE	if the call is successful and the mutex has been created.
OS_ERR_CREATE_ISR	if attempting to create a mutex from an ISR.
OS_ERR_OBJ_CREATED	if p_mutex already points to a mutex. This indicates that the mutex is already created.
OS_ERR_OBJ_PTR_NULL	if p_mutex is a NULL pointer.
OS_ERR_OBJ_TYPE	if p_mutex points to a different type of object (semaphore, message queue or timer).

Returned Value

None

Notes/Warnings

1. Mutexes must be created before they are used.

Example

```
OS_MUTEX  DispMutex;


void main (void)
{
    OS_ERR  err;


    :
    OSInit(&err);                       /* Initialize µC/OS-III       */
    :
    :
    OSMutexCreate(&DispMutex,           /* Create Display Mutex       */
                  "Display Mutex",
                  &err);
    /* Check "err" */


    :
    :
    OSStart(&err);                      /* Start Multitasking         */
}
```

OSMutexDel()

```
void  OSMutexDel (OS_MUTEX  *p_mutex,
                  OS_OPT     opt,
                  OS_ERR    *p_err)
```

File	Called from	Code enabled by
OS_MUTEX.C	Task	OS_CFG_MUTEX_EN and OS_CFG_MUTEX_DEL_EN

OSMutexDel() is used to delete a mutex. This function should be used with care because multiple tasks may rely on the presence of the mutex. Generally speaking, before deleting a mutex, first delete all the tasks that access the mutex. However, as a general rule, do not delete kernel objects at run-time.

Arguments

p_mutex   is a pointer to the mutex to delete.

opt   specifies whether to delete the mutex only if there are no pending tasks (OS_OPT_DEL_NO_PEND), or whether to always delete the mutex regardless of whether tasks are pending or not (OS_OPT_DEL_ALWAYS). In this case, all pending task are readied.

p_err   is a pointer to a variable that is used to hold an error code:

OS_ERR_NONE	if the call is successful and the mutex has been deleted.
OS_ERR_DEL_ISR	if attempting to delete a mutex from an ISR.
OS_ERR_OBJ_PTR_NULL	if p_mutex is a NULL pointer.
OS_ERR_OBJ_TYPE	if p_mutex is not pointing to a mutex.
OS_ERR_OPT_INVALID	if the user does not specify one of the two options mentioned in the opt argument.
OS_ERR_TASK_WAITING	if one or more task are waiting on the mutex and OS_OPT_DEL_NO_PEND is specified.

Returned Value

The number of tasks that were waiting for the mutex and 0 if an error occurred.

Notes/Warnings

1. Use this call with care as other tasks may expect the presence of the mutex.

Example

```
OS_MUTEX  DispMutex;


void Task (void *p_arg)
{
    OS_ERR  err;


    (void)&p_arg;
    while (DEF_ON) {
        :
        :
        OSMutexDel(&DispMutex,
                   OS_OPT_DEL_ALWAYS,
                   &err);
        /* Check "err" */
        :
        :
    }
}
```

OSMutexPend()

```
void   OSMutexPend (OS_MUTEX    *p_mutex,
                    OS_TICK      timeout,
                    OS_OPT       opt,
                    CPU_TS      *p_ts,
                    OS_ERR      *p_err)
```

File	Called from	Code enabled by
OS_MUTEX.C	Task only	OS_CFG_MUTEX_EN

OSMutexPend() is used when a task requires exclusive access to a resource. If a task calls OSMutexPend() and the mutex is available, OSMutexPend() gives the mutex to the caller and returns to its caller. Note that nothing is actually given to the caller except that if p_err is set to OS_ERR_NONE, the caller can assume that it owns the mutex.

However, if the mutex is already owned by another task, OSMutexPend() places the calling task in the wait list for the mutex. The task waits until the task that owns the mutex releases the mutex and therefore the resource, or until the specified timeout expires. If the mutex is signaled before the timeout expires, μC/OS-III resumes the highest-priority task that is waiting for the mutex.

Note that if the mutex is owned by a lower-priority task, OSMutexPend() raises the priority of the task that owns the mutex to the same priority as the task requesting the mutex. The priority of the owner will be returned to its original priority when the owner releases the mutex (see OSMutexPost()).

OSMutexPend() allows nesting. The same task can call OSMutexPend() multiple times. However, the same task must then call OSMutexPost() an equivalent number of times to release the mutex.

Arguments

p_mutex   is a pointer to the mutex.

timeout   specifies a timeout value (in clock ticks) and is used to allow the task to resume execution if the mutex is not signaled (i.e., posted to) within the specified timeout. A timeout value of 0 indicates that the task wants to wait forever for the mutex. The timeout value is not synchronized with the clock tick. The timeout count is decremented on the next clock tick, which could potentially occur immediately.

opt   determines whether the user wants to block if the mutex is not available or not. This argument must be set to either:

            OS_OPT_PEND_BLOCKING, or

            OS_OPT_PEND_NON_BLOCKING

            Note that the timeout argument should be set to 0 when specifying OS_OPT_PEND_NON_BLOCKING since the timeout value is irrelevant using this option.

p_ts   is a pointer to a timestamp indicating when the mutex was posted, the pend was aborted, or the mutex was deleted. If passing a NULL pointer (i.e., (CPU_TS *)0), the user will not receive the timestamp. In other words, passing a NULL pointer is valid and indicates that the timestamp is not required.

            A timestamp is useful when it is important for a task to know when the mutex was posted, or how long it took for the task to resume after the mutex was posted. In the latter case, the user must call OS_TS_GET() and compute the difference between the current value of the timestamp and *p_ts. In other words:

            delta = OS_TS_GET() - *p_ts;

p_err   is a pointer to a variable that is used to hold an error code:

OS_ERR_NONE	if the call is successful and the mutex is available.
OS_ERR_MUTEX_NESTING	if the calling task already owns the mutex and it has not posted all nested values.
OS_ERR_MUTEX_OWNER	if the calling task already owns the mutex.
OS_ERR_OBJ_PTR_NULL	if p_mutex is a NULL pointer.

OS_ERR_OBJ_TYPE	if the user did not pass a pointer to a mutex.
OS_ERR_OPT_INVALID	if a valid option is not specified.
OS_ERR_PEND_ISR	if attempting to acquire the mutex from an ISR.
OS_ERR_SCHED_LOCKED	if calling this function when the scheduler is locked
OS_ERR_TIMEOUT	if the mutex is not available within the specified timeout.

Returned Value

None

Notes/Warnings

1. Mutexes must be created before they are used.

2. Do not suspend the task that owns the mutex. Also, do not have the mutex owner wait on any other µC/OS-III objects (i.e., semaphore, event flag, or queue), and delay the task that owns the mutex. The code should release the resource as quickly as possible.

Example

```
OS_MUTEX  DispMutex;


void  DispTask (void *p_arg)
{
    OS_ERR  err;
    CPU_TS  ts;


    (void)&p_arg;
    while (DEF_ON) {
        :
        OSMutexPend(&DispMutex,
                    0,
                    OS_OPT_PEND_BLOCKING,
                    &ts,
                    &err);
        /* Check "err" */
    }
}
```

OSMutexPendAbort()

```
void OSMutexPendAbort (OS_MUTEX  *p_mutex,
                       OS_OPT     opt,
                       OS_ERR    *p_err)
```

File	Called from	Code enabled by
OS_MUTEX.C	Task	OS_CFG_MUTEX_EN and OS_CFG_MUTEX_PEND_ABORT_EN

OSMutexPendAbort() aborts and readies any tasks currently waiting on a mutex. This function should be used to fault-abort the wait on the mutex rather than to normally signal the mutex via OSMutexPost().

Arguments

p_mutex   is a pointer to the mutex.

opt   specifies whether to abort only the highest-priority task waiting on the mutex or all tasks waiting on the mutex:

OS_OPT_PEND_ABORT_1   to abort only the highest-priority task waiting on the mutex.

OS_OPT_PEND_ABORT_ALL   to abort all tasks waiting on the mutex.

OS_OPT_POST_NO_SCHED   specifies that the scheduler should not be called even if the pend of a higher-priority task has been aborted. Scheduling will need to occur from another function.

The user would select this option if the task calling OSMutexPendAbort() will be doing additional pend aborts, rescheduling should not take place until all tasks are completed, and multiple pend aborts should take place simultaneously.

p_err   is a pointer to a variable that is used to hold an error code:

OS_ERR_NONE	if at least one task was aborted. Check the return value for the number of tasks aborted.
OS_ERR_OBJ_PTR_NULL	if **p_mutex** is a **NULL** pointer.
OS_ERR_OBJ_TYPE	if the user does not pass a pointer to a mutex.
OS_ERR_OPT_INVALID	if the user specified an invalid option.
OS_ERR_PEND_ABORT_ISR	if attempting to call this function from an ISR
OS_ERR_PEND_ABORT_NONE	if no tasks were aborted.

Returned Value

OSMutexPendAbort() returns the number of tasks made ready to run by this function. Zero indicates that no tasks were pending on the mutex and therefore this function had no effect.

Notes/Warnings

1. Mutexes must be created before they are used.

Example

```
OS_MUTEX  DispMutex;


void  DispTask (void *p_arg)
{
    OS_ERR     err;
    OS_OBJ_QTY qty;


    (void)&p_arg;
    while (DEF_ON) {
        :
        :
        qty = OSMutexPendAbort(&DispMutex,
                               OS_OPT_PEND_ABORT_ALL,
                               &err);
        /* Check "err" */
    }
}
```

OSMutexPost()

```
void OSMutexPost (OS_MUTEX   *p_mutex,
                  OS_OPT      opt,
                  OS_ERR     *p_err);
```

File	Called from	Code enabled by
OS_MUTEX.C	Task	OS_CFG_MUTEX_EN

A mutex is signaled (i.e., released) by calling **OSMutexPost()**. Call this function only if acquiring the mutex by first calling **OSMutexPend()**. If the priority of the task that owns the mutex has been raised when a higher priority task attempted to acquire the mutex, at that point, the original task priority of the task is restored. If one or more tasks are waiting for the mutex, the mutex is given to the highest-priority task waiting on the mutex. The scheduler is then called to determine if the awakened task is now the highest-priority task ready to run, and if so, a context switch is done to run the readied task. If no task is waiting for the mutex, the mutex value is simply set to available (**DEF_TRUE**).

Arguments

p_mutex   is a pointer to the mutex.

opt   determines the type of POST performed.

OS_OPT_POST_NONE	No special option selected.
OS_OPT_POST_NO_SCHED	Do not call the scheduler after the post, therefore the caller is resumed even if the mutex was posted and tasks of higher priority are waiting for the mutex.
	Use this option if the task calling **OSMutexPost()** will be doing additional posts, if the user does not want to reschedule until all is complete, and multiple posts should take effect simultaneously.

p_err   is a pointer to a variable that is used to hold an error code:

OS_ERR_NONE	if the call is successful and the mutex is available.
OS_ERR_MUTEX_NESTING	if the owner of the mutex has the mutex nested and it has not fully un-nested the mutex yet.
OS_ERR_MUTEX_NOT_OWNER	if the caller is not the owner of the mutex and therefore is not allowed to release it.
OS_ERR_OBJ_PTR_NULL	if **p_mutex** is a **NULL** pointer.
OS_ERR_OBJ_TYPE	if not passing a pointer to a mutex.
OS_ERR_POST_ISR	if attempting to post the mutex from an ISR.

Returned Value
None

Notes/Warnings
1. Mutexes must be created before they are used.

2. Do not call this function from an ISR.

Example

```
OS_MUTEX  DispMutex;


void  TaskX (void *p_arg)
{
    OS_ERR  err;



    (void)&p_arg;
    while (DEF_ON) {
        :
        OSMutexPost(&DispMutex,
                    OS_OPT_POST_NONE,
                    &err);
        /* Check "err" */
        :
    }
}
```

OSPendMulti()

```
OS_OBJ_QTY  OSPendMulti(OS_PEND_DATA  *p_pend_data_tbl,
                        OS_OBJ_QTY     tbl_size,
                        OS_TICK        timeout,
                        OS_OPT         opt,
                        OS_ERR         *p_err);
```

File	Called from	Code enabled by
OS_PEND_MULTI.C	Task	OS_CFG_PEND_MULTI_EN && (OS_CFG_Q_EN || OS_CFG_SEM_EN)

OSPendMulti() is used when a task expects to wait on multiple kernel objects, specifically semaphores or message queues. If more than one such object is ready when **OSPendMulti()** is called, then all available objects and messages, if any, are returned as ready to the caller. If no objects are ready, **OSPendMulti()** suspends the current task until either:

■ an object becomes ready,

■ a timeout occurs,

■ one or more of the tasks are deleted or pend aborted or,

■ one or more of the objects are deleted.

If an object becomes ready, and multiple tasks are waiting for the object, µC/OS-III resumes the highest-priority task waiting on that object.

A pended task suspended with **OSTaskSuspend()** can still receive a message from a multi-pended message queue, or obtain a signal from a multi-pended semaphore. However, the task remains suspended until it is resumed by calling **OSTaskResume()**.

Arguments

p_pend_data_tbl is a pointer to an **OS_PEND_DATA** table. This table will be used by the caller to understand the outcome of this call. Also, the caller *must* initialize the **.PendObjPtr** field of the **OS_PEND_DATA** field for each object that the caller wants to pend on (see example below).

tbl_size   is the number of entries in the **OS_PEND_DATA** table pointed to by
            p_pend_data_tbl. This value indicates how many objects the task will be
            pending on.

timeout   specifies the amount of time (in clock ticks) that the calling task is willing to
            wait for objects to be posted. A timeout value of 0 indicates that the task wants
            to wait forever for any of the multi-pended objects. The timeout value is not
            synchronized with the clock tick. The timeout count begins decrementing on
            the next clock tick, which could potentially occur immediately.

p_err   is a pointer to a variable that holds an error code:

OS_ERR_NONE	if any of the multi-pended objects are ready.
OS_ERR_OBJ_TYPE	if any of the **.PendObjPtr** in the **p_pend_data_tbl** is a **NULL** pointer, not a semaphore, or not a message queue.
OS_ERR_OPT_INVALID	if specifying an invalid option.
OS_ERR_PEND_ABORT	indicates that a multi-pended object was aborted; check the **.RdyObjPtr** of the **p_pend_data_tbl** to know which object was aborted. The first non-**NULL** **.RdyObjPtr** is the object that was aborted.
OS_ERR_PEND_DEL	indicates that a multi-pended object was deleted; check the **.RdyObjPtr** of the **p_pend_data_tbl** to know which object was deleted. The first non-**NULL** **.RdyObjPtr** is the object that was deleted.
OS_ERR_PEND_ISR	if calling this function from an ISR.
OS_ERR_PEND_LOCKED	if calling this function when the scheduler is locked.
OS_ERR_PEND_WOULD_BLOCK	if the caller does not want to block and no object is ready.
OS_ERR_PTR_INVALID	if **p_pend_data_tbl** is a **NULL** pointer.
OS_ERR_TIMEOUT	if no multi-pended object is ready within the specified timeout.

Returned Value

OSPendMulti() returns the number of multi-pended objects that are ready. If an object is pend aborted or deleted, the return value will be 1. Examine the value of *p_err to know the exact outcome of this call. If no multi-pended object is ready within the specified timeout period, or because of any error, the .RdyObjPtr in the p_pend_data_tbl array will all be NULL.

When objects are posted, the OS_PEND_DATA fields of p_pend_data_tbl contains additional information about the posted objects:

.RdyObjPtr   Contains a pointer to the object ready or posted to, or NULL pointer if the object was not ready or posted to.

.RdyMsgPtr   If the object pended on was a message queue and the queue was posted to, this field contains the message.

.RdyMsgSize   If the object pended on was a message queue and the queue was posted to, this field contains the size of the message (in number of bytes).

.RdyTS   If the object pended on was posted to, this field contains the timestamp as to when the object was posted. Note that if the object is deleted or pend-aborted, this field contains the timestamp of when the condition occurred.

Notes/Warnings

1. Message queue or semaphore objects must be created before they are used.

2. Do call OSPendMulti() from an ISR.

3. The user cannot multi-pend on event flags and mutexes.

Example

```
OS_SEM   Sem1;
OS_SEM   Sem2;
OS_Q     Q1;
OS_Q     Q2;


void Task(void *p_arg)
{
    OS_PEND_DATA  pend_data_tbl[4];
    OS_ERR        err;
    OS_OBJ_QTY    nbr_rdy;


    (void)&p_arg;
    while (DEF_ON) {
        :
        pend_data_tbl[0].PendObjPtr = (OS_PEND_OBJ *)Sem1;
        pend_data_tbl[1].PendObjPtr = (OS_PEND_OBJ *)Sem2;
        pend_data_tbl[2].PendObjPtr = (OS_PEND_OBJ *)Q1;
        pend_data_tbl[3].PendObjPtr = (OS_PEND_OBJ *)Q2;
        nbr_rdy = OSPendMulti(&pend_data_tbl[0],
                              4,
                              0,
                              OS_OPT_PEND_BLOCKING,
                              &err);
        /* Check "err" */
        :
        :
    }
}
```

OSQCreate()

```
void  OSQCreate (OS_Q        *p_q,
                 CPU_CHAR     *p_name,
                 OS_MSG_QTY    max_qty,
                 OS_ERR       *p_err)
```

File	Called from	Code enabled by
OS_Q.C	Task or startup code	OS_CFG_Q_EN and OS_CFG_MSG_EN

OSQCreate() creates a message queue. A message queue allows tasks or ISRs to send pointer-sized variables (messages) to one or more tasks. The meaning of the messages sent are application specific.

Arguments

p_q   is a pointer to the message queue control block. It is assumed that storage for the message queue will be allocated in the application. The user will need to declare a "global" variable as follows, and pass a pointer to this variable to OSQCreate():

OS_Q MyMsgQ;

p_name   is a pointer to an ASCII string used to name the message queue. The name can be displayed by debuggers or μC/Probe.

msg_size   indicates the maximum size of the message queue (must be non-zero). If the user intends to not limit the size of the queue, simply pass a very large number. Of course, if there are not enough OS_MSGs in the pool of OS_MSGs, the post call (i.e., OSQPost()) will simply fail and an error code will indicate that there are no more OS_MSGs to use.

p_err   is a pointer to a variable that is used to hold an error code:

OS_ERR_NONE	if the call is successful and the mutex has been created.
OS_ERR_CREATE_ISR	if attempting to create the message queue from an ISR.
OS_ERR_NAME	if **p_name** is a **NULL** pointer.
OS_ERR_OBJ_CREATED	if **p_q** is already pointing to a message queue. In other words, the user is trying to create a message queue that has already been created.
OS_ERR_OBJ_PTR_NULL	if **p_q** is a **NULL** pointer.
OS_ERR_Q_SIZE	if the size specified is 0.

Returned Value

None

Notes/Warnings

1. Queues must be created before they are used.

Example

```
OS_Q    CommQ;



void main (void)
{
    OS_ERR   err;



    OSInit(&err);                    /* Initialize µC/OS-III */
    :
    :
    OSQCreate(&CommQ,
             "Comm Queue",
             10,
             &err);                  /* Create COMM Q        */
    /* Check "err" */
    :
    :
    OSStart();                       /* Start Multitasking   */
}
```

OSQDel()

```
OS_OBJ_QTY  OSQDel (OS_Q    *p_q,
                    OS_OPT   opt,
                    OS_ERR   *p_err)
```

File	Called from	Code enabled by
OS_Q.C	Task	OS_CFG_Q_EN and OS_CFG_Q_DEL_EN

OSQDel() is used to delete a message queue. This function should be used with care since multiple tasks may rely on the presence of the message queue. Generally speaking, before deleting a message queue, first delete all the tasks that can access the message queue. However, it is highly recommended that you do not delete kernel objects at run time.

Arguments

p_q   is a pointer to the message queue to delete.

opt   specifies whether to delete the queue only if there are no pending tasks (OS_OPT_DEL_NO_PEND), or always delete the queue regardless of whether tasks are pending or not (OS_OPT_DEL_ALWAYS). In this case, all pending task are readied.

p_err   is a pointer to a variable that is used to hold an error code. The error code can be one of the following:

OS_ERR_NONE	if the call is successful and the message queue has been deleted.
OS_ERR_DEL_ISR	if the user attempts to delete the message queue from an ISR.
OS_ERR_OBJ_PTR_NULL	if passing a NULL pointer for p_q.
OS_ERR_OBJ_TYPE	if p_q is not pointing to a queue.
OS_ERR_OPT_INVALID	if not specifying one of the two options mentioned in the opt argument.
OS_ERR_TASK_WAITING	if one or more tasks are waiting for messages at the message queue and it is specified to only delete if no task is pending.

Returned Value

The number of tasks that were waiting on the message queue and 0 if an error is detected.

Notes/Warnings

1. Message queues must be created before they can be used.

2. This function must be used with care. Tasks that would normally expect the presence of the queue *must* check the return code of OSQPend( ).

Example

```
OS_Q  DispQ;


void Task (void *p_arg)
{
    OS_ERR  err;


    (void)&p_arg;
    while (DEF_ON) {
        :
        :
        OSQDel(&DispQ,
               OS_OPT_DEL_ALWAYS,
               &err);
        /* Check "err" */
        :
        :
    }
}
```

OSQFlush()

```
OS_MSG_QTY  OSQFlush (OS_Q    *p_q,
                      OS_ERR  *p_err)
```

File	Called from	Code enabled by
OS_Q.C	Task	OS_CFG_Q_EN and OS_CFG_Q_FLUSH_EN

OSQFlush() empties the contents of the message queue and eliminates all messages sent to the queue. This function takes the same amount of time to execute regardless of whether tasks are waiting on the queue (and thus no messages are present), or the queue contains one or more messages. OS_MSGs from the queue are simply returned to the free pool of OS_MSGs.

Arguments

p_q   is a pointer to the message queue.

p_err   is a pointer to a variable that will contain an error code returned by this function.

OS_ERR_NONE	if the message queue is flushed.
OS_ERR_FLUSH_ISR	if calling this function from an ISR
OS_ERR_OBJ_PTR_NULL	if p_q is a NULL pointer.
OS_ERR_OBJ_TYPE	if you attempt to flush an object other than a message queue.

Returned Value

The number of OS_MSG entries freed from the message queue. Note that the OS_MSG entries are returned to the free pool of OS_MSGs.

Notes/Warnings

1. Queues must be created before they are used.

2. Use this function with great care. When flushing a queue, you lose the references to what the queue entries are pointing to, potentially causing 'memory leaks'. The data that the user is pointing to that is referenced by the queue entries should, most likely, be de-allocated (i.e., freed). To flush a queue that contains entries, instead use `OSQPend()` with the `OS_OPT_PEND_NON_BLOCKING` option.

Example

```
OS_Q   CommQ;


void Task (void *p_arg)
{
    OS_ERR   err;


    (void)&p_arg;
    while (DEF_ON) {
        :
        :
        entries = OSQFlush(&CommQ,
                           &err);
        /* Check "err" */
        :
        :
    }
}
```

OSQPend()

```
void  *OSQPend (OS_Q          *p_q,
                OS_TICK        timeout,
                OS_OPT         opt,
                OS_MSG_SIZE   *p_msg_size,
                CPU_TS        *p_ts,
                OS_ERR        *p_err)
```

File	Called from	Code enabled by
OS_Q.C	Task	OS_CFG_Q_EN and OS_CFG_MSG_EN

OSQPend() is used when a task wants to receive messages from a message queue. The messages are sent to the task via the message queue either by an ISR, or by another task using the OSQPost() call. The messages received are pointer-sized variables, and their use is application specific. If at least one message is already present in the message queue when OSQPend() is called, the message is retrieved and returned to the caller.

If no message is present in the message queue and OS_OPT_PEND_BLOCKING is specified for the opt argument, OSQPend() suspends the current task (assuming the scheduler is not locked) until either a message is received, or a user-specified timeout expires. If a message is sent to the message queue and multiple tasks are waiting for such a message, µC/OS-III resumes the highest priority task that is waiting.

A pended task suspended with OSTaskSuspend() can receive a message. However, the task remains suspended until it is resumed by calling OSTaskResume().

If no message is present in the queue and OS_OPT_PEND_NON_BLOCKING is specifed for the opt argument, OSQPend() returns to the caller with an appropriate error code, and returns a NULL pointer.

Arguments

p_q   is a pointer to the queue from which the messages are received.

timeout   allows the task to resume execution if a message is not received from the
            message queue within the specified number of clock ticks. A timeout value of 0
            indicates that the task is willing to wait forever for a message. The timeout
            value is not synchronized with the clock tick. The timeout count starts
            decrementing on the next clock tick, which could potentially occur
            immediately.

opt   determines whether or not to block if a message is not available in the queue.
            This argument must be set to either:

            OS_OPT_PEND_BLOCKING, or

            OS_OPT_PEND_NON_BLOCKING

            Note that the timeout argument should be set to 0 when specifying
            OS_OPT_PEND_NON_BLOCKING, since the timeout value is irrelevant using this
            option.

p_msg_size is a pointer to a variable that will receive the size of the message (in number of
            bytes).

p_ts   is a pointer to a variable that will receive the timestamp of when the message
            was received. If passing a **NULL** pointer (i.e., (**CPU_TS** *)0), the timestamp will
            not be returned. Passing a **NULL** pointer is valid, and indicates that the user
            does not need the timestamp.

            A timestamp is useful when the user wants the task to know when the message
            queue was posted, or how long it took for the task to resume after the message
            queue was posted. In the latter case, call **OS_TS_GET()** and compute the
            difference between the current value of the timestamp and *p_ts. In other
            words:

            delta = OS_TS_GET() - *p_ts;

p_err	is a pointer to a variable used to hold an error code.

OS_ERR_NONE	if a message is received.
OS_ERR_OBJ_PTR_NULL	if **p_q** is a **NULL** pointer.
OS_ERR_OBJ_TYPE	if **p_q** is not pointing to a message queue.
OS_ERR_PEND_ABORT	if the pend was aborted because another task called **OSQPendAbort()**.
OS_ERR_PEND_ISR	if the function is called from an ISR.
OS_ERR_PEND_WOULD_BLOCK	if this function is called with the opt argument set to OS_OPT_PEND_NON_BLOCKING, and no message is in the queue.
OS_ERR_SCHED_LOCKED	if calling this function when the scheduler is locked.
OS_ERR_TIMEOUT	if a message is not received within the specified timeout.

Returned Value

The message (i.e., a pointer) or a **NULL** pointer if no messages has been received. Note that it is possible for the actual message to be **NULL** pointers, so check the returned error code instead of relying on the returned value.

Notes/Warnings

1. Queues must be created before they are used.

2. The user cannot call **OSQPend()** from an ISR.

Example

```
OS_Q   CommQ;


void CommTask (void *p_arg)
{
    OS_ERR       err;
    void         *p_msg;
    OS_MSG_SIZE  msg_size;
    CPU_TS       ts;


    (void)&p_arg;
    while (DEF_ON) {
        :
        :
        p_msg = OSQPend(CommQ,
                        100,
                        OS_OPT_PEND_BLOCKING,
                        &msg_size,
                        &ts,
                        &err);
        /* Check "err" */
        :
        :
    }
}
```

OSQPendAbort()

```
OS_OBJ_QTY  OSQPendAbort (OS_Q     *p_q,
                          OS_OPT   opt,
                          OS_ERR   *p_err)
```

File	Called from	Code enabled by
OS_Q.C	Task only	OS_CFG_Q_EN and OS_CFG_Q_PEND_ABORT_EN

OSQPendAbort() aborts and readies any tasks currently waiting on a message queue. This function should be used to fault-abort the wait on the message queue, rather than to signal the message queue via OSQPost().

Arguments

p_q   is a pointer to the queue for which pend(s) need to be aborted.

opt   determines the type of abort to be performed.

OS_OPT_PEND_ABORT_1	Aborts the pend of only the highest-priority task waiting on the message queue.
OS_OPT_PEND_ABORT_ALL	Aborts the pend of all tasks waiting on the message queue.
OS_OPT_POST_NO_SCHED	specifies that the scheduler should not be called, even if the pend of a higher-priority task has been aborted. Scheduling will need to occur from another function.
	Use this option if the task calling OSQPendAbort() is doing additional pend aborts, rescheduling is not performed until completion, and multiple pend aborts are to take effect simultaneously.

p_err   is a pointer to a variable that holds an error code:

OS_ERR_NONE	at least one task waiting on the message queue was readied and informed of the aborted wait. Check the return value for the number of tasks whose wait on the message queue was aborted.
OS_ERR_PEND_ABORT_ISR	if called from an ISR
OS_ERR_PEND_ABORT_NONE	if no task was pending on the message queue
OS_ERR_OBJ_PTR_NULL	if **p_q** is a **NULL** pointer.
OS_ERR_OBJ_TYPE	if **p_q** is not pointing to a message queue.
OS_ERR_OPT_INVALID	if an invalid option is specified.

Returned Value

OSQPendAbort() returns the number of tasks made ready to run by this function. Zero indicates that no tasks were pending on the message queue, therefore this function had no effect.

Notes/Warnings

1. Queues must be created before they are used.

Example

```
OS_Q  CommQ;


void CommTask(void *p_arg)
{
    OS_ERR      err;
    OS_OBJ_QTY  nbr_tasks;


    (void)&p_arg;
    while (DEF_ON) {
        :
        :
        nbr_tasks = OSQPendAbort(&CommQ,
                                 OS_OPT_PEND_ABORT_ALL,
                                 &err);
        /* Check "err" */
        :
        :
    }
}
```

OSQPost()

```
void   OSQPost (OS_Q         *p_q,
               void          *p_void,
               OS_MSG_SIZE   msg_size,
               OS_OPT        opt,
               OS_ERR        *p_err)
```

File	Called from	Code enabled by
OS_Q.C	Task or ISR	OS_CFG_Q_EN

OSQPost() sends a message to a task through a message queue. A message is a pointer-sized variable, and its use is application specific. If the message queue is full, an error code is returned to the caller. In this case, OSQPost() immediately returns to its caller, and the message is not placed in the message queue.

If any task is waiting for a message to be posted to the message queue, the highest-priority task receives the message. If the task waiting for the message has a higher priority than the task sending the message, the higher-priority task resumes, and the task sending the message is suspended; that is, a context switch occurs. Message queues can be first-in first-out (OS_OPT_POST_FIFO), or last-in-first-out (OS_OPT_POST_LIFO) depending of the value specified in the opt argument.

If any task is waiting for a message at the message queue, OSQPost() allows the user to either post the message to the highest-priority task waiting at the queue (opt set to OS_OPT_POST_FIFO or OS_OPT_POST_LIFO), or to all tasks waiting at the message queue (opt is set to OS_OPT_POST_ALL). In either case, scheduling occurs unless opt is also set to OS_OPT_POST_NO_SCHED.

Arguments

p_q   is a pointer to the message queue being posted to.

p_void   is the actual message posted. **p_void** is a pointer-sized variable. Its meaning is application specific.

msg_size   specifies the size of the message (in number of bytes).

opt   determines the type of POST performed. The last two options may be added to either OS_OPT_POST_FIFO or OS_OPT_POST_LIFO to create different combinations:

OS_OPT_POST_FIFO	POST message to the end of the queue (FIFO), or send message to a single waiting task.
OS_OPT_POST_LIFO	POST message to the front of the queue (LIFO), or send message to a single waiting task
OS_OPT_POST_ALL	POST message to ALL tasks that are waiting on the queue. This option can be added to either OS_OPT_POST_FIFO or OS_OPT_POST_LIFO.
OS_OPT_POST_NO_SCHED	Do not call the scheduler after the post and therefore the caller is resumed, even if the message was posted to a message queue with tasks having a higher priority than the caller. Use this option if the task (or ISR) calling OSQPost() will do additional posts, the user does not want to reschedule until finished, and, multiple posts are to take effect simultaneously.

p_err   is a pointer to a variable that will contain an error code returned by this function.

OS_ERR_NONE	if no tasks were waiting on the queue. In this case, the return value is also 0.
OS_ERR_MSG_POOL_EMPTY	if there are no more OS_MSG structures to use to store the message.
OS_ERR_OBJ_PTR_NULL	if p_q is a NULL pointer.
OS_ERR_OBJ_TYPE	if p_q is not pointing to a message queue.
OS_ERR_Q_MAX	if the queue is full and therefore cannot accept more messages.

Returned Value

None

Notes/Warnings

1. Queues must be created before they are used.

2. Possible combinations of options are:

> OS_OPT_POST_FIFO
>
> OS_OPT_POST_LIFO
>
> OS_OPT_POST_FIFO + OS_OPT_POST_ALL
>
> OS_OPT_POST_LIFO + OS_OPT_POST_ALL
>
> OS_OPT_POST_FIFO + OS_OPT_POST_NO_SCHED
>
> OS_OPT_POST_LIFO + OS_OPT_POST_NO_SCHED
>
> OS_OPT_POST_FIFO + OS_OPT_POST_ALL + OS_OPT_POST_NO_SCHED
>
> OS_OPT_POST_LIFO + OS_OPT_POST_ALL + OS_OPT_POST_NO_SCHED

3. Although the example below shows calling OSQPost() from a task, it can also be called from an ISR.

Example

```
OS_Q          CommQ;
CPU_INT08U    CommRxBuf[100];


void CommTaskRx (void *p_arg)
{
    OS_ERR  err;


    (void)&p_arg;
    while (DEF_ON) {
        :
        :
        OSQPost(&CommQ,
                &CommRxBuf[0],
                sizeof(CommRxBuf),
                OS_OPT_POST_OPT_FIFO + OS_OPT_POST_ALL + OS_OPT_POST_NO_SCHED,
                &err);
        /* Check "err" */
        :
        :
    }
}
```

OSSafetyCriticalStart()

void OSSafetyCriticalStart (void)

File	Called from	Code enabled by
OS_CORE.C	Task	OS_SAFETY_CRITICAL_IEC61508

OSSafetyCriticalStart() allows your code to notify µC/OS-III that you are done initializing and creating all kernel objects. After calling OSSafetyCriticalStart(), your application code will no longer be allowed to create kernel objects.

Arguments

None

Returned Value

None

Notes/Warnings

None

Example

```
void AppStartTask (void *p_arg)
{
    (void)&p_arg;
    /* Create tasks and other kernel objects          */
    OSSafetyCriticalStart();
    /* Your code is no longer allowed to create kernel objects */
    while (DEF_ON) {
        :
        :
    }
}
```

OSSched()

void OSSched (void)

File	Called from	Code enabled by
OS_CORE.C	Task	N/A

OSSched() allows a task to call the scheduler. Use this function if creating a series of "posts" and specifing OS_OPT_POST_NO_SCHED as a post option.

OSSched() can only be called by task-level code. Also, if the scheduler is locked (i.e., OSSchedLock() was previously called), then OSSched() will have no effect.

If a higher-priority task than the calling task is ready to run, OSSched() will context switch to that task.

Arguments
None

Returned Value
None

Notes/Warnings
None

Example

```
void TaskX (void *p_arg)
{
    (void)&p_arg;
    while (DEF_ON) {
        :
        OS??Post(…);          /* Posts with OS_OPT_POST_NO_SCHED option    */
        /* Check "err" */
        OS??Post(…);
        /* Check "err" */
        OS??Post(…);
        /* Check "err" */
        :
        OSSched();            /* Run the scheduler                         */
        :
    }
}
```

OSSchedLock()

`void OSSchedLock (OS_ERR *p_err)`

File	Called from	Code enabled by
OS_CORE.C	Task or ISR	N/A

OSSchedLock() prevents task rescheduling until its counterpart, OSSchedUnlock(), is called. The task that calls OSSchedLock() retains control of the CPU, even though other higher-priority tasks are ready to run. However, interrupts are still recognized and serviced (assuming interrupts are enabled). OSSchedLock() and OSSchedUnlock() must be used in pairs.

μC/OS-III allows OSSchedLock() to be nested up to 250 levels deep. Scheduling is enabled when an equal number of OSSchedUnlock() calls have been made.

Arguments

p_err   is a pointer to a variable that will contain an error code returned by this function.

OS_ERR_NONE	the scheduler is locked.
OS_ERR_LOCK_NESTING_OVF	if the user called this function too many times.
OS_ERR_OS_NOT_RUNNING	if the function is called before calling OSStart().

Returned Value

None

Notes/Warnings

1. After calling OSSchedLock(), the application must not make system calls that suspend execution of the current task; that is, the application cannot call OSTimeDly(), OSTimeDlyHMSM(), OSFlagPend(), OSSemPend(), OSMutexPend(), or OSQPend(). Since the scheduler is locked out, no other task is allowed to run, and the system will lock up.

Example

```
void TaskX (void *p_arg)
{
    OS_ERR   err;


    (void)&p_arg;
    while (DEF_ON) {
        :
        OSSchedLock(&err);      /* Prevent other tasks to run          */
        /* Check "err" */
        :                       /* Code protected from context switch */
        OSSchedUnlock(&err);    /* Enable other tasks to run           */
        /* Check "err" */
        :
    }
}
```

OSSchedRoundRobinCfg()

```
void  OSSchedRoundRobinCfg (CPU_BOOLEAN  en,
                            OS_TICK       dflt_time_quanta,
                            OS_ERR        *p_err)
```

File	Called from	Code enabled by
OS_CORE.C	Task or startup code	OS_CFG_SCHED_ROUND_ROBIN_EN

OSSchedRoundRobinCfg() is used to enable or disable round-robin scheduling.

Arguments

en   when set to **DEF_ENABLED** enables round-robin scheduling, and when set to **DEF_DISABLED** disables it.

dflt_time_quanta   is the default time quanta given to a task. This value is used when a task was created and specified a value of 0 for the time quanta. In other words, if the user did not specify a non-zero for the task's time quanta, this is the value that will be used. If passing 0 for this argument, µC/OS-III will assume a time quanta of 1/10 the tick rate. For example, if the tick rate is 1000 Hz and 0 for dflt_time_quanta is specified, µC/OS-III will set the time quanta to 10 milliseconds.

p_err   is a pointer to a variable that is used to hold an error code:

OS_ERR_NONE   if the call is successful.

Returned Value
None

Notes/Warnings
None

Example

```
void main (void)
{
    OS_ERR  err;


    :
    OSInit(&err);                    /* Initialize µC/OS-III        */
    :
    :
    OSSchedRoundRobinCfg(DEF_ENABLED,
                     10,
                     &err);
    /* Check "err" */
    :
    :
    OSStart(&err);                   /* Start Multitasking          */
}
```

OSSchedRoundRobinYield()

void OSSchedRoundRobinYield (OS_ERR *p_err);

File	Called from	Code enabled by
OS_CORE.C	Task	OS_CFG_SCHED_ROUND_ROBIN_EN

OSSchedRoundRobinYield() is used to voluntarily give up a task's time slot, assuming that there are other tasks running at the same priority.

Arguments

p_err   is a pointer to a variable used to hold an error code:

> OS_ERR_NONE   if the call was successful.
>
> OS_ERR_ROUND_ROBIN_1   if there is only one task at the current priority level that is ready to run.
>
> OS_ERR_ROUND_ROBIN_DISABLED if round-robin scheduling has not been enabled. See OSSchedRoundRobinCfg() to enable or disable.
>
> OS_ERR_SCHED_LOCKED   if the scheduler is locked and µC/OS-III cannot switch tasks.
>
> OS_ERR_YIELD_ISR   if calling this function from an ISR.

Returned Value

None

Notes/Warnings

None

Example

```
void Task (void *p_arg)
{
    OS_ERR   err;


    (void)&p_arg;
    while (DEF_ON) {
        :
        :
        OSSchedRoundRobinYield(&err); /* Give up the CPU to the next task at same priority */
        /* Check "err" */
        :
        :
    }
}
```

OSSchedUnlock()

void OSSchedUnlock(OS_ERR *p_err);

File	Called from	Code enabled by
OS_CORE.C	Task or ISR	N/A

OSSchedUnlock() re-enables task scheduling whenever it is paired with OSSchedLock().

Arguments

p_err   is a pointer to a variable that will contain an error code returned by this function.

<table>
<tr><td>OS_ERR_NONE</td><td>the call is successful and the scheduler is no longer locked.</td></tr>
<tr><td>OS_ERR_OS_NOT_RUNNING</td><td>if calling this function before calling OSStart().</td></tr>
<tr><td>OS_ERR_SCHED_LOCKED</td><td>if the scheduler is still locked. This would indicate that scheduler lock has not fully unnested</td></tr>
<tr><td>OS_ERR_SCHED_NOT_LOCKED</td><td>if the user did not call OSSchedLock().</td></tr>
</table>

Returned Value

None

Notes/Warnings

None

Example

```
void TaskX (void *p_arg)
{
    OS_ERR   err;


    (void)&p_arg;
    while (DEF_ON) {
        :
        OSSchedLock(&err);      /* Prevent other tasks to run          */
        /* Check "err" */
        :                       /* Code protected from context switch */
        OSSchedUnlock(&err);    /* Enable other tasks to run           */
        /* Check "err" */
        :
    }
}
```

OSSemCreate()

```
void  OSSemCreate (OS_SEM      *p_sem,
                   CPU_CHAR    *p_name,
                   OS_SEM_CTR  cnt,
                   OS_ERR      *p_err)
```

File	Called from	Code enabled by
OS_SEM.C	Task or startup code	OS_CFG_SEM_EN

OSSemCreate() initializes a semaphore. Semaphores are used when a task wants exclusive access to a resource, needs to synchronize its activities with an ISR or a task, or is waiting until an event occurs. Use a semaphore to signal the occurrence of an event to one or multiple tasks, and use mutexes to guard share resources. However, technically, semaphores allow for both.

Arguments

p_sem   is a pointer to the semaphore control block. It is assumed that storage for the semaphore will be allocated in the application. In other words, declare a "global" variable as follows, and pass a pointer to this variable to OSSemCreate():

OS_SEM MySem;

p_name   is a pointer to an ASCII string used to assign a name to the semaphore. The name can be displayed by debuggers or μC/Probe.

cnt   specifies the initial value of the semaphore.

If the semaphore is used for resource sharing, set the initial value of the semaphore to the number of identical resources guarded by the semaphore. If there is only one resource, the value should be set to 1 (this is called a binary semaphore). For multiple resources, set the value to the number of resources (this is called a counting semaphore).

If using a semaphore as a signaling mechanism, set the initial value to 0.

p_err   is a pointer to a variable used to hold an error code:

OS_ERR_NONE	if the call is successful and the semaphore has been created.
OS_ERR_CREATE_ISR	if calling this function from an ISR.
OS_ERR_NAME	if **p_name** is a **NULL** pointer.
OS_ERR_OBJ_CREATED	if the semaphore is already created.
OS_ERR_OBJ_PTR_NULL	if **p_q** is a **NULL** pointer.
OS_ERR_OBJ_TYPE	if **p_sem** has been initialized to a different object type.

Returned Value

None

Notes/Warnings

Semaphores must be created before they are used.

Example

```
OS_SEM  SwSem;


void main (void)
{
    OS_ERR  err;


    :
    OSInit(&err);                  /* Initialize μC/OS-III        */
    :
    :
    OSSemCreate(&SwSem,            /* Create Switch Semaphore     */
                "Switch Semaphore",
                0,
                &err);
    /* Check "err" */
    :
    :
    OSStart(&err);                 /* Start Multitasking          */
}
```

OSSemDel()

```
void  OSSemDel (OS_SEM   *p_sem,
               OS_OPT    opt,
               OS_ERR    *p_err)
```

File	Called from	Code enabled by
OS_SEM.C	Task	OS_CFG_SEM_EN and OS_CFG_SEM_DEL_EN

OSSemDel() is used to delete a semaphore. This function should be used with care as multiple tasks may rely on the presence of the semaphore. Generally speaking, before deleting a semaphore, first delete all the tasks that access the semaphore. As a rule, it is highly recommended to not delete kernel objects at run time.

Deleting the semaphore will not de-allocate the object. In other words, storage for the variable will still remain at the same location unless the semaphore is allocated dynamically from the heap. The dynamic allocation of objects has its own set of problems. Specifically, it is not recommended for embedded systems to allocate (and de-allocate) objects from the heap given the high likelihood of fragmentation.

Arguments

p_sem   is a pointer to the semaphore.

opt   specifies one of two options: **OS_OPT_DEL_NO_PEND** or **OS_OPT_DEL_ALWAYS**.

OS_OPT_DEL_NO_PEND specifies to delete the semaphore only if no task is waiting on the semaphore. Because no task is "currently" waiting on the semaphore does not mean that a task will not attempt to wait for the semaphore later. How would such a task handle the situation waiting for a semaphore that was deleted? The application code will have to deal with this eventuality.

OS_OPT_DEL_ALWAYS specifies deleting the semaphore, regardless of whether tasks are waiting on the semaphore or not. If there are tasks waiting on the semaphore, these tasks will be made ready to run and informed (through an appropriate error code) that the reason the task is readied is that the semaphore it was waiting on was deleted. The same reasoning applies with the other option, how will the tasks handle the fact that the semaphore they want to wait for is no longer available?

p_err   is a pointer to a variable used to hold an error code. The error code may be one of the following:

OS_ERR_NONE	if the call is successful and the semaphore has been deleted.
OS_ERR_DEL_ISR	if attempting to delete the semaphore from an ISR.
OS_ERR_OBJ_PTR_NULL	if **p_sem** is a **NULL** pointer.
OS_ERR_OBJ_TYPE	if **p_sem** is not pointing to a semaphore.
OS_ERR_OPT_INVALID	if one of the two options mentioned in the opt argument is not specified.
OS_ERR_TASK_WAITING	if one or more tasks are waiting on the semaphore.

Returned Value

None

Notes/Warnings

Use this call with care because other tasks might expect the presence of the semaphore.

Example

```
OS_SEM   SwSem;


void Task (void *p_arg)
{
    OS_ERR   err;


    (void)&p_arg;
    while (DEF_ON) {
        :
        :
        OSSemDel(&SwSem,
                 OS_OPT_DEL_ALWAYS,
                 &err);
        /* Check "err" */
        :
        :
    }
}
```

OSSemPend()

```
OS_SEM_CTR  OSSemPend (OS_SEM      *p_sem,
                       OS_TICK     timeout,
                       OS_OPT      opt,
                       CPU_TS      *p_ts,
                       OS_ERR      *p_err)
```

File	Called from	Code enabled by
OS_SEM.C	Task only	OS_CFG_SEM_EN

OSSemPend() is used when a task wants exclusive access to a resource, needs to synchronize its activities with an ISR or task, or is waiting until an event occurs.

When the semaphore is used for resource sharing, if a task calls OSSemPend() and the value of the semaphore is greater than 0, OSSemPend() decrements the semaphore and returns to its caller. However, if the value of the semaphore is 0, OSSemPend() places the calling task in the waiting list for the semaphore. The task waits until the owner of the semaphore (which is always a task in this case) releases the semaphore by calling OSSemPost(), or the specified timeout expires. If the semaphore is signaled before the timeout expires, μC/OS-III resumes the highest-priority task waiting for the semaphore.

When the semaphore is used as a signaling mechanism, the calling task waits until a task or an ISR signals the semaphore by calling OSSemPost(), or the specified timeout expires. If the semaphore is signaled before the timeout expires, μC/OS-III resumes the highest-priority task waiting for the semaphore.

A pended task that has been suspended with OSTaskSuspend() can obtain the semaphore. However, the task remains suspended until it is resumed by calling OSTaskResume().

OSSemPend() also returns if the pend is aborted or, the semaphore is deleted.

Arguments

p_sem   is a pointer to the semaphore.

timeout allows the task to resume execution if a semaphore is not posted within the specified number of clock ticks. A timeout value of 0 indicates that the task waits forever for the semaphore. The timeout value is not synchronized with the clock tick. The timeout count begins decrementing on the next clock tick, which could potentially occur immediately.

opt specifies whether the call is to block if the semaphore is not available, or not block.

  OS_OPT_PEND_BLOCKING to block the caller until the semaphore is available or a timeout occurs.

  OS_OPT_PEND_NON_BLOCKING if the semaphore is not available, **OSSemPend()** will not block but return to the caller with an appropriate error code.

p_ts is a pointer to a variable that will receive a timestamp of when the semaphore was posted, pend aborted, or deleted. Passing a **NULL** pointer is valid and indicates that a timestamp is not required.

  A timestamp is useful when the task must know when the semaphore was posted or, how long it took for the task to resume after the semaphore was posted. In the latter case, call **CPU_BOOLEAN()** and compute the difference between the current value of the timestamp and ***p_ts**. In other words:

  delta = OS_TS_GET() - *p_ts;

p_err is a pointer to a variable used to hold an error code:

OS_ERR_NONE	if the semaphore is available.
OS_ERR_OBJ_DEL	if the semaphore was deleted.
OS_ERR_OBJ_PTR_NULL	if **p_sem** is a **NULL** pointer.
OS_ERR_OBJ_TYPE	if **p_sem** is not pointing to a semaphore.
OS_ERR_PEND_ABORT	if the pend was aborted
OS_ERR_PEND_ISR	if this function is called from an ISR.
OS_ERR_PEND_WOULD_BLOCK	if this function is called as specified OS_OPT_PEND_NON_BLOCKING, and the semaphore was not available.
OS_ERR_SCHED_LOCKED	if calling this function when the scheduler is locked.

        OS_ERR_TIMEOUT   if the semaphore is not signaled within the specified timeout.

Returned Value

The new value of the semaphore count.

Notes/Warnings

1. Semaphores must be created before they are used.

Example

```
OS_SEM  SwSem;


void DispTask (void *p_arg)
{
    OS_ERR   err;
    CPU_TS   ts;


    (void)&p_arg;
    while (DEF_ON) {
        :
        :
        OSSemPend(&SwSem,
                  0,
                  OS_OPT_PEND_BLOCKING,
                  &ts,
                  &err);
        /* Check "err" */
    }
}
```

OSSemPendAbort()

```
OS_OBJ_QTY  OSSemPendAbort (OS_SEM  *p_sem,
                            OS_OPT   opt,
                            OS_ERR  *p_err)
```

File	Called from	Code enabled by
OS_SEM.C	Task only	OS_CFG_SEM_EN and OS_CFG_SEM_PEND_ABORT_EN

OSSemPendAbort() aborts and readies any task currently waiting on a semaphore. This function should be used to fault-abort the wait on the semaphore, rather than to normally signal the semaphore via OSSemPost().

Arguments

p_sem   is a pointer to the semaphore for which pend(s) need to be aborted.

opt   determines the type of abort performed.

OS_OPT_PEND_ABORT_1	Aborts the pend of only the highest-priority task waiting on the semaphore.
OS_OPT_PEND_ABORT_ALL	Aborts the pend of all the tasks waiting on the semaphore.
OS_OPT_POST_NO_SCHED	Specifies that the scheduler should not be called, even if the pend of a higher-priority task has been aborted. Scheduling will need to occur from another function. Use this option if the task calling OSSemPendAbort() will be doing additional pend aborts, reschedule takes place when finished, and multiple pend aborts are to take effect simultaneously.
p_err	Is a pointer to a variable that holds an error code. OSSemPendAbort() sets *p_err to one of the following:

OS_ERR_NONE	At least one task waiting on the semaphore was readied and informed of the aborted wait. Check the return value for the number of tasks whose wait on the semaphore was aborted.
OS_ERR_OBJ_PTR_NULL	if p_sem is a NULL pointer.
OS_ERR_OBJ_TYPE	if p_sem is not pointing to a semaphore.
OS_ERR_OPT_INVALID	if an invalid option is specified.
OS_ERR_PEND_ABORT_ISR	This function is called from an ISR.
OS_ERR_PEND_ABORT_NONE	No task was aborted because no task was waiting.

Returned Value

OSSemPendAbort() returns the number of tasks made ready to run by this function. Zero indicates that no tasks were pending on the semaphore and therefore, the function had no effect.

Notes/Warnings

Semaphores must be created before they are used.

Example

```
OS_SEM  SwSem;


void CommTask(void *p_arg)
{
    OS_ERR      err;
    OS_OBJ_QTY  nbr_tasks;


    (void)&p_arg;
    while (DEF_ON) {
        :
        :
        nbr_tasks = OSSemPendAbort(&SwSem,
                                   OS_OPT_PEND_ABORT_ALL,
                                   &err);
        /* Check "err" */
        :
        :
    }
}
```

OSSemPost()

```
OS_SEM_CTR  OSSemPost (OS_SEM  *p_sem,
                       OS_OPT   opt,
                       OS_ERR  *p_err)
```

File	Called from	Code enabled by
OS_SEM.C	Task or ISR	OS_CFG_SEM_EN

A semaphore is signaled by calling **OSSemPost()**. If the semaphore value is 0 or more, it is incremented, and **OSSemPost()** returns to its caller. If tasks are waiting for the semaphore to be signaled, **OSSemPost()** removes the highest-priority task pending for the semaphore from the waiting list and makes this task ready to run. The scheduler is then called to determine if the awakened task is now the highest-priority task that is ready to run.

Arguments

p_sem   is a pointer to the semaphore.

opt   determines the type of post performed.

OS_OPT_POST_1	Post and ready only the highest-priority task waiting on the semaphore.
OS_OPT_POST_ALL	Post to all tasks waiting on the semaphore. ONLY use this option if the semaphore is used as a signaling mechanism and NEVER when the semaphore is used to guard a shared resource. It does not make sense to tell all tasks that are sharing a resource that they can all access the resource.
OS_OPT_POST_NO_SCHED	This option indicates that the caller does not want the scheduler to be called after the post. This option can be used in combination with ONE of the two previous options.

	Use this option if the task (or ISR) calling **OSSemPost()** will be doing additional, the user does not want to reschedule until all done, and multiple posts are to take effect simultaneously.
p_err	is a pointer to a variable that holds an error code:

OS_ERR_NONE	if no tasks are waiting on the semaphore. In this case, the return value is also 0.
OS_ERR_OBJ_PTR_NULL	if **p_sem** is a **NULL** pointer.
OS_ERR_OBJ_TYPE	if **p_sem** is not pointing to a semaphore.
OS_ERR_SEM_OVF	if the post would have caused the semaphore counter to overflow.

Returned Value

The current value of the semaphore count

Notes/Warnings

1. Semaphores must be created before they are used.

2. You can also post to a semaphore from an ISR but the semaphore must be used as a signaling mechanism and not to protect a shared resource.

Example

```
OS_SEM  SwSem;


void TaskX (void *p_arg)
{
    OS_ERR      err;
    OS_SEM_CTR  ctr;


    (void)&p_arg;
    while (DEF_ON) {
        :
        :
        ctr = OSSemPost(&SwSem,
                        OS_OPT_POST_1 + OS_OPT_POST_NO_SCHED,
                        &err);
        /* Check "err" */
        :
        :
    }
}
```

OSSemSet()

```
void  OSSemSet (OS_SEM     *p_sem,
               OS_SEM_CTR  cnt,
               OS_ERR      *p_err)
```

File	Called from	Code enabled by
OS_SEM.C	Task	OS_CFG_SEM_EN and OS_CFG_SEM_SET_EN

OSSemSet() is used to change the current value of the semaphore count. This function is normally selected when a semaphore is used as a signaling mechanism. OSSemSet() can then be used to reset the count to any value. If the semaphore count is already 0, the count is only changed if there are no tasks waiting on the semaphore.

Arguments

p_sem   is a pointer to the semaphore that is used as a signaling mechanism.

cnt   is the desired count that the semaphore should be set to.

p_err   is a pointer to a variable used to hold an error code:

OS_ERR_NONE	if the count was changed or, not changed, because one or more tasks was waiting on the semaphore.
OS_ERR_OBJ_PTR_NULL	if **p_sem** is a **NULL** pointer.
OS_ERR_OBJ_TYPE	if **p_sem** is not pointing to a semaphore.
OS_ERR_SET_ISR	if this function was called from an ISR.
OS_ERR_TASK_WAITING	if tasks are waiting on the semaphore.

Returned Value

None

Notes/Warnings

Do not use this function if the semaphore is used to protect a shared resource.

Appendix A

Example

```
OS_SEM  SwSem;


void Task (void *p_arg)
{
    OS_ERR  err;


    (void)&p_arg;
    while (DEF_ON) {
        OSSemSet(&SwSem,        /* Reset the semaphore count */
                 0,
                 &err);
        /* Check "err" */
        :
        :
    }
}
```

OSStart()

```
void  OSStart (OS_ERR  *p_err)
```

File	Called from	Code enabled by
OS_CORE.C	Startup code only	N/A

OSStart() starts multitasking under µC/OS-III. This function is typically called from startup code after calling OSInit(). OSStart() will not return to the caller. Once µC/OS-III is running, calling OSStart() again will have no effect.

Arguments

p_err   is a pointer to a variable used to hold an error code:

> OS_ERR_FATAL_RETURN   if we ever return to this function.
>
> OS_ERR_OS_RUNNING   if the kernel is already running. In other words, if this function has already been called.

Returned Value

None

Notes/Warnings

OSInit() must be called prior to calling OSStart(). OSStart() should only be called once by the application code. However, if calling OSStart() more than once, nothing happens on the second and subsequent calls.

Example

```
void main (void)
{
    OS_ERR  err;

                                        /* User Code              */

    :
    OSInit(&err);                       /* Initialize µC/OS-III */
    /* Check "err" */
    :                                   /* User Code              */

    :
    OSStart(&err);                      /* Start Multitasking   */
    /* Any code here should NEVER be executed! */
}
```

OSStartHighRdy()

`void  OSStartHighRdy (void)`

File	Called from	Code enabled by
OS_CPU_A.ASM	OSStart()	N/A

`OSStartHighRdy()` is responsible for starting the highest-priority task that was created prior to calling `OSStart()`.

Arguments

None

Returned Values

None

Notes/Warnings

None

Example

The pseudocode for `OSStartHighRdy()` is shown below.

```
void  OSStartHighRdy (void)
{
    OSTaskSwHook();                         (1)
    SP = OSTCBHighRdyPtr->StkPtr;           (2)
    Pop CPU registers off the task's stack; (3)
    Return from interrupt;                  (4)
}
```

(1)   `OSStartHighRdy()` must call `OSTaskSwHook()`.

When called, `OSTCBCurPtr` and `OSTCBHighRdyPtr` both point to the `OS_TCB` of the highest-priority task created.

`OSTaskSwHook()` should check that `OSTCBCurPtr` is not equal to `OSTCBHighRdyPtr` as this is the first time `OSTaskSwHook()` is called and there is not a task that is switched out.

(2)   Load the CPU stack pointer register with the top-of-stack (TOS) of the task being started. The TOS is found in the **.StkPtr** field of the **OS_TCB**. For convenience, the **.StkPtr** field is the very first field of the **OS_TCB** data structure. This makes it easily accessible from assembly language.

(3)   Pop the registers from the task's stack frame. Recall that the registers should have been placed on the stack frame in the same order as if they were pushed at the beginning of an interrupt service routine.

(4)   Perform a return from interrupt, which starts the task as if it was resumed when returning from a real interrupt.

OSStatReset()

void OSStatReset (OS_ERR *p_err)

File	Called from	Code enabled by
OS_STAT.C	Task Level Only	OS_CFG_STAT_TASK_EN

OSStatReset() is used to reset statistical variables maintained by µC/OS-III. Specifically, the per-task maximum interrupt disable time, maximum scheduler lock time, maximum amount of time a message takes to reach a task queue, the maximum amount of time it takes a signal to reach a task and more.

Arguments

p_err   is a pointer to a variable used to hold an error code:

OS_ERR_NONE	the call was successful.
OS_ERR_STAT_RESET_ISR	if the call was attempted from an ISR.

Returned Value

None

Notes/Warnings

None

Example

```
void TaskX (void *p_arg)
{
    OS_ERR    err;

    (void)&p_arg;
    while (DEF_ON) {
        :
        :
        OSStatReset(&err);
        /* Check "err" */
        :
        :
    }
}
```

OSStatTaskCPUUsageInit()

void OSStatTaskCPUUsageInit (void)

File	Called from	Code enabled by
OS_STAT.C	Startup code only	OS_CFG_TASK_STAT_EN

OSStatTaskCPUUsageInit() determines the maximum value that a 32-bit counter can reach when no other task is executing. This function must be called when only one task is created in the application and when multitasking has started. This function must be called from the first and only task created by the application.

Arguments

p_err   is a pointer to a variable used to hold an error code:

OS_ERR_NONE   Always returns this value.

Returned Value

None

Notes/Warnings

None

Example

```
void FirstAndOnlyTask (void *p_arg)
{
    :
    :
#if OS_CFG_TASK_STAT_EN > 0
    OSStatTaskCPUUsageInit(); /* Compute CPU capacity with no task running */
#endif
    :
    OSTaskCreate(_);              /* Create the other tasks                    */
    OSTaskCreate(_);
    :
    while (DEF_ON) {
        :
        :
    }
}
```

OSStatTaskHook()

```
void OSStatTaskHook (void);
```

File	Called from	Code enabled by
OS_CPU_C.C	OSStatTask()	Always enabled

OSStatTaskHook() is a function called by µC/OS-III's statistic task, OSStatTask(). OSStatTaskHook() is generally implemented by the port implementer for the processor used. This hook allows the port to perform additional statistics for the processor used.

Arguments

None

Returned Values

None

Notes/Warnings

None

Example

The code below calls an application-specific hook that an application programmer can define. For this, the user can simply set the value of OS_AppStatTaskHookPtr to point to the desired hook function (see App_OS_SetAllHooks() in OS_APP_HOOKS.C).

In the example below, OSStatTaskHook() calls App_OS_StatTaskHook() if the pointer OS_AppStatTaskHookPtr is set to that function.

```
void  App_OS_StatTaskHook (void)                        /* OS_APP_HOOKS.C       */
{
    /* Your code goes here! */
}


void App_OS_SetAllHooks (void)                          /* OS_APP_HOOKS.C       */
{
    CPU_SR_ALLOC();

    CPU_CRITICAL_ENTER();
    :
    OS_AppStatTaskHookPtr = App_OS_StatTaskHook;
    :
    CPU_CRITICAL_EXIT();
}


void  OSStatTaskHook (void)                             /* OS_CPU_C.C           */
{
#if OS_CFG_APP_HOOKS_EN > 0u
    if (OS_AppStatTaskHookPtr != (OS_APP_HOOK_VOID)0) {   /* Call application hook */
        (*OS_AppStatTaskHookPtr)();
    }
#endif
}
```

OSTaskChangePrio()

```
void  OSTaskChangePrio (OS_TCB    *p_tcb,
                        OS_PRIO   prio_new,
                        OS_ERR    *p_err)
```

File	Called from	Code enabled by
OS_TASK.C	Task	OS_CFG_TASK_CHANGE_PRIO_EN

When you creating a task (see **OSTaskCreate()**), you also specify the priority of the task being created. In most cases, it is not necessary to change the priority of the task at run time. However, it is sometimes useful to do so, and **OSTaskChangePrio()** allows this to take place.

If the task is ready to run, **OSTaskChangePrio()** simply changes the position of the task in µC/OS-III's ready list. If the task is waiting on an event, **OSTaskChangePrio()** will change the position of the task in the pend list of the corresponding object, so that the pend list remains sorted by priority.

Because µC/OS-III supports multiple tasks at the same priority, there are no restrictions on the priority that a task can have, except that task priority zero (0) is reserved by µC/OS-III, and priority **OS_PRIO_MAX-1** is used by the idle task.

Note that a task priority cannot be changed from an ISR.

Arguments

p_tcb   is a pointer to the **OS_TCB** of the task for which the priority is being changed. If passing a **NULL** pointer, the priority of the current task is changed.

prio_new   is the new task's priority. This value must never be set to **OS_CFG_PRIO_MAX-1**, or higher and you must not use priority 0 since they are reserved for µC/OS-III.

p_err   is a pointer to a variable that will receive an error code:

OS_ERR_NONE	if the task's priority is changed.
OS_ERR_TASK_CHANGE_PRIO_ISR	if attempting to change the task's priority from an ISR.

OS_ERR_PRIO_INVALID if the priority of the task specified is invalid. By specifying a priority greater than or equal to **OS_PRIO_MAX-1**, or 0.

Returned Value

None

Notes/Warnings

None

Example

```
OS_TCB   MyTaskTCB;


void TaskX (void *p_arg)
{
    OS_ERR   err;


    while (DEF_ON) {
        :
        :
        OSTaskChangePrio(&MyTaskTCB,      /* Change the priority of "MyTask" to 10 */
                         10,
                         &err);
        /* Check "err" */
        :
    }
}
```

OSTaskCreate()

```
void   OSTaskCreate (OS_TCB          *p_tcb,
                     CPU_CHAR        *p_name,
                     OS_TASK_PTR      p_task,
                     void            *p_arg,
                     OS_PRIO          prio,
                     CPU_STK         *p_stk_base,
                     CPU_STK_SIZE     stk_limit,
                     CPU_STK_SIZE     stk_size,
                     OS_MSG_QTY       q_size,
                     OS_TICK          time_quanta,
                     void            *p_ext,
                     OS_OPT           opt,
                     OS_ERR          *p_err)
```

File	Called from	Code enabled by
OS_TASK.C	Task or startup code	N/A

Tasks must be created in order for µC/OS-III to recognize them as tasks. Create a task by calling **OSTaskCreate()** and provide arguments specifying to µC/OS-III how the task will be managed. Tasks are always created in the ready-to-run state.

Tasks can be created either prior to the start of multitasking (i.e., before calling **OSStart()**), or by a running task. A task cannot be created by an ISR. A task must either be written as an infinite loop, or delete itself once completed. If the task code returns by mistake, µC/OS-III will terminate the task by calling **OSTaskDel((OS_TCB *)0, &err))**. At Micrium, we like the "**while (DEF_ON)**" to implement infinite loops because, by convention, we use a **while** loop when we don't know how many iterations a loop will do. This is the case of an infinite loop. We use **for** loops when we know how many iterations a loop will do.

Task as an infinite loop:

```
void MyTask (void *p_arg)
{
    /* Local variables                                          */


    /* Do something with 'p_arg'                                */
    /* Task initialization                                      */
    while (DEF_ON) {       /* Task body, as an infinite loop.   */
        :
        :
        /* Must call one of the following services:             */
        /*    OSFlagPend()                                       */
        /*    OSMutexPend()                                      */
        /*    OSQPend()                                          */
        /*    OSSemPend()                                        */
        /*    OSTimeDly()                                        */
        /*    OSTimeDlyHMSM()                                    */
        /*    OSTaskQPend()                                      */
        /*    OSTaskSemPend()                                    */
        /*    OSTaskSuspend()     (Suspend self)                 */
        /*    OSTaskDel()         (Delete  self)                 */
        :
        :
    }
}
```

Run to completion task:

```
void MyTask (void *p_arg)
{
    OS_ERR  err;
    /* Local variables                                          */


    /* Do something with 'p_arg'                                */
    /* Task initialization                                      */
    /* Task body (do some work)                                 */
    OSTaskDel((OS_TCB *)0, &err);
    /* Check 'err"                                              */
}
```

Arguments

p_tcb   is a pointer to the task's **OS_TCB** to use. It is assumed that storage for the TCB of the task will be allocated by the user code. Declare a "global" variable as follows, and pass a pointer to this variable to **OSTaskCreate()**:

```
OS_TCB MyTaskTCB;
```

p_name   is a pointer to an ASCII string (NUL terminated) to assign a name to the task. The name can be displayed by debuggers or by µC/Probe.

p_task   is a pointer to the task (i.e., the name of the function).

p_arg   is a pointer to an optional data area, which is used to pass parameters to the task when it is created. When µC/OS-III runs the task for the first time, the task will think that it was invoked, and passed the argument **p_arg**. For example, create a generic task that handles an asynchronous serial port. **p_arg** can be used to pass task information about the serial port it will manage: the port address, baud rate, number of bits, parity, and more. **p_arg** is the argument received by the task shown below.

```
void MyTask (void *p_arg)
{
    while (DEF_ON) {
        Task code;
    }
}
```

prio   is the task priority. The lower the number, the higher the priority (i.e., the importance) of the task. If **OS_CFG_ISR_POST_DEFERRED_EN** is set to 1, the user may not use priority 0.

Task priority must also have a lower number than **OS_CFG_PRIO_MAX-1**. Priorities 0, 1, **OS_CFG_PRIO_MAX-2** and **OS_CFG_PRIO_MAX-1** are reserved. In other words, a task should have a priority between 2 and **OOS_CFG_PRIO_MAX-3**, inclusively.

p_stk_base is a pointer to the task's stack base address. The task's stack is used to store local variables, function parameters, return addresses, and possibly CPU registers during an interrupt.

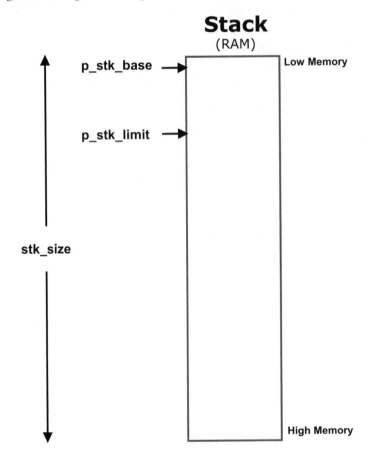

The task stack must be declared as follows:

```
CPU_STK MyTaskStk[xxx];
```

The user would then pass **p_stk_base** the address of the first element of this array or, &MyTaskStk[0]. "xxx" represents the size of the stack.

The size of this stack is determined by the task's requirements and the anticipated interrupt nesting (unless the processor has a separate stack just for interrupts). Determining the size of the stack involves knowing how many bytes are required for storage of local variables for the task itself and all nested functions, as well as requirements for interrupts (accounting for nesting).

Note that you can allocate stack space for a task from the heap but, in this case, never delete the task and free the stack space as this can cause the heap to fragment, which is not desirable in embedded systems.

stk_limit is used to locate, within the task's stack, a watermark limit that can be used to monitor and ensure that the stack does not overflow.

If the processor does not have hardware stack overflow detection, or this feature is not implemented in software by the port developer, this value may be used for other purposes. For example, some processors have two stacks, a hardware and a software stack. The hardware stack typically keeps track of function call nesting and the software stack is used to pass function arguments. **stk_limit** may be used to set the size of the hardware stack as shown below.

stk_size   specifies the size of the task's stack in number of elements. If **CPU_STK** is set to **CPU_INT08U** (see **OS_TYPE.H**), stk_size corresponds to the number of bytes available on the stack. If **CPU_STK** is set to **CPU_INT16U**, then stk_size contains the number of 16-bit entries available on the stack. Finally, if **CPU_STK** is set to **CPU_INT32U**, stk_size contains the number of 32-bit entries available on the stack.

q_size   A μC/OS-III task contains an optional internal message queue (if **OS_TASK_Q_EN > 0**). This argument specifies the maximum number of messages that the task can receive through this message queue. The user may specify that the task is unable to receive messages by setting the argument to 0.

time_quanta   the amount of time (in clock ticks) for the time quanta when round robin is enabled. If you specify 0, then the default time quanta will be used which is the tick rate divided by 10.

p_ext   is a pointer to a user-supplied memory location (typically a data structure) used as a TCB extension. For example, the user memory can hold the contents of floating-point registers during a context switch.

opt   contains task-specific options. Each option consists of one bit. The option is selected when the bit is set. The current version of µC/OS-III supports the following options:

> OS_OPT_TASK_NONE   specifies that there are no options.
>
> OS_OPT_TASK_STK_CHK   specifies whether stack checking is allowed for the task.
>
> OS_OPT_TASK_STK_CLR   specifies whether the stack needs to be cleared.
>
> OS_OPT_TASK_SAVE_FP   specifies whether floating-point registers are saved. This option is only valid if the processor has floating-point hardware and the processor-specific code saves the floating-point registers.

p_err   is a pointer to a variable that will receive an error code:

> OS_ERR_NONE   if the function is successful.
>
> OS_ERR_NAME   if **p_name** is a **NULL** pointer.
>
> OS_ERR_PRIO_INVALID   if prio is higher than the maximum value allowed (i.e., > **OS_PRIO_MAX-1**). Also, if the user set **OS_CFG_ISR_POST_DEFERRED_EN** to 1 and tried to use priority 0.
>
> OS_ERR_STK_INVALID   if specifying a **NULL** pointer for **p_stk_base**.
>
> OS_ERR_STK_SIZE_INVALID   if specifying a stack size smaller than what is currently specified by **OS_CFG_STK_SIZE_MIN** (see the **OS_CFG.H**).
>
> OS_ERR_TASK_CREATE_ISR   if attempting to create the task from an ISR.
>
> OS_ERR_TASK_INVALID   if specifying a **NULL** pointer for **p_task**
>
> OS_ERR_TCB_INVALID   if specifying a **NULL** pointer for **p_tcb**.

Returned Value

None

Notes/Warnings

1. The stack must be declared with the CPU_STK type.

2. A task must always invoke one of the services provided by µC/OS-III to wait for time to expire, suspend the task, or wait on an object (wait on a message queue, event flag, mutex, semaphore, a signal or a message to be sent directly to the task). This allows other tasks to gain control of the CPU.

3. Do not use task priorities 0, 1, OS_PRIO_MAX-2 and OS_PRIO_MAX-1 because they are reserved for use by µC/OS-III.

Example

OSTaskCreate() can be called from **main()** (in C), or a previously created task.

```
OS_TCB  MyTaskTCB;                    /*  (1) Storage for task's TCB                    */
CPU_STK MyTaskStk[200];


void  MyTask (void *p_arg)            /*  (3) The address of the task is its name       */
{
    while (DEF_ON) {
            /* Wait for an event */
            /* My task body       */
    }
}


void SomeCode (void)
{
    OS_ERR  err;
    :
    :

    OSTaskCreate (&MyTaskTCB,                 /*  (1) Address of TCB assigned to the task       */
                  "My Task",                  /*  (2) Name you want to give the task            */
                  MyTask,                     /*  (3) Address of the task itself                */
                  (void *)0,                  /*  (4) "p_arg" is not used                       */
                  12,                         /*  (5) Priority you want to assign to the task   */
                  &MyTaskStk[0],              /*  (6) Base address of task's stack              */
                  10,                         /*  (7) Watermark limit for stack growth          */
                  200,                        /*  (8) Stack size in number of CPU_STK elements  */
                  5,                          /*  (9) Size of task message queue                */
                  10,                         /* (10) Time quanta (in number of ticks)          */
                  (void *)0,                  /* (11) Extension pointer is not used             */
                  OS_OPT_TASK_STK_CHK + OS_OPT_TASK_STK_CLR, /* (12) Options                    */
                  &err);                      /* (13) Error code                                */
    /* Check "err"                             (14)                                             */
    :
    :
}
```

(1)   In order to create a task, allocate storage for a TCB and pass a pointer to this TCB to **OSTaskCreate()**.

(2)   Assign an ASCII name to the task by passing a pointer to an ASCII string. The ASCII string may be allocated in code space (i.e., ROM), or data space (i.e., RAM). In either case, it is assumed that the code can access that memory.

(3)   Pass the address of the task to **OSTaskCreate()**. In C, the address of a function is simply the name of the function.

(4)   To provide additional data to **MyTask()**, simply pass a pointer to such data. In this case, **MyTask()** did not need such data and therefore, a **NULL** pointer is passed.

(5)   The user must assign a priority to the task. The priority specifies the importance of this task with respect to other tasks. A low-priority value indicates a high priority. Priority 0 is the highest priority (reserved for an internal task) and a priority up to **OS_PRIO_MAX-2** can be specified (see **OS_CFG.H**). Note that **OS_PRIO_MAX-1** is also reserved for an internal task, the idle task.

(6)   The next argument specifies the "base address" of the task's stack. In this case, it is simply the base address of the array **MyTaskStk[]**. Note that it is possible to simply specify the name of the array. I prefer to make it clear by writing **&MyTaskStk[0]**.

(7)   Set the watermark limit for stack growth. If the processor port does not use this field then either set this value to **0**.

(8)   µC/OS-III also needs to know the size of the stack for the task. This allows µC/OS-III to perform stack checking at run time.

(9)   µC/OS-III allows tasks or ISRs to send messages directly to a task. This argument specifies how many such messages can be received by this task.

(10)   This argument specifies how much time (in number of ticks) this task will run on the CPU before µC/OS-III will force the CPU away from this task and run the next task at the same priority (if there are more than one task at the same priority that is ready to run).

(11)   µC/OS-III allows the user to "extend" the capabilities of the TCB by allowing passing a pointer to some memory location that could contain additional information about the task. For example, there may be a CPU that supports floating-point math and the user would likely need to save the floating-point registers during a context switch. This pointer could point to the storage area for these registers.

(12)   When creating a task, options must be specified. Specifically, such options as, whether the stack of the task will be cleared (i.e., filled with 0x00) when the task is created (**OS_OPT_TASK_STK_CLR**), whether µC/OS-III will be allowed to check for stack usage (**OS_OPT_TASK_STK_CHK**), whether the CPU supports floating-point math, and whether the task will make use of the floating-point registers and therefore need to save and restore them during a context switch (**OS_OPT_TASK_SAVE_FP**). The options are additive.

(13)   Most of µC/OS-III's services return an error code indicating the outcome of the call. The error code is always returned as a pointer to a variable of type **OS_ERR**. The user must allocate storage for this variable prior to calling **OSTaskCreate()**. By the way, a pointer to an error variable is always the last argument, which makes it easy to remember.

(14)   It is highly recommended that the user examine the error code whenever calling a µC/OS-III function. If the call is successful, the error code will always be **OS_ERR_NONE**. If the call is not successful, the returned code will indicate the reason for the failure (see **OS_ERR_???** in **OS.H**).

OSTaskCreateHook()

void   OSTaskCreateHook (OS_TCB   *p_tcb)

File	Called from	Code enabled by
OS_CPU_C.C	OSTaskCreate() ONLY	N/A

This function is called by **OSTaskCreate()** just before adding the task to the ready list. When **OSTaskCreateHook()** is called, all of the **OS_TCB** fields are assumed to be initialized. **OSTaskCreateHook()** is called after initializing the **OS_TCB** fields and setting up the stack frame for the task, before the task is placed in the ready list.

OSTaskCreateHook() is part of the CPU port code and this function *must not* be called by the application code. **OSTaskCreateHook()** is actually used by the µC/OS-III port developer.

Use this hook to initialize and store the contents of floating-point registers, MMU registers, or anything else that can be associated with a task. Typically, store this additional information in memory allocated by the application.

Arguments

p_tcb   is a pointer to the TCB of the task being created. Note that the **OS_TCB** has been validated by **OSTaskCreate()** and is guaranteed to not be a **NULL** pointer when **OSTaskCreateHook()** is called.

Returned Value

None

Notes/Warnings

Do not call this function from the application.

Example

The code below calls an application-specific hook that the application programmer can define. The user can simply set the value of **OS_AppTaskCreateHookPtr** to point to the desired hook function as shown in the example. **OSTaskCreate()** calls

`OSTaskCreateHook()` which in turns calls **App_OS_TaskCreateHook()** through **OS_AppTaskCreateHookPtr**. As can be seen, when called, the application hook is passed the address of the **OS_TCB** of the newly created task.

```
void  App_OS_TaskCreateHook (OS_TCB *p_tcb)              /* OS_APP_HOOKS.C     */
{
    /* Your code goes here! */
}


void App_OS_SetAllHooks (void)                          /* OS_APP_HOOKS.C     */
{
    CPU_SR_ALLOC();

    CPU_CRITICAL_ENTER();
    :
    OS_AppTaskCreateHookPtr = App_OS_TaskCreateHook;
    :
    CPU_CRITICAL_EXIT();
}


void  OSTaskCreateHook (OS_TCB *p_tcb)                   /* OS_CPU_C.C         */
{
#if OS_CFG_APP_HOOKS_EN > 0u
    if (OS_AppTaskCreateHookPtr != (OS_APP_HOOK_TCB)0) {   /* Call application hook */
        (*OS_AppTaskCreateHookPtr)(p_tcb);
    }
#endif
}
```

OSTaskDel()

```
void   OSTaskDel (OS_TCB   *p_tcb,
                  OS_ERR   *p_err)
```

File	Called from	Code enabled by
OS_TASK.C	Task	OS_CFG_TASK_DEL_EN

When a task is no longer needed, it can be deleted. Deleting a task does not mean that the code is removed, but that the task code is no longer managed by µC/OS-III. **OSTaskDel()** can be used when creating a task that will only run once. In this case, the task must not return but instead call **OSTaskDel((OS_TCB *)0, &err)**, specifying to µC/OS-III to delete the currently running task.

A task may also delete another task by specifying to **OSTaskDel()** the address of the **OS_TCB** of the task to delete.

Once a task is deleted, its **OS_TCB** and stack may be reused to create another task. This assumes that the task's stack requirement of the new task is satisfied by the stack size of the deleted task.

Even though µC/OS-III allows the user to delete tasks at run time, it is recommend that such actions be avoided. Why? Because a task can "own" resources that are shared with other tasks. Deleting the task that owns resource(s) without first relinquishing the resources could lead to strange behaviors and possible deadlocks.

Arguments

p_tcb   is a pointer to the TCB of the task to delete or, a **NULL** pointer for the calling task to delete itself. If deleting the calling task, the scheduler will be invoked so that the next highest-priority task is executed.

p_err   is a pointer to a variable that will receive an error code:

OS_ERR_NONE	if the desired task was deleted (unless the task deleted itself in which case there are no errors to return).
OS_ERR_TASK_DEL_IDLE	if attempting to delete the ilde task.

OS_ERR_TASK_DEL_ISR   if calling **OSTaskDel()** from an ISR.

OS_ERR_TASK_DEL_INVALID   if attempting to delete the ISR Handler task while **OS_CFG_ISR_POST_DEFERRED_EN** is set to 1.

Returned Value

None

Notes/Warnings

1. **OSTaskDel()** verifies that the user is not attempting to delete the µC/OS-III idle task and the ISR handler task.

2. Be careful when deleting a task that owns resources.

Example

```
OS_TCB  MyTaskTCB;


void TaskX (void *p_arg)
{
    OS_ERR  err;


    while (DEF_ON) {
        :
        :
        OSTaskDel(&MyTaskTCB,
                  &err);
        /* Check "err" */
        :
        :
    }
}
```

OSTaskDelHook()

```
void   OSTaskDelHook (OS_TCB   *p_tcb);
```

File	Called from	Code enabled by
OS_CPU_C.C	OSTaskDel() ONLY	N/A

This function is called by **OSTaskDel()** after the task is removed from the ready list or any pend list.

Use this hook to deallocate storage assigned to the task.

OSTaskDelHook() is part of the CPU port code and this function *must not* be called by the application code. **OSTaskDelHook()** is actually used by the µC/OS-III port developer.

Arguments

p_tcb   is a pointer to the TCB of the task being created. Note that the **OS_TCB** has been validated by **OSTaskDel()** and is guaranteed to not be a **NULL** pointer when **OSTaskDelHook()** is called.

Returned Value

None

Notes/Warnings

Do not call this function from the application.

Example

The code below calls an application-specific hook that the application programmer can define. The user can simply set the value of **OS_AppTaskDelHookPtr** to point to the desired hook function. **OSTaskDel()** calls **OSTaskDelHook()** which in turns calls **App_OS_TaskDelHook()** through **OS_AppTaskDelHookPtr**. As can be seen, when called, the application hook is passed the address of the **OS_TCB** of the task being deleted.

```
void  App_OS_TaskDelHook (OS_TCB *p_tcb)                /* OS_APP_HOOKS.C      */
{
    /* Your code goes here! */
}


void App_OS_SetAllHooks (void)                          /* OS_APP_HOOKS.C      */
{
    CPU_SR_ALLOC();

    CPU_CRITICAL_ENTER();
    :
    OS_AppTaskDelHookPtr = App_OS_TaskDelHook;
    :
    CPU_CRITICAL_EXIT();
}



void  OSTaskDelHook (OS_TCB *p_tcb)                      /* OS_CPU_C.C          */
{
#if OS_CFG_APP_HOOKS_EN > 0u
    if (OS_AppTaskDelHookPtr != (OS_APP_HOOK_TCB)0) {    /* Call application hook */
        (*OS_AppTaskDelHookPtr)(p_tcb);
    }
#endif
}
```

OSTaskQPend()

```
void   *OSTaskQPend (OS_TICK        timeout,
                     OS_OPT         opt,
                     OS_MSG_SIZE    *p_msg_size,
                     CPU_TS         *p_ts,
                     OS_ERR         *p_err)
```

File	Called from	Code enabled by
OS_TASK.C	Task	OS_CFG_TASK_Q_EN and OS_CFG_MSG_EN

OSTaskQPend() allows a task to receive messages directly from an ISR or another task, without going through an intermediate message queue. In fact, each task has a built-in message queue if the configuration constant **OS_TASK_Q_EN** is set to 1. The messages received are pointer-sized variables, and their use is application specific. If at least one message is already present in the message queue when OSTaskQPend() is called, the message is retrieved and returned to the caller.

If no message is present in the task's message queue and **OS_OPT_PEND_BLOCKING** is specified for the **opt** argument, OSTaskQPend() suspends the current task (assuming the scheduler is not locked) until either a message is received, or a user-specified timeout expires. A pended task that is suspended with OSTaskSuspend() can receive messages. However, the task remains suspended until it is resumed by calling OSTaskResume().

If no message is present in the task's message queue and **OS_OPT_PEND_NON_BLOCKING** is specified for the opt argument, OSTaskQPend() returns to the caller with an appropriate error code and returns a **NULL** pointer.

Arguments

timeout   allows the task to resume execution if a message is not received from a task or an ISR within the specified number of clock ticks. A timeout value of 0 indicates that the task wants to wait forever for a message. The timeout value is not synchronized with the clock tick. The timeout count starts decrementing on the next clock tick, which could potentially occur immediately.

opt   determines whether or not the user wants to block if a message is not available in the task's queue. This argument must be set to either:

OS_OPT_PEND_BLOCKING, or

OS_OPT_PEND_NON_BLOCKING

Note that the timeout argument should be set to 0 when OS_OPT_PEND_NON_BLOCKING is specified, since the timeout value is irrelevant using this option.

p_msg_size is a pointer to a variable that will receive the size of the message.

p_ts   is a pointer to a timestamp indicating when the task's queue was posted, or the pend aborted. If passing a **NULL** pointer (i.e., (CPU_TS *)0), the timestamp will not returned. In other words, passing a **NULL** pointer is valid and indicates that the timestamp is not necessary.

A timestamp is useful when the task must know when the task message queue was posted, or how long it took for the task to resume after the task message queue was posted. In the latter case, call OS_TS_GET() and compute the difference between the current value of the timestamp and *p_ts. In other words:

delta = OS_TS_GET() - *p_ts;

p_err   is a pointer to a variable used to hold an error code.

OS_ERR_NONE	if a message is received.
OS_ERR_PEND_ABORT	if the pend was aborted because another task called OSTaskQPendAbort().
OS_ERR_PEND_ISR	if calling this function from an ISR.
OS_ERR_PEND_WOULD_BLOCK	if calling this function with the opt argument set to OS_OPT_PEND_NON_BLOCKING and no message is in the task's message queue.
OS_ERR_SCHED_LOCKED	if calling this function when the scheduler is locked and the user wanted to block.

OS_ERR_TIMEOUT	if a message is not received within the specified timeout.

Returned Value

The message if no error or a **NULL** pointer upon error. Examine the error code since it is possible to send **NULL** pointer messages. In other words, a **NULL** pointer does not mean an error occurred. *p_err must be examined to determine the reason for the error.

Notes/Warnings

Do not call **OSTaskQPend()** from an ISR.

Example

```
void CommTask (void *p_arg)
{
    OS_ERR       err;
    void        *p_msg;
    OS_MSG_SIZE  msg_size;
    CPU_TS       ts;


    (void)&p_arg;
    while (DEF_ON) {
        :
        :
        p_msg = OSTaskQPend(100,
                            OS_OPT_PEND_BLOCKING,
                            &msg_size,
                            &ts,
                            &err);
        /* Check "err" */
        :
        :
    }
}
```

OSTaskQPendAbort()

```
CPU_BOOLEAN  OSTaskQPendAbort (OS_TCB  *p_tcb,
                               OS_OPT   opt,
                               OS_ERR  *p_err)
```

File	Called from	Code enabled by
OS_Q.C	Task	OS_CFG_TASK_Q_EN and OS_CFG_TASK_Q_PEND_ABORT_EN

OSTaskQPendAbort() aborts and readies a task currently waiting on its built-in message queue. This function should be used to fault-abort the wait on the task's message queue, rather than to normally signal the message queue via **OSTaskQPost()**.

Arguments

p_tcb   is a pointer to the task for which the pend needs to be aborted. Note that it doesn't make sense to pass a **NULL** pointer or the address of the calling task's TCB since, by definition, the calling task cannot be pending.

opt   provides options for this function.

OS_OPT_POST_NONE	No option specified.
OS_OPT_POST_NO_SCHED	specifies that the scheduler should not be called even if the pend of a higher priority task has been aborted. Scheduling will need to occur from another function.
	Use this option if the task calling **OSTaskQPendAbort()** will do additional pend aborts, rescheduling will take place when completed, and multiple pend aborts should take effect simultaneously.

p_err   is a pointer to a variable that holds an error code:

OS_ERR_NONE	the task was readied by another task and it was informed of the aborted wait.
OS_ERR_PEND_ABORT_ISR	if called from an ISR

OS_ERR_PEND_ABORT_NONE	if the task was not pending on the task's message queue.
OS_ERR_PEND_ABORT_SELF	if p_tcb is a **NULL** pointer. The user is attempting to pend abort the calling task which makes no sense as the caller, by definition, is not pending.

Returned Value

OSTaskQPendAbort() returns DEF_TRUE if the task was made ready to run by this function. DEF_FALSE indicates that the task was not pending, or an error occurred.

Notes/Warnings

None

Example

```
OS_TCB  CommRxTaskTCB;


void CommTask (void *p_arg)
{
    OS_ERR       err;
    CPU_BOOLEAN  aborted;


    (void)&p_arg;
    while (DEF_ON) {
        :
        :
        aborted = OSTaskQPendAbort(&CommRxTaskTCB,
                                   OS_OPT_POST_NONE,
                                   &err);
        /* Check "err" */
        :
        :
    }
}
```

OSTaskQPost()

```
void  OSTaskQPost (OS_TCB       *p_tcb,
                   void         *p_void,
                   OS_MSG_SIZE  msg_size,
                   OS_OPT       opt,
                   OS_ERR       *p_err)
```

File	Called from	Code enabled by
OS_Q.C	Task or ISR	OS_CFG_TASK_Q_EN and OS_CFG_MSG_EN

OSTaskQPost() sends a message to a task through its local message queue. A message is a pointer-sized variable, and its use is application specific. If the task's message queue is full, an error code is returned to the caller. In this case, OSTaskQPost() immediately returns to its caller, and the message is not placed in the message queue.

If the task receiving the message is waiting for a message to arrive, it will be made ready to run. If the receiving task has a higher priority than the task sending the message, the higher-priority task resumes, and the task sending the message is suspended; that is, a context switch occurs. A message can be posted as first-in first-out (FIFO), or last-in-first-out (LIFO), depending on the value specified in the opt argument. In either case, scheduling occurs unless opt is set to OS_OPT_POST_NO_SCHED.

Arguments

p_tcb   is a pointer to the TCB of the task. Note that it is possible to post a message to the calling task (i.e., self) by specifying a NULL pointer, or the address of its TCB.

p_void   is the actual message sent to the task. p_void is a pointer-sized variable and its meaning is application specific.

msg_size   specifies the size of the message posted (in number of bytes).

opt   determines the type of POST performed. Of course, it does not make sense to post LIFO and FIFO simultaneously, so these options are exclusive:

OS_OPT_POST_FIFO	POST message to task, or place at the end of the queue if the task is not waiting for messages.
OS_OPT_POST_LIFO	POST message to task, or place at the front of the queue if the task is not waiting for messages.
OS_OPT_POST_NO_SCHED	Do not call the scheduler after the post and therefore the caller is resumed.
	Use this option if the task (or ISR) calling **OSTaskQPost()** will be doing additional posts, the user does not want to reschedule until all done, and multiple posts are to take effect simultaneously. **p_err** is a pointer to a variable that will contain an error code returned by this function.
OS_ERR_NONE	if the call was successful and the message was posted to the task's message queue.
OS_ERR_MSG_POOL_EMPTY	if running out of **OS_MSG** to hold the message being posted.
OS_ERR_Q_MAX	if the task's message queue is full and cannot accept more messages.

Returned Value

None

Notes/Warnings

None

Example

```
OS_TCB      CommRxTaskTCB;
CPU_INT08U  CommRxBuf[100];


void CommTaskRx (void *p_arg)
{
    OS_ERR  err;


    (void)&p_arg;
    while (DEF_ON) {
        :
        OSTaskQPost(&CommRxTaskTCB,
                    (void *)&CommRxBuf[0],
                    sizeof(CommRxBuf),
                    OS_OPT_POST_FIFO,
                    &err);
        /* Check "err" */
        :
    }
}
```

OSTaskRegGet()

```
OS_REG   OSTaskRegGet (OS_TCB      *p_tcb,
                       OS_REG_ID   id,
                       OS_ERR      *p_err)
```

File	Called from	Code enabled by
OS_TASK.C	Task	OS_CFG_TASK_REG_TBL_SIZE > 0

μC/OS-III allows the user to store task-specific values in task registers. Task registers are different than CPU registers and are used to save such information as "errno," which are common in software components. Task registers can also store task-related data to be associated with the task at run time such as I/O register settings, configuration values, etc. A task may have as many as **OS_CFG_TASK_REG_TBL_SIZE** registers, and all registers have a data type of **OS_REG**. However, **OS_REG** can be declared at compile time (see **OS_TYPE.H**) to be nearly anything (8-, 16-, 32-, 64-bit signed or unsigned integer, or floating-point).

As shown below, a task is register is changed by calling **OSTaskRegSet()** and read by calling **OSTaskRegGet()**. The desired task register is specified as an argument to these functions and can take a value between 0 and **OS_CFG_TASK_REG_TBL_SIZE-1**.

Arguments

p_tcb
is a pointer to the TCB of the task the user is receiving a task-register value from. A **NULL** pointer indicates that the user wants the value of a task register of the calling task.

id
is the identifier of the task register and valid values are from 0 to OS_CFG_TASK_REG_TBL_SIZE-1.

p_err
is a pointer to a variable that will contain an error code returned by this function.

OS_ERR_NONE	if the call was successful and the function returned the value of the desired task register.
OS_ERR_REG_ID_INVALID	if a valid task register identifier is not specified.

Returned Value

The current value of the task register.

Notes/Warnings

None

Example

```
OS_TCB  MyTaskTCB;


void TaskX (void *p_arg)
{
    OS_ERR  err;
    OS_REG  reg;


    while (DEF_ON) {
        :
        reg = OSTaskRegGet(&MyTaskTCB,
                           5,
                           &err);
        /* Check "err" */
        :
    }
}
```

OSTaskRegSet()

```
void  OSTaskRegSet (OS_TCB     *p_tcb,
                    OS_REG_ID  id,
                    OS_REG     value,
                    OS_ERR     *p_err)
```

File	Called from	Code enabled by
OS_TASK.C	Task	OS_CFG_TASK_REG_TBL_SIZE > 0

μC/OS-III allows the user to store task-specific values in task registers. Task registers are different than CPU registers and are used to save such information as "errno," which are common in software components. Task registers can also store task-related data to be associated with the task at run time such as I/O register settings, configuration values, etc. A task may have as many as OS_CFG_TASK_REG_TBL_SIZE registers, and all registers have a data type of OS_REG. However, OS_REG can be declared at compile time to be nearly anything (8-, 16-, 32-, 64-bit signed or unsigned integer, or floating-point).

As shown below, a task is register is changed by calling OSTaskRegSet(), and read by calling OSTaskRegGet(). The desired task register is specified as an argument to these functions and can take a value between 0 and OS_CFG_TASK_REG_TBL_SIZE-1.

Arguments

p_tcb   is a pointer to the TCB of the task you are setting. A **NULL** pointer indicates that the user wants to set the value of a task register of the calling task.

id   is the identifier of the task register and valid values are from 0 to **OS_CFG_TASK_REG_TBL_SIZE-1**.

value   is the new value of the task register specified by **id**.

p_err   is a pointer to a variable that will contain an error code returned by this function.

OS_ERR_NONE	if the call was successful, and the function set the value of the desired task register.
OS_ERR_REG_ID_INVALID	if a valid task register identifier is not specified.

Returned Value

None

Notes/Warnings

None

Example

```
OS_TCB   MyTaskTCB;


void TaskX (void *p_arg)
{
    OS_ERR   err;


    while (DEF_ON) {
        :
        reg = OSTaskRegSet(&MyTaskTCB,
                           5,
                           23,
                           &err);
        /* Check "err" */
        :
    }
}
```

OSTaskReturnHook()

```
void  OSTaskReturnHook (void);
```

File	Called from	Code enabled by
OS_CPU_C.C	OS_TaskReturn() ONLY	N/A

This function is called by OS_TaskReturn(). OS_TaskReturn() is called if the user accidentally returns from the task code. In other words, the task should either be implemented as an infinite loop and never return, or the task must call OSTaskDel((OS_TCB *)0, &err) to delete itself to prevent it from exiting.

OSTaskReturnHook() is part of the CPU port code and this function *must not* be called by the application code. OSTaskReturnHook() is actually used by the µC/OS-III port developer.

Note that after calling OSTaskReturnHook(), OS_TaskReturn() will actually delete the task by calling:

```
OSTaskDel((OS_TCB *)0,
          &err)
```

Arguments

p_tcb   is a pointer to the TCB of the task that is not behaving as expected. Note that the OS_TCB is validated by OS_TaskReturn(), and is guaranteed to not be a NULL pointer when OSTaskReturnHook() is called.

Returned Value

None

Notes/Warnings

Do not call this function from the application.

Example

The code below calls an application-specific hook that the application programmer can define. For this, the user can simply set the value of OS_AppTaskReturnHookPtr to point to the desired hook function as shown in the example. If a task returns and forgets to call

OSTaskDel((OS_TCB *)0, &err) then µC/OS-III will call OSTaskReturnHook() which in turns calls App_OS_TaskReturnHook() through OS_AppTaskReturnHookPtr. When called, the application hook is passed the address of the OS_TCB of the task returning.

```
void  App_OS_TaskReturnHook (OS_TCB  *p_tcb)              /* OS_APP_HOOKS.C      */
{
    /* Your code goes here! */
}


void App_OS_SetAllHooks (void)                            /* OS_APP_HOOKS.C      */
{
    CPU_SR_ALLOC();

    CPU_CRITICAL_ENTER();
    :
    OS_AppTaskReturnHookPtr = App_OS_TaskReturnHook;
    :
    CPU_CRITICAL_EXIT();
}


void  OSTaskReturnHook (OS_TCB *p_tcb)                    /* OS_CPU_C.C          */
{
#if OS_CFG_APP_HOOKS_EN > 0u
    if (OS_AppTaskReturnHookPtr != (OS_APP_HOOK_TCB)0) {  /* Call application hook */
        (*OS_AppTaskReturnHookPtr)(p_tcb);
    }
#endif
}
```

OSTaskResume()

```
void   OSTaskResume (OS_TCB   *p_tcb,
                     OS_ERR   *p_err)
```

File	Called from	Code enabled by
OS_TASK.C	Task	OS_CFG_TASK_SUSPEND_EN

OSTaskResume() resumes a task suspended through the OSTaskSuspend() function. In fact, OSTaskResume() is the only function that can unsuspend a suspended task. Obviously, the suspended task can only be resumed by another task. If the suspended task is also waiting on another kernel object such as an event flag, semaphore, mutex, message queue etc., the suspension will simply be lifted (i.e., removed), but the task will continue waiting for the object.

The user can "nest" suspension of a task by calling OSTaskSuspend() and therefore must call OSTaskResume() an equivalent number of times to resume such a task. In other words, if suspending a task five times, it is necessary to unsuspend the same task five times to remove the suspension of the task.

Arguments

p_tcb   is a pointer to the TCB of the task that is resuming. A NULL pointer is not a valid value as one cannot resume the calling task because, by definition, the calling task is running and is not suspended.

p_err   is a pointer to a variable that will contain an error code returned by this function.

OS_ERR_NONE	if the call was successful and the desired task is resumed.
OS_ERR_TASK_RESUME_ISR	if calling this function from an ISR.
OS_ERR_TASK_RESUME_SELF	if passing a NULL pointer for p_tcb. It is not possible to resume the calling task since, if suspended, it cannot be executing.
OS_ERR_TASK_NOT_SUSPENDED	if the task attempting to be resumed is not suspended.

Returned Value

None

Notes/Warnings

None

Example

```
OS_TCB    TaskY;


void TaskX (void *p_arg)
{
    OS_ERR err;


    while (DEF_ON) {
        :
        :
        OSTaskResume(&TaskY,
                     &err);           /* Resume suspended task      */
        /* Check "err" */
        :
        :
    }
}
```

OSTaskSemPend()

```
OS_SEM_CTR  OSTaskSemPend (OS_TICK    timeout,
                           OS_OPT     opt,
                           CPU_TS    *p_ts,
                           OS_ERR    *p_err)
```

File	Called from	Code enabled by
OS_TASK.C	Task	Always enabled

OSTaskSemPend() allows a task to wait for a signal to be sent by another task or ISR without going through an intermediate object such as a semaphore. If the task was previously signaled when OSTaskSemPend() is called then, the caller resumes.

If no signal was received by the task and OS_OPT_PEND_BLOCKING is specified for the opt argument, OSTaskSemPend() suspends the current task (assuming the scheduler is not locked) until either a signal is received, or a user-specified timeout expires. A pended task suspended with OSTaskSuspend() can receive signals. However, the task remains suspended until it is resumed by calling OSTaskResume().

If no signals were sent to the task and OS_OPT_PEND_NON_BLOCKING was specified for the opt argument, OSTaskSemPend() returns to the caller with an appropriate error code and returns a signal count of 0.

Arguments

timeout   allows the task to resume execution if a signal is not received from a task or an ISR within the specified number of clock ticks. A timeout value of 0 indicates that the task wants to wait forever for a signal. The timeout value is not synchronized with the clock tick. The timeout count starts decrementing on the next clock tick, which could potentially occur immediately.

opt   determines whether the user wants to block or not, if a signal was not sent to the task. Set this argument to either:

     OS_OPT_PEND_BLOCKING, or

     OS_OPT_PEND_NON_BLOCKING

Note that the timeout argument should be set to 0 when specifying **OS_OPT_PEND_NON_BLOCKING**, since the timeout value is irrelevant using this option.

p_ts   is a pointer to a timestamp indicating when the task's semaphore was posted, or the pend was aborted. If passing a **NULL** pointer (i.e., (CPU_TS *)0) the timestamp will not be returned. In other words, passing a **NULL** pointer is valid and indicates that the timestamp is not necessary.

A timestamp is useful when the task is to know when the semaphore was posted, or how long it took for the task to resume after the semaphore was posted. In the latter case, call **OS_TS_GET()** and compute the difference between the current value of the timestamp and *p_ts. In other words:

```
delta = OS_TS_GET() - *p_ts;
```

p_err   is a pointer to a variable used to hold an error code.

OS_ERR_NONE	if a signal is received.
OS_ERR_PEND_ABORT	if the pend was aborted because another task called **OSTaskSemPendAbort()**.
OS_ERR_PEND_ISR	if calling this function from an ISR.
OS_ERR_PEND_WOULD_BLOCK	if calling this function with the opt argument set to **OS_OPT_PEND_NON_BLOCKING**, and no signal was received.
OS_ERR_SCHED_LOCKED	if calling this function when the scheduler is locked and the user wanted the task to block.
OS_ERR_TIMEOUT	if a signal is not received within the specified timeout.

Returned Value

The current value of the signal counter after it has been decremented. In other words, the number of signals still remaining in the signal counter.

Notes/Warnings

Do not call **OSTaskSemPend()** from an ISR.

Example

```
void CommTask(void *p_arg)
{
    OS_ERR      err;
    OS_SEM_CTR  ctr;
    CPU_TS      ts;


    (void)&p_arg;
    while (DEF_ON) {
        :
        ctr = OSTaskSemPend(100,
                            OS_OPT_PEND_BLOCKING,
                            &ts,
                            &err);
        /* Check "err" */
        :
    }
}
```

OSTaskSemPendAbort()

```
CPU_BOOLEAN  OSTaskSemPendAbort (OS_TCB  *p_tcb,
                                 OS_OPT   opt,
                                 OS_ERR  *p_err)
```

File	Called from	Code enabled by
OS_TASK.C	Task	OS_CFG_TASK_SEM_PEND_ABORT_EN

OSTaskSemPendAbort() aborts and readies a task currently waiting on its built-in semaphore. This function should be used to fault-abort the wait on the task's semaphore, rather than to normally signal the task via OSTaskSemPost().

Arguments

p_tcb   is a pointer to the task for which the pend must be aborted. Note that it does not make sense to pass a NULL pointer or the address of the calling task's TCB since, by definition, the calling task cannot be pending.

opt   provides options for this function.

OS_OPT_POST_NONE	no option specified, call the scheduler by default.
OS_OPT_POST_NO_SCHED	specifies that the scheduler should not be called even if the pend of a higher-priority task has been aborted. Scheduling will need to occur from another function.
	Use this option if the task calling OSTaskSemPendAbort() will be doing additional pend aborts, rescheduling will not take place until finished, and multiple pend aborts are to take effect simultaneously.

p_err   is a pointer to a variable that holds an error code:

OS_ERR_NONE	the pend was aborted for the specified task.
OS_ERR_PEND_ABORT_ISR	if called from an ISR
OS_ERR_PEND_ABORT_NONE	if the task was not waiting for a signal.
OS_ERR_PEND_ABORT_SELF	if p_tcb is a **NULL** pointer or the TCB of the calling task is specified. The user is attempting to pend abort the calling task, which makes no sense since, by definition, the calling task is not pending.

Returned Value

OSTaskSemPendAbort() returns DEF_TRUE if the task was made ready to run by this function. DEF_FALSE indicates that the task was not pending, or an error occurred.

Notes/Warnings

None

Example

```
OS_TCB   CommRxTaskTCB;


void CommTask (void *p_arg)
{
    OS_ERR      err;
    CPU_BOOLEAN aborted;


    (void)&p_arg;
    while (DEF_ON) {
        :
        :
        aborted = OSTaskSemPendAbort(&CommRxTaskTCB,
                                     OS_OPT_POST_NONE,
                                     &err);
        /* Check "err" */
        :
        :
    }
}
```

OSTaskSemPost()

```
OS_SEM_CTR  OSTaskSemPost (OS_TCB    *p_tcb,
                           OS_OPT     opt,
                           OS_ERR    *p_err)
```

File	Called from	Code enabled by
OS_TASK.C	Task or ISR	Always enabled

OSTaskSemPost() sends a signal to a task through it's local semaphore.

If the task receiving the signal is actually waiting for a signal to be received, it will be made ready to run and, if the receiving task has a higher priority than the task sending the signal, the higher-priority task resumes, and the task sending the signal is suspended; that is, a context switch occurs. Note that scheduling only occurs if opt is set to OS_OPT_POST_NONE, because the OS_OPT_POST_NO_SCHED option does not cause the scheduler to be called.

Arguments

p_tcb   is a pointer to the TCB of the task being signaled. A NULL pointer indicates that the user is sending a signal to itself.

opt   provides options to the call.

OS_OPT_POST_NONE	No option, by default the scheduler will be called.
OS_OPT_POST_NO_SCHED	Do not call the scheduler after the post, therefore the caller is resumed. Use this option if the task (or ISR) calling OSTaskSemPost() will be doing additional posts, reschedule waits until all is done, and multiple posts are to take effect simultaneously.

p_err   is a pointer to a variable that will contain an error code returned by this function.

OS_ERR_NONE	if the call was successful and the signal was sent.

| OS_ERR_SEM_OVF | the post would have caused the semaphore counter to overflow. |

Returned Value

The current value of the task's signal counter, or 0 if called from an ISR and OS_CFG_ISR_POST_DEFERRED_EN is set to 1.

Notes/Warnings

None

Example

```
OS_TCB          CommRxTaskTCB;


void CommTaskRx (void *p_arg)
{
    OS_ERR      err;
    OS_SEM_CTR  ctr;


    (void)&p_arg;
    while (DEF_ON) {
        :
        ctr = OSTaskSemPost(&CommRxTaskTCB,
                            OS_OPT_POST_NONE,
                            &err);
        /* Check "err" */
        :
    }
}
```

OSTaskSemSet()

```
OS_SEM_CTR  OSTaskSemSet (OS_TCB      *p_tcb,
                          OS_SEM_CTR  cnt;
                          OS_ERR      *p_err)
```

File	Called from	Code enabled by
OS_TASK.C	Task or ISR	Always Enabled

OSTaskSemSet() allows the user to set the value of the task's signal counter. Set the signal counter of the calling task by passing a **NULL** pointer for p_tcb.

Arguments

p_tcb   is a pointer to the task's **OS_TCB** to clear the signal counter. A **NULL** pointer indicates that the user wants to clear the caller's signal counter.

cnt   the desired value for the task semaphore counter.

p_err   is a pointer to a variable that will contain an error code returned by this function.

OS_ERR_NONE	if the call was successful and the signal counter was cleared.
OS_ERR_SET_ISR	if calling this function from an ISR

Returned Value

The value of the signal counter prior to setting it.

Notes/Warnings

None

Example

```
OS_TCB   TaskY;


void TaskX (void *p_arg)
{
    OS_ERR err;


    while (DEF_ON) {
        :
        :
        OSTaskSemSet(&TaskY,
                     0,
                     &err);
        /* Check "err" */
        :
        :
    }
}
```

OSTaskStatHook()

```
void  OSTaskStatHook (void);
```

File	Called from	Code enabled by
OS_CPU_C.C	OS_TaskStat() ONLY	OS_CFG_TASK_STAT_EN

This function is called by **OS_TaskStat()**.

OSTaskStatHook() is part of the CPU port code and *must not* be called by the application code. **OSTaskStatHook()** is actually used by the µC/OS-III port developer.

Arguments
None

Returned Value
None

Notes/Warnings
Do not call this function from the application.

Example
The code below calls an application-specific hook that the application programmer can define. The user can simply set the value of **OS_AppStatTaskHookPtr** to point to the desired hook function as shown in the example. The statistic task calls **OSStatTaskHook()** which in turns calls **App_OS_StatTaskHook()** through **OS_AppStatTaskHookPtr**.

```
void  App_OS_StatTaskHook (void)                          /* OS_APP_HOOKS.C        */
{
    /* Your code goes here! */
}


void App_OS_SetAllHooks (void)                            /* OS_APP_HOOKS.C        */
{
    CPU_SR_ALLOC();

    CPU_CRITICAL_ENTER();
    :
    OS_AppStatTaskHookPtr = App_OS_StatTaskHook;
    :
    CPU_CRITICAL_EXIT();
}


void  OSStatTaskHook (void)                               /* OS_CPU_C.C            */
{
#if OS_CFG_APP_HOOKS_EN > 0u
    if (OS_AppStatTaskHookPtr != (OS_APP_HOOK_VOID)0) {   /* Call application hook */
        (*OS_AppStatTaskHookPtr)();
    }
#endif
}
```

OSTaskStkChk()

```
void   OSTaskStkChk (OS_TCB        *p_tcb,
                     CPU_STK_SIZE  *p_free,
                     CPU_STK_SIZE  *p_used,
                     OS_ERR        *p_err)
```

File	Called from	Code enabled by
OS_TASK.C	Task	OS_CFG_TASK_STAT_CHK_EN

OSTaskStkChk() determines a task's stack statistics. Specifically, it computes the amount of free stack space, as well as the amount of stack space used by the specified task. This function requires that the task be created with the OS_TASK_OPT_STK_CHK and OS_TASK_OPT_STK_CLR options.

Stack sizing is accomplished by walking from the bottom of the stack and counting the number of 0 entries on the stack until a non-zero value is found. It is possible to not set the OS_TASK_OPT_STK_CLR when creating the task if the startup code clears all RAM, and tasks are not deleted (this reduces the execution time of OSTaskCreate()).

μC/OS-III's statistic task calls OSTaskStkChk() for each task created and stores the results in each task's OS_TCB so your application doesn't need to call this function if the statistic task is enabled.

Arguments

p_tcb   is a pointer to the TCB of the task where the stack is being checked. A NULL pointer indicates that the user is checking the calling task's stack.

p_free   is a pointer to a variable of type CPU_STK_SIZE and will contain the number of free "bytes" on the stack of the task being inquired about.

p_used   is a pointer to a variable of type CPU_STK_SIZE and will contain the number of used "bytes" on the stack of the task being inquired about.

p_err   is a pointer to a variable that will contain an error code returned by this function.

OS_ERR_NONE	if the call was successful.
OS_ERR_PTR_INVALID	if either p_free or p_used are **NULL** pointers.
OS_ERR_TASK_NOT_EXIST	if the stack pointer of the task is a **NULL** pointer.
OS_ERR_TASK_OPT	if **OS_OPT_TASK_STK_CHK** is not specififed whencreating the task being checked.
OS_ERR_TASK_STK_CHK_ISR	if calling this function from an ISR.

Returned Value

None

Notes/Warnings

1. Execution time of this task depends on the size of the task's stack.

2. The application can determine the total task stack space (in number of bytes) by adding the value of *p_free and *p_used.

3. The **#define CPU_CFG_STK_GROWTH** must be declared (typically from **OS_CPU.H**). When this **#define** is set to **CPU_STK_GROWTH_LO_TO_HI**, the stack grows from low memory to high memory. When this **#define** is set to **CPU_STK_GROWTH_HI_TO_LO**, the stack grows from high memory to low memory.

Example

```
OS_TCB  MyTaskTCB;


void Task (void *p_arg)
{
    OS_ERR        err;
    CPU_STK_SIZE  n_free;
    CPU_STK_SIZE  n_used;


    (void)&p_arg;
    while (DEF_ON) {
        :
        :
        OSTaskStkChk(&MyTaskTCB,
                     &n_free,
                     &n_used,
                     &err);
        /* Check "err" */
        :
        :
    }
}
```

OSTaskStkInit()

```
void OSTaskStkInit (OS_TASK_PTR    p_task,
                    void           *p_arg,
                    CPU_STK        *p_stk_base,
                    CPU_STK        *p_stk_limit,
                    CPU_STK_SIZE   stk_size,
                    OS_OPT         opt);
```

File	Called from	Code enabled by
OS_CPU_C.C	OSTaskCreate() ONLY	N/A

This function is called by **OSTaskCreate()** to setup the stack frame of the task being created. Typically, the stack frame will look as if an interrupt just occurred, and all CPU registers were pushed onto the task's stack. The stacking order of CPU registers is very CPU specific.

OSTaskStkInit() is part of the CPU port code and this function *must not* be called by the application code. **OSTaskStkInit()** is actually defined by the µC/OS-III port developer.

Arguments

p_task   is the address of the task being created (see MyTask below). Tasks must be declared as follows:

```
void   MyTask (void  *p_arg)
{
    /* Do something with "p_arg" (optional) */
    while (DEF_ON) {
        /* Wait for an event to occur */
        /* Do some work             */
    }
}
```

Or,

```
void    MyTask (void  *p_arg)
{
    OS_ERR  err;


    /* Do something with "p_arg" (optional) */
    /* Do some work                          */
    OSTaskDel((OS_TCB *)0,
            &err);
}
```

p_arg   is the argument that the task will receive when the task first start (see code above).

p_stk_base is the base address of the task's stack. This is typically the lowest address of the area of storage reserved for the task stack. In other words, if declaring the task's stack as follows:

```
CPU_STK  MyTaskStk[100];
```

OSTaskCreate() would pass **&OSMyTaskStk[0]** to **p_stk_base**.

p_stk_limit is the address of the task's stack limit watermark. This pointer is the same pointer passed to **OSTaskCreate()**.

stk_size is the size of the task's stack in number of **CPU_STK** elements. In the example above, the stack size is 100.

opt   is the options pass to **OSTaskCreate()** for the task being created.

Returned Value

The new top of stack after the task's stack is initialized. **OSTaskStkInit()** will place values on the task's stack and will return the new pointer of the stack pointer for the task. The value returned is very processor specific. For some processors, the returned value will point to the last value placed on the stack while, with other processors, the returned value will point at the next free stack entry.

Notes/Warnings
Do not call this function from the application.

Example
The pseudo code below shows the typical steps performed by this function. Consult an existing μC/OS-III port for examples. Here it is assumed that the stack grows from high memory to low memory.

```
CPU_STK  *OSTaskStkInit (OS_TASK_PTR   p_task,
                         void          *p_arg,
                         CPU_STK       *p_stk_base,
                         CPU_STK       *p_stk_limit,
                         CPU_STK_SIZE  stk_size,
                         OS_OPT        opt)
{
    CPU_STK  *p_stk;


    p_stk  = &p_stk_base[stk_size - 1u];                        (1)
    *p_stk-- = Initialize the stack as if an interrupt just occurred; (2)
    return (p_stk);                                            (3)
}
```

(1)   'p_stk" is set to the top-of-stack. It is assumed that the stack grows from high memory locations to lower ones. If the stack of the CPU grew from low memory locations to higher ones, the user would simply set "p_stk" to point at the base. However, this also means that it would be necessary to initialize the stack frame in the opposite direction.

(2)   Store the CPU registers onto the stack using the same stacking order as used when an interrupt service routine (ISR) saves the registers at the beginning of the ISR. The value of the register contents on the stack is typically not important. However, there are some values that are critical. Specifically, place the address of the task in the proper location on the stack frame and it may be important to load the value of the CPU register and possibly pass the value of "p_arg" in one of the CPU registers. Finally, if the task is to return by mistake, it is a good idea to place the address of "OS_TaskReturn()" in the proper location on the stack frame. This ensures that a faulty returning task is intercepted by μC/OS-III.

(3)   Finally, return the value of the stack pointer at the new top-of-stack frame. Some processors point to the last stored location, while others point to the next empty location. Consult the processor documentation so that the return value points at the proper location.

Below is a complete example showing **OSTaskCreate()** which calls **OSTaskStkInit()** with the proper arguments.

```
CPU_STK  MyTaskStk[100];
OS_TCB   MyTaskTCB;


void  MyTask (void *p_arg)
{
    /* Do something with "parg" (optional) */
}



void  main (void)
{
    OS_ERR  err;
    :
    :
    OSInit(&err);
    /* Check "err" */
    :
    OSTaskCreate ((OS_TCB        *)&MyTaskTCB,
                  (CPU_CHAR      *)"My Task",
                  (OS_TASK_PTR   )MyTask,           /* "p_task"      of OSTaskStkInit() */
                  (void          *)0,               /* "p_arg"       of OSTaskStkInit() */
                  (OS_PRIO       )prio,
                  (CPU_STK       *)&MyTaskStk[0],    /* "p_stk_base"  of OSTaskStkInit() */
                  (CPU_STK_SIZE  )10,               /* "p_stk_limit" of OSTaskStkInit() */
                  (CPU_STK_SIZE  )100,              /* "stk_size"    of OSTaskStkInit() */
                  (OS_MSG_QTY    )0,
                  (OS_TICK       )0,
                  (void          *)0,
                  (OS_OPT        )(OS_OPT_TASK_STK_CLR + OS_OPT_TASK_STK_CHK),   /* "opt" */
                  (OS_ERR        *)&err);
    /* Check "err" */
    :
    :
    OSStart(&err);
    /* Check "err" */
}
```

OSTaskSuspend()

```
void    OSTaskSuspend (OS_TCB   *p_tcb,
                       OS_ERR    *p_err)
```

File	Called from	Code enabled by
OS_TASK.C	Task	OS_CFG_TASK_SUSPEND_EN

OSTaskSuspend() suspends (or blocks) execution of a task unconditionally. The calling task may be suspended by specifying a NULL pointer for p_tcb, or simply by passing the address of its OS_TCB. In this case, another task needs to resume the suspended task. If the current task is suspended, rescheduling occurs, and µC/OS-III runs the next highest priority task ready to run. The only way to resume a suspended task is to call OSTaskResume().

Task suspension is additive, which means that if the task being suspended is delayed until n ticks expire, the task is resumed only when both the time expires and the suspension is removed. Also, if the suspended task is waiting for a semaphore and the semaphore is signaled, the task is removed from the semaphore wait list (if it is the highest-priority task waiting for the semaphore), but execution is not resumed until the suspension is removed.

The user can "nest" suspension of a task by calling OSTaskSuspend() and therefore it is important to call OSTaskResume() an equivalent number of times to resume the task. If suspending a task five times, it is necessary to unsuspend the same task five times to remove the suspension of the task.

Arguments

p_tcb   is a pointer to the TCB of the task the user is suspending. A NULL pointer indicates suspension of the calling task.

p_err   is a pointer to a variable that will contain an error code returned by this function.

> OS_ERR_NONE   if the call was successful and the desired task was suspended.
>
> OS_ERR_TASK_SUSPEND_ISR   if the function is called from an ISR.

OS_ERR_TASK_SUSPEND_IDLE   if attempting to suspend the idle task. This is not allowed since the idle task must always exist.

OS_ERR_TASK_SUSPEND_INT_HANDLER if attempting to suspend the ISR handler task. This is not allowed since the ISR handler task is a µC/OS-III internal task.

Returned Value

None

Notes/Warnings

1. OSTaskSuspend() and OSTaskResume() must be used in pairs.

2. A suspended task can only be resumed by OSTaskResume().

Example

```
void TaskX (void *p_arg)
{
    OS_ERR  err;

    (void)&p_arg;
    while (DEF_ON) {
        :
        :
        OSTaskSuspend((OS_TCB *)0,
                      &err);        /* Suspend current task              */
        /* Check "err" */
        :
    }
}
```

OSTaskSwHook()

void   OSTaskSwHook (void)

File	Called from	Code enabled by
OS_CPU_C.C	OSCtxSw() or OSIntCtxSw()	N/A

OSTaskSwHook() is always called by either OSCtxSw() or OSIntCtxSw() (see OS_CPU_A.ASM), just after saving the CPU registers onto the task being switched out. This hook function allows the port developer to perform additional operations (if needed) when μC/OS-III performs a context switch.

Before calling OSTaskSwHook(), OSTCBCurPtr is set to point at the OS_TCB of the task being switched out, and OSTCBHighRdyPtr points at the OS_TCB of the new task being switched in.

The code shown in the example below should be included in all implementations of OSTaskSwHook(), and is used for performance measurements. This code is written in C for portability.

Arguments
None

Returned Values
None

Notes/Warnings
None

Example
The code below calls an application specific hook that the application programmer can define. The user can simply set the value of OS_AppTaskSwHookPtr to point to the desired hook function. When μC/OS-III performs a context switch, it calls OSTaskSwitchHook() which in turn calls App_OS_TaskSwHook() through OS_AppTaskSwHookPtr.

```
void  App_OS_TaskSwHook (void)                          /* OS_APP_HOOKS.C        */
{
    /* Your code goes here! */
}


void App_OS_SetAllHooks (void)                          /* OS_APP_HOOKS.C        */
{
    CPU_SR_ALLOC();

    CPU_CRITICAL_ENTER();
    :
    OS_AppTaskSwHookPtr = App_OS_TaskSwHook;
    :
    CPU_CRITICAL_EXIT();
}
```

```
void  OSTaskSwHook (void)                              /* OS_CPU_C.C              */
{
#if OS_CFG_TASK_PROFILE_EN > 0u
    CPU_TS    ts;
#endif
#ifdef  CPU_CFG_TIME_MEAS_INT_DIS_EN
    CPU_TS    int_dis_time;
#endif


#if OS_CFG_APP_HOOKS_EN > 0u
    if (OS_AppTaskSwHookPtr != (OS_APP_HOOK_VOID)0) {
        (*OS_AppTaskSwHookPtr)();
    }
#endif
#if OS_CFG_TASK_PROFILE_EN > 0u
    ts = OS_TS_GET();
    if (OSTCBCurPtr != OSTCBHighRdyPtr) {
        OSTCBCurPtr->CyclesDelta = ts - OSTCBCurPtr->CyclesStart;
        OSTCBCurPtr->CyclesTotal = OSTCBCurPtr->CyclesTotal + OSTCBCurPtr->CyclesDelta;
    }
    OSTCBHighRdyPtr->CyclesStart = ts;
#ifdef  CPU_CFG_INT_DIS_MEAS_EN
    int_dis_time = CPU_IntDisMeasMaxCurReset();
    if (int_dis_time > OSTCBCurPtr->IntDisTimeMax) {
        OSTCBCurPtr->IntDisTimeMax = int_dis_time;
    }
#endif
#if OS_CFG_SCHED_LOCK_TIME_MEAS_EN > 0u
    if (OSSchedLockTimeMaxCur > OSTCBCurPtr->SchedLockTimeMax) {
        OSTCBCurPtr->SchedLockTimeMax = OSSchedLockTimeMaxCur;
        OSSchedLockTimeMaxCur         = (CPU_TS)0;
    }
#endif
#endif
}
```

OSTaskTimeQuantaSet()

```
void    OSTaskTimeQuantaSet (OS_TCB   *p_tcb,
                             OS_TICK  time_quanta,
                             OS_ERR   *p_err)
```

File	Called from	Code enabled by
OS_TASK.C	Task only	OS_CFG_SCHED_ROUND_ROBIN_EN

OSTaskTimeQuantaSet() is used to change the amount of time a task is given when time slicing multiple tasks running at the same priority.

Arguments

p_tcb   is a pointer to the TCB of the task for which the time quanta is being set. A **NULL** pointer indicates that the user is changing the time quanta for the calling task.

time_quanta   specifies the amount of time (in ticks) that the task will run when µC/OS-III is time slicing between tasks at the same priority. Specifying 0 indicates that the default time as specified will be used when calling the function OSSchedRoundRobinCfg(), or OS_CFG_TICK_RATE_HZ / 10 if you never called OSSchedRoundRobinCfg().

Do not specify a "large" value for this argument as this means that the task will execute for that amount of time when multiple tasks are ready to run at the same priority. The concept of time slicing is to allow other equal-priority tasks a chance to run. Typical time quanta periods should be approximately 10 mS. A too small value results in more overhead because of the additional context switches.

p_err   is a pointer to a variable that will contain an error code returned by this function.

OS_ERR_NONE   if the call was successful and the time quanta for the task was changed.

OS_ERR_SET_ISR   if calling this function from an ISR.

Returned Value

None

Notes/Warnings

Do not specify a large value for time_quanta.

Example

```
void TaskX (void *p_arg)
{
    OS_ERR  err;


    while (DEF_ON) {
        :
        :
        OSTaskTimeQuantaSet((OS_TCB *)0,
                            OS_CFG_TICK_RATE_HZ / 4;
                            &err);
        /* Check "err" */
        :
    }
}
```

OSTickISR()

void   OSTickISR (void)

File	Called from	Code enabled by
OS_CPU_A.ASM	Tick interrupt	N/A

OSTickISR() is invoked by the tick interrupt, and the function is generally written in assembly language. However, this depends on how interrupts are handled by the processor. (see Chapter 9, "Interrupt Management" on page 165).

Arguments

None

Returned Values

None

Notes/Warnings

None

Example

The code below indicates how to write OSTickISR() if all interrupts vector to a common location, and the interrupt handler simply calls OSTickISR(). As indicated, this code can be written completely in C and can be placed either in OS_CPU_C.C of the µC/OS-III port, or in the board support package (BSP.C) and be reused by applications using the same BSP.

```
void  OSTickISR (void)
{
    Clear the tick interrupt;
    OSTimeTick();
}
```

The pseudo code below shows how to write OSTickISR() if each interrupt directly vectors to its own interrupt handler. The code, in this case, would be written in assembly language and placed either in OS_CPU_A.ASM of the µC/OS-III port, or in the board support package (BSP.C).

```
void  OSTickISR (void)
{
    Save all the CPU registers onto the current task's stack;
    if (OSIntNestingCtr == 0) {
        OSTCBCurPtr->StkPtr = SP;
    }
    OSIntNestingCtr++;
    Clear the tick interrupt;
    OSTimeTick();
    OSIntExit();
    Restore the CPU registers from the stack;
    Return from interrupt;
}
```

OSTimeDly()

```
void OSTimeDly (OS_TICK  dly,
                OS_OPT   opt,
                OS_ERR   *p_err)
```

File	Called from	Code enabled by
OS_TIME.C	Task only	N/A

OSTimeDly() allows a task to delay itself for an integral number of clock ticks. The delay can either be relative (delay from current time), periodic (delay occurs at fixed intervals) or absolute (delay until we reach some time).

In relative mode, rescheduling always occurs when the number of clock ticks is greater than zero. A delay of 0 means that the task is not delayed, and OSTimeDly() returns immediately to the caller.

In periodic mode, you must specify a non-zero period otherwise the function returns immediately with an appropriate error code. The period is specified in "ticks".

In absolute mode, rescheduling always occurs since all delay values are valid.

The actual delay time depends on the tick rate (see **OS_CFG_TICK_RATE_HZ**).

Arguments

dly   is the desired delay expressed in number of clock ticks. Depending on the value of the **opt** field, delays can be relative or absolute.

A relative delay means that the delay is started from the "**current time + dly**".

A periodic delay means the period (in number of ticks).

An absolute delay means that the task will wake up when OSTaskTickCtr reaches the value specified by **dly**.

opt   is used to indicate whether the delay is absolute or relative:

OS_OPT_TIME_DLY	Specifies a relative delay.
OS_OPT_TIME_PERIODIC	Specifies periodic mode.
OS_OPT_TIME_MATCH	Specifies that the task will wake up when OSTaskTickCtr reaches the value specified by dly

p_err   is a pointer to a variable that will contain an error code returned by this function.

OS_ERR_NONE	if the call was successful, and the task has returned from the desired delay.
OS_ERR_OPT_INVALID	if a valid option is not specified.
OS_ERR_TIME_DLY_ISR	if calling this function from an ISR.
OS_ERR_TIME_ZERO_DLY	if specifying a delay of 0 when the option was set to OS_OPT_TIME_DLY. Note that a value of 0 is valid when setting the option to OS_OPT_TIME_MATCH.

Returned Value

None

Notes/Warnings

None

Example

```
void TaskX (void *p_arg)
{
  OS_ERR  err;


  while (DEF_ON) {
    :
    :
    OSTimeDly(10,
              OS_OPT_TIME_PERIODIC,
              &err);
    /* Check "err" */
    :
    :
  }
}
```

OSTimeDlyHMSM()

```
void   OSTimeDlyHMSM (CPU_INT16U   hours,
                      CPU_INT16U   minutes,
                      CPU_INT16U   seconds,
                      CPU_INT32U   milli,
                      OS_OPT       opt,
                      OS_ERR       *p_err)
```

File	Called from	Code enabled by
OS_TIME.C	Task only	OS_CFG_TIME_DLY_HMSM_EN

OSTimeDlyHMSM() allows a task to delay itself for a user-specified period that is specified in hours, minutes, seconds, and milliseconds. This format is more convenient and natural than simply specifying ticks as is true in the case of OSTimeDly(). Rescheduling always occurs when at least one of the parameters is non-zero. The delay is relative from the time this function is called.

µC/OS-III allows the user to specify nearly any value when indicating that this function is not to be strict about the values being passed (opt == OS_OPT_TIME_HMSM_NON_STRICT). This is a useful feature, for example, to delay a task for thousands of milliseconds.

Arguments

hours   is the number of hours the task is delayed. Depending on the opt value, the valid range is 0..99 (OS_OPT_TIME_HMSM_STRICT), or 0..999 (OS_OPT_TIME_HMSM_NON_STRICT). Please note that it *not* recommended to delay a task for many hours because feedback from the task will not be available for such a long period of time.

minutes   is the number of minutes the task is delayed. The valid range of values is 0 to 59 (OS_OPT_TIME_HMSM_STRICT), or 0..9,999 (OS_OPT_TIME_HMSM_NON_STRICT). Please note that it *not* recommended to delay a task for tens to hundreds of minutes because feedback from the task will not be available for such a long period of time.

seconds   is the number of seconds the task is delayed. The valid range of values is 0 to 59 (OS_OPT_TIME_HMSM_STRICT), or 0..65,535 (OS_OPT_TIME_HMSM_NON_STRICT).

milli   is the number of milliseconds the task is delayed. The valid range of values is 0 to 999 (`OS_OPT_TIME_HMSM_STRICT`), or 0..4,294,967,295 (`OS_OPT_TIME_HMSM_NON_STRICT`). Note that the resolution of this argument is in multiples of the tick rate. For instance, if the tick rate is set to 100Hz, a delay of 4 ms results in no delay. Also, the delay is rounded to the nearest tick. Thus, a delay of 15 ms actually results in a delay of 20 ms.

opt   is the desired mode and can be either:

         `OS_OPT_TIME_HMSM_STRICT`   (see above)
         `OS_OPT_TIME_HMSM_NON_STRICT`(see above)

p_err   is a pointer to a variable that contains an error code returned by this function.

`OS_ERR_NONE`	if the call was successful and the task has returned from the desired delay.
`OS_ERR_TIME_DLY_ISR`	if calling this function from an ISR.
`OS_ERR_TIME_INVALID_HOURS`	if not specifying a valid value for hours.
`OS_ERR_TIME_INVALID_MINUTES`	if not specifying a valid value for minutes.
`OS_ERR_TIME_INVALID_SECONDS`	if not specifying a valid value for seconds.
`OS_ERR_TIME_INVALID_MILLISECONDS`	if not specifying a valid value for milliseconds.
`OS_ERR_TIME_ZERO_DLY`	if specifying a delay of 0 because all the time arguments are 0.

Returned Value

None

Notes/Warnings

1. Note that `OSTimeDlyHMSM(0,0,0,0,OS_OPT_TIME_HMSM_???,&err)` (i.e., hours, minutes, seconds, milliseconds are 0) results in no delay, and the function returns to the caller.

2. The total delay (in ticks) must not exceed the maximum acceptable value that an `OS_TICK` variable can hold. Typically `OS_TICK` is a 32-bit value.

Example

```
void TaskX (void *p_arg)
{
    OS_ERR  err;


    while (DEF_ON) {
        :
        :
        OSTimeDlyHMSM(0,
                      0,
                      1,
                      0,
                      OS_OPT_TIME_HMSM_STRICT,
                      &err);                /* Delay task for 1 second */
        /* Check "err" */
        :
        :
    }
}
```

OSTimeDlyResume()

```
void  OSTimeDlyResume (OS_TCB  *p_tcb,
                       OS_ERR  *p_err)
```

File	Called from	Code enabled by
OS_TIME.C	Task only	OS_CFG_TIME_DLY_RESUME_EN

OSTimeDlyResume() resumes a task that has been delayed through a call to either OSTimeDly(), or OSTimeDlyHMSM().

Arguments

p_tcb   is a pointer to the TCB of the task that is resuming. A **NULL** pointer is not valid since it would indicate that the user is attempting to resume the current task and that is not possible as the caller cannot possibly be delayed.

p_err   is a pointer to a variable that contains an error code returned by this function.

OS_ERR_NONE	if the call was successful and the task was resumed.
OS_ERR_STATE_INVALID	if the task is in an invalid state.
OS_ERR_TIME_DLY_RESUME_ISR	if calling this function from an ISR.
OS_ERR_TIME_NOT_DLY	if the task was not delayed.
OS_ERR_TASK_SUSPENDED	if the task to resume is suspended and will remain suspended.

Returned Value

None

Notes/Warnings

Do not call this function to resume a task that is waiting for an event with timeout.

Example

```
OS_TCB  AnotherTaskTCB;


void TaskX (void *p_arg)
{
    OS_ERR  err;


    while (DEF_ON) {
        :
        OSTimeDlyResume(&AnotherTaskTCB,
                        &err);
        /* Check "err" */
        :
    }
}
```

OSTimeGet()

`OS_TICK  OSTimeGet (OS_ERR  *p_err)`

File	Called from	Code enabled by
OS_TIME.C	Task + ISR	N/A

`OSTimeGet()` obtains the current value of the system clock. Specifically, it returns a snapshot of the variable `OSTaskTickCtr`. The system clock is a counter of type `OS_TICK` that counts the number of clock ticks since power was applied, or since `OSTaskTickCtr` was last set by `OSTimeSet()`.

Arguments

`p_err`   is a pointer to a variable that contains an error code returned by this function.

OS_ERR_NONE   if the call was successful.

Returned Value

The current value of `OSTaskTickCtr` (in number of ticks).

Notes/Warnings

None

Example

```c
void TaskX (void *p_arg)
{
    OS_TICK   clk;
    OS_ERR    err;


    while (DEF_ON) {
        :
        :
        clk = OSTimeGet(&err);   /* Get current value of system clock */
        /* Check "err" */
        :
        :
    }
}
```

OSTimeSet()

```
void  OSTimeSet (OS_TICK  ticks,
                 OS_ERR   *p_err)
```

File	Called from	Code enabled by
OS_TIME.C	Task + ISR	N/A

OSTimeSet() sets the system clock. The system clock is a counter, which has a data type of OS_TICK, and it counts the number of clock ticks since power was applied. or since the system clock was last set.

Arguments

ticks   is the desired value for the system clock, in ticks.

p_err   is a pointer to a variable that will contain an error code returned by this function.

      OS_ERR_NONE   if the call was successful.

Returned Value

None

Notes/Warnings

You should be careful when using this function because other tasks may depend on the current value of the tick counter (OSTickCtr). Specifically, a task may delay itself (see OSTimeDly() and specify to wake up when OSTickCtr reaches a specific value.

Example

```
void TaskX (void *p_arg)
{
    OS_ERR   err;


    while (DEF_ON) {
        :
        :
        OSTimeSet(0,
                  &err);        /* Reset the system clock  */
        /* Check "err" */
        :
        :
    }
}
```

OSTimeTick()

void OSTimeTick (void)

File	Called from	Code enabled by
OS_TIME.C	ISR	N/A

OSTimeTick() "announces" that a tick has just occurred, and that time delays and timeouts need to be updated. This function must be called from the tick ISR.

Arguments

None

Returned Value

None

Notes/Warnings

None

Example

```
void MyTickISR (void)
{
    /* Clear interrupt source */
    OSTimeTick();
    :
    :
}
```

OSTimeTickHook()

void OSTimeTickHook (void);

File	Called from	Code enabled by
OS_CPU_C.C	OSTimeTick() ONLY	N/A

This function is called by **OSTimeTick()**, which is assumed to be called from an ISR. **OSTimeTickHook()** is called at the very beginning of **OSTimeTick()** to give priority to user or port-specific code when the tick interrupt occurs.

If the **#define OS_APP_HOOKS_EN** is set to 1 in **OS_CFG.H**, **OSTimeTickHook()** will call **AppTimeTickHook()**.

OSTimeTickHook() is part of the CPU port code and the function *must not* be called by the application code. **OSTimeTickHook()** is actually used by the µC/OS-III port developer.

Arguments

None

Returned Value

None

Notes/Warnings

Do not call this function from the application.

Example

The code below calls an application-specific hook that the application programmer can define. The user can simply set the value of **OS_AppTimeTickHookPtr** to point to the desired hook function **OSTimeTickHook()** is called by **OSTimeTick()** which in turn calls **App_OS_TimeTickHook()** through the pointer **OS_AppTimeTickHookPtr**.

```c
void  App_OS_TimeTickHook (void)                          /* OS_APP_HOOKS.C        */
{
    /* Your code goes here! */
}


void App_OS_SetAllHooks (void)                            /* OS_APP_HOOKS.C        */
{
    CPU_SR_ALLOC();

    CPU_CRITICAL_ENTER();
    :
    OS_AppTimeTickHookPtr = App_OS_TimeTickHook;
    :
    CPU_CRITICAL_EXIT();
}


void  OSTimeTickHook (void)                               /* OS_CPU_C.C            */
{
#if OS_CFG_APP_HOOKS_EN > 0u
    if (OS_AppTimeTickHookPtr != (OS_APP_HOOK_VOID)0) {   /* Call application hook */
        (*OS_AppTimeTickHookPtr)();
    }
#endif
}
```

OSTmrCreate()

```
void   OSTmrCreate (OS_TMR                 *p_tmr,
                    CPU_CHAR               *p_name,
                    OS_TICK                 dly,
                    OS_TICK                 period,
                    OS_OPT                  opt,
                    OS_TMR_CALLBACK_PTR     p_callback,
                    void                   *p_callback_arg,
                    OS_ERR                 *p_err)
```

File	Called from	Code enabled by
OS_TMR.C	Task Only	OS_CFG_TMR_EN

OSTmrCreate() allows the user to create a software timer. The timer can be configured to run continuously (opt set to OS_TMR_OPT_PERIODIC), or only once (opt set to OS_TMR_OPT_ONE_SHOT). When the timer counts down to 0 (from the value specified in period), an optional "callback" function can be executed. The callback can be used to signal a task that the timer expired, or perform any other function. However, it is recommended to keep the callback function as short as possible.

The timer is created in the "stop" mode and therefore the user *must* call OSTmrStart() to actually start the timer. If configuring the timer for ONE-SHOT mode, and the timer expires, call OSTmrStart() to retrigger the timer, or OSTmrDel() to delete the timer if it is not necessary to retrigger it, or not use the timer anymore. Note: use the callback function to delete the timer if using the ONE-SHOT mode.

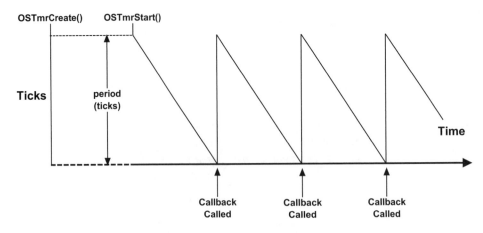

PERIODIC MODE (see "opt") – dly > 0, period > 0

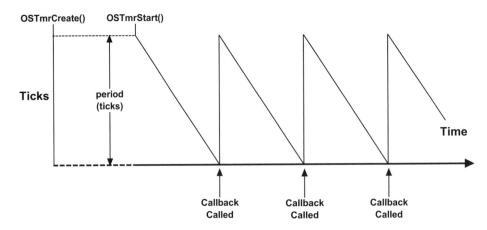

PERIODIC MODE (see "opt") – " == 0

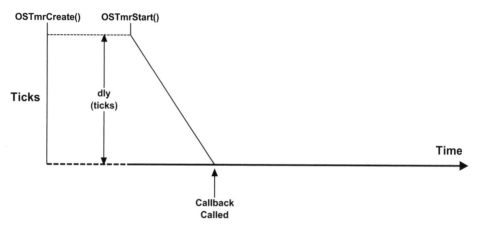

ONE-SHOT MODE (see "**opt**") – **dly** > 0, **period** == 0

Arguments

p_tmr   is a pointer to the timer-control block of the desired timer. It is assumed that
storage for the timer will be allocated in the application. In other words, declare a
"global" variable as follows, and pass a pointer to this variable to **OSTmrCreate()**:

```
OS_TMR MyTmr;
```

p_name   is a pointer to an ASCII string (NUL terminated) used to assign a name to the
timer. The name can be displayed by debuggers or µC/Probe.

dly   specifies the initial delay (specified in timer tick units) used by the timer (see
drawing above). If the timer is configured for ONE-SHOT mode, this is the
timeout used. If the timer is configured for PERIODIC mode, this is the timeout
to wait before the timer enters periodic mode. The units of this time depends
on how often the user will call **OSTmrSignal()** (see **OSTimeTick()**). If
OSTmrSignal() is called every 1/10 of a second (i.e.,
OS_CFG_TMR_TASK_RATE_HZ set to 10), **dly** specifies the number of 1/10 of a
second before the delay expires. Note that the timer is *not* started when it is
created.

period   specifies the period repeated by the timer if configured for PERIODIC mode. Set the "period" to 0 when using ONE-SHOT mode. The units of time depend on how often **OSTmrSignal()** is called. If **OSTmrSignal()** is called every 1/10 of a second (i.e., **OS_CFG_TMR_TASK_RATE_HZ** set to 10), the period specifies the number of 1/10 of a second before the timer times out.

opt   is used to specify whether the timer is to be ONE-SHOT or PERIODIC:

    OS_OPT_TMR_ONE_SHOT ONE-SHOT mode
    OS_OPT_TMR_PERIODIC PERIODIC mode

p_callback is a pointer to a function that will execute when the timer expires (ONE-SHOT mode), or every time the period expires (PERIODIC mode). A **NULL** pointer indicates that no action is to be performed upon timer expiration. The callback function must be declared as follows:

    void MyCallback (OS_TMR *p_tmr, void *p_arg);

When called, the callback will be passed the pointer to the timer as well as an argument (**p_callback_arg**), which can be used to indicate to the callback what to do. Note that the user is allowed to call all of the timer related functions (i.e., **OSTmrCreate()**, **OSTmrDel()**, **OSTmrStateGet()**, **OSTmrRemainGet()**, **OSTmrStart()**, and **OSTmrStop()**) from the callback function.

Do not make blocking calls within callback functions.

p_callback_arg   is an argument passed to the callback function when the timer expires (ONE-SHOT mode), or every time the period expires (PERIODIC mode). The pointer is declared as a "**void ***" so it can point to any data.

p_err   is a pointer to a variable that contains an error code returned by this function.

OS_ERR_NONE	if the call was successful.
OS_ERR_OBJ_CREATED	if the timer was already created
OS_ERR_OBJ_PTR_NULL	if p_tmr is a NULL pointer
OS_ERR_TMR_INVALID_DLY	if specifying an invalid delay in ONE-SHOT mode. In other words, it is not allowed to delay for 0 in ONE-SHOT mode.

OS_ERR_TMR_INVALID_PERIOD	if specifying an invalid period in PERIODIC mode. It is not allowed to have a 0 period in PERIODIC.
OS_ERR_TMR_INVALID_OPT	if not specifying a valid options.
OS_ERR_TMR_ISR	if calling this function from an ISR.

Returned Values

None.

Notes/Warnings

1. *Do not* call this function from an ISR.

2. The timer is *not* started when it is created. To start the timer, call **OSTmrStart()**.

3. *Do not* make blocking calls within callback functions.

4. Keep callback functions as short as possible.

Example

```
OS_TMR  CloseDoorTmr;


void Task (void *p_arg)
{
    OS_ERR   err;


    (void)&p_arg;
    while (DEF_ON) {
        OSTmrCreate(&CloseDoorTmr,         /* p_tmr          */
                    "Door close"           /* p_name         */
                     10,                    /* dly            */
                     100,                   /* period         */
                     OS_OPT_TMR_PERIODIC,   /* opt            */
                     DoorCloseFnct,         /* p_callback     */
                     0,                     /* p_callback_arg */
                     &err);                 /* p_err          */
        /* Check "err" */
    }
}


void  DoorCloseFnct (void *p_arg)
{
    /* Close the door! */
}
```

OSTmrDel()

```
CPU_BOOLEAN   OSTmrDel(OS_TMR    *p_tmr,
                       OS_ERR     *p_err)
```

File	Called from	Code enabled by
OS_TMR.C	Task only	OS_CFG_TMR_EN and OS_CFG_TMR_DEL_EN

OSTmrDel() allows the user to delete a timer. If a timer was running it will be stopped, then deleted. If the timer has already timed out and is therefore stopped, it will simply be deleted.

It is up to the user to delete unused timers. If deleting a timer, *Do not* reference it again.

Arguments

p_tmr   is a pointer to the timer to be deleted.

p_err   a pointer to an error code and can be any of the following:

OS_ERR_NONE	if the timer was deleted.
OS_ERR_OBJ_TYPE	if the user did not pass a pointer to a timer.
OS_ERR_TMR_INVALID	if p_tmr is a NULL pointer.
OS_ERR_TMR_ISR	This function is called from an ISR, which is *not* allowed.
OS_ERR_TMR_INACTIVE	p_tmr is pointing to an inactive timer. In other words, this error appears when pointing to a timer that has been deleted or was not created.
OS_ERR_TMR_INVALID_STATE	the timer is in an invalid state.

Returned Values

DEF_TRUE if the timer was deleted, DEF_FALSE if not.

Notes/Warnings

1. Examine the return value to make sure what is received from this function is valid.

2. *Do not* call this function from an ISR.

3. When deleting a timer, *do not* reference it again.

Example

```
OS_TMR  CloseDoorTmr;


void Task (void *p_arg)
{
    OS_ERR       err;
    CPU_BOOLEAN  deleted;


    (void)&p_arg;
    while (DEF_ON) {
        deleted = OSTmrDel(&CloseDoorTmr,
                           &err);
        /* Check "err" */
    }
}
```

OSTmrRemainGet()

```
OS_TICK  OSTmrRemainGet(OS_TMR *p_tmr,
                        OS_ERR *p_err);
```

File	Called from	Code enabled by
OS_TMR.C	Task only	OS_CFG_TMR_EN

OSTmrRemainGet() allows the user to obtain the time remaining (before timeout) of the specified timer. The value returned depends on the rate (in Hz) at which the timer task is signaled (see OS_CFG_TMR_TASK_RATE_HZ). If OS_CFG_TMR_TASK_RATE_HZ is set to 10, the value returned is the number of 1/10 of a second before the timer times out. If the timer has timed out, the value returned is 0.

Arguments

p_tmr   is a pointer to the timer the user is inquiring about.

p_err   a pointer to an error code and can be any of the following:

OS_ERR_NONE	if the function returned the time remaining for the timer.
OS_ERR_OBJ_TYPE	'p_tmr" is not pointing to a timer.
OS_ERR_TMR_INVALID	if p_tmr is a NULL pointer.
OS_ERR_TMR_ISR	This function is called from an ISR, which is *not* allowed.
OS_ERR_TMR_INACTIVE	p_tmr is pointing to an inactive timer. In other words, this error will appear when pointing to a timer that has been deleted or was not created.
OS_ERR_TMR_INVALID_STATE	the timer is in an invalid state.

Returned Values

The time remaining for the timer. The value returned depends on the rate (in Hz) at which the timer task is signaled (see OS_CFG_TMR_TASK_RATE_HZ). If OS_CFG_TMR_TASK_RATE_HZ is set to 10 the value returned is the number of 1/10 of a second before the timer times out. If specifying an invalid timer, the returned value will be 0. If the timer expired, the returned value will be 0.

Notes/Warnings

1. Examine the returned error code to ensure the results from this function are valid.

2. *Do not* call this function from an ISR.

Example

```c
OS_TICK    TimeRemainToCloseDoor;
OS_TMR     CloseDoorTmr;


void Task (void *p_arg)
{
    OS_ERR     err;


    (void)&p_arg;
    while (DEF_ON) {
        TimeRemainToCloseDoor = OSTmrRemainGet(&CloseDoorTmr,
                                               &err);

        /* Check "err" */
    }
}
```

OSTmrStart()

```
CPU_BOOLEAN   OSTmrStart (OS_TMR   *p_tmr,
                          OS_ERR   *p_err);
```

File	Called from	Code enabled by
OS_TMR.C	Task	OS_CFG_TMR_EN

OSTmrStart() allows the user to start (or restart) the countdown process of a timer. The timer *must* have previously been created.

Arguments

p_tmr   is a pointer to the timer to start (or restart).

p_err   a pointer to an error code and can be any of the following:

OS_ERR_NONE	if the timer was started.
OS_ERR_OBJ_TYPE	'p_tmr" is not pointing to a timer.
OS_ERR_TMR_INVALID	if p_tmr is a NULL pointer.
OS_ERR_TMR_INACTIVE	p_tmr is pointing to an inactive timer. In other words, this error occurs if pointing to a timer that has been deleted or was not created.
OS_ERR_TMR_INVALID_STATE	the timer is in an invalid state.
OS_ERR_TMR_ISR	This function was called from an ISR, which is *not* allowed.

Returned Values

DEF_TRUE   if the timer was started

DEF_FALSE   if an error occurred.

Notes/Warnings

1. *Do not* call this function from an ISR.

2. The timer *must* have previously been created.

Example

```
OS_TMR      CloseDoorTmr;


void Task (void *p_arg)
{
    OS_ERR      err;
    CPU_BOOLEAN status;


    (void)&p_arg;
    while (DEF_ON) {
        status = OSTmrStart(&CloseDoorTmr,
                            &err);
        /* Check "err" */
    }
}
```

OSTmrStateGet()

```
OS_STATE  OSTmrStateGet(OS_TMR  *p_tmr,
                        OS_ERR  *p_err);
```

File	Called from	Code enabled by
OS_TMR.C	Task only	OS_CFG_TMR_EN

OSTmrStateGet() allows the user to obtain the current state of a timer. A timer can be in one of four states:

OS_TMR_STATE_UNUSED	the timer has not been created
OS_TMR_STATE_STOPPED	the timer is created but has not yet started, or has been stopped.
OS_TMR_STATE_COMPLETED	the timer is in *one-shot* mode, and has completed its delay.
OS_TMR_STATE_RUNNING	the timer is currently running

Arguments

p_tmr   is a pointer to the timer that the user is inquiring about. This pointer is returned when the timer is created (see OSTmrCreate()).

p_err   a pointer to an error code and can be any of the following:

OS_ERR_NONE	if the function returned the state of the timer.
OS_ERR_OBJ_TYPE	p_tmr is not pointing to a timer.
OS_ERR_TMR_INVALID	if p_tmr is a NULL pointer.
OS_ERR_TMR_INVALID_STATE	the timer is in an invalid state.
OS_ERR_TMR_ISR	This function was called from an ISR, which is *not* allowed.

Returned Values

The state of the timer (see description).

Notes/Warnings

1. Examine the return value to ensure the results from this function are valid.

2. *Do not* call this function from an ISR.

Example

```
OS_STATE    CloseDoorTmrState;
OS_TMR      CloseDoorTmr;


void Task (void *p_arg)
{
    OS_ERR  err;


    (void)&p_arg;
    while (DEF_ON) {
        CloseDoorTmrState = OSTmrStateGet(&CloseDoorTmr,
                                          &err);
        /* Check "err" */
    }
}
```

OSTmrStop()

```
CPU_BOOLEAN    OSTmrStop (OS_TMR    *p_tmr,
                         OS_OPT     opt,
                         void       *p_callback_arg,
                         OS_ERR     *p_err)
```

File	Called from	Code enabled by
OS_TMR.C	Task	OS_CFG_TMR_EN

OSTmrStop() allows the user to stop a timer. The user may execute the callback function of the timer when it is stopped, and pass this callback function a different argument than was specified when the timer was started. This allows the callback function to know that the timer was stopped since the callback argument can be set to indicate this (this is application specific). If the timer is already stopped, the callback function is not called.

Arguments

p_tmr   is a pointer to the timer control block of the desired timer.

opt   is used to specify options:

OS_OPT_TMR_NONE	No option
OS_OPT_TMR_CALLBACK	Run the callback function with the argument specified when the timer was created.
OS_OPT_TMR_CALLBACK_ARG	Run the callback function, but use the argument passed in OSTmrStop() instead of the one specified when the task was created.

p_callback_arg   is a new argument to pass the callback functions (see options above).

p_err   is a pointer to a variable that contains an error code returned by this function.

OS_ERR_NONE	if the call was successful.
OS_ERR_OBJ_TYPE	if p_tmr is not pointing to a timer object.
OS_ERR_TMR_INACTIVE	the timer cannot be stopped since it is inactive.

OS_ERR_TMR_INVALID	When passing a **NULL** pointer for the **p_tmr** argument.
OS_ERR_TMR_INVALID_OPT	if the user did not specify a valid option.
OS_ERR_TMR_INVALID_STATE	the timer is in an invalid state.
OS_ERR_TMR_ISR	if calling this function from an ISR.
OS_ERR_TMR_NO_CALLBACK	if the timer lacks a callback function. This should be specified when the timer is created.
OS_ERR_TMR_STOPPED	if the timer is currently stopped.

Returned Values

DEF_TRUE   if the timer was stopped (even if it was already stopped).

DEF_FALSE if an error occurred.

Notes/Warnings

1. Examine the returned error code to make ensure the results from this function are valid.

2. *Do not* call this function from an ISR.

3. The callback function is *not* called if the timer is already stopped.

Example

```
OS_TMR  CloseDoorTmr;


void Task (void *p_arg)
{
    OS_ERR      err;


    (void)&p_arg;
    while (DEF_ON) {
        OSTmrStop(&CloseDoorTmr,
                  OS_TMR_OPT_CALLBACK,
                  (void *)0,
                  &err);
        /* Check "err" */
    }
}
```

OSVersion()

```
CPU_INT16U OSVersion (OS_ERR  *p_err);
```

File	Called from	Code enabled by
OS_CORE.C	Task or ISR	N/A

OSVersion() obtains the current version of µC/OS-III.

Arguments

p_err   is a pointer to a variable that contains an error code returned by this function. Currently, OSVersion() always return:

      OS_ERR_NONE

Returned Value

The version is returned as x.yy multiplied by 1000. For example, v3.00.0 is returned as 3000.

Notes/Warnings

None

Example

```
void TaskX (void *p_arg)
{
    CPU_INT16U  os_version;
    OS_ERR      err;


    while (DEF_ON) {
        :
        :
        os_version = OSVersion(&err);  /* Obtain µC/OS-III's version      */
        /* Check "err" */
        :
        :
    }
}
```

Appendix A

B

µC/OS-III Configuration Manual

Three (3) files are used to configure µC/OS-III as highlighted in Figure B-1: **OS_CFG.H**, **OS_TYPE.H**, and **OS_CFG_APP.H**.

Table B-1 shows where these files are typically located on your on a computer.

File	Directory
OS_CFG.H	\Micrium\Software\uCOS-III\Cfg\Template
OS_CFG_APP.H	\Micrium\Software\uCOS-III\Cfg\Template
OS_TYPE.H	\Micrium\Software\uCOS-III\Source

Table B-1 **Configuration files and directories**

µC/OS-III Configuration	**Application Code**
(1) `OS_CFG.H` **(3)** `OS_CFG_APP.H`	`APP.C` `APP.H`

µC/OS-III
CPU Independent

```
    OS_CFG_APP.C
(2) OS_TYPE.H
    OS_CORE.C
    OS_DBG.C
    OS_FLAG.C
    OS_INT.C
    OS_MEM.C
    OS_MSG.C
    OS_MUTEX.C
 OS_PEND_MULTI.C
    OS_PRIO.C
    OS_Q.C
    OS_SEM.C
    OS_STAT.C
    OS_TASK.C
    OS_TICK.C
    OS_TIME.C
    OS_TMR.C
    OS.H
```

µC/LIB
Libraries

```
    LIB_ASCII.C
    LIB_ASCII.H
    LIB_DEF.H
    LIB_MATH.C
    LIB_MATH.H
 LIB_MEM_A.ASM
    LIB_MEM.C
    LIB_MEM.H
    LIB_STR.C
    LIB_STR.H
```

µC/OS-III CPU Specific	**µC/CPU** CPU Specific	**BSP** Board Support Package	**CPU**

`OS_CPU.H`
`OS_CPU_A.ASM`
`OS_CPU_C.C`
	`CPU.H`
	`CPU_A.ASM`
	`CPU_CORE.C`
		`BSP.C`
		`BSP.H`
			`*.C`
			`*.H`

Software/Firmware

- -

Hardware

CPU	**Timer**	**Interrupt Controller**

Figure B-1 **Task pending on multiple objects**

FB-1(1)   **µC/OS-III Features (OS_CFG.H):**

OS_CFG.H is used to determine which features are needed from µC/OS-III for an application (i.e., product). Specifically, this file allows a user to determine whether to include semaphores, mutexes, event flags, run-time argument checking, etc. If µC/OS-III is provided in linkable object form, the available features are determined in advanced.

If using a pre-compiled µC/OS-III library, make sure to use the same OS_CFG.H file used to build this library so that all the data types properly match up.

FB-1(2)   **µC/OS-III Data Types (OS_TYPE.H):**

OS_TYPE.H establishes µC/OS-III-specific data types used when building an application. It specifies the size of variables used to represent task priorities, the size of a semaphore count, and more. This file contains recommended data types for µC/OS-III, however these can be altered to make better use of the CPU's natural word size. For example, on some 32-bit CPUs, it is better to declare boolean variables as 32-bit values for performance considerations, even though an 8-bit quantity is more space efficient (assuming performance is more important than footprint).

The port developer typically makes those decisions, since altering the contents of the file requires a deep understanding of the CPU and, most important, how data sizes affect µC/OS-III.

If using a pre-compiled µC/OS-III library, make sure to use the same OS_TYPE.H file used to build this library so that all the data types properly match up.

FB-1(3)   **µC/OS-III Stacks, Pools and other data sizes (OS_CFG_APP.H):**

µC/OS-III can be configured at the application level through #**define** constants in OS_CFG_APP.H even if µC/OS-III is provided in linkable object form. The #**defines** allows a user to specify stack sizes for all µC/OS-III internal tasks: the idle task, statistic task, tick task, timer task, and the ISR handler task. OS_CFG_APP.H also allows users to specify task priorities (except for the idle task since it is always the lowest priority), the tick rate, tick wheel size, the timer wheel size, and more.

You can simply copy **OS_CFG_APP.H** into the project directory and alter the contents of this file for the application. Once altered, simply re-compile **OS_CFG_APP.C**, and link the object file produced by the compiler with the rest of the µC/OS-III application. **OS_CFG_APP.C** "maps" the **#define** constants defined in **OS_CFG_APP.H** to variables (placed in code space, i.e., ROM) that µC/OS-III uses at initialization. This process is necessary to allow using µC/OS-III in linkable object form. µC/OS-III licensees will have full source code for µC/OS-III.

The contents of the three configuration files will be described in the following sections.

B-1 µC/OS-III FEATURES (OS_CFG.H)

Compile-time configuration allows users to determine which features to enable and those features that are not needed. This assumes that the user has the µC/OS-III source code. With compile-time configuration, the code and data sizes of µC/OS-III (i.e., its footprint) can be reduced by enabling only the desired functionality.

Compile-time configuration is accomplished by setting a number of **#define** constants in a file called **OS_CFG.H** that the application is expected to provide. With the full source code for µC/OS-III, simply copy **OS_CFG.H** into the application directory and change the copied file to satisfy the application's requirements. This way, **OS_CFG.H** is not recreated from scratch.

The compile-time configuration **#defines** are listed below in alphabetic order and are not necessarily found in this order in **OS_CFG.H**.

OS_CFG_APP_HOOKS_EN
When set to 1, this **#define** specifies that application-defined hooks can be called from µC/OS-III's hooks. This allows the application code to extend the functionality of µC/OS-III. Specifically:

The µC/OS-III hook ...	Calls the Application-define hook through...
OSIdleTaskHook()	OS_AppIdleTaskHookPtr
OSInitHook()	None
OSStatTaskHook()	OS_AppStatTaskHookPtr
OSTaskCreateHook()	OS_AppTaskCreateHookPtr

The µC/OS-III hook ...	Calls the Application-define hook through...
OSTaskDelHook()	OS_AppTaskDelHookPtr
OSTaskReturnHook()	OS_AppTaskReturnHookPtr
OSTaskSwHook()	OS_AppTaskSwHookPtr
OSTimeTickHook()	OS_AppTimeTickHookPtr

Application hook functions could be declared as shown in the code below.

```
void  App_OS_TaskCreateHook (OS_TCB *p_tcb)
{
    /* Your code here */
}


void  App_OS_TaskDelHook (OS_TCB *p_tcb)
{
    /* Your code here */
}


void  App_OS_TaskReturnHook (OS_TCB *p_tcb)
{
    /* Your code here */
}


void  App_OS_IdleTaskHook (void)
{
    /* Your code here */
}


void  App_OS_StatTaskHook (void)
{
    /* Your code here */
}


void  App_OS_TaskSwHook (void)
{
    /* Your code here */
}


void  App_OS_TimeTickHook (void)
{
    /* Your code here */
}
```

It's also up to a user to set the value of the pointers so that they point to the appropriate functions as shown below. The pointers do not have to be set in **main()** but, set them after calling OSInit().

```
void  main (void)
{
    OS_ERR  err;


    OSInit(&err);
    :
    :
    OS_AppTaskCreateHookPtr = (OS_APP_HOOK_TCB )App_OS_TaskCreateHook;
    OS_AppTaskDelHookPtr    = (OS_APP_HOOK_TCB )App_OS_TaskDelHook;
    OS_AppTaskReturnHookPtr = (OS_APP_HOOK_TCB )App_OS_TaskReturnHook;
    OS_AppIdleTaskHookPtr   = (OS_APP_HOOK_VOID)App_OS_IdleTaskHook;
    OS_AppStatTaskHookPtr   = (OS_APP_HOOK_VOID)App_OS_StatTaskHook;
    OS_AppTaskSwHookPtr     = (OS_APP_HOOK_VOID)App_OS_TaskSwHook;
    OS_AppTimeTickHookPtr   = (OS_APP_HOOK_VOID)App_OS_TimeTickHook;
    :
    :
    OSStart(&err);
}
```

Note that not every hook function need to be defined, only the ones the user wants to place in the application code.

Also, if you don't intend to extend μC/OS-III's hook through these application hooks, set OS_CFG_APP_HOOKS_EN to 0 to save RAM (i.e., the pointers).

OS_CFG_ARG_CHK_EN

OS_CFG_ARG_CHK_EN determines whether the user wants most of μC/OS-III functions to perform argument checking. When set to 1, μC/OS-III ensures that pointers passed to functions are non-NULL, that arguments passed are within allowable range, that options are valid, and more. When set to 0, OS_CFG_ARG_CHK_EN reduces the amount of code space and processing time required by μC/OS-III. Set OS_CFG_ARG_CHK_EN to 0 if you are certain that the arguments are correct.

μC/OS-III performs argument checking in over 40 functions. Therefore, you can save a few hundred bytes of code space by disabling this check. However, always enable argument checking until you are certain the code can be trusted.

OS_CFG_CALLED_FROM_ISR_CHK_EN

OS_CFG_CALLED_FROM_ISR_CHK_EN determines whether most of µC/OS-III functions are to confirm that the function is not called from an ISR. In other words, most of the functions from µC/OS-III should be called by task-level code except "post" type functions (which can also be called from ISRs). By setting this **#define** to 1 µC/OS-III is told to make sure that functions that are only supposed to be called by tasks are not called by ISRs. It's highly recommended to set this **#define** to 1 until absolutely certain that the code is behaving correctly and that task-level functions are always called from tasks. Set this **#define** to 0 to save code space and, of course, processing time.

µC/OS-III performs this check in approximately 50 functions. Therefore, you can save a few hundred bytes of code space by disabling this check.

OS_CFG_DBG_EN

When set to 1, this **#define** adds ROM constants located in **OS_DBG.C** to help support kernel aware debuggers. Specifically, a number of named ROM variables can be queried by a debugger to find out about compiled-in options. For example, a debugger can find out the size of an **OS_TCB**, µC/OS-III's version number, the size of an event flag group (**OS_FLAG_GRP**), and much more.

OS_CFG_FLAG_EN

OS_CFG_FLAG_EN enables (when set to 1) or disables (when set to 0) code generation of event flag services and data structures. This reduces the amount of code and data space needed when an application does not require event flags. When **OS_CFG_FLAG_EN** is set to 0, it is not necessary to enable or disable any of the other **OS_CFG_FLAG_xxx #define** constants in this section.

OS_CFG_FLAG_DEL_EN

OS_CFG_FLAG_DEL_EN enables (when set to 1) or disables (when set to 0) code generation of the function OSFlagDel().

OS_CFG_FLAG_MODE_CLR_EN

OS_CFG_FLAG_MODE_CLR_EN enables (when set to 1) or disables (when set to 0) code generation used to wait for event flags to be 0 instead of 1. Generally, wait for event flags to be set. However, the user may also want to wait for event flags to be clear and in this case, enable this option.

OS_CFG_FLAG_PEND_ABORT_EN

OS_CFG_FLAG_PEND_ABORT_EN enables (when set to 1) or disables (when set to 0) code generation of the function OSFlagPendAbort().

OS_CFG_ISR_POST_DEFERRED_EN

When set to 1, OS_CFG_ISR_POST_DEFERRED_EN reduces interrupt latency since interrupts are not disabled during most critical sections of code within µC/OS-III. Instead, the scheduler is locked during the processing of these critical sections. The advantage of setting OS_CFG_ISR_POST_DEFERRED_EN to 1 is that interrupt latency is lower, however, ISR to task response is slightly higher. It is recommended to set

OS_CFG_ISR_POST_DEFERRED_EN to 1 when enabling the following services, as setting this #define to 0 would potentially make interrupt latency unacceptably high:

µC/OS-III Services	Enabled by ...
Event Flags	OS_CFG_FLAG_EN
Multiple Pend	OS_CFG_PEND_MULTI_EN
OS???Post() with broadcast	
OS???Del() with OS_OPT_DEL_ALWAYS	
OS???PendAbort()	

The compromise to make is:

> OS_CFG_ISR_POST_DEFERRED_EN set to 1
> Short interrupt latency, longer ISR-to-task response.

> OS_CFG_ISR_POST_DEFERRED_EN set to 0
> Long interrupt latency (see table above), shorter ISR-to-task response.

OS_CFG_MEM_EN

OS_CFG_MEM_EN enables (when set to 1) or disables (when set to 0) code generation of the µC/OS-III partition memory manager and its associated data structures. This feature allows users to reduce the amount of code and data space needed when an application does not require the use of memory partitions.

OS_CFG_MUTEX_EN

OS_CFG_MUTEX_EN enables (when set to 1) or disables (when set to 0) the code generation of all mutual exclusion semaphore services and data structures. This feature allows users to reduce the amount of code and data space needed when an application does not require the use of mutexes. When OS_CFG_MUTEX_EN is set to 0, there is no need to enable or disable any of the other OS_CFG_MUTEX_XXX #define constants in this section.

OS_CFG_MUTEX_DEL_EN

OS_CFG_MUTEX_DEL_EN enables (when set to 1) or disables (when set to 0) code generation of the function OSMutexDel().

OS_CFG_MUTEX_PEND_ABORT_EN

OS_CFG_MUTEX_PEND_ABORT_EN enables (when set to 1) or disables (when set to 0) code generation of the function OSMutexPendAbort().

OS_CFG_OBJ_TYPE_CHK_EN

OS_CFG_OBJ_TYPE_CHK_EN determines whether most of µC/OS-III functions should check to see if the function is manipulating the proper object. In other words, if attempting to post to a semaphore, is the user in fact passing a semaphore object or another object by mistake? It is recommended to set this #define to 1 until absolutely certain that the code is behaving correctly and the user code is always pointing to the proper objects. Set this #define to 0 to save code space as well as data space. µC/OS-III object type checking is done nearly 30 times, and it is possible to save a few hundred bytes of code space and processing time by disabling this check.

OS_CFG_PEND_MULTI_EN

This constant determines whether the code to support pending on multiple events (i.e., semaphores or message queues) will be enabled (1) or not (0).

OS_CFG_PRIO_MAX

OS_CFG_PRIO_MAX specifies the maximum number of priorities available in the application. Specifying OS_CFG_PRIO_MAX to just the number of priorities the user intends to use, reduces the amount of RAM needed by µC/OS-III.

In µC/OS-III, task priorities can range from 0 (highest priority) to a maximum of 255 (lowest possible priority) when the data type OS_PRIO is defined as a CPU_INT08U. However, in µC/OS-III, there is no practical limit to the number of available priorities. Specifically, if defining OS_PRIO as a CPU_INT16U, there can be up to 65536 priority levels. It is recommended to leave OS_PRIO defined as a CPU_INT08U and use only 256 different priority levels (i.e., 0..255), which is generally sufficient for every application. Always set the value of OS_CFG_PRIO_MAX to even multiples of 8 (8, 16, 32, 64, 128, 256, etc.). The higher the number of different priorities, the more RAM µC/OS-III will consume.

An application cannot create tasks with a priority number higher than or equal to

OS_CFG_PRIO_MAX. In fact, µC/OS-III reserves priority OS_CFG_PRIO_MAX-1 for itself; OS_CFG_PRIO_MAX-1 is reserved for the idle task OS_IdleTask(). Additionally, do not use priority 0 for an application since it is reserved by µC/OS-III's ISR handler task. The priorities of the application tasks can therefore take a value between 1 and OS_CFG_PRIO_MAX-2 (inclusive).

To summarize, there are two priority levels to avoid in an application:

Priority	Reserved by µC/OS-III for ...
0	The ISR Handler Task (OS_IntQTask())
1	Reserved
2	Reserved
OS_CFG_PRIO_MAX-2	Reserved
OS_CFG_PRIO_MAX-1	The idle task (OS_IdleTask())

OS_CFG_Q_EN

OS_CFG_Q_EN enables (when set to 1) or disables (when set to 0) code generation of message queue services and data structures. This reduces the amount of code space needed when an application does not require the use of message queues. When OS_CFG_Q_EN is set to 0, do not enable or disable any of the other OS_CFG_Q_XXX #define constants in this section.

OS_CFG_Q_DEL_EN

OS_CFG_Q_DEL_EN enables (when set to 1) or disables (when set to 0) code generation of the function OSQDel().

OS_CFG_Q_FLUSH_EN

OS_CFG_Q_FLUSH_EN enables (when set to 1) or disables (when set to 0) code generation of the function OSQFlush().

OS_CFG_Q_PEND_ABORT_EN

OS_CFG_Q_PEND_ABORT_EN enables (when set to 1) or disables (when set to 0) code generation of the function OSQPendAbort().

OS_CFG_SCHED_LOCK_TIME_MEAS_EN

This constant enables (when set to 1) or disables (when set to 0) code generation to measure the amount of time the scheduler is locked. This is useful when determining task latency.

OS_CFG_SCHED_ROUND_ROBIN_EN

This constant enables (when set to 1) or disables (when set to 0) code generation for the round-robin feature of µC/OS-III.

OS_CFG_SEM_EN

OS_CFG_SEM_EN enables (when set to 1) or disables (when set to 0) code generation of the semaphore manager and associated data structures. This reduces the amount of code and data space needed when an application does not require the use of semaphores. When OS_CFG_SEM_EN is set to 0, it is not necessary to enable or disable any of the other OS_CFG_SEM_XXX #define constants in this section.

OS_CFG_SEM_DEL_EN

OS_CFG_SEM_DEL_EN enables (when set to 1) or disables (when set to 0) code generation of the function OSSemDel().

OS_CFG_SEM_PEND_ABORT_EN

OS_CFG_SEM_PEND_ABORT_EN enables (when set to 1) or disables (when set to 0) code generation of the function OSSemPendAbort().

OS_CFG_SEM_SET_EN

OS_CFG_SEM_SET_EN enables (when set to 1) or disables (when set to 0) code generation of the function OSSemSet().

OS_CFG_STAT_TASK_EN

OS_CFG_STAT_TASK_EN specifies whether or not to enable µC/OS-III's statistic task, as well as its initialization function. When set to 1, the statistic task OS_StatTask() and statistic task initialization function are enabled. OS_StatTask() computes the CPU usage of an application, stack usage of each task, the CPU usage of each task at run time and more.

When enabled, OS_StatTask() executes at a rate of OS_CFG_STAT_TASK_RATE_HZ (see OS_CFG_APP.H), and computes the value of OSStatTaskCPUUsage, which is a variable that contains the percentage of CPU used by the application. OS_StatTask() calls OSStatTaskHook() every time it executes so that the user can add their own statistics as needed. See OS_STAT.C for details on the statistic task. The priority of OS_StatTask() is configurable by the application code (see OS_CFG_APP.H).

OS_StatTask() also computes stack usage of each task created when the #define

OS_CFG_STAT_TASK_STK_CHK_EN is set to 1. In this case, OS_StatTask() calls OSTaskStkChk() for each task and the result is placed in the task's TCB. The .StkFree and .StkUsed field of the task's TCB represents the amount of free space (in bytes) and amount of used space, respectively.

When OS_CFG_STAT_TASK_EN is set to 0, all variables used by the statistic task are not declared (see OS.H). This, of course, reduces the amount of RAM needed by µC/OS-III when not enabling the statistic task. When setting OS_CFG_STAT_TASK_EN to 1, statistics will be determined at a rate of OS_CFG_STAT_TASK_RATE_HZ (see OS_CFG_APP.H).

OS_CFG_STAT_TASK_STK_CHK_EN

This constant allows the statistic task to call OSTaskStkChk() for each task created. For this to happen, OS_CFG_STAT_TASK_EN needs to be set to 1 (i.e., the statistic task needs to be enabled). However, call OSStatStkChk() from one of the tasks to obtain this information about the task(s).

OS_CFG_STK_SIZE_MIN

This #define specifies the minimum stack size (in CPU_STK elements) for each task. This is used by µC/OS-III to verify that sufficient stack space is provided for when each task is created. Suppose the full context of a processor consists of 16 registers of 32 bits. Also, suppose CPU_STK is declared as being of type CPU_INT32U, at a bare minimum, set OS_CFG_STK_SIZE_MIN to 16. However, it would be quite unwise to not accommodate for storage of local variables, function call returns, and possibly nested ISRs. Refer to the "port" of the processor used to see how to set this minimum. Again, this is a safeguard to make sure task stacks have sufficient stack space.

OS_CFG_TASK_CHANGE_PRIO_EN

OS_CFG_TASK_CHANGE_PRIO_EN enables (when set to 1) or disables (when set to 0) code generation of the function OSTaskChangePrio().

OS_CFG_TASK_DEL_EN

OS_CFG_TASK_DEL_EN enables (when set to 1) or disables (when set to 0) code generation of the function OSTaskDel().

OS_CFG_TASK_Q_EN

OS_CFG_TASK_Q_EN enables (when set to 1) or disables (when set to 0) code generation of the OSTaskQXXX() functions used to send and receive messages directly to/from tasks and ISRs. Sending messages directly to a task is more efficient than sending messages using a message queue because there is no pend list associated with messages sent to a task.

OS_CFG_TASK_Q_PEND_ABORT_EN

OS_CFG_TASK_Q_PEND_ABORT_EN enables (when set to 1) or disables (when set to 0) code generation of code for the function OSTaskQPendAbort().

OS_CFG_TASK_PROFILE_EN

This constant allows variables to be allocated in each task's OS_TCB to hold performance data about each task. If OS_CFG_TASK_PROFILE_EN is set to 1, each task will have a variable to keep track of the number of times a task is switched to, the task execution time, the percent CPU usage of the task relative to the other tasks and more. The information made available with this feature is highly useful when debugging, but requires extra RAM.

OS_CFG_TASK_REG_TBL_SIZE

This constant allows each task to have task context variables. Use task variables to store such elements as "errno", task identifiers and other task-specific values. The number of variables that a task contains is set by this constant. Each variable is identified by a unique identifier from 0 to OS_CFG_TASK_REG_TBL_SIZE-1. Also, each variable is declared as having an OS_REG data type (see OS_TYPE.H). If OS_REG is a CPU_INT08U, all variables in this table are of this type.

OS_CFG_TASK_SEM_PEND_ABORT_EN

OS_CFG_TASK_SEM_PEND_ABORT_EN enables (when set to 1) or disables (when set to 0) code generation of code for the function OSTaskSemPendAbort().

OS_CFG_TASK_SUSPEND_EN

OS_CFG_TASK_SUSPEND_EN enables (when set to 1) or disables (when set to 0) code generation of the functions OSTaskSuspend() and OSTaskResume(), which allows the application to explicitly suspend and resume tasks, respectively. Suspending and resuming a task is useful when debugging, especially if calling these functions via a terminal interface at run time.

OS_CFG_TIME_DLY_HMSM_EN

OS_CFG_TIME_DLY_HMSM_EN enables (when set to 1) or disables (when set to 0) the code generation of the function OSTimeDlyHMSM(), which is used to delay a task for a specified number of hours, minutes, seconds, and milliseconds.

OS_CFG_TIME_DLY_RESUME_EN

OS_CFG_TIME_DLY_RESUME_EN enables (when set to 1) or disables (when set to 0) the code generation of the function OSTimeDlyResume().

OS_CFG_TMR_EN

Enables (when set to 1) or disables (when set to 0) the code generation of timer management services.

OS_CFG_TMR_DEL_EN

OS_CFG_TMR_DEL_EN enables (when set to 1) or disables (when set to 0) the code generation of the function OSTmrDel().

B-2 DATA TYPES (OS_TYPE.H)

OS_TYPE.H contains the data types used by µC/OS-III, which should only be altered by the implementer of the µC/OS-III port. If the user only has access to a compiled µC/OS-III library or object code, make sure to use the same OS_TYPE.H used to compile the library in order to use µC/OS-III. Of course, if there is access to the source code of both the port and µC/OS-III, you can alter the contents of OS_TYPE.H. However, it is important to understand how each of the data types that are being changed will affect the operation of µC/OS-III-based applications.

The reason to change OS_TYPE.H is that processors may work better with specific word sizes. For example, a 16-bit processor will likely be more efficient at manipulating 16-bit values and a 32-bit processor more comfortable with 32-bit values, even at the cost of extra RAM. In other words, the user may need to choose between processor performance and RAM footprint.

If changing "any" of the data types, copy OS_TYPE.H in the project directory and change that file (not the original OS_TYPE.H that comes with the µC/OS-III release). Of course, to change the data types, the user must have the full source code for µC/OS-III and recompile all of the code using the new data types.

Recommended data type sizes are specified in comments in OS_TYPE.H.

B-3 µC/OS-III STACKS, POOLS AND OTHER (OS_CFG_APP.H)

µC/OS-III allows the user to configure the sizes of the idle task stack, statistic task stack, message pool, tick wheel, timer wheel, debug tables, and more. This is done through OS_CFG_APP.H.

OS_CFG_TASK_STK_LIMIT_PCT_EMPTY
This #define sets the position (as a percentage to empty) of the stack limit for the idle, statistic, tick, interrupt queue handler, and timer tasks stacks. In other words, the amount of space to leave before the stack is empty. For example if the stack contains 1000 CPU_STK entries and the user declares OS_CFG_TASK_STK_LIMIT_PCT_EMPTY to 10, the stack limit will be set when the stack reaches 90% full, or 10% empty.

If the stack of the processor grows from high memory to low memory, the limit would be set towards the "base address" of the stack, i.e., closer to element 0 of the stack.

If the processor used does not offer automatic stack limit checking, set this #define to 0.

OS_CFG_IDLE_TASK_STK_SIZE
This #define sets the size of the idle task's stack as follows:

```
CPU_STK OSCfg_IdleTaskStk[OS_CFG_IDLE_TASK_STK_SIZE];
```

Note that the stack size needs to be at least greater than OS_CFG_STK_SIZE_MIN.

OS_CFG_INT_Q_SIZE

If OS_CFG_ISR_POST_DEFERRED_EN is set to 1 (see OS_CFG.H), this #define specifies the number of entries that can be placed in the interrupt queue. The size of this queue depends on how many interrupts could occur in the time it takes to process interrupts by the ISR Handler Task. The size also depends on whether or not to allow interrupt nesting. A good start point is approximately 10 entries.

OS_CFG_INT_Q_TASK_STK_SIZE

If OS_CFG_ISR_POST_DEFERRED_EN is set to 1 (see OS_CFG.H) then this #define sets the size of the ISR handler task's stack as follows:

```
CPU_STK OSCfg_IntQTaskStk[OS_CFG_INT_Q_TASK_STK_SIZE];
```

Note that the stack size needs to be at least greater than OS_CFG_STK_SIZE_MIN.

OS_CFG_ISR_STK_SIZE

This specifies the size of µC/OS-III's interrupt stack (in CPU_STK elements, see OS_TYPE.H). Note that the stack size needs to accommodate for worst case interrupt nesting, assuming the processor supports interrupt nesting.

OS_CFG_MSG_POOL_SIZE

This entry specifies the number of OS_MSGs available in the pool of OS_MSGs. The size is specified in number of OS_MSG elements. The message pool is declared in OS_CFG_APP.C as follows:

```
OS_MSG   OSCfg_MsgPool[OS_CFG_MSG_POOL_SIZE];
```

OS_CFG_STAT_TASK_PRIO

This #define allows a user to specify the priority assigned to the µC/OS-III statistic task. It is recommended to make this task a very low priority and possibly even one priority level just above the idle task, or, OS_CFG_PRIO_MAX-2.

OS_CFG_STAT_TASK_RATE_HZ

This #define defines the execution rate (in Hz) of the statistic task. It is recommended to make this rate an even multiple of the tick rate (see OS_CFG_TICK_RATE_HZ).

OS_CFG_STAT_TASK_STK_SIZE

This #define sets the size of the statistic task's stack as follows:

    CPU_STK OSCfg_StatTaskStk[OS_CFG_STAT_TASK_STK_SIZE];

Note that the stack size needs to be at least greater than OS_CFG_STK_SIZE_MIN.

OS_CFG_TICK_RATE_HZ

This #define specifies the rate in Hertz of µC/OS-III's tick interrupt. The tick rate should be set between 10 and 1000 Hz. The higher the rate, the more overhead it will impose on the processor. The desired rate depends on the granularity required for time delays and timeouts.

OS_CFG_TICK_TASK_PRIO

This #define specifies the priority to assign to the µC/OS-III tick task. It is recommended to make this task a fairly high priority, but it does not need to be the highest. The priority assigned to this task must be greater than 0 and less than OS_CFG_PRIO_MAX-1.

OS_CFG_TICK_TASK_STK_SIZE

This entry specifies the size of µC/OS-III's tick task stack (in CPU_STK elements). Note that the stack size must be at least greater than OS_CFG_STK_SIZE_MIN.

OS_CFG_TICK_WHEEL_SIZE

This #define determines the number of entries in the OSTickWheel[] table. This "wheel" reduces the number of tasks to be updated by the tick task. The size of the wheel should be a fraction of the number of tasks expected in the application.

This value should be a number between 4 and 1024. Task management overhead is somewhat determined by the size of the wheel. A large number of entries might reduce the overhead for tick management but would require more RAM. Each entry requires a pointer and a counter of the number of entries in each "spoke" of the wheel. This counter is typically a 16-bit value. It is recommended that OS_CFG_TICK_WHEEL_SIZE not be a multiple of the tick rate. If the application has many tasks, a large wheel size is recommended. As a starting value, use a prime number (3, 5, 7, 11, 13, 17, 19, 23, etc.).

OS_CFG_TMR_TASK_PRIO

This **#define** allows a user to specify the priority to assign to the µC/OS-III timer task. It is recommended to make this task a medium-to-low priority, depending on how fast the timer task will execute (see **OS_CFG_TMR_TASK_RATE_HZ**), how many timers running in the application, and the size of the timer wheel, etc. The priority assigned to this task must be greater than 0 and less than **OS_CFG_PRIO_MAX-1**.

Start with these simple rules:

■ The faster the timer rate, the higher the priority to assign to this task.

■ The higher the timer wheel size, the higher the priority to assign this task.

■ The higher the number of timers in the system, the lower the priority.

In other words:

High Timer Rate	Higher Priority
High Timer Wheel Size	Higher Priority
High Number of Timers	Lower Priority

OS_CFG_TMR_TASK_RATE_HZ

This **#define** specifies the rate in Hertz of µC/OS-III's timer task. The timer task rate should typically be set to 10 Hz. However, timers can run at a faster rate at the price of higher processor overhead. Note that **OS_CFG_TMR_TASK_RATE_HZ** MUST be an integer multiple of **OS_CFG_TICK_TASK_RATE_HZ**. In other words, if setting **OS_CFG_TICK_TASK_RATE_HZ** to 1000, do not set **OS_CFG_TMR_TASK_RATE_HZ** to 11 since 90.91 ticks would be required for every timer update, and 90.91 is not an integer multiple. Use approximately 10 Hz in this example.

OS_CFG_TMR_TASK_STK_SIZE

This **#define** sets the size of the timer task's stack as follows:

```
CPU_STK OSCfg_TmrTaskStk[OS_CFG_TMR_TASK_STK_SIZE];
```

Note that the stack size needs to be at least greater than **OS_CFG_STK_SIZE_MIN**.

OS_CFG_TMR_WHEEL_SIZE

Timers are updated using a rotating wheel mechanism. This "wheel" reduces the number of timers to be updated by the timer manager task. The size of the wheel should be a fraction of the number of timers in the application.

This value should be a number between 4 and 1024. Timer management overhead is somewhat determined by the size of the wheel. A large number of entries might reduce the overhead for timer management but would require more RAM. Each entry requires a pointer and a counter of the number of entries in each "spoke" of the wheel. This counter is typically a 16-bit value. It is recommended that this value *not* be a multiple of the tick rate. If an application has many timers a large wheel size is recommended. As a starting value, use a prime number (3, 5, 7, 11, 13, 17, 19, 23, etc.).

C

Migrating from μC/OS-II to μC/OS-III

μC/OS-III is a completely new real-time kernel with roots in μC/OS-II. Portions of the μC/OS-II Application Programming Interface (API) function names are the same, but the arguments passed to the functions have, in some places, drastically changed.

Appendix C explains several differences between the two real-time kernels. However, access to μC/OS-II and μC/OS-III source files best highlights the differences.

Table C-1 is a feature-comparison chart for µC/OS-II and µC/OS-III.

Feature	µC/OS-II	µC/OS-III
Year of introduction	1998/2002	2009
Book	Yes	Yes
Source code available (Licensees only)	Yes	Yes
Preemptive Multitasking	Yes	Yes
Maximum number of tasks	255	Unlimited
Number of tasks at each priority level	1	Unlimited
Round Robin Scheduling	No	Yes
Semaphores	Yes	Yes
Mutual Exclusion Semaphores (Nestable)	Yes	Yes
Event Flags	Yes	Yes
Message Mailboxes (not needed)	Yes	No
Message Queues	Yes	Yes
Fixed Sized Memory Management	Yes	Yes
Signal a task without requiring a semaphore	No	Yes
Send messages to a task without requiring a message queue	No	Yes
Software Timers	Yes	Yes
Task suspend/resume (Nestable)	Yes	Yes
Deadlock prevention	Yes	Yes
Scalable	Yes	Yes
Code Footprint	6K to 26K	6K to 20K
Data Footprint	1K+	1K+
ROMable	Yes	Yes
Run-time configurable	No	Yes
Feature	µC/OS-II	µC/OS-III
Compile-time configurable	Yes	Yes

Feature	µC/OS-II	µC/OS-III
ASCII names for each kernel object	Yes	Yes
Interrupt Latency	1200~	< 1000~
Pend on multiple objects	Yes	Yes
Task registers	Yes	Yes
Built-in performance measurements	Limited	Extensive
User definable hook functions	Yes	Yes
Time stamps on posts	No	Yes
Built-in Kernel Awareness support	Yes	Yes
Optimizable Scheduler in assembly language	No	Yes
Tick handling at task level	No	Yes
Source code available	Yes	Yes
Number of services	~90	~70
MISRA-C:1998 (except 5 rules)	Yes	N/A
MISRA-C:2004 (except 5 rules)	No	Yes
DO178B Level A and EUROCAE ED-12B	Yes	In progress
Medical FDA pre-market notification (510(k)) and pre-market approval (PMA)	Yes	In progress
SIL3/SIL4 IEC for transportation and nuclear systems	Yes	In progress
IEC-61508	Yes	In progress

Table C-1 **µC/OS-II and µC/OS-III features comparison chart**

C-1 DIFFERENCES IN SOURCE FILE NAMES AND CONTENTS

Table C-2 shows the source files used in both kernels. Note that a few of the files have the same or similar name. Even though µC/OS-III has more source files, the final compiled footprint is actually smaller for a full configuration.

µC/OS-II	µC/OS-III	Note
	OS_APP_HOOKS.C	(1)
	OS_CFG_APP.C	(2)
	OS_CFG_APP.H	(3)
OS_CFG_R.H	OS_CFG.H	(4)
OS_CORE.C	OS_CORE.C	
OS_CPU.H	OS_CPU.H	(5)
OS_CPU_A.ASM	OS_CPU_A.ASM	(5)
OS_CPU_C.C	OS_CPU_C.C	(5)
OS_DBG_R.C	OS_DBG.C	(6)
OS_FLAG.C	OS_FLAG.C	
	OS_INT.C	(7)
	OS_PEND_MULTI.C	(8)
	OS_PRIO.C	(9)
OS_MBOX.C		(10)
OS_MEM.C	OS_MEM.C	
	OS_MSG.C	(11)
OS_MUTEX.C	OS_MUTEX.C	
OS_Q.C	OS_Q.C	
OS_SEM.C	OS_SEM.C	
	OS_STAT.C	(12)
OS_TASK.C	OS_TASK.C	
OS_TIME.C	OS_TIME.C	
OS_TMR.C	OS_TMR.C	
	OS_VAR.C	(13)
	OS_TYPE.H	(14)
UCOS_II.H	OS.H	(15)

Table C-2 µC/OS-II and µC/OS-III files

TC-2(1)   µC/OS-II does not have this file, which is now provided for convenience so the user can add application hooks. Copy this file to the application directory and edit the contents of the file.

TC-2(2)   **OS_CFG_APP.C** did not exist in µC/OS-II. This file needs to be added to a project build for µC/OS-III.

TC-2(3)   In µC/OS-II, all configuration constants were placed in **OS_CFG.H**. In µC/OS-III, some of the configuration constants are placed in this file, while others are in **OS_CFG.H**. **OS_CFG_APP.H** contains application-specific configurations such as the size of the idle task stack, tick rate, and others.

TC-2(4)   In µC/OS-III, **OS_CFG.H** is reserved for configuring certain features of the kernel. For example, are any of the semaphore services required, and will the application have fixed-sized memory partition management?

TC-2(5)   These are the port files and a few variables and functions will need to be changed when using a µC/OS-II port as a starting point for the µC/OS-III port.

µC/OS-II variable changes to ...	... in µC/OS-III
OSIntNesting	OSIntNestingCtr
OSTCBCur	OSTCBCurPtr
OSTCBHighRdy	OSTCBHighRdyPtr
µC/OS-II function changes to ...	**... in µC/OS-III**
OSInitHookBegin()	OSInitHook()
OSInitHookEnd()	N/A
OSTaskStatHook()	OSStatTaskHook()
OSTaskIdleHook()	OSIdleTaskHook()
OSTCBInitHook()	N/A
OSTaskStkInit()	OSTaskStkInit()

The name of **OSTaskStkInit()** is the same but it is listed here since the code for it needs to be changed slightly as several arguments passed to this function are different. Specifically, instead of passing the top-of-stack as in µC/OS-II, **OSTaskStkInit()** is passed the base address and the size of the task stack.

TC-2(6)   In µC/OS-III, **OS_DBG.C** should always be part of the build. In µC/OS-II, the equivalent file (**OS_DBG_R.C**) was optional.

TC-2(7)   **OS_INT.C** contains the code for the Interrupt Queue handler, which is a new feature in µC/OS-III, allowing post calls from ISRs to be deferred to a task-level handler. This is done to reduce interrupt latency (see Chapter 9, "Interrupt Management" on page 165).

TC-2(8)   Both kernels allow tasks to pend on multiple kernel objects. In µC/OS-II, this code is found in **OS_CORE.C**, while in µC/OS-III, the code is placed in a separate file.

TC-2(9)   The code to determine the highest priority ready-to-run task is isolated in µC/OS-III and placed in **OS_PRIO.C**. This allows the port developer to replace this file by an assembly language equivalent file, especially if the CPU used supports certain bit manipulation instructions and a count leading zeros (CLZ) instruction.

TC-2(10)   µC/OS-II provides message mailbox services. A message mailbox is identical to a message queue of size one. µC/OS-III does not have these services since they can be easily emulated by message queues.

TC-2(11)   Management of messages for message queues is encapsulated in **OS_MSG.C** in µC/OS-III.

TC-2(12)   The statistics task and its support functions have been extracted out of **OS_CORE.C** and placed in **OS_STAT.C** for µC/OS-III.

TC-2(13)   All the µC/OS-III variables are instantiated in a file called **OS_VAR.C**.

TC-2(14)   In µC/OS-III, the size of most data types is better adapted to the CPU architecture used. In µC/OS-II, the size of a number of these data types was assumed.

TC-2(15)   In µC/OS-II, the main header file is called **UCOS_II.H**. In µC/OS-III, it is renamed to **OS.H**.

C-2 CONVENTION CHANGES

There are a number of convention changes from µC/OS-II to µC/OS-III. The most notable is the use of CPU-specific data types. Table C-3 shows the differences between the data types used in both kernels.

µC/OS-II (OS_CPU.H)	µC/CPU (CPU.H)	Note
BOOLEAN	CPU_BOOLEAN	
INT8S	CPU_INT8S	
INT8U	CPU_INT8U	
INT16S	CPU_INT16S	
INT16U	CPU_INT16U	
INT32S	CPU_INT32S	
INT32U	CPU_INT32U	
OS_STK	CPU_OS_STK	(1)
OS_CPU_SR	CPU_SR	(2)
µC/OS-II (OS_CFG.H)	**µC/CPU (CPU.H)**	
OS_STK_GROWTH	CPU_CFG_STK_GROWTH	(3)

Table C-3 **µC/OS-II vs. µC/OS-III basic data types**

TC-3(1)   A task stack in µC/OS-II is declared as an **OS_STK**, which is now replaced by a CPU specific data type **CPU_STK**. These two data types are equivalent, except that defining the width of the CPU stack in µC/CPU makes more sense.

TC-3(2)   It also makes sense to declare the CPU's status register in µC/CPU.

TC-3(3)   Stack growth (high-to-low or low-to-high memory) is declared in µC/CPU since stack growth is a CPU feature and not an OS one.

Another convention change is the use of the acronym "**cfg**" which stands for configuration. Now, all **#define** configuration constants and variables have the "**CFG**" or "**Cfg**" acronym in them as shown in Table C-4. Table C-4 shows the configuration constants that have been moved from **OS_CFG.H** to **OS_CFG_APP.H**. This is done because µC/OS-III is configurable at the application level instead of just at compile time as with µC/OS-II.

µC/OS-II (OS_CFG.H)	µC/OS-III (OS_CFG_APP.H)	Note
	OS_CFG_MSG_POOL_SIZE	
	OS_CFG_ISR_STK_SIZE	
	OS_CFG_TASK_STK_LIMIT_PCT_EMPTY	
OS_TASK_IDLE_STK_SIZE	OS_CFG_IDLE_TASK_STK_SIZE	
	OS_CFG_INT_Q_SIZE	
	OS_CFG_INT_Q_TASK_STK_SIZE	
	OS_CFG_STAT_TASK_PRIO	
	OS_CFG_STAT_TASK_RATE_HZ	
OS_TASK_STAT_SIZE	OS_CFG_STAT_TASK_STK_SIZE	
OS_TICKS_PER_SEC	OS_CFG_TICK_RATE_HZ	(1)
	OS_CFG_TICK_TASK_PRIO	
	OS_CFG_TICK_TASK_STK_SIZE	
	OS_CFG_TICK_WHEEL_SIZE	
	OS_CFG_TMR_TASK_PRIO	
OS_TMR_CFG_TICKS_PER_SEC	OS_CFG_TMR_TASK_RATE_HZ	
OS_TASK_TMR_STK_SIZE	OS_CFG_TMR_TASK_STK_SIZE	
OS_TMR_CFG_WHEEL_SIZE	OS_CFG_TMR_WHEEL_SIZE	

Table C-4 µC/OS-III uses "CFG" in configuration

TC-4(1)   The very useful **OS_TICKS_PER_SEC** in µC/OS-II was renamed to **OS_CFG_TICK_RATE_HZ** in µC/OS-III. The "**HZ**" indicates that this **#define** represents Hertz (i.e., ticks per second).

Table C-5 shows additional configuration constants added to **OS_CFG.H**, while several µC/OS-II constants were either removed or renamed.

µC/OS-II (OS_CFG.H)	µC/OS-III (OS_CFG.H)	Note
OS_APP_HOOKS_EN	OS_CFG_APP_HOOKS_EN	
OS_ARG_CHK_EN	OS_CFG_ARG_CHK_EN	
	OS_CFG_CALLED_FROM_ISR_CHK_EN	
OS_DEBUG_EN	OS_CFG_DBG_EN	(1)
OS_EVENT_MULTI_EN	OS_CFG_PEND_MULTI_EN	
OS_EVENT_NAME_EN		(2)
	OS_CFG_ISR_POST_DEFERRED_EN	
OS_MAX_EVENTS		(3)
OS_MAX_FLAGS		(3)
OS_MAX_MEM_PART		(3)
OS_MAX_QS		(3)
OS_MAX_TASKS		(3)
	OS_CFG_OBJ_TYPE_CHK_EN	
OS_LOWEST_PRIO	OS_CFG_PRIO_MAX	
	OS_CFG_SCHED_LOCK_TIME_MEAS_EN	
	OS_CFG_SCHED_ROUND_ROBIN_EN	
	OS_CFG_STK_SIZE_MIN	
OS_FLAG_EN	OS_CFG_FLAG_EN	
OS_FLAG_ACCEPT_EN		(6)
OS_FLAG_DEL_EN	OS_CFG_FLAG_DEL_EN	
OS_FLAG_WAIT_CLR_EN	OS_CFG_FLAG_MODE_CLR_EN	
OS_FLAG_NAME_EN		(2)
OS_FLAG_NBITS		(4)
OS_FLAG_QUERY_EN		(5)
	OS_CFG_PEND_ABORT_EN	
OS_MBOX_EN		
OS_MBOX_ACCEPT_EN		(6)

µC/OS-II (OS_CFG.H)	µC/OS-III (OS_CFG.H)	Note
OS_MBOX_DEL_EN		
OS_MBOX_PEND_ABORT_EN		
OS_MBOX_POST_EN		
OS_MBOX_POST_OPT_EN		
OS_MBOX_QUERY_EN		(5)
OS_MEM_EN	OS_CFG_MEM_EN	
OS_MEM_NAME_EN		(2)
OS_MEM_QUERY_EN		(5)
OS_MUTEX_EN	OS_CFG_MUTEX_EN	
OS_MUTEX_ACCEPT_EN		(6)
OS_MUTEX_DEL_EN	OS_CFG_MUTEX_DEL_EN	
	OS_CFG_MUTEX_PEND_ABORT_EN	
OS_MUTEX_QUERY_EN		(5)
OS_Q_EN	OS_CFG_Q_EN	
OS_Q_ACCEPT_EN		(6)
OS_Q_DEL_EN	OS_CFG_Q_DEL_EN	
OS_Q_FLUSH_EN	OS_CFG_Q_FLUSH_EN	
	OS_CFG_Q_PEND_ABORT_EN	
OS_Q_POST_EN		(7)
OS_Q_POST_FRONT_EN		(7)
OS_Q_POST_OPT_EN		(7)
OS_Q_QUERY_EN		(5)
OS_SCHED_LOCK_EN		
OS_SEM_EN	OS_CFG_SEM_EN	
OS_SEM_ACCEPT_EN		(6)
OS_SEM_DEL_EN	OS_CFG_SEM_DEL_EN	
OS_SEM_PEND_ABORT_EN	OS_CFG_SEM_PEND_ABORT_EN	

µC/OS-II (OS_CFG.H)	µC/OS-III (OS_CFG.H)	Note
OS_SEM_QUERY_EN		(5)
OS_SEM_SET_EN	OS_CFG_SEM_SET_EN	
OS_TASK_STAT_EN	OS_CFG_STAT_TASK_EN	
OS_TASK_STK_CHK_EN	OS_CFG_STAT_TASK_STK_CHK_EN	
OS_TASK_CHANGE_PRIO_EN	OS_CFG_TASK_CHANGE_PRIO_EN	
OS_TASK_CREATE_EN		
OS_TASK_CREATE_EXT_EN		
OS_TASK_DEL_EN	OS_CFG_TASK_DEL_EN	
OS_TASK_NAME_EN		(2)
	OS_CFG_TASK_Q_EN	
	OS_CFG_TASK_Q_PEND_ABORT_EN	
OS_TASK_QUERY_EN		(5)
OS_TASK_PROFILE_EN	OS_CFG_TASK_PROFILE_EN	
	OS_CFG_TASK_REG_TBL_SIZE	
	OS_CFG_TASK_SEM_PEND_ABORT_EN	
OS_TASK_SUSPEND_EN	OS_CFG_TASK_SUSPEND_EN	
OS_TASK_SW_HOOK_EN		
OS_TICK_STEP_EN		(8)
OS_TIME_DLY_HMSM_EN	OS_CFG_TIME_DLY_HMSM_EN	
OS_TIME_DLY_RESUME_EN	OS_CFG_TIME_DLY_RESUME_EN	
OS_TIME_GET_SET_EN		
OS_TIME_TICK_HOOK_EN		
OS_TMR_EN	OS_CFG_TMR_EN	
OS_TMR_CFG_NAME_EN		(2)
OS_TMR_DEL_EN	OS_CFG_TMR_DEL_EN	

Table C-5 **µC/OS-III uses "CFG" in configuration**

617

TC-5(1)   **DEBUG** is replaced with **DBG**.

TC-5(2)   In μC/OS-II, all kernel objects have ASCII names after creation. In μC/OS-III, ASCII names are assigned when the object is created.

TC-5(3)   In μC/OS-II, it is necessary to declare the maximum number of kernel objects (number of tasks, number of event flag groups, message queues, etc.) at compile time. In μC/OS-III, all kernel objects are allocated at run time so it is no longer necessary to specify the maximum number of these objects. This feature saves valuable RAM as it is no longer necessary to over allocate objects.

TC-5(4)   In μC/OS-II, event-flag width must be declared at compile time through **OS_FLAG_NBITS**. In μC/OS-III, this is accomplished by defining the width (i.e., number of bits) in **OS_TYPE.H** through the data type **OS_FLAG**. The default is typically 32 bits.

TC-5(5)   μC/OS-III does not provide query services to the application.

TC-5(6)   μC/OS-III does not directly provide "**accept**" function calls as with μC/OS-II. Instead, **OS???Pend()** functions provide an option that emulates the "**accept**" functionality.

TC-5(7)   In μC/OS-II, there are a number of "**post**" functions. The features offered are now combined in the **OS???Post()** functions in μC/OS-III.

TC-5(8)   The μC/OS-View feature **OS_TICK_STEP_EN** is not present in μC/OS-III since μC/OS-View is an obsolete product.

C-3 VARIABLE NAME CHANGES

Some of the variable names in µC/OS-II are changed for µC/OS-III to be more consistent with coding conventions. Significant variables are shown in Table C-6.

µC/OS-II (uCOS_II.H)	µC/OS-III (OS.H)	Note
OSCtxSwCtr	OSTaskCtxSwCtr	
OSCPUUsage	OSStatTaskCPUUsage	(1)
OSIdleCtr	OSIdleTaskCtr	
OSIdleCtrMax	OSIdleTaskCtrMax	
OSIntNesting	OSIntNestingCtr	(2)
OSPrioCur	OSPrioCur	
OSPrioHighRdy	OSPrioHighRdy	
OSRunning	OSRunning	
OSSchedNesting	OSSchedLockNestingCtr	(3)
	OSSchedLockTimeMax	
OSTaskCtr	OSTaskQty	
OSTCBCur	OSTCBCurPtr	(4)
OSTCBHighRdy	OSTCBHighRdyPtr	(4)
OSTime	OSTickCtr	(5)
OSTmrTime	OSTmrTickCtr	

Table C-6 **Changes in variable naming**

TC-6(1) In µC/OS-II, **OSCPUUsage** contains the total CPU utilization in percentage format. If the CPU is busy 12% of the time, **OSCPUUsage** has the value 12. In µC/OS-III, the same information is provided in **OSStatTaskCPUUsage**.

TC-6(2) In µC/OS-II, **OSIntNesting** keeps track of the number of interrupts nesting. µC/OS-III uses **OSIntNestingCtr**. The "**Ctr**" has been added to indicate that this variable is a counter.

TC-6(3)   OSSchedNesting represents the number of times OSSchedLock() is called. µC/OS-III renames this variable to OSSchedLockNestingCtr to better represent the variable's meaning.

TC-6(4)   In µC/OS-II, OSTCBCur and OSTCBHighRdy are pointers to the OS_TCB of the current task, and to the OS_TCB of the highest-priority task that is ready to run. In µC/OS-III, these are renamed by adding the "Ptr" to indicate that they are pointers.

TC-6(5)   The internal counter of the number of ticks since power up, or the last time the variable was changed through OSTimeSet(), has been renamed to better reflect its function.

C-4 API CHANGES

The most significant change from µC/OS-II to µC/OS-III occurs in the API. In order to port a µC/OS-II-based application to µC/OS-III, it is necessary to change the way services are invoked.

Table C-7 shows changes in the way critical sections in µC/OS-III are handled. Specifically, µC/OS-II defines macros to disable interrupts, and they are moved to µC/CPU since they are CPU specific functions.

µC/OS-II (OS_CPU.H)	µC/CPU (CPU.H)	Note
OS_ENTER_CRITICAL()	CPU_CRITICAL_ENTER()	
OS_EXIT_CRITICAL()	CPU_CRITICAL_EXIT()	

Table C-7 **Changes in variable naming**

One of the biggest changes in the µC/OS-III API is its consistency. In fact, based on the function performed, it is possible to guess which arguments are needed, and in what order. For example, "*p_err" is a pointer to an error-returned variable. When present, "*p_err" is always the last argument of a function. In µC/OS-II, error-returned values are at times returned as a "*perr," and at other times as the return value of the function.

C-4-1 EVENT FLAGS

Table C-8 shows the API for event-flag management.

µC/OS-II (OS_FLAG.C)	µC/OS-III (OS_FLAG.C)	Note

OS_FLAGS
OSFlagAccept(
    OS_FLAG_GRP *pgrp,
    OS_FLAGS   flags,
    INT8U   wait_type,
    INT8U   *perr);
		(1)

OS_FLAG_GRP *
OSFlagCreate(
    OS_FLAGS   flags,
    INT8U   *perr);
	void
	OSFlagCreate(
	    OS_FLAG_GRP *p_grp,
	    CPU_CHAR *p_name,
	    OS_FLAGS flags,
	    OS_ERR *p_err);
		(2)

OS_FLAG_GRP *
OSFlagDel(
    OS_FLAG_GRP *pgrp,
    INT8U   opt,
    INT8U   *perr);
	OS_OBJ_QTY
	OSFlagDel(
	    OS_FLAG_GRP *p_grp,
	    OS_OPT opt,
	    OS_ERR *p_err);	

INT8U
OSFlagNameGet(
    OS_FLAG_GRP *pgrp,
    INT8U   **pname,
    INT8U *perr);		

void
OSFlagNameSet(
    OS_FLAG_GRP *pgrp,
    INT8U   *pname,
    INT8U   *perr);
		(3)

OS_FLAGS
OSFlagPend(
    OS_FLAG_GRP *pgrp,
    OS_FLAGS   flags,
    INT8U   wait_type,
    INT32U   timeout,
    INT8U   *perr);
	OS_FLAGS
	OSFlagPend(
	    OS_FLAG_GRP *p_grp,
	    OS_FLAGS flags,
	    OS_TICK timeout,
	    OS_OPT opt,
	    OS_TS *p_ts,
	    OS_ERR *p_err);	

μC/OS-II (OS_FLAG.C)	μC/OS-III (OS_FLAG.C)	Note

OS_FLAGS
OSFlagPendGetFlagsRdy(
    void);
	OS_FLAGS
	OSFlagPendGetFlagsRdy(
	    OS_ERR *p_err);	

OS_FLAGS
OSFlagPost(
    OS_FLAG_GRP *pgrp,
    OS_FLAGS   flags,
    INT8U   opt,
    INT8U   *perr);
	OS_FLAGS
	OSFlagPost(
	    OS_FLAG_GRP *p_grp,
	    OS_FLAGS flags,
	    OS_OPT opt,
	    OS_ERR *p_err);	

OS_FLAGS
OSFlagQuery(
    OS_FLAG_GRP *pgrp,
    INT8U   *perr);
		(4)

Table C-8 **Event Flags API**

TC-8(1)   In μC/OS-III, there is no "accept" API. This feature is actually built-in the `OSFlagPend()` by specifying the `OS_OPT_PEND_NON_BLOCKING` option.

TC-8(2)   In μC/OS-II, `OSFlagCreate()` returns the address of an `OS_FLAG_GRP`, which is used as the "handle" to the event-flag group. In μC/OS-III, the application must allocate storage for an `OS_FLAG_GRP`, which serves the same purpose as the `OS_EVENT`. The benefit in μC/OS-III is that it is not necessary to predetermine the number of event flags at compile time.

TC-8(3)   In μC/OS-II, the user may assign a name to an event-flag group after the group is created. This functionality is built-into `OSFlagCreate()` for μC/OS-III.

TC-8(4)   μC/OS-III does not provide query services, as they are typically rarely used.

C-4-2 MESSAGE MAILBOXES

Table C-9 shows the API for message mailbox management. Note that µC/OS-III does not directly provide services for managing message mailboxes. Given that a message mailbox is a message queue of size one, µC/OS-III can easily emulate message mailboxes.

µC/OS-II (OS_MBOX.C)		µC/OS-III (OS_Q.C)		Note
void * OSMboxAccept(OS_EVENT *pevent);				(1)

OS_EVENT *
OSMboxCreate(
    void   *pmsg);
		void
		OSQCreate(
		    OS_Q *p_q,
		    CPU_CHAR *p_name,
		    OS_MSG_QTY max_qty,
		    OS_ERR *p_err);
				(2)

void *
OSMboxDel(
    OS_EVENT   *pevent,
    INT8U   opt,
    INT8U   *perr);
		OS_OBJ_QTY,
		OSQDel(
		    OS_Q *p_q,
		    OS_OPT opt,
		    OS_ERR *p_err);		

void *
OSMboxPend(
    OS_EVENT   *pevent,
    INT32U   timeout,
    INT8U   *perr);
		void *
		OSQPend(
		    OS_Q *p_q,
		    OS_TICK timeout,
		    OS_OPT opt,
		    OS_MSG_SIZE *p_msg_size,
		    CPU_TS *p_ts,
		    OS_ERR *p_err);
				(3)

INT8U
OSMBoxPendAbort(
    OS_EVENT   *pevent,
    INT8U   opt,
    INT8U   *perr);
		OS_OBJ_QTY
		OSQPendAbort(
		    OS_Q *p_q,
		    OS_OPT opt
		    OS_ERR *p_err);		

µC/OS-II (os_MBOX.c)	µC/OS-III (os_Q.c)	Note

INT8U
OSMboxPost(
    OS_EVENT   *pevent,
    void   *pmsg);
	void
	OSQPost(
	    OS_Q *p_q,
	    Void *p_void,
	    OS_MSG_SIZE msg_size,
	    OS_OPT opt,
	    OS_ERR *p_err);
		(4)

INT8U
OSMboxPostOpt(
    OS_EVENT   *pevent,
    void   *pmsg,
    INT8U   opt);
		(4)

INT8U
OSMboxQuery(
    OS_EVENT   *pevent,
    OS_MBOX_DATA *p_mbox_data);
		(5)

Table C-9 **Message Mailbox API**

TC-9(1)   In µC/OS-III, there is no "accept" API since this feature is built into the OSQPend() by specifying the OS_OPT_PEND_NON_BLOCKING option.

TC-9(2)   In µC/OS-II, OSMboxCreate() returns the address of an OS_EVENT, which is used as the "handle" to the message mailbox. In µC/OS-III, the application must allocate storage for an OS_Q, which serves the same purpose as the OS_EVENT. The benefit in µC/OS-III is that it is not necessary to predetermine the number of message queues at compile time.

TC-9(3)   µC/OS-III returns additional information about the message received. Specifically, the sender specifies the size of the message as a snapshot of the current timestamp is taken and stored as part of the message. The receiver of the message therefore knows when the message was sent.

TC-9(4)   In µC/OS-III, OSQPost() offers a number of options that replaces the two post functions provided in µC/OS-II.

TC-9(5)   µC/OS-III does not provide query services, as they were rarely used.

C-4-3 MEMORY MANAGEMENT

Table C-10 shows the difference in API for memory management.

µC/OS-II (OS_MEM.C)		µC/OS-III (OS_MEM.C)		Note

`OS_MEM *`
`OSMemCreate(`
   `void          *addr,`
   `INT32U        nblks,`
   `INT32U        blksize,`
   `INT8U         *perr);`
		`void`
		`OSMemCreate(`
		   `OS_MEM        *p_mem,`
		   `CPU_CHAR      *p_name,`
		   `void          *p_addr,`
		   `OS_MEM_QTY    n_blks,`
		   `OS_MEM_SIZE   blk_size,`
		   `OS_ERR        *p_err);`
				(1)

`void *`
`OSMemGet(`
   `OS_MEM        *pmem,`
   `INT8U         *perr);`
		`void *`
		`OSMemGet(`
		   `OS_MEM        *p_mem,`
		   `OS_ERR        *p_err);`		

`INT8U`
`OSMemNameGet(`
   `OS_MEM        *pmem,`
   `INT8U         **pname,`
   `INT8U         *perr);`				

`void`
`OSMemNameSet(`
   `OS_MEM        *pmem,`
   `INT8U         *pname,`
   `INT8U         *perr);`
		`void`
		`OSMemPut(`
		   `OS_MEM        *p_mem,`
		   `void          *p_blk,`
		   `OS_ERR        *p_err);`
				(2)

`INT8U`
`OSMemPut(`
   `OS_MEM        *pmem,`
   `void          *pblk);`
				(3)

`INT8U`
`OSMemQuery(`
   `OS_MEM        *pmem,`
   `OS_MEM_DATA   *p_mem_data);`				

Table C-10 **Memory Management API**

TC-10(1)   In µC/OS-II, `OSMemCreate()` returns the address of an `OS_MEM` object, which is used as the "handle" to the newly created memory partition. In µC/OS-III, the application must allocate storage for an `OS_MEM`, which serves the same purpose. The benefit in µC/OS-III is that it is not necessary to predetermine the number of memory partitions at compile time.

TC-10(2)   µC/OS-III does not need an **OSMemNameSet()** since the name of the memory partition is passed as an argument to **OSMemCreate()**.

TC-10(3)   µC/OS-III does not support query calls.

C-4-4 MUTUAL EXCLUSION SEMAPHORES

Table C-11 shows the difference in API for mutual exclusion semaphore management.

µC/OS-II (OS_MUTEX.C)		µC/OS-III (OS_MUTEX.C)		Note

BOOLEAN
OSMutexAccept(
    OS_EVENT   *pevent,
    INT8U   *perr);
				(1)

OS_EVENT *
OSMutexCreate(
    INT8U   prio,
    INT8U   *perr);
		void
		OSMutexCreate(
		    OS_MUTEX *p_mutex,
		    CPU_CHAR *p_name,
		    OS_ERR *p_err);
				(2)

OS_EVENT *
OSMutexDel(
    OS_EVENT   *pevent,
    INT8U   opt,
    INT8U   *perr);
		void
		OSMutexDel(
		    OS_MUTEX *p_mutex,
		    OS_OPT opt,
		    OS_ERR *p_err);		

void
OSMutexPend(
    OS_EVENT   *pevent,
    INT32U   timeout,
    INT8U   *perr);
		void
		OSMutexPend(
		    OS_MUTEX *p_mutex,
		    OS_TICK timeout,
		    OS_OPT opt,
		    CPU_TS *p_ts,
		    OS_ERR *p_err);
				(3)

		OS_OBJ_QTY
		OSMutexPendAbort(
		    OS_MUTEX *p_mutex,
		    OS_OPT opt,
		    OS_ERR *p_err);		

µC/OS-II (OS_MUTEX.C)	µC/OS-III (OS_MUTEX.C)	Note

`INT8U`
`OSMutexPost(`
`    OS_EVENT        *pevent);`
	`void`
	`OSMutexPost(`
	`    OS_MUTEX    *p_mutex,`
	`    OS_OPT      opt,`
	`    OS_ERR      *p_err);`	

`INT8U`
`OSMutexQuery(`
`    OS_EVENT        *pevent,`
`    OS_MUTEX_DATA  *p_mutex_data);`		

Table C-11 **Mutual Exclusion Semaphore Management API**

TC-11(1)   In µC/OS-III, there is no "accept" API, since this feature is built into the `OSMutexPend()` by specifying the `OS_OPT_PEND_NON_BLOCKING` option.

TC-11(2)   In µC/OS-II, `OSMutexCreate()` returns the address of an `OS_EVENT`, which is used as the "handle" to the message mailbox. In µC/OS-III, the application must allocate storage for an `OS_MUTEX`, which serves the same purpose as the `OS_EVENT`. The benefit in µC/OS-III is that it is not necessary to predetermine the number of mutual-exclusion semaphores at compile time.

TC-11(3)   µC/OS-III returns additional information when a mutex is released. The releaser takes a snapshot of the current time stamp and stores it in the `OS_MUTEX`. The new owner of the mutex therefore knows when the mutex was released.

TC-11(4)   µC/OS-III does not provide query services as they were rarely used.

C-4-5 MESSAGE QUEUES

Table C-12 shows the difference in API for message-queue management.

µC/OS-II (os_q.c)	µC/OS-III (os_q.c)	Note

void *
OSQAccept(
    OS_EVENT *pevent,
    INT8U   *perr);
		(1)

OS_EVENT *
OSQCreate(
    void   **start,
    INT16U size);
	void
	OSQCreate(
	    OS_Q *p_q,
	    CPU_CHAR *p_name,
	    OS_MSG_QTY max_qty,
	    OS_ERR *p_err);
		(2)

OS_EVENT *
OSQDel(
    OS_EVENT *pevent,
    INT8U   opt,
    INT8U   *perr);
	OS_OBJ_QTY,
	OSQDel(
	    OS_Q *p_q,
	    OS_OPT opt,
	    OS_ERR *p_err);	

INT8U
OSQFlush(
    OS_EVENT *pevent);
	OS_MSG_QTY
	OSQFlush(
	    OS_Q *p_q,
	    OS_ERR *p_err);	

void *
OSQPend(
    OS_EVENT *pevent,
    INT32U timeout,
    INT8U   *perr);
	void *
	OSQPend(
	    OS_Q *p_q,
	    OS_MSG_SIZE *p_msg_size,
	    OS_TICK timeout,
	    OS_OPT opt,
	    CPU_TS *p_ts,
	    OS_ERR *p_err);
		(3)

INT8U
OSQPendAbort(
    OS_EVENT *pevent,
    INT8U   opt,
    INT8U   *perr);
	OS_OBJ_QTY
	OSQPendAbort(
	    OS_Q *p_q,
	    OS_OPT opt,
	    OS_ERR *p_err);	

INT8U
OSQPost(
    OS_EVENT *pevent,
    void   *pmsg);
	void
	OSQPost(
	    OS_Q *p_q,
	    void *p_void,
	    OS_MSG_SIZE msg_size,
	    OS_OPT opt,
	    OS_ERR *p_err);
		(4)

µC/OS-II (os_q.c)	µC/OS-III (os_q.c)	Note

INT8U
OSQPostFront(
    OS_EVENT *pevent,
    void *pmsg);		

INT8U
OSQPostOpt(
    OS_EVENT *pevent,
    void   *pmsg,
    INT8U   opt);
		(4)

INT8U
OSQQuery(
    OS_EVENT *pevent,
    OS_Q_DATA *p_q_data);
		(5)

Table C-12 **Message Queue Management API**

TC-12(1)   In µC/OS-III, there is no "accept" API as this feature is built into the OSQPend()
by specifying the OS_OPT_PEND_NON_BLOCKING option.

TC-12(2)   In µC/OS-II, OSQCreate() returns the address of an OS_EVENT, which is used
as the "handle" to the message queue. In µC/OS-III, the application must
allocate storage for an OS_Q object, which serves the same purpose as the
OS_EVENT. The benefit in µC/OS-III is that it is not necessary to predetermine at
compile time, the number of message queues.

TC-12(3)   µC/OS-III returns additional information when a message queue is posted.
Specifically, the sender includes the size of the message and takes a snapshot
of the current timestamp and stores it in the message. The receiver of the
message therefore knows when the message was posted.

TC-12(4)   In µC/OS-III, OSQPost() offers a number of options that replaces the three
post functions provided in µC/OS-II.

TC-12(5)   µC/OS-III does not provide query services as they were rarely used.

C-4-6 SEMAPHORES

Table C-13 shows the difference in API for semaphore management.

µC/OS-II (os_sem.c)	µC/OS-III (os_sem.c)	Note
INT16U OSSemAccept(OS_EVENT *pevent);		(1)

OS_EVENT *
OSSemCreate(
    INT16U   cnt);
	void
	OSSemCreate(
	    OS_SEM *p_sem,
	    CPU_CHAR *p_name,
	    OS_SEM_CTR cnt,
	    OS_ERR *p_err);
		(2)

OS_EVENT *
OSSemDel(
    OS_EVENT   *pevent,
    INT8U   opt,
    INT8U   *perr);
	OS_OBJ_QTY,
	OSSemDel(
	    OS_SEM *p_sem,
	    OS_OPT opt,
	    OS_ERR *p_err);	

void
OSSemPend(
    OS_EVENT   *pevent,
    INT32U   timeout,
    INT8U   *perr);
	OS_SEM_CTR
	OSSemPend(
	    OS_SEM *p_sem,
	    OS_TICK timeout,
	    OS_OPT opt,
	    CPU_TS *p_ts,
	    OS_ERR *p_err);
		(3)

INT8U
OSSemPendAbort(
    OS_EVENT   *pevent,
    INT8U   opt,
    INT8U   *perr);
	OS_OBJ_QTY
	OSSemPendAbort(
	    OS_SEM *p_sem,
	    OS_OPT opt,
	    OS_ERR *p_err);	

void
OSSemPost(
    OS_EVENT   *pevent);
	void
	OSSemPost(
	    OS_SEM *p_sem,
	    OS_OPT opt,
	    OS_ERR *p_err);	

INT8U
OSSemQuery(
    OS_EVENT   *pevent,
    OS_SEM_DATA *p_sem_data);
		(4)

µC/OS-II (os_sem.c)		µC/OS-III (os_sem.c)		Note
void OSSemSet(		void OSSemSet(		
OS_EVENT	*pevent,	OS_SEM	*p_sem,	
INT16U	cnt,	OS_SEM_CTR	cnt,	
INT8U	*perr);	OS_ERR	*p_err);	

Table C-13 **Semaphore Management API**

TC-13(1)   In µC/OS-III, there is no "accept" API since this feature is built into the OSSemPend() by specifying the OS_OPT_PEND_NON_BLOCKING option.

TC-13(2)   In µC/OS-II, **OSSemCreate()** returns the address of an **OS_EVENT**, which is used as the "handle" to the semaphore. In µC/OS-III, the application must allocate storage for an **OS_SEM** object, which serves the same purpose as the **OS_EVENT**. The benefit in µC/OS-III is that it is not necessary to predetermine the number of semaphores at compile time.

TC-13(3)   µC/OS-III returns additional information when a semaphore is signaled. The ISR or task that signals the semaphore takes a snapshot of the current timestamp and stores this in the **OS_SEM** object signaled. The receiver of the signal therefore knows when the signal was sent.

TC-13(5)   µC/OS-III does not provide query services, as they were rarely used.

C

C-4-7 TASK MANAGEMENT

Table C-14 shows the difference in API for task-management services.

µC/OS-II (OS_TASK.C)	µC/OS-III (OS_TASK.C)	Note

INT8U
OSTaskChangePrio(
    INT8U   oldprio,
    INT8U   newprio);
	void
	OSTaskChangePrio(
	    OS_TCB *p_tcb,
	    OS_PRIO prio,
	    OS_ERR *p_err);
		(1)

INT8U
OSTaskCreate(
    void   (*task)(void *p_arg),
    void   *p_arg,
    OS_STK   *ptos,
    INT8U   prio);
	void
	OSTaskCreate(
	    OS_TCB *p_tcb,
	    CPU_CHAR *p_name,
	    OS_TASK_PTR *p_task,
	    void *p_arg,
	    OS_PRIO prio,
	    CPU_STK *p_stk_base,
	    CPU_STK_SIZE stk_limit,
	    CPU_STK_SIZE stk_size,
	    OS_MSG_QTY q_size,
	    OS_TICK time_quanta,
	    void *p_ext,
	    OS_OPT opt,
	    OS_ERR *p_err);
		(2)

INT8U
OSTaskCreateExt(
    void   (*task)(void *p_arg),
    void   *p_arg,
    OS_STK   *ptos,
    INT8U   prio,
    INT16U   id,
    OS_STK   *pbos,
    INT32U   stk_size,
    void   *pext,
    INT16U   opt);
	void
	OSTaskCreate(
	    OS_TCB *p_tcb,
	    CPU_CHAR *p_name,
	    OS_TASK_PTR *p_task,
	    void *p_arg,
	    OS_PRIO prio,
	    CPU_STK *p_stk_base,
	    CPU_STK_SIZE stk_limit,
	    CPU_STK_SIZE stk_size,
	    OS_MSG_QTY q_size,
	    OS_TICK time_quanta,
	    void *p_ext,
	    OS_OPT opt,
	    OS_ERR *p_err);
		(2)

INT8U
OSTaskDel(
    INT8U   prio);
	void
	OSTaskDel(
	    OS_TCB *p_tcb,
	    OS_ERR *p_err);	

µC/OS-II (os_task.c)	µC/OS-III (os_task.c)	Note
| ```
INT8U
OSTaskDelReq(
    INT8U      prio);
``` | | |
| ```
INT8U
OSTaskNameGet(
    INT8U      prio,
    INT8U      **pname,
    INT8U      *perr);
``` | | |
| ```
void
OSTaskNameSet(
    INT8U      prio,
    INT8U      *pname,
    INT8U      *perr);
``` | | (3) |
| | ```
OS_MSG_QTY
OSTaskQFlush(
    OS_TCB     *p_tcb,
    OS_ERR     *p_err);
``` | (4) |
| | ```
void *
OSTaskQPend(
    OS_TICK       timeout,
    OS_OPT        opt,
    OS_MSG_SIZE *p_msg_size,
    CPU_TS        *p_ts,
    OS_ERR        *p_err);
``` | (4) |
| | ```
CPU_BOOLEAN
OSTaskQPendAbort(
    OS_TCB     *p_tcb,
    OS_OPT       opt,
    OS_ERR     *p_err);
``` | (4) |
| | ```
void
OSTaskQPost(
    OS_TCB       *p_tcb,
    void         *p_void,
    OS_MSG_SIZE  msg_size,
    OS_OPT       opt,
    OS_ERR       *p_err);
``` | (4) |
| ```
INT32U
OSTaskRegGet(
    INT8U      prio,
    INT8U      id,
    INT8U      *perr);
``` | ```
OS_REG
OSTaskRegGet(
    OS_TCB     *p_tcb,
    OS_REG_ID  id,
    OS_ERR     *p_err);
``` | |
```

µC/OS-II (OS_TASK.C)	µC/OS-III (OS_TASK.C)	Note

`void`
`OSTaskRegSet(`
    `INT8U`   `prio,`
    `INT8U`   `id,`
    `INT32U`   `value,`
    `INT8U`   `*perr);`
	`void`
	`OSTaskRegGet(`
	    `OS_TCB` `*p_tcb,`
	    `OS_REG_ID` `id,`
	    `OS_REG` `value,`
	    `OS_ERR` `*p_err);`	

`INT8U`
`OSTaskResume(`
    `INT8U`   `prio);`
	`void`
	`OSTaskResume(`
	    `OS_TCB` `*p_tcb,`
	    `OS_ERR` `*p_err);`	

	`OS_SEM_CTR`
	`OSTaskSemPend(`
	    `OS_TICK` `timeout,`
	    `OS_OPT` `opt,`
	    `CPU_TS` `*p_ts,`
	    `OS_ERR` `*p_err);`
		(5)

	`CPU_BOOLEAN`
	`OSTaskSemPendAbort(`
	    `OS_TCB` `*p_tcb,`
	    `OS_OPT` `opt,`
	    `OS_ERR` `*p_err);`
		(5)

	`CPU_BOOLEAN`
	`OSTaskSemPendAbort(`
	    `OS_TCB` `*p_tcb,`
	    `OS_OPT` `opt,`
	    `OS_ERR` `*p_err);`
		(5)

	`OS_SEM_CTR`
	`OSTaskSemPost(`
	    `OS_TCB` `*p_tcb,`
	    `OS_OPT` `opt,`
	    `OS_ERR` `*p_err);`
		(5)

	`OS_SEM_CTR`
	`OSTaskSemSet(`
	    `OS_TCB` `*p_tcb,`
	    `OS_SEM_CTR` `cnt,`
	    `OS_ERR` `*p_err);`
		(5)

`INT8U`
`OSTaskSuspend(`
    `INT8U`   `prio);`
	`void`
	`OSTaskSuspend(`
	    `OS_TCB` `*p_tcb,`
	    `OS_ERR` `*p_err);`	

µC/OS-II (OS_TASK.C)	µC/OS-III (OS_TASK.C)	Note
```INT8U OSTaskStkChk(INT8U prio, OS_STK_DATA *p_stk_data);```	```void OSTaskStkChk(OS_TCB *p_tcb, CPU_STK_SIZE *p_free, CPU_STK_SIZE *p_used, OS_ERR *p_err);```	(6)
	```void OSTaskTimeQuantaSet(OS_TCB *p_tcb, OS_TICK time_quanta, OS_ERR *p_err);```	(7)
```INT8U OSTaskQuery(INT8U prio, OS_TCB *p_task_data);```		(8)

Table C-14 **Task Management API**

TC-14(1)   In µC/OS-II, each task must have a unique priority. The priority of a task can be changed at run-time, however it can only be changed to an unused priority. This is generally not a problem since µC/OS-II supports up to 255 different priority levels and is rare for an application to require all levels. Since µC/OS-III supports an unlimited number of tasks at each priority, the user can change the priority of a task to any available level.

TC-14(2)   µC/OS-II provides two functions to create a task: **OSTaskCreate()** and **OSTaskCreateExt()**. **OSTaskCreateExt()** is recommended since it offers more flexibility. In µC/OS-III, only one API is used to create a task, **OSTaskCreate()**, which offers similar features to **OSTaskCreateExt()** and provides additional ones.

TC-14(3)   µC/OS-III does not need an **OSTaskNameSet()** since an ASCII name for the task is passed as an argument to **OSTaskCreate()**.

TC-14(4)   µC/OS-III allows tasks or ISRs to send messages directly to a task instead of having to pass through a mailbox or a message queue as does µC/OS-II.

TC-14(5)   µC/OS-III allows tasks or ISRs to directly signal a task instead of having to pass through a semaphore as does µC/OS-II.

635

TC-14(6)   In µC/OS-II, the user must allocate storage for a special data structure called **OS_STK_DATA**, which is used to place the result of a stack check of a task. This data structure contains only two fields: **.OSFree** and **.OSUsed**. In µC/OS-III, it is required that the caller pass pointers to destination variables where those values will be placed.

TC-14(7)   µC/OS-III allows users to specify the time quanta of each task on a per-task basis. This is available since µC/OS-III supports multiple tasks at the same priority, and allows for round robin scheduling. The time quanta for a task is specified when the task is created, but it can be changed by the API at run time.

TC-14(8)   µC/OS-III does not provide query services as they were rarely used.

C-4-8 TIME MANAGEMENT

Table C-15 shows the difference in API for time-management services.

µC/OS-II (os_time.c)	µC/OS-III (os_time.c)	Note
```void OSTimeDly(INT32U ticks);```	```void OSTimeDly(OS_TICK dly, OS_OPT opt, OS_ERR *p_err);```	(1)
```INT8U OSTimeDlyHMSM(INT8U hours, INT8U minutes, INT8U seconds, INT16U ms);```	```void OSTimeDlyHMSM(CPU_INT16U hours, CPU_INT16U minutes, CPU_INT16U seconds CPU_INT32U milli, OS_OPT opt, OS_ERR *p_err);```	(2)
```INT8U OSTimeDlyResume(INT8U prio);```	```void OSTimeDlyResume(OS_TCB *p_tcb, OS_ERR *p_err);```	
```INT32U OSTimeGet(void);```	```OS_TICK OSTimeGet(OS_ERR *p_err);```	

µC/OS-II (OS_TIME.C)	µC/OS-III (OS_TIME.C)	Note

void
OSTimeSet(
    INT32U   ticks);
	void
	OSTimeSet(
	    OS_TICK ticks,
	    OS_ERR *p_err);	

void OSTimeTick(void)	void OSTimeTick(void)	

Table C-15 **Time Management API**

TC-15(1)   µC/OS-III includes an option argument, which allows the user to delay a task for a certain number of ticks, or wait until the tick counter reaches a certain value. In µC/OS-II, only the former is available.

TC-15(2)   **OSTimeDlyHMSM()** in µC/OS-III is more flexible as it allows a user to specify whether to be "strict" about the ranges of hours (0 to 999), minutes (0 to 59), seconds (0 to 59), and milliseconds (0 to 999), or whether to allow any values such as 200 minutes, 75 seconds, or 20,000 milliseconds.

C-4-9 TIMER MANAGEMENT

Table C-16 shows the difference in API for timer-management services. The timer management in µC/OS-III is similar to that of µC/OS-II except for minor changes in arguments in OSTmrCreate().

µC/OS-II (OS_TMR.C)	µC/OS-III (OS_TMR.C)	Note

OS_TMR *
OSTmrCreate(
    INT32U   dly,
    INT32U   period,
    INT8U   opt,
    OS_TMR_CALLBACK callback,
    void   *callback_arg,
    INT8U   *pname,
    INT8U   *perr);
	void
	OSTmrCreate(
	    OS_TMR *p_tmr,
	    CPU_CHAR *p_name,
	    OS_TICK dly,
	    OS_TICK period,
	    OS_OPT opt,
	    OS_TMR_CALLBACK_PTR *p_callback,
	    void *p_callback_arg,
	    OS_ERR *p_err);	

µC/OS-II (OS_TMR.C)		µC/OS-III (OS_TMR.C)		Note

BOOLEAN
OSTmrDel(
    OS_TMR   *ptmr,
    INT8U   *perr);
		CPU_BOOLEAN
		OSTmrDel(
		    OS_TMR *p_tmr,
		    OS_ERR *p_err);		

INT8U
OSTmrNameGet(
    OS_TMR   *ptmr,
    INT8U   **pdest,
    INT8U *perr);				

INT32U
OSTmrRemainGet(
    OS_TMR   *ptmr,
    INT8U   *perr);
		OS_TICK
		OSTmrRemainGet(
		    OS_TMR *p_tmr,
		    OS_ERR *p_err);		

INT8U
OSTmrStateGet(
    OS_TMR   *ptmr,
    INT8U   *perr);
		OS_STATE
		OSTmrStateGet(
		    OS_TMR *p_tmr,
		    OS_ERR *p_err);		

BOOLEAN
OSTmrStart(
    OS_TMR   *ptmr,
    INT8U   *perr);
		CPU_BOOLEAN
		OSTmrStart(
		    OS_TMR *p_tmr,
		    OS_ERR *p_err);		

BOOLEAN
OSTmrStop(
    OS_TMR   *ptmr,
    INT8U   opt,
    void   *callback_arg,
    INT8U   *perr);
		CPU_BOOLEAN
		OSTmrStop(
		    OS_TMR *p_tmr,
		    OS_OPT opt,
		    void *p_callback_arg,
		    OS_ERR *p_err);		

INT8U OSTmrSignal(void);				

Table C-16 **Timer Management API**

C-4-10 MISCELLANEOUS

Table C-17 shows the difference in API for miscellaneous services.

µC/OS-II (OS_CORE.C)	µC/OS-III (OS_CORE.C)	Note
```INT8U OSEventNameGet(OS_EVENT *pevent, INT8U **pname, INT8U *perr);```		
```void OSEventNameSet(OS_EVENT *pevent, INT8U *pname, INT8U *perr);```		(1)
```INT16U OSEventPendMulti(OS_EVENT **pevent_pend, OS_EVENT **pevent_rdy, void **pmsgs_rdy, INT32U timeout, INT8U *perr);```	```OS_OBJ_QTY OSPendMulti(OS_PEND_DATA *p_pend_data_tbl, OS_OBJ_QTY tbl_size, OS_TICK timeout, OS_OPT opt, OS_ERR *p_err);```	(2)
```void OSInit(void)```	```void OSInit(OS_ERR *p_err);```	(3)
```void OSIntEnter(void)```	```void OSIntEnter(void);```	
```void OSIntExit(void)```	```void OSIntExit(void)```	
	```void OSSched(void);```	
```void OSSchedLock(void)```	```void OSSchedLock(OS_ERR *p_err);```	(4)
	```void OSSchedRoundRobinCfg(CPU_BOOLEAN en, OS_TICK dflt_time_quanta, OS_ERR *p_err);```	(5)
	```void OSSchedRoundRobinYield(OS_ERR *p_err);```	(6)

µC/OS-II (OS_CORE.C)	µC/OS-III (OS_CORE.C)	Note
void OSSchedUnlock(void)	void OSSchedUnlock(OS_ERR *p_err);	(7)
void OSStart(void)	void OSStart(void);	
void OSStatInit(void)	void OSStatTaskCPUUsageInit(OS_ERR *p_err);	(8)
INT16U OSVersion(void)	CPU_INT16U OSVersion(OS_ERR *p_err);	(9)

Table C-17 **Miscellaneous API**

TC-17(1)   Objects in µC/OS-III are named when they are created and these functions are not required in µC/OS-III.

TC-17(2)   The implementation of the multi-pend functionality is changed from µC/OS-II. However, the purpose of multi-pend is the same, to allow a task to pend (or wait) on multiple objects. In µC/OS-III, however, it is possible to only multi-pend on semaphores and message queues and not event flags and mutexes.

TC-17(3)   An error code is returned in µC/OS-III for this function. Initialization is successful if **OS_ERR_NONE** is received back from **OSInit()**. In µC/OS-II, there is no way of knowing whether there is an error in the configuration that caused **OSInit()** to fail.

TC-17(4)   An error code is returned in µC/OS-III for this function.

TC-17(5)   Enable or disable µC/OS-III's round-robin scheduling at run time, as well as change the default time quanta.

TC-17(6)   A task that completes its work before its time quanta expires may yield the CPU to another task at the same priority.

TC-17(7)   An error code is returned in µC/OS-III for this function.

TC-17(8)   Note the change in name for the function that computes the "capacity" of the CPU for the purpose of computing CPU usage at run-time.

TC-17(9)   An error code is returned in µC/OS-III for this function.

C-4-11 HOOKS AND PORT

Table C-18 shows the difference in APIs used to port µC/OS-II to µC/OS-III.

µC/OS-II (OS_CPU*.C/H)	µC/OS-III (OS_CPU*.C/H)	Note
	OS_TS OSGetTS(void);	(1)
void OSInitHookBegin(void);	void OSInitHook(void);	
void OSInitHookEnd(void);		

void
OSTaskCreateHook(
    OS_TCB   *ptcb);
	void
	OSTaskCreateHook(
	    OS_TCB *p_tcb);	

void
OSTaskDelHook(
    OS_TCB   *ptcb);
	void
	OSTaskDelHook(
	    OS_TCB *p_tcb);	

void OSTaskIdleHook(void);	void OSIdleTaskHook(void);	
	void OSTaskReturnHook(OS_TCB *p_tcb);	(2)
void OSTaskStatHook(void)	void OSStatTaskHook(void);	

void
OSTaskStkInit(
    void   (*task)(void *p_arg),
    void   *p_arg,
    OS_STK   *ptos,
    INT16U   opt);
	CPU_STK *
	OSTaskStkInit(
	    OS_TASK_PTR p_task,
	    void *p_arg,
	    CPU_STK *p_stk_base,
	    CPU_STK *p_stk_limit,
	    CPU_STK_SIZE size,
	    OS_OPT opt);
		(3)

void OSTaskSwHook(void)	void OSTaskSwHook(void);	

641

µC/OS-II (os_cpu*.c/h)	µC/OS-III (os_cpu*.c/h)	Note
void OSTCBInitHook(OS_TCB *ptcb);		(4)
void OSTimeTickHook(void);	void OSTimeTickHook(void);	
void OSStartHighRdy(void);	void OSStartHighRdy(void);	(5)
void OSIntCtxSw(void);	void OSIntCtxSw(void);	(5)
void OSCtxSw(void);	void OSCtxSw(void);	(5)

Table C-18 **Hooks and Port API**

TC-18(1)   µC/OS-III requires that the Board Support Package (BSP) provide a 32-bit free-running counter (from **0x00000000** to **0xFFFFFFFF** and rolls back to **0x00000000**) for the purpose of performing time measurements. When a signal is sent, or a message is posted, this counter is read and sent to the recipient. This allows the recipient to know when the message was sent. If a 32-bit free-running counter is not available, simulate one using a 16-bit counter.

TC-18(2)   µC/OS-III is able to terminate a task that returns. Recall that tasks should not return since they should be either implemented as an infinite loop, or deleted if implemented as run once.

TC-18(3)   The code for **OSTaskStkInit()** must be changed slightly in µC/OS-III since several arguments passed to this function are different than in µC/OS-II. Instead of passing the top-of-stack as in µC/OS-II, **OSTaskStkInit()** is passed the base address of the task stack, as well as the size of the stack.

TC-18(4)   This function is not needed in µC/OS-III.

TC-18(5)   These functions are a part of **OS_CPU_A.ASM**, and should only require name changes for the following variables:

µC/OS-II variable changes to ...	... in µC/OS-III
OSIntNesting	OSIntNestingCtr
OSTCBCur	OSTCBCurPtr
OSTCBHighRdy	OSTCBHighRdyPtr

Appendix

D

MISRA-C:2004 and μC/OS-III

MISRA C is a software development standard for the C programming language developed by the Motor Industry Software Reliability Association (MISRA). Its aims are to facilitate code safety, portability, and reliability in the context of embedded systems, specifically those systems programmed in ANSI C. There is also a set of guidelines for MISRA C++.

There are now more MISRA users outside of the automotive industry than within it. MISRA has evolved into a widely accepted model of best practices by leading developers in such sectors as aerospace, telecom, medical devices, defense, railway, and others.

The first edition of the MISRA C standard, "Guidelines for the use of the C language in vehicle based software," was produced in 1998 and is officially known as MISRA-C:1998. MISRA-C:1998 had 127 rules, of which 93 were required and 34 advisory. The rules were numbered in sequence from 1 to 127.

In 2004, a second edition "Guidelines for the use of the C language in critical systems," or MISRA-C:2004 was produced with many substantial changes, including a complete renumbering of the rules.

The MISRA-C:2004 document contains 141 rules, of which 121 are "required" and 20 are "advisory," divided into 21 topical categories, from "Environment" to "Run-time failures."

μC/OS-III follows most of the MISRA-C:2004 except that five (5) of the required rules were suppressed. The reasoning behind this is discussed within this appendix.

IAR Embedded Workbench for ARM (EWARM) V5.40 was used to verify MISRA-C:2004 compliance, which required suppressing the rules to achieve a clean build.

D

D-1 MISRA-C:2004, RULE 8.5 (REQUIRED)

Rule Description

There shall be no definitions of objects or functions in a header file.

Offending code appears as

```
OS_EXT    OS_IDLE_CTR    OSIdleTaskCtr;
```

`OS_EXT` allows us to declare "extern" and storage using a single declaration in `OS.H` but allocation of storage actually occurs in `OS_VAR.C`.

Rule suppressed

The method used in µC/OS-III is an improved scheme as it avoids declaring variables in multiple files. Storage for a variable must be declared in one file (such as `OS_VAR.C`) and another file needs to extern the variables in a separate file (such as `OS.H`).

Occurs in

OS.H

D-2 MISRA-C:2004, RULE 8.12 (REQUIRED)

Rule Description:

When an array is declared with external linkage, its size shall be stated explicitly or defined implicitly by initialization.

Offending code appears as

```
extern   CPU_STK        OSCfg_IdleTaskStk[];
```

µC/OS-III can be provided in object form (linkable object), but requires that the value and size of known variables and arrays be declared in application code. It is not possible to know the size of the arrays.

Rule suppressed

There is no choice other than to suppress or add a fictitious size, which would not be proper. For example, we could specify a size of 1 and the MISRA-C:2004 would pass.

Occurs in:

OS.H

D-3 MISRA-C:2004, RULE 14.7 (REQUIRED)

Rule Description

A function shall have a single point of exit at the end of the function.

Offending code appears as

```
if (argument is invalid) {
    Set error code;
    return;
}
```

Rule suppressed

We prefer to exit immediately upon finding an invalid argument rather than create nested "if" statements.

Occurs in

OS_CORE.C

OS_FLAG.C

OS_INT.C

OS_MEM.C

OS_MSG.C

OS_MUTEX.C

OS_PEND_MULTI.C

OS_PRIO.C

OS_Q.C

OS_SEM.C

OS_STAT.C

OS_TASK.C

OS_TICK.C

OS_TIME.C

OS_TMR.C

D

D-4 MISRA-C:2004, RULE 15.2 (REQUIRED)

Rule Description
An unconditional break statement shall terminate every non-empty switch clause.

Offending code appears as

```
switch (value) {
    case constant_value:
        /* Code */
        return;
}
```

Rule suppressed
The problem involves using a return statement to exit the function instead of using a break. When adding a "break" statement after the return, the compiler complains about the unreachable code of the "break" statement.

Occurs in
OS_FLAG.C
OS_MUTEX.C
OS_Q.C
OS_TMR.C

D-5 MISRA-C:2004, RULE 17.4 (REQUIRED)

Rule Description

Array indexing shall be the only allowed form of pointer arithmetic.

Offending code appears as

```
    :
  p_tcb++;
    :
```

Rule suppressed

It is common practice in C to increment a pointer instead of using array indexing to accomplish the same thing. This common practice is not in agreement with this rule.

Occurs in

OS_CORE.C

OS_CPU_C.C

OS_INT.C

OS_MSG.C

OS_PEND_MULTI.C

OS_PRIO.C

OS_TASK.C

OS_TICK.C

OS_TMR.C

D

Appendix

E

Bibliography

Bal Sathe, Dhananjay. 1988. *Fast Algorithm Determines Priority.* EDN (India), September, p. 237.

Comer, Douglas. 1984. *Operating System Design, The XINU Approach.* Englewood Cliffs, New Jersey: Prentice-Hall. ISBN 0-13-637539-1.

Kernighan, Brian W. and Dennis M. Ritchie. 1988. *The C Programming Language, 2nd edition.* Englewood Cliffs, New Jersey: Prentice Hall. ISBN 0-13-110362-8.

Klein, Mark H., Thomas Ralya, Bill Pollak, Ray Harbour Obenza, and Michael Gonzlez. 1993. *A Practioner's Handbook for Real-Time Analysis: Guide to Rate Monotonic Analysis for Real-Time Systems.* Norwell, Massachusetts: Kluwer Academic Publishers Group. ISBN 0-7923-9361-9.

Labrosse, Jean J. 2002, *MicroC/OS-II, The Real-Time Kernel,* CMP Books, 2002, ISBN 1-57820-103-9.

Li, Qing. *Real-Time Concepts for Embedded Systems,* CMP Books, July 2003, ISBN 1-57820-124-1.

The Motor Industry Software Reliability Association, *MISRA-C:2004,* Guidelines for the Use of the C Language in Critical Systems, October 2004. www.misra-c.com.

E

Appendix

F

Licensing Policy

This book contains µC/OS-III, precompiled in linkable object form, and is accompanied by an evaluation board and tools (compiler/assembler/linker/debugger). The user may use µC/OS-III with the evaluation board that accompanied the book and it is not necessary to purchase anything else as long as the initial purchase is used for educational purposes. Once the code is used to create a commercial project/product for profit, however, it is necessary to purchase a license.

It is necessary to purchase this license when the decision to use µC/OS-III in a design is made, not when the design is ready to go to production.

If you are unsure about whether you need to obtain a license for your application, please contact Micriµm and discuss the intended use with a sales representative.

Contact Micriµm

Micriµm
1290 Weston Road, Suite 306
Weston, FL 33326

+1 954 217 2036
+1 954 217 2037 (FAX)

E-Mail : sales@micrium.com
Website : www.micrium.com

F

µC/OS-III™
The Real-Time Kernel

and the
Texas Instruments
LM3S9B92

Jean J. Labrosse
and
The Stellaris Team

Micriµm
Press

Weston, FL 33326

Micriµm Press
1290 Weston Road, Suite 306
Weston, FL 33326
USA
www.micrium.com

Library of Congress Control Number: 2010922732

Library of Congress subject headings:

1. Embedded computer systems
2. Real-time data processing
3. Computer software - Development

For bulk orders, please contact Micriµm Press at: +1 954 217 2036

ISBN: 978-0-9823375-6-1

100-uCOS-III-TI-LM3S9B92-001

Foreword

In the almost 30 years that I have been active in the embedded systems industry, I have worked with everything from the smallest 8-bit processor to the latest of five generations of 32-bit processors. I have spent a great deal of time developing embedded processing boards, devices, and ASICs, as well as software tools, libraries, and real-time operating systems (RTOSs). During the first part of my tenure, commercial RTOSs were not widely used because they were very expensive, required royalty payments (read: access to your books), were only available in object form, and never had the BSP (HAL) you needed. Most developers wrote their own homegrown RTOS, the functions of which ranged from an event-loop to a simple scheduler to a monstrosity that no one understood anymore (the author left, and his four total comments apparently were not quite enough to decipher it).

In 1992, Jean Labrosse shocked the industry by writing an article in *Embedded Systems Programming* magazine explaining and showing the code to a really nice RTOS that was efficient and easy to understand. This groundbreaking event led to a new generation of RTOS vendors who licensed their products with source code and without royalties—finally making a commercial RTOS a reasonable option for many. It also opened the door to an open-source model for RTOS that has proved to be very successful. His follow-on book, *MicroC/OS-II: The Real-Time Kernel*, accomplished two interesting feats: it allowed users of RTOSs to better understand how they work as well as the trade-offs involved, resulting in better applications and implementations; and it laid bare many of the essentials of RTOS design to a larger number of developers, similar to the "dragon" book for compiler writers (*Principles of Compiler Design*, by Alfred Aho and Jeffrey D. Ullman). Prior to this book, most OS books gave RTOSs short shrift at best and were generally unreadable.

When I worked at ARM designing ARMv7-M (Cortex™-M3/M4), embedded operating systems were very much on my mind. I put a great deal of effort into ensuring that the new processor core would be able to work efficiently with RTOSs, knowing that the processor's system handling was usually the enemy of real-time OSs. I worked with Jean Labrosse as well as a few others to ensure that any instructions and facilities I added would be useful and optimal. µC/OS was quick to exploit most of those features, probably faster and more fully than any other RTOS. From the CLZ instruction (count leading zeros) to find the highest priority ready task, to PendSV/SVC (pended system call/system service call) for scheduling, to knowing that SysTick will be there for the base tick feature, µC/OS was able to immediately gain major advantage in performance and determinism. Micrium also was quick to take advantage of debug and test facilities to not only optimize the kernel but also allow the developer to optimize the application, including use of the specialized hardware in Cortex-M3.

Texas Instruments' Stellaris® family of microcontrollers, the first Cortex™-M3 implementation, was a natural fit for µC/OS. The StellarisWare® Peripheral Driver Library was leveraged by µC/OS from early on (so avoiding the dreaded BSP/HAL porting problem). As StellarisWare® added advanced communication facilities, µC/OS was quick to support these capabilities, greatly increasing the productivity of application developers by providing a stable base for development and allowing them to focus on their actual applications instead of middleware. I look forward to µC/OS taking advantage of even more capabilities of Cortex™-M3/M4 and Stellaris® products over the next few years.

As you read this book, I believe you will gain a good understanding of how your application and µC/OS work together, how to get the best determinism, how to avoid the pitfalls of high jitter and priority inversion, how to streamline data and task flow, and how to take advantage of the hardware and OS facilities to get the most from your application.

Paul Kimelman
Chief Architect, Stellaris Business Unit
Texas Instruments

Acknowledgements

STELLARIS® TEAM

■ Jonathan Guy—circuit design, *EVALBOT User's Guide*

■ David Yanoshak—mechanical design and board layout

■ Dan Nakoneczny, Kyle Norman, and Eric Ocasio—software examples

■ Wendell Smith—project planning

■ Rebecca Rostetter—board packaging

■ Sue Cozart, Denise Fischer—Part II Stellaris material

MICRIUM

■ Fabiano Kovalski—Code example setup and tests

Acknowledgements

1

Introduction

Part II of this book provides an example project that highlights the features of µC/OS-III with interactive hardware and software examples, IAR Embedded Workbench tools, and detailed instructions. The EVALBOT project is packaged with this book and contains everything you need to get the project running quickly.

1-1 EVALBOT OVERVIEW

The EVALBOT is a small robotic device that features a board with a Stellaris® LM3S9B92 microcontroller with Ethernet, USB OTG (On-The-Go), and I^{2}S. The kit contains wheels that are easy to attach to the board, a display, batteries, a USB cable, and a CD with the IAR tools, the StellarisWare® software, and all the necessary documentation. Figure 1-1 shows the top-side of the EVALBOT.

Figure 1-1 **Stellaris® EVALBOT Robot**

The board features include:

- Stellaris® LM3S9B92-IQC80 microcontroller

  - 256 KB Flash memory/96 KB SRAM

  - Ethernet

  - USB OTG

  - I^2S

- microSD card support

- I^2S audio codec with speaker

- USB 2.0 Host and Device connectors

- Ethernet 10/100 port with two LED indicators

- OLED graphics display

- Wireless communication expansion port

- On/Reset and Off buttons and power indicator LED

- Two application-defined buttons

- Left and right bump sensors

- Standard ARM® 10-pin JTAG debug connector for use as an In-Circuit Debug Interface (ICDI)

- I/O signal break-out pads for hardware prototyping

- Battery power through 3 AAA batteries or power through USB

The LM3S9B92 features high performance along with industrial connectivity, expanded peripheral interface connectivity, and low-power optimization for battery-backed applications. The LM3S9B92 provides a fully-integrated Ethernet with both MAC and PHY layers, 2 CAN 2.0 A/B controllers, and USB full-speed OTG or Host/Device with integrated PHY. Also included are two separate ADC units along with extended StellarisWare software in ROM, including the Peripheral Driver Library and Boot Loader, AES cryptography tables, and CRC error-detection functionality. The LM3S9B92 includes additional enhancements such as an internal 16-MHz precision oscillator with software trim capability, a second watchdog timer on an independent clock domain, and a uniquely flexible external peripheral interface (EPI), which is a 32-bit dedicated parallel bus for external peripherals that supports SDRAM, SRAM/Flash, and machine-to-machine up to 150 Mbytes/sec usage.

The StellarisWare software included in ROM is an extensive suite of software designed to simplify and speed development of Stellaris-based microcontroller applications and contains:

- Stellaris Peripheral Driver Library for peripheral initialization and control functions

- Stellaris® Boot Loader and vector table

- Advanced Encryption Standard (AES) cryptography tables

- Cyclic Redundancy Check (CRC) error detection functionality

StellarisWare also includes a wide array of example code and applications and can be used royalty-free on any Stellaris microcontroller.

1-2 CONTENTS OF PART II

Chapter 2, The ARM Cortex-M3 and Stellaris® Microcontrollers. This chapter provides an overview of the Stellaris implementation of the ARM Cortex-M3 CPU.

Chapter 3, Getting Started with the Stellaris® EVALBOT Evaluation Kit. This chapter explains how to connect the board to your PC and how to download the 32 K Kickstart version of the IAR Systems Embedded Workbench for ARM tools and how to run the example code.

Chapter 4, Stellaris® Robotic Evaluation Board (EVALBOT) User's Manual. This chapter provides a description of the EVALBOT evaluation board as well as complete schematics.

Chapter 5, Using the EVALBOT Examples. This chapter describes the steps you need to follow to get started with the examples for the EVALBOT. Once you have completed these basic steps, you can then get started with any of the examples that follow in the subsequent chapters.

Chapter 6, Simple Display Example with the EVALBOT. The example described in this chapter provides a simple example that displays various strings on the OLED display on a rotational basis. This simple project is designed to familiarize the user with the basic structure of µC/OS-III operating on the EVALBOT evaluation board.

Chapter 7, Using Audio with the EVALBOT. The example described in this chapter uses the EVALBOT evaluation board to play WAV files stored in the internal Flash memory of the LM3S9B92 microcontroller. This project demonstrates how µC/OS-III, in conjunction with the EVALBOT evaluation board, can be used to create an audio control application. Several small audio tracks are loaded into the Flash memory when this example is downloaded onto the board.

Chapter 8, Simple Control of the EVALBOT. This example shows how to control each motor independently using the user buttons. The motors are turned on and off using the buttons. If the bump sensor is pressed while the motor on that side is running, the motor turns off. µC/Probe can be used to turn the motors on and off, monitor the bump sensors, and variables such as CPU usage and motor speed.

Chapter 9, Autonomous Control of the EVALBOT. In this example, the EVALBOT is allowed to roam in an area. If the robot runs into anything, it will rotate and drive straight again. At random intervals, the robot rotates a random amount and then continues driving straight.

Appendix A, μC/OS-III Port for the Cortex-M3. This appendix explains how μC/OS-III was adapted to the Cortex-M3 CPU. The Cortex-M3 contains interesting features specifically designed for real-time kernels which μC/OS-III fully leverages.

Appendix B, μC/CPU Port to the Cortex-M3. This appendix describes how μC/CPU was adapted for the Cortex-M3.

Appendix C, IAR Systems Embedded Workbench for ARM. This appendix provides a description of IAR Systems Embedded Workbench for the ARM architecture (EWARM).

Appendix D, μC/Probe. This appendix provides a brief descriptions of Micriµm's award-winning μC/Probe, which easily allows users to display and change target variables at run time.

Appendix E, Bibliography

Appendix F, Licensing μC/OS-III

2

The ARM Cortex-M3 and Stellaris® Microcontrollers

The ARM Cortex family is a new generation of processor that provides a standard architecture for a wide range of technological demands. Unlike other ARM CPUs, the Cortex family is a complete processor core that provides a standard CPU and system architecture. The Cortex-M3 family is designed for cost-sensitive and microcontroller applications.

This chapter provides a brief summary of the Cortex-M3 architecture. Additional reference material is provided in Appendix E, "Bibliography" on page 839.

While ARM7 and ARM9 CPUs are successfully integrated into standard microcontrollers, they do show their SoC heritage. Each specific manufacturer has designed an interrupt handling solution. However, the Cortex-M3 provides a standardized microcontroller core, which goes beyond the CPU to provide the complete heart of a microcontroller (including the interrupt system, SysTick timer, debug system and memory map). The 4 Gbyte address space of Cortex-M3 is split into well-defined regions for code, SRAM, peripherals, and system peripherals. Unlike the ARM7, the Cortex-M3 is a Harvard architecture with multiple busses that allow it to perform operations in parallel, boosting overall performance. Unlike earlier ARM architectures, the Cortex family allows unaligned data access. This ensures the most efficient use of the internal SRAM. The Cortex family also supports setting and clearing of bits within two 1Mbyte regions of memory by a method called bit banding. This allows efficient access to peripheral registers and flags located in SRAM memory, without the need for a full Boolean processor.

One of the key components of the Cortex-M3 core is the Nested Vector Interrupt Controller (NVIC). The NVIC provides a standard interrupt structure for all Cortex-based microcontrollers and exceptional interrupt handling. The NVIC provides dedicated interrupt vectors for up to 240 peripheral sources so that each interrupt source can be individually prioritized. In the case of back-to-back interrupts, the NVIC uses a "tail chaining" method that allows successive interrupts to be serviced with minimal overhead. During the interrupt-stacking phase, a high-priority interrupt can preempt a low-priority interrupt without incurring additional CPU cycles. The interrupt structure is also tightly coupled to the low-power modes within the Cortex-M3 core.

Although the Cortex-M3 is designed as a low cost core, it is still a 32-bit CPU with support for two operating modes: Thread mode and Handler mode, which can be configured with their own stacks. This allows more sophisticated software design and support for such real-time kernels as μC/OS-II and μC/OS-III.

The Cortex core also includes a 24-bit auto reload timer that is intended to provide a periodic interrupt for the kernel. While the ARM7 and ARM9 CPUs have two instruction sets (the ARM 32-bit and Thumb 16-bit), the Cortex family is designed to support the ARM Thumb-2 instruction set. This blends both 16-bit and 32-bit instructions to deliver the performance of the ARM 32-bit instruction set with the code density of the Thumb 16-bit instruction set. The Thumb-2 is a rich instruction set designed as a target for C/C++ compilers. This means that a Cortex application can be entirely coded in C.

2-1 THE CORTEX CPU

The Cortex CPU is a 32-bit RISC CPU. This CPU has a simplified version of the ARM7/9 programmer's model, but a richer instruction set with good integer math support, better bit manipulation, and 'harder' real-time performance.

The Cortex CPU executes most instructions in a single cycle, which is achieved with a three-stage pipeline.

The Cortex CPU is a RISC processor featuring a load and store architecture. In order to perform data processing instructions, the operands must be loaded into CPU registers, the data operation must be performed on these registers, and the results saved back to memory. Consequently, all program activity focuses on the CPU registers.

As shown in Figure 2-1, the CPU registers consists of sixteen 32-bit wide registers. Registers R0-R12 can be used to hold variables or addresses. Registers R13-R15 have special functions within the Cortex CPU. Register R13 is used as a stack pointer. This register is banked, which allows the Cortex CPU to have two operating modes, each with their own separate stack space. In the Cortex CPU the two stacks are called the main stack (ISR stack) and the process stack (Task stack). The next register R14 is called the link register, and it is used to store the return address when a call is made to a function. This allows the Cortex CPU to make a fast entry and exit to a function. If the code calls several levels of subroutines, the compiler automatically stores R14 onto the stack. The final register R15 is the program counter. Since R15 is part of the CPU registers it can be read and manipulated like any other register.

Figure 2-1 **The Cortex-M3 CPU Registers**

2-1-1 THE PROGRAM STATUS REGISTER

In addition to the CPU registers there is a separate register called the Program Status Register (PSR). The PSR is not part of the main CPU registers and is only accessible through two dedicated instructions. The PSR contains a number of fields that influence the execution of the Cortex CPU. Refer to the Cortex-M3 Technical Reference Manual for details.

Figure 2-2 **The Cortex-M3 PSR Register**

While most Thumb-2 instructions execute in a single cycle, some (such as load and store instructions) take multiple cycles. To enable the Cortex CPU to have a deterministic interrupt response time, these instructions are interruptible.

2-1-2 STACKING AND INTERRUPTS

Tasks execute in Thread mode using the process stack; interrupts execute in Handler mode using the main stack. The task context is automatically saved on the process stack when an exception occurs, whereupon the processor moves to Handler mode, making the main stack active. On return from the exception, the task context is restored and Thread mode reinstated.

Figure 2-3 shows the stacking order of the CPU registers during an exception or interrupt. The software only needs to save/restore registers R4-R11 (if required by the Interrupt Service Routine); the other registers are saved automatically by hardware upon accepting the interrupt.

| R13 (SP_{process}) | Top-Of-Stack → |

Figure 2-3 **Cortex-M3 Register Stacking Order**

2-2 NESTED VECTOR INTERRUPT CONTROLLER (NVIC)

The Cortex-M3 includes not only the core CPU (ALU, control logic, data interface, instruction decoding, etc.), but also several integrated peripherals. Most important is the Nested Vectored Interrupt Controller (NVIC), designed for low latency, efficiency and configurability.

The NVIC saves half of the processor registers automatically upon interrupt, restoring them upon exit, which allows for efficient interrupt handling. Moreover, back-to-back interrupts are handled without saving/restoring registers (since that is unnecessary). This is called Tail Chaining.

The Stellaris implementation of the NVIC offers 8 priority levels, with dynamic priority assignment. The NVIC also is capable of handling between 1 and 240 external interrupt sources.

The NVIC is a standard unit within the Cortex core. This means that all Cortex-based microcontrollers have the same interrupt structure, regardless of the manufacturer. Therefore, application code and operating systems can be easily ported from one microcontroller to another, and the programmer does not need to learn a new set of registers. The NVIC is also designed to have very low interrupt latency. This is both a feature of the NVIC itself and of the Thumb-2 instruction set, which allows such multi-cycle instructions as load and store multiple to be interruptible.

The NVIC peripheral eases the migration between Cortex-M3 processors. This is particularly true for µC/OS-III.

2-3 EXCEPTION VECTOR TABLE

The Cortex vector table starts at the bottom of the address range. However, rather than start at zero, the vector table starts at address 0x00000004 and the first four bytes are used to store the starting address of the stack pointer. The vector table is shown in Table 2-1.

Each of the interrupt vector entries is four bytes wide and holds the start address of each service routine associated with the interrupt. The first 15 entries are for exceptions that occur within the Cortex core. These include the reset vector, non-maskable interrupt, fault and error management, debug exceptions, and the SysTick timer interrupt. The Thumb-2 instruction set also includes system service call instructions which, when executed, generate an exception. The user peripheral interrupts start from entry 16, and will be linked to peripherals as defined for the specific Stellaris microcontroller. In software, the vector table is usually maintained in the startup by locating the service routine addresses at the base of memory.

No.	Type	Priority	Description
1	Reset	-3	Reset
2	NMI	-2	Non-Maskable Interrupts
3	Hard Fault	-1	Default fault if other handler not implemented
4	MemManageFault	programmable	MPU violation
5	Bus Fault	programmable	Fault if AHB error
6	Usage Fault	programmable	Program error exception
7-10	Reserved		
11	SV Call	programmable	System Call Service

No.	Type	Priority	Description
12	Debug Monitor	programmable	Breakpoints, watchpoints, external debug
13	Reserved	N/A	
14	PendSV	programmable	Pendable request
15	SysTick	programmable	System tick timer
16	Interrupt #0	programmable	External interrupt #0
:	:	:	:
:	:	:	:
256	Interrupt #240	programmable	External interrupt #240

Table 2-1 **The Cortex-M3 Exception Table**

The PendSV vector is used by µC/OS-III to perform a context switch, while the SysTick vector is used by µC/OS-III for the clock tick interrupt.

2-4 SYSTICK (SYSTEM TICK)

The Cortex core includes a 24-bit down counter with auto reload and end of count interrupt, called the SysTick. The SysTick was designed to be used as an RTOS clock tick interrupt, and it is present in all Cortex implementations.

The SysTick timer has three registers. The current value and reload value should be initialized with the count period. The control and status register contains an ENABLE bit to start the timer running, and a TICKINT bit to enable its interrupt line.

The SysTick peripheral eases the migration between Cortex-M3 processors, which is particularly true for µC/OS-III.

2-5 MEMORY MAP

Unlike most previous ARM processors, the Cortex-M3 has a fixed-memory map as shown in Figure 2-4.

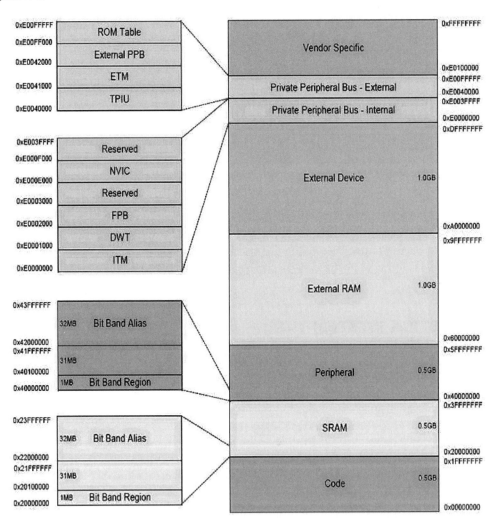

Figure 2-4 **Cortex-M3 Memory Map**

The first 1.0 Gbyte of memory is split evenly between a code region and an SRAM region. Although code can be loaded and executed from the SRAM, instructions would be fetched using the system bus, which incurs an extra wait state. It is likely that code would run slower from SRAM than from on-chip FLASH memory located in the code region.

The next 0.5 Gbyte of memory is the on-chip peripheral region. All user peripherals provided by the microcontroller vendor are located in this region.

The first Mbyte of both the SRAM and Peripheral regions is bit-addressable using a technique called bit banding. Since all SRAM and user peripherals on the processor are located in these regions, every memory location of the processor can be manipulated in a word-wide or bitwise fashion.

The next 2.0 Gbytes of address space is allocated to external memory-mapped SRAM and peripherals.

The final 0.5 Gbyte is allocated to the internal Cortex processor peripherals and a region for future vendor-specific enhancements to the Cortex processor. All Cortex processor registers are at fixed locations for all Cortex-based microcontrollers.

2-6 INSTRUCTION SET

The ARM7 and ARM9 CPUs execute two instruction sets: the ARM 32-bit instruction set and the Thumb 16-bit instruction set. This allows developers to optimize a program by selecting the instruction set used for different procedures: for example, 32-bit instructions for speed, and 16-bit instructions for code compression.

The Cortex CPU is designed to execute the Thumb-2 instruction set, which is a blend of 16-bit and 32-bit instructions. The Thumb-2 instruction set yields a 26% code density improvement over the ARM 32-bit instruction set, and a 25% improvement in performance over the Thumb 16-bit instruction set.

The Thumb-2 instruction set has improved multiply instructions, which can execute in a single cycle, and a hardware divide that takes between 2 – 7 cycles.

Of special interest to μC/OS-III is the Count Leading Zeros (CLZ) instruction, which greatly improves the scheduling algorithm, See Chapter 6, "The Ready List" on page 131 in Part I of this book.

2-7 DEBUGGING FEATURES

The Cortex core has a debug system called CoreSight as shown in Figure 2-5. The full CoreSight debug system has a Debug Access Port (DAP), which allows connection to the microcontroller by a JTAG tool. The debug tool can connect using the standard 4-pin JTAG interface or a serial 2-wire interface.

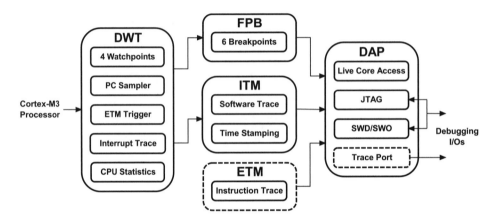

Figure 2-5 **Cortex-M3 CoreSight Debug System**

In addition to the JTAG debug features, the full CoreSight debug system contains a Data Watch Trace (DWT) and an Embedded Trace Macrocell (ETM). For software testing, there is Instrumentation Trace Macrocell (ITM) and Flash Patch Block (FPB). Stellaris microcontrollers implement the CoreSight debug system, but do not include the Embedded Trace Macrocell.

The CoreSight debug system provides six hardware breakpoints which can be non-intrusively set and cleared while the Cortex CPU is running. In addition, the Data Watch Trace allows you to view the contents of memory locations non-intrusively while the Cortex CPU runs. The CoreSight debug system can stay active when the Cortex core enters a low power or sleep mode. This makes a world of difference when debugging a low-power application. Additionally, the Stellaris timers can be halted when the CPU is halted by the CoreSight system. This allows you to single-step the code and keep the timers in synchronization with the instructions executing on the Cortex CPU.

The Data Watch Trace module also contains a 32-bit CPU cycle counter, which can be used to make time measurements. This is particularly interesting for µC/CPU, which can use this cycle counter for time stamping.

2-8 TEXAS INSTRUMENTS' STELLARIS® MICROCONTROLLERS

Stellaris® 32-bit microcontrollers combine sophisticated, flexible, mixed-signal system-on-chip integration with unparalleled real-time multi-tasking capabilities. Complex applications previously impossible with legacy microcontrollers can now be accommodated with ease by powerful, cost-effective, and simple-to-program Stellaris microcontrollers. With entry-level pricing at $1.00, the Stellaris product line allows for standardization that eliminates future architectural upgrades or software tools changes.

With single-cycle access to on-chip flash at speeds up to 50 MHz, Stellaris microcontrollers deliver 1.25 DMIPS/MHz – better than ARM7 and ARM9. In addition, Stellaris micro-controllers provide all the typical peripherals, such as timers, dual ADC modules, CAN 2.0, full speed USB Device/Host/OTG, I^2C, SPI, I^2S, Ethernet, QEI, and PWM modules. But the capabilities of these peripherals are far from typical. For example, Stellaris devices provide an Ethernet controller that has an integrated MAC and PHY, saving design time, board space, and cost. The GPIOs are highly capable with programmable drive strength, bit-addressable access, fast toggle speed (up to ½ the system clock), and various configurations. The External Peripheral Interface (EPI) extends these capabilities, offering efficient communication to off-chip SDRAM, Host-Bus devices, and FPGAs. The ADC modules have highly flexible digital comparators and can be closely linked to the powerful PWM units, enabling sophisticated motor control applications.

For safety-critical industrial and consumer applications, Stellaris microcontrollers offer integrated features such as high-reliability, automotive-grade Flash memory, up to two watchdog timers that take advantage of the non-maskable interrupt (NMI) handler safety feature of the ARM® Cortex™-M3 processor, and deterministic, fast interrupt processing through the nested vectored interrupt controller (NVIC). Some Stellaris family members also offer an integrated precision oscillator to supply an independent time base when periodic safety tests are executed. In addition, select Stellaris microcontrollers include ROM preloaded with a cyclic redundancy check (CRC) function, which is especially useful in verifying the contents of the Stellaris microcontroller's memory.

With Stellaris microcontrollers, all programming can be in C/C++, even interrupt service routines and startup code. StellarisWare® software support makes code development even easier with code and royalty-free libraries for applications support. The Stellaris Peripheral Driver Library provides a royalty-free set of peripheral drivers and can be used as applications examples or directly included in user applications as-is. In addition, all Stellaris microcontrollers ship with either a serial flash loader programmed into flash or a boot loader in ROM, providing maximum flexibility for production programming options. The royalty-free boot loader facilitates in-field updates for end applications, with flexible interface options and program signaling.

With all that is offered by Stellaris microcontrollers based on the Cortex™-M3, you may never have to switch architectures again!

Getting Started with the Stellaris® EVALBOT Evaluation Kit

The Stellaris EVALBOT Evaluation Kit provides a low-cost way to start designing simple robotic applications with Stellaris microcontrollers. The EVALBOT Evaluation Board (EVB) functions as a complete evaluation target that also includes a debugger interface that can be used to program and debug the evaluation board as well as any other external Stellaris device. The included USB cable is all that is needed to provide power and communication to the host PC. Three included AA batteries provide power for mobile applications.

3-1 REQUIREMENTS

■   You have a PC, with a USB interface, running Microsoft® Windows 2000, Windows XP, Windows Vista or Windows 7.

■   You have an Internet connection.

SOFTWARE DOWNLOAD

Before connecting the EVALBOT to your PC, download and install the supporting software and device drivers for the board. These can be found at `http://micrium.com/page/downloads/os-iii_files` listed under "µC/OS-III for TI Stellaris."

After downloading the file **Micrium-Book-uCOS-III-LM3S9B92.exe**, run it and unzip the contents to a directory on your hard disk.

3-2 DOWNLOADING µC/PROBE

µC/Probe is an award-winning Microsoft Windows-based application that allows users to display or change the value (at run time) of virtually any variable or memory location on a connected embedded target. See Appendix D, "Micriµm's µC/Probe" on page 773 for a brief introduction.

µC/Probe is used in all of the examples described in Chapter 3 to gain run-time visibility. There are two versions of µC/Probe:

The *Full Version* of µC/Probe is included with all µC/OS-III licenses. The Full Version supports J-Link, RS-232C, TCP/IP, USB, and other interfaces.

The *Full Version* allows users to display or change an unlimited number of variables.

The Trial Version is not time limited, but only allows users to display or change up to eight application variables. However, the trial version allows users to monitor any µC/OS-III variables because µC/Probe is µC/OS-III aware.

Both versions are available from Micriµm's website. Simply point your favorite browser to:

`www.Micrium.com/Books/Micrium-uCOS-III`

Follow the links to download the desired version (or both). If not already registered on the Micriµm website, you will be asked to do so. Once downloaded, execute the appropriate µC/Probe setup file:

`Micrium-uC-Probe-Setup-Full.exe`
`Micrium-uC-Probe-Setup-Trial.exe`

3-3 DOWNLOADING THE IAR EMBEDDED WORKBENCH FOR ARM

Examples provided with this book were tested using the IAR Embedded Workbench for ARM V5.5. You can download the 32K Kickstart version from the IAR website. This version allows users to create applications up to 32 Kbytes in size (excluding µC/OS-III). The file from IAR is about 400 MBytes. If you have a slow Internet connection or are planning to install a new version of Windows, you might want to consider archiving this file on a CD or even a USB drive.

You can download IAR tools from (case sensitive):

www.iar.com/MicriumuCOSIII

■ Click on the *Download IAR Embedded Workbench* >> link in the middle of the page. This will bring you to the '*Download Evaluation Software*' page on the IAR website.

■ Locate the "ARM" processor row and go to the "Kickstart edition" column on that same row and clock on the link for *v5.50 (32K)* link (or newer version if that's available). A page titled *KickStart edition of IAR Embedded Workbench* will be displayed.

■ After reading this page, simply click on *Continue....*

■ You will again be required to register. Unfortunately, the information you provided to register with Micriµm is not transferred to IAR and vice-versa. Fill out the form and click *Submit*.

■ Save the file to a convenient location.

■ You should receive a *License number and Key for EWARM-KS32* from IAR.

■ Double click on the IAR executable file (**EWARM-KS-WEB-5505.exe**) (or a similar file if newer) and install the files on the disk drive of your choice, at the root.

You can use the full version of the IAR Embedded Workbench if you are already a licensee.

3-4 BOARD SET-UP

Assuming you followed the assembly instructions you will, by now, have seen the EVALBOT driving around under battery power. The board can also be powered via a USB connection. This configuration would typically be used when downloading or debugging software on the board. To connect the EVALBOT to a PC, use the USB-miniB to USB-A cable supplied in the kit. Connect the miniB (smaller) end of the USB cable to the connector labeled "ICDI." Connect the other end (Type A) to a free USB port on your host PC. The USB is capable of sourcing up to 500 mA for each attached device, which is sufficient for the evaluation board. If connecting the board through a USB hub, it must be a powered hub. Once the board is connected to the PC, press the button marked "ON/RESET" next to the display on EVALBOT.

Important Note: The next step explains how to install the FTDI drivers for the board. Some customers with previous installations of the FTDI drivers may experience trouble when installing newer (2.02.04 and later) versions of the driver. The problem only seems to affect users of Windows XP, and not Windows Vista. If you have any problems with the driver installation, go to `http://www.ti.com/lm_ftdi_driver` for more information.

When you plug in the EVALBOT for the first time, Windows starts the Found New Hardware Wizard and asks if Windows can connect to Windows Update to search for software. Select "No, not this time" and then click Next.

Figure 3-1 **Found New Hardware Wizard**

Next, the Found New Hardware Wizard asks from where to install the software. Select "Install from a list or specific location (Advanced)" and click Next.

Figure 3-2 **Install from a specific location**

Select "Search for the best driver in these locations," and check the "Include this location in the search" option. Click the Browse button and navigate to the **FTDI-Stellaris** directory that was created when you unzipped the downloaded software package. If you unzipped the software into the root of your C: drive, for example, this would be **C:\Stellaris_FTDI-2_06_00**. Click Next.

Figure 3-3 **Search the CD-ROM**

Windows finishes installing the drivers for "Stellaris Evaluation Board A." When the driver install is finished, the Found New Hardware Wizard window appears like the one below. Click Finish to close the dialog box.

Figure 3-4 **Finished installing**

You have just installed the drivers for "Stellaris Evaluation Board A." The USB device built into the EVALBOT is a composite USB device. After you click Finish, Windows will automatically install a driver for the "Luminary Micro ICDI Stellaris Evaluation Board B" part of the composite USB device. Follow the same instructions as above to install the drivers for this device.

The Found New Hardware Wizard appears one last time. This is to install the drivers for the "Stellaris Virtual COM Port." Again, follow the same instructions to install the drivers for this device.

Now all of the FTDI drivers for the EVALBOT Evaluation Board have been installed. These drivers give the debugger access to the JTAG/SWD interface and the host PC access to the Virtual COM Port.

With the drivers installed, Windows will automatically detect any new Stellaris boards that you attach, and install the drivers for you.

3-5 QUICKSTART APPLICATION

The EVALBOT Evaluation Board comes preprogrammed with a quickstart application. Once you have powered the board by pressing the ON/RESET button, this application runs automatically. Press SWITCH1 to start the robot moving and SWITCH2 to stop the motion. The quickstart application provides autonomous control of the EVALBOT evaluation board using the motors and bump sensors on the board. This project demonstrates how µC/OS-III, in conjunction with the EVALBOT evaluation board, can be used to create an autonomous motor control application. The robot drives forward until either the robot bumps into something or a bounded random time value expires. If either of these events occur, the robot turns in a random direction and then continues driving forward.

The bump sensors on the front of the EVALBOT board are used to detect the robot bumping into something while driving forward. If the left bump sensor is triggered, the robot turns to the right and then continues driving forward. Conversely, if the right bump sensor is triggered, the robot turns to the left and then continues driving forward.

In addition to the bump sensors, a timer expiration event causes the robot to change directions while driving forward. A timer is configured to expire in a bounded random amount of time when the robot begins to drive forward. If the timer expires prior to bumping into something, the robot randomly chooses to turn to the left or right, and then continues driving forward.

For more information on how the application works, see Chapter 9, "Autonomous Control of the EVALBOT" on page 765.

3-6 SOFTWARE DEVELOPMENT TOOLS

The next step is to install and run the software development tools included in the development kit. For more information, see Chapter 5, "Using the EVALBOT Examples" on page 713. Additional tools may be available through the www.ti.com/stellaris web site.

3-7 REFERENCES

The following references are available for download at www.ti.com/stellaris:

- *StellarisWare® Peripheral Driver Library User's Manual*

- *Stellaris® LM3S9B92 Microcontroller Data Sheet*

Chapter

4

Stellaris® Robotic Evaluation Board (EVALBOT) User's Manual

4-1 BOARD OVERVIEW

The Stellaris® Robotic Evaluation Board (EVALBOT) is a robotic evaluation platform for the Stellaris LM3S9B92 microcontroller. The board also uses a range of Texas Instruments analog components for motor drive, power supply, and communications functions. The EVALBOT's electronics arrive ready-to-run. The board's robotics capabilities require less than 30 minutes of mechanical assembly. Figure 4-1 shows a photo of the EVALBOT.

Figure 4-1 **Stellaris® EVALBOT Robot**

4

When roaming, three AA batteries supply power to the EVALBOT. The EVALBOT automatically selects USB power when tethered to a PC as a USB device or when debugging. Test points are provided to all key EVALBOT signals. Two 20-pin headers enable future wireless communications using standardized Texas Instruments' low-power embedded radio modules (EM boards). Additional uncommitted microcontroller signals are available on break-out pads arranged in rows adjacent to the microcontroller.

The EVALBOT has factory-installed quickstart software resident in on-chip Flash memory. For software debugging and Flash programming, an integrated In-Circuit Debug Interface (ICDI) requires only a single USB cable for debug and serial port functions.

4-1-1 FEATURES

The EVALBOT board includes the following features:

■ Evaluation board with robotic capabilities

■ Mechanical components assembled by user

■ Stellaris® LM3S9B92-IQC80 microcontroller

■ MicroSD card connector

■ I^2S audio codec with speaker

■ USB Host and Device connectors

■ RJ45 Ethernet connector

■ Bright 96 x 6 Blue OLED display

■ On-board In-Circuit Debug Interface (ICDI)

■ Battery power (3 AA batteries) or power through USB

■ Wireless communication expansion port

■ Robot features

   ■ Two DC gear-motors provide drive and steering

   ■ Opto-sensors detect wheel rotation with 45° resolution

   ■ Sensors for "bump" detection

4-1-2 BLOCK DIAGRAM

The EVALBOT evaluation board uses the Stellaris® LM3S9B92 microcontroller and includes a 10/100 Ethernet port and a USB 2.0 full-speed On-the-Go (OTG) port. The EVALBOT combines all mechanical and electrical components on a single circuit board. Figure 4-2 shows a block diagram of the electrical section of the EVALBOT.

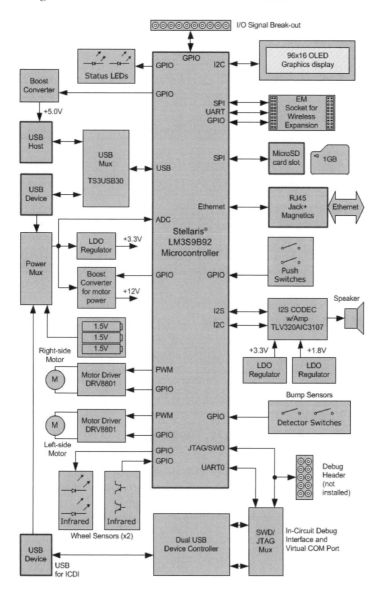

Figure 4-2 **EVALBOT Block Diagram**

4

4-1-3 SPECIFICATIONS

Table 4-1 shows the specifications for the EVALBOT.

Parameter	Min	Typical	Max
Battery Supply Voltage	3.5 V	4.5 V	5.0 V
USB Supply Voltage	4.0 V	5.0 V	5.25 V
Battery current (typical stationary)	–	100 mA	–
Battery current (typical in motion)	–	200 mA	–
Power down supply current		0.5 uA	
AA Alkaline Battery Capacity (typ)	–	2.5 A/Hr*	–
Reverse Battery Protection		No	
Allowable Battery/USB Current			0.5A

* From Energizer E91 data sheet.

Table 4-1 **EVALBOT Specifications**

4-2 HARDWARE DESCRIPTION

The EVALBOT consists of a 4-inch diameter circuit board populated with a Stellaris LM3S9B92 microcontroller and 14 additional Texas Instruments analog and digital semiconductors.

4-2-1 LM3S9B92 MICROCONTROLLER

The Stellaris LM3S9B92 is an ARM® Cortex™-M3-based microcontroller with 256-KB flash memory, 96-KB SRAM, 80-MHz operation, Ethernet MAC/PHY, USB Host/Device/OTG, and a wide range of other peripherals. See the LM3S9B92 microcontroller data sheet (order number DS-LM3S9B92) for complete device details.

Unused microcontroller signals are routed to either the 20-pin EM expansion headers or to 0.1" pitch break-out pads which are labeled with their GPIO reference. An internal multiplexer allows different peripheral functions to be assigned to each of these GPIO pads. When adding external circuitry, consideration should be given to the additional load on the EVALBOT's power rails.

The reference design may include additional components necessary to address silicon errata. For details of those circuit functions, see the LM3S9B92 Errata document.

4-2-2 CLOCKING

The EVALBOT uses a 16.0-MHz crystal (Y3) to complete the LM3S9B92 microcontroller's main internal clock circuit. An internal PLL, configured in software, multiples this clock to higher frequencies for core and peripheral timing.

A 25.0 MHz (Y1) crystal provides an accurate timebase for the Ethernet PHY.

4-2-3 RESET

The RESET signal into the LM3S9B92 microcontroller connects to the Reset/On switch (SW6) and to the ICDI circuit for a debugger-controlled reset.

External reset is asserted (active low) under any one of three conditions:

- Power-on reset (filtered by an R-C network)

- Reset/On push switch SW6 held down

- By the ICDI circuit when instructed by the debugger (this capability is optional, and may not be supported by all debuggers).

The OLED Module and Audio CODEC have special Reset timing requirements requiring a dedicated control line from the microcontroller.

4

4-2-4 POWER SUPPLIES

The EVALBOT can be powered either from batteries, the ICDI USB cable, or a USB device cable. The power source is determined by a Texas Instruments TPS2113 Auto Switching Power Mux and two Schottky diodes. Battery power is selected automatically when USB power is not present.

Table 4-2 shows the EVALBOT's power supplies. Each supply is generated directly or indirectly from the main power bus, +VS, using either a linear regulator or boost converter.

Name	Voltage	Max Current	Use
+VS	3.5 – 5.0 V	0.5 A	Main power distribution bus to other power rails
+3.3V	+3.3 V	150 mA	Logic power supply for main MCU, digital, and ICDI functions
+3.3VA	+3.3 V	150 mA	Analog and I/O power for audio CODEC
+1.8V	+1.8 V	25 mA	Digital/core power for audio CODEC
+5V_HVBUS	+5.25 V	100 mA	USB Host power supply
+12V	+12 V	100 mA	Motor driver power supply
+10V	+10 V	5 mA	OLED bias power supply

Table 4-2 **EVALBOT Power Supplies**

The board's on/off feature uses two push switches (SW5, SW6) and a simple feedback circuit through the inverter created by MOSFET Q3. An internal 1uA constant current source on the TPS2113's Enable pin (ENn) ensures that the TPS2113 is initially powered on when power is connected. Resistor R47 sets the overcurrent protection to 0.5 A.

4-2-5 ORGANIC LED DISPLAY

The user interface consists of a 96 x 16 OLED display and two push switches. The OLED display has an integrated controller IC with a parallel, SPI, and I^2C interfaces. In this design, the I^2C interface is used. The OLED display is limited to 'write-only' in this mode, so pixel data cannot be read back from the display

4-2-6 MICROSD CARD

EVALBOT includes a microSD card interface, which interfaces to the MCU using an SPI interface. Because power to the SD card is not controlled, removing or inserting the card while power is applied is not recommended.

4-2-7 AUDIO

A Texas Instruments TLV320AIC3107 CODEC adds a high performance audio stage to the EVALBOT. An integrated mono class-D amplifier drives an on-board speaker, with other audio inputs and outputs available on break-out header pads. An I2S interface carries the output (and input) audio data streams, while an I2C interface configures the CODEC. Most unused audio pins are available on nearby pads (0.05" pitch).

4-2-8 ETHERNET

With its fully integrated 10/100 Ethernet MAC and PHY, the LM3S9B92 requires only a standard Jack with integrated magnetics and a few passive components. The TX and RX signals are routed to the jack as a differential pair. The PHY incorporates MDI/MDI-X cross-over, so the function of the TX and RX pairs can be swapped in software.

4-2-9 USB

The LM3S9B92 microcontroller has Host, Device and OTG USB capabilities. EVALBOT supports USB Host and Device with dedicated connectors and a Texas Instruments T3USB30E high-speed USB multiplexer to select between them.

4-2-10 ROBOTIC FEATURES

Two 12-V gear motors provide locomotion to the EVALBOT. A Texas Instruments' DRV8801 Full-Bridge motor driver IC controls each motor; providing direction control, over-current and short-circuit protection, dead-time insertion and several switching schemes.

Each EVALBOT wheel has two infra-red optical sensors which generate a quadrature signal as the wheel rotates. The IR emitters (D2, D3, D11, and D12) each connect to a GPIO signal so that the MCU can turn off the LEDs for power saving when not in motion. The GPIO outputs should be configured for 8 mA drive-strength to ensure the IR emitters have sufficient intensity.

4

Left and right bumpers detect collisions using simple detector switches. The GPIO inputs should have internal pull-up resistors enabled and may optionally be configured to generate an interrupt when a collision occurs.

4-2-11 EXPANSION

The EM port on EVALBOT enables RF connectivity using a range of Low-Power RF Evaluation Modules (EM boards) from Texas Instruments. EM boards cover both sub 1-GHz and 2.4 GHz bands and are a supported by several different protocol stacks.

The EM port can also be used for general-purpose expansion. SPI, UART and GPIO signals are available. Table 4-3 lists the connector part numbers. Two identical connectors should be installed on a 1.20" pitch.

Supplier	Part Number	Description	Use
Samtec	TFM-110-02-S-D	SMT Header 20-pos 0.050" pitch	EVALBOT EM port
Samtec	SFM-110-02-S-D	SMT Socket 20-pos 0.050" pitch	EM board

Table 4-3 **Connector Part Numbers**

In additional to the EM port, EVALBOT also has 9 GPIO (PJ0..7, PE7), Power and GND connections on a 0.1" grid.

4-2-12 DEBUGGING

EVALBOT includes an integrated In-Circuit Debug Interface (ICDI) for debugging, serial communication and power over a single USB cable. Based on an FTDI FT2232 USB controller, the ICDI supports all major Cortex-M3 development environments.

Stellaris microcontrollers support programming and debugging using either JTAG or SWD. JTAG uses the signals TCK, TMS, TDI, and TDO. SWD requires fewer signals (SWCLK, SWDIO, and, optionally, SWO for trace). The debugger determines which debug protocol is used.

An external debug interface can be used with EVALBOT if connector J4 is installed by the user.

JTAG/SWD

The FT2232 is factory-configured by Texas Instruments to implement a JTAG/SWD port (synchronous serial) on channel A and a Virtual COM Port (VCP) on channel B. This feature allows two simultaneous communications links between the host computer and the target device using a single USB cable. Separate Windows drivers for each function can be found in the directory created by downloading, unzipping, and running the `Micrium-Book-uCOS-III-LM3S9B92.exe` file, see section 3-1 "Requirements" on page 679

The In-Circuit Debug Interface USB capabilities are completely independent from the LM3S9B92's on-chip USB functionality.

A small serial EEPROM holds the FT2232 configuration data. The EEPROM is not accessible by the LM3S9B92 microcontroller. For full details on FT2232 operation, go to www.ftdichip.com.

The FT2232 USB device performs JTAG/SWD serial operations under the control of the debugger. A simple logic circuit multiplexes SWD and JTAG functions and, when working in SWD mode, provides direction control for the bidirectional data line.

VIRTUAL COM PORT

The Virtual COM Port (VCP) allows Windows applications (such as HyperTerminal) to communicate with UART0 on the LM3S9B92 over USB. Once the FT2232 VCP driver is installed, Windows assigns a COM port number to the VCP channel.

SERIAL WIRE OUT

EVALBOT also supports the Cortex-M3 Serial-Wire Output (SWO) trace capabilities. Under debugger control, on-board logic can route the SWO data stream to the VCP transmit channel. The debugger software can then decode and interpret the trace information received from the Virtual Com Port. The normal VCP connection to UART0 is interrupted when using SWO. Not all debuggers support SWO.

See the *Stellaris LM3S9B92 Microcontroller Data Sheet* for additional information on the Trace Port Interface Unit (TPIU).

4

4-3 SCHEMATICS

Schematics for the EVALBOT board follow.

Figure 4-3 **EVALBOT Schematic (page 1)**

Figure 4-4 **EVALBOT Schematic (page 2)**

Figure 4-5 **EVALBOT Schematic (page 3)**

Figure 4-6 **EVALBOT Schematic (page 4)**

Figure 4-7 **EVALBOT** Schematic (page 5)

4

4-4 COMPONENT LOCATIONS

Plots of the top-side and bottom-side component locations are shown in Figure 4-8.

Figure 4-8 **EVALBOT Component Locations**

4

4-5 BILL OF MATERIALS (BOM)

Table 4-4 shows the Bill of Materials for the EVALBOT board design.

Item	Reference	Qty	Part Number	Description	Mfg	Supplier	Stock
1	BAT1-3	3	1028	Compact AA Battery holder, through-hole	Keystone	Digikey	1028K-ND
2	C1 C11 C24-25 C27 C33-34 C39 C43 C54 C55 C56 C62	13	C2012X5R1E105K	Capacitor, 1.0uF 25V 10% X5R 0805	TDK	Digikey	445-1419-2-ND
3	C15 C35 C41 C44 C48	5	C0603C103J5RACTU	Capacitor, 0.01uF 50V 5% 0603 X7R	Kemet	Mouser	80-C0603C103J5R
4	C2	1	C0603C102J5RACTU	Capacitor , 0.001uF 50V 5% 0603 X7R	Kemet	Mouser	80-C0603C102J5R
5	C3 C5-6 C8-10 C12-14 C16-19 C21-23 C26 C30-31 C36-37 C46 C49-50 C52-53 C57-59 C61 C65	31	GRM188R71H104KA93D	Capacitor, 0.1uF 50V 10% 0603 X7R	TDK	Digikey	490-1519-2-ND
6	C4 C28-29 C38 C40 C42 C45 C47 C51 C60	10	C0603C100J5GACTU	Capacitor 10pF 50V 5% Ceramic NPO/COG 0603	Kemet	Mouser	80-C0603C100J5G

Item	Reference	Qty	Part Number	Description	Mfg	Supplier	Stock
7	C20 C32	2	C0603C270J5GACTU	Capacitor 27pF 50V 5% Ceramic NPO/COG 0603	Kemet	Mouser	80-C0603C270J5G
8	C7 C63-64	3	C3225X5R1C106M	Capacitor, 10uF 16V 20% X5R 1210	TDK	Digikey	445-1400-2-ND
9	D5 D8-9	3	LTST-C171GKT	LED, 0805 SMT Green	LiteOn	Mouser / Arrow	LTST-C171GKT
10	D2-3 D11-12	4	APECVA3010F3C	LED, Infrared, Right Angle in 3.0 x 1.0mm SMT	Kingbright	Digikey	754-1363-2-ND
11	D4 D6-7	4	SS12	Diode, Schottky 20V 1A SMA	Taiwan Semi	Mouser	821-SS12
12	D10	1	BAS40-05-7-F	Diode, Schottky 40V 100mA SOT23	Diodes	Digikey	BAS40-05-FDICT-ND
13	J1	1	HR961160C J3011G21DNLT	Connector, RJ45 with 10/100 magnetics, shielded SMT	Hanrun Pulse	Hanrun Arrow Mouser	HR961160C J3011G21DNL
14	J2	1	2908-05WB-MG	Connector, Micro SD card, push-push SMT	3M	Mouser	517-2908-05WB-MG
15	J3 J6	2	54819-0572	Connector, USB Mini-B SMT 5pin	Molex	Mouser	538-54819-0572
16	J7	1	AU-Y1006-R 154-UAR42-E	Connector, USB Type A	Assmann Kobiconn	Digikey Mouser	AE9924-ND 154-UAR42-E
17	J8 J13	2	DF13C-2P-1.25V(20)	Connector, Header 2 pos, 1.25mm SMD Tin	Hirose	Digikey	H3419-ND
18	K1	1	AST-01508MR-R	Speaker, 8 ohm 0.3W 15mm PCB mount	Projects Unlimited	Digikey	668-1132-ND
19	L1-2	2	VLF4012AT-4R7M1R1	Inductor 3.7x3.5 SMT 1.1A	TDK	Digikey	445-3235-2-ND
20	Q1-2 Q4-5	4	APA3010P3BT	Phototransistor, Infrared, Right Angle in 3.0 x 1.0mm SMT	Kingbright	Digikey	754-1067-2-ND

Item	Reference	Qty	Part Number	Description	Mfg	Supplier	Stock
21	Q3 Q6	2	BSS123LT1	MOSFET, N-Channel 100V 170mA SOT-23	On Semi	Digikey	BSS123LT1GOSTR-ND
22	R11 R52	2		Resistor 1 ohms 1% 0603	Generic	Digikey	311-1.00HRTR-ND
23	R19, R22	2		Resistor 27 ohms 5% 0603	Generic	Digikey	311-27GRTR-ND
24	R1-2 R57-58	4		Resistor 2.7K 5% 0603	Generic	Digikey	311-2.7KGRTR-ND
24	R13	1		Resistor 22.6K 1% 0603	Generic	Digikey	311-22.6KHRTR-ND
25	R14 R18 R23-24 R36 R40 R44-45 R49 R60-62	12		Resistor 10K 5% 0606	Generic	Digikey	311-10KGRTR-ND
26	R39	1		Resistor 9.10K 1% 0603	Generic	Digikey	311-9.10KHRTR-ND
27	R21 R25	2		Resistor 1.0M 1% 0603	Generic	Digikey	311-1.00MHRTR-ND
28	R26 R53	2		Resistor 137K 1% 0603	Generic	Digikey	311-137KHRTR-ND
29	R29	1		Resistor 12.4K 1% 0603	Generic	Digikey	311-12.4KHRTR-ND
30	R5, R64	2		Resistor, 10 ohms 5% 0603	Generic	Digikey	311-10GRTR-ND
31	R31-33 R35 R43	5		Resistor 49.9 ohms 1% 0603	Generic	Digikey	311-49.9HRTR-ND
32	R3-4 R54-55	4		Resistor 120 ohms 1% 0603	Generic	Digikey	311-120HRTR-ND
33	R10, R12, R38	3		Resistor 0 ohms 0603	Generic	Digikey	311-0.0GRTR-ND

Item	Reference	Qty	Part Number	Description	Mfg	Supplier	Stock
34	R16-17 R34 R37 R47 R63	6		Resistor 1K 5% 0603	Generic	Digikey	311-1.0KGRTR-ND
35	R7, R59	2		Resistor 1.5K 5% 0603	Generic	Digikey	311-1.5KGRTR-ND
36	R15 R20 R30 R41 R48 R50	6		Resistor 330 ohms 5% 0603	Generic	Digikey	311-330GRTR-ND
37	R56	1		Resistor 1.30M 1% 0603	Generic	Digikey	P1.30MHTR-ND
38	R6	1		Resistor 47K 5% 0603	Generic	Digikey	311-47KGRTR-ND
39	R8 R27-28	3		Resistor 200K 1% 0603	Generic	Digikey	311-200KGRTR-ND
40	R9 R42 R46 R51	4		Resistor 100K 1% 0603	Generic	Digikey	P100KHTR-ND
41	SW3	1	ESE-22MH22	Switch, Detector-style Horizontal - Right/top actuation	Panasonic	Digikey	P13583STR-ND
42	SW4	1	ESE-22MH24	Switch, Detector-style Horizontal - Left/top actuation	Panasonic	Digikey	P13584STR-ND
43	SW1-2 SW5-6	2	EVQ-Q2B02W	Switch, Tact 6mm SMT, 50gf	Panasonic	Digikey	P12931STR-ND
44	U3	1	FT2232D	IC, USB to Serial Interface TQFP48	Ftdi	Ftdi	FT2232D
45	U15	1	CAT93C46YI-G / AT93C46A-10TU-2.7	IC, Serial Eeprom 1Kbit TSSOP8	Catalyst Atmel	Mouser Digikey	CAT93C46YI-G
46	Y1	1	NX5032GA-25.000000MHZ 8B48-25.000MHZ TR	Crystal, 25.00MHz 5.0x3.2mm SMT	NDK Suntsu	Digikey	644-1041-2-ND
47	Y2	1	FOXSDLF/060-20	Crystal, 6.00MHz HC49US SMT	Fox	Mouser /Digikey	559-FOXSD060-20-LF 631-1008-2-ND

4

Item	Reference	Qty	Part Number	Description	Mfg	Supplier	Stock
48	Y3	1	NX5032GA-16.000000MHZ	Crystal, 16.00MHz 5.0x3.2mm SMT	tbd	Digikey	644-1037-2-ND
49	J5 J33	2	TFM-110-02-S-D-K-A	Connector, 20 pos 1.27mm pitch, SMT	Samtec	Samtec	TFM-110-02-S-D-K-A
50	U1	1	LM3S9B92-IQC80	IC, ARM Cortex-M3 Microcontroller TQFP100	TI	TI	LM3S9B92-IQC80
51	U2 U13	2	DRV8801RTY	IC, Full-Bridge Motor Driver	TI	TI	DRV8801RTY
52	U4	1	TLV320AIC3107IRSBR	IC, Audio CODEC with class D amplifier WQFN	TI	TI	TLV320AIC3107IRSBR
53	U5	1	TLV70018DDCT	IC, 1.8V 200mA Low-dropout voltage regulator	TI	TI	TLV70018DDCT
54	U6 U10	2	TLV70033DDCT	IC, 3.3V 200mA Low-dropout voltage regulator	TI	TI	TLV70033DDCT
55	U7	1	TPS71501DCKR	IC, Adjustable 50mA Low-dropout voltage regulator, SC70	TI	TI	TPS71501DCKR
56	U8	1	RGS08096016BW001	OLED display, 96x16 Blue 13701	RiT	RiT	13701
57	U9	1	TPS61085PWR	IC, Step-up DC-DC Converter	TI	TI	TPS61085PWR
58	U11	1	TS3USB30EDGSR	IC, High Speed USB 2.0 1:2 Mux/Demux Switch SSOP	TI	TI	TS3USB30EDGSR
59	U12	1	TPS2113PW	IC, 2-Ch Auto-switching power mux	TI	TI	TPS2113PW
60	U14	1	TPS61073DDC	IC, Synchronous Boost Converter with 600-mA switch	TI	TI	TPS61073DDC
61	U17	1	SN74LVC126ARGY	IC, Quad tri-state line driver act lo TSSOP14	TI	Digikey	296-8458-1-ND
62	U19 U20	2	SN74LVC125ARGY	IC, Quad tri-state line driver act hi TSSOP14	TI	Digikey	296-1222-1-ND
63	PCB1	1	PCB-EVALBOT-A	PCB, 4-layer 5.200x6.850"			

Item	Reference	Qty	Part Number	Description	Mfg	Supplier	Stock
64	LABEL1	1	LABEL-EVALBOT	Label, 2.90" x 0.50" "Learn more at www.ti.com/EvalBot". Place on robot underside.			
		189					
	Do not fit these components:		J4, U16				

Mechanical Items

Item	Reference	Qty	Part Number	Description	Mfg	Supplier	Stock No
M1		2	KM-12FN20	Motor, 100RPM 12V with Gearbox	Kinmore	Kinmore	KM-12FN20
M2		4	621K-ND	L-bracket Steel 4-40 threaded	Keystone	Digikey	621K-ND
M3		2	FC4532-440-A	Hex Standoff 3/8" 4-40 Male-Female	Fascomp	Mouser	728-FC4532-440-A
M4		2	90003A005	Acorn Nut 4-40 9/32" Black Nylon	McMaster	McMaster	90003A005
M5		8	90272A103	Screw 4-40 Steel 1/8" Phillips	McMaster	McMaster	90272A103
M6		2	90272A105	Screw 4-40 Steel 3/16" Phillips	McMaster	McMaster	90272A105
M7		2	90272A106	Screw 4-40 Steel 1/4" Phillips	McMaster	McMaster	90272A106
M8		4	92005A002	Screw M1.6 x 3mm Steel Phillips	McMaster	McMaster	92005A002
M9		2	90633A005	Nut 4-40 Thin Nylock for bumpers	McMaster	McMaster	90633A005
M10		2	9452K72	O-Ring 1/16" x 3/4" Size -018 Buna 70	McMaster	McMaster	9452K72
M11		6	91375A105	Set Screw, 4-40 Steel 3/16" Hex	McMaster	McMaster	91375A105
M12		1	7122A13	Hex L-Key 0.050"	McMaster	McMaster	7122A13

Item	Reference	Qty	Part Number	Description	Mfg	Supplier	Stock
M13		2	H4BBT-10103-R8-ND	Wire, Red 3" 28 AWG with DF13 contact one end	Digikey	Digikey	H4BBT-10103-R8-ND
M14		2	H4BBT-10103-B8-ND	Wire, Black 3" 28 AWG with DF13 contact one end	Digikey	Digikey	H4BBT-10103-R8-ND
M15		2	DF13-2S-1.25C	Connector Socket Housing DF13 2 pos 1.25MM	Digikey	Digikey	H2179-ND

Table 4-4 **Bill of Materials**

4-6 REFERENCES

In addition to this document, the following references are available for download at www.ti.com/stellaris.

- *Stellaris LM3S9B92 Microcontroller Data Sheet*

- *DMOS Full-Bridge Motor Drivers Data Sheet (DRV8801RTY)*

- *Low-Power Stereo CODEC with Integrated Mono Class-D Amplifier Data Sheet (TLV320AIC3107)*

- *200mA, Low IQ, Low Dropout Regulator for Portables Data Sheet (TLV70018)*

- *200mA, Low IQ, Low Dropout Regulator for Portables Data Sheet (TLV70033)*

- *50mA, 24V, 3.2-μA Supply Current, Low-Dropout Linear Regulator in SC70 Package Data Sheet (TPS71501)*

- *650 kHz/1.2MHz Step-Up DC-DC Converter w/ Forced PWM Mode Data Sheet (TPS61085)*

- *High-Speed USB 2.0 (480 Mbps) 1:2 Multiplexer/Demultiplexer Switch With Single Enable Data Sheet (TS3USB30)*

- *Dual In/Single Out Autoswitching Power MUX Data Sheet (TPS2113)*

- *Adjustable, 600-mA Switch, 90% Efficient PFM/PWM Boost Converter in ThinSOT Data Sheet (TPS61073)*

The following data sheets can be obtained from the manufacturer:

- *P13701 OLED Display Data Sheet from RiT Display Corporation*

- *SSD1300 OLED Controller Data Sheet from Solomon Systech Limited*

Using the EVALBOT Examples

This chapter describes the steps you need to follow to get started with the examples for the EVALBOT. Once you have completed these basic steps, you can then get started with any of the following examples:

- Chapter 6, "Simple Display Example with the EVALBOT" on page 723

- Chapter 7, "Using Audio with the EVALBOT" on page 733

- Chapter 8, "Simple Control of the EVALBOT" on page 749

- Chapter 9, "Autonomous Control of the EVALBOT" on page 765

See section 1-8 "Conventions" on page 35 for details on the conventions used for the code listings in this book.

5-1 OPENING THE PROJECT

Start the IAR Embedded Workbench for ARM IDE. Select File > Open > Workspace as shown in Figure 5-1 to open the following workspace:

\Micrium\Software\EvalBoards\TI\LM3S9B92-EVALBOT\IAR\uCOS-LM3S9B92-EVALBOT.eww

Figure 5-1 **Open the uCOS-LM3S9B92-EVALBOT.eww Workspace**

In the workspace explorer window, select the tab for the project you want to open. This example shows the uCOS-III-Ex3 tab. The workspace window shows all of the files in the corresponding project. The files within the project are sorted into groups represented by folder icons in the workspace window. Figure 5-2 shows the project files for uCOS-III-Ex3 in the workspace explorer window.

Figure 5-2 **uCOS-III-Ex3 Project in Workspace Explorer Window**

F5-2(1)   The **APP** group includes all of the application files for this example. The subgroup **CFG** includes the header files used to configure the application.

F5-2(2)   The **BSP** group contains the files that comprise the board support package. The board support package includes the code used to control the peripherals on the board. For this example, the software to control the LEDs, pushbuttons, bump sensors, and motors will be used.

F5-2(3)   The **CFG – LIBRARIES** group includes the header files used to configure the µC/CPU, µC/LIB, and µC/OS-III libraries included in this project.

F5-2(4)   The **CPU** group includes the Stellaris family's peripheral driver library. The peripheral driver library contains the drivers and header files needed to control all of the peripherals for the Stellaris family of microcontrollers.

F5-2(5)   The **uC/CPU** group contains the µC/CPU precompiled library as well as the header files used to describe the contents of the library.

F5-2(6)   The **uC/LIB** group contains the µC/LIB precompiled library as well as the header files used to describe the contents of the library.

F5-2(7)   The **µC/OS-III** group contains the µCOS-III precompiled library and the header files used to describe the contents of the library. In addition, the **OS_CFG_APP.C** and **OS_DBG.C** files are included in this group to allow certain behavior to be defined at compile time.

F5-2(8)   The **µC/Probe** group includes the source code that defines how the application communicates with µC/Probe. µC/Probe will be discussed later in this chapter.

F5-2(9)   The **Output** group contains the files generated by the compiler/linker.

5-2 RUNNING THE PROJECT

Note: To run this project, raise the EVALBOT so that the wheels are not touching any surface. Doing so will keep the EVALBOT from moving, while still testing the functionality of the project.

You can run this project in one of two ways:

■ **Connected to the PC when using the IAR Embedded Workbench debugger or µC/Probe**
When doing this, raise the EVALBOT so that the wheels are not touching any surface. Doing so keeps the EVALBOT from moving around while running the project.

- **Disconnected from the PC**

  The EVALBOT must first be connected to the PC to program the example application into the LM3S9B92 microcontroller using IAR Embedded Workbench. After this, the EVALBOT can be disconnected from the PC and placed on the ground so that it can move around freely.

To run the project using either of these methods, you must do the following steps which are described in more detail on the following pages.

STEP 1: CONNECT THE EVALBOT TO YOUR PC

Connect the EVALBOT to your PC. Connect the Mini-B end of the USB cable provided in the kit to the ICDI USB connector on the EVALBOT. Connect the other end of the USB cable to a free USB port on your PC.

STEP 2: BUILD THE PROJECT

Select Project > Make in IAR Embedded Workbench as shown in Figure 5-3.

Figure 5-3 **Building the Project**

5

STEP 3: RUN AND DEBUG THE APPLICATION

Start the debugger by clicking the "Download and Debug" icon as shown in Figure 5-4. The application is programmed to the internal Flash of the LM3S9B92 microcontroller and the debugger starts. The code automatically starts executing and stops at the **main()** function in the **APP.C** file.

Figure 5-4 **Downloading the Application and Starting the Debugger**

If you want to run the EVALBOT while disconnected from the PC, stop the debugger by clicking the "Stop" icon, as shown in Figure 5-5, now that the internal flash has been programmed. You can disconnect the EVALBOT board from the PC and place it on the floor. Press the SWITCH1 pushbutton to start moving the EVALBOT. To learn how the project works, move on to the next section.

If you want to continue using the debugger or μC/Probe, leave the EVALBOT connected to the PC while raised so that the wheels are not touching any surface.

Start the application by clicking the "Go" icon as shown in Figure 5-5. Once the application is running, use the SWITCH1 pushbutton to start running the motors. Push the button again to stop the motors. You can trigger the bump sensors which simulates the EVALBOT bumping into something to test the behavior.

Click the "Stop" icon to stop the application. To reset the application, click the "Reset" icon. See Figure 5-5 and Figure 5-6 for details. The other icons can be used to step through the application.

Figure 5-5 **Go and Reset Icons**

Figure 5-6 **Stop Icon**

5-3 MONITORING VARIABLES USING μC/PROBE

Click the "Go" icon in IAR Embedded Workbench (see Figure 5-5) to run the application.

Start μC/Probe and open the μC/Probe workspace for your project. The workspace filenames end with **.wsp**. You can find the workspace files in the following directory:

`\Micrium\Software\EvalBoards\TI\LM3S9B92-EVALBOT\IAR\`

After µC/Probe starts, click the run button. Once µC/Probe is running, you will see a screen similar to the one shown in Figure 5-7.

Figure 5-7 **µC/Probe Monitoring Example 3 Application**

The µC/Probe workspace is configured to allow monitoring of the CPU usage, the current state of both the left and right motors, and the state of the LEDs on the board. In addition, the operating system statistics can be viewed in real time using the µC/OS-III tab as shown in Figure 5-8 on page 721.

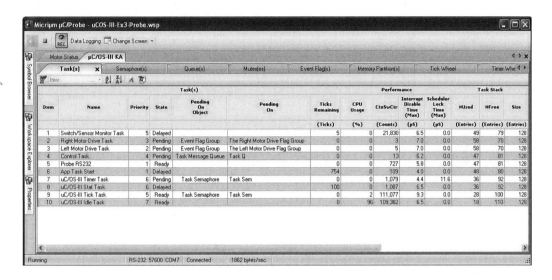

Figure 5-8 **µC/Probe Monitoring Example 3 OS Statistics**

5-4 SUMMARY

You are now ready to start using the following Stellaris examples:

- Chapter 6, "Simple Display Example with the EVALBOT" on page 723

- Chapter 7, "Using Audio with the EVALBOT" on page 733

- Chapter 8, "Simple Control of the EVALBOT" on page 749

- Chapter 9, "Autonomous Control of the EVALBOT" on page 765

6

Simple Display Example with the EVALBOT

The example described in this chapter provides a simple example that displays various strings on the OLED display on a rotational basis. This simple project is designed to familiarize the user with the basic structure of µC/OS-III operating on the EVALBOT evaluation board.

This example uses one task to toggle the LEDs once per second and a second task to display one of three messages for 5 seconds, clear the display for 1 second, and then display the next message.

6-1 HOW THE PROJECT WORKS

The code for the **main()** function is shown in Listing 6-1.

```
void  main (void)
{
    OS_ERR  err;


    BSP_IntDisAll();                                              (1)


    OSInit(&err);                                                 (2)

    OSTaskCreate((OS_TCB     *)&AppTaskStartTCB,                  (3)
                 (CPU_CHAR    *)"App Task Start",
                 (OS_TASK_PTR ) AppTaskStart,
                 (void        *) 0,
                 (OS_PRIO     ) APP_TASK_START_PRIO,
                 (CPU_STK     *)&AppTaskStartStk[0],
                 (CPU_STK_SIZE) APP_TASK_START_STK_SIZE / 10u,
                 (CPU_STK_SIZE) APP_TASK_START_STK_SIZE,
                 (OS_MSG_QTY  ) 0u,
                 (OS_TICK     ) 0u,
                 (void        *) 0,
                 (OS_OPT      )(OS_OPT_TASK_STK_CHK | OS_OPT_TASK_STK_CLR),
                 (OS_ERR      *)&err);

    OSStart(&err);                                                (4)
}
```

Listing 6-1 **main() in APP.C**

L6-1(1)   The first step in the **main()** function calls the **BSP_IntDisAll()** function. The code for this function is located in the **BSP_INT.C** file and simply calls the **CPU_IntDis()** function to disable all of the interrupts to the CPU.

L6-1(2)   The **OSInit()** function is then called to initialize the µC/OS-III operating system.

L6-1(3)   The **OSTaskCreate()** function is called to create the **AppTaskStart** task.

L6-1(4)   The **OSStart()** function is called to start operation of the multitasking operating system.

Listing 6-2 shows the code for the **AppTaskStart()** task and Figure 6-1 on page 727 shows a diagram for the application tasks interaction.

```
static  void  AppTaskStart (void  *p_arg)
{
    CPU_INT32U  clk_freq;
    CPU_INT32U  cnts;
    OS_ERR      err;


    BSP_Init();                                              (1)
    CPU_Init();                                              (2)

    clk_freq = BSP_CPU_ClkFreq();                            (3)
    cnts     = clk_freq / (CPU_INT32U)OSCfg_TickRate_Hz;
    OS_CPU_SysTickInit(cnts);

#if (OS_CFG_STAT_TASK_EN > 0u)
    OSStatTaskCPUUsageInit(&err);                            (4)
#endif

    CPU_IntDisMeasMaxCurReset();                             (5)

    App_ProbeInit();                                         (6)

    BSP_LED_On(1);                                           (7)
    BSP_LED_Off(2);

    AppDisplayTaskCreate();                                  (8)

    while (DEF_ON) {                                         (9)
        OSTimeDlyHMSM(0u, 0u, 1u, 0u,                        (10)
                      OS_OPT_TIME_HMSM_STRICT,
                      &err);
        BSP_LED_Toggle(0);                                   (11)
    }
}
```

Listing 6-2 **AppTaskRobotStart() in APP.C**

L6-2(1)   The **BSP_Init()** function initializes the CPU peripherals and signals used with this board.

L6-2(2)   The **CPU_Init()** function initializes the µC/CPU services.

725

6

L6-2(3)   These three lines of code are used to set up the SysTick timer built into the Cortex™-M3 core. This timer provides the system tick used by µC/OS-III.

L6-2(4)   The **OSStatTaskCPUUsageInit()** function computes the CPU capacity which is used by the operating system's statistic task.

L6-2(5)   The **CPU_IntDisMeasMaxCurReset()** function initializes the measurement of the amount of time that interrupts are disabled.

L6-2(6)   The **App_ProbeInit()** function initializes the µC/Probe modules.

L6-2(7)   Initializes the LEDs on the board. One LED is initially lit while the other is off.

L6-2(8)   The **AppDisplayTaskCreate()** function initializes the other task and objects used by the application.

L6-2(9)   Sets the infinite loop for this task.

L6-2(10)   The **OSTimeDlyHMSM()** function delays the task from being ready to run for 1 second. This delay causes the code within the main task loop to execute approximately every 1 second.

L6-2(11)   Toggles the LEDs on the board once per second.

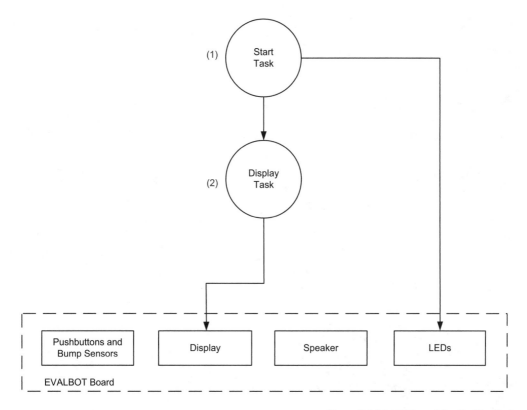

Figure 6-1 **Interaction of Application Tasks**

F6-1(1)   The Start Task initializes the timer and also initializes the LED status and then toggles the LEDs once per second.

F6-1(2)   The Display Task shows the possible strings in a rotation.

The code for the Robot DisplayTask is shown in Listing 6-3.

```
static void AppTaskRobotDisplay(void *p_arg)
{
    CPU_INT08U  state;
    CPU_INT16U  sec;
    OS_ERR      err;


    sec   = 1u;
    state = 0u;

    while (DEF_ON) {                                                    (1)
        OSTimeDlyHMSM(0u, 0u, sec, 300u,                               (2)
                      OS_OPT_TIME_HMSM_STRICT,
                      &err);

        switch (state) {                                               (3)
            case 0:
                 BSP_DisplayStringDraw("TEXAS",        29u, 0u);
                 BSP_DisplayStringDraw("INSTRUMENTS", 11u, 1u);
                 sec   = 5u;
                 state = 1u;
                 break;

            case 1:
                 BSP_DisplayClear();
                 sec   = 1u;
                 state = 2u;
                 break;

            case 2:
                 BSP_DisplayStringDraw("STELLARIS", 21u, 0u);
                 sec   = 5u;
                 state = 3u;
                 break;

            case 3:
                 BSP_DisplayClear();
                 sec   = 1u;
                 state = 4u;
                 break;

            case 4:
                 BSP_DisplayStringDraw("MICRIUM",   27u, 0u);
                 BSP_DisplayStringDraw("uC/OS-III", 21u, 1u);
                 sec   = 5u;
                 state = 5u;
                 break;
```

```
            case 5:
                 BSP_DisplayClear();
                 sec   = 1u;
                 state = 0u;
                 break;

            default:
                 sec   = 1u;
                 state = 0u;
                 break;
        }
    }
}
```

Listing 6-3 **Input Monitor Task in APP.C**

L6-3(1)   Sets the infinite loop for this task.

L6-3(2)   The **OSTimeDlyHMSM( )** function delays the task from being ready to run for
           5 milliseconds. This delay causes the code within the main task loop to execute
           approximately every 5 milliseconds.

L6-3(3)   Rotates through the screen display options.

6-2 MONITORING VARIABLES USING μC/PROBE

Click the "Go" icon in IAR Embedded Workbench (see Figure 5-5 on page 719) to start the
application.

Start μC/Probe and open the μC/Probe workspace for this project, uCOS-III-Ex4-Probe.wsp.
You can find this file in the following directory:

\Micrium\Software\EvalBoards\TI\LM3S9B92-EVALBOT\IAR\uCOS-III-Ex1

After µC/Probe starts, click the run button. Once µC/Probe is running, you will see a screen that looks like Figure 6-2.

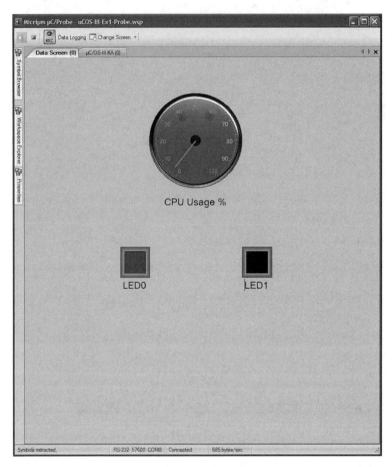

Figure 6-2 **µC/Probe Monitoring Example 4 Application**

The µC/Probe workspace is set to allow monitoring of the CPU usage and the state of the LEDs on the board. In addition, the operating system statistics can be viewed in real time using the µC/OS-III tab.

6-3 SUMMARY

This example application demonstrates the most basic μC/OS-III example. The concept of tasks is introduced using two simple tasks that are independent from one another. One task toggles the on-board LEDs while the second one diplays various strings on the OLED screen on a rotating basis.

A μC/Probe workspace is also supplied with this example. This workspace demonstrates μC/Probe's ability to visually demonstrate the inner workings of the RTOS and the application.

Chapter

7

Using Audio with the EVALBOT

The example described in this chapter uses the EVALBOT evaluation board to play WAV files stored in the internal Flash memory of the LM3S9B92 microcontroller. This project demonstrates how µC/OS-III, in conjunction with the EVALBOT evaluation board, can be used to create an audio control application. Several small audio tracks are loaded into the Flash memory when this example is downloaded onto the board. The application uses the bump sensors to select an audio track: the left bump sensor selects the previous track and the right bump sensor selects the next track. The two user pushbuttons (SWITCH1 and SWITCH2) are used to control audio playback: SWITCH2 begins audio playback, and SWITCH1 stops audio playback. Most WAV file formats are supported by the included sound driver, so alternate audio tracks can be linked into the example application, providing that the size of all the files combined is not larger than 200 kB.

When audio is playing, the EVALBOT flashes the on-board LEDs at a 5 Hz rate to indicate that audio playback is active. In addition, the on-board display shows the title of the current track, which is defined by the user in the application, as well as the playback time status.

7-1 HOW THE PROJECT WORKS

The code for the **main()** function is shown in Listing 7-1.

```
void  main (void)
{
    OS_ERR  err;


    BSP_IntDisAll();                                                      (1)

    OSInit(&err);                                                         (2)

    OSTaskCreate((OS_TCB      *)&AppTaskStartTCB,                         (3)
                 (CPU_CHAR    *)"App Task Start",
                 (OS_TASK_PTR ) AppTaskStart,
                 (void        *) 0,
                 (OS_PRIO     ) APP_TASK_START_PRIO,
                 (CPU_STK     *)&AppTaskStartStk[0],
                 (CPU_STK_SIZE) APP_TASK_START_STK_SIZE / 10u,
                 (CPU_STK_SIZE) APP_TASK_START_STK_SIZE,
                 (OS_MSG_QTY  ) 0u,
                 (OS_TICK     ) 0u,
                 (void        *) 0,
                 (OS_OPT      )(OS_OPT_TASK_STK_CHK | OS_OPT_TASK_STK_CLR),
                 (OS_ERR      *)&err);

    OSStart(&err);                                                       (4)
}
```

Listing 7-1 **main() in APP.C**

L7-1(1)   The first step in the **main()** function calls the **BSP_IntDisAll()** function. The
            code for this function is located in the **BSP_INT.C** file and simply calls the
            CPU_IntDis() function to disable all of the interrupts to the CPU.

L7-1(2)   The **OSInit()** function is then called to initialize the µC/OS-III operating
            system.

L7-1(3)   The **OSTaskCreate()** function is called to create the **AppTaskStart** task.

L7-1(4)   The **OSStart()** function is called to start operation of the multitasking
            operating system.

Listing 7-2 shows the code for the **AppTaskRobotStart()** task and Figure 7-1 on page 738 shows a diagram for the application tasks interaction.

```
static  void  AppTaskRobotStart (void  *p_arg)
{
    CPU_INT32U  clk_freq;
    CPU_INT32U  cnts;
    OS_ERR      err;
    CPU_TS      ts;


    BSP_Init();                                                     (1)
    CPU_Init();                                                     (2)

    clk_freq = BSP_CPU_ClkFreq();                                  (3)
    cnts     = clk_freq / (CPU_INT32U)OSCfg_TickRate_Hz;
    OS_CPU_SysTickInit(cnts);

#if (OS_CFG_STAT_TASK_EN > 0u)
    OSStatTaskCPUUsageInit(&err);                                  (4)
#endif

    CPU_IntDisMeasMaxCurReset();                                   (5)

    App_ProbeInit();                                               (6)

    AppRobotTasksCreate();                                         (7)

    AppRobotDisplayTmrInit();                                      (8)

    while (DEF_ON) {
        OSFlagPend(&AppRobotControlFlagGroup,                      (9)
                   FLAG_AUDIO_PLAY,
                   0u,
                   OS_OPT_PEND_FLAG_SET_ANY + OS_OPT_PEND_FLAG_CONSUME,
                   &ts,
                   &err);
```

```
        OSTaskResume(&AppTaskRobotPlaybackLEDTCB, &err);                    (10)

        OSFlagPend(&AppRobotControlFlagGroup,                               (11)
                   FLAG_AUDIO_STOP,
                   0u,
                   OS_OPT_PEND_FLAG_SET_ANY + OS_OPT_PEND_FLAG_CONSUME,
                   &ts,
                   &err);

        OSTaskSuspend(&AppTaskRobotPlaybackLEDTCB, &err);                   (12)
    }
}
```

Listing 7-2 **AppTaskRobotStart() in APP.C**

L7-2(1)   The **BSP_Init()** function initializes the CPU peripherals and signals used with this board.

L7-2(2)   The **CPU_Init()** function initializes the µC/CPU services.

L7-2(3)   These three lines of code are used to set up the SysTick timer built into the Cortex™-M3 core. This timer provides the system tick used by µC/OS-III.

L7-2(4)   The **OSStatTaskCPUUsageInit()** function computes the CPU capacity used by the operating system's statistic task.

L7-2(5)   The **CPU_IntDisMeasMaxCurReset()** function initializes the measurement of the amount of time that interrupts are disabled.

L7-2(6)   The **App_ProbeInit()** function initializes the µC/Probe modules.

L7-2(7)   The **AppRobotTasksCreate()** function initializes the tasks and objects used by the application.

L7-2(8)   The **AppRobotDisplayTmrInit()** function initializes a periodic timer that updates the display.

L7-2(9)   The **OSFlagPend()** function waits until audio playback has been initiated by SWITCH2. When playback begins, the LED blink task is started.

L7-2(10)   The **OSTaskResume()** function resumes the LED blink task so that the LEDs flash while playback is running.

L7-2(11)   The **OSFlagPend()** function waits until audio playback has ended before suspending the LED blink task.

L7-2(12)   The **OSTaskSuspend()** function suspends the LED blink task.

The **AppRobotTasksCreate()** function creates all of the tasks that make up the application. The following four application tasks are created:

- **AppTaskRobotAudioPlayback** – play WAV files through the DAC.

- **AppTaskRobotInputMonitor** – monitor button and bump sensor events.

- **AppTaskRobotDisplay** – display track title and playback status on the display.

- **AppTaskRobotPlaybackLED** – blink LEDs while playback is active.

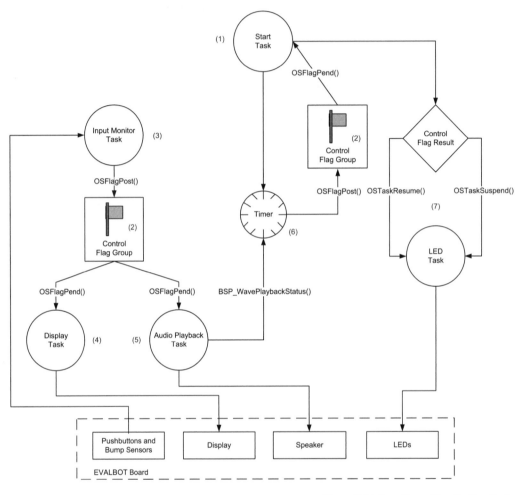

Figure 7-1 **Interaction of Application Tasks**

F7-1(1)   The Start Task initializes the timer and also uses the Control Flag Group information to provide information to the LED task.

F7-1(2)   The Control Flag Group contains four flags; one for the pushbuttons, one for the right bump sensor, one for the left bump sensor, and one for timer expiration.

F7-1(3)   The Input Monitor Task takes the data from the pushbuttons and bump sensors and posts to the Control Flag Group.

F7-1(4)   The Display Task uses the Control Flag Group information to control the data shown on the display.

F7-1(5)   The Audio Playback task uses the Control Flag Group information to start or stop playback and to advance to the next track or go back to the previous track.

F7-1(6)   The playback status is used by the Timer function to update the Control Flag Group.

F7-1(7)   Based on the Control Flag Group status, the LED Task either starts or stops toggling the LEDs.

The code for the Audio Playback Task is shown in Listing 7-3.

```
static  void  AppTaskRobotAudioPlayback (void  *p_arg)
{
    OS_ERR  err;
    CPU_TS  ts;


    g_psWaveFiles[0].pucFilePtr = __section_begin("wave_1");        (1)
    g_psWaveFiles[1].pucFilePtr = __section_begin("wave_2");
    g_psWaveFiles[2].pucFilePtr = __section_begin("wave_3");
    g_psWaveFiles[3].pucFilePtr = __section_begin("wave_4");
    g_psWaveFiles[4].pucFilePtr = __section_begin("wave_5");

    sprintf(g_psWaveFiles[0].pcFilename, "Intro");                  (2)
    sprintf(g_psWaveFiles[1].pcFilename, "Boing");
    sprintf(g_psWaveFiles[2].pcFilename, "Crash");
    sprintf(g_psWaveFiles[3].pcFilename, "Horn");
    sprintf(g_psWaveFiles[4].pcFilename, "Note");

    g_ucCurrentWaveIdx = 0;                                         (3)
    strcpy(pcCurrentWaveTitle, g_psWaveFiles[0].pcFilename);
```

```
    while (DEF_ON) {
        OSFlagPend(&AppRobotControlFlagGroup,                               (4)
                FLAG_PUSH_BUTTON,
                0u,
                OS_OPT_PEND_FLAG_SET_ANY + OS_OPT_PEND_FLAG_CONSUME,
                &ts,
                &err);

        BSP_WaveOpen(g_psWaveFiles[g_ucCurrentWaveIdx].pucFilePtr, &g_sWaveHeader);   (5)

        BSP_WavePlay(&g_sWaveHeader);                                       (6)
    }
}
```

Listing 7-3 Audio Playback Task in APP.C

L7-3(1) These five lines of code get pointers from IAR to the WAV files. The information is obtained from the memory map at compile/link time.

L7-3(2) These five lines of code name the WAV files. Because the WAV files don't contain track titles in the file, the tracks can be assigned any name.

L7-3(3) These two lines of code set the default WAV file and update the variable used by μC/Probe that stores the active track title.

L7-3(4) The **OSFlagPend()** function waits for SWITCH2 to be pressed before beginning playback.

L7-3(5) The **BSP_WaveOpen()** function opens the desired WAV file and checks that the file is in a valid format. If the format is not valid, the file will not play.

L7-3(6) The **BSP_WavePlay()** function plays the WAV file. The function "sleeps" the playback task after configuring the DMA to transmit 1KB of data to the I^2S. The function then waits for 40 ms using the **OSTimeDlyHMSM()** function, allowing the CPU to allocate bandwidth for the display and LED tasks.

The code for the Robot Input Monitor task is shown in Listing 7-4.

```
static  void  AppTaskInputMonitor (void  *p_arg)
{
    CPU_INT08U  ucData;
    OS_ERR      err;
    CPU_INT08U  ucSwitches;
    CPU_INT08U  ucDelta;
    CPU_INT08U  ucSwitchesClockA;
    CPU_INT08U  ucSwitchesClockB;


    ucSwitches       = 0x0Fu;                                       (1)
    ucSwitchesClockA =    0u;
    ucSwitchesClockB =    0u;

    while (DEF_ON) {                                                (2)
        OSTimeDlyHMSM(0u, 0u, 0u, 5u,                              (3)
                      OS_OPT_TIME_HMSM_STRICT,
                      &err);

        ucData =  BSP_PushButtonGetStatus(1u)        | // Top    Push Button   (4)
                 (BSP_PushButtonGetStatus(2u) << 1u) | // Bottom Push Button
                 (BSP_BumpSensorGetStatus(1u) << 2u) | // Right  Bump Sensor
                 (BSP_BumpSensorGetStatus(2u) << 3u); // Left   Bump Sensor

        ucDelta = ucData ^ ucSwitches;                             (5)

        ucSwitchesClockA ^=  ucSwitchesClockB;
        ucSwitchesClockB  = ~ucSwitchesClockB;

        ucSwitchesClockA &=  ucDelta;
        ucSwitchesClockB &=  ucDelta;

        ucSwitches &=    ucSwitchesClockA | ucSwitchesClockB;
        ucSwitches |= (~(ucSwitchesClockA | ucSwitchesClockB)) & ucData;

        ucDelta ^= ucSwitchesClockA | ucSwitchesClockB;

        if ((ucDelta & 0x01u) && (~ucSwitches & 0x01u)) {          (6)
            BSP_WaveStop();
        }
```

```
        if ((ucDelta & 0x02u) && (~ucSwitches & 0x02u)) {                    (7)
            OSFlagPost(&AppRobotControlFlagGroup,
                       FLAG_PUSH_BUTTON,
                       OS_OPT_POST_FLAG_SET,
                       &err);
        }


        if ((ucDelta & 0x04u) && (~ucSwitches & 0x04u)) {                    (8)
            OSFlagPost(&AppRobotControlFlagGroup,
                       FLAG_RIGHT_BUMP_SENSOR,
                       OS_OPT_POST_FLAG_SET,
                       &err);

            BSP_WaveStop();

            if (g_ucCurrentWaveIdx < (NUM_WAVE_FILES - 1u)) {
                g_ucCurrentWaveIdx++;
            } else {
                // Do nothing.
            }
        }


        if ((ucDelta & 0x08u) && (~ucSwitches & 0x08u)) {                    (9)
            OSFlagPost(&AppRobotControlFlagGroup,
                       FLAG_LEFT_BUMP_SENSOR,
                       OS_OPT_POST_FLAG_SET,
                       &err);

            BSP_WaveStop();

            if (g_ucCurrentWaveIdx > 0u) {
                g_ucCurrentWaveIdx--;
            } else {
                // Do nothing.
            }
        }


        strcpy(pcCurrentWaveTitle, g_psWaveFiles[g_ucCurrentWaveIdx].pcFilename);
    }
}
```

Listing 7-4 **Input MonitorTask in APP.C**

L7-4(1)   Initializes the variables that require initialization.

L7-4(2)   Sets the infinite loop for this task.

L7-4(3)   The **OSTimeDlyHMSM( )** function delays the task from being ready to run for 5 milliseconds. This delay causes the code within the main task loop to execute approximately every 5 milliseconds.

L7-4(4)   The current state of the pushbuttons and the bump sensors are read and stored to a bit-mapped variable where each bit indicates the state of a single pushbutton or bump sensor.

L7-4(5)   These 8 lines of code handle the debouncing of the pushbuttons and bump sensors.

L7-4(6)   Check the status of SWITCH1 and stop playback if the button has been pressed.

L7-4(7)   Check the status of SWITCH2 and begin playback if the button has been pressed.

L7-4(8)   Check the status of the right bumper and advance to the next track if the bumper has been pressed. If the current track is the last one, keep the track number on the last track. Playback stops and does not continue until SWITCH1 is pressed again.

L7-4(9)   Check the status of the left bumper and go back to the previous track if the bumper has been pressed. If the current track is the first one, keep the track number on the first track. Playback stops and does not continue until SWITCH1 is pressed again.

The Display Task controls the output to the display. The code for this task is shown in Listing 7-5.

7

```
static  void  AppTaskRobotDisplay (void *p_arg)
{
    CPU_INT32U  ulFileNameSize;
    OS_ERR      err;
    CPU_TS      ts;


    BSP_DisplayStringDraw("TEXAS",        29u, 0u);                         (1)
    BSP_DisplayStringDraw("INSTRUMENTS", 11u, 1u);

    OSTimeDlyHMSM(0u, 0u, 2u, 0u,
                  OS_OPT_TIME_HMSM_STRICT,
                  &err);

    while (DEF_ON) {
        BSP_DisplayClear();                                                (2)

        ulFileNameSize = strlen(g_psWaveFiles[g_ucCurrentWaveIdx].pcFilename);  (3)

        BSP_DisplayStringDraw(g_psWaveFiles[g_ucCurrentWaveIdx].pcFilename,     (4)
                              ((16 - ulFileNameSize) / 2u) * 6u, 0u);

        if (!BSP_WavePlaybackStatus()) {                                   (5)
            BSP_DisplayStringDraw("0:00/0:00", 18u, 1u);
        }

        OSFlagPend(&AppRobotControlFlagGroup,                              (6)
                   FLAG_PUSH_BUTTON +
                   FLAG_LEFT_BUMP_SENSOR +
                   FLAG_RIGHT_BUMP_SENSOR,
                   0u,
                   OS_OPT_PEND_FLAG_SET_ANY + OS_OPT_PEND_FLAG_CONSUME,
                   &ts,
                   &err);
    }
}
```

Listing 7-5 **Display Task in APP.C**

L7-5(1)   Displays the initial Texas Instruments splash screen for 2 seconds.

L7-5(2)   Clears the screen to prepare for displaying the name of the first track.

L7-5(3)   Determines the length of the file name.

L7-5(4)   Displays the file name, centered on the screen.

744

L7-5(5)   If nothing is playing, a zero'd play time indicator is displayed.

L7-5(6)   Wait until the play button or bump sensors are pressed. This task is used to update track information only. Playback time is not updated with this task, other than to zero out the playback time if nothing is playing.

The Playback LED Task is used to control the LEDs during playback.. The code for this task is shown in Listing 7-6.

```c
static void AppTaskRobotPlaybackLED (void *p_arg)
{
    OS_ERR  err;


    OSTaskSuspend(&AppTaskRobotPlaybackLEDTCB, &err);          (1)

    BSP_LED_On(1);                                            (2)
    BSP_LED_Off(2);

    while (DEF_ON) {
        OSTimeDlyHMSM(0u, 0u, 0u, 200u,                       (3)
                      OS_OPT_TIME_HMSM_STRICT,
                      &err);
        BSP_LED_Toggle(0);                                   (4)
    }
}
```

Listing 7-6 **Playback LED Task in APP.C**

L7-6(1)   This task is initially suspended because there is no playback at startup.

L7-6(2)   Initializes the LEDs on the board. One LED is initially lit while the other is off.

L7-6(3)   Delay for 200 ms in between LED toggles.

L7-6(4)   Toggle the LEDs at a 5 Hz rate and update the variables that are used in µC/Probe.

7-2 MONITORING VARIABLES USING μC/PROBE

Click the "Go" icon in IAR Embedded Workbench (see Figure 5-5 on page 719) to start the application.

Start μC/Probe and open the μC/Probe workspace for this project, uCOS-III-Ex2-Probe.wsp. You can find this file in the following directory:

`\Micrium\Software\EvalBoards\TI\LM3S9B92-EVALBOT\IAR\uCOS-III-Ex2`

After μC/Probe starts, click the run button. Once μC/Probe is running, you will see a screen that looks like Figure 7-2.

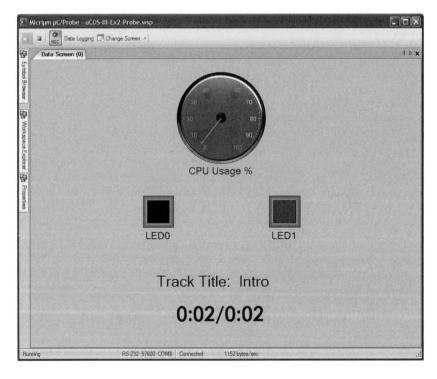

Figure 7-2 **μC/Probe Monitoring Example 2 Application**

The μC/Probe workspace is set to allow monitoring of the CPU usage and the state of the LEDs on the board.

7-3 SUMMARY

This example application demonstrates several key features of μC/OS-III. Specifically, it illustrates how to achieve audio control using a multitasking approach. One task is used for audio playback. A second task is used to monitor the input from the two pushbuttons and two bump sensors on the board. Additional tasks are used to control the information that is displayed on the screen and the on-board LEDs. The state of the pushbuttons and bump sensors is used to change the track that is played as well as the display data. Information is passed among the tasks using the flag mechanism built into the RTOS.

A μC/Probe workspace is also supplied with this example. This workspace demonstrates μC/Probe's ability to visually demonstrate the inner workings of the RTOS and the application.

Chapter

8

Simple Control of the EVALBOT

The example described in this chapter provides simple control of the two motors on the EVALBOT evaluation board using the two pushbuttons and two bump sensors on the EVALBOT. Figure 8-1 shows the top side of the EVALBOT board.

Figure 8-1 **EVALBOT (top view)**

You can control each motor by using a combination of one pushbutton and one bump sensor. The SWITCH1 pushbutton controls the left motor and the SWITCH2 pushbutton controls the right motor. Each bump sensor on the front of the EVALBOT controls the motor on the corresponding side of the board (for example, the front right bump sensor controls the right motor). Press the pushbutton once to spin the motor in the forward direction. Press the pushbutton again to stop the motor. Press the pushbutton a third time to spin the motor in reverse. Press the pushbutton a fourth time to stop the motor. Repeat these steps to control the motor. If you press the bump sensor while the motor is spinning in either direction, the motor stops spinning. When you release the bump sensor, the motor resumes spinning in the same direction.

8-1 HOW THE PROJECT WORKS

Listing 8-1 shows the code for the **main()** function.

```
int  main (void)
{
    OS_ERR  err;


    BSP_IntDisAll();                                                    (1)

    OSInit(&err);                                                       (2)

    OSTaskCreate((OS_TCB      *)&AppTaskStartTCB,                       (3)
                 (CPU_CHAR    *)"App Task Start",
                 (OS_TASK_PTR ) AppTaskStart,
                 (void        *) 0,
                 (OS_PRIO     ) APP_TASK_START_PRIO,
                 (CPU_STK     *)&AppTaskStartStk[0],
                 (CPU_STK_SIZE) APP_TASK_START_STK_SIZE / 10u,
                 (CPU_STK_SIZE) APP_TASK_START_STK_SIZE,
                 (OS_MSG_QTY  ) 0u,
                 (OS_TICK     ) 0u,
                 (void        *) 0,
                 (OS_OPT       )(OS_OPT_TASK_STK_CHK | OS_OPT_TASK_STK_CLR),
                 (OS_ERR      *)&err);

    OSStart(&err);                                                      (4)
}
```

Listing 8-1 **main() in APP.C**

L8-1(1)   The first step in the **main()** function calls the **BSP_IntDisAll()** function. The code for this function is located in the **BSP_INT.C** file and simply calls the **CPU_IntDis()** function to disable all of the interrupts to the CPU.

L8-1(2)   The **OSInit()** function is then called to initialize the µC/OS-III operating system.

L8-1(3)   The **OSTaskCreate()** function is called to create the **AppTaskStart** task.

L8-1(4)   The **OSStart()** function is called to start operation of the multitasking operating system.

Listing 8-2 shows the code for the **AppTaskStart()** task.

```
static  void  AppTaskStart (void  *p_arg)
{
    CPU_INT32U  clk_freq;
    CPU_INT32U  cnts;
    OS_ERR      err;


    BSP_Init();                                              (1)
    CPU_Init();                                              (2)


    clk_freq = BSP_CPU_ClkFreq();                            (3)
    cnts     = clk_freq / (CPU_INT32U)OSCfg_TickRate_Hz;
    OS_CPU_SysTickInit(cnts);

#if (OS_CFG_STAT_TASK_EN > 0u)
    OSStatTaskCPUUsageInit(&err);                            (4)
#endif

    CPU_IntDisMeasMaxCurReset();                             (5)

    App_ProbeInit();                                         (6)

    AppTasksInit();                                          (7)

    BSP_LED_On(1);                                           (8)
    BSP_LED_Off(2);

    while (DEF_ON) {                                         (9)
        OSTimeDlyHMSM(0u, 0u, 1u, 0u,                        (10)
                      OS_OPT_TIME_HMSM_STRICT,
                     &err);
        BSP_LED_Toggle(0);                                   (11)
    }
}
```

Listing 8-2 **AppTaskStart() in APP.C**

L8-2(1)   The **BSP_Init()** function initializes the CPU peripherals and signals used with this board.

L8-2(2)   The **CPU_Init()** function initializes the μC/CPU services.

L8-2(3)   These three lines of code are used to set up the Cortex™-M3 core's built-in SysTick timer. This timer provides the system tick used by μC/OS-III.

L8-2(4)   The `OSStatTaskCPUUsageInit()` function computes the CPU capacity which is used by the operating system's statistic task.

L8-2(5)   The `CPU_IntDisMeasMaxCurReset()` function initializes the measurement of the amount of time that interrupts are disabled.

L8-2(6)   The `App_ProbeInit()` function initializes the µC/Probe modules.

L8-2(7)   The `AppTasksInit()` function initializes the tasks and objects used by the application.

L8-2(8)   Initializes the LEDs on the board. One LED is lit while the other LED is off.

L8-2(9)   Sets the infinite loop for this task.

L8-2(10)   The `OSTimeDlyHMSM()` function delays the task from being ready to run for 1 second. This delay causes the code within the main task loop to execute approximately every 1 second.

L8-2(11)   Toggles the LEDs on the board.

The `AppTasksInit()` function creates all of the tasks and objects used by the application including the following four application tasks:

■ `AppTaskControl` – the main control task.

■ `AppTaskLeftMotorDrive` – the left motor control task.

■ `AppTaskRightMotorDrive` – the right motor control task.

■ `AppTaskInputMonitor` – the monitor button and bump sensor events task.

In addition, the `AppTasksInit()` function creates the following flag groups:

■ `AppLeftMotorDriveFlagGroup` – the flag group used by the left motor control task.

■ `AppRightMotorDriveFlagGroup` – the flag group used by the right motor control task.

8

Figure 8-2 shows how the tasks interact for this application.

Figure 8-2 **Interaction of Application Tasks**

F8-2(1)   The Input Monitor Task monitors the state of the pushbuttons and bump sensors. If the state of the input changes, a message with the current state and delta information for all of the input is posted to the Main Control Task Queue.

F8-2(2)   The Main Control Task Queue is the task queue defined when creating the task.

8

F8-2(3)   The Main Control Task waits for a message to arrive in the Main Control Task Queue. When a message is received, the message is processed and a flag is posted to the corresponding Left Motor Drive Flag Group or Right Motor Drive Flag Group.

F8-2(4)   The Left Motor Flag Group contains three flags: one for a pushbutton press, one for a bump sensor press, and one for a bump sensor release.

F8-2(5)   The Left Motor Drive Task waits for a flag to be posted to the Left Motor Flag Group. When a flag is posted, the task determines which flag is posted and drives the left motor accordingly.

F8-2(6)   The Right Motor Flag Group contains three flags: one for a pushbutton press, one for a bump sensor press, and one for a bump sensor release.

F8-2(7)   The Right Motor Drive Task waits for a flag to be posted to the Right Motor Flag Group. When a flag is posted, the task determines which flag is posted and drives the right motor accordingly.

Listing 8-3 shows the code for the Input Monitor Task.

```
static  void  AppTaskInputMonitor (void  *p_arg)
{
    CPU_INT08U  pucMsg[2];
    CPU_INT08U  ucData;
    OS_ERR      err;
    CPU_INT08U  ucSwitches;
    CPU_INT08U  ucDelta;
    CPU_INT08U  ucSwitchesClockA;
    CPU_INT08U  ucSwitchesClockB;


    ucSwitches       = 0x0Fu;                                    (1)
    ucSwitchesClockA =    0u;
    ucSwitchesClockB =    0u;
```

```
    while (DEF_ON) {                                               (2)
        OSTimeDlyHMSM(0u, 0u, 0u, 5u,                             (3)
                    OS_OPT_TIME_HMSM_STRICT,
                   &err);

        ucData =  BSP_PushButtonGetStatus(1u)       |            (4)
                 (BSP_PushButtonGetStatus(2u) << 1u) |
                 (BSP_BumpSensorGetStatus(1u) << 2u) |
                 (BSP_BumpSensorGetStatus(2u) << 3u);

        ucDelta =  ucData ^ ucSwitches;                          (5)

        ucSwitchesClockA ^=  ucSwitchesClockB;
        ucSwitchesClockB  = ~ucSwitchesClockB;

        ucSwitchesClockA &= ucDelta;
        ucSwitchesClockB &= ucDelta;

        ucSwitches &=    ucSwitchesClockA | ucSwitchesClockB;
        ucSwitches |= (~(ucSwitchesClockA | ucSwitchesClockB)) & ucData;

        ucDelta ^= ucSwitchesClockA | ucSwitchesClockB;

        if (ucDelta & 0x0Fu) {                                   (6)
            pucMsg[0] = ucSwitches;                              (7)
            pucMsg[1] = ucDelta;

            OSTaskQPost((OS_TCB    *)&AppTaskControlTCB,         (8)
                        (void      *)&pucMsg[0],
                        (OS_MSG_SIZE) 2u,
                        (OS_OPT     ) OS_OPT_POST_FIFO,
                        (OS_ERR    *)&err);
        }
    }
}
```

Listing 8-3 **Input Monitor Task in APP.C**

L8-3(1)   Initializes the variables that require initialization.

L8-3(2)   Sets the infinite loop for this task.

L8-3(3)   The **OSTimeDlyHMSM()** function delays the task from being ready to run for 5 milliseconds. This causes the code within the main task loop to execute approximately every 5 milliseconds.

L8-3(4)   Reads and stores the current state of the pushbuttons and the bump sensors to a bit-mapped variable where each bit indicates the state of a single pushbutton or bump sensor.

L8-3(5)   Handles the debouncing of the pushbuttons and bump sensors (the next 8 lines of code).

L8-3(6)   Checks to see if any of the pushbuttons or bump sensors have changed state.

L8-3(7)   Configures the message to be sent to the Main Control Task.

L8-3(8)   Posts the message to the Main Control Task's queue.

Listing 8-4 shows the code for the Main Control Task.

```
static  void  AppTaskControl (void  *p_arg)
{
    OS_MSG_SIZE     msg_size;
    CPU_INT08U      ucSwitches;
    CPU_INT08U      ucDelta;
    CPU_INT08U      *pucMsg;
    CPU_TS          ts;
    OS_ERR          err;


    while (DEF_ON) {                                            (1)
        pucMsg = (CPU_INT08U *)OSTaskQPend(0u,                  (2)
                                  OS_OPT_PEND_BLOCKING,
                                  &msg_size,
                                  &ts,
                                  &err);

        ucSwitches = pucMsg[0];                                (3)
        ucDelta    = pucMsg[1];

        if ((ucDelta & 0x01u) && !(ucSwitches & 0x01u)) {
            OSFlagPost(&AppRightMotorDriveFlagGroup,           (4)
                    FLAG_PUSH_BUTTON_PRESSED,
                    OS_OPT_POST_FLAG_SET,
                    &err);
    }
```

8

```
        if ((ucDelta & 0x02u) && !(ucSwitches & 0x02u)) {
            OSFlagPost(&AppLeftMotorDriveFlagGroup,                    (5)
                    FLAG_PUSH_BUTTON_PRESSED,
                    OS_OPT_POST_FLAG_SET,
                    &err);
        }

        if ((ucDelta & 0x04u) && !(ucSwitches & 0x04u)) {
            OSFlagPost(&AppRightMotorDriveFlagGroup,                   (6)
                    FLAG_BUMP_SENSOR_PRESSED,
                    OS_OPT_POST_FLAG_SET,
                    &err);
        }

        if ((ucDelta & 0x04u) && (ucSwitches & 0x04u)) {
            OSFlagPost(&AppRightMotorDriveFlagGroup,                   (7)
                    FLAG_BUMP_SENSOR_RELEASED,
                    OS_OPT_POST_FLAG_SET,
                    &err);
        }

        if((ucDelta & 0x08u) && !(ucSwitches & 0x08u)) {
            OSFlagPost(&AppLeftMotorDriveFlagGroup,                    (8)
                    FLAG_BUMP_SENSOR_PRESSED,
                    OS_OPT_POST_FLAG_SET,
                    &err);
        }

        if((ucDelta & 0x08u) && (ucSwitches & 0x08u)) {
            OSFlagPost(&AppLeftMotorDriveFlagGroup,                    (9)
                    FLAG_BUMP_SENSOR_RELEASED,
                    OS_OPT_POST_FLAG_SET,
                    &err);
        }
    }
}
```

Listing 8-4 **Main Control Task in APP.C**

L8-4(1)   Sets the infinite loop for this task.

L8-4(2)   The **OSTaskQPend()** function causes the task to delay from being ready run until a message has been posted to its queue. This causes the code within the main task loop to execute every time a new message is posted.

L8-4(3)   Reads the message into local variables.

L8-4(4) If the right pushbutton is pressed, posts the button-pressed flag to the Right Motor Drive Task.

L8-4(5) If the left pushbutton is pressed, posts the button-pressed flag to the Left Motor Drive Task.

L8-4(6) If the right bump sensor is pressed, posts the bump sensor-pressed flag to the Right Motor Drive Task.

L8-4(7) If the right bump sensor is released, posts the bump sensor-released flag to the Right Motor Drive Task.

L8-4(8) If the left bump sensor is pressed, posts the bump sensor-pressed flag to the Left Motor Drive Task.

L8-4(9) If the left bump sensor is released, posts the bump sensor-released flag to the Left Motor Drive Task.

The Left Motor Drive Task and the Right Motor Drive Task are independent tasks that execute the same function. Listing 8-5 shows the code for these tasks.

```
static  void  AppTaskMotorDrive (void  *p_arg)
{
    OS_FLAGS   flags;
    tSide      eSide;
    tState     eState;


    eSide  = *(tSide *)p_arg;                                (1)
    eState = MOTOR_DRIVE_OFF_FORW_NEXT;                      (2)

    BSP_MotorStop(eSide);                                    (3)
    BSP_MotorSpeed(eSide, 50u << 8u);                        (4)
```

```
    while (DEF_ON) {                                        (5)
        flags = AppMotorDriveFlagPend(eSide);              (6)
        if (flags & FLAG_PUSH_BUTTON_PRESSED) {            (7)
            switch (eState) {                              (8)
                case MOTOR_DRIVE_OFF_FORW_NEXT:
                    eState = MOTOR_DRIVE_FORW;             (9)
                    BSP_MotorDir(eSide, FORWARD);
                    BSP_MotorRun(eSide);
                    break;


                case MOTOR_DRIVE_OFF_REV_NEXT:
                    eState = MOTOR_DRIVE_REV;              (10)
                    BSP_MotorDir(eSide, REVERSE);
                    BSP_MotorRun(eSide);
                    break;


                case MOTOR_DRIVE_FORW:
                    eState = MOTOR_DRIVE_OFF_REV_NEXT;     (11)
                    BSP_MotorStop(eSide);
                    break;


                case MOTOR_DRIVE_REV:
                    eState = MOTOR_DRIVE_OFF_FORW_NEXT;    (12)
                    BSP_MotorStop(eSide);
                    break;


                default:
                    break;
            }

        } else {

            if ((eState == MOTOR_DRIVE_FORW) ||            (13)
                (eState == MOTOR_DRIVE_REV)) {

                if(flags & FLAG_BUMP_SENSOR_PRESSED) {
                    BSP_MotorStop(eSide);                 (14)
                }
```

```
            if(flags & FLAG_BUMP_SENSOR_RELEASED) {
                BSP_MotorRun(eSide);                          (15)
            }
        }
    }
  }
}
```

Listing 8-5 **Left Motor Drive Task and Right Motor Drive Task in APP.C**

L8-5(1)   The motor that this task is intended for (left or right) is passed to the function in **p_arg**. The value of **p_arg** is defined when the task is created. **eSide** is initialized with the intended motor (left or right).

L8-5(2)   The initial state of the motor is off, and the next state is the drive forward state.

L8-5(3)   Stops the motor initially.

L8-5(4)   Sets the motor speed to 50 percent of the maximum speed. The desired speed is left-shifted 8 bits because the parameter that defines the speed is an 8.8 fixed-point formatted variable.

L8-5(5)   Sets the infinite loop for this task.

L8-5(6)   The **AppMotorDriveFlagPend()** function does not return until a flag has been posted to the task by the Main Control Task. When it does return, it returns the value of the flags.

L8-5(7)   Checks to see if the pushbutton-pressed flag is set.

L8-5(8)   Switches based on the motor's current state.

L8-5(9)   The motor is currently in the off state with forward next. This case switches to the forward state, sets the direction of the motor to be forward, and runs the motor.

8

L8-5(10)   The motor is currently in the off state with reverse next. This case switches to the reverse state, sets the direction of the motor to be reverse, and runs the motor.

L8-5(11)   The motor is currently in the forward state. This case switches to the off state with reverse next and stops the motor.

L8-5(12)   The motor is currently in the reverse state. This case switches to the off state with forward next and stops the motor.

L8-5(13)   Checks to see if we are currently in a forward or reverse state. Ignores the bump sensors unless the motor is running.

L8-5(14)   Stops the motor if the bump sensor pressed flag is set. The state of the motor remains the same.

L8-5(15)   Runs the motor if the bump sensor released flag is set. The direction is determined by the current state of the motor.

8-2 MONITORING VARIABLES USING µC/PROBE

Click the "Go" icon in IAR Embedded Workbench (see Figure 5-5 on page 719) to run the application.

Start µC/Probe and open the µC/Probe workspace for this project, uCOS-III-Ex3-Probe.wsp. You will find this file in the following directory:

\Micrium\Software\EvalBoards\TI\LM3S9B92-EVALBOT\IAR\uCOS-III-Ex3

After μC/Probe starts, click the run button. Once μC/Probe is running, you will see a screen that looks like Figure 8-3.

Figure 8-3 **μC/Probe Monitoring Example 3 Application**

The µC/Probe workspace is configured to allow monitoring of the CPU usage, the current state of both the left and right motors, and the state of the LEDs on the board. In addition, the operating system statistics can be viewed in real time using the µC/OS-III tab as shown in Figure 8-4.

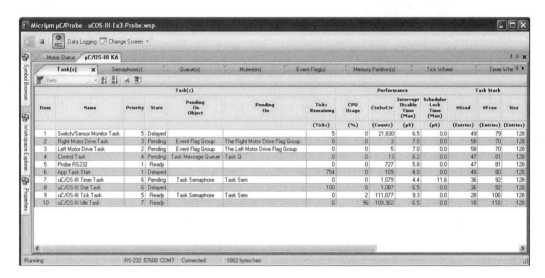

Figure 8-4 **µC/Probe Monitoring Example 3 OS Statistics**

8-3 SUMMARY

This example application demonstrates several key features of µC/OS-III. Specifically, it illustrates how to achieve basic motor control using a multitasking approach. One task is used to monitor the input from the two pushbuttons and two bump sensors on the board. Information on the state of these buttons and bump sensors is sent to the main control task using the message queue mechanism built into the RTOS. The main control task is then responsible for relaying the appropriate information to the two motor drive tasks using the flag mechanism built into the RTOS.

A µC/Probe workspace is also supplied with this example. This workspace demonstrates µC/Probe's ability to display real-time information about the internal state of an application and RTOS as they run on the target board.

9

Autonomous Control of the EVALBOT

The example described in this chapter provides autonomous control of the EVALBOT evaluation board using the motors and bump sensors on the board. This project demonstrates how µC/OS-III, in conjunction with the EVALBOT evaluation board, can be used to create an autonomous motor control application. The robot drives forward until either the robot bumps into something or a bounded random time value expires. If either of these events occur, the robot turns some bounded random amount and then continues driving forward.

The bump sensors on the front of the EVALBOT board are used to detect the robot bumping into something while driving forward. If the left bump sensor is triggered, the robot turns to the right and then continues driving forward. Conversely, if the right bump sensor is triggered, the robot turns to the left and then continues driving forward.

In addition to the bump sensors, a timer expiration event causes the robot to change directions while driving forward. A timer is configured to expire in a bounded random amount of time when the robot begins to drive forward. If the timer expires prior to bumping into something, the robot chooses to turn to the left or right direction, turns a bounded random amount in that direction, and then continues driving forward.

9-1 HOW THE PROJECT WORKS

The code for the **main()** function is shown in Listing 9-1.

```
int  main (void)
{
    OS_ERR  err;


    BSP_IntDisAll();                                              (1)

    OSInit(&err);                                                 (2)

    OSTaskCreate((OS_TCB      *)&AppTaskStartTCB,                 (3)
                 (CPU_CHAR    *)"App Task Start",
                 (OS_TASK_PTR ) AppTaskStart,
                 (void        *) 0,
                 (OS_PRIO     ) APP_TASK_START_PRIO,
                 (CPU_STK     *)&AppTaskStartStk[0],
                 (CPU_STK_SIZE) APP_TASK_START_STK_SIZE / 10u,
                 (CPU_STK_SIZE) APP_TASK_START_STK_SIZE,
                 (OS_MSG_QTY  ) 0u,
                 (OS_TICK     ) 0u,
                 (void        *) 0,
                 (OS_OPT      )(OS_OPT_TASK_STK_CHK | OS_OPT_TASK_STK_CLR),
                 (OS_ERR      *)&err);

    OSStart(&err);                                                (4)
}
```

Listing 9-1 **main() in APP.C**

L9-1(1)   The first step in the **main()** function calls the **BSP_IntDisAll()** function. The code for this function is located in the **BSP_INT.C** file and simply calls the **CPU_IntDis()** function to disable all of the interrupts to the CPU.

L9-1(2)   The **OSInit()** function is then called to initialize the µC/OS-III operating system.

L9-1(3)   The **OSTaskCreate()** function is called to create the **AppTaskStart** task.

L9-1(4)   The **OSStart()** function is called to start operation of the multitasking operating system.

Listing 9-2 shows the code for the **AppTaskRobotStart()** task and Figure 9-1 on page 769 shows a diagram for the application tasks interaction..

```
static  void  AppTaskRobotStart (void  *p_arg)
{
    CPU_INT32U  clk_freq;
    CPU_INT32U  cnts;
    OS_ERR      err;


    BSP_Init();                                              (1)
    CPU_Init();                                              (2)

    clk_freq = BSP_CPU_ClkFreq();                            (3)
    cnts     = clk_freq / (CPU_INT32U)OSCfg_TickRate_Hz;
    OS_CPU_SysTickInit(cnts);

#if (OS_CFG_STAT_TASK_EN > 0u)
    OSStatTaskCPUUsageInit(&err);                            (4)
#endif

    CPU_IntDisMeasMaxCurReset();                             (5)

    App_ProbeInit();                                         (6)

    AppRobotTasksCreate();                                   (7)

    BSP_LED_On(1);                                           (8)
    BSP_LED_Off(2);

    while (DEF_TRUE) {                                       (9)
        OSTimeDlyHMSM(0u, 0u, 1u, 0u,                        (10)
                      OS_OPT_TIME_HMSM_STRICT,
                      &err);
        BSP_LED_Toggle(0);                                   (11)
    }
}
```

Listing 9-2 **AppTaskRobotStart() in APP.C**

L9-2(1)   The **BSP_Init()** function initializes the CPU peripherals and signals used with this board.

L9-2(2)   The **CPU_Init()** function initializes the µC/CPU services.

9

L9-2(3)   These three lines of code are used to set up the SysTick timer built into the Cortex™-M3 core. This timer provides the system tick used by μC/OS-III.

L9-2(4)   The `OSStatTaskCPUUsageInit()` function computes the CPU capacity. This is used by the operating system's statistic task.

L9-2(5)   The `CPU_IntDisMeasMaxCurReset()` function initializes the measurement of the amount of time that interrupts are disabled.

L9-2(6)   The `App_ProbeInit()` function initializes the μC/Probe modules.

L9-2(7)   The `AppRobotTasksCreate()` function initializes the tasks and objects used by the application.

L9-2(8)   Initializes the LEDs on the board. One LED is initially lit while the other is off.

L9-2(9)   Sets the infinite loop for this task.

L9-2(10)   The `OSTimeDlyHMSM()` function delays the task from being ready to run for 1 second. This delay causes the code within the main task loop to execute approximately every 1 second.

L9-2(11)   Toggles the LEDs on the board.

The `AppRobotTasksCreate()` function creates all of the tasks that make up the application. The following six application tasks are created:

■   `AppTaskRobotControl` – the main control task.

■   `AppTaskRobotLeftMotorDrive` – the left motor control task.

■   `AppTaskRobotRightMotorDrive` – the right motor control task.

■   `AppTaskRobotLeftMotorPID` – the left motor PID controller task.

■   `AppTaskRobotRightMotorPID` – the right motor PID controller task.

■   `AppTaskRobotInputMonitor` – the task to monitor button and bump sensor events.

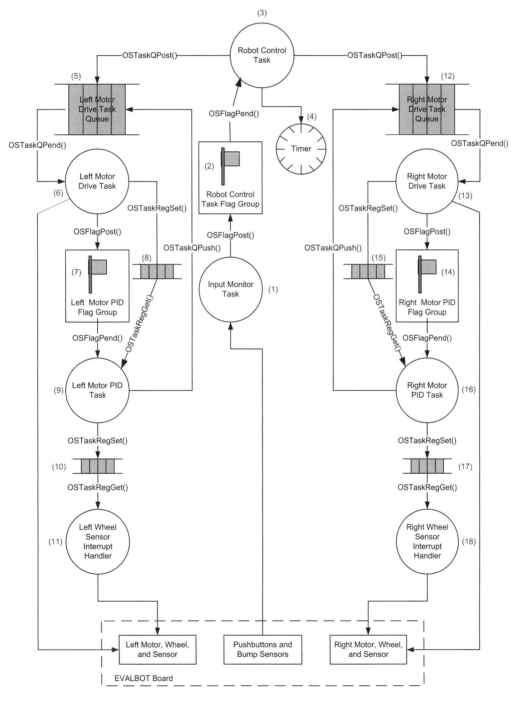

Figure 9-1 **Interaction of Application Tasks**

9

F9-1(1)   The Input Monitor Task monitors the state of the pushbuttons and bump sensors. A flag is posted to the Robot Control Task Queue if the state of the input changes. The flag indicates which input has changed.

F9-1(2)   The Robot Control Task Flag Group contains four flags; one for the pushbuttons, one for the right bump sensor, one for the left bump sensor, and one for timer expiration.

F9-1(3)   The Robot Control Task transitions between states based on flags being posted to its flag group. It will post messages to the Left Motor Task and the Right Motor Task as appropriate.

F9-1(4)   A timer is used for the amount of time to turn and the amount of time to drive forward without making a random turn if a bump sensor is not triggered.

F9-1(5)   The Left Motor Drive Task Queue passes messages to the Left Motor Drive Task.

F9-1(6)   The Left Motor Drive Task waits to receive a message. When a message is received, the Left Motor Drive Task drives the left motor accordingly.

F9-1(7)   The Left Motor PID Task Flag Group consists of two flags; one to start the PID controller, and one to stop the PID controller.

F9-1(8)   The Left Motor PID Task Register sets the target speed from the Left Motor Drive Task.

F9-1(9)   The Left Motor PID Task reacts to flags posted from the Left Motor Drive Task as well as its register contents being set by the Left Motor Drive Task and the Left Wheel Sensor Interrupt Handler.

F9-1(10)   The Left Motor PID Task Register sets the actual speed from the Left Wheel Sensor Interrupt Handler.

F9-1(11)   The Left Wheel Sensor Interrupt Handler handles edge interrupts generated by the left wheel sensor and calculates the speed. This speed information is then shared with the Left Motor PID Task.

F9-1(12)   The Right Motor Drive Task Queue passes messages to the Right Motor Drive Task.

F9-1(13)   The Right Motor Drive Task waits to receive a message. When a message has been received, it drives the right motor accordingly.

F9-1(14)   The Right Motor PID Task Flag Group consists of two flags; one to start the PID controller, and one to stop the PID controller.

F9-1(15)   The Right Motor PID Task Register sets the target speed from the Right Motor Drive Task.

F9-1(16)   The Right Motor PID Task reacts to flags posted from the Right Motor Drive Task as well as its register contents being set by the Right Motor Drive Task and the Right Wheel Sensor Interrupt Handler.

F9-1(17)   The Right Motor PID Task Register sets the actual speed from the Right Wheel Sensor Interrupt Handler.

F9-1(18)   The Right Wheel Sensor Interrupt Handler handles edge interrupts generated by the right wheel sensor and calculates the speed. This speed information is then shared with the Right Motor PID Task.

The code for the Input Monitor Task is shown in Listing 9-3.

```
static  void  AppTaskRobotInputMonitor (void  *p_arg)
{
    CPU_INT08U  ucData;
    OS_ERR      err;
    CPU_INT08U  ucSwitches;
    CPU_INT08U  ucDelta;
    CPU_INT08U  ucSwitchesClockA;
    CPU_INT08U  ucSwitchesClockB;


    ucSwitches       = 0x0Fu;                                    (1)
    ucSwitchesClockA =   0u;
    ucSwitchesClockB =   0u;
```

```
    while (DEF_ON) {                                             (2)
        OSTimeDlyHMSM(0u, 0u, 0u, 5u,                           (3)
                    OS_OPT_TIME_HMSM_STRICT,
                 &err);


        ucData =  BSP_PushButtonGetStatus(1u)         |          (4)
              (BSP_PushButtonGetStatus(2u) << 1u) |
              (BSP_BumpSensorGetStatus(1u) << 2u) |
              (BSP_BumpSensorGetStatus(2u) << 3u);

        ucDelta = ucData ^ ucSwitches;                          (5)


        ucSwitchesClockA ^= ucSwitchesClockB;
        ucSwitchesClockB  = ~ucSwitchesClockB;


        ucSwitchesClockA &= ucDelta;
        ucSwitchesClockB &= ucDelta;


        ucSwitches &=   ucSwitchesClockA | ucSwitchesClockB;
        ucSwitches |= (~(ucSwitchesClockA | ucSwitchesClockB)) & ucData;


        ucDelta ^= ucSwitchesClockA | ucSwitchesClockB;

        if ((ucDelta & 0x0Fu) && (~ucSwitches & 0x0Fu)) {       (6)
            RandomAddEntropy(OSTimeGet(&err));                  (7)
            RandomSeed();                                       (8)
        }


        if ((ucDelta & 0x03u) && (~ucSwitches & 0x03u)) {
            OSFlagPost(&AppRobotControlFlagGroup,               (9)
                    FLAG_PUSH_BUTTON,
                     OS_OPT_POST_FLAG_SET,
                     &err);
        }


        if ((ucDelta & 0x04u) && (~ucSwitches & 0x04u)) {
            OSFlagPost(&AppRobotControlFlagGroup,               (10)
                    FLAG_RIGHT_BUMP_SENSOR,
                     OS_OPT_POST_FLAG_SET,
                     &err);
        }
```

```
        if ((ucDelta & 0x08u) && (~ucSwitches & 0x08u)) {
            OSFlagPost(&AppRobotControlFlagGroup,                    (11)
                    FLAG_LEFT_BUMP_SENSOR,
                    OS_OPT_POST_FLAG_SET,
                    &err);
        }
    }
}
```

Listing 9-3 **Input Monitor Task in APP.C**

L9-3(1)   Initializes the variables that require initialization.

L9-3(2)   Sets the infinite loop for this task.

L9-3(3)   The `OSTimeDlyHMSM()` function delays the task from being ready to run for 5 milliseconds. This delay causes the code within the main task loop to execute approximately every 5 milliseconds.

L9-3(4)   The current state of the pushbuttons and the bump sensors are read and stored to a bit-mapped variable where each bit indicates the state of a single pushbutton or bump sensor.

L9-3(5)   The next 8 lines of code handle the debouncing of the pushbuttons and bump sensors.

L9-3(6)   Checks to see if any of the pushbuttons or bump sensors were just pressed.

L9-3(7)   Adds the current time to the random number generator's entropy pool.

L9-3(8)   Seeds the random number generator using the updated entropy pool.

L9-3(9)   Posts the pushbutton flag to the Robot Control Task Flag Group if either pushbutton is pressed.

L9-3(10)   Posts the right bump sensor flag to the Robot Control Task Flag Group if the right bump sensor is pressed.

L9-3(11)   Posts the left bump sensor flag to the Robot Control Task Flag Group if the left bump sensor is pressed.

The code for the Robot Control Task is shown in Listing 9-4.

```c
static void AppTaskRobotControl (void *p_arg)
{
    CPU_INT16U        usDriveTimeWindow;
    CPU_INT08U        pucMotorSpeed[2];
    tControlTaskState eState;
    OS_FLAGS          flags;
    OS_ERR            err;
    CPU_TS            ts;


    OSFlagCreate(&AppRobotControlFlagGroup,                      (1)
                 "Robot Control Task Flag Group",
                 (OS_FLAGS)0,
                 &err);

    eState             = CONTROL_IDLE;                           (2)
    usDriveTimeWindow = INIT_DRIVE_TIME_WINDOW;                  (3)

    while (DEF_ON) {                                             (4)
        switch (eState) {                                       (5)
            case CONTROL_IDLE:                                  (6)
                OSFlagPend(&AppRobotControlFlagGroup,
                           FLAG_PUSH_BUTTON      +
                           FLAG_LEFT_BUMP_SENSOR +
                           FLAG_RIGHT_BUMP_SENSOR,
                           0u,
                           OS_OPT_PEND_FLAG_SET_ANY + OS_OPT_PEND_FLAG_CONSUME,
                           &ts,
                           &err);
                flags = OSFlagPendGetFlagsRdy(&err);
                if ((flags & FLAG_LEFT_BUMP_SENSOR) ||
                    (flags & FLAG_RIGHT_BUMP_SENSOR)) {
                    break;
                }
                eState = CONTROL_DRIVE_FORWARD;
                break;
```

```
        case CONTROL_DRIVE_FORWARD:                              (7)
            if ((((RandomNumber() >> 16u) * 100u) >> 16u) < 75u) {
                AppRobotDriveForward(65u, 65u);
            } else {
                pucMotorSpeed[0] = (((RandomNumber() >> 16u) * 10u) >> 16u) + 60u;
                pucMotorSpeed[1] = (((RandomNumber() >> 16u) * 10u) >> 16u) + 45u;
                if (RandomNumber() & 0x80000000u) {
                    AppRobotDriveForward(pucMotorSpeed[1], pucMotorSpeed[0]);
                } else {
                    AppRobotDriveForward(pucMotorSpeed[0], pucMotorSpeed[1]);
                }
            }
            AppRobotDriveTmrInit(usDriveTimeWindow);
            eState = CONTROL_DRIVING_FORWARD;
            break;

        case CONTROL_DRIVING_FORWARD:                            (8)
            OSFlagPend(&AppRobotControlFlagGroup,
                       FLAG_PUSH_BUTTON        +
                       FLAG_RIGHT_BUMP_SENSOR +
                       FLAG_LEFT_BUMP_SENSOR  +
                       FLAG_TIMER_EXPIRATION,
                       0u,
                       OS_OPT_PEND_FLAG_SET_ANY + OS_OPT_PEND_FLAG_CONSUME,
                       &ts,
                       &err);
            AppRobotDriveTmrDel();
            AppRobotStop();
            flags = OSFlagPendGetFlagsRdy(&err);
            if (flags & FLAG_PUSH_BUTTON) {
                eState = CONTROL_IDLE;
            } else if (flags & FLAG_TIMER_EXPIRATION) {
                usDriveTimeWindow = INIT_DRIVE_TIME_WINDOW;
                if (RandomNumber() & 0x80000000u) {
                    eState = CONTROL_TURN_LEFT;
                } else {
                    eState = CONTROL_TURN_RIGHT;
                }
            } else if (flags & FLAG_RIGHT_BUMP_SENSOR) {
                usDriveTimeWindow = (usDriveTimeWindow * 3u) / 4u;
                eState = CONTROL_TURN_LEFT;
            } else if (flags & FLAG_LEFT_BUMP_SENSOR) {
                usDriveTimeWindow = (usDriveTimeWindow * u3) / 4u;
                eState = CONTROL_TURN_RIGHT;
            }
            break;
```

9

```
        case CONTROL_TURN_LEFT:                                (9)
            AppRobotTurnLeft();
            AppRobotTurnTmrInit();
            eState = CONTROL_TURNING;
            break;

        case CONTROL_TURN_RIGHT:                               (10)
            AppRobotTurnRight();
            AppRobotTurnTmrInit();
            eState = CONTROL_TURNING;
            break;

        case CONTROL_TURNING:                                  (11)
            OSFlagPend(&AppRobotControlFlagGroup,
                       FLAG_PUSH_BUTTON        +
                       FLAG_LEFT_BUMP_SENSOR   +
                       FLAG_RIGHT_BUMP_SENSOR  +
                       FLAG_TIMER_EXPIRATION,
                       0u,
                       OS_OPT_PEND_FLAG_SET_ANY + OS_OPT_PEND_FLAG_CONSUME,
                       &ts,
                       &err);
            flags = OSFlagPendGetFlagsRdy(&err);
            if ((flags & FLAG_LEFT_BUMP_SENSOR) ||
                (flags & FLAG_RIGHT_BUMP_SENSOR)) {
                break;
            }
            AppRobotTurnTmrDel();
            AppRobotStop();
            if (flags & FLAG_PUSH_BUTTON) {
                eState = CONTROL_IDLE;
            } else if (flags & FLAG_TIMER_EXPIRATION) {
                eState = CONTROL_DRIVE_FORWARD;
            }
            break;
        }
    }
}
```

Listing 9-4 **Robot Control Task in APP.C**

L9-4(1)   Creates the Robot Control Flag Group used by this task.

L9-4(2)   Sets the state of the Robot Control Task to idle.

L9-4(3)   Configures the drive time window in which the robot can make a random turn to its initial value. This window is reduced each time a bump sensor is pressed, increasing the probability of making a random turn. This window is reset to its initial value when a random turn is made.

L9-4(4)   Sets the infinite loop for this task.

L9-4(5)   Switches the EVALBOT's state based on the current state.

L9-4(6)   Defines the idle state. Gets the flag that caused the task to be ready to run. If one of the bump sensors is triggered, break causes the state to be reentered and pended again. This is needed so that the bump sensor flags are consumed if they are posted. Otherwise, a pushbutton was pressed. When it is pressed, changes the state to the drive forward state.

L9-4(7)   Defines the drive forward state. In this state, the robot is set up to start driving forward. Approximately 75% of the time, the robot drives straight. The other 25% of the time, the robot veers either to the left or right. The drive timer, which can expire if a bump sensor is not triggered first, is created and started. Finally, the state changes to the driving forward state.

L9-4(8)   Defines the driving forward state. Pends until a pushbutton is pressed, a bump sensor is triggered, or the timer expires. Deletes the drive timer and stops the robot. Gets the flag that caused the task to be ready to run. If a pushbutton was pressed, moves to the idle state. If the timer expired, resets the drive time window and moves to the turn left or turn right state. If the right bump sensor is triggered, reduces the drive time window by 25% and moves to the turn left state. If the left bump sensor was triggered, reduces the drive time window by 25% and moves to the turn right state.

L9-4(9)   Defines the turn left state. In this state, the robot is set to start turning to the left, the turn timer is created and started, and the state is moved to the turning state.

L9-4(10)   Defines the turn right state. In this state, the robot is set to start turning to the right, the turn timer is created and started, and the state is moved to the turning state.

L9-4(11)   Defines the turning state. Pends until a pushbutton is pressed, a bump sensor is triggered, or the timer expires. Gets the flag that caused the task to be ready to run. If one of the bump sensors was triggered, break causes the state to be reentered and pended again. This is needed so that the bump sensor flags will be consumed if they were posted. Delete the turn timer and stop the robot. If a pushbutton is pressed, moves to the idle state.

The Left Motor Drive Task and the Right Motor Drive Task are independent tasks that execute the same function. The code for these tasks is shown in Listing 9-5 below.

```
static  void  AppTaskRobotMotorDrive (void  *p_arg)
{
    CPU_INT08U   *pucMsg;
    OS_MSG_SIZE  msg_size;
    CPU_INT16U   usPercent;
    tSide        eSide;
    OS_ERR       err;
    CPU_TS       ts;


    eSide = *(tSide *)p_arg;                                          (1)

    while (DEF_ON) {                                                  (2)
        pucMsg = (CPU_INT08U *)OSTaskQPend(0u,                        (3)
                                  OS_OPT_PEND_BLOCKING,
                                  &msg_size,
                                  &ts,
                                  &err);
        switch (pucMsg[0]) {                                         (4)
            case MSG_TYPE_MOTOR_DRIVE_START:                          (5)
                if (pucMsg[1] == MOTOR_DRIVE_FORWARD) {
                    BSP_MotorDir(eSide, FORWARD);
                } else {
                    BSP_MotorDir(eSide, REVERSE);
                }
                BSP_MotorSpeed(eSide, 0u);
                BSP_MotorRun(eSide);
                AppRobotMotorDriveSensorEnable(eSide);
                AppRobotMotorPIDTaskActualSpeedSet(eSide, 0u);
                AppRobotMotorPIDTaskTargetSpeedSet(eSide, pucMsg[2]);
                AppRobotMotorPIDTaskStart(eSide);
                break;
```

```
        case MSG_TYPE_MOTOR_STOP:                          (6)
            BSP_MotorStop(eSide);
            AppRobotMotorDriveSensorDisable(eSide);
            AppRobotMotorPIDTaskStop(eSide);
            break;

        case MSG_TYPE_MOTOR_DRIVE:                         (7)
            usPercent = (pucMsg[1] << 8u) | (pucMsg[2]);
            BSP_MotorSpeed(eSide, usPercent);
            break;

        default:
            break;
        }
    }
}
```

Listing 9-5 **Left Motor Drive Task and Right Motor Drive Task in APP.C**

L9-5(1)   The motor that this task is intended for (left or right) is passed to the function
           in p_arg. The value of p_arg is defined when the task is created. eSide is
           initialized with which motor this task is intended for.

L9-5(2)   Sets the infinite loop for this task.

L9-5(3)   Pends until a message is received.

L9-5(4)   Switches based on the message type. The message type is defined by the first
           byte of the message.

L9-5(5)   Sets the motor drive start message that comes from the Robot Control Task.
           Gets the drive direction from the second byte of the message and sets the
           direction of the motor accordingly. Sets the message speed to 0. This is updated
           by messages sent from the PID task. Enables the motor to run. Resets and
           enables capturing of the edge detection from the wheel sensor. Clears the
           actual speed value and sets the desired speed value, both used by the PID task.
           Finally, starts the PID task.

L9-5(6)   Sets the motor drive stop message that comes from the Robot Control Task.
           Stops the motor. Disables capturing of the edge detection from the wheel
           sensor and stops the PID task.

779

L9-5(7)   Sets the motor drive message that comes from the PID task. The new drive strength to drive the motor with is read from the second and third bytes of the message, and the motor speed is updated according to that value.

The Left Motor PID Task and the Right Motor PID Task are independent tasks that execute the same function. The code for these tasks is shown in Listing 9-6.

```
static  void  AppTaskRobotMotorPID (void  *p_arg)
{
    CPU_INT32S      lDelta;
    CPU_INT32U      ulPercent;
    CPU_INT08U      ucTargetSpeed;
    CPU_INT08U      ucActualSpeed;
    CPU_INT08U      pucMotorMsg[3];
    tPIDState       sSpeedState;
    tPIDTaskState   eState;
    tSide           eSide;
    OS_ERR          err;


    eSide  = *(tSide *)p_arg;                               (1)
    AppRobotMotorPIDTaskFlagCreate(eSide);                  (2)
    eState = PID_IDLE;                                      (3)
    while (DEF_ON) {                                        (4)
        switch (eState) {                                  (5)
            case PID_IDLE:                                 (6)
                AppRobotMotorPIDTaskStartFlagPend(eSide);
                eState = PID_START;
                break;

            case PID_START:                                (7)
                PIDInitialize(&sSpeedState,
                              (100u << 16u) / 3277,
                              0u,
                              0u,
                              3277u << 16u,
                              0u);
                eState = PID_RUNNING;
                break;
```

```
        case PID_RUNNING:                                          (8)
            if (AppRobotMotorPIDTaskStopFlagPend(eSide) == OS_ERR_TIMEOUT) {
                ucTargetSpeed  = AppRobotMotorPIDTaskTargetSpeedGet(eSide);
                ucActualSpeed  = AppRobotMotorPIDTaskActualSpeedGet(eSide);
                lDelta         = ((CPU_INT32S)ucTargetSpeed) -
                                 ((CPU_INT32S)ucActualSpeed);
                ulPercent      = PIDUpdate(&sSpeedState, lDelta);

                if (ulPercent > (100u << 16u)) {
                    ulPercent =  100u << 16u;
                }

                pucMotorMsg[0] = MSG_TYPE_MOTOR_DRIVE;
                pucMotorMsg[1] =   ulPercent >> 16u; // upper byte of 8.8 percentage
                pucMotorMsg[2] = ((ulPercent & 0xFF00u) >> 8u);
                OSTaskQPost((eSide == LEFT_SIDE) ?
                            (OS_TCB   *)&AppTaskRobotLeftMotorDriveTCB :
                            (OS_TCB   *)&AppTaskRobotRightMotorDriveTCB,
                            (void     *)&pucMotorMsg[0],
                            (OS_MSG_SIZE) 3u,
                            (OS_OPT    ) OS_OPT_POST_FIFO,
                            (OS_ERR   *)&err);
            } else {
                eState = PID_IDLE;
            }
            break;

        default:
            break;
        }
    }
}
```

Listing 9-6 **Left Motor PID Task and Right Motor PID Task in APP.C**

L9-6(1)   The motor that this task is intended for (left or right) is passed to the function in **p_arg**. The value of **p_arg** is defined when the task is created. eSide is initialized with the intended motor.

L9-6(2)   Creates the flag group for this task.

L9-6(3)   Sets the state of the Motor PID Task to idle.

L9-6(4)   Sets the infinite loop for this task.

L9-6(5)   Switches the EVALBOT's state based on the current state.

L9-6(6)   Defines the idle state. Pends until the start flag has been posted. After the start
           flag has been posted, moves to the start state.

L9-6(7)   Defines the start state. Initializes the PID controller with a P of 0, I of 0.05, and
           D of 0. The P, I, and D parameter values are in 16.16 fixed-point format. Moves
           to the running state.

L9-6(8)   Defines the running state. Pends until the stop flag is set or the 10 ms timeout
           occurs. This allows the PID Task to run approximately every 10 ms while also
           monitoring the stop flag. If the timeout occurs, gets the target and actual
           speeds, calculates the difference, gets the new motor drive value from the PID
           controller, and posts the motor drive message to the Motor Drive Task. If the
           stop flag is posted, then moves to the idle state.

The Left Wheel Sensor Interrupt and the Right Wheel Sensor Interrupt share the same
interrupt handler. The code for this interrupt handler is shown in Listing 9-7 below.

```
static  void  AppRobotWheelSensorIntHandler (void)
{
    static CPU_INT32U  ulRightEdgePrevTime;
    static CPU_INT32U  ulLeftEdgePrevTime;
    CPU_INT32U         ulRightEdgeDiff;
    CPU_INT32U         ulLeftEdgeDiff;
    CPU_INT32U         ulRightEdgeTime;
    CPU_INT32U         ulLeftEdgeTime;
    CPU_INT08U         ucRightRPM;
    CPU_INT08U         ucLeftRPM;
    CPU_INT32U         ulStatus;
    OS_ERR             err;


    ulStatus = GPIOPinIntStatus(LEFT_SIDE_SENSOR_PORT, DEF_TRUE);       (1)
    if (ulStatus & LEFT_SIDE_SENSOR_PIN) {
        GPIOPinIntClear(LEFT_SIDE_SENSOR_PORT,                          (2)
                        LEFT_SIDE_SENSOR_PIN);
        if (AppRobotLeftWheelFirstEdge) {
            ulLeftEdgePrevTime = OSTimeGet(&err);                      (3)
            AppRobotLeftWheelFirstEdge = DEF_FALSE;
```

```
        } else {
            ulLeftEdgeTime = OSTimeGet(&err);                      (4)
            if (ulLeftEdgeTime <= ulLeftEdgePrevTime) {
                ulLeftEdgeDiff  = ulLeftEdgeTime +
                                (0xFFFFFFFFu - ulLeftEdgePrevTime) + 1u;
            } else {
                ulLeftEdgeDiff  = ulLeftEdgeTime - ulLeftEdgePrevTime;
            }
            ucLeftRPM = (60u * OSCfg_TickRate_Hz) /
                        (16u * ulLeftEdgeDiff);
            ulLeftEdgePrevTime = ulLeftEdgeTime;
            AppRobotMotorPIDTaskActualSpeedSet(LEFT_SIDE, ucLeftRPM);
        }
    }
    ulStatus = GPIOPinIntStatus(RIGHT_SIDE_SENSOR_PORT, DEF_TRUE);   (5)
    if (ulStatus & RIGHT_SIDE_SENSOR_PIN) {
        GPIOPinIntClear(RIGHT_SIDE_SENSOR_PORT,                     (6)
                        RIGHT_SIDE_SENSOR_PIN);
        if (AppRobotRightWheelFirstEdge) {
            ulRightEdgePrevTime        = OSTimeGet(&err);           (7)
            AppRobotRightWheelFirstEdge = DEF_FALSE;
        } else {
            ulRightEdgeTime = OSTimeGet(&err);                     (8)
            if (ulRightEdgeTime <= ulRightEdgePrevTime) {
                ulRightEdgeDiff  = ulRightEdgeTime +
                                (0xFFFFFFFFu - ulRightEdgePrevTime) + 1u;
            } else {
                ulRightEdgeDiff  = ulRightEdgeTime - ulRightEdgePrevTime;
            }
            ucRightRPM            = (60u * OSCfg_TickRate_Hz) /
                                    (16u * ulRightEdgeDiff);
            ulRightEdgePrevTime = ulRightEdgeTime;
            AppRobotMotorPIDTaskActualSpeedSet(RIGHT_SIDE, ucRightRPM);
        }
    }
}
```

Listing 9-7 **Left Wheel and Right Wheel Sensor Interrupt Handler in APP.C**

L9-7(1)   Gets the interrupt state for the left-side sensor GPIO port.

L9-7(2)   Clears the left sensor interrupt status flag which was set.

L9-7(3)   If this is the first edge, then speed cannot yet be calculated. Saves the current time to the previous time variable and indicates that we are no longer looking for the first edge.

L9-7(4)   This interrupt was not due to the first edge. Gets the current time. Calculates the difference between the current time and the previous time. Uses the difference in time to calculate the wheel RPM and then copies the current time to the previous time. Gives the actual speed to the Left Motor PID Task.

L9-7(5)   Gets the interrupt state for the right-side sensor GPIO port.

L9-7(6)   Clears the right sensor interrupt status flag which was set.

L9-7(7)   If this is the first edge, then speed cannot yet be calculated. Saves the current time to the previous time variable and indicates that we are no longer looking for the first edge.

L9-7(8)   This interrupt was not due to the first edge. Gets the current time. Calculates the difference between the current time and the previous time. Uses the difference in time to calculate the wheel RPM and then copies the current time to the previous time. Gives the actual speed to the Right Motor PID Task.

9-2 MONITORING VARIABLES USING µC/PROBE

Click the "Go" icon in IAR Embedded Workbench (see Figure 5-5 on page 719) to start the application.

Start µC/Probe and open the µC/Probe workspace for this project, uCOS-III-Ex4-Probe.wsp. You can find this file in the following directory:

\Micrium\Software\EvalBoards\TI\LM3S9B92–EVALBOT\IAR\uCOS–III–Ex4

After μC/Probe starts, click the run button. Once μC/Probe is running, you will see a screen that looks like Figure 9-2.

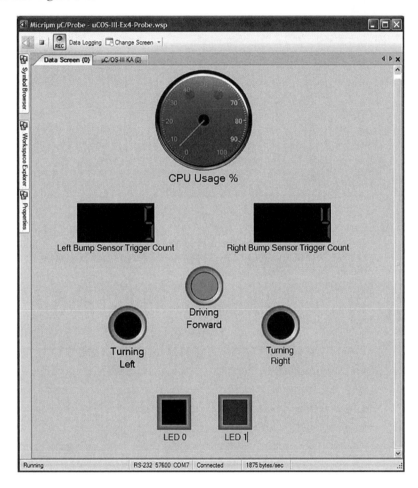

Figure 9-2 **μC/Probe Monitoring Example 4 Application**

The μC/Probe workspace is set to allow monitoring of the CPU usage, whether the robot is driving forward, turning left, or turning right, and the state of the LEDs on the board. In addition, the operating system statistics can be viewed in real time using the μC/OS-III tab as shown in Figure 9-3.

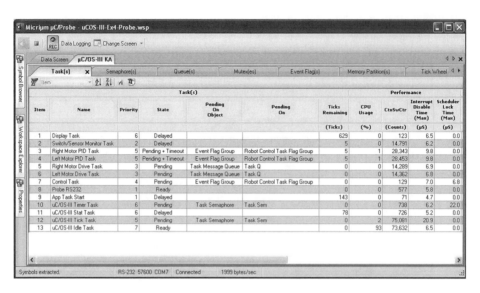

Figure 9-3 **µC/Probe Monitoring Example 4 OS Statistics**

9-3 SUMMARY

This example application demonstrates several key features of µC/OS-III. Specifically, it shows how to achieve autonomous robot control using a multitasking approach. One task is used to monitor the input from the two pushbuttons and two bump sensors on the board. Information on the state of these buttons and bump sensors is sent to the robot control task using the flag mechanism built into the RTOS. The robot control task is then responsible for relaying the appropriate information to the two motor drive tasks using the message queue mechanism built into the RTOS. Each motor drive task starts and stops the PID task for that motor using flags, and relays the target speed information to the PID task using the PID task's register. Additionally, both the left and right wheel sensors are tied to an interrupt which is responsible for calculating actual speed and sharing this information with the associated PID task using the PID task's register.

A µC/Probe workspace is also supplied with this example. This workspace demonstrates µC/Probe's ability to visually demonstrate the inner workings of the RTOS and the application.

Appendix

A

µC/OS-III Port for the Cortex-M3

This appendix describes the adaptation of µC/OS-III to the Cortex-M3 which is called a *Port*.

The port files are found in the following directory:

\Micrium\Software\uCOS-III\Ports\ARM-Cortex-M3\Generic\IAR

The port consists of three files:

    OS_CPU.H
    OS_CPU_C.C
    OS_CPU_A.ASM

A-1 OS_CPU.H

OS_CPU.H contains processor- and implementation-specific **#defines** constants, macros, and typedefs. OS_CPU.H is shown in listing A-1.

```
#ifndef  OS_CPU_H                                                    (1)
#define  OS_CPU_H
#ifdef   OS_CPU_GLOBALS                                              (2)
#define  OS_CPU_EXT
#else
#define  OS_CPU_EXT    extern
#endif
/*
*****************************************************************************************
**
*                                      MACROS
*****************************************************************************************
**
*/
#define  OS_TASK_SW()               OSCtxSw()                        (3)
#define  OS_TS_GET()                CPU_TS_TmrRd()                   (4)
/*
*****************************************************************************************
**
*                                     PROTOTYPES
*****************************************************************************************
**
*/
void  OSCtxSw              (void);                                   (5)
void  OSIntCtxSw           (void);
void  OSStartHighRdy       (void);
void  OS_CPU_PendSVHandler (void);                                  (6)
void  OS_CPU_SysTickHandler (void);                                 (7)
void  OS_CPU_SysTickInit   (CPU_INT32U  cnts);
#endif
```

Listing A-1 **OS_CPU.H**

LA-1(1)   Typical multiple header file inclusion protection.

LA-1(2)   **OS_CPU_GLOBALS** and **OS_CPU_EXT** allow us to declare global variables that are specific to this port. However, the port doesn't contain any global variables and thus these statements are just included for completeness and consistency.

LA-1(3)   The task level context switch code is performed by **OSCtxSw()**. This function is actually implemented in **OS_CPU_A.ASM**.

LA-1(4)   Timestamps are obtained by calling **CPU_TS_TmrRd()**. On the Cortex-M3, **CPU_TS_TmrRd()** reads the **DWT_CYCCNT** register which is a 32-bit free-running up counter.

LA-1(5)   The prototypes of mandatory µC/OS-III functions.

LA-1(6)   The Cortex-M3 processor provides a special interrupt handler specifically designed for use by context switch code. This is called the PendSV Handler and is implemented by **OS_CPU_PendSVHandler()**. The function is found in **OS_CPU_A.ASM.**

LA-1(7)   The Cortex-M3 has a timer dedicated for RTOS use called the SysTick. The code to initialize and handle the SysTick interrupt is found in **OS_CPU_C.C**. Note that this code is part of the µC/OS-III port file and not the Board Support Package (BSP), because the SysTick is available to all Cortex-M3 implementations and is always handled the same by µC/OS-III.

A-2 OS_CPU_C.C

A µC/OS-III port requires that the following functions be declared:

```
OSIdleTaskHook()
OSInitHook()
OSStatTaskHook()
OSTaskCreateHook()
OSTaslDelHook()
OSTaskReturnHook()
OSTaskStkInit()
OSTaskSwHook()
OSTimeTickHook()
```

The Cortex-M3 port implements two additional functions as described in the previous sections:

```
OS_CPU_SysTickHandler()
OS_CPU_SysTickInit()
```

A-2-1 OS_CPU_C.C — OSIdleTaskHook()

The idle task hook allows the port developer to extend the functionality of the idle task. For example, you can place the processor in low power mode when no other higher-priority tasks are running. This is especially useful in battery-powered applications. Listing A-2 shows the typical code for OSIdleTaskHook().

```
void  OSIdleTaskHook (void)
{
#if OS_CFG_APP_HOOKS_EN > 0u                                     (1)
    if (OS_AppIdleTaskHookPtr != (OS_APP_HOOK_VOID)0) {         (2)
        (*OS_AppIdleTaskHookPtr)();                              (3)
    }
#endif
}
```

Listing A-2 **OS_CPU_C.C – OSIdleTaskHook()**

LA-2(1)   Application level hook functions are enabled by OS_CFG_APP_HOOKS_EN.

LA-2(2)   If the application developer wants his/her own function to be called on every iteration of the idle task, the developer needs to initialize the value of OS_AppIdleTaskHookPtr to point to the desired function to call.

Note that µC/OS-III initializes OS_AppIdleTaskHookPtr to NULL when OSInit() is called and therefore, the code must set this pointer only after calling OSInit().

The application hook function *must not* make any blocking calls because the idle task must never block. In other words, it cannot call OSTimeDly(), OSTimeDlyHMSM(), or OSTaskSuspend() (to suspend 'self'), and any of the OS???Pend() functions.

Examples of application hooks are found in OS_APP_HOOKS.C.

LA-2(3)   The application level idle task hook is called without any argument.

A-2-2 OS_CPU_C.C — OSInitHook()

Listing A-3 shows the typical code for OSInitHook().

```
void  OSInitHook (void)
{
}
```

OSInitHook() does not call any application-level hook functions because it can't, and thus there is no application hook function pointer. The reason for this is that OSInit() initializes all the application hook pointers to **NULL** and because of that, it would not be possible to redefine the application init hook pointer before OSInit() returns.

A-2-3 OS_CPU_C.C — OSStatTaskHook()

OSTaskStatHook() allows the port developer to extend the functionality of the statistic task by allowing him/her to add additional statistics. OSStatTaskHook() is called after computing the total CPU usage (see OS_StatTask() in OS_STAT.C). Listing A-4 shows the typical code for OSStatTaskHook().

```
void  OSStatTaskHook (void)
{
#if OS_CFG_APP_HOOKS_EN > 0u
    if (OS_AppStatTaskHookPtr != (OS_APP_HOOK_VOID)0) {       (1)
        (*OS_AppStatTaskHookPtr)();                           (2)
    }
#endif
}
```

Listing A-4 **OS_CPU_C.C – OSStatTaskHook()**

LA-4(1)   If the application developer wants his/her own function to be called by µC/OS-III's statistic task (i.e., OS_StatTask()) then he/she needs to initialize the value of OS_AppStatTaskHookPtr to point to the desired function to call.

Note that μC/OS-III initializes **OS_AppStatTaskHookPtr** to **NULL** when **OSInit()** is called and therefore, the code must set this pointer only after calling **OSInit()**.

The application hook function *must not* make any blocking calls because it would affect the behavior of the statistic task. Examples of application hooks are found in **OS_APP_HOOKS.C**.

LA-4(2)   The application level statistic task hook is called without any argument.

A-2-4 OS_CPU_C.C — OSTaskCreateHook()

OSTaskCreateHook() gives the port developer the opportunity to add code specific to the port when a task is created. **OSTaskCreateHook()** is called once the **OS_TCB** fields are initialized, but prior to making the task ready to run. Listing A-5 shows the typical code for **OSTaskCreateHook()**.

```
void  OSTaskCreateHook (OS_TCB *p_tcb)
{
#if OS_CFG_APP_HOOKS_EN > 0u
    if (OS_AppTaskCreateHookPtr != (OS_APP_HOOK_TCB)0) {         (1)
        (*OS_AppTaskCreateHookPtr)(p_tcb);                      (2)
    }
#else
    (void)&p_tcb;          /* Prevent compiler warning */
#endif
}
```

Listing A-5 **OS_CPU_C.C – OSTaskCreateHook()**

LA-5(1)   If the application developer wants his/her own function to be called when a task is created, the developer needs to initialize the value of **OS_AppTaskCreateHookPtr** to point to the desired function to call.

The application hook function *must not* make any blocking calls and should perform its function as quickly as possible.

Note that μC/OS-III initializes **OS_AppTaskCreateHookPtr** to **NULL** when **OSInit()** is called. The code must set this pointer only after calling **OSInit()**.

Examples of application hooks are found in OS_APP_HOOKS.C.

LA-5(2)   The application level task create hook is passed the address of the OS_TCB of the task being created.

A-2-5 OS_CPU_C.C — OSTaskDelHook()

OSTaskDelHook() gives the port developer the opportunity to add code specific to the port when a task is deleted. OSTaskDelHook() is called once the task has been removed from all lists (the ready list, the tick list or a pend list). Listing A-6 shows the typical code for OSTaskDelHook().

```
void  OSTaskDelHook (OS_TCB *p_tcb)
{
#if OS_CFG_APP_HOOKS_EN > 0u
    if (OS_AppTaskDelHookPtr != (OS_APP_HOOK_TCB)0) {        (1)
        (*OS_AppTaskDelHookPtr)(p_tcb);                     (2)
    }
#else
    (void)&p_tcb;        /* Prevent compiler warning */
#endif
}
```

Listing A-6 **OS_CPU_C.C – OSTaskDelHook()**

LA-6(1)   If the application developer wants his/her own function to be called when a task is deleted, the developer needs to initialize the value of OS_AppTaskDelHookPtr to point to the desired function to call.

The application hook function *must not* make any blocking calls, and should perform its function as quickly as possible.

Note that μC/OS-III initializes OS_AppTaskDelHookPtr to NULL when OSInit() is called and the code must set this pointer only after calling OSInit().

Examples of application hooks are found in OS_APP_HOOKS.C.

LA-6(2)   The application level task delete hook is passed the address of the OS_TCB of the task being created.

A-2-6 OS_CPU_C.C — OSTaskReturnHook()

With µC/OS-III, a task is never allowed to return. However, if this happens accidentally, µC/OS-III will catch this and delete the offending task. However, **OSTaskDelHook()** will be called before the task is deleted. Listing A-7 shows the typical code for OSTaskReturnHook().

```c
void  OSTaskReturnHook (OS_TCB *p_tcb)
{
#if OS_CFG_APP_HOOKS_EN > 0u
    if (OS_AppTaskReturnHookPtr != (OS_APP_HOOK_TCB)0) {          (1)
        (*OS_AppTaskReturnHookPtr)(p_tcb);                        (2)
    }
#else
    (void)&p_tcb;          /* Prevent compiler warning */
#endif
}
```

Listing A-7 **OS_CPU_C.C – OSTaskReturnHook()**

LA-7(1)   If the application developer wants his/her own function to be called when a task returns, the developer needs to initialize the value of OS_AppTaskReturnHookPtr to point to the desired function to call.

The application hook function *must not* make any blocking calls and should perform its function as quickly as possible.

Note that µC/OS-III initializes OS_AppTaskReturnHookPtr to NULL when OSInit() is called and the code must set this pointer only after calling OSInit().

Examples of application hooks are found in OS_APP_HOOKS.C.

LA-7(2)   The application level task return hook is passed the address of the OS_TCB of the task being created.

A-2-7 OS_CPU_C.C — OSTaskStkInit()

This function initializes the stack frame of a task being created. When μC/OS-III creates a task it makes its stack look as if an interrupt just occurred and simulates pushing the context of the task onto the task stack. **OSTaskStkInit()** is called by **OSTaskCreate()**.

Listing A-8 shows the Cortex-M3 code for **OSTaskStkInit()**.

```
CPU_STK *OSTaskStkInit (OS_TASK_PTR    p_task,                (1)
                        void           *p_arg,
                        CPU_STK        *p_stk_base,
                        CPU_STK        *p_stk_limit,
                        CPU_STK_SIZE   stk_size,
                        OS_OPT         opt)
{
    CPU_STK  *p_stk;


    (void)&opt;
    (void)&p_stk_limit;
    p_stk    = &p_stk_base[stk_size - 1u];                    (2)
   *p_stk-- = (CPU_INT32U)0x01000000L;                        (3)
   *p_stk-- = (CPU_INT32U)p_task;                             (4)
   *p_stk-- = (CPU_INT32U)OS_TaskReturn;                      (5)
   *p_stk-- = (CPU_INT32U)0x12121212L;                        (6)
   *p_stk-- = (CPU_INT32U)0x03030303L;
   *p_stk-- = (CPU_INT32U)0x02020202L;
   *p_stk-- = (CPU_INT32U)0x01010101L;
   *p_stk-- = (CPU_INT32U)p_arg;                              (7)
   *p_stk-- = (CPU_INT32U)0x11111111L;                        (8)
   *p_stk-- = (CPU_INT32U)0x10101010L;
   *p_stk-- = (CPU_INT32U)0x09090909L;
   *p_stk-- = (CPU_INT32U)0x08080808L;
   *p_stk-- = (CPU_INT32U)0x07070707L;
   *p_stk-- = (CPU_INT32U)0x06060606L;
   *p_stk-- = (CPU_INT32U)0x05050505L;
   *p_stk  = (CPU_INT32U)0x04040404L;
    return (p_stk);                                           (9)
}
```

Listing A-8 **OS_CPU_C.C – OSTaskStkInit()**

LA-8(1)   **OSTaskStkInit()** is called by **OSTaskCreate()** and is passed six arguments:

     1   The task's entry point (i.e., the address of the task).

     2   A pointer to an argument that will be passed to the task when the task starts, i.e., **p_arg**.

     3   The base address of the storage area in RAM of the stack. Typically a stack is declared as an array of **CPU_STKs** as shown below.

           CPU_STK MyTaskStk[stk_size];

         In this case, the base address is simply **&MyTaskStk[0]**.

     4   The address of where the stack limit is to point to. This assumes that the CPU supports stack limit checking. If not then this pointer is not used.

     5   The size of the stack is also passed to **OSTaskStkInit()**.

     6   Finally, the 'opt' argument of **OSTaskCreate()** is passed to **OSTaskStkInit()** in case any of these are needed by **OSTaskStkInit()** for special options.

LA-8(2)   A local pointer is initialized to the top-of-stack to initialize. In the case of the Cortex-M3, the stack grows from high memory to low memory and therefore, the top-of-stack is at the highest address of the stack storage area.

LA-8(3)   The Cortex-M3's PSR register is initialized. The initial value sets the 'T' bit in the PSR, which causes the Cortex-M3 to use Thumb instructions (this should always be the case).

LA-8(4)   This register corresponds to R15 which is the program counter. We initialize this register to point to the task entry point.

LA-8(5)   This register corresponds to R14 (the link register), which contains the return address of the task. As previously mentioned, a task is not supposed to return. This pointer allows us, therefore, to catch this fault and properly terminate the task. μC/OS-III provides a function just for that purpose, **OS_TaskReturn()**.

LA-8(6)   Registers R12, R3, R2 and R1 are initialized to a value that makes it easy for them to be identified when a debugger performs a memory dump.

LA-8(7)   R0 is the register used by the C compiler to pass the first argument to a function. Recall that the prototype for a task looks as shown below.

void MyTask (void *p_arg);

In this case, '**p_arg**' is simply passed in R0 so that when the task starts, it will think it was called as with any other function.

LA-8(8)   Registers R11, R10, R9 and R8, R7, R6, R5 and R4 are initialized to a value that makes it easy for them to be identified when a debugger performs a memory dump.

LA-8(9)   Notice that the stack pointer is not decremented after the last register is placed onto the stack. This is because the Cortex-M3 assumes that the stack pointer points to the last element pushed onto the stack.

OSTaskStkInit() returns the new top-of-stack pointer to **OSTaskCreate()**, which will save this value in the task's **OS_TCB** in the **.StkPtr** field.

The stack frame of the task being created is shown in Figure A-1.

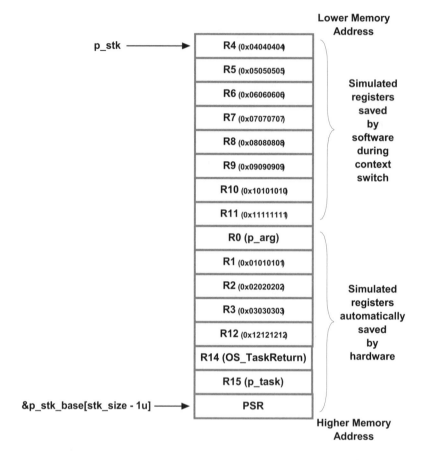

p_stk

| R4 (0x04040404) |
| R5 (0x05050505) |
| R6 (0x06060606) |
| R7 (0x07070707) |
| R8 (0x08080808) |
| R9 (0x09090909) |
| R10 (0x10101010) |
| R11 (0x11111111) |

Simulated
registers
saved
by
software
during
context
switch

| R0 (p_arg) |
| R1 (0x01010101) |
| R2 (0x02020202) |
| R3 (0x03030303) |
| R12 (0x12121212) |
| R14 (OS_TaskReturn) |
| R15 (p_task) |

Simulated
registers
automatically
saved
by
hardware

&p_stk_base[stk_size - 1u]

| PSR |

Higher Memory
Address

Figure A-1 **Stack frame of task being created**

A-2-8 OS_CPU_C.C — OSTaskSwHook()

OSTaskSwHook() is called when µC/OS-III performs a context switch. If fact, OSTaskSwHook() is called after saving the context of the task being suspended. Also, OSTaskSwHook() is called with interrupts disabled.

Listing A-9 shows the code for OSTaskSwHook(). This function is fairly complex and contains a lot of conditional compilation.

```
void  OSTaskSwHook (void)
{
#if OS_CFG_TASK_PROFILE_EN > 0u
    CPU_TS      ts;
#ifdef  CPU_CFG_INT_DIS_MEAS_EN
    CPU_TS      int_dis_time;
#endif
#endif
#if OS_CFG_APP_HOOKS_EN > 0u
    if (OS_AppTaskSwHookPtr != (OS_APP_HOOK_VOID)0) {                    (1)
        (*OS_AppTaskSwHookPtr)();                                       (2)
    }
#endif
#if OS_CFG_TASK_PROFILE_EN > 0u
    ts = OS_TS_GET();                                                   (3)
    if (OSTCBCurPtr != OSTCBHighRdyPtr) {
        OSTCBCurPtr->CyclesDelta  = ts - OSTCBCurPtr->CyclesStart;
        OSTCBCurPtr->CyclesTotal += (OS_CYCLES)OSTCBCurPtr->CyclesDelta;
    }
    OSTCBHighRdyPtr->CyclesStart  = ts;                                (4)
#ifdef  CPU_CFG_INT_DIS_MEAS_EN
    int_dis_time = CPU_IntDisMeasMaxCurReset();                         (5)
    if (int_dis_time > OSTCBCurPtr->IntDisTimeMax) {
        OSTCBCurPtr->IntDisTimeMax = int_dis_time;
    }
#if OS_CFG_SCHED_LOCK_TIME_MEAS_EN > 0u
    if (OSSchedLockTimeMaxCur > OSTCBCurPtr->SchedLockTimeMax) {        (6)
        OSTCBCurPtr->SchedLockTimeMax = OSSchedLockTimeMaxCur;
        OSSchedLockTimeMaxCur         = (CPU_TS)0;
    }
#endif
#endif
#endif
}
```

Listing A-9 **OS_CPU_C.C – OSTaskSwHook()**

LA-9(1)   If the application developer wants his/her own function to be called when a context switch occurs, the developer needs to initialize the value of **OS_AppTaskSwHookPtr** to point to the desired function to call.

The application hook function *must not* make any blocking calls and should perform its function as quickly as possible.

Note that µC/OS-III initializes **OS_AppTaskSwHookPtr** to **NULL** when **OSInit()** is called and your code must set this pointer only after calling **OSInit()**.

Examples of application hooks are found in **OS_APP_HOOKS.C**.

LA-9(2) The application level task switch hook is not passed any arguments. However, the global µC/OS-III variables **OSTCBCurPtr** and **OSTCBHighRdyPtr** will point to the **OS_TCB** of the task being switched out and the **OS_TCB** of the task being switched in, respectively.

LA-9(3) This code measures the execution time of each task. This will be used by the statistic task to compute the relative CPU usage (in percentage) that each task uses.

If task profiling is enabled (i.e., **OS_CFG_TASK_PROFILE_EN** is set to 1) then we obtain the current timestamp. If we are switching to a new task, we simply compute how long the task that is being switched out ran for. We then accumulate this in the **.CyclesTotal** field (64 bits) of the **OS_TCB** for that task.

LA-9(4) **OSTaskSwHook()** stores the timestamp read as the beginning time of the new task being switched in.

Note is that the execution time of each task also includes the execution time of any interrupt that occurred while the task was executing. It would be possible to exclude this, but it would require more overhead on the CPU.

LA-9(5) If **CPU_CFG_INT_DIS_MEAS_EN** is set to 1, µC/CPU measures the interrupt disable time on a per-task basis. The code simply detects the maximum amount of interrupt disable time for each task and stores it in the **.IntDisTimeMax** field of the **OS_TCB** for the task being switched out.

LA-9(6) If **OS_CFG_SCHED_LOCK_TIME_MEAS_EN** is set to 1, µC/OS-III keeps track of the maximum amount of time a task will have the scheduler locked for critical sections. This value is saved in the **.SchedLockTimeMax** field of the **OS_TCB** of the task being switched out.

A-2-9 OS_CPU_C.C — OSTimeTickHook()

OSTimeTickHook() gives the port developer the opportunity to add code that will be called by OSTimeTick(). OSTimeTickHook() is called from the tick ISR and must not make any blocking calls (it would be allowed to anyway) and must execute as quickly as possible.

Listing A-10 shows the typical code for OSTimeTickHook().

```
void  OSTimeTickHook (void)
{
#if OS_CFG_APP_HOOKS_EN > 0u
    if (OS_AppTimeTickHookPtr != (OS_APP_HOOK_VOID)0) {       (1)
        (*OS_AppTimeTickHookPtr)();                           (2)
    }
#else
    (void)&p_tcb;        /* Prevent compiler warning */
#endif
}
```

Listing A-10 **OS_CPU_C.C – OSTimeTickHook()**

LA-10(1)   If the application developer wants his/her own function to be called when a tick interrupt occurs, the developer needs to initialize the value of OS_AppTimeTickHookPtr to point to the desired function to call.

Note that µC/OS-III initializes OS_AppTimeTickHookPtr to NULL when OSInit() is called and the code must set this pointer only after calling OSInit().

Examples of application hooks are found in OS_APP_HOOKS.C.

LA-10(2)   The application level time tick hook is not passed any arguments.

A-2-10 OS_CPU_C.C — OS_CPU_SysTickHandler()

OS_CPU_SysTickHandler() is automatically invoked by the Cortex-M3 when a SysTick interrupt occurs and interrupts are enabled. For this to happen, however, the address of OS_CPU_SysTickHandler() must be placed in the interrupt vector table at the SysTick entry (the 15th entry in the vector table of the Cortex-M3).

Listing A-11 shows the Cortex-M3 code for OS_CPU_SysTickHandler().

```
void  OS_CPU_SysTickHandler (void)                    (1)
{
    CPU_SR_ALLOC();


    CPU_CRITICAL_ENTER();
    OSIntNestingCtr++;                                (2)
    CPU_CRITICAL_EXIT();
    OSTimeTick();                                     (3)
    OSIntExit();                                      (4)
}
```

Listing A-11 **OS_CPU_C.C – OS_CPU_SysTickHandler()**

LA-11(1)   When the Cortex-M3 enters an interrupt, the CPU automatically saves critical registers (R0, R1, R2, R3, R12, PC, LR and XPSR) onto the current task's stack and switches to the Main Stack (MSP) to handle the interrupt.

This means that R4 through R11 are not saved when the interrupt starts and the ARM Architecture Procedure Call Standard (AAPCS) requires that all interrupt handlers preserve the values of the other registers, if they are required during the ISR.

LA-11(2)   The interrupt nesting counter is incremented in a critical section because the **SysTick** interrupt handler could be interrupted by a higher priority interrupt.

LA-11(3)   The μC/OS-III tick interrupt needs to call **OSTimeTick()**.

LA-11(4)   Every interrupt handler must call **OSIntExit()** at the end of the handler.

A-2-11 OS_CPU_C.C — OS_CPU_SysTickinit()

OS_CPU_SysTickInit() is called by your application code to initialize the SysTick interrupt.

Listing A-12 shows the Cortex-M3 code for OS_CPU_SysTickInit().

```
void  OS_CPU_SysTickInit (CPU_INT32U  cnts)                      (1)
{
    CPU_REG_NVIC_ST_RELOAD = cnts - 1u;                          (1)
    CPU_REG_NVIC_SHPRI3    |= 0xFF000000u;                       (2)
    CPU_REG_NVIC_ST_CTRL   |= CPU_REG_NVIC_ST_CTRL_CLKSOURCE
                            | CPU_REG_NVIC_ST_CTRL_ENABLE;
    CPU_REG_NVIC_ST_CTRL   |= CPU_REG_NVIC_ST_CTRL_TICKINT;
}
```

Listing A-12 **OS_CPU_C.C – OS_CPU_SysTickInit()**

LA-12(1)   OS_CPU_SysTickInit() must be informed about the counts to reload into the SysTick timer. The counts to reload depend on the CPU clock frequency and the configured tick rate (i.e., OS_CFG_TICK_RATE_HZ in OS_CFG_APP.H).

The reload value is typically computed by the first application task to run as follows:

```
cpu_clk_freq = BSP_CPU_ClkFreq();
cnts         = cpu_clk_freq / (CPU_INT32U)OS_CFG_TICK_RATE_HZ;
```

BSP_CPU_ClkFreq() is a BSP function that returns the CPU clock frequency. We then compute reload counts from the tick rate.

LA-12(2)   The SysTick interrupt is set to the lowest priority because ticks are mostly used for coarse time delays and timeouts, and we want application interrupts to be handled first.

A-3 OS_CPU_A.ASM

OS_CPU_A.ASM contains processor-specific code for three functions that must be written in assembly language:

```
OSStartHighRdy()
OSCtxSw()
OSIntCtxSw()
```

In addition, the Cortex-M3 requires the definition of a function to handle the PendSV exception.

```
OS_CPU_PendSVHandler()
```

A-3-1 OS_CPU_A.ASM − OSStartHighRdy()

OSStartHighRdy() is called by OSStart() to start the process of multitasking. µC/OS-III will switch to the highest priority task that is ready to run.

Listing A-13 shows the Cortex-M3 code for OSStartHighRdy().

```
OSStartHighRdy
        LDR     R0, =NVIC_SYSPRI14              (1)
        LDR     R1, =NVIC_PENDSV_PRI
        STRB    R1, [R0]
        MOVS    R0, #0
        MSR     PSP, R0
        LDR     R0, =NVIC_INT_CTRL             (2)
        LDR     R1, =NVIC_PENDSVSET
        STR     R1, [R0]
        CPSIE   I                              (3)
OSStartHang
        B       OSStartHang                    (4)
```

Listing A-13 **OS_CPU_A.ASM − OSStartHighRdy()**

LA-13(1)   OSStartHighRdy() starts by setting the priority level of the PendSV handler. The PendSV handler is used to perform all context switches and is always set at the lowest priority so that it executes after the last nested ISR.

LA-13(2)   The PendSV handler is invoked by 'triggering' it. However, the PendSV will not execute immediately because it is assumed that interrupts are disabled.

LA-13(3)   Interrupts are enabled and this should cause the Cortex-M3 processor to vector to the PendSV handler (described later).

LA-13(4)   The PendSV handler should pass control to the highest-priority task that was created and the code should never come back to OSStartHighRdy().

A-3-2 OS_CPU_A.ASM — OSCtxSw() **AND** OSIntCtxSw()

OSCtxSw() is called by OSSched() and OS_Sched0() to perform a context switch from a task.

OSIntCtxSw() is called by OSIntExit() to perform a context switch after an ISR has completed.

Both of these functions simply 'trigger' the PendSV exception handler, which does the actual context switching.

Listing A-14 shows the Cortex-M3 code for OSCtxSw() and OSIntCtxSw().

```
OSCtxSw
        LDR     R0, =NVIC_INT_CTRL
        LDR     R1, =NVIC_PENDSVSET
        STR     R1, [R0]
        BX      LR
OSIntCtxSw
        LDR     R0, =NVIC_INT_CTRL
        LDR     R1, =NVIC_PENDSVSET
        STR     R1, [R0]
        BX      LR
```

Listing A-14 **OS_CPU_A.ASM – OSCtxSw() and OSIntCtxSw()**

A-3-3 OS_CPU_A.ASM — OS_CPU_PendSVHandler()

OS_CPU_PendSVHandler() is the code that performs a context switch initiated by a task, or at the completion of an ISR. OS_CPU_PendSVHandler() is invoked by OSStartHighRdy(), OSCtxSw() and OSIntCtxSw().

Listing A-15 shows the Cortex-M3 code for OS_CPU_PendSVHandler().

```
OS_CPU_PendSVHandler
    CPSID   I                                       (1)
    MRS     R0, PSP                                  (2)
    CBZ     R0, OS_CPU_PendSVHandler_nosave
    SUBS    R0, R0, #0x20                            (3)
    STM     R0, {R4-R11}
    LDR     R1, =OSTCBCurPtr                         (4)
    LDR     R1, [R1]
    STR     R0, [R1]

OS_CPU_PendSVHandler_nosave
    PUSH    {R14}                                    (5)
    LDR     R0, =OSTaskSwHook
    BLX     R0
    POP     {R14}
    LDR     R0, =OSPrioCur                           (6)
    LDR     R1, =OSPrioHighRdy
    LDRB    R2, [R1]
    STRB    R2, [R0]
    LDR     R0, =OSTCBCurPtr                         (7)
    LDR     R1, =OSTCBHighRdyPtr
    LDR     R2, [R1]
    STR     R2, [R0]
    LDR     R0, [R2]                                 (8)
    LDM     R0, {R4-R11}                             (9)
    ADDS    R0, R0, #0x20
    MSR     PSP, R0                                  (10)
    ORR     LR, LR, #0x04
    CPSIE   I                                        (11)
    BX      LR                                       (12)
```

Listing A-15 **OS_CPU_A.ASM – OS_CPU_PendSVHandler()**

LA-15(1)   OS_CPU_PendSVHandler() starts by disabling all interrupts because interrupt
              should not occur during a context switch.

LA-15(2)   This code skips saving the remaining eight registers if this is the first time the
              PendSV is called. In other words, when OSStartHighRdy() triggers the
              PendSV handler, there is nothing to save from the 'previous task' as there is no
              previous task.

LA-15(3)   If OS_CPU_PendSVHandler() is invoked from either OSCtxSw() or
              OSIntCtxSw(), the PendSV handler saves the remaining eight CPU registers
              (R4 through R11) onto the stack of the task switched out.

LA-15(4)   OS_CPU_PendSVHandler() saves the stack pointer of the task switched out into
              that task's OS_TCB. Note that the first field of an OS_TCB is .StkPtr (the task's
              stack pointer), which makes it convenient for assembly language code since
              there are no offsets to determine.

LA-15(5)   The task switch hook (OSTaskSwHook()) is then called.

LA-15(6)   OS_CPU_PendSVHandler() copies the priority of the new task into the priority
              of the current task, i.e.:

              OSPrioCur = OSPrioHighRdy;

LA-15(7)   OS_CPU_PendSVHandler() copies the pointer to the new task's OS_TCB into the
              pointer to the current task's OS_TCB, i.e.,:

              OSTCBCurPtr = OSTCBHighRdyPtr;

LA-15(8)   OS_CPU_PendSVHandler() retrieves the stack pointer from the new task's
              OS_TCB.

LA-15(9)   CPU registers R4 through R11 from the new task are loaded into the CPU.

LA-15(10)   The task stack pointer is updated with the new top-of-stack pointer.

LA-15(11) Interrupts are re-enabled since we are finished performing the critical portion of the context switch. If another interrupt occurs before we return from the PendSV handler, the Cortex-M3 knows that there are eight registers still saved on the stack, and there would be no need for it to save them. This is called Tail Chaining and it makes servicing back-to-back interrupts quite efficient on the Cortex-M3.

LA-15(12) By performing a return from the PendSV handler, the Cortex-M3 processors knows that it is returning from interrupt and will thus restore the remaining registers.

B

µC/CPU Port for the Cortex-M3

µC/CPU consists of files that encapsulate common CPU-specific functionality and CPU compiler-specific data types. Appendix B describes the adaptation of µC/CPU to the Cortex-M3 as it relates to µC/OS-III.

Notice how each variable, function, **#define** constant, or macro is prefixed with **CPU_**. This makes it easier to identify them as belonging to the µC/CPU module when invoked by other modules, or application code.

The µC/CPU files are found in the following three directories:

```
\Micrium\Software\uC-CPU\CPU_CORE.C
\Micrium\Software\uC-CPU\CPU_CORE.H
\Micrium\Software\uC-CPU\CPU_DEF.H
\Micrium\Software\uC-CPU\Cfg\Template\CPU_CFG.H
\Micrium\Software\uC-CPU\ARM-Cortex-M3\IAR\CPU.H
\Micrium\Software\uC-CPU\ARM-Cortex-M3\IAR\CPU_A.ASM
\Micrium\Software\uC-CPU\ARM-Cortex-M3\IAR\CPU_C.C
```

B-1 CPU_CORE.C

CPU_CORE.C contains C code that is common to all CPU architectures and this file must not be changed. Specifically, CPU_CORE.C contains functions to allow μC/OS-III and your application to obtain time stamps, measure the interrupt disable time of the CPU_CRITICAL_ENTER() and CPU_CRITICAL_EXIT() macros, a function that emulates a count leading zeros instruction (if the processor does not have that instruction built-in), and a few other functions.

The application code must call CPU_Init() before it calls any other μC/CPU function. This call can be placed in main() before calling μC/OS-III's OSInit().

B-2 CPU_CORE.H

CPU_CORE.H contains function prototypes for the functions provided in CPU_CORE.C and allocation of the variables used by the module to measure interrupt disable time. This file must not be modified.

B-3 CPU_DEF.H

CPU_DEF.H contains miscellaneous #define constants used by the μC/CPU module. This file must not be modified.

B-4 CPU_CFG.H

CPU_CFG.H contains a template to configure μC/CPU for an actual project. CPU_CFG.H determines whether to enable measurement of the interrupt disable time, whether the CPU implements a count leading zeros instruction in assembly language, or whether it will be emulated in C, and more.

You should copy CPU_CFG.H to the application directory for a project and modify this file as necessary. This obviously assumes that you have access to the source code. The source code is provided to μC/OS-III licensees.

Listing B-1 shows the recommended values for the Cortex-M3.

```
#define   CPU_CFG_NAME_EN                    DEF_ENABLED            (1)
#define   CPU_CFG_NAME_SIZE                          16u            (2)
#define   CPU_CFG_TS_EN                      DEF_ENABLED            (3)
#define   CPU_CFG_INT_DIS_MEAS_EN            DEF_ENABLED            (4)
#define   CPU_CFG_INT_DIS_MEAS_OVRHD_NBR             1u            (5)
#define   CPU_CFG_LEAD_ZEROS_ASM_PRESENT    DEF_ENABLED            (6)
```

Listing B-1 **CPU_CFG.H recommended values**

LB-1(1)   Assign an ASCII name to the CPU by calling **CPU_NameSet()**. This is useful for debugging purposes.

LB-1(2)   The name of the CPU should be limited to 15 characters plus a NUL, unless this value is changed.

LB-1(3)   This **#define** enables the code to measure timestamps. It is a feature required by µC/OS-III, and should always be set to **DEF_ENABLED**.

LB-1(4)   This **#define** determines whether to measure interrupt disable time. This is a useful feature during development but it may be turned off when deploying a system as measuring interrupt disable time adds measurement artifacts (i.e., overhead).

LB-1(5)   This **#define** determines how many iterations will be performed when determining the overhead involved in measuring interrupt disable time. For the Cortex-M3, the recommended value is 1.

LB-1(6)   The ARMv7 instruction set of the Cortex-M3 contains a Count Leading Zeros (CLZ) instruction, which significantly improves the performance of the µC/OS-III scheduler and, therefore, this option always needs to be enabled.

B-5 μC/CPU FUNCTIONS IN BSP.C

μC/CPU also requires two Board Support Package (BSP) specific functions:

    CPU_TS_TmrInit()
    CPU_TS_TmrRd()

These functions are typically implemented in **BSP.C** of the evaluation or target board.

The Cortex-M3's Debug Watch Trace (DWT) contains a 32-bit CPU cycle counter (CYCCNT) that is used by μC/CPU for time stamping. The 32-bit counter is incremented at the CPU clock rate which provides excellent time measurement accuracy. The CYCCNT will overflow and reset from 0 after counting 4,294,967,296 CPU clock cycles. This is not a problem since μC/CPU maintains a 64-bit timestamp using two 32-bit values. The overflows are therefore accounted for. However, for μC/OS-III, we only need the lower 32 bits because that offers sufficient resolution for what μC/OS-III needs to do with it.

A 64-bit timestamp is unlikely to ever overflow for the life of a product. For example, if the Cortex-M3 is clocked at 1 GHz (this is not possible at this time), the 64-bit timestamp would overflow after approximately 585 years!

B-5-1 μC/CPU FUNCTIONS IN BSP.C, CPU_TS_TmrInit()

Listing B-2 shows how to initialize the DWT's cycle counter.

```
#if (CPU_CFG_TS_TMR_EN == DEF_ENABLED)
CPU_INT16U  CPU_TS_TmrInit (void)
{
    DEM_CR    |= (CPU_INT32U)DEM_CR_TRCENA;                      (1)
    DWT_CYCCNT = (CPU_INT32U)0;
    DWT_CR    |= (CPU_INT32U)0x00000001;                        (2)
    return ((CPU_INT16U)0);                                     (3)
}
#endif
```

Listing B-2 **BSP.C, CPU_TS_TmrInit()**

LB-2(1)   We need to enable the trace module.

LB-2(2)   To initialize the DWT's CYCCNT set bit 0 in the DWT's Control Register (DWT_CR). A read-modify-write avoids altering the other bits in the DWT_CR.

LB-2(3)   **CPU_TS_TmrInit()** requires that the function returns the number of left shifts needed to make **CPU_TS_TmrRd()** (described below) return a 32-bit value. Since CYCCNT is already a 32-bit counter, no shifts are needed, and this value is 0.

B-5-2 µC/CPU FUNCTIONS IN BSP.C, CPU_TS_TmrRd()

The DWT's CYCCNT register is read by calling **CPU_TS_TmrRd()**. This function is implemented as shown in Listing B-3.

```
#if (CPU_CFG_TS_TMR_EN == DEF_ENABLED)
CPU_TS  CPU_TS_TmrRd (void)
{
    return ((CPU_TS)DWT_CYCCNT);
}
#endif
```

Listing B-3 **BSP.C, CPU_TS_TmrRd()**

B-6 CPU.H

CPU.H contains processor- and implementation-specific #defines constants, macros and typedefs.

B-6-1 CPU.H — #DEFINES

CPU.H declares a number of processor specific #define constants and macros. The most important ones related to µC/OS-III are shown in Listing B-4.

```
#define  CPU_CFG_STK_GROWTH            CPU_STK_GROWTH_HI_TO_LO            (1)
#define  CPU_CFG_LEAD_ZEROS_ASM_PRESENT                                  (2)
#define  CPU_SR_ALLOC()               CPU_SR  cpu_sr = (CPU_SR)0;        (3)
#define  CPU_CRITICAL_ENTER()         { cpu_sr = CPU_SR_Save(); }        (4)
#define  CPU_CRITICAL_EXIT()          { CPU_SR_Restore(cpu_sr);}         (5)
```

Listing B-4 **CPU.H, #defines**

LB-4(1)   This **#define** specifies that the Cortex-M3 stack grows from high memory to lower-memory addresses.

LB-4(2)   This **#define** indicates that the Cortex-M3 has an assembly language instruction that counts leading zeros in a data word. This feature significantly speeds up µC/OS-III's scheduling algorithm.

LB-4(3)   The macro is used to allocate a local variable in a function that needs to protect a critical section by disabling interrupts. µC/OS-III uses **CPU_SR_ALLOC()** as follows:

```
void  OSFunction (void)
{
    CPU_SR_ALLOC();
    CPU_CRITICAL_ENTER();
    /* Code protected by critical section */
    CPU_CRITICAL_EXIT();
    :
}
```

The macro might not appear necessary if we are only declaring a single variable, but the actual code in **CPU.H** is slightly more complex. Therefore the macro hides this complexity from the user.

LB-4(4)   **CPU_CRITICAL_ENTER()** is invoked by µC/OS-III to disable interrupts. As shown, the macro calls **CPU_SR_Save()**, which is declared in **CPU_A.ASM** (described later). **CPU_SR_Save()** saves the current state of the Cortex-M3's PSR and then disables interrupts. The saved value of the PSR is returned to the function that invokes **CPU_CRITICAL_ENTER()**. The PSR is saved in the local variable allocated by **CPU_SR_ALLOC()**. **CPU_SR_Save()** is implemented in assembly language because C cannot access CPU registers.

LB-4(5)   **CPU_CRITICAL_EXIT()** calls the function **CPU_SR_Restore()** (See **CPU_A.ASM**) to restore the previously saved state of the PSR. The reason the PSR was saved in the first place is because interrupts might already be disabled before invoking **CPU_CRITICAL_ENTER()** and we want to keep them disabled when we exit the critical section. If interrupts were enabled before calling **CPU_CRITICAL_ENTER()**, they will be re-enabled by **CPU_CRITICAL_EXIT()**.

B-6-2 CPU.H – DATA TYPES

Micriµm does not make use of the standard C data types. Instead, data types are declared that are highly portable and intuitive. In addition, all data types are always declared in upper case, which follows Micriµm's coding standard.

Listing B-5 shows the data types used by Micriµm specific to the Cortex-M3 (assuming the IAR C compiler).

```
typedef            void      CPU_VOID;
typedef            char      CPU_CHAR;              /*  8-bit character         */  (1)
typedef   unsigned char      CPU_BOOLEAN;          /*  8-bit boolean or logical */  (2)
typedef   unsigned char      CPU_INT08U;           /*  8-bit unsigned integer   */  (3)
typedef   signed   char      CPU_INT08S;           /*  8-bit   signed integer   */
typedef   unsigned short     CPU_INT16U;           /* 16-bit unsigned integer   */
typedef   signed   short     CPU_INT16S;           /* 16-bit   signed integer   */
typedef   unsigned int       CPU_INT32U;           /* 32-bit unsigned integer   */
typedef   signed   int       CPU_INT32S;           /* 32-bit   signed integer   */
typedef   unsigned long long CPU_INT64U;           /* 64-bit unsigned integer   */  (4)
typedef   signed   long long CPU_INT64S;           /* 64-bit   signed integer   */
typedef            float     CPU_FP32;             /* 32-bit floating point     */  (5)
typedef            double    CPU_FP64;             /* 64-bit floating point     */
typedef   volatile CPU_INT08U CPU_REG08;           /*  8-bit register           */
typedef   volatile CPU_INT16U CPU_REG16;           /* 16-bit register           */
typedef   volatile CPU_INT32U CPU_REG32;           /* 32-bit register           */
typedef   volatile CPU_INT64U CPU_REG64;           /* 64-bit register           */
typedef            void      (*CPU_FNCT_VOID)(void);
typedef            void      (*CPU_FNCT_PTR )(void *);
```

Listing B-5 **CPU.H, Data Types**

LB-5(1)   Characters are assumed to be 8-bit quantities on the Cortex-M3.

LB-5(2)   It is often convenient to declare Boolean variables. However, even though a Boolean represents either 1 or 0, a whole byte is used. This is done because ANSI C does not define single bit variables.

LB-5(3)   The signed and unsigned integer data types are declared for 8, 16 and 32-bit quantities.

LB-5(4)   µC/OS-III requires that the compiler defines 64-bit data types. These are used when computing CPU usage on a per-task basis. The 64-bit data types are used when declaring **OS_CYCLES** in **OS_TYPE.H**.

LB-5(5)   Most of Micrium's software components do not use floating-point values. These data types are declared for consistency and to provide portable data types to the application developer.

```
#define  CPU_CFG_ADDR_SIZE       CPU_WORD_SIZE_32                          (6)
#define  CPU_CFG_DATA_SIZE       CPU_WORD_SIZE_32
#if      (CPU_CFG_ADDR_SIZE == CPU_WORD_SIZE_32)
typedef  CPU_INT32U              CPU_ADDR;
#elif    (CPU_CFG_ADDR_SIZE == CPU_WORD_SIZE_16)
typedef  CPU_INT16U              CPU_ADDR;
#else
typedef  CPU_INT08U              CPU_ADDR;
#endif
#if      (CPU_CFG_DATA_SIZE == CPU_WORD_SIZE_32)
typedef  CPU_INT32U              CPU_DATA;
#elif    (CPU_CFG_DATA_SIZE == CPU_WORD_SIZE_16)
typedef  CPU_INT16U              CPU_DATA;
#else
typedef  CPU_INT08U              CPU_DATA;
#endif
typedef  CPU_DATA               CPU_ALIGN;
typedef  CPU_ADDR               CPU_SIZE_T;
typedef  CPU_INT16U             CPU_ERR;
typedef  CPU_INT32U             CPU_STK;                                   (7)
typedef  CPU_ADDR               CPU_STK_SIZE;
typedef  CPU_INT32U             CPU_SR;                                    (8)
```

Listing B-6 **CPU.H, Data Type (Continued)**

LB-6(6)   Miscellaneous types are declared.

LB-6(7)   **CPU_STK** declares the width of a CPU stack entry and they are 32-bits wide on the Cortex-M3. All µC/OS-III stacks must be declared using **CPU_STK**.

LB-6(8)   µC/CPU provides code to protect critical sections by disabling interrupts. This is implemented by **CPU_CRITICAL_ENTER()** and **CPU_CRITICAL_EXIT()**. When **CPU_CRITICAL_ENTER()** is invoked, the current state of the Cortex-M3's Program Status Register (PSR) is saved in a local variable so that it can be restored when **CPU_CRITICAL_EXIT()** is invoked. The local variable that holds the saved PSR is declared as a **CPU_SR**.

B-6-3 CPU.H – FUNCTION PROTOTYPES

CPU.H also contains a number of data types. The most significant prototypes related to µC/OS-III are shown in Listing B-6.

```
CPU_SR      CPU_SR_Save     (void);
void        CPU_SR_Restore  (CPU_SR    cpu_sr);
CPU_DATA    CPU_CntLeadZeros (CPU_DATA  val);
```

Listing B-7 **CPU.H, Data Type**

B-7 CPU_A.ASM

CPU_A.ASM contains assembly language functions provided by µC/CPU. Three functions of particular importance to µC/OS-III are shown in Listing B-7.

CPU_SR_Save( ) obtains the current value of the Cortex-M3 PSR and then disables all CPU interrupts. The value of the saved PSR is returned to the caller.

CPU_SR_Restore( ) reverses the process and restores the PSR to the value passed to

CPU_SR_Restored( ) as an argument.

CPU_CntLeadZeros( ) counts the number of zero bits starting from the most significant bit position. This function is implemented in assembly language because the ARMv7 instruction incorporates this functionality.

In all of the functions below, R0 contains the value passed to the function, as well as the returned value.

```
CPU_SR_Save
        MRS     R0, PRIMASK
        CPSID   I
        BX      LR


CPU_SR_Restore
        MSR     PRIMASK, R0
        BX      LR


CPU_CntLeadZeros
        CLZ     R0, R0
        BX      LR
```

Listing B-8 **CPU_A.ASM**

C

Micriµm's µC/Probe

µC/Probe is an award-winning Microsoft Windows™-based application that allows a user to display or change the value (at run time) of virtually any variable or memory location on a connected embedded target. The user simply populates µC/Probe's graphical environment with gauges, numeric indicators, tables, graphs, virtual LEDs, bar graphs, sliders, switches, push buttons, and other components, and associates each of these to a variable or memory location.

With µC/Probe, it is not necessary to instrument the target code in order to display or change variables at run time. In fact, there is no need to add `printf()` statements, hardware such as Light Emitting Diodes (LEDs), Liquid Crystal Displays (LCDs), or use any other means to get visibility inside an embedded target at run time.

Two versions of µC/Probe are available from Micriµm (See section C-1 "Downloading µC/Probe" on page 823).

µC/OS-III licensees will receive one free license of the full version of µC/Probe. This full version supports J-Link, RS-232C, TCP/IP, USB, and other interfaces, and allows you to display or change an unlimited number of variables. The trial version only allows you to display or change up to eight application variables. However, it allows you to monitor any µC/OS-III variables since µC/Probe is µC/OS-III aware.

The examples provided with this book assume that you have downloaded and installed one of these two versions of µC/Probe.

This appendix provides a brief introduction to µC/Probe.

Figure C-1 shows a block diagram of a typical development environment with the addition of µC/Probe as used with the LM3S9B92, available with this book.

Figure C-1 **Development environment using the LM3S9B92**

FC-1(1)   This is the application code you are developing. It is assumed that you are using μC/OS-III provided with this book. However, μC/Probe does not require an RTOS, and can work with or without an RTOS.

FC-1(2)   The examples provided with this book assumes the IAR Embedded Workbench for ARM, but μC/Probe works with any toolchain as long as the linker/locator is able to produce an .ELF or .IEEE695 output file.

FC-1(3)   The LM3S9B92-based evaluation board available with this book is able to interface to a J-Link SWD provided by Segger. The J-Link allows the C-SPY™ debugger to download Flash code onto the on-board LM3S9B92 Cortex-M3-based Micro Controller Unit (MCU). C-SPY also allows you to debug application code.

FC-1(4)   μC/Probe reads the exact same .ELF or .IEEE695 output file produced by the linker/locator. From this file, μC/Probe is able to extract names, data types and addresses of all the global variables of the application code. This information allows μC/Probe to display any of the values of the variables using the display objects available in μC/Probe (gauges, meters, virtual LEDs, bar graphs, numeric indicators, graphs, and more.

FC-1(5)   μC/Probe is able to interface to the Cortex-M3 processor via the SWD interface of the J-Link. In fact, both the C-SPY debugger and μC/Probe can access the target through the J-Link at the same time. This allows μC/Probe to monitor or change any target variable while you are stepping through the code using the

C-SPY debugger. Interfacing through the J-Link also has the advantage of not requiring any target resident code to interface to µC/Probe.

FC-1(6)   µC/Probe can also interface to the LM3S9B92-based evaluation board using RS-232C, Ethernet (using TCP/IP) or USB.

Target resident code must be added when using RS-232C. This code is however provided by Micriµm, and the user needs only to add it to the application code as part of the build. Also, unlike when using the J-Link, target data can only be displayed or changed by µC/Probe when the target is running. However, the RS-232C interface allows data to be collected faster than through the onboard J-Link.

Target resident code is also required if using the Ethernet port on the LM3S9B92-based evaluation board. In fact, you'll need a full TCP/IP stack such as Micriµm's µC/TCP-IP. Again, data can only be displayed and changed when the target is running. However, the Ethernet interface provides the best throughput and data update rates for µC/Probe.

Finally, µC/Probe can also works over the onboard USB-Device connector and requires a USB-Device (HID) stack such as Micriµm's µC/USB-Device with HID option. As with the RS-232C and TCP/IP, data can only be displayed or changed when the target is running when using this interface.

C-1 DOWNLOADING µC/PROBE

The Full Version of µC/Probe is included with all µC/OS-III licenses. The full version supports J-Link, RS-232C, TCP/IP, USB, and other interfaces, and allows users to display or change an unlimited number of variables. The Trial Version is not time limited, but only allows users to display or change up to eight application variables. Both versions are available from Micriµm's website. Simply point your favorite browser to:

www.Micrium.com/Books/Micrium-uCOS-III

Follow the links to download the desired version (or both). If not already registered on the Micriµm website, you will be asked to do so. Once downloaded, execute the appropriate µC/Probe setup file:

Micrium-uC-Probe-Setup-Full.exe Micrium-uC-Probe-Setup-Trial.exe

C-2 µC/PROBE IS A WINDOWS™-BASED APPLICATION

As previously mentioned, µC/Probe is a Microsoft Windows-based application. When opening µC/Probe you will see the environment shown in Figure C-2.

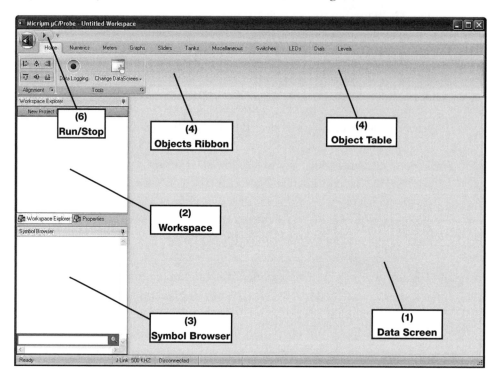

Figure C-2 **Empty µC/Probe project**

FC-2(1)   µC/Probe's main focus is the *Data Screen*. This is where you drag and drop such *Objects* as gauges, meters, graphs, virtual LEDs, sliders, switches, and more, which are used to display or change the value of target variables at run time. µC/Probe allows you to define any number of Data Screens and each Data Screen can be assigned a name. Each data screen is selected by using a *Tab* at the top of the data screen area.

FC-2(2)   When data screens are created, their names also appear in the *Workspace* area. The Workspace defines the structure of the µC/Probe project. Data screens can be imported from other projects, and can be exported.

FC-2(3)   The *Symbol Browser* contains a list of all the variables that can be displayed or changed in the target by µC/Probe. The variables are organized alphabetically by compile modules (i.e., source files). You can expand each of those files and view all the variables defined in that module, and search symbols by using the search box.

FC-2(4)   The *Object Ribbon* is where to find the objects (gauges, meters, numeric indicators, sliders, graphs, etc.) to drag and drop onto the data screen.

FC-2(5)   Similar objects are grouped together. Each group is selected by clicking on the appropriate tab. Drag and drop any object onto a data screen of your choice, and associate a variable to the instantiated object. Some objects even allow you to associate multiple variables.

Figure C-3 shows a group of *Meter* objects and Figure C-4 shows a group of *Level* objects.

Figure C-3 **µC/Probe meter objects**

Figure C-4 **µC/Probe level objects**

Figure C-5 shows a group of Slider objects, which can be used to modify target variables.

Figure C-5 **µC/Probe slider objects**

825

C-3 ASSIGNING A VARIABLE TO AN OBJECT

Assigning a variable to an object is quite simple as illustrated in Figure C-6. It is assumed that the code has been downloaded to the target and the target is running.

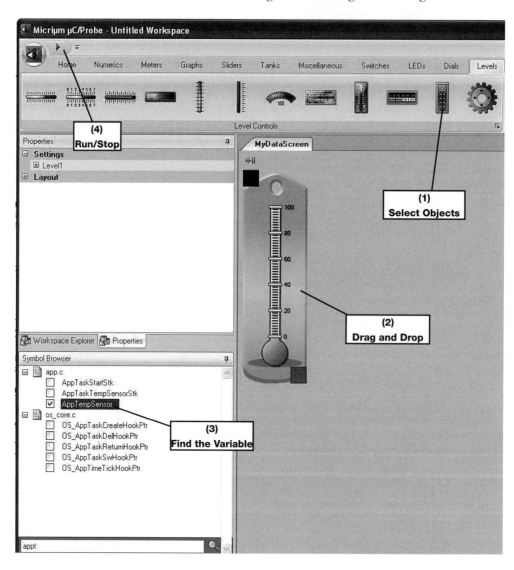

Figure C-6 **Assigning a variable to an object**

FC-6(1)   Select the object that will allow you to better visualize the variable (a meter, a thermometer, an LED, etc.).

FC-6(2)   Drag and drop the object onto the data screen.

FC-6(3)   Find the variable in the symbol browser. Simply type the first few letters of the variable and µC/Probe will narrow down the search. Click on the small box to the left of the variable.

FC-6(4)   When you want to see the value of the variable, simply click on the 'Run/Stop' button on the upper left corner.

Add as many objects as you want to each data screen and use as many data screens as you want. However, remember that the trial-version of µC/Probe only allows you to have a total of eight application variables, but enables the display of any µC/OS-III variable.

C

IAR Systems IAR Embedded Workbench for ARM

IAR Embedded Workbench is a set of highly sophisticated and easy-to-use development tools for embedded applications. It integrates the IAR C/C++ Compiler™, assembler, linker, librarian, text editor, project manager and C-SPY® Debugger in an integrated development environment (IDE).

With its built-in chip-specific code optimizer, IAR Embedded Workbench generates very efficient and reliable FLASH/ROMable code for ARM devices. In addition to this solid technology, the IAR Systems also provides professional world-wide technical support.

The KickStart™ edition of IAR Embedded Workbench is free of charge and you may use it for as long as you want. KickStart tools are ideal for creating small applications, or for getting started fast on a new project. The only requirement is that you register to obtain a license key.

The KickStart edition is code-size limited, but a fully functional integrated development environment that includes a project manager, editor, compiler, assembler, linker, librarian, and debugger tools. A complete set of user guides is included in PDF format.

The KickStart edition corresponds to the latest release of the full edition of IAR Embedded Workbench, with the following exceptions:

■ It has a code size limitation (32 Kbytes).

■ It does not include source code for runtime libraries.

■ It does not include support for MISRA C.

■ There is limited technical support.

The KickStart edition of IAR Embedded Workbench allows you to run all of the examples provided in this book.

D

D-1 IAR EMBEDDED WORKBENCH FOR ARM – HIGHLIGHTS

The full version of the IAR Embedded Workbench for ARM offers the following features.

- Support for:

  - ARM7™

  - ARM9™

  - ARM9E™

  - ARM10™

  - ARM11

  - SecurCore

  - Cortex-M0

  - Cortex-M1

  - Cortex-M

  - Cortex-R4

  - Intel® XScale™

- Most compact and efficient code

- ARM Embedded Application Binary Interface (EABI)

- Extensive support for hardware and RTOS-aware debugging

- Total solutions for ARM

- New Cortex-M3 debug features

- Function profiler

- Interrupt graph window

- Data log window

■ MISRA C:2004 support

■ Extensive device support

■ Over 1400 example projects

■ μC/OS-II Kernel Awareness built-into the C-Spy debugger

Figure D-1 shows a block diagram of the major EWARM components.

Figure D-1 **IAR Embedded Workbench**

D-2 MODULAR AND EXTENSIBLE IDE

■ A seamlessly Integrated Development Environment (IDE) for building and debugging embedded applications

■ Powerful project management allowing multiple projects in one workspace

■ Build integration with IAR visualSTATE

■ Hierarchical project representation

■ Dockable and floating windows management

- Smart source browser

- Tool options configurable on global, group of source files, or individual source files level

- Multi-file compilation support for even better code optimization

- Flexible project building via batch build, pre/post-build or custom build with access to external tools in the build process.

- Integration with source code control systems

Figure D-2 **IAR Embedded Workbench IDE**

D-3 HIGHLY OPTIMIZING C/C++ COMPILER

■ Support for C, EC++ and extended EC++ including templates, namespace, standard template library (STL) etc.

■ ARM Embedded Application Binary Interface (EABI) and ARM Cortex Microcontroller Software Interface Standard (CMSIS) compliant

■ Interoperability and binary compatibility with other EABI compliant tools

■ Automatic checking of MISRA C rules

■ Support for ARM, Thumb1 and Thumb2 processor modes

■ Support for 4 Gbyte applications in all processor modes

■ Support for 64-bit long

■ Reentrant code

■ 32- and 64-bit floating-point types in standard IEEE format

■ Multiple levels of optimizations on code size and execution speed allowing different transformations enabled, such as function inlining, loop unrolling etc.

■ Advanced global and target-specific optimizer generating the most compact and stable code

■ Compressed initializers

■ Support for ARM7, ARM7E, ARM9, ARM9E, ARM10E, ARM11, Cortex-M0, Cortex-M1, Cortex-M3, Cortex-R4 and Intel XScale

■ Support for ARM, Thumb1 and Thumb2 processor modes

■ Generates code for ARM VFP series of floating-point coprocessors

■ Little/big endian mode

D-4 DEVICE SUPPORT

Device support on five levels:

- Core support - instruction set, debugger interface (for all supported devices)

- Header/DDF files - peripheral register names in C/asm source and debugger (for all supported devices)

- Flash loader for on-chip flash or off-chip EVB flash (for most of our supported devices)

- Project examples - varies from simple to fairly complex applications (for most of our supported devices)

- Detailed device support list at www.iar.com/ewarm

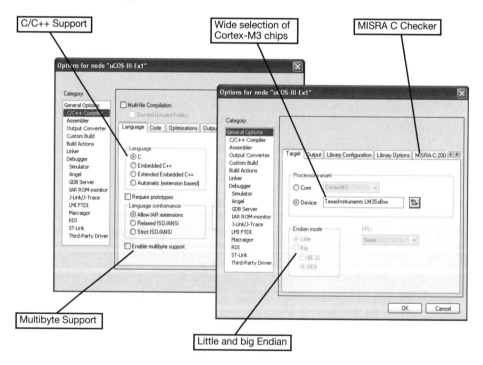

Figure D-3 **Device Support**

D-5 STATE-OF-THE-ART C-SPY® DEBUGGER

■ Cortex-M3 SWV/SWO debugger support

■ Complex code and data breakpoints

■ User selectable breakpoint types (hardware/software)

■ Unlimited number of breakpoints in flash via optional license for J-Link

■ Runtime stack analysis - stack window to monitor the memory consumption and integrity of the stack

■ Complete support for stack unwinding even at high optimization levels

■ Profiling and code coverage performance analysis tools

■ Trace utility with expressions, such as variables and register values, to examine execution history

■ Versatile monitoring of registers, structures, call chain, locals, global variables and peripheral registers

■ Smart STL container display in Watch window

■ Symbolic memory window and static watch window

■ I/O and interrupt simulation

■ True editing-while-debugging

■ Drag and drop model

■ Target access to host file system via file I/O

■ Built-in µC/OS-II Kernel Awareness

D-6 C-SPY DEBUGGER AND TARGET SYSTEM SUPPORT

The C-SPY Debugger for the ARM core is available with drivers for the following target systems:

■ Simulator

■ Emulator (JTAG/SWD)

  ■ IAR J-Link probe, JTAG and SWD support, connection via USB or TCP/IP server

  ■ RDI (Remote Debug Interface), such as Abatron BDI1000 & BDI2000, EPI Majic, Ashling Opella, Aiji OpenICE, Signum JTAGjet, ARM Multi-ICE

  ■ Macraigor JTAG interfaces: Macraigor Raven, Wiggler, mpDemon, usbDemon, usb2Demon and usb2Sprite

  ■ ST ST-LINK JTAG debug probe

D-7 IAR ASSEMBLER

■ A powerful relocating macro assembler with a versatile set of directives and operators

■ Built-in C language preprocessor, accepting all C macro definitions

D-8 IAR J-LINK LINKER

■ Complete linking, relocation and format generation to produce FLASH/PROMable code

■ Flexible commands allowing detailed control of code and data placement

■ Optimized linking removing unused code and data

■ Direct linking of raw binary images, for instance multimedia files

■ Comprehensive cross-reference and dependency memory maps

■ Link compatibility with object files and libraries generated by other EABI compliant tools

D-9 IAR LIBRARY AND LIBRARY TOOLS

■ All required ISO/ANSI C and C++ libraries and source included

■ All low-level routines such as **writechar()** and **readchar()** provided in full source code

■ Lightweight runtime library, user-configurable to match the needs of the application; full source included

■ Library tools for creating and maintaining library projects, libraries and library modules

■ Listings of entry points and symbolic information

D-10 COMPREHENSIVE DOCUMENTATION

■ Efficient coding hints for embedded application

■ Extensive step-by-step tutorials

■ Context sensitive help and hypertext versions of the user documentation available online

D-11 FIRST CLASS TECHNICAL SUPPORT

IAR Systems has a global organization with local presence through branch offices and a worldwide distributor network. Extended, customized technical services are available.

- *ARM® CoreSight Technical Reference Manual*

- *ARM® Cortex™M3 Technical Reference Manual*

- *Stellaris® LM3S9B92 Microcontroller Data Sheet*

- *Stellaris® LM3S9B92 Errata*

- *ARM® Cortex™-M3 Errata*

- *ARM® v7-M Architecture Application Level Reference Manual*

- *Stellaris® Boot Loader User's Guide*

- *Stellaris® Peripheral Driver Library User's Guide*

- *Stellaris® ROM User' Guide*

- *Stellaris® LM3S9B92 Microcontroller Data Sheet*

- *DRV8801RTY Data Sheet*, Literature Number SLVA322
  Full bridge motor driver

- *TLV320AIC3107 Data Sheet*, Literature Number SLOS545
  Low-power Stereo Codec with Integrated Mono Class-D Speaker Amplifier

- *TLV70018 Data Sheet*, Literature Number SLVSA00
  200-mA, Low-I_Q, Low-Dropout Regulator for Portable Devices

- *TLV70033 Data Sheet*, Literature Number SLVSA00
  200-mA, Low-I_Q, Low-Dropout Regulator for Portable Devices

- *TPS71501 Data Sheet,* Literature Number SLVS338
  50mA, 24V, 3.2-µA Supply Current, Low-Dropout Linear Regulator in SC70 Package

- *TPS61085 Data Sheet*, Literature Number SLVS859
  18.5V, 2A, 650kHz, 1.2MHz Step-Up DC-DC Converter with Forced PWM Mode

- *TS3USB30 Data Sheet*, Literature Number SCDS237
  High-Speed USB 2.0 (480 Mbps) 1:2 Multiplexer/Demultiplexer Switch With Single Enable

- *TPS2113 Data Sheet*, Literature Number SLVS446
  Dual In/Single Out Autoswitching Power MUX

- *TPS61073 Data Sheet*, Literature Number SLVS510
  Adjustable, 600-mA Switch, 90% Efficient PFM/PWM Boost Converter in ThinSOT-23

The following data sheets can be obtained from the manufacturer:

- *P13701 OLED Display Data Sheet from RiT Display Corporation*

- *SSD1300 OLED Controller Data Sheet from Solomon Systech Limited*

Licensing Policy

This book contains µC/OS-III, precompiled in linkable object form, and is accompanied by an evaluation board and tools (compiler/assembler/linker/debugger). The user may use µC/OS-III with the evaluation board that accompanied the book and it is not necessary to purchase anything else as long as the initial purchase is used for educational purposes. Once the code is used to create a commercial project/product for profit, however, it is necessary to purchase a license.

It is necessary to purchase this license when the decision to use µC/OS-III in a design is made, not when the design is ready to go to production.

If you are unsure about whether you need to obtain a license for your application, please contact Micriµm and discuss the intended use with a sales representative.

Contact Micriµm
Micriµm
1290 Weston Road, Suite 306
Weston, FL 33326

+1 954 217 2036
+1 954 217 2037 (FAX)

E-Mail : sales@micrium.com
Website : www.micrium.com

F

Index

Stellaris®

Connected. Versatile. Cost-effective.

Stellaris LM3S9B90 Ethernet Evaluation Kit

featuring USB, Ethernet and CAN

$99

Stellaris LM3S8962 Evaluation Kit

featuring integrated Ethernet and CAN

$89

Stellaris LM3S3748 Evaluation Kit

featuring USB Host/Device

$109

Stellaris® Means:

- Deterministic ARM® Cortex™-M3 cores
- Real-time multi-tasking MCUs
- Advanced interrupt-driven software with Stellarisware® software

Stellaris LM3S6965 Ethernet Evaluation Kit

demonstrating an embedded web server out-of-the-box

$69

Stellaris LM3S811 Evaluation Kit

featuring basic embedded control

$49

Stellaris LM3S2965 CAN Evaluation Kit

demonstrating a CAN network out-of-the-box

$79